W9-BYG-883

IMPORTANT:

HERE IS YOUR REGISTRATION CODE TO ACCESS
YOUR PREMIUM McGRAW-HILL ONLINE RESOURCES.

For key premium online resources you need THIS CODE to gain access. Once the code is entered, you will be able to use the Web resources for the length of your course.

If your course is using **WebCT** or **Blackboard**, you'll be able to use this code to access the McGraw-Hill content within your instructor's online course.

Access is provided if you have purchased a new book. If the registration code is missing from this book, the registration screen on our Website, and within your WebCT or Blackboard course, will tell you how to obtain your new code.

Registering for McGraw-Hill Online Resources

To gain access to your McGraw-Hill web resources simply follow the steps below:

(1) USE YOUR WEB BROWSER TO GO TO: **www.mhhe.com/unfinishednation4**

(2) CLICK ON **FIRST TIME USER**.

(3) ENTER THE REGISTRATION CODE* PRINTED ON THE TEAR-OFF BOOKMARK ON THE RIGHT.

(4) AFTER YOU HAVE ENTERED YOUR REGISTRATION CODE, CLICK **REGISTER**.

(5) FOLLOW THE INSTRUCTIONS TO SET-UP YOUR PERSONAL UserID AND PASSWORD.

(6) WRITE YOUR UserID AND PASSWORD DOWN FOR FUTURE REFERENCE.
KEEP IT IN A SAFE PLACE.

TO GAIN ACCESS to the McGraw-Hill content in your instructor's **WebCT** or **Blackboard** course simply log in to the course with the UserID and Password provided by your instructor. Enter the registration code exactly as it appears in the box to the right when prompted by the system. You will only need to use the code the first time you click on McGraw-Hill content.

Thank you, and welcome to your McGraw-Hill Online Resources!

Mc Graw Hill **Higher Education**

REGISTRATION CODE

exchangers-63193054

0-07-293249-X T/A BRINKLEY:THE UNFINISHED NATION:A CONCISE HISTORY OF THE AMERICAN PEOPLE

THE UNFINISHED NATION

A Concise History of the American People
Volume II: From 1865

THE UNFINISHED NATION

A Concise History of the American People
Volume II: From 1865

Fourth Edition

ALAN BRINKLEY
Columbia University

Boston Burr Ridge, IL Dubuque, IA Madison, WI New York
San Francisco St. Louis Bangkok Bogotá Caracas Kuala Lumpur
Lisbon London Madrid Mexico City Milan Montreal New Delhi
Santiago Seoul Singapore Sydney Taipei Toronto

Higher Education

THE UNFINISHED NATION: A CONCISE HISTORY OF THE AMERICAN PEOPLE
VOLUME II: FROM 1865
Published by McGraw-Hill, a business unit of The McGraw-Hill Companies, Inc., 1221 Avenue of the Americas, New York, NY, 10020. Copyright © 2004, 2000, 1997, 1993, by The McGraw-Hill Companies, Inc. All rights reserved. No part of this publication may be reproduced or distributed in any form or by any means, or stored in a database or retrieval system, without the prior written consent of The McGraw-Hill Companies, Inc., including, but not limited to, in any network or other electronic storage or transmission, or broadcast for distance learning.
Some ancillaries, including electronic and print components, may not be available to customers outside the United States.

This book is printed on acid-free paper.

1 2 3 4 5 6 7 8 9 0 DOC/DOC 0 9 8 7 6 5 4 3

ISBN   0-07-256563-2

Publisher: *Lyn Uhl*
Senior sponsoring editor: *Steve Drummond*
Senior developmental editor: *Jim Strandberg*
Editorial assistant: *Kimberly McGrath*
Marketing manager: *Katherine Bates*
Senior media producer: *Sean Crowley*
Lead project manager: *Susan Trentacosti*
Production supervisor: *Carol A. Bielski*
Freelance design coordinator: *Gino Cieslik*
Supplement associate: *Kathleen Boylan*
Supplement developmental editor: *Kate Scheinman*
Associate photo research coordinator: *Natalia Peschiera*
Associate art editor: *Cristin Yancey*
Photo researcher: *PhotoSearch, Inc.*
Cover and interior design: *Maureen McCutcheon*
Typeface: *10.5/12 Janson*
Compositor: *Shepherd Inc.*
Printer: *R.R. Donnelley and Sons, Inc.*

Library of Congress Cataloging-in-Publication Data

Brinkley, Alan.
    The unfinished nation : a concise history of the American people / Alan Brinkley.—4th ed.
    p. cm.
    Includes bibliographical references and index.
    Contents: v. 1. To 1877 — v. 2. From 1865.
    ISBN 0-07-256554-3 (softcover : alk. paper) — ISBN 0-07-256562-4 (v. 1 : softcover : alk. paper) — ISBN 0-07-256563-2 (v. 2 : softcover : alk. paper)
    1. United States—History. I. Title
E178.1B827 2004
973—dc21   2003046457

www.mhhe.com

About the Author

❧

ALAN BRINKLEY is the Allan Nevins Professor of History at Columbia University. He is the author of *Voices of Protest: Huey Long, Father Coughlin, and the Great Depression*, which won the 1983 National Book Award; *American History: A Survey*; *The End of Reform: New Deal Liberalism in Recession and War*; and *Liberalism and Its Discontents*. He was educated at Princeton and Harvard, and he has taught at Harvard (where he was awarded the Joseph R. Levenson Memorial Teaching Award), Princeton, the City University of New York Graduate School, and Oxford University, where he was the Harmsworth Professor of American History. He is a member of the American Academy of Arts and Sciences, a member of the board of the New York Council for the Humanities, and chairman of the board of the Century Foundation.

Brief Contents

Contents

The New Deal   676

The Global Crisis, 1921–1941   702

List of Illustrations

LIST OF ILLUSTRATIONS

List of Maps and Charts

Preface

The story of the American past, which is the subject of this book, has undergone many transformations in recent decades. The past itself has not changed, of course, but the way Americans understand it has changed dramatically. And in the wake of those changes have come both new forms of presentation and bitter controversies.

In one sense, American history is thriving as almost never before as a part of American popular culture. Historical museums and exhibitions have multiplied and have attracted large audiences. Popular writing on history—both nonfiction and novels—has grown in popularity. History is a continuing presence on television, in films, and increasingly on the Internet. The popular appetite for American history seems to be almost boundless. At the same time, however, historical scholarship has become the source of increasing debate—among historians themselves, among the various publics historians try to reach, and among politicians, some of whom attack the historical profession for what they claim is an excessively critical view of the past.

Both the growing popularity of history and the growing controversies surrounding it reflect the character of our time. Ours is an era of rapid and bewildering change, which encourages people—particularly in the aftermath of the attacks of September 11, 2001—to look to the past for guidance, reassurance, and for reminders of what many believe were simpler, stabler times. But the turbulence of our age has also encouraged historians to ask new questions of the past—and thus to reinterpret it—in an effort to understand the tensions and contests that preoccupy us today. As the population of the United States has become more diverse and as groups that once stood outside the view of scholarship have thrust themselves into its center, historians have labored to reveal the immense complexity of their country's past. As America's economy and culture and power become more deeply involved in the life of the rest of the world, historians struggle to see the ways in which global forces have shaped the nation's development. Historical narratives once recounted little beyond the experiences of great men and the unfolding of great public events. Today, they attempt to tell a more complicated story—one that includes private as well as public lives, ordinary people as well as celebrated ones, differences as well as unity, international phenomena as well as national ones. This newer history seems fragmented at times, because it attempts to embrace so many more areas of human experience than the older narratives. It is often disturbing, because it reveals failures and injustices as well as triumphs. But it is also richer, fuller, and better suited to helping us understand our own diverse and contentious world.

I have tried in this book to consider both the diversity and the unity that have characterized the American experience. The United States is, and has always been, a nation of many cultures. To understand its history, we must understand the experiences of the many groups who have shaped American society—the many worlds that have developed within it based on region, religion, class, ideology, race, gender, and ethnicity.

But the United States is not simply a collection of different cultures. It is also a great nation. And as important as understanding its diversity is understanding the forces that have drawn it together and allowed it to survive and flourish despite division. The United States has constructed a remarkably stable and enduring political system, which touches the lives of all Americans. It has developed an immense and highly productive national economy that affects the working and consuming lives of virtually everyone and reaches all across the globe. It has created a mass popular culture that colors the experiences and assumptions of almost all Americans, and of the people of much of the rest of the world as well. One can admire these unifying forces for their contributions to America's considerable success as a nation, or condemn them for creating—or failing to address—injustices. But no one proposing to understand the history of the United States can afford to ignore them.

In this fourth edition of *The Unfinished Nation,* I have tried to tell the complicated and fascinating story of America for students of history and for general readers. Those familiar with earlier editions will find a thorough editing and updating of all chapters, reflecting recent scholarship. Beyond that, there are three areas of special emphasis in this revision:

1. Greater attention to the global context of United States history, including a new feature called "America in the World."
2. Expanded coverage of science and technology.
3. Extensive new material on environmental history.

In addition, new chapter introductions and marginal notes throughout the text should make it more accessible to readers. And the most visible change is the introduction of full color maps, images, and other graphics to the book—and an expanded map and illustration program to take advantage of this change.

I trust that this edition will introduce readers to enough different aspects of American history to make them aware of its extraordinary richness and complexity. But I hope, too, that it will provide readers some sense of the shared experiences of Americans and of the forces that have sustained the United States as a nation.

My thanks to Kevin Murphy for his assistance on this edition. I am, as always, grateful to the many people at McGraw-Hill who have helped with the editing and production of this book: Lyn Uhl, Steve Drummond, Jim Strandberg, Susan Trentacosti, Gino Cieslik, Kim McGrath, Carol Bielski, Holly Rudelitsch, Natalia Peschiera, and Cristin Yancey. I am also grateful to the teachers and scholars who reviewed the manuscript and offered suggestions for revision: S. Charles Bolton, *University of Arkansas,*

Little Rock; Steven Boyd, *University of Texas, San Antonio;* Mike Haridopolos, *Brevard Community College;* Mark D. Van Ells, *Queensborough Community College;* B. R. Burg, *Arizona State University;* Yolanda Chávaz Leyva, *University of Texas, El Paso;* Gregory Wilson, *University of Akron;* Beverly Garrison, *Oral Roberts University;* Kenneth W. Townsend, *Coastal Carolina University;* Joanne Kropp, *University of Texas, El Paso;* Anita Ashendel, *Texas A & M University;* Donald Rakestraw, *Georgia Southern University;* Josh Rothman, *University of Alabama;* David Freligh, *Phillips Community College;* Victor Triary, *Middlesex Community College;* Alex Wellek, *Quinnipiac University;* Margaret Orelup, *Keene State College;* Dr. Robert Tracy McKenzie, *University of Washington;* Jeffrey A. Kaufmann, *Muscatine Community College;* Jack Hammersmith, *West Virginia University;* Wendy Gunderson, *Collin County Community College;* Elizabeth Osborn, *Indiana University;* Alexander Knott, *University of Northern Colorado;* William Virden, *University of Northern Colorado;* and David Cullin, *Collin County Community College.*

I am grateful, finally, to those readers of the book who have offered me unsolicited comments, criticisms, and corrections. I hope they will continue to do so. Suggestions can be sent to me at the Department of History, Columbia University, New York, NY 10027, or by e-mail at ab65@columbia.edu.

Alan Brinkley

THE GENIUS OF FREEDOM This 1874 lithograph portrays a series of important moments in the history of African Americans in the South during Reconstruction—among them the participation of black soldiers in the Civil War, a speech by a black representative in the South Carolina legislature, and the movement of African-American workers from slavery into a system of free labor. It also portrays some of the white leaders (among them Lincoln and Charles Sumner) who had promoted the cause of the freedman. *(Chicago Historical Society)*

TIME LINE

1863	1864	1865	1866	1867	1868	1869
Lincoln announces Reconstruction plan	Lincoln vetoes Wade-Davis bill	Lincoln assassinated; Johnson is president	Republicans gain in congressional elections	Congressional Reconstruction begins	Grant elected president	Congress passes 15th Amendment
		Freedmen's Bureau			Johnson impeached and acquitted	
		Joint Committee on Reconstruction			14th Amendment ratified	

RECONSTRUCTION AND THE NEW SOUTH

The Problems of Peacemaking
Radical Reconstruction
The South in Reconstruction
The Grant Administration
The Abandonment of Reconstruction
The New South

F ew periods in the history of the United States have produced as much bitterness or created such enduring controversy as the era of Reconstruction—the years following the Civil War during which Americans attempted to reunite their shattered nation. To many white Southerners, Reconstruction was a vicious and destructive experience—a period when vindictive Northerners inflicted humiliation and revenge on the prostrate South. Northern defenders of Reconstruction, in contrast, argued that their policies were the only way to prevent unrepentant Confederates from restoring Southern society to what it had been before the war.

To most African Americans at the time, and to many people of all races since, Reconstruction was notable for other reasons. Neither a vicious tyranny, as white Southerners charged, nor a thoroughgoing reform, as many Northerners hoped, it was, rather, a small but important first step in the effort to secure civil rights and economic power for the former slaves. Reconstruction did not provide African Americans with either the legal protections or the material resources to assure them anything like real equality. Most black men and women who continued to live in what came to be known as the New South had little power to resist their oppression for many decades.

And yet for all its shortcomings, Reconstruction did help African Americans create some new institutions and some important legal precedents that helped them survive and that ultimately, well into the twentieth century, became the basis of later efforts to win freedom and equality.

1872	1873	1875	1877	1883	1890s	1895	1896	
Grant reelected	Panic and depression	"Whiskey ring" scandal	Hayes wins disputed election	Supreme Court upholds segregation	Jim Crow laws in South	Atlanta Compromise	*Plessy* v. *Ferguson*	
			Compromise of 1877 ends Reconstruction					

THE PROBLEMS OF PEACEMAKING

In 1865, when it became clear that the war was almost over, no one in Washington was certain about what to do. Abraham Lincoln could not negotiate a treaty with the defeated government; he continued to insist that the Confederate government had no legal right to exist. Yet neither could he simply readmit the Southern states into the Union.

The Aftermath of War and Emancipation

The Devastated South　　The South after the Civil War was a desolate place. Towns had been gutted, plantations burned, fields neglected, bridges and railroads destroyed. Many white Southerners—stripped of their slaves through emancipation and stripped of the capital they had invested in now worthless Confederate bonds and currency—had almost no personal property. More than 258,000 Confederate soldiers had died in the war, and thousands more returned home wounded or sick. Some white Southerners faced starvation and homelessness.

If conditions were bad for Southern whites, they were far worse for Southern blacks—the three and a half million men and women now emerging from bondage. As soon as the war ended, hundreds of thousands of them left their plantations in search of a new life in freedom. But most had nowhere to go, and few had any possessions except the clothes they wore.

Competing Notions of Freedom

For blacks and whites alike, Reconstruction became a struggle to define the meaning of freedom. But the former slaves and the defeated whites had very different conceptions of what freedom meant.

Some blacks believed the only way to secure freedom was to have the government take land away from white people, who owned virtually all of it, and give it to black people, who owned virtually none. Others asked only for legal equality, confident that they could advance successfully in American society once the formal obstacles to their advancement disap-

Black Desire for Independence　　peared. But whatever their particular demands, virtually all former slaves were united in their desire for independence from white control. Throughout the post-Civil War South, African Americans separated themselves from white institutions—pulling out of white-controlled churches and establishing their own, creating clubs and societies for their own people, and in some cases starting their own schools.

For most white Southerners, freedom meant something very different. It meant the ability to control their own destinies without interference from the North or the federal government. And in the immediate af-

RICHMOND, 1865 By the time Union forces captured Richmond in early 1865, the Confederate capital had been under siege for months and much of the city lay in ruins, as this photograph reveals. On April 4, President Lincoln, accompanied by his son Tad, visited Richmond. As he walked through the streets of the shattered city, hundreds of former slaves emerged from the rubble to watch him pass. "No triumphal march of a conqueror could have equalled in moral sublimity the humble manner in which he entered Richmond," a black soldier serving with the Union army wrote. "It was a great deliverer among the delivered. No wonder tears came to his eyes." *(The Library of Congress)*

termath of the war, they attempted to exercise this version of freedom by trying to restore their society to its antebellum form. When these white Southerners fought for what they considered freedom, they were fighting above all to preserve local and regional autonomy and white supremacy.

In the immediate aftermath of the war, the federal government's contribution to solving the question of the future of the South was modest. Federal troops remained in the South to preserve order and protect the freedmen. And in March 1865, Congress established the Freedmen's Bureau, an agency of the army directed by General Oliver O. Howard. The Freedmen's Bureau distributed food to millions *The Freedmen's Bureau* of former slaves. It established schools, staffed by missionaries and teachers who had been sent to the South by Freedmen's Aid Societies and other private and church groups in the North. It made a modest effort to settle blacks on lands of their own. But the Freedmen's Bureau was not a permanent solution. It had authority to operate for only one year, and it was, in any case, far too small to deal effectively with the enormous problems facing Southern society. By the time the war ended, other proposals for reconstructing the defeated South were emerging.

A MONUMENT TO THE CONFEDERATE DEAD This monument in the town square of Greenwood, South Carolina, was typical of many such memorials erected all across the South in the aftermath of the Civil War. They served to commemorate the soldiers who had died in the struggle, but also to remind white Southerners of what was by the 1870s already widely known and romanticized as the "Lost Cause." *(Museum of the Confederacy, Richmond, Virginia)*

Plans for Reconstruction

Control of Reconstruction was in the hands of the Republicans, who were divided in their approach to the issue. Conservatives within the party insisted that the South accept the abolition of slavery, but they proposed few other conditions for the readmission of the seceded states. The Radicals, led by Representative Thaddeus Stevens of Pennsylvania and Senator Charles Sumner of Massachusetts, urged a much harsher course, including dis-

Thaddeus Stevens and Charles Sumner

enfranchising large numbers of Southern whites, protecting black civil rights, and confiscating the property of wealthy white Southerners who had aided the Confederacy and distributing the land among the freedmen. There was also a group of Republican Moderates, who rejected the most stringent demands of the Radicals but supported extracting at least some concessions from the South on black rights.

President Lincoln favored a lenient Reconstruction policy, and he believed that Southern Unionists (mostly former Whigs) could become the nucleus of new, loyal state governments in the South. Lincoln announced his Reconstruction plan in December 1863, more than a year before the war ended. It offered a general amnesty to white Southerners—other than high officials of the Confederacy—who would pledge an oath of loyalty to the government and accept the elimination of slavery. When 10 percent of a state's total number of voters in 1860 took the oath, those loyal voters could set up a state government. Lincoln also proposed extending suffrage to those African Americans who were educated, owned property, and had served in the Union army. Three Southern states—Louisiana, Arkansas, and Tennessee, all under Union occupation—reestablished loyal governments under the Lincoln formula in 1864.

The Radical Republicans were outraged at the mildness of Lincoln's program and refused to admit representatives from the three "reconstructed" states to Congress. In July 1864, they pushed their own plan through Congress in the form of the Wade-Davis Bill. It called for the president to appoint a provi-   *Wade-Davis Bill*
sional governor for each conquered state. When a majority of the white males of a state pledged their allegiance to the Union, the governor could summon a state constitutional convention, whose delegates were to be elected by voters who had never borne arms against the United States. The new state constitutions would be required to abolish slavery, disenfranchise Confederate civil and military leaders, and repudiate debts accumulated by the state governments during the war. Only then would Congress readmit the states to the Union. Like the president's proposal, the Wade-Davis Bill left the question of political rights for blacks up to the states.

Congress passed the bill a few days before it adjourned in 1864, and Lincoln disposed of it with a pocket veto. His action enraged the Radical leaders, and the pragmatic Lincoln realized he would have to accept at least some of the Radical demands.

The Death of Lincoln

What plan he might have produced no one can say. On the night of April 14, 1865, Lincoln and his wife attended a play at Ford's Theater in Washington. As they sat in the theater, John Wilkes Booth, an   *John Wilkes Booth*
actor fervently committed to the Southern cause, entered the presidential box from the rear and shot Lincoln in the head. Early the next morning, the president died.

ABRAHAM LINCOLN This haunting photograph of Abraham Lincoln, showing clearly the weariness and aging that four years as a war president had created, was taken in Washington only four days before his assassination in 1865. *(The Library of Congress)*

The circumstances of Lincoln's death earned him immediate martyr-dom. They also produced something close to hysteria throughout the North, especially because it quickly became clear that Booth had been the leader of a conspiracy. One of his associates shot and wounded Secretary of State William Seward on the night of the assassination, and another abandoned at the last moment a scheme to murder Vice President Andrew Johnson. Booth himself escaped on horseback into the Maryland country-side, where, on April 26, he was cornered by Union troops and shot to death in a blazing barn. Eight other people were convicted by a military tribunal of participating in the conspiracy. Four were hanged.

To many Northerners, however, the murder of the president seemed evidence of an even greater conspiracy—one masterminded and directed by the unrepentant leaders of the defeated South. Militant Republicans exploited such suspicions relentlessly in the ensuing months.

Johnson and "Restoration"

Leadership of the Moderates and Conservatives fell to Lincoln's successor, Andrew Johnson of Tennessee. A Democrat until he had joined the Union ticket with Lincoln in 1864, he became president at a time of growing partisan passions.

Johnson revealed his plan for Reconstruction— *Johnson's Reconstruction Plan* or "Restoration," as he preferred to call it—soon after he took office, and he implemented it during the summer of 1865 when Congress was in recess. Like Lincoln, he offered some form of amnesty to Southerners who would take an oath of allegiance. In most other respects, however, his plan resembled the Wade-Davis Bill. The president appointed a provisional governor in each state and charged him with inviting qualified voters to elect delegates to a constitutional convention. In order to win readmission to Congress, a state had to revoke its ordinance of secession, abolish slavery and ratify the Thirteenth Amendment, and repudiate Confederate and state war debts.

By the end of 1865, all the seceded states had formed new governments—some under Lincoln's plan, some under Johnson's—and awaited congressional approval of them. But Radicals in Congress vowed not to recognize the Johnson governments, for, by now, Northern opinion had become more hostile toward the South than it had *Hardening Northern Attitudes* been a year earlier when Congress had passed the Wade-Davis Bill. Delegates to the Southern conventions had angered much of the North by their apparent reluctance to abolish slavery and by their refusal to grant suffrage to any blacks. Southern states had also seemed to defy the North by electing prominent Confederate leaders to represent them in Congress.

RADICAL RECONSTRUCTION

Reconstruction under Johnson's plan—often known as "presidential Reconstruction"—continued only until Congress reconvened in December 1865. At that point, Congress refused to seat the representatives of the "restored" states and created a new Joint Committee on Reconstruction to frame a Reconstruction policy of its own. The period of "congressional" or "Radical" Reconstruction had begun.

The Black Codes

Meanwhile, events in the South were driving Northern opinion in even more radical directions. Throughout the South in 1865 and early 1866, state legislatures were enacting sets of laws known as the Black Codes, which authorized local officials to apprehend unemployed blacks, fine

RECONSTRUCTION

Debate over the nature of Reconstruction has been unusually intense. Indeed, few issues in American history have raised such deep and enduring passions.

Beginning in the late nineteenth century and continuing well into the twentieth, a relatively uniform and highly critical view of Reconstruction prevailed among historians. William A. Dunning's *Reconstruction, Political and Economic* (1907) was the principal scholarly expression of this prevailing view. Dunning portrayed Reconstruction as a corrupt and oppressive outrage imposed on a prostrate South by a vindictive group of Northern Republican Radicals. Unscrupulous carpetbaggers flooded the South and plundered the region. Ignorant African Americans were thrust into political offices for which they were unfit. Reconstruction governments were awash in corruption and compiled enormous levels of debt. The Dunning interpretation dominated several generations of historical scholarship. It also helped shape such popular images of Reconstruction as those in the novel and film *Gone with the Wind.*

W. E. B. Du Bois, the great African-American scholar, offered one of the first alternative views in *Black Reconstruction* (1935). To Du Bois, Reconstruction was an effort by freed blacks (and their white allies) to create a more democratic society in the South, and it was responsible for many valuable social innovations. In the early 1960s, John Hope Franklin and Kenneth Stampp, building on a generation of work by other scholars, published new histories of Reconstruction that also radically revised the Dunning interpretation. Reconstruction, they argued, was a genuine, if flawed, effort to solve the problem of race in the South. Congressional Radicals were not saints, but they were genuinely concerned with protecting the rights of former slaves. Reconstruction had brought important, if temporary, progress to the South and had created no more corruption there than governments were creating in the North at the same time. What was tragic about Reconstruction, the revisionists claimed, was not what it did to Southern whites but what it failed to do for Southern blacks. It was, in the end, too weak and too short-lived to guarantee African Americans genuine equality.

In more recent years, some historians have begun to question the assessment of the first revisionists that, in the end, Reconstruction accomplished relatively little. Leon Litwack argued in *Been in the Storm So Long* (1979) that former slaves used the protections Reconstruction offered them to carve out a certain level of independence for themselves within Southern society: strengthening churches, reuniting families, and resisting the efforts of white planters to revive the gang labor system.

Eric Foner's *Reconstruction: America's Unfinished Revolution* (1988) also emphasized how far African Americans moved toward freedom and independence in a short time and how important they were in shaping the execution of Reconstruction policies. Reconstruction, he argues, "can only be judged a failure" as an effort to secure "blacks' rights as citizens and free laborers." But it "closed off even more oppressive alternatives. . . . The post-Reconstruction labor system embodied neither a return to the closely supervised gang labor of antebellum days, nor the complete dispossession and immobilization of the black labor force and coercive apprenticeship systems envisioned by white Southerners in 1865 and 1866. Nor were blacks, as in twentieth-century South Africa, barred from citizenship, herded into labor reserves, or prohibited by law from moving from one part of the country to another. . . . The doors of economic opportunity that had opened could never be completely closed."

(text continued from page 403)

them for vagrancy, and hire them out to private employers to satisfy the fine. Some of the codes forbade blacks to own or lease farms or to take any jobs other than as plantation workers or domestic servants.

Congress first responded to the Black Codes by passing an act extending the life of the Freedmen's Bureau and widening its powers so that it could nullify work agreements forced on freedmen under the Black Codes. Then, in April 1866, Congress passed the first Civil Rights Act, which declared blacks to be citizens of the United States and gave the federal government power to intervene in state affairs to protect the rights of citizens. Johnson vetoed both bills, but Congress overrode him on each of them.

Johnson's Vetoes

The Fourteenth Amendment

In April 1866, the Joint Committee on Reconstruction proposed a new amendment to the Constitution, which Congress approved in early summer and sent to the states for ratification. The Fourteenth Amendment offered the first constitutional definition of American citizenship. Everyone born in the United States, and everyone naturalized, was automatically a citizen and entitled to all the "privileges and immunities" guaranteed by the Constitution, including equal protection of the laws by both the state and national governments. There could be no other requirements for citizenship. The amendment also imposed penalties on states that denied suffrage to any adult male inhabitants. (The wording reflected the prevailing view in Congress and elsewhere that the franchise was properly restricted to men.) Finally, it prohibited former members of Congress or other former federal officials who had aided the Confederacy from holding any state or federal office unless two-thirds of Congress voted to pardon them.

Citizenship for African Americans

Congressional Radicals offered to readmit to the Union any state whose legislature ratified the Fourteenth Amendment. Only Tennessee did so. All the other former Confederate states, along with Delaware and Kentucky, refused, leaving the amendment temporarily without the necessary approval of three-fourths of the states.

But by now, the Radicals were growing more confident and determined. Bloody race riots in New Orleans and other Southern cities were among the events that strengthened their hand. In the 1866 congressional elections, Johnson actively campaigned for Conservative candidates, but he did his own cause more harm than good with his intemperate speeches. The voters returned an overwhelming majority of Republicans, most of them Radicals, to Congress. In the Senate, there were now 42 Republicans to 11 Democrats; in the House, 143 Republicans to 49 Democrats. Congressional Republicans were now strong enough to enact a plan of their own even over the president's objections.

Radicals Ascendant

The Congressional Plan

The Radicals passed three Reconstruction bills early in 1867 and overrode Johnson's vetoes of all of them. These bills finally established, nearly two years after the end of the war, a coherent plan for Reconstruction.

Under the congressional plan, Tennessee, which had ratified the Fourteenth Amendment, was promptly readmitted. But Congress rejected the Lincoln-Johnson governments of the other ten Confederate states and, instead, combined those states into five military districts. A military commander governed each district and had orders to register qualified voters (defined as all adult black males and those white males who had not participated in the rebellion). Once registered, voters would elect conventions to prepare new state constitutions, which had to include provisions for black suffrage. Once voters ratified the new constitutions, they could elect state governments. Congress had to approve a state's constitution, and the state legislature had to ratify the Fourteenth Amendment. Once that happened, and once enough states ratified the amendment to make it part of the Constitution, then the former Confederate states could be restored to the Union.

By 1868, seven of the ten former Confederate states (Arkansas, North Carolina, South Carolina, Louisiana, Alabama, Georgia, and Florida) had fulfilled these conditions (including ratification of the Fourteenth Amendment, which now became part of the Constitution) and were readmitted to the Union. Conservative whites held up the return of Virginia and Texas until 1869 and Mississippi until 1870. By then, Congress had added an additional requirement for readmission—ratification of another consti-

Fifteenth Amendment   tutional amendment, the Fifteenth, which forbade the states and the federal government to deny suffrage to any citizen on account of "race, color, or previous condition of servitude." Ratification by the states was completed in 1870.

To stop the president from interfering with their plans, the congressional Radicals passed two remarkable laws of dubious constitutionality in

Tenure of Office Act   1867. One, the Tenure of Office Act, forbade the president to remove civil officials, including members of his own cabinet, without the consent of the Senate. The principal purpose of the law was to protect the job of Secretary of War Edwin M. Stanton, who was cooperating with the Radicals. The other law, the Command of the Army Act, prohibited the president from issuing military orders except through the commanding general of the army (General Grant), who could not be relieved or assigned elsewhere without the consent of the Senate.

The congressional Radicals also took action to stop the Supreme Court from interfering with their plans. In 1866, the Court had declared in the case of *Ex parte Milligan* that military tribunals were unconstitutional in places where civil courts were functioning. Radicals in Congress immediately proposed several bills that would require two-thirds of the justices to support any decision overruling a law of Congress, would deny

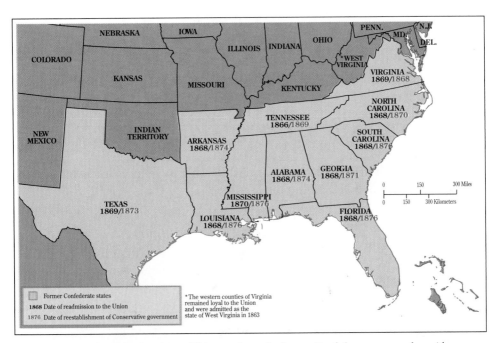

RECONSTRUCTION, 1866–1877 This map shows the former Confederate states and provides the dates when each was readmitted to the Union as well as a subsequent date when each state managed to return political power to traditional white, conservative elites—a process white southerners liked to call "redemption." • *What had to happen for a state to be readmitted to the Union? What had to happen before a state could experience "redemption"?*

the Court jurisdiction in Reconstruction cases, would reduce its membership to three, and would even abolish it. The justices apparently took notice. Over the next two years, the Court refused to accept jurisdiction in any cases involving Reconstruction.

The Impeachment of the President

President Johnson had long since ceased to be a serious obstacle to the passage of Radical legislation, but he was still the official charged with administering the Reconstruction programs. As such, the Radicals believed, he remained a major impediment to their plans. Early in 1867, they began looking for a way to impeach him and remove him from office. A search for grounds for impeachment began. Republicans found them, they believed, when Johnson dismissed Secretary of War Stanton despite Congress's refusal to agree. Elated Radicals in the House quickly impeached the president and sent the case to the Senate for trial.

The trial before the Senate lasted throughout April and May 1868. The Radicals put heavy pressure on all the Republican senators, but the Moderates vacillated. On the first three charges to come to a vote, seven Republi-

The President Acquitted cans joined the Democrats and independents to support acquittal. The vote was 35 to 19, one short of the constitutionally required two-thirds majority. After that, the Radicals dropped the impeachment effort.

THE SOUTH IN RECONSTRUCTION

Reconstruction may not have accomplished what its framers intended, but it did have profound effects on the South.

The Reconstruction Governments

"Scalawags" and "Carpetbaggers" Critics labeled Southern white Republicans with the derogatory terms "scalawags" and "carpetbaggers." Many of the "scalawags" were former Whigs who had never felt comfortable in the Democratic Party or farmers who lived in remote areas where there had been little or no slavery. The "carpetbaggers" were white men from the North, most of them veterans of the Union army who looked on the South as a new frontier, more promising than the West. They had settled there at war's end as hopeful planters, businessmen, or professionals.

Freedmen The most numerous Republicans in the South were the black freedmen, most of whom had no previous experience in politics and tried, therefore, to build institutions through which they could learn to exercise their power. In several states, African-American voters held their own conventions to chart their future course. Freedmen had created their own churches after emancipation, and this religious independence also helped give them unity and self-confidence.

African Americans played a significant role in the politics of the Reconstruction South. They served as delegates to the constitutional conventions. They held public offices of practically every kind. Between 1869 and 1901, twenty blacks served in the United States House of Representatives, two in the Senate. They served, too, in state legislatures and in various other state offices. Southern whites complained loudly about "Negro rule" during Reconstruction, but in the South as a whole, the percentage of black officeholders was always far lower than the percentage of blacks in the population.

The record of the Reconstruction governments is mixed. Critics at the time and later denounced them for corruption and financial extravagance, and there is some truth to both charges. But the corruption in the South, real as it was, was hardly unique to the Reconstruction governments. Corruption had been rife in some antebellum and Confederate governments, and it was at least as rampant in the Northern states. And the large state expenditures of the Reconstruction years were huge only in

A CELEBRATION OF RECONSTRUCTION The celebrated cartoonist Thomas Nast—best known for his savage caricatures of machine politicians in New York's Tammany Hall—drew this celebratory, and optimistic, image of Reconstruction not long after the end of the Civil War: a classical goddess restoring the former Confederate states to their rightful place within a symbolic fasces that represented union. In fact, the Reconstruction process proved much more difficult than this hopeful image suggested. *(North Wind Picture Archives)*

comparison with the meager budgets of the antebellum era. They represented an effort to provide the South with desperately needed services that antebellum governments had never offered.

Education

Perhaps the most important of the accomplishments of the Reconstruction governments was a dramatic improvement in Southern education. In the first years of Reconstruction, much of the impetus for educational reform in the South came from outside groups—from the Freedmen's Bureau, from Northern private philanthropic organizations, from the many Northern white women who traveled to the South to teach in freedmen's schools—and from African Americans themselves. Over the opposition of many Southern whites, who feared that education *Establishment of Black Schools* would give blacks "false notions of equality," these reformers established a large network of schools for former slaves—4,000 schools by 1870, staffed by 9,000 teachers (half of them black), teaching 200,000 students. In the 1870s, Reconstruction governments began to build a comprehensive public school system in the South. By 1876, more than half of all white children and about 40 percent of all black children were attending schools in the South (although almost all such schools were racially segregated). Several black "academies," offering more advanced education, also began operating. Gradually, these academies grew into an important network of black colleges and universities.

Landownership and Tenancy

The most ambitious goal of the Freedmen's Bureau, and of some Republican Radicals in Congress, was to reform landownership in the South. The effort failed. By June 1865, the bureau had settled nearly 10,000 black families on their own land—most of it drawn from abandoned plantations in areas occupied by the Union armies. By the end of that year, however, Southern plantation owners were returning and demanding the restoration of their property. President Johnson supported their demands, and the government eventually returned most of the confiscated lands to their original white owners.

Land Reform Thwarted

Even so, the distribution of landownership in the South changed considerably in the postwar years. Among whites, there was a striking decline in landownership, from 80 percent before the war to 67 percent by the end of Reconstruction. Some whites lost their land because of unpaid debt or increased taxes; some left the marginal lands they had owned to move to more fertile areas, where they rented. Among blacks, during the same period, the proportion who owned land rose from virtually none to more than 20 percent.

Still, most blacks, and a growing minority of whites, did not own their own land during Reconstruction, and some who acquired land in the 1860s had lost it by the 1890s. Instead, they worked for others in one form or another. Many black agricultural laborers—perhaps 25 percent of the total—simply worked for wages. Most, however, became tenants of white landowners—that is, they worked their own plots of land and paid their landlords either a fixed rent or a share of their crop (hence the term "sharecropping"). As tenants and sharecroppers, blacks enjoyed at least a physical independence from their landlords and had the sense of working their own land, even if in most cases they could never hope to buy it. But tenantry also benefited landlords in some ways, relieving them of the cost of purchasing slaves and of responsibility for the physical well-being of their workers.

Rapid Growth of Sharecropping

Incomes and Credit

In some respects, the postwar years were a period of remarkable economic progress for African Americans in the South. The per capita income of blacks (when the material benefits of slavery are counted as income) rose 46 percent between 1857 and 1879, while the per capita income of whites declined 35 percent. African Americans were also able to work less than they had under slavery. Women and children were less likely to labor in the fields, and adult men tended to work shorter days. In all, the black labor force worked about one-third fewer hours during Reconstruction than it had been compelled to work under slavery—a reduction that brought the working schedule of blacks roughly into accord with that of white farm laborers.

But other developments were limiting these gains. While the black share of profits was increasing, the total profits of Southern agriculture were declining. Nor did the income redistribution of the postwar years lift many blacks out of poverty. Black per capita in- *Persistent Black Poverty* come rose from about one-quarter of white per capita income (which was itself low) to about one-half in the first few years after the war. After this initial increase, however, it rose hardly at all.

Blacks and poor whites alike often found themselves virtually imprisoned by the crop-lien system. Few of the traditional institutions of credit in the South—the "factors" and banks—returned after the war. In their stead emerged a new system of credit, centered in large part on local country stores—some of them owned by planters, others owned by independent merchants. Blacks and whites, landowners *The "Crop-lien System"* and tenants—all depended on these stores. And since farmers did not have the same steady cash flow as other workers, customers usually had to rely on credit from these merchants in order to purchase what they needed. Most local stores had no competition. As a result, they were able to set interest rates as high as 50 or 60 percent. Farmers had to give the merchants a lien (or claim) on their crops as collateral for the loans (thus the term "crop-lien system," generally used to describe Southern farming in this period). Farmers who suffered a few bad years in a row, as many did, could become trapped in a cycle of debt from which they could never escape.

One effect of this burdensome credit system was that some blacks who had acquired land during the early years of Reconstruction gradually lost it as they fell into debt. Another was that Southern farmers became almost wholly dependent on cash crops—and most of all on cotton—because only such marketable commodities seemed to offer any possibility of escape from debt. The relentless planting of cotton contributed to an exhaustion of the soil. The crop-lien system, in other words, was not only helping to impoverish small farmers; it was also contributing to a general decline in the Southern agricultural economy.

AFTER SLAVERY Although most freed slaves remained agricultural laborers after Emancipation, a considerable number moved off the land in search of new occupations and new homes. For many, that meant living for some time without stable employment or a permanent home. This photograph from the late 1860s shows a group of former slaves at a county almshouse in the South. *(Bettmann/Corbis)*

The African-American Family in Freedom

A major reason for the rapid departure of so many blacks from plantations was the desire to find lost relatives and reunite families. Thousands of African Americans wandered through the South looking for husbands, wives, children, or other relatives from whom they had been separated. Former slaves rushed to have their marriages, previously without legal standing, sanctified by church and law.

Families Reunited

Within the black family, the definition of male and female roles quickly came to resemble that within white families. Many women and children ceased working in the fields. Such work, they believed, was a badge of slavery. Instead, many women restricted themselves largely to domestic tasks. Still, economic necessity often compelled black women to engage in income-producing activities: working as domestic servants, taking in laundry, or helping their husbands in the fields. By the end of Reconstruction, half of all black women over the age of sixteen were working for wages.

THE GRANT ADMINISTRATION

American voters in 1868 yearned for a strong, stable figure to guide them through the troubled years of Reconstruction. They turned trustingly to General Ulysses S. Grant.

The Soldier President

Grant could have had the nomination of either party in 1868. But believing that Republican Re- *Grant Elected* construction policies were more popular in the North, he accepted the Republican nomination. The Democrats nominated former governor Horatio Seymour of New York. The campaign was a bitter one, and Grant's triumph was surprisingly narrow. Without the 500,000 new black Republican voters in the South, he would have had a minority of the popular vote.

Grant entered the White House with no political experience, and his performance was clumsy and ineffectual from the start. Except for Hamilton Fish, whom Grant appointed secretary of state, most members of the cabinet were ill-equipped for their tasks. Grant relied chiefly on established party leaders—the group most ardently devoted to patronage, and his administration used the spoils system even more blatantly than most of its predecessors. Grant also alienated the many Northerners who were growing disillusioned with the Radical Reconstruction policies, which the president continued to support. Some Republicans suspected, correctly, that there was also corruption in the Grant administration itself.

By the end of Grant's first term, therefore, members of a substantial faction of the party—who referred to themselves as *Liberal Republicans* Liberal Republicans—had come to oppose what they called "Grantism." In 1872, hoping to prevent Grant's reelection, they bolted the party and nominated their own presidential candidate: Horace Greeley, veteran editor and publisher of the *New York Tribune*. The Democrats, somewhat reluctantly, named Greeley their candidate as well, hoping that the alliance with the Liberals would enable them to defeat Grant. But the effort was in vain. Grant won a substantial victory, polling 286 electoral votes to Greeley's 66.

The Grant Scandals

During the 1872 campaign, the first of a series of political scandals came to light that would plague Grant and the Republicans for the next eight years. It involved the French-owned Crédit Mobilier construction company, which had helped build the Union Pacific Railroad. The heads of Crédit Mobilier had used their positions as Union Pacific stockholders to steer large fraudulent contracts to their construction company, thus bilking the Union Pacific of millions. To prevent investigations, the directors had given Crédit Mobilier stock to key members of Congress. But in 1872, Congress did conduct an investigation, which revealed that some highly placed Republicans—including Schuyler Colfax, now Grant's vice president—had accepted stock.

One dreary episode followed another in Grant's second term. Benjamin H. Bristow, Grant's third Treasury secretary, discovered that some of his officials and a group of distillers operating as a "whiskey ring" were cheating the government *The "Whiskey Ring"* out of taxes by filing false reports. Then a House investigation revealed that William W. Belknap, secretary of war, had accepted bribes to retain an Indian-post trader in office (the so-called Indian ring). Other, lesser scandals added to the growing impression that "Grantism" had brought rampant corruption to government.

The Greenback Question

Compounding Grant's, and the nation's, problems was a financial crisis, known as the Panic of 1873. It began with the failure of a leading investment banking firm, Jay Cooke and Company, which had invested too heavily in postwar railroad building. There had been panics before—in 1819, 1837, and 1857—but this was the worst one yet.

Debtors now pressured the government to redeem federal war bonds with greenbacks, which would increase the amount of money in circulation. But Grant and most Republicans wanted a "sound" currency—based solidly on gold reserves—which would favor the interests of banks and other creditors. There was approximately $356 million in paper currency issued during the Civil War that was still in circulation. In 1873, the Treasury issued more in response to the panic. But in 1875, Republican leaders

Specie Resumption Act   in Congress passed the Specie Resumption Act. It provided that after January 1, 1879, the greenback dollars would be redeemed by the government and replaced with new certificates, firmly pegged to the price of gold. The law satisfied creditors, who had worried that debts would be repaid in paper currency of uncertain value. But "resumption" made things more difficult for debtors, because the gold-based money supply could not easily expand.

National Greenback Party   In 1875, the "greenbackers" formed their own political organization: the National Greenback Party. It failed to gain widespread support, but it did keep the money issue alive. The question of the proper composition of the currency was to remain one of the most controversial and enduring issues in late-nineteenth-century American politics.

Republican Diplomacy

The Johnson and Grant administrations achieved their greatest successes in foreign affairs. The accomplishments were the work not of the presidents themselves but of two outstanding secretaries of state: William H. Seward and Hamilton Fish.

An ardent expansionist, Seward acted with as much daring as the demands of Reconstruction politics and the Republican hatred of President

Purchase of Alaska   Johnson would permit. Seward accepted a Russian offer to sell Alaska to the United States for $7.2 million, despite criticism from many who derided the purchase as "Seward's Folly." In 1867, Seward also engineered the American annexation of the tiny Midway Islands, west of Hawaii.

Hamilton Fish's first major challenge was resolving the longstanding controversy with England over the American claims that it had violated neutrality laws during the Civil War by permitting English shipyards to build ships (among them the *Alabama*) for the Confederacy. American demands that England pay for the damage these vessels had caused became known as the *"Alabama* claims." In 1871, after a number of failed efforts, Fish forged an agreement, *"Alabama Claims" Resolved* the Treaty of Washington, which provided for international arbitration.

THE ABANDONMENT OF RECONSTRUCTION

As the North grew increasingly preoccupied with its own political and economic problems, interest in Reconstruction began to wane. By the time Grant left office, Democrats had taken back seven of the governments of the former Confederate states. For three other states—South Carolina, Louisiana, and Florida—the end of Reconstruction had to wait for the withdrawal of the last federal troops in 1877.

The Southern States "Redeemed"

In the states where whites constituted a majority—the states of the upper South—overthrowing Republican control was relatively simple. By 1872, all but a handful of Southern whites had regained suffrage. Now a clear majority, they needed only to organize and elect their candidates.

In other states, where blacks were a majority or where the populations of the two races were almost equal, whites used intimidation and violence to undermine the Reconstruction regimes. Secret societies—the Ku Klux Klan, the Knights of the *Ku Klux Klan* White Camellia, and others—used terrorism to frighten or physically bar blacks from voting. Paramilitary organizations—the Red Shirts and White Leagues—armed themselves to "police" elections and worked to force all white males to join the Democratic Party. Strongest of all, however, was the simple weapon of economic pressure. Some planters refused to rent land to Republican blacks; storekeepers refused to extend them credit; employers refused to give them work.

The Republican Congress responded to this wave of repression with the Enforcement Acts of 1870 and 1871 (better known as the Ku Klux Klan Acts), which prohibited states from discriminating against voters on the basis of race and gave the national government the authority to prosecute crimes by individuals under federal law. The laws also authorized the president to use federal troops to protect civil rights—a provision President Grant used in 1871 in nine counties of South Carolina. The Enforcement Acts, although seldom enforced, discouraged Klan violence, which declined by 1872.

Waning Northern Commitment

But this Northern commitment to civil rights in the South did not last very long. After the adoption of the Fifteenth Amendment in 1870, some reformers convinced themselves that their long campaign on behalf of black people was now over, that with the vote blacks ought to be able to take care of themselves. Former Radical leaders such as Charles Sumner and Horace Greeley now began calling themselves Liberals, cooperating with the Democrats, and denouncing what they viewed as black-and-carpetbag misgovernment. Within the South itself, many white Republicans now moved into the Democratic Party.

Flagging Interest in Civil Rights

The Panic of 1873 further undermined support for Reconstruction. In the congressional elections of 1874, the Democrats won control of the House of Representatives for the first time since 1861. Grant reduced the use of military force to prop up the Republican regimes in the South.

By the end of 1876, only three states were left in the hands of the Republicans—South Carolina, Louisiana, and Florida. In the state elections that year, Democrats (after using terrorist tactics) claimed victory in all three. But the Republicans claimed victory as well and were able to remain in office because of the presence of federal troops.

The Compromise of 1877

Grant had hoped to run for another term in 1876, but most Republican leaders—shaken by recent Democratic successes and the scandals with which Grant was associated—resisted. Instead, they settled on Rutherford B. Hayes, three-time governor of Ohio and a champion of civil service reform. The Democrats united behind Samuel J. Tilden, the reform governor of New York, who had been instrumental in overthrowing the corrupt Tweed Ring of New York City's Tammany Hall.

Although the campaign was a bitter one, there were few differences of principle between the candidates. The November election produced an apparent Democratic victory. Tilden carried the South and several large Northern states, and his popular margin over Hayes was nearly 300,000 votes. But disputed returns from Louisiana, South Carolina, Florida, and Oregon, whose electoral votes totaled 20, threw the election in doubt. Hayes could still win if he managed to receive all 20 disputed votes.

Disputed Election

The Constitution had established no method to determine the validity of disputed returns. The decision clearly lay with Congress, but it was not clear with which house or through what method. (The Senate was Republican, and the House was Democratic.) Members of each party naturally supported a solution that would yield them the victory. Finally, late in January 1877, Congress tried to break the deadlock by creating a special electoral commission composed of five senators, five representatives, and five justices of the Supreme

Special Electoral Commission

AFRICAN-AMERICAN WORK AFTER SLAVERY Black men and women engaged in a wide range of economic activities in the aftermath of slavery. But discrimination by white Southerners and the former slaves' own lack of education limited most of them to relatively menial jobs. Many black women (including this former slave) earned money for their families by working as "washer women," doing laundry for white people. *(Historic New Orleans Collection)*

Court. The congressional delegation would consist of five Republicans and five Democrats. The Court delegation would include two Republicans, two Democrats, and the only independent, Justice David Davis. But when the Illinois legislature elected Davis to the United States Senate, the justice resigned from the commission. His seat went instead to a Republican justice. The commission voted along straight party lines, 8 to 7, awarding every disputed vote to Hayes.

Behind the resolution of the deadlock, however, lay a series of elaborate compromises among leaders of both parties. When a Democratic filibuster threatened to derail the commission's report, Republican Senate leaders met secretly with Southern Democratic leaders to work out terms by which the Democrats would support Hayes. As the price of their cooperation, the Southern Democrats exacted several pledges from the Republicans: the appointment of at least one Southerner to the Hayes cabinet, control of federal patronage in their areas, generous internal improvements, federal aid for the Texas and Pacific Railroad, and withdrawal of the troops. Many powerful Southern Democrats believed that Republican programs of federal support for business and industry would help their region develop economically.

In his inaugural address, Hayes announced that the South's most pressing need was the restoration of "wise, honest, and peaceful local self-
Federal Troops Withdrawn   government," and he soon withdrew the troops and let white Democrats take over the remaining southern state governments. That produced charges that he was paying off the South for acquiescing in his election. But the election had already created such bitterness that not even Hayes's promise to serve only one term could mollify his critics.

The president and his party hoped to build up a "new Republican" organization in the South committed to modest support for black rights. But although many white Southern leaders sympathized with Republican economic policies, resentment of Reconstruction was so deep that supporting the party was politically impossible. The "solid" Democratic South, which would survive until the mid-twentieth century, was taking shape.

The Legacy of Reconstruction

Reconstruction made important contributions to the efforts of former slaves to achieve dignity and equality in American life. There was a significant redistribution of income. There was a more limited but not unim-
Lasting Contributions   portant redistribution of landownership. Perhaps most important, there was a large, and largely successful, effort by African Americans themselves to carve out a society and culture of their own and to create or strengthen their own institutions.

Reconstruction was not as disastrous an experience for Southern white elites as most believed at the time. Within little more than a decade after the end of a devastating war, the white South had regained control of its own institutions and, to a great extent, restored its traditional ruling class to power. The federal government imposed no drastic economic reforms on the region, and indeed few lasting political changes of any kind other than the abolition of slavery.

Reconstruction was notable, finally, for its limitations. For in those years the United States failed in its first serious effort to resolve its oldest and deepest social problem—the problem of race. What was more, the ex-

perience so disillusioned white Americans that it
would be nearly a century before they would try
again to combat racial injustice.

Limits of Reconstruction

Given the odds confronting them, however, African Americans had
reason for considerable pride in the gains they were able to make during
Reconstruction. And future generations could be grateful for two great
charters of freedom—the Fourteenth and Fifteenth Amendments to the
Constitution—which, although widely ignored at the time, would one day
serve as the basis for a "Second Reconstruction" that would renew the
drive to bring freedom to all Americans.

THE NEW SOUTH

The agreement between southern Democrats and northern Republicans
that helped settle the disputed election of 1876 was supposed to be the
first step toward developing a stable, permanent Republican Party in the
South. In that respect, at least, it failed. In the years following the end of
Reconstruction, white southerners established the Democratic Party as
the only viable political organization for the region's whites. Even so, the
South did change in some of the ways the framers of the Compromise of
1877 had hoped.

The "Redeemers"

Many white southerners rejoiced at the restoration
of what they liked to call "home rule." But in real-

"Home Rule"

ity, political power in the region was soon more restricted than at any time
since the Civil War. Once again, most of the South fell under the control
of a powerful, conservative oligarchy, whose members were known vari-
ously as the "Redeemers" or the "Bourbons."

In some places, this post-Reconstruction ruling class was much the
same as the ruling class of the antebellum period. In Alabama, for example, the old planter elite retained much of its former power. In other areas,
however, the Redeemers constituted a genuinely new ruling class. They
were merchants, industrialists, railroad developers, and financiers. Some
of them were former planters, some of them northern immigrants, some
of them ambitious, upwardly mobile white southerners from the region's
lower social tiers. They combined a commitment to "home rule" and social conservatism with a commitment to economic development.

The various Bourbon governments of the New South behaved in
many respects quite similarly. Virtually all the new Democratic regimes
lowered taxes, reduced spending, and drastically diminished state services.
One state after another eliminated or reduced its support for public school
systems.

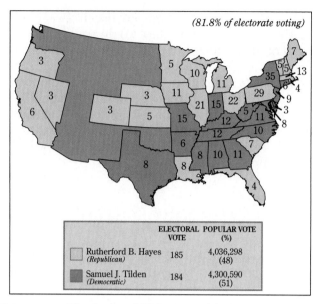

(81.8% of electorate voting)

	ELECTORAL VOTE	POPULAR VOTE (%)
Rutherford B. Hayes *(Republican)*	185	4,036,298 (48)
Samuel J. Tilden *(Democratic)*	184	4,300,590 (51)

THE ELECTION OF 1876 The election of 1876 was one of the most controversial in American history. As in the elections of 1824, 1888, and 2000, the winner of the popular vote—Samuel J. Tilden—was not the winner of the electoral college, which he lost by one vote. The final decision as to who would be president was not made until the day before the official Inauguration in March. ◆ *How did the Republicans turn this apparent defeat into a victory?*

For an interactive version of this map go to www.mhhe.com/unfinishednation4ch15maps

Industrialization and the "New South"

Many white southern leaders in the post-Reconstruction era hoped to see their region become the home of a vigorous industrial economy, a "New South." Henry Grady, editor of the *Atlanta Constitution*, and other New South advocates seldom challenged white supremacy, but they did promote the virtues of thrift, industry, and progress—qualities that prewar southerners had often denounced in northern society.

Henry Grady

Southern industry did expand dramatically in the years after Reconstruction. Most visible was the growth in textile manufacturing. In the past, southern planters had usually shipped their cotton out of the region to manufacturers in the North or in Europe. Now textile factories appeared in the South itself—many of them drawn to the region from New England by the abundance of water power, the ready supply of cheap labor, the low taxes, and the accommodating conservative governments. The tobacco-processing industry, similarly, established an important foothold in the region. In the lower South, and particularly in Birmingham, Alabama, the iron (and, later, steel) industry grew rapidly.

Substantial Railroad Development

Railroad development also increased substantially in the post-Reconstruction years. Between 1880 and 1890, trackage in the South more than doubled. And in 1886, the South changed the gauge (width) of its trackage to correspond with the standards of the North. No longer would it be necessary for cargoes heading into the South to be transferred from one train to another at the borders of the region.

Yet southern industry developed within strict limits, and its effects on the region were never even remotely comparable to the effects of industrialization on the North. The southern share of national manufacturing doubled in the last twenty years of the century, but it was still only 10 percent of the total. The region's per capita income increased 21 percent in the same period, but average income in the South was still only 40 percent of that in the North; in 1860 it had been more than 60 percent. And even in those industries where development had been most rapid—textiles, iron, railroads—much of the capital had come from, and many of the profits thus flowed to, the North.

The growth of industry in the South required the region to recruit a substantial industrial work force for the first time. From the beginning, a high percentage of the factory workers were women. Heavy male casualties in the Civil War had helped create a large population of unmarried women who desperately needed employment. *Worker Exploitation* Hours were long (often as much as twelve hours a day), and wages were far below the northern equivalent; indeed, one of the greatest attractions of the South to industrialists was that employers were able to pay workers there as little as one-half what northern workers received. Life in most mill towns was rigidly controlled by the owners and managers of the factories. They rigorously suppressed attempts at protest or union organization. Company stores sold goods to workers at inflated prices and issued credit at exorbitant rates (much like country stores in agrarian areas), and mill owners ensured that no competing merchants were able to establish themselves in the community.

Some industries, such as textiles, offered virtually no opportunities to African-American workers. Others—tobacco, iron, and lumber, for example—did provide some employment for blacks. Some mill towns, therefore, were places where the black and white cultures came into close contact. This juxtaposition of cultures inhibited the growth of racial harmony and increased the determination of white leaders to take additional measures to protect white supremacy.

Tenants and Sharecroppers

The most important economic reality in the post-Reconstruction South was the impoverished state of agriculture. The *Impoverished Agriculture* 1870s and 1880s saw an acceleration of the process that had begun in the immediate postwar years: the imposition of systems of tenantry and debt peonage on much of the region; the reliance on a few cash crops rather than on a diversified agricultural system; and increasing absentee ownership of valuable farmlands. During Reconstruction, perhaps a third or more of the farmers in the South were tenants; by 1900 the figure had increased to 70 percent.

Tenantry took several forms. Farmers who owned tools, equipment, and farm animals usually paid an annual cash rent for their land. But many farmers (including most black ones) had no money or equipment at all. Landlords would supply them with land, a crude house, a few tools, seed, and sometimes a mule. In return, the farmers would promise the landlord a large share of the annual crop. After paying their landlords and their local furnishing merchants (who were often the same people), these "sharecroppers" seldom had anything left to sell on their own.

African Americans and the New South

The "New South creed" was not the property of whites alone. Many African Americans were attracted to the vision of progress and self-improvement as well. Some blacks succeeded in elevating themselves into a distinct middle class. These were former slaves (and, as the decades passed, their offspring) who managed to acquire property, establish small businesses, or enter professions. This rising group of African Americans believed strongly that education was vital to the future of their people, and they expanded the network of black colleges and institutes that had taken root during Reconstruction into an important educational system.

Booker T. Washington

The chief spokesman for this commitment to education was Booker T. Washington, founder and president of the Tuskegee Institute in Alabama. Born into slavery, Washington had worked his way out of poverty after acquiring an education (at Virginia's Hampton Institute). He urged other blacks to follow the same road to self-improvement.

Washington's message was both cautious and hopeful. African Americans should attend school, learn skills, and establish a solid footing in agriculture and the trades. Industrial, not classical, education should be their goal. Blacks should, moreover, refine their speech, improve their dress, and adopt habits of thrift and personal cleanliness; they should, in short, adopt the standards of the white middle class. Only thus, he claimed, could they win the respect of the white population.

In a famous speech in Georgia in 1895, Washington outlined a controversial philosophy of race relations that became widely known as the

Atlanta Compromise

Atlanta Compromise. Blacks, he said, should forgo agitating for political rights and concentrate on self-improvement and preparation for equality. Washington offered a powerful challenge to those whites who wanted to discourage African Americans from acquiring an education or winning any economic gains. But his message was also intended to assure whites that blacks would not challenge the system of segregation, which southern governments were in the process of creating.

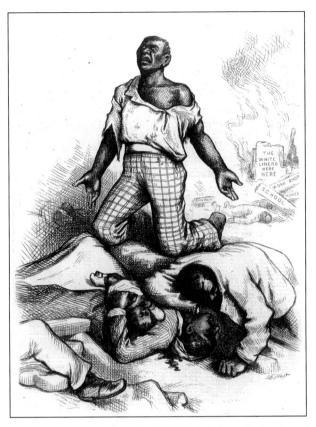

"IS THIS A REPUBLICAN FORM OF GOVERNMENT?" The New York artist and cartoonist
Thomas Nast marked the end of Reconstruction in 1876 with this biting cartoon in *Harper's
Weekly*, expressing his dismay at what he considered the nation's betrayal of the former slaves,
who still had not received adequate guarantees of their rights. The caption of the cartoon
continued: "Is *this* protecting life, liberty, or property? Is *this* equal protection of the laws?"
(The Newberry Library, Chicago, Illinois)

The Birth of Jim Crow

Few white southerners had ever accepted the idea of racial equality. That
the former slaves acquired any legal and political rights at all after emancipation was in large part the result of their own efforts and critical federal
support. That outside support all but vanished after 1877, when federal
troops withdrew and the Supreme Court stripped the Fourteenth and Fifteenth Amendments of much of their significance. In the so-called civil
rights cases of 1883, the Court ruled that the Fourteenth Amendment prohibited state governments from discriminating against people because of
race but did not restrict private organizations or individuals from doing so.

Eventually, the Court also validated state legislation that institutionalized
the separation of the races. In *Plessy* v. *Ferguson*
(1896), a case involving a Louisiana law that required

Plessy v. Ferguson

TUSKEGEE INSTITUTE, 1881 From these modest beginnings, Booker T. Washington's Tuskegee Institute in Alabama became the preeminent academy offering technical and industrial training to black men. It deliberately de-emphasized the traditional liberal arts curricula of most colleges. Washington considered such training less important than developing practical skills. *(Bettmann/Corbis)*

separate seating arrangements for the races on railroads, the Court held that separate accommodations did not deprive blacks of equal rights if the accommodations were equal. In *Cumming* v. *County Board of Education* (1899), the Court ruled that communities could establish schools for whites only, even if there were no comparable schools for blacks.

Even before these decisions, white southerners were working to separate the races to the greatest extent possible. They were particularly determined to strip African Americans of the right to vote. In some states, disenfranchisement had begun almost as soon as Reconstruction ended. But in other areas, black voting continued for some time after Reconstruction—largely because conservative whites believed they could control the black electorate and use it to beat back the attempts of poor white farmers to take control of the Democratic Party.

In the 1890s, however, franchise restrictions became much more rigid. During those years, some small white farmers began to demand complete

Black Disenfranchisement black disenfranchisement—because they objected to the black vote being used against them by the Bourbons. At the same time, many members of the conservative elite began to fear that poor whites might unite politically with poor blacks to challenge them.

In devising laws to disenfranchise black males, the southern states had to find ways to evade the Fifteenth Amendment, which prohibited states from denying anyone the right to vote because of race. Two devices emerged before 1900 to accomplish this goal. One was the poll tax or some form of property qualification; few blacks were prosperous enough to meet such requirements. Another was the "literacy" or "understanding" test, which required voters to demonstrate an ability to read and to interpret the Constitution. Even those African Americans who could read had a hard time passing the difficult test white officials gave them. The laws affected poor white voters as well as blacks. By the late 1890s, the black vote had decreased by 62 percent, the white vote by 26 percent.

Laws restricting the franchise and segregating schools were only part of a network of state and local statutes—known as the Jim Crow laws—that by the first years of the *Jim Crow Laws* twentieth century had institutionalized an elaborate system of segregation reaching into almost every area of southern life. Blacks and whites could not ride together in the same railroad cars, sit in the same waiting rooms, use the same washrooms, eat in the same restaurants, or sit in the same theaters. Blacks had no access to many public parks, beaches, or picnic areas; they could not be patients in many hospitals. Much of the new legal structure did no more than confirm what had already been widespread social practice in the South. But the Jim Crow laws also stripped blacks of many of the modest social, economic, and political gains they had made in the late nineteenth century.

More than legal efforts were involved in this process. The 1890s witnessed a dramatic increase in white violence against blacks, which, along with the Jim Crow laws, served to inhibit black agitation for equal rights. The worst such violence—lynching of blacks by white mobs—reached appalling levels. In the nation as a whole in the 1890s, there was an average of 187 lynchings each year, more than 80 percent of them in the South. The vast majority of victims were black. Those who participated in lynchings often saw their actions as a legitimate form of law enforcement, and some victims of lynchings had in fact committed crimes. But lynchings were also a means by which whites controlled the black population through terror and intimidation.

The rise of lynchings shocked the conscience of many white Americans in a way that other forms of racial injustice did not. *Ida B. Wells* In 1892 Ida B. Wells, a committed black journalist, launched what became an international anti-lynching movement with a series of impassioned articles after the lynching of three of her friends in Memphis, Tennessee, her home. The movement gradually gathered strength in the first years of the twentieth century, attracting substantial support from whites in both the North and South (particularly from white women). Its goal was a federal anti-lynching law, which would allow the national government to do what state and local governments in the South were generally unwilling to do: punish those responsible for lynchings.

But the substantial southern white opposition to lynchings stood as an exception to the general white support for suppression of African Americans. Indeed, just as in the antebellum period, the shared commitment to white supremacy helped dilute class animosities between poorer whites and the Bourbon oligarchies. Economic issues tended to play a secondary role to race in southern politics, distracting people from the glaring social inequalities that afflicted blacks and whites alike.

CONCLUSION

Reconstruction was a profoundly important moment in American history. Despite the bitter political battles in Washington and throughout the South, culminating in the unsuccessful effort to remove President Andrew Johnson from office, the most important result of the effort to reunite the nation after its long and bloody war was a reshaping of the lives of ordinary people in all regions of the nation.

In the North, Reconstruction solidified the power of the Republican Party. The rapid expansion of the northern economy continued and accelerated, drawing more and more of its residents into a burgeoning commercial world.

In the South, Reconstruction fundamentally rearranged the relationship between the region's white and black citizens. Only for a while did Reconstruction permit African Americans to participate actively and effectively in southern politics. After a few years of widespread black voting and significant black officeholding, the forces of white supremacy forced most African Americans to the margins of the southern political world, where they would mostly remain until the 1960s.

In other ways, the lives of southern blacks changed dramatically and permanently. Overwhelmingly, they left the plantations. Some sought work in towns and cities. Some left the region altogether. But the great majority began farming on small farms of their own—not as landowners, except in rare cases, but as tenants and sharecroppers on land owned by whites. The result was a form of economic bondage, driven by debt, only scarcely less oppressive than the legal bondage of slavery. Within this system, however, African Americans managed to carve out a much larger sphere of social and cultural activity than they had ever been able to create under slavery. Black churches proliferated in great numbers. African-American schools emerged in some communities, and black colleges began to operate in the region. Some former slaves owned businesses and flourished.

Strenuous efforts by "New South" advocates to advance industry and commerce in the region produced significant results in a few areas. But the South on the whole remained what it had always been: an overwhelmingly rural society with a sharply defined class structure. It was also a region with a deep commitment among its white citizens to the subordination of African Americans—a commitment solidified in the 1890s and the early twentieth century when white southerners erected an elaborate legal system of segregation (the "Jim Crow" laws). The promise of the great Reconstruction amendments to the Constitution—the Fourteenth and Fifteenth—remained largely unfulfilled in the South as the century drew to its close.

FOR FURTHER REFERENCE

Eric Foner, *Reconstruction: America's Unfinished Revolution, 1863–1877* (1988), the most important modern synthesis of Reconstruction scholarship, emphasizes the radicalism of Reconstruction and the agency of freed people in the process of political and economic renovation. David W. Blight, *Race and Reunion: The Civil War in American Memory* (2001) is an excellent study of the ways in which Americans reinterpreted the Civil War in the late nineteenth century. Amy Dru Stanley, *From Bondage to Contract: Wage Labor, Marriage, and the Market in the Age of Slave Emancipation* (1998) and Jeffrey R. Kerr-Ritchie, *Freedpeople in the Tobacco South: Virginia, 1860–1900* (1999) are important examinations of African-American labor during and after Emancipation. Thomas Holt, *Black over White: Negro Political Leadership in South Carolina During Reconstruction* (1977) examines Reconstruction in the state where black political power reached its apex. C. Vann Woodward, *Origins of the New South* (1951), a classic work on the history of the South after Reconstruction, argues that a rising middle class defined the economic and political transformation of the New South. Edward Ayers, *The Promise of the New South* (1992) offers a rich portrait of social and cultural life in the New South. Jacqueline Jones, *Labor of Love, Labor of Sorrow* (1985) examines the lives of African-American women after Emancipation. Mia Bay, *The White Image in the Black Mind: African-American Ideas about White People, 1830–1925* (2000) is a valuable study of African-American attitudes toward white society. Leon Litwack, *Been in the Storm So Long: The Aftermath of Slavery* (1979) is a major study of the experiences of freed slaves. C. Vann Woodward, *The Strange Career of Jim Crow* (rev. 1974) claims that segregation emerged only gradually across the South after Reconstruction. The "Woodward Thesis" has been challenged by, among others, Joel Williamson, *After Slavery: The Negro in South Carolina During Reconstruction* (1965); John W. Cell, *The Highest Stage of White Supremacy: The Origins of Segregation in South Africa and the American South* (1982); and Howard N. Rabinowitz, *Race Relations in the Urban South, 1865–1890* (1978).

For quizzes, Internet resources, references to additional books and films, and more, consult this book's Online Learning Center site at www.mhhe.com/unfinishednation4.

***AMERICAN PROGRESS*, 1872**   John Gast, an artist in Brooklyn, New York, painted this tribute to westward expansion—a picture of hardy pioneers marching toward the frontier, protected by the goddess of progress—at the request of a publisher of travel guides. Engravings adapted from the painting appeared in one guidebook, and color reproductions were offered to customers as a bonus for subscribing to others. It is an example of the wide-ranging promotional effort—by railroads, landowners, farm-equipment manufacturers, even guidebook publishers—designed to persuade Americans to move into the western territories in the late nineteenth century.
(Oil on canvas, American Progress, *1872, by John Gast; Autry Museum of Western Heritage, Los Angeles)*

TIME LINE

1862	1865-1867	1866	1869	1873	1874	1876	
Homestead Act	Sioux Wars	Western cattle bonanza begins	Transcontinental railroad completed	Barbed wire invented	Black Hills gold rush	Battle of Little Bighorn	

~&~

THE CONQUEST
OF THE FAR WEST

The Societies of the Far West
The Changing Western Economy
The Romance of the West
The Dispersal of the Tribes
The Rise and Decline of the Western Farmer

B y the mid-1840s migrants from the eastern regions of the nation had
settled in the West in substantial numbers. Farmers, ranchers, and
miners all found opportunity in the western lands. By the end of the
Civil War, the West had become legendary in the eastern states. No
longer the Great American Desert, it was now the "frontier": an empty
land awaiting settlement and civilization; a place of wealth, adventure, opportunity, and untrammeled individualism.

In fact, the real West of the mid-nineteenth century bore little resem-
blance to its popular image. It was a diverse land, with many different regions, many different climates, many different stores of natural resources. And it was extensively populated. The English-speaking migrants
of the late nineteenth century did not find an empty, desolate land. They
found Indians, Mexicans, French and British Canadians, Asians, and others, some of whose families had been living in the West for generations.

1877	1882	1885	1887	1889	1890	1893	
Desert Land Act	Chinese Exclusion Act	Twain's *Huckleberry Finn*	Dawes Act	Oklahoma opened to white settlement	Battle of Wounded Knee	Turner's "Frontier Thesis"	

THE SOCIETIES OF THE FAR WEST

The Far West was in fact many lands. It contained some of the most arid territory in the United States, and some of the wettest and lushest. It contained the flattest plains and the highest mountains. And it contained many peoples.

The Western Tribes

The largest and most important western population group before the great white migration from the East was the Indian tribes. Some were members of eastern tribes who had been forcibly resettled west of the Mississippi. But most were members of tribes indigenous to the West.

The western tribes had developed a number of patterns of civilization. More than 300,000 Indians (among them the Serrano, Chumash, Pomo, Maidu, Yurok, and Chinook) had lived on the Pacific coast before the arrival of Spanish settlers, supporting themselves through a combination of fishing, foraging, and simple agriculture. The Pueblos of the Southwest had long lived largely as farmers and had established permanent settlements there.

Plains Indians   The most widespread Indian groups in the West were the Plains Indians. They were, in fact, made up of many different tribal and language groups. Some lived more or less sedentary lives as farmers. But many of the Plains tribes subsisted largely through hunting buffalo. Riding small but powerful horses, the tribes moved through the grasslands following the herds. When a band halted, it constructed tepees as temporary dwellings. The buffalo, or bison, provided the economic basis for the Plains Indians' way of life. The flesh of the large animal was their principal source of food, and its skin supplied materials for clothing, shoes, tepees, blankets, robes, and utensils. "Buffalo chips"—dried manure—provided fuel; buffalo bones became knives and arrow tips; buffalo tendons formed the strings of bows.

The Plains warriors proved to be the most formidable foes white settlers had encountered. But the various tribes were usually unable to unite against white aggression. At times, tribal warriors faced white forces who were being assisted by guides and even fighters from other, usually rival, tribes. Some tribes, however, were able to overcome their divisions and unite effectively. By the mid-nineteenth century, for example, the Sioux, Arapaho, and Cheyenne had forged a powerful alliance that dominated the northern plains. That proved no protection, however, against the greatest danger to the tribes: ecological and economic decline. Indians were highly vulnerable to eastern infectious diseases. Smallpox epidemics, for example, decimated the Pawnees in Nebraska in the 1840s. And the tribes were, of

Indian Disadvantages   course, at a considerable disadvantage in any long-term battle with an economically and industrially advanced people. They were, in the end, outmanned and outgunned.

Hispanic New Mexico

For centuries, much of the Far West had been part of, first, the Spanish Empire and, later, the Mexican Republic. When the United States acquired its new lands there in the 1840s, it acquired many Mexican residents at the same time.

In New Mexico, the centers of Spanish-speaking society were the farming and trading communities the Spanish had established in the seventeenth century. Descendants of the original Spanish settlers (and more recent migrants from Mexico) engaged primarily in cattle and sheep ranching. When the United States acquired title to New Mexico in the aftermath of the Mexican War, General Stephen Kearny—who had commanded the American troops in the region during the conflict—tried to establish a territorial government out of the approximately 1,000 Anglo-Americans in the region, ignoring the over 50,000 Hispanics. There were widespread fears among the Hispanics and Indians that the new American rulers of the region would confiscate their lands. In 1847, before the new government had established itself, Taos Indians re- *Taos Indian Rebellion* belled; they killed the new governor and other Anglo-American officials before being subdued by United States Army forces. New Mexico remained under military rule for three years, until the United States finally organized a territorial government there in 1850. The United States Army finally broke the power of the Navajo, Apache, and other tribes in the region. The defeat of the tribes led to substantial Hispanic migration into other areas of the Southwest and as far north as Colorado.

The Anglo-American presence in the Southwest grew rapidly once the railroads established lines into the region in the 1880s and early 1890s. With the railroads came extensive new ranching, farming, and mining. The expansion of economic activity in the region attracted a new wave of Mexican immigrants, who moved across the border in search of work. The English-speaking proprietors of the new enterprises restricted most Mexicans to the lowest-paying and least stable jobs.

Hispanic California and Texas

In California, Spanish settlement began in the eighteenth century with a string of Christian missions along the Pacific coast. The missionaries and the soldiers who accompanied them gathered most of the coastal Indians into their communities, some forcibly and some by persuasion. In the 1830s, after the new Mexican government began reducing the power of the church, the mission society largely collapsed. In its place emerged a secular Mexican aristocracy, which controlled a chain of large estates in the fertile lands west of the Sierra mountains. For them, the acquisition of California by the United States was disastrous. So vast were the numbers of English-speaking immigrants that the *californios* *Anglo-American Onslaught* (as the Hispanic residents of the region were known) had little power to resist the onslaught. English-speaking prospectors organized to exclude them, sometimes violently, from the mines during the gold rush. Many *californios* also lost their lands—either through corrupt business deals or through outright seizure.

Increasingly, Mexicans and Mexican Americans became part of the lower end of the state's working class, clustered in *barrios* in Los Angeles or elsewhere or laboring as migrant farmworkers. Even small Hispanic landowners who managed to hang on to their farms found themselves unable to raise livestock, as once-communal grazing lands fell under the control of powerful Anglo ranchers.

Hispanics Oppressed   A similar pattern occurred in Texas after it joined the United States. Many Mexican landowners lost their land—some as a result of fraud and coercion, some because even the most substantial Mexican ranchers could not compete with the enormous Anglo-American ranching kingdoms that were emerging. In 1859, angry Mexicans, led by the rancher Juan Cortina, raided the jail in Brownsville and freed all the Mexican prisoners inside. But such resistance had little long-term effect. As in California, Mexicans in southern Texas became an increasingly impoverished working class relegated largely to unskilled farm or industrial labor.

The Chinese Migration

At the same time that ambitious or impoverished Europeans were crossing the Atlantic in search of opportunities in the New World, many Chinese were crossing the Pacific in hopes of better lives. Not all came to the United States. Many Chinese moved to Hawaii, Australia, Latin America, South Africa, and even the Caribbean—some as "coolies" (indentured servants whose condition was close to slavery).

Increasing Chinese Immigration   A few Chinese traveled to the American West even before the gold rush, but after 1848 the flow increased dramatically. By 1880, more than 200,000 Chinese had settled in the United States. Almost all came as free laborers. For a time, white Americans welcomed the Chinese as a conscientious, hardworking people. Very quickly, however, white opinion turned hostile—in part because the Chinese were so industrious and successful that some white Americans began considering them rivals.

In the early 1850s, large numbers of Chinese immigrants joined the hunt for gold. Many of them were well-organized, hardworking prospectors, and for a time some of them enjoyed considerable success. But opportunities for Chinese to prosper in the mines were fleeting. In 1852, the California legislature began trying to exclude the Chinese from gold mining by enacting a "foreign miners" tax. Gradually, the effect of the discriminatory laws, the hostility of white miners, and the declining profitability of the surface mines drove most Chinese out of prospecting.

A CHINESE FAMILY IN SAN FRANCISCO Like many other Americans, Chinese families liked to pose for photographic portraits in the late nineteenth century. And like many other immigrants, they often sent them back to relatives in China. This portrait of Chun Duck Chin and his seven-year-old son Chun Jan Yut was taken in a studio in San Francisco in the 1870s. Both father and son appear to have dressed up for the occasion, in traditional Chinese garb, and the studio—which likely took many such portraits of Chinese families—provided a formal Chinese backdrop. The son is holding what appears to be a chicken, perhaps to impress relatives in China with the family's prosperity. *(The National Archives and Records Administration)*

As mining declined as a source of wealth and jobs for the Chinese, railroad employment grew. Beginning in 1865, over 12,000 Chinese found work building the transcontinental railroad. In fact, *Transcontinental Railroad* Chinese workers formed 90 percent of the labor force of the Central Pacific. The company preferred them to white laborers because they worked hard, made few demands, and accepted relatively low wages.

Work on the Central Pacific was arduous and often dangerous. In the winter, many Chinese tunneled into snow banks at night to create warm sleeping areas for themselves, even though such tunnels frequently collapsed, suffocating those inside. In the spring of 1866, 5,000 Chinese railroad workers rebelled against the terrible conditions of their work and went on strike demanding higher wages and a shorter workday. The company isolated them, surrounded them with strikebreakers, and starved them into submission. The strike failed, and most of the workers returned to their jobs.

In 1869 the transcontinental railroad was completed, and thousands of Chinese lost their jobs. Some moved into agricultural work, usually in menial positions. Increasingly, however, the Chinese flocked to cities. By far the largest single Chinese community was in San Francisco. Much of

"Chinatowns" community life there, and in other "Chinatowns" throughout the West, revolved around organizations that functioned as something like benevolent societies and filled many of the roles that political machines often served in immigrant communities in eastern cities. They were often led by prominent merchants. (In San Francisco, the leading merchants—known as the "Six Companies"—often worked together to advance their interests in the larger community of the city and state.) These organizations became, in effect, employment brokers, unions, arbitrators of disputes, defenders of the community against outside persecution, and dispensers of social services. They also organized the elaborate festivals and celebrations that were such a conspicuous and important part of life in Chinatowns.

Other Chinese organizations were secret societies, known as "tongs." And some of the tongs were violent criminal organizations, involved in the opium trade and prostitution. Few people outside the Chinese communities were aware of their existence, except when rival tongs engaged in violent conflict (or "tong wars").

In San Francisco and other western cities, the Chinese usually occupied the lower rungs of the employment ladder. Many worked as common laborers, servants, and unskilled factory hands. Some established their own small businesses, especially laundries. They moved into this business not because of experience—there were few commercial laundries in China—but because laundries could be started with very little capital and required only limited command of English. By the 1890s, Chinese constituted over two-thirds of all the laundry workers in California.

Growing Gender Balance During the earliest Chinese migrations to California, virtually all the relatively small number of women who made the journey did so because they had been sold into prostitution in China. As late as 1880, nearly half the Chinese women in California were prostitutes. Gradually, however, the number of Chinese women increased, and Chinese men in America became more likely to seek companionship in families.

Anti-Chinese Sentiments

As Chinese communities grew larger and more conspicuous, anti-Chinese sentiment among white residents became increasingly strong. Anti-Chinese activities, some of them violent, reflected the resentment of many white workers toward Chinese laborers for accepting low wages and thus undercutting union members. As the political value of attacking the Chinese grew in California, the Democratic Party took up the call. So did the Workingmen's Party of California—created in 1878 by Denis Kearney, an Irish immigrant—which gained significant political power in the state in large part on the basis of its hostility to the Chinese. By the mid-1880s, anti-Chinese agitation and violence had spread up and down the Pacific coast and into other areas of the West.

In 1882, Congress responded to the political pressure and the growing violence by passing the Chinese Exclusion Act, *Chinese Exclusion Act* which banned Chinese immigration into the United States for ten years and barred Chinese already in the country from becoming naturalized citizens. Congress renewed the law for another ten years in 1892 and made it permanent in 1902. It had a dramatic effect on the Chinese population, which declined by more than 40 percent in the forty years after the act's passage.

Migration from the East

The scale of the post–Civil War migration to the American West dwarfed everything that had preceded it. In previous decades, the settlers had come in thousands. Now they came in millions. Most of the new settlers were from the established Anglo-American societies of the eastern United States, but substantial numbers—over 2 million between 1870 and 1900—were foreign-born immigrants from Europe: Scandinavians, Germans, Irish, Russians, Czechs, and others.

They came to the West for many reasons. Settlers were attracted by gold and silver deposits, by the shortgrass pasture for cattle and sheep, and ultimately by the sod of the plains and the meadowlands of the mountains. The completion of the great transcontinental railroad line in 1869, and the construction of the many subsidiary lines that spread out from it, encouraged settlement. So did the land policies of the federal government. The Homestead Act of 1862 permitted settlers to *Homestead Act of 1862* buy plots of 160 acres for a small fee if they occupied the land they purchased for five years and improved it.

Supporters of the Homestead Act believed it would create new markets and new outposts of commercial agriculture for the nation's growing economy. But a unit of 160 acres, while ample in much of the East, was too small for the grazing and grain farming of the Great Plains. Eventually, the federal government provided some relief. The Timber Culture Act (1873) permitted homesteaders to receive grants of 160 additional acres if they planted 40 acres of trees on them. The Desert Land Act (1877) provided that claimants could buy 640 acres at $1.25 an acre provided they irrigated part of their holdings within three years. These and other laws ultimately made it possible for individuals to acquire as much as 1,280 acres of land at little cost.

Political organization followed on the heels of settlement. By the mid-1860s, territorial governments were in operation in the new provinces of *New Western States* Nevada, Colorado, Dakota, Arizona, Idaho, Montana, and Wyoming. Statehood rapidly followed. Nevada became a state in 1864, Nebraska in 1867, and Colorado in 1876. In 1889, North and South Dakota, Montana, and Washington won admission; Wyoming and Idaho entered the next year. Congress denied Utah statehood until its Mormon leaders convinced the government in 1896 that polygamy (the practice of men taking several wives) had been abandoned. At the turn of the century, only Arizona, New Mexico, and Oklahoma remained outside the Union.

THE CHANGING WESTERN ECONOMY

Among many other things, the great wave of Anglo-American and European settlement transformed the economy of the Far West. The new American settlers tied the West firmly to the growing industrial economy of the East.

Labor in the West

As commercial activity increased, many farmers, ranchers, and miners found it necessary to recruit a paid labor force—not an easy task for people far away from major population centers. The labor shortage of the region led to higher wages for some workers than were typical in most areas of the East. But working conditions were often arduous, and job security was almost nonexistent. Once a railroad was built, a crop harvested, a herd sent to market, a mine played out, hundreds and even thousands of workers could find themselves suddenly unemployed. Competition from Chinese immigrants also forced some Anglo-Americans and Europeans out of work.

Multiracial Working Class Even more than in many parts of the East, the western working class was highly multiracial. English-speaking whites worked alongside African Americans and immigrants from southern and eastern Europe, as they did in the East. Even more, they worked with Chinese, Filipinos, Mexicans, and Indians. But the work force was highly stratified along racial lines. In almost every area of the western economy, white workers (whatever their ethnicity) occupied the upper tiers of employment: management and skilled labor. The lower tiers—unskilled work in the mines, on the railroads, or in agriculture—consisted overwhelmingly of nonwhites.

COLORADO BOOM TOWN After a prospector discovered silver nearby in 1890, miners flocked to the town of Creede, Colorado. For a time in the early 1890s, 150 to 300 people arrived there daily. Although the town was located in a canyon so narrow that there was room for only one street, buildings sprouted rapidly to serve the growing community. Like other such boom towns, however, Creede's prosperity was short-lived. In 1893 the price of silver collapsed, and by the end of the century, Creede was almost deserted. *(Henry Ford Museum and Greenfield Village)*

The western economy was, however, no more a single entity than the economy of the East. In the late nineteenth century, the region produced three major industries, each with a distinctive history and distinctive characteristics: mining, ranching, and commercial farming.

The Arrival of the Miners

The first economic boom in the Far West came in mining. The mining boom began around 1860 and flourished until the 1890s. Then it abruptly declined.

News of a gold or silver strike in an area would start a stampede reminiscent of the California gold *Mining Booms* rush of 1849, followed by several stages of settlement. Individual prospectors would exploit the first shallow deposits of ore largely by hand, with pan and placer mining. After these surface deposits dwindled, corporations moved in to engage in lode or quartz mining, which dug deeper beneath the surface. Then, as those deposits dwindled, commercial mining either disappeared or continued on a restricted basis, and ranchers and farmers moved in and established a more permanent economy.

The first great mineral strikes (other than the California gold rush) occurred just before the Civil War. In 1858, gold was discovered in the Pike's Peak district of what would soon be the territory of Colorado; the following year, 50,000 prospectors stormed in. Denver and other mining camps blossomed into "cities" overnight. Almost as rapidly as it had developed, the boom ended. Later, the discovery of silver near Leadville supplied a new source of mineral wealth.

While the Colorado rush of 1859 was still in progress, news of another strike drew miners to Nevada. Gold had been found in the Washoe district. But even more plentiful and more valuable was the silver found in *Comstock Lode Discovered* the great Comstock Lode (first discovered in 1858 by Henry Comstock) and other Washoe veins. The first prospectors to reach the Washoe fields came from California, and from the beginning, Californians dominated the settlement and development of Nevada. In a remote desert without railroad transportation, the territory produced no supplies of its own, and everything had to be shipped from California to Virginia City, Carson City, and other roaring camp towns. When the first placer (or surface) deposits ran out, Californian and eastern capitalists bought the claims of the pioneer prospectors and began to use the more difficult process of quartz mining, which enabled them to retrieve silver from deeper veins. For a few years these outside owners reaped tremendous profits: from 1860 to 1880 the Nevada lodes yielded bullion worth $306 million. After that, the mines quickly played out.

The next important mineral discoveries came in 1874, when gold was found in the Black Hills of southwestern Dakota Territory. Prospectors swarmed into the remote area. Like the others, the boom flared for a time, until surface resources faded and corporations took over from the miners. One enormous company, the Homestake, came to dominate the fields. The Dakotas, like other boom areas of the mineral empire, ultimately developed a largely agricultural economy.

Although the gold and silver discoveries generated the most popular excitement, in the long run other, less glamorous natural resources proved more important to the development of the West. The great Anaconda copper mine launched by William Clark in 1881 marked the beginning of an industry that would remain important to Montana for many decades. In other areas, mining operations had significant success with lead, tin, quartz, and zinc.

Gender Disparity Men greatly outnumbered women in the mining towns, and younger men in particular had difficulty finding female companions of comparable age. Those women who did gravitate to the new communities often came with their husbands. Single women, or women whose husbands were earning no money, did work for wages at times, as cooks, laundresses, and tavern keepers. And in the sexually imbalanced mining communities, there was always a ready market for prostitutes.

The thousands of people who flocked to the mining towns in search of quick wealth and failed to find it often remained as wage laborers in corporate mines after the boom period, working in almost uniformly terrible conditions. In the 1870s, one worker in every thirty was disabled in the mines, and one in every eighty was killed. That rate fell later in the nineteenth century, but mining remained one of the most dangerous and arduous working environments in the United States.

The Cattle Kingdom

A second important element of the changing economy of the Far West was cattle ranching. The open range—the vast grasslands of the public domain—provided a huge area on the Great Plains where cattle raisers could graze their herds.

The western cattle industry was Mexican and Texan by ancestry. Long before citizens of the *Mexican Roots* United States entered the Southwest, Mexican ranchers had developed the techniques and equipment that the cattlemen and cowboys of the Great Plains later employed: branding, roundups, roping, and the gear of the herders—their lariats, saddles, leather chaps, and spurs. Americans in Texas adopted these methods and carried them to the northernmost ranges of the cattle kingdom. Texas also had the largest herds of cattle in the country. From Texas, too, came the small, muscular horses (broncos and mustangs) that enabled cowboys to control the herds.

At the end of the Civil War, an estimated 5 million cattle roamed the Texas ranges. Eastern markets were offering good prices for steers in any condition, and the challenge facing the cattle industry was getting the animals from the range to the railroad centers. Early in 1866, some Texas cattle ranchers began driving their combined herds, some 260,000 head, north to Sedalia, Missouri, on the Missouri Pacific Railroad. The caravan suffered heavy losses. But the drive proved that cattle could be driven to distant markets and pastured along the trail. This earliest of the "long drives," in other words, established the first, tentative link between the isolated cattle breeders of west Texas and the booming urban markets of the East.

With the precedent of the long drive established, the next step was to find an easier route through more accessible country. Market facilities grew up at Abilene, Kansas, on the Kansas Pacific Railroad, and for years the town reigned as the railhead of the cattle kingdom. But by the mid-1870s, agricultural development in western Kansas was eating away at the open-range land. Cattlemen had to develop other trails and other market outlets. As the railroads began to reach farther west, Dodge City and Wichita in Kansas, Ogallala and Sidney in Nebraska, Cheyenne and Laramie in Wyoming, and Miles City and Glendive in Montana all began to rival Abilene as major centers of stock herding.

There had always been an element of risk and speculation in the open-range cattle business. Rustlers and Indians frequently seized large numbers of animals. But as settlement of the plains increased, new forms of competition arose. Sheep breeders from California and Oregon brought their flocks onto the range to compete for grass. Farmers ("nesters") from the

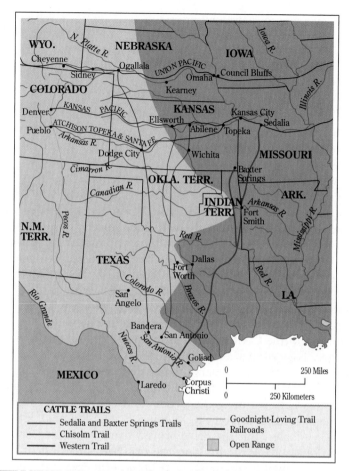

THE CATTLE KINGDOM, c. 1866–1887 Cattle ranching and cattle drives are among the most romanticized features of the nineteenth-century West. But they were also hard-headed business ventures, made possible by the growing eastern market for beef and the availability of reasonably inexpensive transportation to take cattle to urban markets. This map shows two important characteristics of the "cattle kingdom" in the 1860s and 1870s. One is the vast expanse of "open range." ◆ *Why was that necessary for the great cattle drives, and what eventually ended it?* The other is the dense network of trails and railroads that together made possible the commerce in cattle.

For an interactive version of this map go to www.mhhe.com/unfinishednation4ch16maps

East threw fences around their claims, blocking trails and breaking up the open range. A series of "range wars"—between sheepmen and cattlemen, between ranchers and farmers—erupted out of the tensions between these competing groups.

"Range Wars"

Accounts of the lofty profits to be made in the cattle business tempted eastern, English, and Scottish capital to the plains. Increasingly, the structure of the cattle economy became corporate; in one year, twenty corporations with a combined capital of $12 million were chartered in Wyoming.

The result of this frenzied, speculative expansion was that the ranges, already severed and shrunk by the railroads and the farmers, became overstocked. There was not enough grass to support the crowding herds or sustain the long drives. Two severe winters, in 1885–1886 and 1886–1887, with a searing summer between them, stung and scorched the plains. Hundreds of thousands of cattle died; streams and grass dried up; princely ranches and costly investments disappeared in a season.

The open-range industry never recovered; the long drive finally disappeared for good. Railroads displaced the trail as the route to market for livestock. But established *Decline of the Open-range Industry* cattle ranches survived, grew, and prospered, eventually producing more beef than ever.

THE ROMANCE OF THE WEST

The West occupied a special place in the Anglo-American imagination in the nineteenth century. Many white Americans continued to consider it a romantic place, a wilderness where individuals could experience true freedom.

The Western Landscape and the Cowboy

Part of the reason was the spectacular natural landscape of the West. Painters of the new "Rocky *"Rocky Mountain School"* Mountain School"—of whom the best known were Albert Bierstadt and Thomas Moran—celebrated the new West in grandiose canvases, some of which were taken on tours around the eastern and midwestern states and attracted enormous crowds, eager for a vision of the Great West.

Gradually, the interest in paintings of the West inspired a growing wave of tourism among people eager to see the natural wonders of the region. In the 1880s and 1890s, resort hotels began to spring up near some of the most spectacular landscapes in the region.

Even more appealing than the landscape was the rugged, free-spirited lifestyle that many Americans associated with the West. Many nineteenth-century Americans came to romanticize, especially, *Cowboys Mythologized* the figure of the cowboy. Western novels such as Owen Wister's *The Virginian* (1902) romanticized the cowboy's supposed freedom from traditional social constraints, his affinity with nature, even his supposed propensity for violence. Wister's character—one of the most enduring in popular American literature—was a semi-educated man whose natural decency, courage, and compassion made him a powerful symbol of the supposed virtues of the "frontier." But *The Virginian* was only the most famous example of a type of literature that soon swept throughout the United States: novels and stories about the West, and about the lives of cowboys in particular, that appeared in boys' magazines, pulp novels, theater, and even serious literature.

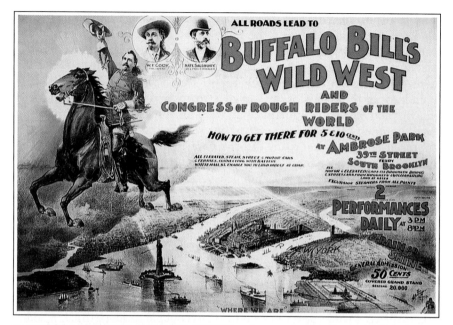

PROMOTING THE WEST Buffalo Bill's Wild West show was popular all over the United States, and indeed through much of the world. He was so familiar a figure that many of his posters contained only his picture with the words "He is Coming." This more conventional poster announces a visit of the show to Brooklyn. *(Culver Pictures, Inc.)*

One reason for the widespread admiration of the cowboy was the remarkable popularity of the Wild West shows that traveled throughout the United States and Europe. The most successful were the shows of Buffalo Bill Cody, a former Pony Express rider and Indian fighter, and the hero of popular dime novels for children. Cody's Wild West show, which had dozens of imitators, exploited his own fame. But it was mainly popular for its romanticization of the West and of the life of the cowboy. It included re-enactments of Indian battles and displays of horsemanship and riflery (many of them by the famous sharpshooter Annie Oakley). Buffalo Bill and his imitators confirmed the popular image of the West as a place of romance and glamour and helped keep that image alive for later generations.

The Idea of the Frontier

Yet it was not simply the particular character of the new West that made it so important to the nation's imagination. It was also that many Americans considered it the last frontier. Since the earliest moments of European settlement in America, the image of uncharted territory to the west had always comforted and inspired those who dreamed of starting life anew.

Mark Twain gave voice to this romantic vision of the frontier in a series of novels and memoirs. In *The Adventures of Tom Sawyer* (1876) and *The Adventures of Huckleberry Finn* (1885), he produced characters who repudiated the constraints of organized society and attempted to escape into a more natural world. For Huck Finn, the vehicle of escape was a small raft on the Mississippi, but the yearning for freedom reflected a larger vision of the West as the last refuge from the constraints of civilization. *Romantic Vision of the Frontier*

The painter and sculptor Frederic Remington also captured the romance of the West. His paintings and sculptures portrayed the cowboy as a natural aristocrat, much like Wister's *Virginian*, living in a natural world in which all the normal supporting structures of "civilization" were missing. Remington became one of the most beloved and successful artists of the nineteenth century.

Theodore Roosevelt also contributed to the romanticizing of the West. He traveled to the Dakota badlands in the mid-1880s to help himself recover from the sudden death of his young wife. In the 1890s, he published a four-volume history, *The Winning of the West*, with a heroic account of the spread of white civilization into the frontier.

The clearest and most influential statement of the romantic vision of the frontier came from the historian Frederick Jackson Turner, in a memorable paper he delivered to a meeting of the American Historical Association in Chicago in 1893 entitled "The Significance of the Frontier in American History." In it he boldly claimed that the experience of expansion into the frontier had stimulated individualism, nationalism, and democracy. It had kept opportunities for advancement alive. It had made Americans the distinctive people that they were. "Now," Turner concluded portentously, "the frontier has gone and with its going has closed the first period of American history." *Frederick Jackson Turner*

In accepting the idea of the "passing of the frontier," many Americans were acknowledging the end of one of their most cherished myths. As long as it had been possible for them to consider the West an empty, open land, it was possible to believe that there were constantly revitalizing opportunities in American life. Now there was a vague and ominous sense of opportunities foreclosed. *"Passing of the Frontier"*

THE DISPERSAL OF THE TRIBES

Having imagined the West as a "virgin land" awaiting civilization by white people, many Americans tried to force the region to match their image of it. That meant, above all, ensuring that the Indian tribes would not remain obstacles to the spread of white society.

White Tribal Policies

The traditional policy of the federal government was to regard the tribes simultaneously as independent nations (with which the United States

The emergence of the history of the American West as an important field of scholarship can be traced to the paper Frederick Jackson Turner delivered at a meeting of the American Historical Association in 1893: "The Significance of the Frontier in American History." Turner stated his thesis simply. The settlement of the West by white Americans—"the existence of an area of free land, its continuous recession, and the advance of American settlement westward"—was the central story of the nation's history. The process of westward expansion had transformed a desolate and savage land into modern civilization. It had also continually renewed American ideas of democracy and individualism.

In the first half of the twentieth century, virtually everyone who wrote about the West echoed at least part of Turner's argument. Ray Allen Billington's *Westward Expansion* (1949) was almost wholly consistent with the Turnerian model. In *The Great Plains* (1931) and *The Great Frontier* (1952), Walter Prescott Webb similarly emphasized the bravery and ingenuity of white settlers in the Southwest.

Serious efforts to displace the Turner thesis as the explanation of western American history began after World War II. In *Virgin Land* (1950), Henry Nash Smith examined many of the same heroic images of the West that Turner and his disciples had presented; but he treated those images less as descriptions of reality than as myths. Earl Pomeroy challenged Turner's notion of the West as a place of individualism, innovation, and democratic renewal. "Conservatism, inheritance, and continuity bulked at least as large," he claimed. Howard Lamar, in *Dakota Territory, 1861–1889* (1956) and *The Far Southwest* (1966), emphasized the highly diverse characters of different areas of the West.

The western historians who began to emerge in the late 1970s launched an even more emphatic attack on the Turner thesis and the idea of the "frontier." "New" western historians such as Richard White, Patricia Nelson Limerick, William Cronon, Donald Worster, Peggy Pascoe, and many others challenged the Turnerians on a number of points.

Turner saw the nineteenth-century West as "free land" awaiting the expansion of Anglo-American settlement and American democracy. The "new western historians" have rejected the concept of an empty "frontier," emphasizing instead the elaborate and highly developed civilizations that already existed in the region. White, English-speaking Americans, they have argued, did not so much settle the West as conquer it. And they continue to share the region not only with the Indians and Hispanics who preceded them there, but also with African Americans, Asians, Latin Americans, and others who flowed into the West at the same time they did.

The Turnerian West was a place of heroism, triumph, and above all progress, dominated by the feats of brave white men. The West the new historians describe is a less triumphant (and less masculine) place in which bravery and success coexist with oppression, greed, and failure; in which decaying ghost towns, bleak Indian reservations, impoverished barrios, and ecologically devastated landscapes are as characteristic of western development as great ranches, rich farms, and prosperous cities.

To Turner and his disciples, the nineteenth-century West was a place where rugged individualism flourished and replenished American democracy. The new scholars point out that the region was inextricably tied to a national and international capitalist economy. Westerners depended on government-subsidized railroads for access to markets, federal troops for protection from Indians, and (later) government-funded dams and canals for irrigating their fields and sustaining their towns.

And while Turner defined the West as a process—a process of settlement that came to an end with the "closing of the frontier" in the late nineteenth century—the new historians see the West as a region. Its history does not end in 1890. It continues into our own time.

(text continued from page 443)

could negotiate treaties) and as wards of the president (who would exercise paternalistic authority over the Indians). The concept of Indian sovereignty had supported the government's attempt before 1860 to erect a permanent frontier between whites and Indians. But the belief in tribal sovereignty, and the treaties or agreements with the Indians, were not strong enough to withstand the pressure of white settlers eager for access to Indian lands.

By the early 1850s, the idea of establishing one great enclave in which many tribes could live gave way to a new reservations policy known as "concentration." In 1851, the government assigned all the tribes their own defined reservations, con-   *"Concentration" Policy*
firmed by individual treaties—treaties often illegitimately negotiated with unauthorized "representatives" chosen by whites, people known sarcastically as "treaty chiefs." The new arrangement had many benefits for whites and few for the Indians. It divided the tribes from one another and made them easier to control. It allowed the government to force tribes into scattered locations and to take over the most desirable lands for white settlement. But it did not survive as the basis of Indian policy for long.

In 1867, Congress established the Indian Peace Commission, composed of both soldiers and civilians, to recommend a new and presumably permanent Indian policy. The commission recommended that the government move all the Plains tribes into two large reservations—one in Indian Territory (Oklahoma), the other in the Dakotas. At a series of meetings with the tribes, government agents cajoled, bribed, and tricked their representatives into agreeing to treaties establishing the new reservations.

But this "solution" worked little better than previous ones. Part of the problem was the abysmal way in which corrupt or incompetent agents of the Bureau of Indian Affairs administered the reservations. But the problem was also a result of the relentless slaughtering   *Buffalo Herds Decimated*
by whites of the buffalo herds that supported the
tribes' way of life. After the Civil War, professional and amateur hunters—even casual visitors shooting from passing trains—swarmed over the plains, killing the huge animals. Some Indian tribes (notably the Blackfeet) also began killing large numbers of buffalo to sell in the booming new market. In 1865, there had been at least 15 million buffalo; a decade later,

HELD UP BY BUFFALO Once among the most numerous creatures in North America, the buffalo became almost extinct as a result of indiscriminate slaughter by white settlers and travelers, who often fired at herds from moving trains simply for the sport of it. This scene was painted around 1880 by N. H. Trotter. *(Held up by Buffalo, by N.H. Trotter, c. 1880. Smithsonian Institution)*

fewer than a thousand of the great beasts survived. By destroying the buffalo herds, whites were destroying the Indians' source of food and supplies and their ability to resist white advance.

The Indian Wars

There was almost incessant fighting between whites and Indians from the 1850s to the 1880s, as Indians struggled against the growing threats to their civilizations. Indian warriors attacked wagon trains, stagecoaches, and isolated ranches, often in retaliation for earlier attacks on them by whites. As the United States Army became more deeply involved in the fighting, the tribes began to focus more of their attacks on white soldiers.

Growing Indian Resistance

At times, this small-scale fighting escalated. During the Civil War, the eastern Sioux in Minnesota, cramped on a small reservation and exploited by corrupt white agents, suddenly rebelled. Led by Little Crow, they killed more than 700 whites before being subdued by a force of regulars and militiamen. Thirty-eight of the Indians were hanged, and the tribe was exiled to the Dakotas.

At the same time, fighting flared up in eastern Colorado, where the Arapaho and Cheyenne were coming into conflict with white miners settling in the region. Bands of Indians attacked stagecoach lines and settlements in an effort to regain territory they had lost. In response to these incidents, whites called up a large territorial militia. The governor urged all friendly Indians to congregate at army posts for protection before the army began its campaign. One Arapaho and Cheyenne band under Black Kettle, apparently in response to the invitation, camped near Fort Lyon on Sand Creek in November 1864. Some members of the party were warriors, but Black Kettle believed he was under official protection and exhibited no hostile intention. Nevertheless, Colonel J. M. Chivington led a volunteer militia force—largely consisting of unemployed miners, many of whom were apparently drunk—to the unsuspecting camp and massacred 133 people, 105 of them women and children. Black Kettle himself escaped the Sand Creek massacre. But four years *Sand Creek Massacre* later, in 1868, he and his Cheyennes, some of whom were now at war with the whites, were caught on the Washita River, near the Texas border, by Colonel George A. Custer. White troops killed the chief and his people.

At the end of the Civil War, white troops stepped up their wars against the western Indians on several fronts. The most serious and sustained conflict was in Montana, where the army was attempting to build a road, the Bozeman Trail, to connect Fort Laramie, Wyoming, to the new mining centers. The western Sioux resented this intrusion into the heart of their buffalo range. Led by one of their great chiefs, Red Cloud, they so harried the soldiers and the construction party that the road could not be used.

But it was not only the United States military that harassed the tribes. It was also unofficial violence by white vigilantes who engaged in what became known as "Indian hunting." Sometimes the *"Indian Hunting"* killing was in response to Indian raids on white communities. But considerable numbers of whites were committed to the goal of literal "elimination" of the tribes whatever their behavior, a goal that rested on the belief in the essential inhumanity of Indians and the impossibility of white coexistence with them. In California, civilians killed close to 5,000 Indians between 1850 and 1880—one of many factors (disease and poverty being the more important) that reduced the Indian population of the state from 150,000 before the Civil War to 30,000 in 1870.

The treaties negotiated in 1867 brought a temporary lull to many of the conflicts. But new forces soon shattered the peace again. In the early 1870s, more waves of white settlers, mostly miners, began to penetrate some of the lands in Dakota Territory supposedly guaranteed to the tribes in 1867. Indian resistance flared anew. In the northern plains, the Sioux rose up in 1875 and left their reservation. When white officials ordered them to return, bands of warriors gathered in Montana and united under two great leaders: Crazy Horse and Sitting Bull. Three army columns set out to round them up and force them back onto the reservation. With the expedition, as colonel of the famous Seventh Cavalry, was the colorful and controversial George A. Custer. At the Battle of *Custer Defeated* the Little Bighorn in southern Montana in 1876, an unprecedentedly large army, perhaps 2,500 tribal warriors, surprised Custer and part of his regiment, surrounded them, and killed every man.

But the Indians did not have the political organization or the supplies to keep their troops united. Soon the warriors drifted off in bands to elude pursuit or search for food, and the army ran them down singly and returned them to Dakota. The power of the Sioux quickly collapsed. They accepted defeat and life on reservations.

One of the most dramatic episodes in Indian history occurred in Idaho in 1877. The Nez Percé were a small and relatively peaceful tribe, some of whose members had managed to live unmolested in Oregon into the 1870s without ever signing a treaty with the United States. But under pressure from white settlers, the government forced them to move onto a reservation. With no realistic prospect of resisting, the Indians began the journey to the reservation; but on the way, several younger Indians, drunk and angry, killed four white settlers.

Chief Joseph   The leader of the band, Chief Joseph, persuaded his followers to flee from the expected retribution. American troops pursued and attacked them, only to be driven off in a battle at White Bird Canyon. After that, the Nez Percé scattered in several directions and became part of a remarkable chase. Joseph moved with 200 warriors and 350 women, children, and old people in an effort to reach Canada. Pursued by four columns of American soldiers, the Indians covered 1,321 miles in seventy-five days, repelling or evading the army time and again. They were finally caught just short of the Canadian boundary. Some escaped and slipped across the border; but Joseph and most of his followers, weary and discouraged, finally gave up. "Hear me, my chiefs," Joseph said after meeting with the American general Nelson Miles. "I am tired. My heart is sick and sad. From where the sun now stands, I will fight no more forever."

The last Indians to maintain organized resistance against the whites were the Chiricahua Apaches. The two ablest chiefs of this fierce tribe were Mangas Colorados and Cochise. Mangas was murdered during the Civil War by white soldiers who tricked him into surrendering, and in 1872 Cochise agreed to peace in exchange for a reservation that included some of the tribe's traditional land. But Cochise died in 1874, and his successor, Geronimo, fought on for more than a decade longer, establishing bases in the mountains of Arizona and Mexico and leading warriors in intermittent raids against white outposts. With each raid, however, the number of warring Apaches dwindled, as some warriors died and others drifted away to the reservation. By 1886, Geronimo's band consisted of only about 30 people, including women and children, while his white pursuers numbered perhaps 10,000. Geronimo recognized the odds and surrendered.

The Apache wars were the most violent of all the Indian conflicts, and they produced brutality on both sides. But it was the whites who committed the most flagrant atrocities. That did not end with the conclusion of the Apache wars. Another tragic encounter occurred in 1890 as a result of a religious revival among the Sioux—a revival that itself symbolized the

THE SURRENDER OF GERONIMO The great Apache warrior Geronimo (front row, third from right) sits with members of his diminished band after surrendering to United States troops in 1886. The two men at front row, left, are Geronimo's half brothers. The young boy in the front row, right, is his son. *(Smithsonian Institution, National Anthropological Archives, Bureau of American Ethnology Collection)*

catastrophic effects of the white assaults on Indian civilization. As other tribes had done in trying times in the past, many of these Indians turned to a prophet who led them in a religious revival.

This time the prophet was Wovoka, a Paiute who inspired a fervent spiritual awakening that began in Nevada and spread quickly to the plains. The new revival emphasized the coming of a messiah, but its most conspicuous feature was a mass, emotional "Ghost Dance," which inspired ecstatic, mystical visions *"Ghost Dance"* among many participants. One of these visions was an image of a retreat of white people from the plains and a restoration of the great buffalo herds. White agents on the Sioux reservation watched the dances in bewilderment and fear; some believed they might be the preliminary to hostilities.

On December 29, 1890, the Seventh Cavalry tried to round up a group of about 350 cold and starving Sioux at *Wounded Knee Massacre* Wounded Knee, South Dakota. Fighting broke out in which about 40 white soldiers and up to 200 of the Indians died. An Indian may have fired the first shot, but the battle soon turned into a one-sided massacre, as the white soldiers turned their new machine guns on the Indians and mowed them down in the snow.

The Dawes Act

Even before the Ghost Dance and the Wounded Knee tragedies, the federal government had moved to destroy forever the tribal structure that had always been the cornerstone of Indian culture. Reversing its policy of nearly fifty years, Congress abolished the practice by which tribes owned reservation lands communally. Some supporters of the new policy believed they were acting for the good of the Indians, whom they considered a "vanishing race" in need of rescue by white society. The action was designed to force Indians to become landowners and farmers, to abandon their collective society and culture and become part of white civilization.

The Dawes Severalty Act of 1887 provided for the gradual elimination of most tribal ownership of land and the allotment of tracts to individual owners: 160 acres to the head of a family, 80 acres to a single adult or orphan, 40 acres to each dependent child. Adult owners were given United States citizenship, but unlike other citizens, they could not gain full title to their property for twenty-five years (supposedly to prevent them from selling the land to speculators).

Assimilation Promoted   In applying the Dawes Act, the Bureau of Indian Affairs relentlessly promoted the idea of assimilation that lay behind it. Not only did agents of the bureau try to move Indian families onto their own plots of land; they also took many Indian children away from their families and sent them to boarding schools run by whites. They moved as well to stop Indian religious rituals and encouraged the spread of Christianity and the creation of Christian churches on the reservations.

Few Indians were prepared for this wrenching change. In any case, white administration of the Dawes Act was so corrupt and inept that ultimately the government simply abandoned most efforts to enforce it. Much of the reservation land, therefore, was never distributed to individual owners.

THE RISE AND DECLINE OF THE WESTERN FARMER

The arrival of the miners, the empire building of the cattle ranchers, the dispersal of the Indian tribes—all served as a prelude to the decisive phase of white settlement of the Far West. Even before the Civil War, farmers had begun moving into the plains region, challenging the dominance of the ranchers and the Indians. By the 1870s, what was once a trickle had become a deluge. Farmers poured into the plains and beyond, enclosed land that had once been hunting territory for Indians and open range for cattle, and established a new agricultural region.

For a time in the late 1870s and early 1880s, the new western farmers flourished, enjoying the fruits of an agricultural economic boom. Beginning in the mid-1880s, however, the boom turned to bust, and the western agricultural economy began a long, steady decline.

From Boom to Bust

Farming on the Plains

Many factors combined to produce the surge of western agricultural settlement, but the most important was the railroads. Before the Civil War, the Great Plains had been accessible only through a difficult journey by wagon. But beginning in the 1860s, a great new network of railroad lines developed. They made huge areas of settlement accessible for the first time.

The building of the transcontinental line—completed in 1869 when the two lines met at Promontory Point, Utah—was a dramatic and monumental achievement. But the construction of subsidiary lines in the following years proved of greater importance to the West. State governments, imitating Washington, subsidized railroad development by offering direct financial aid, favorable loans, and more than 50 million acres of land (on top of the 130 million acres the federal government had already provided). Although built and operated by private corporations, the railroads were in many respects public projects.

The railroads spurred agricultural settlement by making access to the Great Plains easier. But the railroad companies also actively promoted settlement. The companies set rates so low for settlers that almost anyone could afford the trip west. And they sold much of their land at very low prices and with liberal credit to prospective settlers.

Cheap Rail Rates

Contributing further to the great surge of white agricultural expansion was a pronounced but temporary change in the climate of the Great Plains. For several years in succession, beginning in the 1870s, rainfall in the Plains states was well above average. White Americans now rejected the old idea that the region was the Great American Desert.

Even under the most favorable conditions, farming on the plains presented special problems. First was the problem of fencing. Farmers had to enclose their land, but materials for traditional wood or stone fences were unavailable. In the mid-1870s, however, two Illinois farmers, Joseph H. Glidden and I. L. Ellwood, solved this problem by developing and marketing barbed wire, which became standard equipment on the plains and revolutionized fencing practices all over the country and the world.

The second problem was water. Water was scarce even when rainfall was above average. After 1887, a series of dry seasons began, and lands that had been fertile now returned to semidesert. Some farmers dealt with the problem by using deep

Scarce Water

wells pumped by steel windmills, by turning to what was called dryland farming (a system of tillage designed to conserve moisture in the soil by covering it with a dust blanket), or by planting drought-resistant crops. In many areas of the plains, however, only large-scale irrigation could save the endangered farms. But irrigation projects of the necessary magnitude required government assistance, and neither the federal nor the state governments were prepared to fund the projects.

Most of the people who moved into the region had previously been farmers in the Middle West, the East, or Europe. In the booming years of the early 1880s, with land values rising, the new farmers had no problem obtaining extensive and easy credit. But the arid years of the late 1880s—during which crop prices were falling while production was becoming more expensive—changed the farmers' prospects. Tens of thousands of farmers could not pay their debts and were forced to abandon their farms.

Reverse Migration There was, in effect, a reverse migration: white settlers moving back east, sometimes turning once-flourishing communities into desolate ghost towns. Those who remained continued to suffer from falling prices (for example, wheat, which had sold for $1.60 a bushel at the end of the Civil War, dropped to 49 cents in the 1890s) and persistent indebtedness.

Commercial Agriculture

By the late nineteenth century the sturdy, independent farmer of popular myth was being replaced by the commercial farmer—attempting to do in the agricultural economy what industrialists were doing in the manufacturing economy. Commercial farmers specialized in cash crops that were sold in national or world markets. They did not often make their own household supplies or grow their own food but bought them from merchants. This kind of farming, when it was successful, raised farmers' living standards. But it also made them dependent on bankers and interest rates, railroads and freight rates, national and European markets, world supply and demand. And unlike the capitalists of the industrial order, they could not regulate their production or influence the prices of what they sold.

Between 1865 and 1900, farm output increased dramatically, not only in the United States but in Brazil, Argentina, Canada, Australia, New Zealand, Russia, and elsewhere. At the same time, modern forms of communication and transportation—the telephone, the telegraph, steam navigation, railroads—were creating new markets around the world for agricultural goods. Beginning in the 1880s, worldwide overproduction led to a *Overproduction* drop in prices for most agricultural goods and hence to great economic distress for many of the more than 6 million American farm families. By the 1890s, 27 percent of the farms in the country were mortgaged; by 1910, 33 percent. In 1880, 25 percent of all farms had been operated by tenants; by 1910, the proportion had grown to 37 percent. Commercial farming made some people fabulously wealthy. But the farm economy as a whole was suffering a significant decline relative to the rest of the nation.

The Farmers' Grievances

American farmers were painfully aware that something was wrong. But few yet understood the implications of national and world overproduction. Instead, they concentrated their attention and anger on more immediate, more comprehensible—and no less real—problems: inequitable freight rates, high interest charges, and an inadequate currency.

The farmers' first and most burning grievance was against the railroads. In many cases, the railroads charged higher rates for farm goods than for other goods, and higher rates in the South and West than in the Northeast. Railroads also controlled elevator and warehouse facilities in buying centers and charged arbitrary storage rates. *Grievances against Railroads*

Farmers also resented the institutions controlling credit—banks, loan companies, insurance corporations. Since sources of credit in the West and South were few, farmers had to take loans on whatever terms they could get, often at interest rates of from 10 to 25 percent. Many farmers had to pay these loans back in years when prices were dropping and currency was becoming scarce. As a result, expansion of the currency became an increasingly important issue to farmers.

A third grievance concerned prices. A farmer could plant a large crop at a moment when its price was high and find that by the time of the harvest the price had declined. Farmers' fortunes rose and fell in response to unpredictable forces. But many farmers became convinced (often with some reason) that "middlemen"—speculators, bankers, regional and local agents—were conspiring with one another to fix prices so as to benefit themselves at the growers' expense. Many farmers also came to believe (again, not entirely without reason) that manufacturers in the East were colluding to keep the prices of farm goods low and the prices of industrial goods high. Although farmers sold their crops in a competitive world market, they bought manufactured goods in a domestic market protected by tariffs and dominated by trusts and corporations. *Belief in Conspiracy*

The Agrarian Malaise

These economic difficulties helped produce a series of social and cultural resentments. In part, this was a result of the isolation of farm life. Farm families in some parts of the country were virtually cut off from the outside world. During the winter months and spells of bad weather, the loneliness and boredom could become nearly unbearable. Many farmers lacked access to adequate education for their children, to proper medical facilities, to recreational or cultural activities, to virtually anything that might give them a sense of being members of a community. Older farmers felt the sting of watching their children leave the farm for the city. They felt the humiliation of being ridiculed as "hayseeds" by the new urban culture that was coming to dominate American life.

Isolation and Obsolescence   The result of this sense of isolation and obsolescence was a growing malaise among many farmers, a discontent that would help create a great national political movement in the 1890s. It found reflection, too, in the literature that emerged from rural America. Writers in the late nineteenth century might romanticize the rugged life of the cowboy and the western miner. For the farmer, however, the image was usually different. Hamlin Garland, for example, reflected the growing disillusionment in a series of novels and short stories. In the past, Garland wrote in the introduction to his novel *Jason Edwards* (1891), the agrarian frontier had seemed to be "the Golden West, the land of wealth and freedom and happiness." Now, however, the bright promise had faded. The trials of rural life were crushing the human spirit. "So this is the reality of the dream!" a character in *Jason Edwards* exclaims. "A shanty on a barren plain, hot and lone as a desert. My God!" Once, sturdy yeoman farmers had viewed themselves as the backbone of American life. Now they were becoming painfully aware that their position was declining in relation to the rising urban-industrial society to the east.

CONCLUSION

To many Americans in the late nineteenth century, the West seemed an untamed "frontier" in which hardy pioneers were creating a new society. The reality of the West in these years, however, was very different from this enduring image. White Americans were moving into the vast regions west of the Mississippi at a remarkable rate in the years after the Civil War, and many of them were indeed settling in lands far from any civilization they had ever known. But the West was not an empty place. It contained a large population of Indians, with whom the white settlers sometimes lived uneasily and sometimes battled, but almost always in the end pushed aside and (with help from the federal government) relocated onto lands whites did not want. There were significant numbers of Mexicans in some areas, small populations of Asians in others, and African Americans moving in from the South in search of land and freedom. The West was not a barren frontier, but a place of many cultures.

The West was also closely and increasingly tied to the emerging capitalist-industrial economy of the East. The miners who flooded into California, Colorado, Nevada, the Dakotas, and elsewhere were responding to the demand in the East for gold and silver, but even more for iron ore, copper, lead, zinc, and quartz. Cattle and sheep ranchers produced meat, wool, and leather for eastern consumers and manufacturers. Farmers grew crops for sale in national and international commodities markets.

The West certainly looked different from the East. But the growth of the West was very much a part of the growth of the rest of the nation. And the culture of the West, despite the romantic images of pioneering individuals embraced by easterners and westerners alike, was at its heart as much a culture of economic growth and capitalist ambition as was the culture of the rest of the nation.

FOR FURTHER REFERENCE

Frederick Jackson Turner's *The Frontier in American History* (1920) is a classic argument on the centrality of the frontier experience to American democracy, an argument that frames much recent history of the West, which reject the Turner thesis. Patricia Nelson Limerick's *The Legacy of Conquest: The Unbroken Past of the American West* (1987) argues that the West was not a frontier but rather an inhabited place conquered by Anglo-Americans. Richard White, *"It's Your Misfortune and None of My Own": A History of the American West* (1991), is an outstanding general history of the region that revises many myths about the West. Ronald Takaki, *Strangers from a Different Shore: A History of Asian Americans* (1989), surveys the Asian-American experience as immigrants to America's western shore. John Mack Faragher, *Women and Men on the Overland Trail* (1979) examines the social experience of westering migrants and Peggy Pascoe, *Relations of Rescue: The Search for Female Authority in the American West, 1874–1939* (1990) describes the female communities of the West. William Cronon, *Nature's Metropolis and the Great West* (1991) describes the relationships among economies and environments in the West. Jon Gjerde, *The Minds of the West: Ethnocultural Evolution in the Rural Middle West, 1830–1914* (1997) examines the impact of the ethnicity on the shaping of the agrarian West. Robert Wooster, *The Military and United States Indian Policy, 1865–1902* (1988) examines the military campaigns against the Indians in the late nineteenth century. Frederick E. Hoxie, *A Final Promise: The Campaign to Assimilate the Indians, 1880–1920* (1984) examines U.S. policies toward Native Americans in the years after the end of the Indian Wars, and Mark David Spence, *Dispossessing the Wilderness: Indian Removal and the Making of the National Parks* (1999) revises a familiar story. John Mack Faragher, *Daniel Boone* (1992) is a study of one of the West's most fabled figures, and Joy S. Kasson, *Buffalo Bill's Wild West: Celebrity, Memory, and Popular History* (2000) describes one of the regon's most accomplished mythmakers. Richard Slotkin, *The Fatal Environment: The Myth of the Frontier in the Age of Industrialization* (1985) and *Gunfighter Nation* (1992) are provocative cultural studies of the idea of the West. Henry Nash Smith, *Virgin Land* (1950) is a classic study of the West in American culture. *The West* (1996), a documentary film by Stephen Ives and Ken Burns, offers a broad history of the region, along with a companion book of the same title by Geoffrey C. Ward.

For quizzes, Internet resources, references to additional books and films, and more, consult this book's Online Learning Center site at www.mhhe.com/unfinishednation4.

SMELTING WORKS AT DENVER The painter Thomas Moran was best known for his enormous canvases depicting the natural landscapes and rugged outdoor societies of the late-nineteenth-century West. In this 1892 watercolor, however, he captures another, less renowned feature of western life: the emergence of industrial manufacturing in the rapidly developing region. *(Smelting Works at Denver, 1892, by Thomas Moran. Watercolor and gouache over black chalk, 34.9 x 42.2 cm. © Cleveland Museum of Art, 1998, Bequest of Mrs. Henry A. Everett for the Dorothy Burnham Everett Collection, 1938.56)*

TIME LINE

1859	1866	1870	1873	1876	1877	1879	1881	
First oil well drilled	National Labor Union founded	Rockefeller founds Standard Oil	Carnegie Steel founded	Bell invents telephone	Nationwide railroad strike	Edison invents electric light bulb	American Federation of Labor founded	
	First transatlantic cable		Economic panic					

INDUSTRIAL SUPREMACY

Sources of Industrial Growth
Capitalism and Its Critics
The Ordeal of the Worker

"Twenty-five years after the death of Lincoln, America had become, in the quantity and value of her products, the first manufacturing nation of the world. What England had accomplished in a hundred years, the United States had achieved in half the time." So wrote the historians Charles and Mary Beard in the 1920s, expressing the amazement many Americans felt when they considered the remarkable expansion of their industrial economy in the late nineteenth century.

In fact, America's rise to industrial supremacy was not as sudden as such observers suggested. The nation had been building a manufacturing economy since early in the nineteenth century. But Americans were clearly correct in observing that the accomplishments of the last three decades of the nineteenth century overshadowed all the earlier progress.

The remarkable growth did much to increase the wealth and improve the lives of many Americans. But such benefits were very unequally shared. While industrial titans and a growing middle class were enjoying a prosperity without precedent in the nation's history, workers, farmers, and others were experiencing an often painful ordeal that slowly edged the United States toward a great economic and political crisis.

1886	1888	1892	1893	1894	1901	1903	1914	
Haymarket bombing	Bellamy's *Looking Backward*	Homestead steel strike	Depression begins	Pullman strike	Morgan creates U.S. Steel	Wright brothers' airplane flight	Ford introduces factory assembly lines	

SOURCES OF INDUSTRIAL GROWTH

Many factors contributed to the growth of American industry: abundant raw materials; a large and growing labor supply; a surge in technological innovation; the emergence of a talented and often ruthless group of entrepreneurs; a federal government eager to assist the growth of business; and an expanding domestic market for the products of manufacturing.

Industrial Technologies

The rapid emergence of new technologies, together with the discovery of new materials and productive processes, was one of the principal sources of late-nineteenth-century industrial growth. Some of the most important innovations were in communications. In 1866, Cyrus W. Field laid a transatlantic

Alexander Graham Bell   telegraph cable to Europe. During the next decade, Alexander Graham Bell developed the first telephone with commercial capacity. By 1900 there were 1.35 million telephones, and by 1920 13.3 million. And the Italian inventor Guglielmo Marconi was taking the first steps toward the development of radio in the 1890s; the technology he developed quickly found its way to the United States. Other inventions that speeded the pace of business organization were the typewriter (by Christopher L. Sholes in 1868), the cash register (by James Ritty in 1879), and the calculating or adding machine (by William S. Burroughs in 1891).

Among the most revolutionary innovations was the introduction in the 1870s of electricity as a source of light and power. Among the pioneers

Impact of Electric Power   of electric lighting were Charles F. Brush, who devised the arc lamp for street illumination, and Thomas A. Edison, who invented the incandescent lamp (or lightbulb). Edison and others designed improved generators and built large power plants to furnish electricity to whole cities. By the turn of the century, electric power was becoming commonplace in street railway systems, in the elevators of urban skyscrapers, in factories, and increasingly in offices and homes.

Particularly important to trade and industry was the development of new, high-efficiency steam engines capable of powering larger ships at faster speeds than ever imagined in the past. The new high-speed freighters, for example, made it cheaper for Britain to buy wheat grown in Canada and the United States than to grow it at home. The introduction of refrigerated ships in the 1870s made it possible to transport meat from North America and even Australia and Asia to Europe.

The Technology of Iron and Steel Production

Perhaps the most important technological development in a nation whose economy rested so heavily on railroads and urban construction was the revolutionizing of iron and steel production. Iron production had devel-

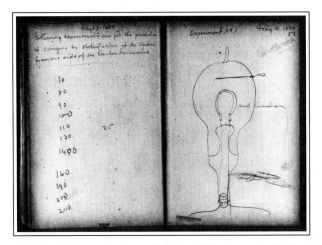

EDISON'S NOTEBOOK This page from one of Thomas Edison's notebooks shows sketches of and notes on some of his early experiments with an incandescent lamp—what we know as an electric lightbulb. Edison was not only the most celebrated inventor of his day, but by the early twentieth century one of the greatest popular heroes in American life in a time when scientific and technological progress was considered the defining feature of the age. *(U.S. Department of the Interior, National Park Service, Edison National Historic Site)*

oped slowly in the United States through most of the nineteenth century, mostly driven by the demand for iron rails for railroads; steel production had developed hardly at all by the end of the Civil War. In the 1870s and 1880s, however, iron production soared as railroads added 40,000 new miles of track, and steel production made great strides toward what would soon be its dominance in the metals industry.

The rise of steel was itself the product of technological discovery. An Englishman, Henry Bessemer, and an American, William Kelly, had developed, almost simultaneously, a process for converting iron into the much more durable and versatile steel. (The *Bessemer Process* process, which took Bessemer's name, consisted of blowing air through molten iron to burn out the impurities and create a much stronger metal.) The Bessemer process also relied on the discovery by the British metallurgist Robert Mushet that ingredients could be added to the iron during conversion to transform it into steel, to give it additional strength. In 1868, the New Jersey ironmaster Abram S. Hewitt introduced from Europe another method of making steel—the open-hearth process. These techniques made possible the production of steel in great quantities and large dimensions, for use in the manufacture of locomotives, steel rails, and girders for the construction of tall buildings.

The steel industry emerged first in western Pennsylvania and eastern Ohio. That was partly because iron ore could be found there in abundance. It was also because the new forms of steel production created a demand for new kinds of fuel—and particularly for the anthracite (or hard) coal that was plentiful in Pennsylvania. Later, new techniques made it possible to use soft bituminous coal, also easily mined in western Pennsylvania. As a result, Pittsburgh quickly became the center of the steel world. But the industry was growing so fast that new sources of ore were soon necessary. The upper peninsula of Michigan, the Mesabi Range in Minnesota, and the area around Birmingham, Alabama, became important ore-producing centers, and new centers of steel production grew up near them: Cleveland, Detroit, Chicago, and Birmingham, among others.

New Blast Furnaces Until the Civil War, iron and steel furnaces were mostly made of stone and usually built against the side of a hill to reduce construction demands. In the 1870s and after, however, furnaces were redesigned as cylindrical iron shells lined with brick. These massive new furnaces were 75 feet tall and higher and could produce over 500 tons a week.

New Transportation Systems As the steel industry spread, new transportation systems emerged to serve it. The steel production in the Great Lakes region was possible only because of the availability of steam freighters that could carry ore on the lakes. The demand for vessels capable of transporting oil and the development of the new and more powerful steam engine encouraged, in turn, the design of larger and heavier freighters. Shippers used new steam engines to speed the unloading of ore, a task that previously had been performed, slowly and laboriously, by men and horses.

There was even a closer relationship between the emerging steel companies and the railroads. Steel manufacturers provided rails and parts for cars to the railroads; railroads were both markets for and transporters of manufactured steel. But the relationship soon became more intimate than that. The Pennsylvania Railroad, for example, literally created the Pennsylvania Steel Company.

The steel industry's need for lubrication for its machines helped create another important new industry in the late nineteenth century—oil. (Not *Rise of the Petroleum Industry* until later did oil become important primarily for its potential as a fuel.) The existence of petroleum reserves in western Pennsylvania had been common knowledge for some time. Not until the 1850s, however, after Pennsylvania businessman George Bissell showed that the substance could be burned in lamps and that it could also yield such products as paraffin, naphtha, and lubricating oil, was there any sense of its commercial value. Bissell raised money to begin drilling; and in 1859, Edwin L. Drake, one of Bissell's employees, established the first oil well near Titusville, Pennsylvania, which was soon producing 500 barrels of oil a month. Demand for petroleum grew quickly, and promoters soon developed other fields in Pennsylvania, Ohio, and West Virginia.

The Airplane and the Automobile

Among the technological innovations that were to have the farthest-reaching impact on the United States was the invention of the automobile. Two technologies were critical to its development. One was the creation of gasoline (or petrol), which was the result of an extraction process developed in the late nineteenth century in the United States by which lubricating oil and fuel oil were removed separately from crude oil. As early as the 1870s, designers in France, Germany, and Austria had begun to develop an "internal combustion engine," which used the expanding power of burning gas to drive pistons. A German, Nicolaus August Otto, created a gas-powered "four-stroke" engine in the mid-1860s, which was a precursor to automobile engines. But he did not develop a way to untether it from gas lines to be used portably in machines. One of Otto's former employees, Gottfried Daimler, later perfected an engine that could be used in automobiles.

The American automobile industry developed rapidly in the aftermath of these breakthroughs. Charles and Frank Duryea built the first gasoline-driven motor vehicle in America in 1903. Three years later, Henry Ford produced the first of the *Henry Ford* famous cars that would bear his name. In 1895, there were only four automobiles on the American highways. By 1917, there were nearly 5 million.

The search for a means of human flight was as old as civilization, and had been almost entirely futile until the late nineteenth century when engineers, scientists, and tinkerers in both the United States and Europe began to experiment with a wide range of aeronautic devices. Balloonists began to consider ways to make dirigibles useful vehicles of transportation. Others experimented with kites and gliders.

Two brothers in Ohio, Wilbur and Orville *The Wright Brothers* Wright, owned a bicycle shop in which they began to construct a glider that could be propelled through the air by an internal-combustion engine. Four years after they began their experiments, Orville made a celebrated test flight near Kitty Hawk, North Carolina, in which an airplane took off by itself and traveled 120 feet in 12 seconds under its own power before settling back to earth. By the fall of 1904, they had improved the plane to the point where they were able to fly over 23 miles, and in the following year they began to take a few passengers on their flights with them.

Although the first working airplane was built in the United States, aviation technology was slow to gain a foothold in America. Most of the early progress in airplane design occurred in France, where there was substantial government funding for research and development. The U.S. government created the National Advisory Committee on Aeronautics in 1915, twelve years after the Wright brothers' flight, and American airplanes became a significant presence in Europe during World War I. But the prospects for commercial flight seemed dim until the 1920s, when Charles Lindbergh's famous solo flight from New York to Paris electrified the nation and the world.

Research and Development

The rapid development of new industrial technologies persuaded many business leaders to sponsor their own research to keep up with the rapid changes in industry. General Electric, fearful of technological competition,

created one of the first corporate laboratories in 1900. The emergence of corporate research and development laboratories coincided with a decline
Corporate Research and Development
in government support for research. That helped corporations to attract skilled researchers who had found themselves without their traditional forms of support. It also decentralized the sources of research funding and ensured that inquiry would move in many different directions, and not just along paths determined by the government.

A rift began to emerge between scientists and engineers. Engineers—both inside and out of universities—became increasingly tied up with the research and development agendas of corporations. Many scientists continued to scorn this "commercialization" of knowledge and preferred to stick to basic research that had no immediate practical applications. Even so, American scientists were more closely connected to practical challenges than were their European counterparts, and some joined engineers in corporate research and development laboratories, which over time began to sponsor not just practical but also basic research.

The Science of Production

Central to the growth of the automobile and other industries were changes in the techniques of production. By the turn of the century, many industrialists were embracing the new principles of "scientific manage-
"Taylorism"
ment," often known as "Taylorism" after its leading theoretician, Frederick Winslow Taylor. Taylor himself, and his many admirers, argued that scientific management made it possible to manage human labor to make it compatible with the demands of the machine age. But scientific management was also a way to increase the employer's control of the workplace. Taylor urged employers to reorganize the production process by subdividing tasks. This would speed up production; it would also make workers more interchangeable and thus diminish a manager's dependence on any particular employee. If properly managed by trained experts, he claimed, workers using modern machines could perform simple tasks at much greater speed, greatly increasing productive efficiency.

The most important change in production technology in the industrial era was the emergence of mass production and, along with it, the moving assembly line, which Henry Ford introduced in his automobile
Assembly Line
plants in 1914. The assembly line was both a particular place—a factory through which automobiles moved as they were being assembled by workers who specialized on particular tasks—and a concept. The concept stressed the complete interchangeability of parts. General Motors adopted the same philosophy, and even proceeded to demonstrate it at a motor works in England in 1906—when three Cadillacs were dismantled, their engines disassembled, the pieces mixed up with one another, and then completely reassembled by

THE ASSEMBLY LINE Workers in the Ford Motor Company's plant in Highland Park, Michigan, guide auto bodies down a ramp onto chassis that have moved into position from below. This was the final stage of the assembly line, which Henry Ford pioneered and which by 1914 (when this photograph was taken) had become common in other industries as well. *(Henry Ford Museum and Greenfield Village)*

several mechanics, who then turned on the engines and drove them onto a track. Automobile production relied on other technologies, too, in particular the intensive use of electricity—to drive the assembly line, to light the factories, and to run the critical ventilating systems to keep dust from interfering with the machines. The revolutionary assembly-line technique enabled Ford to raise the wages and reduce the hours of his workers while cutting the base price of his Model T from $950 in 1914 to $290 in 1929. It became a standard for many other industries.

Railroad Expansion and the Corporation

But the principal agent of industrial development in the late nineteenth century was the expansion of the railroads. Railroads gave industrialists access to distant markets and distant sources of raw materials. They were the nation's largest businesses and created new forms of corporate organization. And they were America's biggest investors, stimulating economic growth through their own enormous expenditures on construction and equipment.

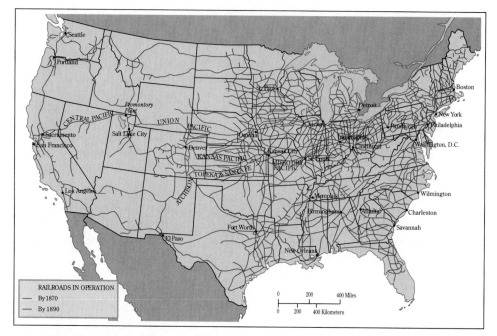

RAILROADS, 1870–1890 This map illustrates the rapid expansion of railroads in the late nineteenth century. In 1870, there was already a dense network of rail lines in the Northeast and Middle West, illustrated here by the red lines. The green lines show the further expansion of rail coverage between 1870 and 1890, much of it in the South and the areas west of the Mississippi River. ◆ *Why were railroads so essential to the nation's economic growth in these years?*

For an interactive version of this map go to www.mhhe.com/unfinishednation4ch17maps

Importance of Government Subsidies

Total railroad trackage increased from 30,000 miles in 1860 to 193,000 in 1900. Subsidies from federal, state, and local governments (along with foreign loans and investments) were vital to this expansion. Equally important was the emergence of great railroad combinations, many of them dominated by one or two individuals. The achievements (and excesses) of these tycoons—Cornelius Vanderbilt, James J. Hill, Collis R. Huntington, and others—became symbols to much of the nation of concentrated economic power. But railroad development was less significant for the individual barons it created than for its contribution to the growth of a new institution: the modern corporation.

There had been various forms of corporations in America since colonial times, but the modern corporation emerged as a major force only after the Civil War. By then, railroad magnates and other industrialists realized that their great ventures could not be financed by any single person.

Under the laws of incorporation passed in many states in the 1830s and 1840s, business organizations could raise money by selling stock to members of the public; after the Civil War, one industry after another began doing so.

What made the stocks more appealing than they had been in the past was that investors now had only "limited liability"—that is, they risked only the amount of their investments; *"Limited Liability"* they were not liable for any debts the corporation might accumulate beyond that point. The ability to sell stock to a broad public made it possible for entrepreneurs to gather vast sums of capital and undertake great projects.

The Pennsylvania and other railroads were among the first to adopt the new corporate form of organization. But incorporation quickly spread beyond the railroad industry. In steel, the central figure was Andrew Carnegie, a Scottish immigrant *U.S. Steel Created* who had worked his way up from modest beginnings and in 1873 opened his own steelworks in Pittsburgh. Soon he dominated the industry. With his associate Henry Clay Frick, he bought up coal mines and leased part of the Mesabi iron range in Minnesota, operated a fleet of ore ships on the Great Lakes, and acquired railroads. He financed his vast undertakings not only out of his own profits but out of the sale of stock. Then, in 1901, he sold out for $450 million to the banker J. Pierpont Morgan, who merged the Carnegie interests with others to create the giant United States Steel Corporation—a $14 billion enterprise that controlled almost two-thirds of the nation's steel production.

There were similar developments in other industries. Gustavus Swift developed a relatively small meatpacking company into a great national corporation. Isaac Singer patented a sewing machine in 1851 and created I. M. Singer and Company—one of the first modern manufacturing corporations.

Large, national business enterprises needed more systematic administrative structures. As a result, corporate leaders introduced a set of managerial techniques that relied on systematic division of responsibilities, a carefully designed hierarchy of control, careful cost-accounting procedures, and perhaps above all a new breed of business executive: the "middle manager," who formed a layer of command between workers and owners. Efficient administrative capabilities helped make possible another major feature of the modern corporation: consolidation.

Businessmen created large, consolidated organizations primarily through two methods. One *"Horizontal Integration" and* was "horizontal integration"—the combining of a *"Vertical Integration"* number of firms engaged in the same enterprise into a single corporation. The consolidation of many different railroad lines into one company was an example. Another method, which became popular in the 1890s, was "vertical integration"—the taking over of all the different businesses on which a company relied for its primary function. Carnegie Steel, which came to control not only steel mills but mines, railroads, and other enterprises, was an example of vertical integration.

The most celebrated corporate empire of the late nineteenth century was John D. Rockefeller's Standard Oil. Shortly after the Civil War, Rockefeller launched a refining company in Cleveland and immediately began trying to eliminate his competition. Allying himself with other wealthy capitalists, he proceeded methodically to buy out competing refineries. In 1870, he formed the Standard Oil Company of Ohio, which in a few years had acquired twenty of the twenty-five refineries in Cleveland, as well as plants in Pittsburgh, Philadelphia, New York, and Baltimore.

So far, Rockefeller had expanded only horizontally. But soon he began expanding vertically as well. He built his own barrel factories, terminal warehouses, and pipelines. Standard Oil owned its own freight cars and developed its own marketing organization. By the 1880s, Rockefeller had established such dominance within the petroleum industry that to much of the nation he served as a leading symbol of monopoly.

Standard Oil

Rockefeller and other industrialists saw consolidation as a way to cope with what they believed was the greatest curse of the modern economy: "cutthroat competition." Most businessmen claimed to believe in free enterprise and a competitive marketplace, but in fact they feared that substantial competition could spell instability and ruin for all.

As the movement toward combination accelerated, new vehicles emerged to facilitate it. The railroads began with so-called pool arrangements—informal agreements among various companies to stabilize rates and divide markets (arrangements that would, in later years, be known as cartels). But if even a few firms in an industry were unwilling to cooperate (as was almost always the case), the pool arrangements collapsed.

The failure of the pools led to new techniques of consolidation. At first, the most successful such technique was the creation of the "trust"—pioneered by Standard Oil in the early 1880s and perfected by the banker J. P. Morgan. Under a trust agreement, stockholders in individual corporations transferred their stocks to a small group of trustees in exchange for shares in the trust itself. Owners of trust certificates often had no direct control over the decisions of the trustees; they simply received a share of the profits of the combination. The trustees themselves, on the other hand, might literally own only a few companies but could exercise effective control over many.

In 1889, the state of New Jersey helped produce a third form of consolidation by changing its laws of incorporation to permit companies to buy up other companies. Other states soon followed. That made the trust unnecessary and permitted actual corporate mergers. Rockefeller, for example, quickly relocated Standard Oil to New Jersey and created there what became known as a "holding company"—a central corporate body that would buy up the stock of various members of the Standard Oil trust and establish direct, formal ownership of the corporations in the trust.

"Holding Company"

By the end of the nineteenth century, 1 percent of the corporations in America were able to control more than 33 percent of the manufacturing. A system of economic organization was emerging that lodged enormous power in the hands of very few men—the great bankers of New York such as J. P. Morgan, industrial titans such as Rockefeller (who himself gained control of a major bank), and others.

The industrial giants of the era were clearly responsible for substantial economic growth. They were also creating the basis for one of the greatest public controversies of their era: a raging debate over concentrated economic and political power that continued well into the twentieth century.

CAPITALISM AND ITS CRITICS

The rise of big business was not without its critics. Farmers and workers saw in the growth of the new corporate power centers a threat to their ability to control their own destinies. Middle-class critics pointed to the corruption that the new industrial titans seemed to produce. The growing criticisms challenged the captains of industry to create a defense of the new corporate economy.

Survival of the Fittest

The new rationale for capitalism rested squarely on an older ideology of individualism. The new industrial economy, its defenders argued, was not shrinking opportunities for individual advance- *Ideology of Individualism* ment. It was providing every individual with a chance to succeed and attain great wealth.

There was an element of truth in such claims, but only a small element. Before the Civil War there had been few millionaires in America; by 1892 there were more than 4,000. Some of them—Carnegie, Rockefeller, and a few others—were in fact "self-made men." But most of the new business tycoons had begun their careers from positions of privilege and wealth. Nor was their rise to power and prominence always a result simply of hard work and ingenuity, as they liked to claim. It was also a result of ruthlessness and, at times, rampant corruption.

Nevertheless, most tycoons continued to claim that they had attained their wealth and power through hard work, acquisitiveness, and thrift. Those who succeeded, they argued, deserved their success, and those who failed had earned their failure through their own laziness, stupidity, or carelessness. Such assumptions became the basis of a popular social theory of the late nineteenth century: Social Darwinism, *Social Darwinism* the application of Charles Darwin's laws of evolution and natural selection among species to human society. Just as only the fittest survived in the process of evolution, the Social Darwinists argued, so in human society only the fittest individuals survived and flourished in the marketplace.

The English philosopher Herbert Spencer was the first and most important proponent of this theory. Society, he argued, benefited from the elimination of the unfit and the survival of the strong and talented. Spencer's teachings found prominent supporters among American intellectuals, most notably William Graham Sumner of Yale, who promoted similar ideas in lectures, articles, and a famous 1906 book, *Folkways*.

Social Darwinism appealed to corporate leaders because it seemed to legitimize their success and confirm their virtues. It was not, however, an *Corporate Wealth Legitimated* ideology that had very much to do with the realities of the corporate economy. At the same time that businessmen were celebrating the virtues of competition and the free market, they were making active efforts to protect themselves from competition and to replace the natural workings of the marketplace with control by great combinations. Vicious competitive battle was in fact the very thing that American businessmen most feared and tried to eliminate.

The Gospel of Wealth

Some businessmen attempted to temper the harsh philosophy of Social Darwinism with a gentler, if in some ways equally self-serving, idea: the "gospel of wealth." People of great wealth, advocates of this idea argued, had not only great power but great responsibilities. It was their duty to use their riches to advance social progress. Andrew Carnegie elaborated on the *Gospel of Wealth* creed in his 1901 book, *The Gospel of Wealth*, in which he wrote that people of wealth should consider all revenues in excess of their own needs "trust funds" to be used for the good of the community. Carnegie was only one of many great industrialists who devoted large parts of their fortunes to philanthropic works.

The notion of private wealth as a public blessing existed alongside another popular concept: the notion of great wealth as something available to all. Russell H. Conwell, a Baptist minister, became the most prominent spokesman for the idea by delivering one lecture, "Acres of Diamonds," more than 6,000 times between 1880 and 1900. Conwell told a series of stories, which he claimed were true, of individuals who had found opportunities for extraordinary wealth in their own backyards. (One such story involved a modest farmer who discovered a vast diamond mine in his own fields in the course of working his land.) Most of the millionaires in the country, Conwell claimed (inaccurately), had begun on the lowest rung of the economic ladder and had worked their way to success.

Horatio Alger Horatio Alger was the most famous promoter of the success story. Alger was originally a minister in a small town in Massachusetts but was driven from his pulpit as a result of a scandal connected to his active, but usually hidden, homosexuality. He moved to New York, where he wrote his celebrated novels: *Ragged Dick*, *Tom the Bootblack*, *Sink or Swim*, and many others, more than 100 in all. The basic story was almost always the same: A young boy, perhaps an orphan, makes his perilous way through life on the rough streets of the city

BOUND TO RISE

ALGER

A NEWSBOY'S STORY Alger's novels were even more popular after his death in 1899 than they had been in his lifetime. This reprint of one of his many "rags-to-riches" stories—about a New York newsboy's rise to wealth and success—was typical of his work. *(Private Collection)*

by selling newspapers or peddling matches. One day, his energy and determination catches the eye of a wealthy man, who gives him a chance to improve himself. Through honesty, charm, hard work, and aggressiveness, the boy rises in the world to become a successful man.

The purpose of writing, Alger claimed, was twofold. He wanted to "exert a salutary influence upon the class of whom [I] was writing, by setting before them inspiring examples of what energy, ambition, and an honest purpose may achieve." He also wanted to show his largely middle-class readers "the life and experiences of the friendless and vagrant children to be found in all our cities."

But Alger's intentions probably had little to do with the success of his books. Most Americans of the late nineteenth and early twentieth centuries were attracted to Alger because his stories helped them to believe that it is possible for individuals to rise in the world with willpower and hard work, that anyone can become a "self-made man." Alger's admirers came to ignore his own misgivings about industrialism and to portray his books purely as a celebration of (and justification for) laissez-faire capitalism and the accumulation of wealth.

Alternative Visions

Alongside the celebrations of competition and the justifications for great wealth stood a group of alternative philosophies, challenging the corporate ethos and at times capitalism itself.

One such philosophy emerged in the work of the sociologist Lester Frank Ward. In *Dynamic Sociology* (1883) and other books, he argued that civilization was not governed by natural selection but by human intelligence, which was capable of shaping society as it wished. In contrast to Sumner, who believed that state intervention to remodel the environment was futile, Ward thought that an active government engaged in positive planning was society's best hope.

Other Americans adopted more radical approaches to reform. Some *Socialist Labor Party* dissenters found a home in the Socialist Labor Party, founded in the 1870s and led for many years by Daniel De Leon, an immigrant from the West Indies. Although De Leon attracted a modest following in the industrial cities, the party never became a major political force and never polled more than 82,000 votes. A dissident faction of De Leon's party, eager to forge stronger ties with organized labor, broke away and in 1901 formed the more enduring American Socialist Party.

Other radicals gained a wider following. Among them was the California writer and activist Henry George. His an-*Henry George's "Single Tax"* grily eloquent *Progress and Poverty*, published in 1879, became one of the best-selling nonfiction works in American publishing history. George blamed social problems on the ability of a few monopolists to grow wealthy as a result of rising land values. An increase in the value of land, he claimed, was not a result of any effort by the owner. It was an "unearned increment," produced by the growth of society around the land. Such profits were rightfully the property of the community. And so George proposed a "single tax" on land, to replace all other taxes, which would return the increment to the people. The tax, he argued, would destroy monopolies, distribute wealth more equally, and eliminate poverty.

Rivaling George in popularity was Edward Bellamy, whose utopian novel *Looking Backward*, published in 1888, sold more than 1 million copies. It described the experiences of a young Bostonian who went into a hypnotic sleep in 1887 and awoke in the year 2000 to find a new social order in which want, politics, and vice were unknown. The new society had emerged through a peaceful, evolutionary process: the large trusts of the late nineteenth century had continued to grow in size and to combine with one another until ultimately they formed a single, great trust, controlled by the government, which distributed the abundance of the industrial economy equally among all the people. "Fraternal cooperation" had replaced competition. Class divisions had disappeared. Bellamy labeled the philosophy behind this vision "nationalism."

"MODERN COLOSSUS OF (RAIL) ROADS" Cornelius Vanderbilt, known as the "Commodore," accumulated one of America's great fortunes by consolidating several large railroad companies under his control in the 1860s. His name became a synonym not only for enormous wealth, but also (in the eyes of many Americans) for excessive corporate power—as suggested in this cartoon, showing him standing astride his empire and manipulating its parts. *(Culver Pictures, Inc.)*

The Problems of Monopoly

Relatively few Americans shared the views of those who questioned capitalism itself. But as time went on, a growing number of people were becoming deeply concerned about the growth of monopoly.

By the end of the century, a wide range of groups had begun to assail monopoly and economic concentration. They blamed monopoly for

Economic Concentration Challenged

creating artificially high prices. In the absence of competition, they argued, monopolistic industries could charge whatever prices they wished; railroads, in particular, charged very high rates along some routes because, in the absence of competition, they knew their customers had no choice but to pay them. Artificially high prices, moreover, contributed to the economy's instability, as production consistently outpaced demand. Beginning in 1873, the economy fluctuated erratically, producing severe recessions every five or six years, each worse than the last.

THE ORDEAL OF THE WORKER

Most workers in the late nineteenth century experienced a real rise in their standard of living. But they did so at the cost of arduous and often dangerous working conditions, diminishing control over their own work, and a growing sense of powerlessness.

The Immigrant Work Force

The industrial work force expanded dramatically in the late nineteenth century. The source of that expansion was a massive migration into industrial cities—immigration of two sorts. The first was the continuing flow of rural Americans into factory towns and cities—people disillusioned with or bankrupted by life on the farm. The second was the great wave of immigration from abroad (primarily from Europe, but also from Asia, Canada, Mexico, and other areas) in the decades following the Civil War—an influx greater than that of any previous era. The 25 million immigrants who arrived in the United States between 1865 and 1915 were more than four times the number who had arrived in the previous fifty years.

Rapidly Expanding Working Class

In the 1870s and 1880s, most of the immigrants came from England, Ireland, and northern Europe. By the end of the century, however, the major sources of immigrants had shifted, with large numbers of southern and eastern Europeans (Italians, Poles, Russians, Greeks, Slavs, and others) moving into the country and into the industrial work force.

The new immigrants were coming to America in part to escape poverty and oppression in their homelands. But they were also lured by expectations of new opportunities. Railroads tried to lure immigrants into their western landholdings by distributing misleading advertisements overseas. Industrial employers actively recruited immigrant workers under the Labor Contract Law, which—until its repeal in 1885—permitted them to pay for the passage of workers in advance and deduct the amount later from their wages. Even after the repeal of the law, employers continued to encourage the immigration of unskilled laborers,

Labor Contract Law

often with the assistance of foreign-born labor brokers, such as the Greek and Italian *padrones*, who recruited work gangs of their fellow nationals.

The arrival of these new groups introduced heightened ethnic tensions into the dynamics of the working class. Low-paid Poles, Greeks, and French Canadians began to displace higher-paid British and Irish workers in the textile factories of New England. Italians, Slavs, and Poles emerged as a major source of labor for the mining industry. Chinese and Mexicans competed with Anglo-Americans and African Americans in mining, farmwork, and factory labor in California, Colorado, and Texas.   *Growing Ethnic Tensions*

Wages and Working Conditions

At the turn of the century, the average income of the American worker was $400 to $500 a year—below the $600 figure that many believed was the minimum required to maintain a reasonable level of comfort. Nor did workers have much job security. All were vulnerable to the boom-and-bust cycle of the industrial economy, and some lost their jobs because of technological advances. Even those who kept their jobs could find their wages suddenly and substantially cut in hard times. Few workers, in other words, were ever very far from poverty.

American laborers faced a wide array of other hardships as well. For first-generation workers accustomed to the patterns of agrarian life, there was a difficult adjustment to the nature of modern industrial labor: the performance of routine, repetitive tasks on a strict and monotonous schedule. To skilled artisans whose once-valued tasks were now performed by machines, the new system was impersonal and demeaning. Most factory laborers worked ten-hour days, six days a week; in the steel industry they worked twelve hours a day. Industrial accidents were frequent.   *Harsh Work Conditions*

The decreasing need for skilled work in factories induced many employers to increase the use of women and children, whom they could hire for lower wages than adult males. By 1900, 20 percent of all manufacturing workers were women. Women worked in all areas of industry, even in some of the most arduous jobs. Most women, however, worked in a few industries where unskilled and semiskilled machine labor (as opposed to heavy manual labor) prevailed. The textile industry remained the largest single industrial employer of women. (Domestic service remained the most common female occupation overall.) Women worked for wages well below the minimum necessary for survival (and well below the wages paid to men working the same jobs).

At least 1.7 million children under sixteen years of age were employed in factories and fields; 10 percent of all girls aged ten to fifteen, and 20 percent of all boys, held jobs. Under public pressure, thirty-eight states passed child labor laws in the   *Child Labor*

SPINDLE BOYS Young boys, some of them barefoot, clamber along the great textile machines in a Georgia cotton mill adjusting spindles. Many of them were the children of women who worked in the plants. The photograph is by Lewis Hine. *(Bettmann/Corbis)*

late nineteenth century. But 60 percent of child workers were employed in agriculture, which was typically exempt from the laws. And even for children employed in factories, the laws merely set a minimum age of twelve years and a maximum workday of ten hours, standards that employers often ignored in any case.

Emerging Unionization

Laborers attempted to fight back against such conditions by creating national unions. By the end of the century, however, their efforts had met with little success.

There had been craft unions in America, representing small groups of skilled workers, since well before the Civil War. Alone, however, individual unions could not hope to exert significant power in the economy. And during the turbulent recession years of the 1870s, unions faced the additional problem of widespread public hostility. When labor disputes with employers turned bitter and violent, as they occasionally did, much of the public instinctively blamed the workers for the trouble, rarely the employ-

"Molly Maguires"

ers. Particularly alarming to middle-class Americans was the emergence of the "Molly Maguires" in the anthracite coal region of western Pennsylvania. This militant labor organization sometimes used violence and even murder in its battle with coal operators. Much of the violence attributed to the Molly Maguires, however, was deliberately instigated by informers and agents employed by the mine owners, who wanted a pretext for ruthless measures to suppress unionization.

Excitement over the Molly Maguires paled beside the near hysteria that gripped the country during the railroad strike of 1877, which began when the eastern railroads *Railroad Strike of 1877* announced a 10 percent wage cut. The strike soon expanded into something approaching a class war. Strikers disrupted rail service from Baltimore to St. Louis, destroyed equipment, and rioted in the streets of Pittsburgh and other cities. State militias were called out, and in July President Hayes ordered federal troops to suppress the disorders in West Virginia. In Baltimore, eleven demonstrators died and forty were wounded in a conflict between workers and militiamen. In Philadelphia, the state militia killed twenty people when the troops opened fire on thousands of workers and their families who were attempting to block the railroad crossings. In all, over 100 people died before the strike finally collapsed several weeks after it had begun. The great railroad strike was America's first major, national labor conflict.

The Knights of Labor

The first major effort to create a genuinely national labor organization was the founding in 1869 of the Noble Order of the Knights of Labor, under the leadership of Uriah S. Stephens. Membership was open to all who "toiled," a definition that included all workers, most business and professional people, and virtually all women—whether they worked in factories, as domestic servants, or in their own homes. The only excluded groups were lawyers, bankers, liquor dealers, and professional gamblers. The Knights of Labor championed an eight-hour workday and the abolition of child labor, but they were more interested in long-range reform of the economy. The Knights hoped to replace the "wage system" with a new "cooperative system," in which workers would themselves control a large part of the economy.

For several years, the Knights remained a secret fraternal organization. But in the late 1870s, under the leadership of Terence V. Powderly, the order moved into the *Terence V. Powderly* open and entered a period of spectacular expansion. By 1886, it claimed a total membership of over 700,000. Local unions or assemblies associated with the Knights launched a series of railroad and other strikes in the 1880s in defiance of Powderly's wishes. Their failure helped discredit the organization. By 1890, the membership of the Knights had shrunk to 100,000. A few years later, the organization disappeared altogether.

The AFL

Even before the Knights began to decline, a rival association appeared. In 1881, representatives of a number of craft unions formed the Federation of Organized Trade and Labor Unions of the United States and Canada. Five years later, this body took the name it has borne ever since, the American Federation of Labor (AFL).

Rejecting the Knights' idea of one big union for everybody, the Federation was an association of essentially autonomous craft unions that rep-

Samuel Gompers

resented mainly skilled workers. Samuel Gompers, the powerful leader of the AFL, concentrated on labor's immediate objectives: wages, hours, and working conditions. As one of its first objectives, the AFL demanded a national eight-hour workday and called for a general strike if the goal was not achieved by May 1, 1886. On that day, strikes and demonstrations for a shorter workday took place all over the country.

In Chicago, a center of labor and radical strength, a strike was already in progress at the McCormick Harvester Company. City police had been harassing the strikers, and labor and radical leaders called a protest meeting

Haymarket Bombing

at Haymarket Square on May 1. When the police ordered the crowd to disperse, someone threw a bomb that killed seven policemen and injured sixty-seven others. The police, who had killed four strikers the day before, fired into the crowd and killed four more people. Conservative, property-conscious Americans—frightened and outraged—demanded retribution. Chicago officials finally rounded up eight anarchists and charged them with murder, on the grounds that their statements had incited whoever had hurled the bomb. All eight scapegoats were found guilty after a remarkably injudicious trial. Seven were sentenced to death. One of them committed suicide, four were executed, and two had their sentences commuted to life imprisonment.

To most middle-class Americans, the Haymarket bombing was an alarming symbol of social chaos and radicalism. "Anarchism" now became in the public mind a code word for terrorism and violence, even though most anarchists were relatively peaceful. For the next thirty years, the specter of anarchism remained one of the most frightening concepts in the American imagination. It was a constant obstacle to the goals of the

Labor Discredited

AFL and other labor organizations, and it did particular damage to the Knights of Labor. However much they tried to distance themselves from radicals, labor leaders were always vulnerable to accusations of anarchism, as the violent strikes of the 1890s occasionally illustrated.

The Homestead Strike

The Amalgamated Association of Iron and Steel Workers was the most powerful trade union in the country. Its members were skilled workers, in great demand by employers, and thus had long been able to exercise sig-

nificant power in the workplace. In the mid-1880s, however, demand for
skilled workers was in decline as new production methods changed the
steelmaking process. In the Carnegie system, which was coming to dominate the steel industry, the union was able to maintain a foothold in only
one of the corporation's three major factories—the Homestead plant near
Pittsburgh.

By 1890, Carnegie and his chief lieutenant,
Henry Clay Frick, had decided that the Amalga-   *Henry Clay Frick*
mated "had to go." Over the next two years, they repeatedly cut wages at
Homestead. At first, the union acquiesced, aware that it was not strong
enough to wage a successful strike. But in 1892, when the company
stopped even discussing its decisions with the union and gave it two days
to accept another wage cut, the Amalgamated called for a strike.

Frick abruptly shut down the plant and called in 300 guards from the
Pinkerton Detective Agency to enable the company to hire nonunion
workers. The hated Pinkertons were well-known strikebreakers. They approached the plant by river, on barges, on July 6, 1892. The strikers
poured gasoline on the water, set it on fire, and then met the Pinkertons at
the docks with guns and dynamite. A pitched battle broke out. After several hours of fighting, which killed three guards and ten strikers and injured many others, the Pinkertons surrendered and were escorted roughly
out of town.

But the workers' victory was temporary. The governor of Pennsylvania, at the company's request, sent the state's entire National Guard con-
tingent, some 8,000 men, to Homestead. Produc-
tion resumed, with strikebreakers now protected by   *Government Intervention*
troops. And public opinion turned against the strikers when a radical
made an attempt to assassinate Frick. Slowly, workers drifted back to their
jobs, and finally—four months after the strike began—the Amalgamated
surrendered. By 1900, every major steel plant in the Northeast had broken with the Amalgamated. Its membership shrank from a high of 24,000
in 1891 (two-thirds of all eligible steelworkers) to fewer than 7,000 a
decade later.

The Pullman Strike

A dispute of greater magnitude, if less violence, was the Pullman strike in
1894. The Pullman Palace Car Company manufactured railroad sleeping
and parlor cars, which it built and repaired at a plant near Chicago. There
the company constructed a 600-acre town, Pullman, and rented its trim,
orderly houses to the employees. George M. Pullman, owner of the company, saw the town as a model—a solution to the problems of industrial
workers. But many residents chafed at the regimentation (and the high
rents). In the winter of 1893–1894, the Pullman Company slashed wages
by about 25 percent, citing its own declining revenues in the depression,
without reducing the rent it charged its employees. Workers went on

BREAKING THE PULLMAN STRIKE Company C of the 15th United States Infantry, called into service by President Grover Cleveland to break a widespread railroad strike in 1894, poses here before a special patrol train near Rock Island, Illinois. The strike began when workers at the Pullman Palace Car Company outside Chicago walked off the job to protest wage cuts and rent increases. Their walkout generated broad support from other railroad workers and even from the governor of Illinois, John Peter Altgeld, who refused to call out the state militia to keep the trains running. Cleveland, however, had little sympathy for striking workers and he used his authority as president to protect the delivery of the mails to call out federal troops to break the strike. *(Bettmann/Corbis)*

American Railway Union strike and persuaded the militant American Railway Union, led by Eugene V. Debs, to support them by refusing to handle Pullman cars and equipment. Within a few days thousands of railroad workers in twenty-seven states and territories were on strike, and transportation from Chicago to the Pacific coast was paralyzed.

Unlike most elected politicians, the governor of Illinois, John Peter Altgeld, was a man with demonstrated sympathies for workers and their grievances. He refused to call out the militia to protect employers. Bypassing Altgeld, railroad operators asked the federal government to send regular army troops to Illinois, using the pretext that the strike was preventing the movement of mail on the trains. In July 1894, President Grover Cleveland ordered 2,000 troops to the Chicago area. A federal court issued an injunction forbidding the union to continue the strike. When Debs and his associates defied it, they were arrested and imprisoned. With federal troops protecting the hiring of new workers and with the union leaders in a federal jail, the strike quickly collapsed.

Sources of Labor Weakness

The last decades of the nineteenth century were years in which labor, despite militant organizing efforts, made few real gains. Industrial wages rose hardly at all. Labor *Few Gains for Labor* leaders won a few legislative victories—the abolition of the Contract Labor Law, the establishment of an eight-hour day for government employees, compensation for some workers injured on the job, and others. But many such laws were not enforced. There were widespread strikes and protests, and many other working-class forms of resistance, large and small, but few real gains. The end of the century found most workers with less political power and less control of the workplace than they had had forty years before.

Workers failed to make greater gains for many reasons. The principal labor organizations represented only a small percentage of the industrial work force; the AFL, the most important, excluded unskilled workers, and along with them most women, blacks, and recent immigrants. Divisions within the work force contributed further to union weakness. Tensions among different ethnic and racial groups kept laborers divided.

Another source of labor weakness was the shifting nature of the work force. Many immigrant *Sources of Labor Weakness* workers came to America intending to earn some money and then return home. The assumption that they had no long-range future in the country eroded their willingness to organize. Other workers were in constant motion, moving from one job to another, one town to another, seldom in a single place long enough to establish any institutional ties or exert any real power.

Above all, perhaps, workers made few gains in the late nineteenth century because they faced corporate organizations of vast wealth and power, which were generally determined to crush any efforts by workers to challenge their prerogatives. And as the Homestead and Pullman strikes suggest, the corporations usually had the support of local, state, and federal authorities, who were willing to send in troops to "preserve order" and crush labor uprisings on demand.

Despite the creation of new labor unions, despite a wave of strikes and protests, workers in the late nineteenth century failed on the whole to create successful organizations or to protect their interests. In the battle for power within the emerging industrial economy, almost all the advantages seemed to lie with capital. *Capital's Strength*

CONCLUSION

In the four decades following the end of the Civil War, the United States propelled itself into the forefront of the industrializing nations of the world. Large areas of the nation remained overwhelmingly rural, to be sure. But even so, America's economy, and along with it the nation's society and culture, was being profoundly transformed.

New technologies, new forms of corporate management, and new supplies of labor helped make possible the rapid growth of the nation's industries and the construction of its railroads. The factory system contributed to the growth of the nation's cities. Immigration provided a steady supply of new workers for the growing industrial economy. The result was a steady increase in national wealth, rising living standards for much of the population, and the creation of great new fortunes.

But industrialization did not spread its fruits evenly. Large areas of the country, most notably the South, and large groups in the population, most notably minorities, women, and recent immigrants, profited relatively little from economic growth. Industrial workers experienced arduous conditions of labor. Small merchants and manufacturers found themselves overmatched by great new combinations.

Industrialists strove to create a rationale for their power and to persuade the public that everyone had something to gain from it. But many Americans remained skeptical of modern capitalism, and some—workers struggling to form unions, reformers denouncing trusts, socialists envisioning a new world, and many others—created broad and powerful critiques of the new economic order. Industrialization brought both progress and pain to late-nineteenth-century America. Controversies over its effects defined the era and would continue to define the first decades of the twentieth century.

FOR FURTHER REFERENCE

Robert Wiebe's *The Search for Order, 1877–1920* (1968) is a classic analysis of America's evolution from a society of island communities to a national urban society. Alfred D. Chandler, Jr., describes the new business practices that made industrialization possible in *The Visible Hand: The Managerial Revolution in American Business* (1977) and *Scale and Scope: The Dynamics of Industrial Capitalism* (1990). Olivier Zunz offers a provocative analysis of the social underpinnings of the new corporate order in *Making America Corporate, 1870–1920* (1990) and *Why the American Century?* (1998). David F. Noble, *America by Design: Science, Technology, and the Rise of Corporate Capitalism* (1977) and David Hounshell, *From the American System to Mass Production, 1800–1932* (1984) discuss the explosion of science and technology in the era of rapid industrialization. Daniel Rodgers, *The Work Ethic in Industrial America, 1850–1920* (1978) is an important intellectual history of the way Americans viewed industrial workers. David Montgomery, *The Fall of the House of Labor: The Workplace, the State, and American Labor Activism, 1865–1925* (1987) analyzes the way industrialization shaped (and was shaped by) the workers, their expertise, and the strong cultural traditions of the shop floor. Kevin Kenny, *Making Sense of the Molly Maguires* (1998) examines labor radicalism and Elliott J. Gorn, *Mother Jones: The Most Dangerous Woman in America* (2001) explores the career of a celebrated labor firebrand. Alice Kessler-Harris documents the tremendous movement of women into the work force in this period in *Out to Work: A History of Wage-Earning Women in the United States* (1982). John L. Thomas, *Alternative America: Henry George, Edward Bellamy, Henry Demarest Lloyd, and the Adversary Tradition* (1983) examines some important critics of corporate capitalism.

For quizzes, Internet resources, references to additional books and films, and more, consult this book's Online Learning Center site at www.mhhe.com/unfinishednation4.

MILWAUKEE, 1900 In the middle years of the nineteenth century, Americans were dazzled by large paintings of the dramatic landscape of the Far West. By the beginning of the twentieth century, they were at least as interested in the new landscape of the city—with its tall buildings, its new technologies, and its dramatic design. This painted photograph of downtown Milwaukee is typical of many images of American city centers in this period, with its focus on a particularly dramatic large building and its presentation of such urban wonders as streetcars and electrical wires. Such images were often reproduced on postcards. *(Photo by William Henry Jackson/Detroit Publishing Company. Reproduced by permission of Christopher Cardozo, Inc.)*

TIME LINE

1869	1870	1871	1872	1876	1882	1884	1890
First intercollegiate football game	NYC opens first elevated railroads	Boston and Chicago fires	Boss Tweed convicted	Baseball's National League founded	Congress restricts Chinese immigration	First "skyscraper" in Chicago	Riis's *How the Other Half Lives*

THE AGE OF THE CITY

The New Urban Growth
The Urban Landscape
Strains of Urban Life
The Rise of Mass Consumption
Leisure in the Consumer Society
High Culture in the Urban Age

The face of American society changed in countless ways in response to the growth of industry and commerce. No change was more profound, however, than the growing size and influence of cities. Having begun its life as a primarily agrarian republic, the United States in the late nineteenth century was becoming an urban nation.

THE NEW URBAN GROWTH

The great movement of people from the countryside to the city was not unique to the United States. But Americans found urbanization particularly jarring. The urban population increased sevenfold in the half-century after the Civil War. And in 1920, the census revealed that for the first time, a majority of the American people lived in "urban" areas—defined as communities of 2,500 people or more.

Natural increase accounted for only a small part of the urban growth. Urban families experienced a high rate of infant mortality, a declining fertility rate, and a high death rate from disease. Without immigration, cities would have grown relatively slowly.

1891	1894	1895	1897	1901	1903	1906	1910	
Basketball invented	Immigration Restriction League formed	Crane's *The Red Badge of Courage*	Boston opens first subway in America	Baseball's American League founded	First World Series	San Franciso earthquake and fire	NCAA founded	
						Sinclair's *The Jungle*		

The Migrations

The late nineteenth century was an age of unprecedented geographical mobility, as Americans left the declining agricultural regions of the East at a dramatic rate. Some of those who left were mov-

Unprecedented Geographical Mobility

ing to the newly developing farmlands of the West. But almost as many were moving to the cities of the East and the Midwest.

Among those leaving rural America for industrial cities in the 1880s were southern blacks. They were escaping the poverty, debt, violence, and oppression they faced in the rural South. They were also seeking new opportunities in cities. Factory jobs for blacks were rare and professional opportunities almost nonexistent. Urban blacks tended to work as cooks, janitors, and domestic servants, as well as in other service occupations. Because many such jobs were considered women's work, black women often outnumbered black men in the cities.

The most important source of urban population growth in the late nineteenth century, however, was the arrival of great numbers of new immigrants from abroad. Some came from Canada,

Southern and Eastern European Immigrants

Latin America, and—particularly on the West Coast—China and Japan. But the greatest number came from Europe. After 1880, the flow of new arrivals began to include large numbers of people from southern and eastern Europe. By the 1890s, more than half of all immigrants came from these regions.

In earlier years, most new immigrants from Europe (particularly Germans and Scandinavians) had arrived with at least some money and education. Most of them arrived at one of the major port cities on the Atlantic coast (the greatest number in New York, through the famous immigrant depot on Ellis Island) and then headed west. But the new immigrants of the late nineteenth century generally lacked the capital to buy farmland and lacked the education to establish themselves in professions. So, like similarly poor Irish immigrants before the Civil War, they settled overwhelmingly in industrial cities, where they worked largely in unskilled jobs.

The Ethnic City

By 1890, most of the population of the major urban areas consisted of immigrants: 87 percent of the population in Chicago, 80 percent in New York, 84 percent in Milwaukee and Detroit.

Diverse Immigrant Populations

Equally striking was the diversity of the new immigrant populations. In other countries experiencing heavy immigration in this period, most of the new arrivals were coming from one or two sources. But in the United States, no single national group dominated.

Most of the new immigrants were rural people, and for many the adjustment to city life was painful. To help ease the transition, some national groups formed close-knit ethnic communities within the cities, neighbor-

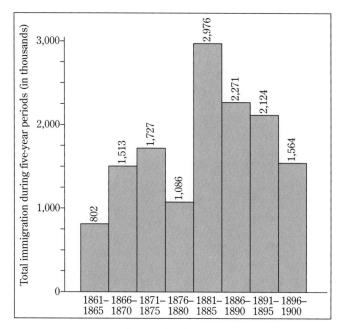

TOTAL IMMIGRATION, 1860–1900 Over 10 million immigrants from abroad entered the United States in the last forty years of the nineteenth century, with particularly high numbers arriving in the 1880s and 1890s. This chart shows the pattern of immigration in five-year intervals. ◆ *What external events might help explain some of the rises and falls in the rates of immigration in these years?*

hoods often called "immigrant ghettoes." Ethnic neighborhoods offered newcomers much that was familiar. They could find newspapers and theaters in their native languages, stores selling their native foods, and church and fraternal organizations that provided links with their national pasts. Many immigrants also maintained close ties with their native countries. They stayed in touch with relatives who had remained behind. Some (perhaps as many as a third in the early years) returned to their homelands after a relatively short time; others helped bring the rest of their families to America.

The cultural cohesiveness of the ethnic communities clearly eased the pain of separation from the immigrants' native lands. What role it played in helping immigrants become absorbed into the economic life of America is a more difficult question to *Importance of Ethnic Ties* answer. Some ethnic groups (Jews and Germans in particular) advanced economically more rapidly than others (for example, the Irish). One explanation is that, by huddling together in ethnic neighborhoods, immigrant groups tended to reinforce the cultural values of their previous societies. When those values were particularly well suited to economic advancement, as was—for example, the high value Jews placed on education—ethnic identification may have helped members of a group to improve their lots. When other values predominated—maintaining community solidarity, strengthening family ties, preserving order—progress could be less rapid.

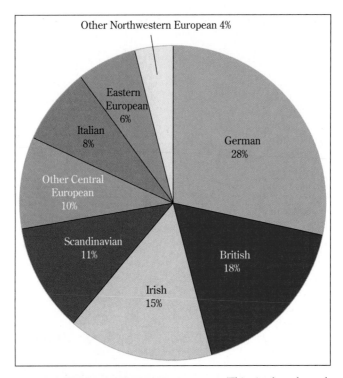

SOURCES OF IMMIGRATION FROM EUROPE, 1860–1900 This pie-chart shows the sources of European immigration in the late nineteenth century. The largest number of immigrants continued to come from traditional sources (Britain, Ireland, Germany, Scandinavia), but the beginnings of what in the early twentieth century would become a major influx of immigrants from new sources—southern and eastern Europe in particular—are already visible here. Immigration from other sources—Mexico, South and Central America, and Asia—was also significant during this period. ◆ *Why would these newer sources of European and other kinds of immigration create controversy among older-stock Americans?*

But other factors were at least as important in determining how well immigrants fared. Immigrants who aroused strong racial prejudice among native-born whites found it very difficult to advance whatever their talents. Those white immigrants who arrived with a valuable skill or with some capital did better than those who did not. And over time, those who lived in cities where people of their own nationality came to predominate—for example, the Irish in New York and Boston, or the Germans in Milwaukee—gained an advantage as they learned to exert their political power.

Assimilation and Exclusion

Despite the many differences among the various immigrant communities, virtually all groups had certain things in common. Most immigrants shared the experience of living in cities. Most were young; the majority of newcomers were between fifteen and forty-five years old. And in most communities of the foreign-born, the strength of ethnic ties had to compete against another powerful force: the desire for assimilation.

Many of the new arrivals had come to America with romantic visions of the New World. And however disillusioning they might find their first contact with the United States, they usually retained the dream of becoming true "Americans." Second-generation immigrants were particularly likely to attempt to break with the old ways. Young women, in particular, sometimes rebelled against parents who tried to arrange (or prevent) marriages or who opposed women entering the workplace.

Native-born Americans encouraged immigrants to assimilate in countless ways. Public *Assimilation Encouraged* schools taught children in English, and employers often insisted that workers speak English on the job. Most non-ethnic stores sold mainly American products, forcing immigrants to adapt their diets, clothing, and lifestyles to American norms. Church leaders were often native-born Americans or more assimilated immigrants who encouraged their parishioners to adopt American ways. Some even embraced reforms to make their religion more compatible with the norms of the new country. Reform Judaism, imported from Germany in the late nineteenth century, was an effort by American Jewish leaders (as it had been by German ones) to make their faith less "foreign" to the dominant culture.

The arrival of these vast numbers of new immigrants, and the way many of them clung to old ways and created distinctive communities, provoked fear and resentment among some native-born Americans in much the same way earlier arrivals had done. The rising nativism provoked political responses. In 1887, Henry Bowers, a self-educated lawyer, founded the American Protective Association, a group committed to stopping immigration. By 1894, membership in the organization reportedly reached 500,000, with chapters throughout the Northeast and Midwest. That same year, five Harvard alumni founded a more genteel organization—the Immigration Restriction *Immigration Restriction League* League—in Boston. They proposed screening immigrants through literacy tests and other standards, to separate the "desirable" from the "undesirable."

The government responded to popular concern about immigration even earlier. In 1882 Congress excluded the Chinese, denied entry to "undesirables"—convicts, paupers, the mentally incompetent—and placed a tax of 50 cents on each person admitted. Later legislation of the 1890s enlarged the list of those barred from immigrating.

But these laws kept out only a small number of aliens, and more ambitious restriction proposals made little progress in Congress. That was because immigration was providing a cheap and plentiful labor supply to the rapidly growing economy, *Cheap Immigrant Labor* and many argued that America's industrial (and indeed agricultural) development would be impossible without it.

The great waves of immigration that transformed American society in the nineteenth and early twentieth centuries were not unique to the United States. They were part of a great, global movement of peoples—unprecedented in history—that affected every continent. These great migrations were the product of two related forces: population growth and industrialization.

The population of Europe grew faster in the second half of the nineteenth century than it had ever grown before and than it has ever grown since—almost doubling between 1850 and the beginning of World War I. The population growth was a result of growing economies able to support more people and of more efficient and productive agriculture that helped end debilitating famines. But the rapid growth nevertheless strained the resources of many parts of Europe and affected, in particular, rural people, who were now too numerous to live off the available land. Many decided to move to other parts of the world where land was more plentiful.

At the same time, industrialization drew millions of people out of the countryside and into cities—sometimes into cities in their own countries, but often to industrial cities in other, more economically advanced nations. Historians of migration speak of "push" factors (pressures on people to leave their homes) and "pull" factors (the lure of new lands) in explaining population movements. The "push" for many nineteenth-century migrants was poverty and inadequate land at home; for others it was political and religious oppression. The "pull" was the availability of land or industrial jobs in other regions or lands—and, for some, the prospect of greater freedom abroad. Faster, cheaper, and easier transportation—railroads and steamships, in particular—also aided large-scale immigration.

From 1800 to the start of World War I, fifty million Europeans migrated to new lands overseas—people from almost all areas of Europe, but in the later years of the century (when migration reached its peak) mostly from poor rural areas in southern and eastern Europe. Italy, Russia, and Poland were among the biggest sources of late-nineteenth-century migrants. Almost two thirds of these immigrants came to the United States. But nearly twenty million Europeans migrated to other lands. Migrants from England and Ireland (among others) moved in large numbers to those areas of the British empire with vast, seemingly open lands: Canada, Australia, New Zealand, and South Africa. Large numbers of Italians moved to Argentina and other parts of South America. Many of these migrants moved to open land in these countries; established themselves as farmers, using the new mechanical farming devices made possible by industrialization; and in many places—Australia, New Zealand, Argentina, South Africa, and the United States—evicted the native residents of their territories and created societies of their own. Many others settled in the industrial cities that were growing up in all these regions and formed distinctive ethnic and national communities within them.

But it was not only Europeans who were transplanting themselves in these years. Tremendous numbers of migrants—usually poor, desperate people—left Asia, Africa, and the Pacific Islands in search of better lives. Most of them could not afford the journey abroad on their own. They moved instead as indentured servants (in much the same way many English migrants moved to America in the seventeenth century), agreeing to a term of servitude in their new land in exchange for food, shelter, and transportation. Recruiters of indentured servants fanned out across China, Japan, areas of Africa and the Pacific Islands, and above all, India. French and British recruiters brought hundreds of thousands of Indian migrants to work in plantations in their own Asian and African colonies. Chinese laborers were recruited to work on plantations in Cuba and Hawaii, mines in Malaya, Peru, South Africa, and Australia, and railroad projects in Canada, Peru, and the United States. African indentured servants moved in large numbers to the Caribbean, and Pacific Islanders tended to move to other islands or to Australia.

The immigration of European peoples to new lands was largely voluntary and brought most migrants to the United States, where indentured servitude was illegal. But the migration of non-European peoples often involved an important element of coercion and brought relatively small numbers of people to the United States. This non-European migration was a function of the growth of European empires, and it was made possible by the imperial system—by its labor recruiters, by its naval resources, by its law, and by its economic needs. Together, these various forms of migration produced one of the greatest population movements in the history of the world and transformed not just the United States, but much of the globe.

(text continued from page 487)

THE URBAN LANDSCAPE

The city was a place of remarkable contrasts. It had homes of almost unimaginable size and grandeur and hovels of indescribable squalor. It had conveniences unknown to earlier generations and problems that seemed beyond the capacity of society to solve.

The Creation of Public Space

In the eighteenth and early nineteenth centuries, cities had generally grown up haphazardly. By the mid-nineteenth century, however, reformers, planners, architects, and others began to call for a more ordered vision of the city.

Among the most important innovations of the mid-nineteenth century were great city parks, which reflected the desire of a growing number of urban leaders to provide an antidote to the congestion of the city landscape. Parks, they argued, would allow city residents a healthy, restorative escape from the strains of urban life by reacquainting them with the natural world. The most successful promoters of this notion of the park as refuge were the landscape designers Frederick Law Olmsted and Calvert Vaux, who together in the late 1850s designed New York's Central Park. They deliberately created a *Central Park* public space that would look as little like the city as possible. Instead of the ordered, formal spaces common in some European cities, they created instead a space that seemed to be entirely natural. Central Park was from the start one of the most popular and admired public spaces in the world.

489

At the same time that cities were creating great parks, they were also creating great public buildings: libraries, art galleries, natural history museums, theaters, concert and opera halls. New York's Metropolitan Museum of Art was only the largest and best known of many great museums taking shape in the late nineteenth century. In one city after another, new and lavish public libraries appeared as if to confirm the city's role as a center of learning and knowledge.

Wealthy residents of cities were the principal force behind the creation of the great art museums, concert halls, opera houses, and at times even parks. As their own material and social aspirations grew, they wanted the public life of the city to provide them with amenities to match their expectations. Becoming an important patron of a major cultural institution was an especially effective route to social distinction.

As both the size and the aspirations of the great cities increased, urban leaders launched monumental projects to remake the way their cities looked. Some cities began to clear away older neighborhoods and streets and create grand, monumental avenues lined with new and more impressive buildings. A particularly important event in inspiring this effort to remake the city was the 1893 Columbian Exposition in Chicago, a world's fair constructed to honor the 400th anniversary of Columbus's first voyage to America. At the center of the wildly popular exposition was a cluster of neoclassical buildings—the "Great White City"—arranged symmetrically around a formal lagoon. It became the inspiration for what became known as the "city beautiful" movement, led by the architect of the Great White City, Daniel Burnham. The movement strove to

Daniel Burnham

impose a similar order and symmetry on the disordered life of cities around the country. Only rarely, however, were planners able to overcome the obstacles of private landowners and complicated urban politics to realize more than a small portion of their dreams.

The effort to remake the city did not focus only on redesigning the existing landscapes. It occasionally led to the creation of entirely new ones. In Boston in the late 1850s, a large area of marshy tidal land was gradually filled in to create the neighborhood

"Back Bay"

known as "Back Bay." The landfill project was one of the largest public works projects ever undertaken in America to that point. But Boston was not alone. Chicago reclaimed large areas from Lake Michigan as it expanded and at one point raised the street level for the entire city to help avoid the problems the marshy land created. In New York and other cities, the response to limited space was not so much creating new land as annexing adjacent territory. A great wave of annexations expanded the boundaries of many American cities in the 1890s and beyond.

The Search for Housing

One of the greatest urban problems was providing housing for the thousands of new residents who were pouring into the cities every day. For the prosperous, housing was seldom a worry. The availability of cheap labor

A TENEMENT LAUNDRY Immigrant families living in tenements, in New York and in many other cities, earned their livelihoods as they could. This woman, shown here with her children, was typical of many working-class mothers who found income-producing activities they could pursue in the home (in this case laundry). The room, dominated by large vats and piles of other people's laundry, is also the family's home, as the crib and religious pictures make clear. *(Bettmann/Corbis)*

reduced the cost of building and permitted anyone with even a moderate income to afford a house. Some of the richest urban residents lived in palatial mansions located in exclusive neighborhoods in the heart of the city—Fifth Avenue in New York, Back Bay and Beacon Hill in Boston, Society Hill in Philadelphia, Lake Shore Drive in Chicago, Nob Hill in San Francisco, and many others.

Many of the moderately well-to-do took advantage of less expensive land on the edges of the city and settled in new suburbs, linked to the downtowns by trains or streetcars. Chicago in the 1870s, for example, connected nearly 100 residential suburbs to the downtown by railroad. Real estate developers *Railroad Suburbs* worked to create and promote suburban communities that would appeal to the nostalgia for the countryside that many city dwellers felt. Affluent suburbs in particular were notable for lawns, trees, and houses designed to look manorial. Even more modest communities strove to emphasize the opportunities suburbs provided for owning land.

Most urban residents, however, could not afford either to own a house in the city or to move to the suburbs. Instead, they stayed in the city centers and rented. Landlords tried to squeeze as many rent-paying residents as possible into the smallest available space. In Manhattan, for example, the average population density in 1894 was 143 people per acre—a rate far higher than that of any other American or European city then or since. In the cities of the South—Charleston, New Orleans, Richmond—poor blacks lived in crumbling former slave quarters. In Boston, immigrants moved into cheap three-story wooden houses ("triple deckers"). In Baltimore and Philadelphia, the new arrivals crowded into narrow brick row houses. And in New York and many other cities, they lived in tenements.

The word "tenement" had originally referred simply to a multiple-family rental building, but by the late nineteenth century it had become a term for slum dwellings only. The first tenements, built in 1850, had been hailed as a great improvement in housing for the poor. But most were, in fact, miserable places, with many windowless rooms and little or no plumbing or heating. Jacob Riis, a Danish immigrant and New York newspaper reporter and photographer, shocked many middle-class Americans with his sensational (and some claimed sensationalized) descriptions and pictures of tenement life in his 1890 book, *How the Other Half Lives*. But the solution reformers often adopted was simply to raze slum dwellings without building any new housing to replace them.

Jacob Riis

Urban Technologies: Transportation and Construction

Urban growth posed monumental transportation challenges. The numbers of people who needed to move every day from one part of the city to another mandated the development of mass transportation. Streetcars drawn on tracks by horses had been introduced into some cities even before the Civil War. But the horsecars were not fast enough, so many communities developed new forms of mass transit. In 1870, New York opened its first elevated railway, whose noisy, steam-powered trains moved rapidly above the city streets on massive iron structures. New York, Chicago, San Francisco, and other cities also experimented with cable cars, towed by continuously moving underground cables. Richmond, Virginia, introduced the first electric trolley line in 1888, and in 1897 Boston opened the first American subway. At the same time, cities were developing new techniques of road and bridge building. One of the great technological marvels of the 1880s was the completion of the Brooklyn Bridge in New York—a dramatic steel-cable suspension span designed by John A. Roebling.

Cities were growing upward as well as outward. In Chicago, the construction in 1884 of the first modern "skyscraper"—by later standards a relatively modest building, ten stories high—launched a new era in urban architecture. Critical to the creation of the skyscraper was a new technology of construction, which emerged as a result of several related developments. One was the creation of new kinds of steel girders, capable of supporting much greater

Skyscrapers

tension than the metals of the past. Still another was the invention and development of the passenger elevator. And another was the search for ways to protect cities from the ravages of great fires, which caused such terrible destruction in wood-frame cities of the late nineteenth century. Steel-frame construction was, among other things, a way to make cities more fireproof. Once the technology existed to permit the construction of tall buildings, there were few obstacles to building taller and taller structures. The early Chicago skyscrapers paved the way for some of the great construction marvels later in the twentieth century: the Chrysler Building and the Empire State Building in New York, the Lasalle Building in Chicago, and ultimately the vast numbers of steel and glass skyscrapers of the post-1945 cities of America and the world.

STRAINS OF URBAN LIFE

The increasing congestion of the city and the absence of adequate public services produced serious hazards. Crime, fire, disease, and indigence all placed strains on the capacities of metropolitan institutions, and both governments and private agencies were for a time poorly equipped to respond.

Fire and Disease

One serious problem was fire. In one major city after another, fires destroyed large downtown areas. Chicago and Boston suffered "great fires" in 1871. Other cities experienced similar disasters. The great fires were terrible experiences, but they were also important events in the development of the cities involved. They encouraged the construction of fireproof buildings and the development of professional fire departments. They also forced cities to rebuild at a time when new technological and architectural innovations were available. Some of the high-rise downtowns of American cities arose out of the rubble of great fires.

An even greater hazard than fire was disease, especially in poor neighborhoods with inadequate sanitation facilities. But an epidemic that began in a poor neighborhood could (and often did) spread easily into other neighborhoods as well. Few municipal officials rec- *Inadequate Sanitation* ognized the relationship of improper sewage disposal and water contamination to such epidemic diseases as typhoid fever and cholera; many cities lacked adequate systems for disposing of human waste until well into the twentieth century. Flush toilets and sewer systems began to appear in the 1870s, but they could not solve the problem as long as sewage continued to flow into open ditches or streams, polluting cities' water supplies.

Environmental Degradation

Modern notions of environmental science were unknown to most Americans in the late nineteenth and early twentieth centuries. But the environmental degradation of many American cities was a visible and disturbing fact of life in those years. The frequency of great fires, the dangers of disease and plague, the extraordinary crowding of working-class neighborhoods were all examples of the environmental costs of industrialization and rapid urbanization.

Improper disposal of human and industrial waste was a common feature of almost all large cities in these years. That contributed to the pollution of rivers and lakes, and also in many cases to the compromising of the city's drinking water. The presence of domestic animals—horses, which were the principal means of transportation until the late nineteenth century, but in poor neighborhoods also cows, pigs, and other animals—contributed as well to the environmental problems.

Air quality in many cities was poor as well. Few Americans had the severe problems that London experienced in these years with its perpetual
Air Pollution   "fogs" created by the debris from the burning of soft coal. But air pollution from factories and from stoves and furnaces in offices, homes, and other buildings was constant and at times severe. The incidence of respiratory infection and related diseases was much higher in cities than it was in rural areas, and it accelerated rapidly in the late nineteenth century.

By the early twentieth century, reformers were actively crusading to improve the environmental conditions of cities and were beginning to achieve some notable successes. New sewage and drainage systems were created to protect drinking water from sewage disposal. By 1910, most large American cities had constructed sewage disposal systems, often at great cost, to protect the drinking water of their inhabitants and to prevent the great bacterial plagues that impure water had helped create in the past—such as the yellow fever epidemic in Memphis that killed 5,000 people.

In 1912, the federal government created the Public Health Service, which was charged with preventing such occupational diseases as tuberculosis and anemia and carbon dioxide poisoning, which were common in the
Public Health Service   garment industry and other trades. It attempted to create common health standards for all factories; but since the agency had few powers of enforcement, it had limited impact. The creation of the Occupational Health and Safety Administration in 1970, which gave government the authority to require employers to create safe and healthy workplaces, was a legacy of the Public Health Service's early work.

Urban Poverty, Crime, and Violence

Above all, perhaps, the expansion of the city spawned widespread and often desperate poverty. Public agencies and private philanthropic organizations offered some relief. But they were generally poorly funded, and in any case dominated by middle-class people who believed that too much assistance would breed dependency. Most tried to restrict aid to the "deserving poor"—those who truly could not help themselves. Charitable organizations conducted elaborate "investigations" to separate the "deserving" from the "undeserving". Other charitable societies—for example, the Salvation Army, which began operating in America in 1879—concentrated more on religious revivalism than on the relief of the homeless and hungry.

Middle-class people grew particularly alarmed over the rising number of poor children in the cities, some of them orphans or runaways. These "street arabs," as they were often called, attracted more attention from reformers than any other group—although that attention produced no lasting solutions to their problems.

Poverty and crowding bred crime and violence. The American murder rate rose rapidly in the late nineteenth century, from 25 murders for every million people in 1880 to over 100 by the *Growing Crime Rate* end of the century. That reflected in part a very high level of violence in some nonurban areas: the American South, where lynching and homicide were particularly high; and the West, where the rootlessness and instability of new communities (cow towns, mining camps, and the like) created much violence. But the cities contributed their share to the increase in crime as well. Native-born Americans liked to believe that crime was a result of the violent proclivities of immigrant groups, and they cited the rise of gangs and criminal organizations in various ethnic communities. But native-born Americans in the cities were as likely to commit crimes as immigrants. The rising crime rates encouraged many cities to develop larger and more professional police forces. But police forces themselves could spawn corruption and brutality, particularly since jobs on them were often filled through political patronage.

Some members of the middle class, fearful of urban insurrections, felt the need for even more substantial forms of protection. Urban national guard groups built imposing armories on the outskirts of affluent neighborhoods and stored large supplies of weapons and ammunition in preparation for uprisings that, in fact, virtually never occurred.

The city was a place of strong allure and great excitement. Yet it was also a place of alienating impersonality and, to some, a place of degradation and exploitation. Theodore Dreiser's novel *Sister Carrie* *Sister Carrie* (1900) exposed one troubling aspect of urban life: the plight of single women (like Dreiser's heroine, Carrie) who moved from the countryside into the city and found themselves without any means of support. Carrie first took an exhausting and ill-paying job in a Chicago shoe factory; then she drifted into a life of "sin," exploited by predatory men.

The Machine and the Boss

Newly arrived immigrants were much in need of institutions to help them adjust to American urban life. For many residents of the inner cities, the principal source of assistance was the political "machine."

The urban machine owed its existence to the power vacuum that the chaotic growth of cities had created. It was also a product of the potential voting power of large immigrant communities. Out of that combination emerged the "urban" bosses. The principal func-

Function of the "Urban" Boss

tion of the political boss was simple: to win votes for his organization. That meant winning the loyalty of his constituents. To do so, a boss might provide them with occasional relief—a basket of groceries or a bag of coal. He might step in to save those arrested for petty crimes from jail. When he could, he found work for the unemployed. Above all, he rewarded many of his followers with patronage: with jobs in city government or in such city agencies as the police (which the machine's elected officials often controlled); with jobs building or operating the new transit systems; and with opportunities to rise in the political organization itself.

Machines were also vehicles for making money. Politicians enriched themselves and their allies through various forms of graft and corruption. A politician might discover in advance where a new road or streetcar line was to be built, buy land near it, and sell it at a profit when property values rose as a result of the construction. There was also covert graft. Officials received kickbacks from contractors in exchange for contracts to build public projects, and they sold franchises for the operation of public

William M. Tweed

utilities. The most famously corrupt city boss was William M. Tweed, boss of New York City's Tammany Hall in the 1860s and 1870s, whose extravagant use of public funds on projects that paid kickbacks to the organization landed him in jail in 1872.

The urban machine was not without competition. Reform groups frequently mobilized public outrage at the corruption of the bosses and often succeeded in driving machine politicians from office. But the reform organizations typically lacked the permanence of the machine.

THE RISE OF MASS CONSUMPTION

In the last decades of the nineteenth century a distinctive middle-class culture began to exert a powerful influence over the whole of American life. Other groups in society advanced less rapidly, or not at all, but almost no one was unaffected by the rise of the new urban, consumer culture.

Patterns of Income and Consumption

Incomes were rising for almost everyone in the industrial era, although at highly uneven rates. The most conspicuous result of the new economy was the creation of vast fortunes, but perhaps the most important result for society as a whole was the growth and increasing prosperity of the middle class. The salaries of clerks, accountants, middle managers, and other "white-collar" workers rose by an average of a third between 1890 and 1910. Doctors, lawyers, and other professionals, for example, experienced a particularly dramatic increase in both the prestige and the profitability of their professions. *Rising Income*

Working-class incomes rose in those years as well, although from a much lower base and often more slowly. The iron and steel industries saw workers' hourly wages increase by a third between 1890 and 1910; but industries with large female work forces—shoes, textiles, and paper—saw more modest increases, as did almost all industries in the South. Wages for African Americans, Mexicans, and Asians also rose more slowly than those for other workers.

Rising incomes created new markets for consumer goods. Affordable products and new merchandising techniques soon made many consumer goods available to this mass market for the first time. A good example of such changes was the *Ready-made Clothing*
emergence of ready-made clothing. In the early nineteenth century, most Americans had made their own clothing. The invention of the sewing machine and the spur that the Civil War (and its demand for uniforms) gave to the manufacture of clothing helped create an enormous industry devoted to producing ready-made garments. By the end of the century, almost all Americans bought their clothing from stores. Partly as a result, much larger numbers of people became concerned with personal style. Interest in women's fashion, for example, had once been a luxury reserved for the relatively affluent. Now middle-class and even working-class women could strive to develop a distinctive style of dress.

Buying and preparing food also became a critical part of the new consumerism. The development and mass production of tin cans in the 1880s created a large new industry devoted to packaging and selling canned food and condensed milk. Refrigerated railroad cars made it possible for perishable foods to be transported over long distances without spoiling. Artificially frozen ice enabled many households to afford iceboxes. The changes brought improved diets and better health. Life expectancy rose six years in the first two decades of the twentieth century.

Chain Stores, Mail-Order Houses, and Department Stores

Changes in marketing also altered the way Americans bought goods. New "chain stores" could usually offer a wider array of goods at lower prices than the small local stores with which they competed. The Atlantic and Pacific Tea Company (the A & P) began a national network of grocery stores in the 1870s. F. W. Woolworth built a chain of dry goods stores. Sears and Roebuck established a large market for its mail-order merchandise by distributing an enormous catalog each year.

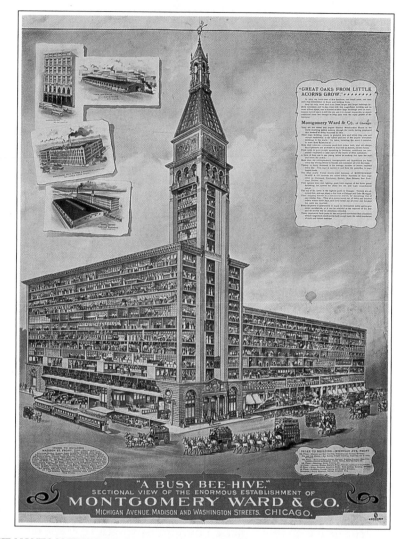

THE MONTGOMERY WARD DEPARTMENT STORE This advertising poster for the Montgomery Ward department store in downtown Chicago dates from about 1880. The designer has stripped away the outside walls to reveal the vast array of goods inside what the poster calls "the enormous establishment." *(Chicago Historical Society)*

In larger cities, the emergence of great department stores helped transform buying habits and turn shopping into a more alluring and glamorous activity. Marshall Field in Chicago created one of the first American department stores—a place deliberately designed to produce a sense of wonder and excitement. Similar stores emerged in New York, Brooklyn, Boston, Philadelphia, and other cities.

Marshall Field

Women as Consumers

The rise of mass consumption had particularly dramatic effects on American women. Women's clothing styles changed much more rapidly and dramatically than men's, which encouraged more frequent purchases. Women generally bought and prepared food for their families, so the availability of new food products changed not only the way everyone ate, but also the way women shopped and cooked. Canning and refrigeration meant greater variety in the diet. It also meant that food did not always have to be eaten on the day it was purchased.

The consumer economy produced new employment opportunities for women as salesclerks and waitresses. And it spawned the creation of a new movement in which women were to play a vital role: the consumer protection movement. The National Consumers League, *National Consumers League* formed in the 1890s under the leadership of Florence Kelley, attempted to mobilize the power of women as consumers to force retailers and manufacturers to improve wages and working conditions.

LEISURE IN THE CONSUMER SOCIETY

Closely related to the growth of consumption was a growing interest in leisure time. Members of the urban middle and professional classes had large blocks of time during which they were not at work—evenings, weekends, even paid vacations. Working hours in many factories declined, from an average of nearly seventy hours a week in 1860 to under sixty in 1900. Even farmers found that the mechanization of agriculture gave them more free time. The lives of many Americans were becoming more compartmentalized, with clear distinctions between work and leisure. The change produced a search for new forms of recreation and entertainment.

Redefining Leisure

It also produced a redefinition of the idea of "leisure." In earlier eras, relatively few Americans had considered leisure a valuable thing. On the contrary, many equated it with laziness or sloth. In the late nineteenth century, however, the beginnings of a redefinition of leisure appeared. The economist Simon Patten was one of the first intel- *Simon Patten* lectuals to articulate this new view of leisure. In *The Theory of Prosperity* (1902), *The New Basis of Civilization* (1910), and other works, he challenged the centuries-old assumption that the normal condition of civilization was a scarcity of goods. In earlier times, Patten argued, fear of scarcity had caused people to place a high value on thrift, self-denial, and restraint. But in modern industrial societies, new economies could create enough wealth to satisfy not just the needs, but also the desires, of all.

As Americans became more accustomed to leisure as a normal part of their lives, they began to look for new experiences with which to entertain themselves. In cities, in particular, the demand for popular entertainment produced a rich mix of spectacles, recreations, and other activities.

Mass entertainment occasionally bridged differences of class, race, or gender. But it could also be sharply divided. Saloons and some sporting events tended to be male preserves. Shopping and going to tea rooms and luncheonettes was more characteristic of female leisure. Theaters, pubs, and clubs were often specific to particular ethnic communities or particular work groups. When the classes did meet in public spaces—as they did, for example, in city parks—there was often considerable conflict over what constituted appropriate public behavior. Elites in New York City, for example, tried to prohibit anything but quiet, "genteel" activities in Central Park, while working-class people wanted to use the public spaces for sports and entertainments.

Spectator Sports

Among the most important responses to the search for entertainment was the rise of organized spectator sports, and especially baseball. A game

Baseball

much like baseball—known as "rounders" and derived from cricket—had enjoyed limited popularity in Great Britain in the early nineteenth century. Versions of the game began to appear in America in the early 1830s. By the end of the Civil War, interest in the game had grown rapidly. More than 200 amateur or semiprofessional teams and clubs existed, many of which joined a national association and proclaimed a set of standard rules. As the game grew in popularity, it offered opportunities for profit. The first salaried team, the Cincinnati Red Stockings, was formed in 1869. Other cities fielded professional teams, and in 1876 the teams banded together in the National League. A rival league, the American Association, soon appeared. It eventually collapsed, but in 1901 the American League emerged to replace it. And in 1903, the first modern World Series was played, in which the American League Boston Red Sox beat the National League Pittsburgh Pirates. By then, baseball had become an important business and a great national preoccupation.

Baseball had great appeal to working-class males. The second most popular game, football, appealed at first to a more elite segment of the male population, in part because it originated in colleges and universities. The first intercollegiate football game in America occurred between Princeton and Rutgers in 1869. Early intercollegiate football bore only an indirect relation to the modern game; it was more similar to what is now known as rugby. By the late 1870s, however, the game was becoming standardized and was taking on the outlines of its modern form.

Basketball was invented in 1891 at Springfield, Massachusetts, by Dr. James A. Naismith, a Cana- dian working as athletic director for a local college. Boxing, which had long been a disreputable activity concentrated primarily among the urban lower classes, became by the 1880s a more popular and, in some places, more reputable sport.

Basketball Invented

Participation in the major sports of the era was almost exclusively the province of men, but several sports emerged in which women became important participants. Golf and tennis both experienced a rapid increase in participation among relatively wealthy men and women. Bicycling and croquet also enjoyed widespread popularity in the 1890s among women as well as men. Women's colleges introduced their students to more strenuous sports as well—track, crew, swimming, and (beginning in the late 1890s) basketball.

Music, Theater, and Movies

Other forms of popular entertainment developed in the cities in response to the large potential markets there. Many ethnic communities maintained their own theaters. Urban theaters also introduced new and distinctively American entertainment forms: the musical comedy, which evolved gradually from the comic operettas of Europe; and vaudeville, a form of theater adapted from French models, which remained the most popular urban entertainment into the first decades of the twentieth century. It consisted of a variety of acts (musicians, comedians, magicians, jugglers, and others) and was, at least in the beginning, inexpensive to produce. As the economic potential of vaudeville grew, some promoters—most prominently Florenz Ziegfeld of New York—staged much more elaborate spectacles.

Vaudeville

Vaudeville was also one of the few entertainment media open to black performers. They brought to it elements of the minstrel shows they had earlier developed for black audiences in the late nineteenth century. Some minstrel singers (including the most famous, Al Jolson) were whites wearing heavy makeup (or "blackface"), but most were black. Entertainers of both races performed music based on the gospel and folk tunes of the plantation and on the jazz and ragtime of black urban communities. Performers of both races also tailored their acts to prevailing white prejudices, ridiculing blacks by acting out demeaning stereotypes.

The most important form of mass entertainment was the movies. Thomas Edison and others had created the technology of the motion picture in the 1880s. Soon after that, short films became available to individual viewers watching peepshows in pool halls, penny arcades, and amusement parks. Soon, larger projectors made it possible to project the images onto big screens, which permitted substantial audiences to see films in

A NICKELODEON, 1905 Before the rise of great movie palaces, urban families flocked to "nickelodeons," smaller theaters that charged five cents for admission and that showed many different films each day, including serials—dramas that drew audiences back into theaters day after day with new episodes of a running story. *(Brown Brothers)*

theaters. By 1900, Americans were becoming attracted in large numbers to these early movies—usually plotless films of trains or waterfalls or other spectacles. The great D. W. Griffith carried the motion picture into a new era with his silent epics—*The Birth of a Nation* (1915), *Intolerance* (1916), and others—which introduced serious (if notoriously racist) plots and elaborate productions to filmmaking. Motion pictures were the first truly mass entertainment medium.

D. W. Griffith

Patterns of Public and Private Leisure

Particularly striking about popular entertainment in the late nineteenth and early twentieth centuries was its public quality. Many Americans spent their leisure time in places where they would find not only entertainment but also other people. Thousands of working-class New Yorkers spent evenings in dance halls, vaudeville houses, and concert halls. More affluent New Yorkers enjoyed afternoons in Central Park, where a principal attraction was seeing other people (and being seen by them). Moviegoers

POSTCARD FROM LUNA PARK Visitors to Coney Island sent postcards to friends and relatives by the millions, and those cards were among the most effective promotional devices for the amusement parks. This one shows the brightly-lit entrance to Luna Park, Coney Island's most popular attraction for many years. *(Bettmann/Corbis)*

were attracted not just by the movies themselves but by the energy of the audiences at lavish new "movie palaces," just as sports fans were drawn by the crowds as well as by the games.

Perhaps the most striking example of popular, public entertainment was Coney Island, the famous and self-consciously fabulous amusement park and resort on a popular beach in Brooklyn. *Coney Island* The greatest of the Coney Island attractions, Luna Park, opened in 1903. It provided rides and stunts, and also lavish reproductions of exotic places and spectacular adventures: Japanese gardens, Venetian canals with gondoliers, a Chinese theater, a simulated trip to the moon, and re-enactments of such disasters as burning buildings and earthquakes. A year later, a competing company opened Dreamland, which tried to outdo even Luna Park with a 375-foot tower, a three-ring circus, chariot races, and a Lilliputian village from *Gulliver's Travels*. The popularity of Coney Island in these years was phenomenal. Thousands of people flocked to the large resort hotels that lined the beaches. Many thousands more made day trips out from the city by train and (after 1920) subway. In 1904, the average daily attendance at Luna Park alone was 90,000 people.

Most people who found Coney Island appealing did so in part because it provided them with an escape from the genteel standards of behavior that governed so much of American life at the time. In the amusement parks of Coney Island, decorum was often forgotten, and people delighted in finding themselves in situations that in any other setting would have seemed embarrassing or improper: women's skirts blown above their heads with hot air; people pummeled with water and rubber paddles by clowns; hints of sexual freedom as strangers were forced to come into physical contact with one another on rides and amusements.

Not all popular entertainment, however, involved public events. Many Americans amused themselves privately by reading novels and poetry. The so-called dime novels, cheaply bound and widely

Dime Novels

circulated, became popular after the Civil War, with detective stories, tales of the "Wild West," sagas of scientific adventure, and novels of "moral uplift." Publishers also distributed sentimental novels of romance, which developed a large audience among women, as did books about animals and about young children growing up. Louisa May Alcott's *Little Women*, most of whose readers were women, sold more than 2 million copies.

The Technologies of Mass Communication

American publishing and journalism experienced an important change in the decades following the Civil War. Between 1870 and 1910, the circulation of daily newspapers increased nearly ninefold (from under 3 million to more than 24 million), a rate three times as great as the rate of population increase. And while standards varied widely from one paper to another, American journalism was developing the beginnings of a professional identity. Salaries of reporters increased; many newspapers began separating the reporting of news from the expression of opinion; and newspapers themselves became important businesses.

The transformation of publishing and journalism was to a large degree a result of new technologies of communication. The emergence of national press services, for example, was a product of the telegraph, which made it possible to supply papers throughout the country with news and features from around the nation and the world. By the turn of the century important newspaper chains had emerged as well, linked together by their own internal wire services. The most powerful was

William Randolph Hearst

owned by William Randolph Hearst, who by 1914 controlled nine newspapers and two magazines. New printing technologies were making possible more elaborate layouts, the publication of color pictures, and, by the end of the century, the printing of photographs. These advances not only helped publishers make their own stories more vivid; they also made it possible for them to attract more advertisers.

The Telephone

The most important new technology of communication was the telephone, which Alexander Graham Bell had first demonstrated in 1876 (see p. 458). In its first years, the telephone was a relatively impractical tool. Those who subscribed to telephone service had to have direct wire links to everyone else they wished to call. In 1878, the first "switchboard" opened in New Haven, Connecticut, opening the way for more practical uses of the telephone. Once there was a switchboard, a telephone subscriber needed only a line to the central telephone office from which connections could be made to any other subscriber. A new occupation—the "telephone operator"—was born. The Bell System, which controlled all American telephone service, hired young white women to work as operators, hoping that a pleasant female voice would make the experience of using the telephone (and the inconvenience of the frequent technological problems that accompanied it) more appealing, or less irritating, to customers. Telephone signals were very weak at first, and callers could seldom reach anyone more than a few miles away. In an effort to increase the range of telephones, engineers created the "repeater," which periodically strengthened the signal as it moved over distances. By 1914, however, the repeaters had improved to the point that it was now practical to envision a transcontinental line.

The Bell System

In its early years, the telephone was an almost entirely commercial instrument. Of the nearly 7,400 telephone customers in the New York-New Jersey area in 1891, 6,000 were businesses and organizations. Even the residential telephones tended to belong to doctors or business managers.

The growing reach of the telephone in the early years of the twentieth century made the Bell System (formally named American Telephone and Telegraph, or AT&T) one of the most powerful corporations in America and a genuine monopoly. Central to its success was an early decision by executives that the company would exclusively build and own all telephone instruments and then lease them to subscribers. That made it possible for AT&T to control both the equipment and the telephone service itself, and to exclude any competitors in either field. It also gave AT&T effective control over the local telephone companies allied with it and made the nation's telephone system into an effective cartel.

HIGH CULTURE IN THE URBAN AGE

In addition to the important changes in popular culture that accompanied the rise of cities and industry, there were profound changes in the realm of "high culture." The distinction between "highbrow" and "lowbrow" culture was largely new to the industrial era. In the early nineteenth century, most cultural activities had targeted people of all classes. By the late nineteenth century, however, elites were developing a cultural and intellectual life quite separate from the popular amusements of the urban masses.

Literature and Art in Urban America

One of the strongest impulses in American literature was the effort to re-create urban social reality. This trend toward realism found an early voice
Literary Realism in Stephen Crane, who—although perhaps best known for his novel of the Civil War, *The Red Badge of Courage* (1895)—created a sensation in 1893 when he published *Maggie: A Girl of the Streets*, a grim picture of urban poverty and slum life. Theodore Dreiser, Frank Norris, and Upton Sinclair were similarly drawn to social issues as themes. Kate Chopin, a southern writer who explored the oppressive features of traditional marriage, encountered widespread public abuse after publication of her shocking novel, *The Awakening*, in 1899. It described a young wife and mother who abandoned her family in search of personal fulfillment. William Dean Howells, in *The Rise of Silas Lapham* and other works, described what he considered the shallowness and corruption in ordinary American lifestyles.

American art through most of the nineteenth century had been over-shadowed by the art of Europe. By 1900, however, a number of American artists broke from the Old World traditions and experimented with new styles. Winslow Homer was vigorously American in his paintings of New England maritime life and other native subjects. James McNeil Whistler was one of the first Western artists to introduce Oriental themes into American and European art.

By the first years of the new century, some American artists were turning decisively away from the traditional academic style (a style per-haps most identified in America by the brilliant portraitist John Singer
Ashcan School Sargent). Members of the so-called Ashcan School produced work startling in its naturalism and stark in its portrayal of the social realities of the era. John Sloan portrayed the dreariness of American urban slums; George Bellows caught the vigor and violence of his time in paintings and drawings of prizefights; Edward Hopper explored the starkness and loneliness of the modern city. The Ashcan artists were also among the first Americans to appreciate expres-sionism and abstraction; and they showed their interest in new forms in 1913 when they helped stage the famous "Armory Show" in New York City, which displayed works of the French postimpressionists and of some American moderns.

The Impact of Darwinism

Perhaps the most profound intellectual development in the late nine-teenth century was the widespread acceptance of the theory of evolution, associated most prominently with the English naturalist Charles Darwin. Darwin argued that the human species had evolved from earlier forms of life through a process of "natural selection." History, Darwin suggested, was not the working out of a divine plan. It was a random process domi-nated by the fiercest or luckiest competitors.

EDWARD HOPPER, *AUTOMAT* Edward Hopper was one of a growing group of American painters in the early twentieth century who chose to chronicle not the world of wealth and power, the characteristic subject of earlier artists, but the harsh, gritty world of the modern city. Hopper's work was distinctive for its evocation of the loneliness of urban life. This 1927 painting of a scene in an "automat" in New York City is characteristic of his work. *(Des Moines Art Center Permanent Collection. Purchased with funds from the Edmundson Art Foundation, Inc., 1958.2. Photo by Michael Tropea, Chicago)*

The theory of evolution met widespread resistance at first from educators, theologians, and even many scientists. By the end of the century, however, the evolutionists had converted most members of the urban professional and educated classes. *Resistance to Evolution* Even many middle-class Protestant religious leaders had accepted the doctrine, making significant alterations in theology to accommodate it. Unseen by most urban Americans at the time, however, the rise of Darwinism was contributing to a deep schism between the new, cosmopolitan culture of the city—which was receptive to new ideas such as evolution—and the more traditional, provincial culture of some rural areas—which remained more wedded to fundamentalist religious beliefs and older values. Thus the late nineteenth century saw not only the rise of a liberal Protestantism in tune with new scientific discoveries but also the beginning of an organized Protestant fundamentalism.

Darwinism helped spawn other new intellectual currents. There was the Social Darwinism of William Graham Sumner and others, which industrialists used so enthusiastically to justify their favored position in American life. But there were also more sophisticated philoso-

"Pragmatism" phies, among them a doctrine that became known as "pragmatism." William James, a Harvard psychologist (and brother of the novelist Henry James), was the most prominent publicist of the new theory, although earlier intellectuals such as Charles S. Peirce and later ones such as John Dewey were also important to its development and dissemination. According to the pragmatists, modern society should rely for guidance not on inherited ideals and moral principles but on the test of scientific inquiry. No idea or institution (not even religious faith) was valid, they claimed, unless it worked, unless it stood the test of experience.

A similar concern for scientific inquiry was influencing the social sciences. Sociologists such as Edward A. Ross and Lester Frank Ward urged applying the scientific method to the solution of social and political problems. Historians such as Frederick Jackson Turner and Charles Beard argued that economic factors more than spiritual ideals had been the governing force in historical development. John Dewey proposed a new approach to education that placed less emphasis on the rote learning of traditional knowledge and more on flexible, democratic schooling.

The implications of Darwinism also promoted the growth of anthropology and encouraged some scholars to begin examining other cultures in new ways. Some white Americans began to look at Indian society, for example, as a coherent culture with its own norms and values that were worthy of respect and preservation, even though they were different from those of white society.

Toward Universal Schooling

The growing demand for specialized skills and scientific knowledge naturally created a growing, and changing, demand for education. The late nineteenth century, therefore, was a time of rapid expansion and reform of American schools and universities.

Spread of Free Public Schooling One example was the spread of free public primary and secondary education. By 1900, compulsory school attendance laws were in effect in thirty-one states and territories. Education was still far from universal. Rural areas lagged far behind urban-industrial ones in funding public education. In the South, many blacks had access to no schools at all. But for many white men and women, educational opportunities were expanding dramatically.

Educational reformers tried to extend educational opportunities to the Indian tribes as well, in an effort to "civilize" them and help them adapt to white society. In the 1870s, reformers recruited small groups of Indians to attend Hampton Institute (a primarily black college). In 1879 they organized the Carlisle Indian Industrial School in Pennsylvania. Like many black colleges, Carlisle emphasized practical "industrial" education. Ultimately, however, these reform efforts failed, in part because it was unpopular with its intended beneficiaries.

Universities and the Growth of Science and Technology

Colleges and universities were also proliferating rapidly in the late nineteenth century. They benefited particularly from the Morrill Land Grant Act of 1862, by which the federal government had donated public land to states for the establishment of colleges. Sixty-nine "land-grant" institutions were established in the last decades of the century—among them the state university systems of California, Illinois, Minnesota, and Wisconsin. Other universities benefited from millions of dollars contributed by business and financial titans. Rockefeller, Carnegie, and others gave generously to such schools as Columbia, Chicago, Harvard, Northwestern, Princeton, Syracuse, and Yale. Other philanthropists founded new universities or reorganized older ones and perpetuated their family names—Vanderbilt, Johns Hopkins, Cornell, Duke, Tulane, and Stanford.

These and other universities played a vital role in the economic development of the United States in the late nineteenth century and beyond. The *Economic Impact of Higher Education* land-grant institutions were specifically mandated to advance knowledge in "agriculture and mechanics." From the beginning, therefore, they were committed not just to abstract knowledge, but to making discoveries that would be of practical use to farmers and manufacturers. As they evolved into great state universities, they retained that tradition and became the source of many of the great technological and scientific discoveries that helped American industry and commerce to advance. Private universities emerged that served many of the same purposes: the Massachusetts Institute of Technology, founded in 1865, which soon became the nation's premier engineering school; Johns Hopkins University in Baltimore, founded in 1876, which did much to advance medical scholarship; the Rockefeller Institute for Medical Research in New York (later Rockefeller University); the Carnegie Institution. By the early twentieth century, even much older and more traditional universities were beginning to form relationships with the private sector and the government, doing research that did not just advance knowledge for its own sake but that was directly applicable to practical problems of the time.

Medical Science

Both the culture of and the scientific basis for medical care was changing rapidly in the early twentieth century. Most doctors were beginning to accept the new medical assumption that there were underlying causes to particular symptoms—that a symptom was not itself a disease. They were also beginning to make use of new or improved technologies—the X-ray, improved microscopes, and other diagnostic devices in laboratories—that made it possible to classify, and distinguish among, different diseases. Laboratory tests could now identify infections such as typhoid and dysentery. That did not in itself help doctors treat diseases, but it was a critical first step toward finding effective treatment. At about the same time, pharmaceutical research was beginning to produce some important new medicines. Aspirin was first synthesized in 1899. Other researchers were beginning to experiment with chemicals that might destroy diseases in the blood, an effort that eventually led to the various forms of chemotherapy that are still widely used in treating cancer. In 1906, an American surgeon, G. W. Crile, became the first physician to use blood transfusion in treatment, which revolutionized surgery. In the past, patients often lost so much blood during operations that extensive surgery could be fatal for that reason alone. With transfusions, it became possible to conduct much longer and more elaborate operations.

Germ Theory Accepted The widespread acceptance by the end of the nineteenth century of the germ theory of disease had important implications. Physicians quickly discovered that exposure to germs did not by itself necessarily cause disease, and they began looking for the other factors that determined who got sick and who did not. Among the factors they eventually discovered were general health, previous medical history, diet and nutrition, and eventually genetic predisposition. The awareness of the importance of infection in spreading disease also encouraged doctors to sterilize their instruments, use surgical gloves, and otherwise purify the medical environment of patients.

By the early twentieth century, American physicians and surgeons were generally recognized as among the best in the world, and American medical education was beginning to attract students from many other countries. These improvements in medical knowledge and training, along with improvements in sanitation and public health, did much to reduce infection and mortality in most American communities.

Education for Women

The post–Civil War era saw an important expansion of educational opportunities for women, although such opportunities continued to lag far behind those available to men and were denied to black women.

Most public high schools accepted women readily, but opportunities for higher education were fewer. At the end of the Civil War, only three American colleges were coeducational. In the years after the war, many of the land-grant colleges and universities in the Midwest and such private universities as Cornell and Wesleyan began to admit women along with men. But coeducation was less crucial to women's education in this period *Women's Colleges* than was the creation of a network of women's colleges. Mount Holyoke in central Massachusetts had begun its life in 1836 as a "seminary" for women; it became a full-fledged college in the 1880s, at about the same time that entirely new female institutions were emerging: Vassar, Wellesley, Smith, Bryn Mawr, Wells, and Goucher. A few of the larger private universities created separate colleges for women on their campuses (Barnard at Columbia and Radcliffe at Harvard, for example).

The female college was part of an important phenomenon in the history of modern American women: the emergence of distinctive women's communities outside the family. Most faculty members and many administrators were women *Emergence of Women's Communities* (usually unmarried). And the life of the college produced a spirit of sorority and commitment among educated women that had important effects in later years. Most female college graduates ultimately married, but they married at a more advanced age than their non-college counterparts. A significant minority, perhaps over 25 percent, did not marry at all, but devoted themselves to careers. The growth of female higher education clearly became for some women a liberating experience, persuading them that they had roles to perform in their rapidly changing urban-industrial society other than those of wives and mothers.

CONCLUSION

The extraordinary growth of American cities in the last decades of the nineteenth century led to both great achievements and enormous problems. Cities became centers of learning, art, and commerce. They produced great advances in technology, transportation, architecture, and communications. They provided their residents—and their many visitors—with varied and dazzling experiences, so much so that people increasingly left the countryside to move to the city.

But cities were also places of congestion, filth, disease, and corruption. With populations expanding too rapidly for services to keep up, most American cities in this era struggled with makeshift techniques to solve the basic problems of providing water, disposing of sewage, building roads, running public transportation, fighting fire, stopping crime, and preventing or curing disease. City governments, many of them dominated by political machines and ruled by party bosses, were often models of inefficiency and corruption—although in their informal way they also provided substantial services to the working-class and immigrant constituencies who needed them most. Yet they also managed to oversee great public projects: the building of parks, museums, opera houses, and theaters, usually in partnership with private developers.

The city brought together races, ethnic groups, and classes of extraordinary variety—from the families of great wealth that the new industrial age was creating to the vast working class, much of it consisting of immigrants, that crowded into densely packed neighborhoods sharply divided by nationality. The city also spawned new forms of popular culture. It created temples of consumerism: shops, boutiques, and above all the great department stores. And it created forums for public recreation and entertainment: parks, theaters, athletic fields, amusement parks, and later movie palaces.

Urban life created anxiety among those who lived within the cities and among those who observed them from afar. But in fact, American cities adapted reasonably successfully over time to the great demands their growth made of them and learned to govern themselves if not entirely honestly and efficiently, at least adequately to allow them to survive and grow.

FOR FURTHER REFERENCE

Lewis Mumford, author of *The City in History* (1961), was America's foremost critic and chronicler of urbanization through the mid-twentieth century. John Bodnar provides a synthetic history of immigration in *The Transplanted: A History of Immigrants in America* (1985), which challenges an earlier classic study by Oscar Handlin, *The Uprooted: The Epic Story of the Great Migrations that Made the American People*, 2nd ed. (1973). Henry Yu, *Thinking Orientals: Migration, Contact, and Exoticism in Modern America* (2001) is a provocative examination of aspects of Asian immigration. Desmond King, *Making Americans: Immigration, Race, and the Origins of Diverse Democracy* (2000) examines responses to immigration. The new urban mass culture of America's cities is the subject of William Leach, *Land of Desire: Merchants, Power, and the Rise of a New American Culture* (1993) and Kathy Peiss, *Cheap Amusements: Working Women and Leisure in Turn-of-the-Century New York* (1986). Sven Beckert, *The Moneyed Metropolis: New York City and the Consolidation of the American Bourgeoisie, 1850–1896* (2001) and Stuart Blumin, *The Emergence of the Middle Class: Social Experience in the American City, 1760–1900* (1989) examine the rise of the urban middle class. Sarah Deutsch, *Women and the City: Gender, Space, and Power in Boston, 1870–1940* (2000), reveals the world of women in the emergence of the modern city. T. J. Jackson Lears, *No Place of Grace: Antimodernism and the Transformation of American Culture, 1880–1920* (1981) chronicles patterns of resistance to the new culture. Roy Rosenzweig and Elizabeth Blackmar, *The Park and the People: A History of Central Park* (1992) studies the creation of America's most famous public park. Edwin G. Burroughs and Mike Wallace, *Gotham: A History of New York City to 1898* (1998) is a thorough history of New York's remarkable growth. Christine Stansell, *American Moderns: Bohemian New York and the Creation of a New Century* (2001) examines the rise of a modern urban sensibility. John F. Kasson, *Amusing the Million: Coney Island at the Turn of the Century* (1978) is an illustrated history and interpretation of the amusement park's place in American culture. *Coney Island* (1991), a film by Ric Burns, presents a colorful history of America's favorite seaside resort. The documentary film *Baseball* (1994) by Ken Burns—and the companion book by the same name, by Geoffrey C. Ward—provide sweeping narratives of the na-

tional pastime, its origins in the age of the city, and its wider social context of race relations, immigration, and popular culture. *New York* (1999–2001), a film by Ric Burns,
is a sweeping documentary history of the city, accompanied by a companion book, Ric
Burns et al., *New York: An Illustrated History* (1999).

For quizzes, Internet resources, references to additional books and films, and more,
consult this book's Online Learning Center site at www.mhhe.com/unfinishednation4.

A PARTY OF PATCHES, *JUDGE* MAGAZINE, JUNE 6, 1891   This political cartoon suggests the contempt and fear with which many easterners, in particular, viewed the emergence of the People's Party in 1891.   *(Kansas State Historical Society)*

TIME LINE

1867	1880	1881	1883	1884	1887	1888
National Grange founded	Garfield elected president	Garfield assassinated	Pendleton Act	Cleveland elected president	Interstate Commerce Act	Benjamin Harrison elected president
		Arthur becomes president				

FROM STALEMATE TO CRISIS

The Politics of Equilibrium
The Agrarian Revolt
The Crisis of the 1890s

The enormous changes America was experiencing in the late nine-teenth century strained not only the nation's traditional social arrangements but its political institutions as well. Industrialization and urbanization had produced considerable progress, but they had also created disorder and despair. Gradually, Americans began to look to government for leadership in their search for stability and social justice. Yet American government during much of this period was ill equipped to deal with the new challenges confronting it. In the face of unprecedented dilemmas, it responded with apparent passivity and confusion. Its leaders, for the most part, seemed political mediocrities. The issue with which it was concerned were often irrelevant to the nation's most serious problems. Rather than taking active leadership of the nation's dramatic transformation, the American political system for nearly two decades after the end of Reconstruction was locked in a rigid stalemate—watching the remarkable changes that were occurring in the nation and doing little to affect them. The result was a set of problems and grievances that festered and grew without any natural outlet. And it was not surprising, under the circumstances, that in the 1890s the United States entered a period of national crisis.

1890	1892	1893	1894	1896	1900	
Sherman Antitrust Act	Cleveland elected president	Economic depression begins	Coxey's Army	McKinley elected president	Gold Standard Act	
Sherman Silver Purchase Act	People's Party formed	Sherman Silver Purchase Act repealed				
McKinley Tariff						

THE POLITICS OF EQUILIBRIUM

To modern eyes, the nature of the American political system in the late nineteenth century appears in many ways paradoxical. The two political parties enjoyed a strength and stability that neither was ever to know again. And yet the federal government was doing relatively little of importance. In fact, most Americans in those years engaged in political activity not because of an interest in particular issues but because of broad regional, ethnic, or religious sentiments.

The Party System

The most striking feature of the late-nineteenth-century party system was its remarkable stability. From the end of Reconstruction until the late 1890s, the electorate was divided almost precisely *Stability and Stalemate* evenly between the Republicans and the Democrats. Sixteen states were solidly and consistently Republican, and fourteen states (most of them in the South) were solidly and consistently Democratic. Only five states were usually in doubt, and their voters generally decided the results of national elections, often on the basis of voter turnout. The Republican Party captured the presidency in all but two of the elections of the era, but the party was not really as dominant as those victories suggest. In the five presidential elections beginning in 1876, the average popular-vote margin separating the Democratic and Republican candidates was 1.5 percent. The congressional balance was similarly stable, with the Republicans generally controlling the Senate and the Democrats generally controlling the House.

As striking as the balance between the parties was the intensity of public loyalty to them. Voter turnout in presidential elections between 1860 and 1900 averaged over 78 percent of all eligible voters (as compared with only about 50 percent in recent decades). Even in *High Turnout* nonpresidential years, from 60 to 80 percent of the voters turned out to cast ballots for congressional and local candidates. Large groups of potential voters were disfranchised in these years: women in most states; almost all blacks and many poor whites in the South. But for adult white males outside the South, there were few franchise restrictions. The remarkable turnout represented a genuinely mass-based politics.

What explains this extraordinary loyalty to the two political parties? It was not, certainly, that the parties took distinct positions on important public issues. They did so rarely. Party loyalties reflected other factors. Region was perhaps the most important. To white southerners, loyalty to the Democratic Party was a matter of unquestioned faith. It was the vehicle by which they had triumphed over Reconstruction, the vehicle by which they preserved white supremacy. To many northerners, Republican loyalties were equally intense. To them, the party of Lincoln remained a bulwark against slavery and treason.

Religious and ethnic differences also shaped party loyalties. The Democratic Party attracted *Cultural Basis of Party Loyalty* most of the Catholic voters, most of the recent immigrants, and most of the poorer workers. The Republican Party appealed to northern Protestants, citizens of old stock, and much of the middle class. Among the few substantive issues on which the parties took clearly different stands were matters connected with immigrants. Republicans tended to support measures restricting immigration and to favor temperance legislation, which many believed would help discipline immigrant communities. Catholics and immigrants viewed such proposals as assaults on them and their cultures; the Democratic Party followed their lead.

Party identification, then, was usually more a reflection of cultural inclinations than a calculation of economic interest. Individuals might affiliate with a party because their parents had done so, or because it was the party of their region, their church, or their ethnic group. Most clung to their party loyalties with great persistence and passion.

The National Government

One reason the two parties managed to avoid substantive issues was that the federal government did relatively little. The *Weak Federal Government* government in Washington was responsible for delivering the mails, for maintaining a national military, for conducting foreign policy, and for collecting tariffs and taxes. It had few other responsibilities and few institutions with which it could have undertaken additional responsibilities even if it had chosen to do so.

There was one significant exception. From the end of the Civil War to the early twentieth century, the federal government administered a system of annual pensions for Union Civil War veterans who had retired from work and for their widows. At its peak, this pension system was making payments to a majority of the male citizens (black and white) of the North and to many women as well. Some reformers hoped to make the system permanent and universal, but their efforts failed, in part because the Civil War pension system was awash in party patronage and corruption. Other reformers—believers in "good government"—saw elimination of the pension system as a way to fight graft, corruption, and party rule. When the Civil War generation died out, the pension system died with it.

In most other respects, the United States in the late nineteenth century was a society without a modern, national government. The most powerful national political institutions were the two political parties. The national leaders of both parties were primarily concerned not with policy but with office—with winning elections and controlling patronage.

Presidents and Patronage

The power of party bosses had an important effect on the power of the presidency. The office had great symbolic importance, but its occupants were unable to do very much except distribute government appointments. A new president and his tiny staff had to make almost 100,000 appointments; and even in that function, presidents had limited latitude, since they had to avoid offending the various factions within their own parties.

Sometimes that proved impossible, as the presidency of Rutherford B. Hayes (1877–1881) demonstrated. By the end of his term, two groups— the Stalwarts, led by Roscoe Conkling of New *Stalwarts and Half-Breeds* York, and the Half-Breeds, captained by James G. Blaine of Maine—were competing for control of the Republican Party. The dispute between the Stalwarts and the Half-Breeds had little basis in substance. Rhetorically, the Stalwarts favored traditional, professional machine politics, while the Half-Breeds favored reform. In fact, both groups were mainly interested in a larger share of the patronage pie. Hayes tried to satisfy both and ended up satisfying neither.

The battle over patronage overshadowed all else during Hayes's unhappy presidency. His one important substantive initiative—an effort to create a civil service system—attracted no support from either party. And his early announcement that he would not seek reelection only weakened him further.

The Republicans managed to retain the presidency in 1880 in part because they agreed on a ticket that included a Stalwart and a Half-Breed. After a long convention deadlock, they nominated James A. Garfield, a veteran congressman from Ohio and a Half-Breed, for president and Chester A. Arthur of New York, a Stalwart and Conkling henchman, for vice president. The Democrats nominated General Winfield Scott Hancock, a minor Civil War commander with no national following. Benefiting from the end of the recession of 1879, Garfield won a decisive electoral victory, although his popular-vote margin was very thin.

Garfield began his presidency by trying to defy the Stalwarts in his appointments and by showing support for civil service reform. He soon found himself embroiled in an ugly public quarrel with both Conkling and other Stalwarts. It was never resolved. On July 2, 1881, only four months after his inauguration, Garfield was shot twice *Garfield Assassinated* while standing in the Washington railroad station by an apparently deranged gunman (and unsuccessful office seeker) who shouted, "I am a Stalwart and Arthur is president now!" Garfield lingered for nearly three months but finally died.

Chester A. Arthur, who succeeded Garfield, had spent a political lifetime as a devoted, skilled, and open spoilsman and a close ally of Roscoe Conkling. But on becoming president, he tried—like Hayes and Garfield before him—to follow an independent course and even to promote reform. To the dismay of the Stalwarts, Arthur kept most of Garfield's appointees in office and supported civil service reform. In 1883, Congress

REVOLT AMONG REPUBLICANS Many Republican reformers, believers in "good government," were aghast when their party nominated James G. Blaine for president in 1884. Blaine, a former Speaker of the House, U.S. senator, and secretary of state, was the leader of the "Half-Breed" faction of the party, the faction that claimed to support cautious reform. But he was controversial even among reformers after a long career of wily political maneuvering and because of the scandals that continually attached themselves to his name. This cartoon by Joseph Keppler in the political magazine *Puck* shows Republican leaders responding with horror to "the writing on the wall," and to the dire consequences they believed would follow the nomination of Blaine. Blaine himself, at left, hides behind the *New York Herald-Tribune*, the principal organ of the reformers and a critic of Blaine. *(New York Public Library)*

passed the first national civil service measure, the *Pendleton Act*
Pendleton Act, which required that some federal jobs be filled by competitive written examinations rather than by patronage. Relatively few offices fell under civil service at first, but its reach extended steadily so that by the mid-twentieth century most federal employees were civil servants.

Cleveland, Harrison, and the Tariff

In the unsavory election of 1884, the Republican candidate for president was Senator James G. Blaine of Maine—known to his adoring admirers as "the Plumed Knight" but to thousands of other Americans as a symbol of seamy party politics. A group of disgruntled "liberal Republicans," known derisively by their critics as the "mugwumps," announced they would bolt the party and support an honest Democrat. Rising to the bait, the Democrats nominated Grover Cleveland, the "reform" governor of New York.

In a campaign filled with personal invective, what may have decided the election was the last-minute introduction of a religious controversy. Shortly before the election, a delegation of Protestant ministers called on

Blaine in New York City; their spokesman, Dr. Samuel Burchard, referred to the Democrats as the party of "rum, Romanism, and rebellion." Blaine was slow to repudiate Burchard's indiscretion, and Democrats quickly

Cleveland Elected spread the news that Blaine had tolerated a slander on the Catholic Church. Cleveland's narrow victory was probably a result of an unusually heavy Catholic vote for the Democrats in New York.

Grover Cleveland was respected, if not often liked, for his stern and righteous opposition to politicians, grafters, pressure groups, and Tammany Hall. He was the embodiment of an era in which few Americans believed the federal government could, or should, do very much. Cleveland had always doubted the wisdom of protective tariffs (taxes on imported goods designed to protect domestic producers). The existing high rates, he believed, were responsible for the annual surplus in federal revenues, which was tempting Congress to pass "reckless" and "extravagant" legislation, which he frequently vetoed. In December 1887, therefore, he asked Congress to reduce the tariff rates. Democrats in the House approved a tariff reduction, but Senate Republicans defiantly passed a bill of their own actually raising the rates. The resulting deadlock made the tariff an issue in the election of 1888.

The Democrats renominated Cleveland and supported tariff reductions. The Republicans settled on former senator Benjamin Harrison of

Election of 1888 Indiana, who was obscure but respectable; and they endorsed protection. The campaign was the first since the Civil War to involve a clear question of economic difference between the parties. It was also one of the most corrupt elections in American history. Harrison won an electoral majority of 233 to 168, but Cleveland's popular vote exceeded Harrison's by 100,000.

New Public Issues

Benjamin Harrison's record as president was little more substantial than that of his grandfather, who had died a month after taking office. Harrison had few visible convictions, and he made no effort to influence Congress. And yet during Harrison's passive administration, public opinion was beginning to force the government to confront some of the pressing social and economic issues of the day. Most notably, perhaps, sentiment was rising in favor of legislation to curb the power of trusts.

By the mid-1880s, fifteen western and southern states had adopted laws prohibiting combinations that restrained competition. But corporations found it easy to escape limitations by incorporating in states such as New Jersey and Delaware that offered them special privileges. If antitrust legislation was to be effective, its supporters believed, it would have to come from the national government. Responding to growing popular demands, both

Sherman Antitrust Act houses of Congress passed the Sherman Antitrust Act in July 1890, almost without dissent. Most members of Congress saw the act as a largely symbolic measure. For over a decade after its passage, the Sherman Act—indifferently enforced and steadily weakened by the courts—had virtually no impact. As of 1901, the Justice Department had instituted many antitrust suits against unions, but only fourteen against business combinations; there had been few convictions.

The Republicans were more interested, however, in the issue they believed had won them the *Tariff Rates Raised* 1888 election: the tariff. Representative William McKinley of Ohio and Senator Nelson W. Aldrich of Rhode Island drafted the highest protective measure ever proposed to Congress. Known as the McKinley Tariff, it became law in October 1890. But Republican leaders apparently misinterpreted public sentiment, for the party suffered a stunning reversal in the 1890 congressional election. The Republicans' substantial Senate majority was slashed to 8; in the House, the party retained only 88 of the 323 seats. Nor were the Republicans able to recover in the course of the next two years. In the presidential election of 1892, Benjamin Harrison once again supported protection; Grover Cleveland, renominated by the Democrats, once again opposed it. A new third party, the People's Party, with James B. Weaver as its candidate, advocated more substantial economic reform. Cleveland won 277 electoral votes to Harrison's 145 and had a popular margin of 380,000. Weaver showed some significant strength, but still ran far behind. For the first time since 1878, the Democrats won a majority of both houses of Congress.

The policies of Cleveland's second term were much like those of his first—hostile to active efforts to deal with social or economic problems. Again, he supported a tariff reduction, which the House approved but the Senate weakened. Cleveland denounced the result but allowed it to become law as the Wilson-Gorman Tariff.

But public pressure was growing in the 1880s for other reforms, among them regulation of the railroads. Farm organizations in the Midwest (most notably the Grangers) had persuaded several state legislatures to pass regulatory legislation in the early 1870s. But in 1886, the Supreme Court—in *Wabash, St. Louis, and Pacific Railway Co. v. Illinois*, known as the *Wabash* case—ruled one of the Granger Laws in Illinois unconstitutional. According to the Court, the law was an attempt to control interstate commerce and thus infringed on the exclusive power of Congress. Later, the courts limited the powers of the states to regulate commerce even within their own boundaries.

Effective railroad regulation, it was now clear, could come only from the federal government. Congress grudgingly responded to public pressure in 1887 with the Interstate *Interstate Commerce Act* Commerce Act, which banned discrimination in rates between long and short hauls, required that railroads publish their rate schedules and file them with the government, and declared that all interstate rail rates must be "reasonable and just." A five-person agency, the Interstate Commerce Commission (ICC), was to administer the act. But it had to rely on the courts to enforce its rulings. For almost twenty years after its passage, the Interstate Commerce Act—which was, like the Sherman Act, haphazardly enforced and narrowly interpreted by the courts—was without much practical effect.

THE AGRARIAN REVOLT

No group watched the performance of the federal government in the 1880s with more dismay than American farmers. The serious problems that afflicted them helped produce one of the most powerful movements of political protest in American history: what became known as Populism.

The Grangers

Farmers had been making efforts to organize politically for several decades before the 1880s. The first major farm organization was the National Grange of the Patrons of Husbandry, founded in 1867. From it emerged a network of local organizations that tried to teach new scientific agricultural techniques to members. But when the depression of 1873 caused a sharp decline in farm prices, membership rapidly increased and the direction of the organization changed. Granges in the Midwest began to organize marketing cooperatives, and they promoted political action to curb the monopolistic practices of the railroads and warehouses. At their peak, Grange supporters controlled the legislatures in most of the midwestern states. The result was the Granger Laws of the early 1870s, by which many states imposed strict regulations on railroad rates and practices. But the destruction of the new regulations by the courts, combined with the political inexperience of many Grange leaders and the return of prosperity in the late 1870s, produced a dramatic decline in the power of the association by the end of the decade.

National Grange of the Patrons of Husbandry

The Alliances

The successor to the Granges began to emerge even before the Granger movement had faded. As early as 1875, farmers in parts of the South were banding together in so-called Farmers' Alliances. By 1880, the Southern Alliance had more than 4 million members; and a comparable Northwestern Alliance was taking root in the plains states and the Midwest.

Like the Granges, the Alliances formed cooperatives and other marketing mechanisms. They established stores, banks, processing plants, and other facilities for their members—to free them from dependence on the hated "furnishing merchants" who kept so many farmers in debt. Some Alliance leaders, however, saw the movement in larger terms: as an effort to

Social Goals of the Farmers' Alliances

build a new kind of society in which economic competition might give way to cooperation. Alliance lecturers traveled throughout rural areas lambasting the concentrated power of the great corporations and financial institutions.

Although the Alliances quickly became far more widespread than the Granges had ever been, they suffered from similar problems. Their cooperatives did not always work well, partly because the market forces operating against them were sometimes too strong to be overcome and partly because the cooperatives themselves were often mismanaged. These economic frustrations helped push the movement into a new phase at the end of the 1880s: the creation of a national political organization.

In 1889, the Southern and Northwestern Alliances agreed to a loose merger. The next year the Alliances held a national convention at Ocala, Florida, and produced a statement of their goals known as the Ocala Demands. In the 1890 off-year elections, candidates supported by the Alliances won partial or complete control of the legislatures in twelve states. They also won six governorships, three seats in the Senate, and approximately fifty in the House of Representatives. Many of the successful Alliance candidates were simply Democrats who had benefited—often passively—from Alliance endorsements. But dissident farmers drew enough encouragement from the results to contemplate further political action.

Alliance leaders discussed plans for a third party at meetings in Cincinnati in May 1891 and St. Louis in February 1892. Then, in July 1892, 1,300 exultant delegates poured into Omaha, Nebraska, to proclaim the creation of the new party, approve an official set of principles, and nominate candidates for the presidency and vice presidency. The new organization's official name was the People's Party, but the movement was more commonly referred to as Populism.

People's Party Established

The election of 1892 demonstrated the potential power of the new movement. The Populist presidential candidate—James B. Weaver of Iowa, a former Greenbacker—polled more than 1 million votes. Nearly 1,500 Populist candidates won election to state legislatures and local offices. The party elected three governors, five senators, and ten congressmen. It could also claim the support of many Republicans and Democrats in Congress who had been elected by appealing to Populist sentiment.

The Populist Constituency

Already, however, there were signs of the limits of Populist strength. Populism had great appeal to farmers, and particularly to small farmers with little long-range economic security. But Populism failed to move much beyond that group. Its leaders made energetic efforts to include labor within the coalition. In addition to courting the Knights of Labor, the new party added a labor plank to its platform—calling for shorter hours for workers and restrictions on immigration, and

Populism's Limited Appeal

POPULISM

The scholarly debates over the nature of Populism have tended to reflect a larger debate over the nature of popular mass movements. To some historians, mass uprisings seem dangerous and potentially antidemocratic; and to them, the Populist movement has usually appeared ominous. To others, such insurgency is evidence of a healthy democratic resistance to oppression; and to them, Populism has generally seemed more appealing.

The latter view shaped the first, and for many years the only, general history of Populism: John D. Hicks's *The Populist Revolt* (1931). Hicks portrayed Populism as an expression of the healthy, democratic sentiments of the West. Populists were reacting rationally and constructively to the harsh impact of eastern industrial growth on agrarian society, and they were proposing potentially valuable reforms to restrict the power of the new financial titans. Populism was, he wrote, "the last phase of a long and perhaps a losing struggle—the struggle to save agricultural America from the devouring jaws of industrial America."

In the early 1950s, scholars sensitive to the nature of European fascism and contemporary communism took a more suspicious view of mass popular politics and a more hostile view of Populism. The leading figure in this reinterpretation was Richard Hofstadter. In *The Age of Reform* (1955), he conceded that the Populists had genuine grievances and advanced some sensible reforms. But he concentrated on revealing what he called the "soft" and "dark" sides of the movement. Populism, Hofstadter claimed, rested on a romanticized and obsolete vision of the role of farmers in American society. And it was permeated with bigotry and ignorance.

Hofstadter's harsh portrait inspired a series of spirited challenges. Norman Pollack, beginning in 1962, argued that the agrarian revolt rested not on nostalgic and romantic concepts but on a sophisticated and even radical vision of reform. A year later, Walter T. K. Nugent attempted to show that Populists were not bigoted, that they not only tolerated but welcomed Jews and other minorities into their party. And in 1976, Lawrence Goodwyn published *Democratic Promise*, which described Populism as a "cooperative crusade" battling against the "coercive potential of the emerging corporate state."

At the same time that historians were debating the meaning of Populism, they were also arguing over who the Populists were. Hicks, Hofstadter, and Goodwyn, for all their many disagreements, shared a belief that Populists were victims of economic distress—usually one-crop farmers in economically marginal regions victimized by drought and debt. Others, however, have suggested that this description is, if not wrong, at least inadequate. Sheldon Hackney maintained in 1969 that Populists in Alabama were not only economically troubled but socially rootless, "only tenuously connected to society by economic function, by personal relationships, by stable community membership, by political participation, or by psychological identification with the South's distinctive myths." Peter Argersinger, Stanley Parsons, James Turner, and others have similarly suggested that Populists tended to be people who were socially and even geographically isolated. Steven Hahn's 1983 study *The Roots of Southern Populism* described the poor farmers of "upcountry" Georgia who became Populists as people almost entirely unconnected to the modern capitalist economy. They were reacting to a real economic threat to their way of life: the intrusion into their world of a new commercial order of which they were not a part and from which they were unlikely to benefit.

There has, finally, been continuing debate over the legacy of Populism. Michael Kazin, in *The Populist Persuasion* (1994), is one of a number of scholars who have argued that a Populist tradition has survived throughout much of the twentieth century, influencing movements as different as those led by Huey Long in the 1930s, George Wallace in the 1960s, and Ross Perot in the 1990s.

(text continued from page 523)

denouncing the use of private detective agencies as strikebreakers in labor disputes. But Populism never attracted any substantial labor support, in part because the economic interests of labor and the interests of farmers were often at odds.

In the South in particular, white Populists struggled with the question of accepting African Americans in the party. Indeed there was an important black component to the movement—a network of "Colored Alliances" that by 1890 numbered over 1.25 million members. But most white Populists were willing to accept the assistance of blacks only as long as it was clear that whites would remain indisputably in control. When southern conservatives began to attack the Populists for undermining white supremacy, the interracial character of the movement quickly faded.

Populist Ideas

The Populists spelled out their program of reform first in the Ocala Demands of 1890 and then, even more clearly, in the Omaha platform of 1892. They proposed a system of "subtreasuries," a network of government-owned warehouses, where farmers could deposit their crops. Using those *The Populists' Reform Program* crops as collateral, growers could then borrow money from the government at low rates of interest and wait for the price of their goods to go up before selling them. In addition, the Populists called for the abolition of national banks, which they believed were dangerous institutions of concentrated power; the end of absentee ownership of land; the direct election of United States senators (which would weaken the power of conservative state legislatures); and other devices to improve the ability of the people to influence the political process. They called as well for regulation and (after 1892) government ownership of railroads, telephones, and telegraphs. And they demanded a system of government-operated postal savings banks, a graduated income tax, the inflation of the currency, and, later, the remonetization of silver.

A POPULIST GATHERING Populism was a response to real economic and political grievances. But like most political movements of its time, it was also important as a cultural experience. For farmers in sparsely settled regions in particular, it provided an antidote to isolation and loneliness. This gathering of Populist farmers in Dickinson County, Kansas, shows how the political purposes of the movement were tightly bound up with its social purposes. *(Kansas State Historical Society)*

Some Populists were openly anti-Semitic. Others were anti-intellectual, antieastern, and antiurban. But bigotry was not the dominant force behind Populism. The movement was a serious and at times highly intelligent effort to find solutions to real problems. Populism was less a critique of industrialization or capitalism than a challenge to what the Populists considered the brutal and chaotic way in which the economy was developing. Progress and growth should continue, they urged, but should be strictly defined by the needs of individuals and communities.

THE CRISIS OF THE 1890S

The rising agrarian protest was only one of many indications of the national political crisis emerging in the 1890s. There was a severe depression, which began in 1893. There was widespread labor unrest and violence. There was the failure of either major party to respond to the growing distress. And there was the rigid conservatism of Grover Cleveland, who took office for the second time just at the moment that the economy collapsed.

The Panic of 1893

The Panic of 1893 precipitated the most severe depression the nation had ever experienced. It began in March 1893, when the Philadelphia and Reading Railroads declared bankruptcy, unable to meet demands for payment by British banks from which they had borrowed large sums. Two months later, the National Cordage Company failed as well. Together, the two corporate failures triggered a collapse of the stock market. And since many of the major New York banks were heavy investors in the market, a wave of bank failures soon began. That caused a contraction of credit, which meant that many of the new, aggressive businesses that had recently begun operations soon went bankrupt.

The depression reflected, among other things, the degree to which all parts of the American economy were now interconnected. And the depression *America's Interconnected Economy* showed how dependent the economy was on the health of the railroads, which remained the nation's most powerful corporate and financial institutions. When the railroads suffered, as they did beginning in 1893, everything suffered.

Once the panic began, its effects spread with startling speed. Within six months, more than 8,000 businesses, 156 railroads, and 400 banks failed. Already low agricultural prices tumbled further. Up to 1 million workers, 20 percent of the labor force, lost their jobs. The depression was unprecedented not only in its severity but also in its persistence. Although there was slight improvement beginning in 1895, prosperity did not fully return until after 1898.

The depression produced widespread social unrest, not least among the enormous numbers of unemployed workers. In 1894, Jacob S. Coxey, an Ohio businessman and Populist, began advocating an inflation of the currency and a massive public works program to create jobs for the unemployed. When it became clear that his proposals were making no progress in Congress, Coxey organized a march of the unemployed (known as "Coxey's Army") to Washington to present his demands to the government. Congress took no action on the demands.

There were major labor upheavals as well during the decade—of which the Homestead and Pullman strikes were only the most prominent examples (see pp. 476–479). To many middle-class Americans, the worker unrest was a sign of danger- *Homestead and Pullman Strikes* ous social instability, even perhaps a revolution. Labor radicalism—some of it real, much of it imagined—was seldom far from the public mind, heightening the general sense of crisis.

The Silver Question

Populists, and many others, blamed the depression on an inadequate supply of money. Conservatives blamed it on a lack of commitment to a "sound currency." The "money question," therefore, became one of the burning issues of the era.

COXEY'S ARMY Jacob S. Coxey's "army" of the unemployed marches toward Washington in 1894 to demand relief from the federal government. Although several thousand people started out from various parts of the country to join the army, only about 400 actually reached the Capital. The protest disbanded after Coxey and several others were arrested for "trespassing" on the grounds of the United States Capitol. *(Culver Pictures, Inc.)*

The heart of the debate was over what would form the basis of the dollar, what would lie behind it and give it value. Today, the value of the dollar rests on little more than public confidence in the government. But in the nineteenth century, most people assumed that currency was worthless if there was not something concrete behind it—precious metal (specie), which holders of paper money could collect if they presented their currency to a bank or to the Treasury.

During most of its existence as a nation, the United States had recognized two metals—gold and silver—as a basis for the dollar, a formula *"Bimetallism"* known as "bimetallism." In the 1870s, however, that had changed. The official ratio of the value of silver to the value of gold for purposes of creating currency (the "mint ratio") was 16 to 1: sixteen ounces of silver equaled one ounce of gold. But the actual commercial value of silver was much higher than that. Owners of silver could get more by selling it for manufacture into jewelry and other objects than they could by taking it to the mint for conversion to coins. So they stopped taking it to the mint, and the mint stopped coining silver.

In 1873, Congress passed a law that seemed simply to recognize the existing situation by officially discontinuing silver coinage. Few objected at the time. But later in the 1870s, the market value of silver fell well below the official mint ratio of 16 to 1. Silver was suddenly available for coinage again, and it soon became clear that Congress had foreclosed a potential method of expanding the currency. Before long, many Americans concluded that a conspiracy of big bankers had been responsible for the "demonetization" of silver, and they referred to the law as the "Crime of '73."

Two groups of Americans were especially determined to undo the "Crime of '73." One consisted of silver-mine owners and their allies, now understandably eager to have the government take their surplus silver and pay them much more than the market price. The other group consisted of discontented farmers, who wanted an increase in the quantity of money—an inflation of the currency—as a means of raising the prices of farm products and easing payment of the farmers' debts. The inflationists demanded that the government return at once to "free silver"—that is, to the "free and unlimited coinage of silver" at *"Free Silver"* the old ratio of 16 to 1. Congress responded weakly to these demands with the Sherman Silver Purchase Act of 1890, which required the government to purchase (but not coin) silver and pay for it in gold.

At the same time, the nation's gold reserves were steadily dropping. And the Panic of 1893 intensified the demands on those reserves. President Cleveland believed that the chief cause of the weakening gold reserves was the Sherman Silver Purchase Act. Early in his second administration, therefore, Congress responded to *Sherman Silver Purchase Act Repealed* his request and repealed the act—although only after a bitter and divisive battle that helped create a permanent split in the Democratic Party.

"A Cross of Gold"

Republicans, watching the failure of Cleveland and the Democrats to deal effectively with the depression, were confident of success in 1896. Party leaders, led by the Ohio boss Marcus A. Hanna, settled on former congressman William McKinley, author of the 1890 *McKinley Nominated* tariff act and now governor of Ohio, as the party's presidential candidate. The tariff, they believed, should be the principal issue in the campaign. But their platform also opposed the free coinage of silver except by agreement with the leading commercial nations (which everyone realized was unlikely). Thirty-four delegates from the mountain and plains states walked out in protest and joined the Democratic Party.

The Democratic convention of 1896 was unusually tumultuous. Southern and western delegates, eager for a way to compete with the Populists, were determined to seize control of the party from conservative easterners and incorporate some Populist demands—among them free silver—into the Democratic platform. They wanted as well to nominate a pro-silver candidate. The divided platform committee presented two reports to the convention. The majority report, the work of westerners and southerners, called for tariff reduction, an income tax, "stricter control" of trusts and railroads, and—most prominently—free silver. The minority report, the product of the party's eastern wing, echoed the Republican platform by opposing the free coinage of silver except by international agreement.

Defenders of the gold standard seemed to prevail in the debate, until the final speech. Then William Jennings Bryan, a handsome, thirty-six-year-old congressman from Nebraska, mounted the podium to address the convention. He delivered a defense of free silver that became one of the most famous political speeches in American history. The closing passage sent his audience into something close to a frenzy: "If they dare to come out in the open and defend the gold standard as a good thing, we will fight them to the uttermost. Having behind us the producing masses of this nation and the world, supported by the commercial interests, the laboring interests and the toilers everywhere, we will answer their demand for a gold standard by saying to them: 'You shall not press down upon the brow of labor this crown of thorns; you shall not crucify mankind upon a cross of gold.'" It became known as the "Cross of Gold" speech.

"Cross of Gold" Speech

In the glow of Bryan's speech, the convention voted to adopt the pro-silver platform. Perhaps more important, the agrarians embraced Bryan as their leader. The following day, Bryan was nominated for president on the fifth ballot.

The Populists had expected both major parties to adopt conservative programs and nominate conservative candidates, leaving the Populists to represent the growing forces of protest. But now the Democrats had stolen much of their thunder. The Populists faced the choice of naming their own candidate and splitting the protest vote or endorsing Bryan and losing their identity as a party. Many Populists argued that "fusion" with the Democrats would destroy their party. But the majority concluded that there was no viable alternative. Amid considerable acrimony, the convention voted to support Bryan. In a feeble effort to maintain their independence, the Populists repudiated the Democratic nominee for vice president and chose their own, Tom Watson of Georgia.

"Fusion"

The Conservative Victory

The campaign of 1896 produced desperation among conservatives. The business and financial community contributed lavishly to the Republican campaign. From his home at Canton, Ohio, McKinley conducted a dignified "front-porch" campaign before pilgrimages of the Republican faithful, customary behavior in an age when many Americans considered it undignified for anyone to campaign too openly for the presidency.

Emergence of Modern Campaigning

Bryan showed no such restraint. He became the first presidential candidate in American history to stump the country systematically. He traveled 18,000 miles (mostly in the West and South) and addressed an estimated 5 million people. His revivalistic, camp-meeting style pleased old-stock Protestants, but it alienated many of the immigrant Catholics and other ethnics who normally voted Democratic. Employers, meanwhile, warned workers that a Bryan victory would cost them their jobs.

On election day, McKinley polled 271 electoral votes to Bryan's 176 and received 51.1 percent of the popular vote to Bryan's 47.7. Bryan car-

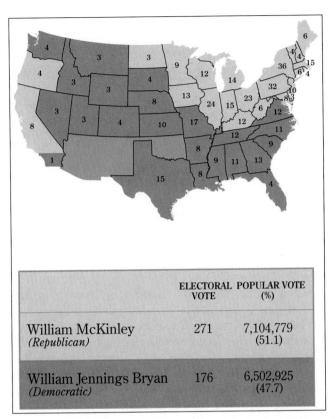

	ELECTORAL VOTE	POPULAR VOTE (%)
William McKinley (Republican)	271	7,104,779 (51.1)
William Jennings Bryan (Democratic)	176	6,502,925 (47.7)

ELECTION OF 1896 The results of the presidential election of 1896 are, as this map shows, striking for the regional differentiation they reveal. William McKinley won the election by a comfortable but not enormous margin, but his victory was not broad-based. He carried all the states of the Northeast and the industrial Midwest, along with California and Oregon, but virtually nothing else. Bryan carried the entire South and almost all of the agrarian West.
◆ *What campaign issues in 1896 help account for the regional character of the results?*

For an interactive version of this map go to www.mhhe.com/unfinishednation4ch19maps

ried only those areas of the South and West where miners or struggling staple farmers predominated. The Democratic program, like that of the Populists, had been too narrow to win a national election.

For the Populists and their allies, the election *Demise of the Populist Party* results were a disaster. They had gambled everything on their "fusion" with the Democratic Party and lost. Within months of the election, the People's Party began to dissolve.

McKinley and Prosperity

The administration of William McKinley saw a return to relative calm. McKinley and his allies worked actively and energetically on only one issue: the need for higher tariff rates. Within weeks of McKinley's inauguration, the administration won approval of the Dingley Tariff, raising duties to the highest point in American history. The administration dealt more gingerly with the explosive silver question (an issue McKinley himself had never considered very important in any case). McKinley sent a commission to Europe to explore the possibility of a silver agreement with Great Britain and France. As he and everyone else anticipated, the effort produced no agreement. The Republicans then enacted the Currency, or Gold Standard, Act of 1900, which confirmed the nation's commitment to the gold standard.

Gold Standard Act

And so the "battle of the standards" ended in victory for the forces of conservatism. Economic developments at the time seemed to vindicate them. Prosperity returned beginning in 1898. Foreign crop failures sent United States farm prices surging upward, and American business entered another cycle of booming expansion. Prosperity and the gold standard, it seemed, were closely allied.

But while the free-silver movement had failed, it had raised an important question for the American economy. In the quarter-century before 1900, the nations of the Western world had experienced a spectacular growth in productive facilities and population. Yet the supply of money had not kept pace with economic progress. Had it not been for a dramatic increase in the gold supply in the late 1890s (a result of new techniques for extracting gold from low-content ores and the discovery of huge new gold deposits in Alaska, South Africa, and Australia), Populist predictions of financial disaster might in fact have proved correct. In 1898, two and a half times as much gold was produced as in 1890, and the currency supply was soon inflated far beyond anything Bryan and the free-silver forces had proposed.

By then, however, Bryan—like many other Americans—was becoming engaged with another major issue: the nation's growing involvement in world affairs and its increasing flirtation with imperialism.

CONCLUSION

For nearly three decades after the battles over Reconstruction, the electorate was relatively evenly divided between the two major parties, which differed with one another on only a few issues. The national government, never fully dominated by either party, remained small and inconsequential. Except for Indian tribes, people engaged in international trade (who were thus subject to tariffs), and the many northern Civil War veterans who received federal pensions, few Americans had any direct contact with the government in Washington except to receive mail from the federal post office. A series of worthy and generally dull presidents presided over this political system as unwitting symbols of its stability and passivity.

Beneath the placid surface of national politics, however, great social issues were creating deep divisions in American life. Battles between employers and workers intensified. American farmers became increasingly resentful of their declining fortunes. Men and women throughout the country grew angry about corruption in government and excessive power in the hands of a few corporate leaders. When a great depression began in 1893, these social tensions exploded to the surface.

The most visible sign of the challenge to politics was the Populist movement. The Populists created their own political party, showed impressive strength in several elections, and then—in 1896—joined with the Democrats to nominate the great Nebraska orator William Jennings Bryan for president. But the forces for insurgency were, in the end, no match for the forces of established institutions. After a campaign notable for its hysterical attacks on Bryan and on the issue with which he was identified ("free silver," making silver a basis for issuing currency in addition to gold), Bryan lost the election to William McKinley. Perhaps more important, the election became the occasion for a great electoral realignment that left the Republicans the clear majority party for the next three decades.

The Republican victory did not, however, end the battle over power and corruption in American life. It simply redirected it into other channels. The challenges to the old politics soon made themselves felt as more conventional reform movements that became known, collectively, as progressivism.

FOR FURTHER REFERENCE

Morton Keller, *Affairs of State: Public Life in Late Nineteenth-Century America* (1977) is an important study of politics and government after Reconstruction. Nell Irvin Painter, *Standing at Armageddon: The United States, 1877–1919* (1987) explores the multicultural dimensions of industrialization, emphasizing the particularly cataclysmic effect of industrialization on minority populations and on race relations. Martin J. Sklar, *The Corporate Reconstruction of American Capitalism, 1890–1916* (1988), offers an interpretation of the evolution of American business practice and, by extension, American politics and society. Two significant books charting the growing capacities of the American state during this period are Theda Skocpol, *Protecting Soldiers and Mothers: The Political Origins of Social Policy in the United States* (1992) and Stephen Skowronek, *Building a New American State: The Expansion of National Administrative Capacities, 1877–1920* (1982). Richard Hofstadter's *The Age of Reform: From Bryan to FDR* (1955) and Lawrence Goodwyn's *The Populist Moment* (1978) offer sharply contrasting characterizations of the Populist and progressive reform movements of this time. Other important studies of Populism include John D. Hicks, *The Populist Revolt* (1931), a classic account, and Steven Hahn, *The Roots of Southern Populism: Yeoman Farmers and the Transformation of the Georgia Upcountry* (1983). Michael Kazin, *The Populist Persuasion: An American History* (1995) places Populist ideas in a broad historical context.

For quizzes, Internet resources, references to additional books and films, and more, consult this book's Online Learning Center site at www.mhhe.com/unfinishednation4.

"MEASURING UNCLE SAM FOR A NEW SUIT," BY J. S. PUGHE, IN *PUCK*
MAGAZINE, **1900** President William McKinley is favorably depicted here as a
tailor, measuring his client for a suit large enough to accommodate the new
possessions the United States obtained in the aftermath of the Spanish-American
War. The cartoon tries to link this expansion with earlier, less controversial ones
such as the Louisiana Purchase. *(Culver Pictures, Inc)*

TIME LINE

1875	1878	1887	1889	1890	1893	1895	
Reciprocity treaty with Hawaii	U.S. gains base at Pago Pago	U.S. gains base at Pearl Harbor	First Pan-American Congress	Mahan's *The Influence of Sea Power upon History*	Revolution in Hawaii	Venezuelan boundary dispute	

THE IMPERIAL REPUBLIC

Stirrings of Imperialism
War with Spain
The Republic as Empire

Throughout the first half of the nineteenth century, as the population of the United States grew and pressed westward, the government, through purchase or conquest, had continually acquired new lands: the trans-Appalachian West, the Louisiana Territory, Florida, Texas, Oregon, California, New Mexico, Alaska. It was the nation's "Manifest Destiny," many Americans believed, to expand into new realms.

In the last years of the nineteenth century, with little room left for territorial growth on the North American continent, those who favored expansion set their eyes beyond the nation's shore. The United States began to consider joining England, France, Germany, and others in the great imperial drive that was bringing much of the nonindustrial world under the control of the industrial powers of the West.

STIRRINGS OF IMPERIALISM

For over two decades after the Civil War, the United States expanded geographically hardly at all. By the 1890s, however, some Americans were ready—indeed, eager—to resume the course of Manifest Destiny that had inspired their ancestors to wrest an empire from Mexico.

1898	1898-1902	1899	1900	1901	1946
Battleship *Maine* sunk	Philippines revolt	Open Door notes	Boxer Rebellion	Platt Amendment	U.S. grants Philippines independence
War with Spain			McKinley reelected		
Treaty of Paris					
U.S. annexes Hawaii, Philippines, Puerto Rico					

The New Manifest Destiny

Several developments helped shift American attention to lands across the seas. The experience of subjugating the Indian tribes had established a

Sources of Imperialism

precedent for exerting colonial control over dependent peoples. The supposed "closing of the frontier" produced fears that natural resources would soon dwindle. The depression that began in 1893 encouraged some businessmen to look for new markets abroad. Americans were, moreover, well aware of the imperialist fever that was raging through Europe. It was leading the major powers to partition most of Africa among themselves and to turn covetous eyes on the Far East and the feeble Chinese Empire. Some Americans feared that their nation would soon be left out, that the Europeans would seize all these potential markets for themselves.

Scholars and others found a philosophic justification for expansionism in Charles Darwin's theories. They contended that nations or "races," like biological species, struggled constantly for existence and that only the fittest could survive. For strong nations to dominate weak ones was, therefore, in accordance with the laws of nature.

Alfred Thayer Mahan

The ablest and most effective advocate of imperialism was Alfred Thayer Mahan, a captain and later admiral in the navy. Mahan's thesis—presented in *The Influence of Sea Power upon History* (1890) and other works—was simple: Countries with sea power were the great nations of history. Effective sea power required, among other things, colonies. Mahan believed America should, at the least, acquire defensive bases in the Caribbean and the Pacific and take possession of Hawaii and other Pacific islands. Mahan feared that the United States did not have a large enough navy to play the great role he envisioned. But during the 1870s and 1880s, the government launched a shipbuilding program that by 1898 had moved the United States to fifth place among the world's naval powers, and by 1900 to third.

Hemispheric Hegemony

James G. Blaine, who served as secretary of state in the Republican administrations of the 1880s, led the early efforts to expand American influence into Latin America. In October 1889, he helped organize the first Pan-American Congress, which attracted delegates from nineteen nations. The delegates agreed to create the Pan-American Union, a weak international organization located in Washington that served as a clearinghouse for distributing information to the member nations. But they rejected Blaine's more substantive proposals: an inter-American customs union and arbitration procedures for hemispheric disputes.

The second Cleveland administration also took a lively interest in Latin

Venezuelan Dispute

America. In 1895, it supported Venezuela in a dispute with Great Britain over the boundary between

LAUNCHING THE *MAINE*, 1889 The battleship *Maine* played a major role in American military history when it blew up in the harbor of Havana, Cuba, in 1898, and help precipitate the Spanish-American War. But it was also significant as part of the growing naval strength the United States was developing in the late nineteenth century. This engraving from *Harper's Weekly* portrays the launching of the *Maine* from the New York Navy Yard in November 1889. *(Naval Historical Center)*

Venezuela and British Guiana. When the British ignored American demands that the matter be submitted to arbitration, the Cleveland administration began threatening England with war. The British government finally realized that it had stumbled into a genuine diplomatic crisis and agreed to arbitration.

Hawaii and Samoa

The islands of Hawaii in the mid-Pacific had been an important way station for American ships in the *Hawaii Coveted* China trade since the early nineteenth century. By the 1880s, officers of the expanding United States Navy were looking covetously at Pearl Harbor on the island of Oahu as a possible permanent base for American ships. Pressure for an increased American presence in Hawaii was emerging from another source as well: the growing number of Americans who had taken up residence on the islands.

Settled by Polynesian people beginning in about 1500 B.C., Hawaii had developed an agricultural and fishing society in which different islands (and different communities on the same islands), each with its own chieftain, lived more or less self-sufficiently. When the first Americans arrived in Hawaii in the 1790s on merchant ships from New England, there were perhaps a half-million people living there.

Empires were not, of course, new to the nineteenth century, when the United States acquired its first overseas colonies. They have existed since the early moments of recorded history—in Greece, Rome, China, and many other parts of the world; and they continued into the sixteenth and seventeenth centuries with vast imperial projects undertaken by Spain, Portugal, France, the Netherlands, and Great Britain in the Americas.

But in the mid- and late-nineteenth century, the construction of empires took on a different form from those of earlier eras, and the word "imperialism" emerged for the first time to describe it. In many places, European powers now created colonies not by sending large numbers of migrants to settle and populate new lands, but instead by creating military, political, and business structures that allowed them to dominate and profit from the existing populations. This new imperialism changed the character of the colonizing nations themselves, enriching them greatly and producing new classes of people whose lives were shaped by the demands of imperial business and administration. It changed the character of colonized societies even more, by drawing them into the vast nexus of global industrial capitalism and by introducing European customs, institutions, and technologies to the subject peoples.

As the popularity of empire grew in the West in the late nineteenth century, efforts to justify it grew as well. Champions of imperialism argued that the acquisition of colonies was essential for the health, even the survival, of their own industrializing nations. Colonies were sources of raw materials vital to industrial production; they were markets for manufactured goods; and they could be suppliers of cheap labor. But defenders of empire also argued that imperialism was good for the colonized people. Many saw colonization as an opportunity to export Christianity to "heathen" lands, and great new missionary movements emerged in Europe and America in response. More secular apologists argued that imperialism helped bring colonized people into the modern world. The British poet Rudyard Kipling was perhaps the most famous spokesman for empire. In his celebrated poem "The White Man's Burden," he spoke of the duty of the colonizers to lift up primitive peoples: to "fill full the mouth of famine and bid the sickness cease."

The growth of empire was not simply a result of need and desire. It was also a result of the new capacities of the imperial powers. The invention of steamships, railroads, telegraphs, and other modern vehicles of transportation and communication; the construction of canals (particular the Suez Canal, completed in 1869, and the Panama Canal, completed in 1914); the birth of new military technologies (repeating rifles, machine guns, and modern artillery): all contributed to the ability of western nations to reach, conquer, and control distant lands.

The greatest imperial power of the nineteenth century, indeed one of the greatest imperial powers in all of human history, was Great Britain. By 1800, despite its recent loss of the colonies that became the United States, it already possessed vast territory in North America, the Caribbean, and the Pacific—most notably Canada and Australia. But in the second half of the nineteenth century, Britain greatly expanded its empire. Its most important acquisition was India, one of the largest and most populous countries in the world. Britain had carried on a substantial trade with India for many years and had gradually increased its economic and military power there. In 1857, when native Indians revolted against British authority, British forces brutally crushed the rebellion and established formal colonial control over India. British officials, backed by substantial military power, now governed India through a large civil service staffed mostly by people from England and Scotland, but with some Indians serving in minor positions. The British invested heavily in railroads, telegraphs, canals, harbors, and agricultural improvements, to enhance the economic opportunities available to them. They created schools for Indian children, in an effort to draw them into British culture and make them supporters of the imperial system.

In those same years, the British extended their empire into Africa and other parts of Asia. The great imperial champion Cecil Rhodes expanded a small existing British colony at Capetown into a substantial colony that included much of what is now South Africa. In 1895, he added new territories to the north, which he named Rhodesia (and which today are Zimbabwe and Zambia). Others spread British authority into Kenya, Uganda, Nigeria, and much of Egypt. British imperialists simultaneously extended the empire into east Asia, with the acquisition of Singapore, Hong Kong, Burma, and Malaya; and they built a substantial presence—although not formal colonial rule—in China.

Other European states, watching the vast expansion of the British empire, quickly jumped into the race for colonies. France created colonies in Indochina (Vietnam and Laos), Algeria, west Africa, and Madagascar. Belgium moved into the Congo in west Africa. Germany established colonies in the Cameroons, Tanganyika, and other parts of Africa, and in the Pacific islands north of Australia. Dutch, Italian, Portuguese, Spanish, Russian, and Japanese imperialists created colonies as well in Africa, Asia, and the Pacific—driven both by a calculation of their own commercial interests and by the frenzied competition that had developed among rival imperial powers. And in 1898, the United States was drawn into the imperial race. Americans entered it in part inadvertently, as an unanticipated result of the Spanish-American War. But they also sought colonies as a result of the deliberate efforts of homegrown proponents of empire (among them Theodore Roosevelt), many of them heavily influenced by British friends and colleagues, who believed that in the modern industrial-imperial world a nation without colonies would have difficulty remaining, or becoming, a true great power.

(text continued from page 537)

Battles among rival communities were frequent, as ambitious chieftains tried to consolidate power over their neighbors. In 1810, after a series of such battles, King Kamehameha I established his dominance over the other chieftains on Hawaii. He welcomed American traders and helped them develop a thriving trade between Hawaii and China. But Americans soon wanted more than trade. Missionaries began settling there in the early nineteenth century, and in the 1830s, William Hooper, a Boston trader, became the first of many Americans to buy land and establish a sugar plantation on the islands.

Growing American Dominance   The arrival of these merchants, missionaries, and planters was devastating to native Hawaiian society. The newcomers inadvertently brought infectious diseases to which the Hawaiians, like the American Indians before them, were tragically vulnerable. By the mid-nineteenth century, more than half the native population had died. But the Americans brought other incursions as well. Missionaries worked to replace native religion with Christianity. Other white settlers introduced liquor, firearms, and a commercial economy, all of which eroded the traditional character of Hawaiian society. By the 1840s, American planters had spread throughout the islands; and an American settler, G. P. Judd, had become prime minister of Hawaii under King Kamehameha III, who had agreed to establish a constitutional monarchy. Judd governed Hawaii for over a decade.

In 1887, the United States negotiated a treaty with Hawaii that permitted it to open a naval base at Pearl Harbor. By then, growing sugar for export to America had become the basis of the Hawaiian economy—as a result of an 1875 agreement allowing Hawaiian sugar to enter the United States duty-free. The American-dominated sugar plantation system displaced native Hawaiians from their lands and relied heavily for workers on Asian immigrants, whom the Americans considered more reliable and more docile than the natives.

Native Hawaiians did not accept these changes without protest. In *Queen Liliuokalani*   1891, they elevated a powerful nationalist to the throne: Queen Liliuokalani. But her brief reign coincided with newly militant efforts by the Americans to seize power, efforts that came as a result of an act of Congress. In 1890, Congress had eliminated the 1875 exemption from tariffs for Hawaiian sugar planters. The result was devastating to the economy of the islands, and American planters concluded that the only way for them to recover was to become part of the United States (and hence exempt from its tariffs). In 1893 they staged a revolution and called on the United States for protection. After the American minister ordered marines from a warship in Honolulu harbor to go ashore to aid the rebels, the queen yielded her authority.

A provisional government, dominated by Americans, immediately sent a delegation to Washington to negotiate a treaty of *Hawaii Annexed*   annexation. Debate over the treaty continued until 1898, when Congress finally approved the agreement.

Three thousand miles south of Hawaii, the Samoan islands had also long served as a port for American ships in the Pacific trade. As American commerce with Asia increased, business groups in the United States regarded Samoa with new interest, and the American navy began eyeing the Samoan harbor at Pago Pago. In 1878, the Hayes administration extracted a treaty from Samoan leaders for an American naval station there. It bound the United States to arbitrate any differences between Samoa and other nations.

But Great Britain and Germany were also interested in the islands, and they too secured treaty rights from the native princes. For the next ten years the three powers jockeyed for dominance in Samoa. Finally, the three powers agreed to create a tripartite protectorate over Samoa, with the native chiefs exercising only nominal authority. The three-way arrangement failed to halt the intrigues and rivalries of its members, and in 1899, the United States and Germany divided the islands between them, compensating Britain with territories elsewhere in the Pacific. The United States retained the harbor at Pago Pago.

Pago Pago Taken

WAR WITH SPAIN

Imperial ambitions had thus begun to stir within the United States well before the late 1890s. But a war with Spain in 1898 turned those stirrings into overt expansionism.

Controversy over Cuba

The Spanish-American War emerged out of events in Cuba. Cubans had been resisting Spanish rule intermittently since at least 1868, when they began a long but ultimately unsuccessful fight for independence. Many Americans had sympathized with the Cubans during that first ten-year struggle, but the United States did not intervene.

In 1895, the Cubans rose up again. This rebellion produced a ferocity on both sides that horrified Americans. The Cubans deliberately devastated the island to force the Spaniards to leave. The Spanish, commanded by General Valeriano Weyler (known in the American press as "Butcher" Weyler), confined civilians in certain areas to hastily prepared concentration camps, where they died by the thousands, victims of disease and malnutrition. The Spanish had used equally savage methods during the earlier struggle in Cuba without shocking American sensibilities. But the revolt of 1895 attracted unprecedented attention in the United States. That was partly because a growing population of Cuban émigrés in the United States—centered in Florida, New York, Philadelphia, and Trenton, New Jersey—gave extensive support to the Cuban Revolutionary Party (whose headquarters was in New York). They helped publicize its leader, José Martí, who was killed in Cuba in 1895. Later, Cuban Americans formed other clubs and associations to support the cause of *Cuba Libre* (Free Cuba).

Cuban Revolt

But it was also because the events in Cuba were reported more fully and flamboyantly by American newspapers, and particularly by the new "yellow press" of William Randolph Hearst and Joseph Pulitzer. Pulitzer's *World*, which began publishing in New York in 1883, launched the age of yellow journalism—a

"Yellow Press"

THE YELLOW PRESS AND THE WRECK OF THE *MAINE* No evidence was ever found tying the Spanish to the explosion in Havana harbor that destroyed the American battleship *Maine* in February 1898. Indeed, most evidence indicated that the blast came from inside the ship, a fact that suggests an accident rather than sabotage. Nevertheless, the newspapers of Joseph Pulitzer and William Randolph Hearst ran sensational stories about the incident that were designed to arouse public sentiment in support of a war against the Spanish. This front-page from Pulitzer's *New York World* is an example of the lurid coverage the event received. Circulation figures at the top of the page indicate, too, how successful the coverage was in selling newspapers. *(The Granger Collection, New York)*

term probably derived originally from the lavish use of color in the *World*, and the color yellow (an especially difficult one to print) in particular. But before long, the term came to be used to describe a sensationalist style of reporting and writing, and a self-conscious effort to reach a mass market. The success of the *World*, whose circulation reached 250,000 by 1886, spawned imitators in New York and elsewhere. Most prominent among them was Hearst's *New York Journal*, which cut its price to one cent after Hearst bought it in 1895 (Pulitzer quickly followed suit), copied many of the *World*'s techniques, and within a year raised its circulation to 400,000. The competition between these two great "yellow" journals soon drove both to new levels of sensationalism. Their success inspired newspapers in other cities around the nation to copy their techniques.

The civil war in Cuba gave both papers their best opportunities yet for combining sensational reporting with shameless appeals to patriotism and moral outrage. They avidly published exaggerated reports of Spanish atrocities against the Cuban rebels, fanning popular anger toward Spain. When the American battleship *Maine* mysteriously exploded in Havana harbor in 1898, both papers immediately blamed Spanish authorities (without any evidence). The *Journal* offered a $50,000 reward for information leading to the conviction of those responsible for the explosion, and it crowded all other stories off its front page. In the three days following the *Maine* explosion, the *Journal* sold over 3 million copies, a new world's record for newspaper circulation. The *World* exploited the destruction of the *Maine* less successfully (although not for lack of trying), but it soon made up for it in its highly sensationalized coverage of the war itself. Hearst boasted at times that the conflict in Cuba was "the *Journal*'s war" and even sent a cable to one of his reporters in Cuba saying: "You furnish the pictures, and I'll furnish the war."

Despite the mounting storm of indignation against Spain, President Cleveland refused to intervene in the conflict. But when McKinley became president in 1897, he formally protested Spain's "uncivilized and inhuman" conduct, causing the Spanish government (fearful of American intervention) to recall Weyler, modify the concentration policy, and grant the island a qualified autonomy.

But whatever chances there were for a peaceful settlement vanished as a result of two dramatic incidents in February 1898. The first occurred when a Cuban agent stole a private letter written by Dupuy de Lôme, the Spanish minister in Washington, and turned it over to the American press. It described McKinley as a weak man and "a bidder for the admiration of the crowd." This was no more than what many Americans, including some Republicans, were saying about their president. But coming from a foreigner, it created intense popular anger. Dupuy de Lôme promptly resigned.

de Lôme Letter

While excitement over the de Lôme letter was still high, the American battleship *Maine* blew up in Havana harbor with a loss of more than 260 people. Many Americans assumed that the Spanish had sunk the ship, particularly when a naval court of inquiry reported that an external explosion by a submarine mine had caused the disaster. (Later evidence suggested that the disaster was actually the result of an accidental explosion inside one of the engine rooms.) War hysteria swept the country, and Congress unanimously appropriated $50 million for military preparations.

The Maine

McKinley still hoped to avoid a conflict. But others in his administration (including Theodore Roosevelt) were clamoring for war. In March 1898, at McKinley's request, Spain agreed to stop the fighting and eliminate its concentration camps; but it refused to negotiate with the rebels and reserved the right to resume hostilities at its discretion. That satisfied neither public opinion nor Congress. A few days later, McKinley asked for and, on April 25, received a congressional declaration of war.

"A Splendid Little War"

Secretary of State John Hay called the Spanish-American conflict "a splendid little war," an opinion that most Americans seemed to share. Declared in April, it was over in August. That was in part because Cuban rebels had already greatly weakened the Spanish resistance, which made the American intervention in many respects little more than a "mopping up" exercise. Only 460 Americans were killed in battle or died of wounds, although some 5,200 perished of disease: malaria, dysentery, and typhoid, among others. Casualties among Cuban insurgents, who continued to bear the brunt of the struggle, were much higher.

Yet the American war effort was not without difficulties. United States soldiers faced serious supply problems: a shortage of modern rifles and *Logistical Difficulties* ammunition, uniforms too heavy for the warm Caribbean weather, inadequate medical services, and skimpy, almost indigestible food. The regular army numbered only 28,000 troops and officers, most of whom had experience in quelling Indian outbreaks but none in larger-scale warfare. That meant that, as in the Civil War, the United States had to rely heavily on National Guard units, organized by local communities and commanded for the most part by local leaders without military experience.

A significant proportion of the American invasion force consisted of black soldiers. Some were volunteer troops put together by black communities. Others were members of the four black regiments in the regular army, who had been stationed on the frontier to defend white settlements against Indians and were now transferred east to fight in Cuba. As the black soldiers traveled through the South toward the training camps, some resisted the rigid segregation to which they were subjected. Black soldiers in Georgia deliberately made use of a "whites only" park; in Florida, they beat a soda-fountain operator for refusing to serve them; in Tampa, white provocations and black retaliation led to a night-long riot that left thirty wounded. *Racial Tensions in the Military* Racial tensions continued in Cuba itself, where African Americans played crucial roles in some of the important battles of the war (including the famous charge at San Juan Hill) and won many medals. Nearly half the Cuban insurgents fighting with the Americans were black, but unlike their American counterparts they were fully integrated into the rebel army. The sight of black Cuban soldiers fighting alongside whites as equals gave African Americans a stronger sense of the injustice of their own position.

Seizing the Philippines

Assistant Secretary of the Navy Theodore Roosevelt was an ardent imperialist and an active proponent of war. As the tension with Spain rose, Roosevelt unilaterally strengthened the navy's Pacific squadron and instructed its commander, Commodore George Dewey, to attack Spanish naval forces in the Philippines, a colony of Spain, in the event of war.

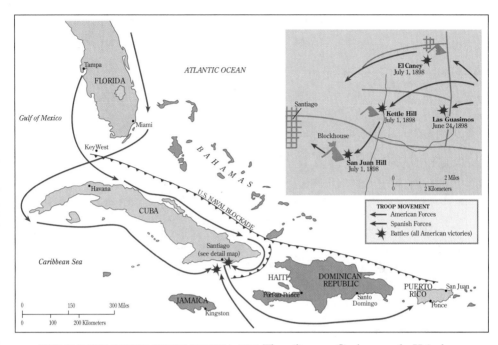

THE SPANISH-AMERICAN WAR IN CUBA, 1898 The military conflict between the United States and Spain in Cuba was a brief affair. The Cuban rebels and an American naval blockade had already brought the Spanish to the brink of defeat. The arrival of American troops was simply the final blow. In the space of about a week, U.S. troops won four decisive battles in the area around Santiago in southeast Cuba—one of them (the Battle of Kettle Hill) the scene of Theodore Roosevelt's famous charge up the adjacent San Juan Hill. This map shows the extent of the American naval blockade, the path of American troops from Florida to Cuba, and the location of the actual fighting. ◆ *What were the implications of the war in Cuba for Puerto Rico?*

For an interactive version of this map go to www.mhhe.com/unfinishednation4ch20maps

Immediately after war was declared, Dewey sailed for the Philippines. On May 1, 1898, he steamed into Manila Bay and completely destroyed the aging Spanish fleet there. Dewey, immediately promoted to admiral, became the first hero of the *Dewey Victorious* war. Several months later, after the arrival of an American expeditionary force, the Spanish surrendered the city of Manila itself.

The Battle for Cuba

Cuba, however, remained the principal focus of American military efforts. At first, the American commanders planned a long period of training before actually sending troops into combat. But when a Spanish fleet under Admiral Pascual Cervera slipped past the American navy into Santiago harbor, on the southern coast of Cuba, plans changed quickly. The American Atlantic fleet quickly bottled Cervera up in the harbor. And the army's

THE ROUGH RIDERS Theodore Roosevelt, center, poses with some of the Rough Riders after their famous charge in the Battle of San Juan Hill. The brigade had an unofficial anthem: "Rough, rough, we're the stuff. We want to fight, and we can't get enough." *(Theodore Roosevelt Association)*

commanding general, Nelson A. Miles, hastily altered his strategy and ordered a force of 17,000 to leave Tampa in June to attack Santiago.

General William R. Shafter, the American commander in Cuba, moved toward Santiago, which he planned to surround and capture. On the way he met and defeated Spanish forces at Las Guasimos and, a week later, in two simultaneous battles, El Caney and San Juan Hill. At the center of the fighting (and on the front pages of the newspapers) during all these engagements was a cavalry unit known as the Rough Riders. Nominally commanded by General Leonard Wood, its real leader was Colonel Theodore Roosevelt, who had resigned from the Navy Department to get into the war. Roosevelt rapidly emerged as a hero of the conflict. His fame rested in large part on his role in leading a bold, if perhaps reckless, charge up Kettle Hill (a charge that was a minor part of the larger battle for the adjacent San Juan Hill) directly into the face of Spanish guns. Roosevelt himself emerged unscathed, but nearly a hundred of his soldiers were killed or wounded. He remembered the battle as "the great day of my life."

Theodore Roosevelt's Rough Riders

Although Shafter was now in position to assault Santiago, his army was so weakened by sickness that he feared he could not go on. Disaster seemed imminent. But unknown to the Americans, the Spanish government had by now decided that Santiago was lost and had ordered Cervera to evacuate. On July 3, Cervera tried to escape the harbor. The waiting American squadron destroyed his entire fleet. On July 16, the commander

of the Spanish ground forces in Santiago surrendered. At about the same
time, an American army landed in Puerto Rico and
occupied it against virtually no opposition. On Au-

Puerto Rico Occupied

gust 12, the United States accepted an end to the war when Spain signed
an armistice recognizing Cuban independence, ceding Puerto Rico to the
United States, and accepting American occupation of Manila until the two
nations reached a final agreement on the Philippines.

Puerto Rico and the United States

The island of Puerto Rico had been a part of the Spanish Empire since
Ponce de León arrived there in 1508. The native people of the island, the
Arawaks, disappeared almost entirely as a result of infectious diseases,
Spanish brutality, and poverty. Puerto Rican society developed, therefore,
with a Spanish ruling class and a large African work force for the coffee
and sugar plantations that came to dominate its economy.

Puerto Rican resistance to Spanish rule began to emerge in the nineteenth century. Uprisings occurred intermittently beginning in the 1820s;
the most important of them—the so-called Lares Rebellion—was, like the
others, effectively crushed by the Spanish in 1868. But the growing resistance did prompt some reforms: the abolition of slavery in 1873, representation in the Spanish parliament, and other changes. Demands for independence continued to grow, and in 1898 Spain granted the island a
degree of independence. But before the changes had any chance to take
effect, control of Puerto Rico shifted to the United States.

American military forces occupied the island during the war. They remained in control until 1900, when the Foraker
Act ended military rule and established a formal

Foraker Act

colonial government. In 1917, Congress passed the Jones Act, which declared Puerto Rico to be United States territory and made all Puerto Ricans American citizens.

The Puerto Rican sugar industry flourished as it took advantage of the
American market that was now open to it without tariffs. As in Hawaii, Americans from the mainland soon established large sugar plantations on the island
and hired natives to work them. The growing emphasis on sugar as a cash
crop and the transformation of many Puerto Rican farmers into paid laborers
led to a reduction in the growing of food for the island and a higher reliance
on imported goods. When international sugar prices were high, Puerto Rico
did well. When they dropped, the island's economy sagged, pushing the many
plantation workers—already desperately poor—into destitution.

The Debate over the Philippines

If the annexation of Puerto Rico produced relatively little controversy, the
annexation of the Philippines occasioned a long
and impassioned debate. Controlling a nearby

Annexation Debated

Caribbean island fit reasonably comfortably into America's sense of itself as the dominant power in the Western Hemisphere. Controlling a large and densely populated territory thousands of miles away seemed different and, to many Americans, more ominous.

McKinley claimed to be reluctant to support annexation. But, according to his own accounts, he emerged from an "agonizing night of prayer" convinced that there were no acceptable alternatives. Returning the Philippines to Spain would be "cowardly and dishonorable," he claimed. Turning the islands over to another imperialist power (France, Germany, or Britain) would be "bad business and discreditable." Granting them independence would be irresponsible; the Filipinos were "unfit for self government." The only solution was "to take them all and to educate the Filipinos, and uplift and Christianize them." Growing popular support for annexation and the pressure of the imperialist leaders of his party undoubtedly helped him reach this decision of conscience.

The Treaty of Paris, signed in December 1898, brought a formal end to the Spanish-American War. It confirmed the terms of the armistice concerning Cuba, Puerto Rico, and Guam. American negotiators had startled the Spanish by demanding that they also cede the Philippines to the United States, but an offer of $20 million for the islands softened Spain's resistance. The Spanish negotiators accepted all the American terms.

In the United States Senate, however, resistance was fierce. During debate over ratification of the treaty, a powerful anti-imperialist movement arose throughout the country to oppose acquisition of the Philippines. Among the anti-imperialists were some of the nation's wealthiest and most influential figures. Some believed simply that imperialism was immoral, a repudiation of America's commitment to human freedom. Some feared "polluting" the American population by introducing "inferior" Asian races into it. Industrial workers feared being undercut by a flood of cheap laborers from the new colonies. Conservatives feared that the large standing army and entangling foreign alliances they thought imperialism would require would threaten American liberties. Sugar growers and others feared unwelcome competition from the new territories. The

Anti-Imperialist League Anti-Imperialist League, established by upper-class Bostonians, New Yorkers, and others late in 1898 to fight against annexation, attracted a widespread following in the Northeast and waged a vigorous campaign against ratification of the Paris treaty.

Supporters of Annexation Favoring ratification was an equally varied group. There were the exuberant imperialists such as Theodore Roosevelt. Some businessmen believed annexation would position the United States to dominate the Asian trade. And most Republicans saw partisan advantages in acquiring valuable new territories through a war fought and won by a Republican administration. Perhaps the strongest argument in favor of annexation, however, was the apparent ease with which it could be accomplished. The United States, after all, already possessed the islands.

When anti-imperialists warned of the danger of acquiring heavily populated territories whose people might have to become citizens, the imperialists had a ready answer: The nation's longstanding policies toward Indians—treating them as dependents rather than as citizens—had created a precedent for annexing land without absorbing people.

The fate of the treaty remained in doubt for weeks, until it received the unexpected support of William Jennings Bryan. Bryan was a fervent anti-imperialist who hoped to move the issue out of the Senate and make annexation the subject of a national referendum in 1900, when he expected to be the Democratic presidential candidate again. Bryan persuaded a number of anti-imperialist Democrats to support the treaty so as to set up the 1900 debate. The Senate ratified it finally on February 6, 1899.

But Bryan miscalculated. If the campaign of 1900 was in fact a debate on the Philippines, as *Election of 1900* Bryan tried to make it, the election proved beyond doubt that the nation had decided in favor of imperialism. Once again, Bryan ran against McKinley, and once again, McKinley won—even more decisively than in 1896. It was not only the issue of the colonies, however, that ensured McKinley's victory. The Republicans were the beneficiaries of growing national prosperity—and also of the colorful personality of their vice presidential candidate, Theodore Roosevelt.

THE REPUBLIC AS EMPIRE

The new American empire was a small one by the standards of the great imperial powers of Europe. But it created large problems. It embroiled the United States in the politics of both Europe and the Far East in ways the nation had always tried to avoid in the past. It also drew Americans into a brutal war in the Philippines.

Governing the Colonies

Three of the new American dependencies—Hawaii, Alaska, and Puerto Rico—presented relatively few problems. They received territorial status (and their residents American citizenship) relatively quickly: Hawaii in 1900, Alaska in 1912, and Puerto Rico (in stages) by 1917. The navy took control of Guam and Tutuila. The United States had also acquired some of the smallest, least populated Pacific islands; it simply left them alone.

Cuba was a thornier problem. American military forces, commanded by General Leonard Wood, remained there until 1902 to prepare the island for independence. They built roads, schools, and hospitals; reorganized the legal, financial, and administrative systems; and introduced medical and sanitation reforms. But when Cuba drew up a constitution that made no reference to the United States, Congress responded by passing

Platt Amendment

the Platt Amendment in 1901 and pressuring Cuba into incorporating the amendment's terms into its constitution. The Platt Amendment barred Cuba from making treaties with other nations; it gave the United States the right to intervene in Cuba to preserve independence, life, and property; and it required Cuba to permit American naval stations on its territory. The amendment left Cuba with only nominal political independence. And American capital made the new nation an American economic appendage as well. American investors poured into Cuba, buying up plantations, factories, railroads, and refineries. Resistance to "Yankee imperialism" produced intermittent revolts against the Cuban government—revolts that at times prompted United States military intervention. American troops occupied the island from 1906 to 1909 after one such rebellion; they returned again in 1912, to suppress a revolt by black plantation workers. As in Puerto Rico and Hawaii, sugar production—spurred by access to the American market—increasingly dominated the island's economic life and subjected it to the same cycle of booms and busts that so plagued other sugar-producing appendages of the United States economy.

The Philippine War

Americans did not like to think of themselves as imperial rulers in the European mold. Yet like other imperial powers, the United States soon discovered that subjugating another people required strength and at times brutality. That, at least, was the lesson of the American experience in the Philippines, where American forces soon became engaged in a long and bloody war.

The conflict in the Philippines is the least remembered of all American wars. It was also one of the longest (it lasted from 1898 to 1902) and one of the most vicious. It involved 200,000 American troops and resulted in 4,300 American deaths. The number of Filipinos killed in the conflict is still in dispute, but it seems likely that at least 50,000 natives (and perhaps many more) died. The American occupiers faced guerrilla tactics in the Philippines very similar to those the Spanish occupiers had faced prior to 1898 in Cuba. And they soon found themselves drawn into the same pattern of brutality that had outraged so many Americans when Weyler had used them in the Caribbean.

The Filipinos had been rebelling against Spanish rule even before 1898. And as soon as they realized the Americans had come to stay, they

Emilio Aguinaldo

rebelled against them as well. Ably led by Emilio Aguinaldo, Filipinos harried the American army of occupation from island to island for more than three years. At first, American commanders believed the rebels had only a small popular following. But by early 1900, General Arthur MacArthur, an American commander in the islands, was writing: "I have been reluctantly compelled to believe that the Filipino masses are loyal to Aguinaldo and the government which he heads."

FILIPINO PRISONERS American troops guard captured Filipino guerrillas in Manila. The suppression of the Filipino insurrection was a much longer and costlier military undertaking than the Spanish-American War, by which the United States first gained possession of the islands. By mid-1900 there were 70,000 American troops in the Philippines, under the command of General Arthur MacArthur (whose son, Douglas, won fame in the Philippines during World War II). *(The Library of Congress)*

To MacArthur and others, that was not a reason to moderate American tactics or conciliate the rebels. It was a reason to adopt more severe measures. Gradually, the American military effort became more systematically vicious and brutal. Captured Filipino guerrillas were summarily executed. On some islands, *The Philippines Brutally Subjugated* entire communities were evacuated—the residents forced into concentration camps while American troops destroyed their villages. A spirit of savagery grew among American soldiers, who came to view the Filipinos as almost sub-human and at times seemed to take pleasure in killing almost arbitrarily.

By 1902, reports of the brutality and of the American casualties had soured the American public on the war. But by then, the occupiers had established control over most of the islands. The key to their victory was the March 1901 capture of Aguinaldo, who later signed a document in which he urged his followers to stop fighting and declared his own allegiance to the United States. Fighting continued intermittently until as late as 1906; but American possession of the Philippines was now secure.

In the summer of 1901, the military transferred authority over the islands to William Howard Taft, who became the first civilian governor. Taft gave the Filipinos broad local autonomy. The Americans also built roads, schools, bridges, and sewers; instituted major administrative and financial reforms; and established a public health system. Filipino self-rule slowly increased. But not until July 4, 1946, did the islands finally gain their independence.

Gradual Shift to Self-rule

The Open Door

The acquisition of the Philippines greatly increased the already strong American interest in Asia. Americans were particularly concerned about the future of China, which was now so enfeebled that it provided a tempting target for exploitation by stronger countries. By 1900, England, France, Germany, Russia, and Japan were beginning to carve up China among themselves, pressuring the Chinese government for "concessions" that gave them effective economic control over various regions. In some cases, they simply seized Chinese territories and claimed them as their own "spheres of influence." Many Americans feared the process would soon cut them out of the China trade altogether.

Eager for a way to protect American interests in China without risking war, McKinley issued a statement in September 1898 saying the United States wanted access to China but no special advantages there: "Asking only the open door for ourselves, we are ready to accord the open door to others." Later, Secretary of State John Hay translated the president's words into policy when he addressed identical messages—which became known as the "Open Door notes"—to England, Germany, Russia, France, Japan, and Italy. He asked them to approve three principles: Each nation with a "sphere of influence" in China was to allow other nations to trade freely and equally in its sphere. The principles he outlined would allow the United States to trade with the Chinese without fear of interference.

Hay's "Open Door Notes"

But the Open Door proposals were coolly received in Europe and Japan. Russia openly rejected them; the other powers claimed to accept them in principle but to be unable to act unless all the powers agreed. Hay, unperturbed, simply announced that all the powers had accepted the principles of the Open Door and that the United States expected them to observe those principles. But unless the United States was willing to resort to war, it could not prevent any nation that wanted to violate the Open Door from doing so.

No sooner had the diplomatic maneuvering over the Open Door ended than the Boxers, a secret Chinese martial-arts society, launched a revolt against foreigners in China. The climax of the Boxer Rebellion was a siege of the entire foreign diplomatic corps in the British embassy in Beijing (Peking). The imperial powers (including the United States) sent an international expedi-

The Boxer Rebellion

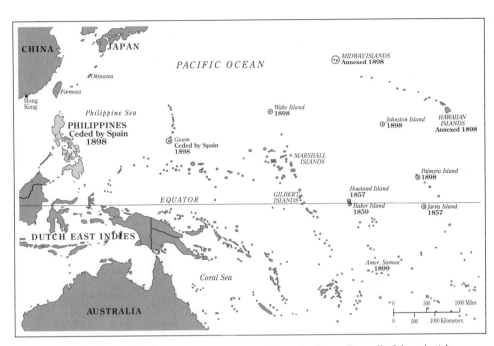

THE AMERICAN SOUTH PACIFIC EMPIRE, 1900 Except for Puerto Rico, all of the colonial acquisitions of the United States in the wake of the Spanish-American War occurred in the Pacific. The new attraction of imperialism persuaded the United States to annex Hawaii in 1898. The war itself gave America control of the Philippines, Guam, and other, smaller Spanish possessions in the Pacific. When added to the small, scattered islands that the United States had acquired as naval bases earlier in the nineteenth century, these new possessions gave the nation a highly far-flung Pacific empire, even if one whose total territory and population remained small by the standards of the other great empires of the age. ◆ *What was the reaction in the United States to the acquisition of this new empire?*

tionary force into China to rescue the diplomats. In August 1900, it fought its way into Beijing and broke the siege.

McKinley and Hay had agreed to American participation so as to secure a voice in the settlement of the uprising and to prevent the partition of China. Hay now won support for his Open Door approach from England and Germany and then induced the other participating powers to accept compensation from the Chinese for the damages the Boxer Rebellion had caused. Chinese territorial integrity survived at least in name, and the United States retained access to its lucrative trade.

A Modern Military System

The war with Spain had revealed glaring deficiencies in the American military system. Had the United States been fighting a more powerful nation, disaster might have resulted. After the war, McKinley appointed Elihu Root, an able New York corporate lawyer, as secretary of war to supervise a major overhaul of the armed forces.

Root's reforms enlarged the maximum size of the regular army from 25,000 to 100,000. They established federal army standards for the National Guard, ensuring that never again would the nation fight a war with volunteer regiments trained and equipped differently from the regular

Creation of the Modern Military

army. They sparked the creation of a system of officer training schools, including the Army Staff College (later the Command and General Staff School) at Fort Leavenworth, Kansas, and the Army War College in Washington, D.C. And in 1903, they established a general staff (named the Joint Chiefs of Staff) to act as military advisers to the secretary of war. As a result of the new reforms, the United States entered the twentieth century with something resembling a modern military system.

CONCLUSION

After more than a century of continual national expansion on the North American continent, the United States joined the community of colonial nations in the 1890s and acquired a substantial empire far from its own shores. But the rise of American imperialism was a halting and contested process, whose purposes were never wholly clear.

In the beginning, America's new internationalism took the form of a supposedly humanitarian intervention in a civil war in Spanish Cuba. The American public, inflamed by lurid journalistic accounts of Spanish atrocities inflicted on innocent Cubans, helped push the United States into a short, victorious war with Spain, fought in theory to secure Cuban independence. But through the efforts of some committed internationalists in the McKinley administration, among them Theodore Roosevelt, the Spanish-American War was soon transformed from a fight to free Cuba into a fight to wrest important colonies from Spain. At its end, the United States found itself in possession of substantial new territories in the Caribbean (including Puerto Rico) and an important territory in the Pacific—the Philippines. A vigorous domestic anti-imperialist movement failed to stop the annexationist drive, and by 1899 the United States found itself in possession of colonies.

Taking the colonies proved easier than holding them. In the Philippines, American forces became bogged down in a four-year war with Filipino rebels. The new colonial rulers soon pacified the Philippines, but not before souring much of the American public on the effort. In part as a result, the territories the United States acquired in the aftermath of the Spanish-American War marked not only the beginning but the end of American territorial imperialism.

FOR FURTHER REFERENCE

Walter LaFeber, *The New Empire: An Interpretation of American Expansion, 1860–1898* (1963) and Ernest May, *Imperial Democracy* (1961) are important introductions to the subject. David F. Healy, *U.S. Expansionism: Imperialist Urge in the 1890s* (1970) is a contrasting view. Walter LaFeber, *The Cambridge History of American Foreign Policy, Vol. 2: The Search for Opportunity, 1865–1913* (1993) is an important overview. William Appleman Williams, *The Tragedy of American Diplomacy*, rev. ed. (1972) is a classic revisionist work on the origins and tragic consequences of American imperialism, supplemented by his *Empire as a Way of Life: An Essay on the Causes and Character of America's Present Predicament* (1982). David M. Pletcher, *The Diplomacy of Trade and Investment: American Economic Expansion in the Hemisphere, 1865–1900* (1998) examines the economic roots of American intervention in Latin America. Anders Stephanson, *Manifest Destiny: American Expansionism and the Empire of Right* (1995) is a short and provocative history of Americans' ideology of expansionism. Robert L. Beisner's *Twelve Against Empire* (1968) chronicles the careers of the leading opponents of imperial expansion. Emily S. Rosenberg, *Spreading the American Dream: American Economic and Cultural Expansion, 1890–1945* (1982) is a provocative cultural interpretation. Gerald F. Linderman, *The Mirror of War: American Society and the Spanish-American War* (1974) examines the social meaning of the war within the United States. Stuart Creighton Miller, *"Benevolent Assimilation": The American Conquest of the Philippines, 1899–1903* (1982) describes the American war in the Philippines. Michael Hunt, *The Making of a Special Relationship: The United States and China to 1914* (1983) is a good introduction to the subject. Matthew Frye Jacobson, *Barbarian Virtues: The United States Encounters Foreign Peoples at Home and Abroad, 1876–1917* (2000) is a broad overview of the interplay between imperialism and immigration.

For quizzes, Internet resources, references to additional books and films, and more, consult this book's Online Learning Center site at www.mhhe.com/unfinishednation4.

"VOTES FOR WOMEN," BY B. M. BOYE   This striking poster was the prize-winning entry in a 1911 contest sponsored by the College Equal Suffrage League of Northern California.   *(Schlesinger Library, Radcliffe Institute, Harvard University)*

TIME LINE

1873	1889	1893	1895	1899	1900
Women's Christian Temperance Union founded	Jane Addams opens Hull House	Anti-Saloon League founded	National Association of Manufacturers founded	Veblen's *A Theory of the Leisure Class*	Galveston, Texas, creates commission government
					Robert La Follette elected Wisconsin governor

CHAPTER TWENTY-ONE

THE RISE OF PROGRESSIVISM

The Progressive Impulse
Women and Reform
The Assault on the Parties
Sources of Progressive Reform
Crusades for Order and Reform

W ell before the turn of the century, many Americans had become convinced that the rapid industrialization and urbanization of their society had created intolerable problems—that the nation's most pressing need was to impose order on the growing chaos and to curb industrial society's most glaring injustices. In the early years of the new century, that outlook acquired a name: progressivism.

Not even those who called themselves progressives could always agree on what the word "progressive" really meant, for it was a phenomenon of great scope and diversity. But it was also one that rested on an identifiable set of central assumptions. It was, first, an optimistic vision. Progressives believed, as their name implies, in the idea of progress. They believed that society was capable of improvement and that continued growth and advancement were the nation's destiny. But progressives believed, too, that growth and progress could not continue to occur recklessly, as they had in the late nineteenth century. The "natural laws" of the marketplace, and the doctrines of laissez-faire and Social Darwinism that celebrated those laws, were not sufficient to create the order and stability that the growing society required. Purposeful human intervention was necessary to solve the nation's problems. Progressives did not always agree on the form that intervention should take, but most believed that government should play an important role in the process.

1902	1909	1911	1912	1919	1920	
Ida Tarbell's exposé of Standard Oil	Croly's *The Promise of American Life* NAACP formed	Triangle Shirtwaist fire	U.S. Chamber of Commerce founded	18th Amendment (prohibition)	19th Amendment (women suffrage)	

THE PROGRESSIVE IMPULSE

෨උ

Beyond these central premises, progressivism flowed outward in a number of different directions. One powerful impulse was the spirit of "antimonopoly," the fear of concentrated power and the urge to limit and disperse authority and wealth. A second progressive impulse was a belief in the importance of social cohesion: the belief that the welfare of any single person is dependent on the welfare of society as a whole. And a third progressive impulse was a belief in organization and efficiency: the belief that social order was a result of intelligent social organization and rational procedures for guiding social and economic life. These varied reform impulses were not entirely incompatible with one another. Many progressives made use of all these ideas at times, and others as well, as they tried to restore order and stability to their turbulent society.

The Muckrakers and the Social Gospel

Among the first to articulate the new spirit of reform was a group of crusading journalists who began to direct public attention toward social, economic, and political injustices. They became known as the "muckrakers" after Theodore Roosevelt accused one of them of raking up muck through his writings. They were committed to exposing scandal, corruption, and injustice.

At first, their major targets were the trusts and particularly the railroads, which the muckrakers considered dangerously powerful and deeply corrupt. Exposés of the great corporate organizations began to appear as early as the 1860s, when Charles Francis Adams, Jr., and others uncovered corruption among the railroad barons. Decades later, Ida Tarbell produced a scorching study of the Standard Oil trust. By the turn of the century, however, many muckrakers were turning their attention to government and particularly to the urban political machines. Among the

Lincoln Steffens — most influential was Lincoln Steffens, a reporter for *McClure's Magazine*. His portraits of "machine government" and "boss rule" in cities had a tone of studied moral outrage that was reflected in the title of his series and of the book that emerged from it, *The Shame of the Cities*. The muckrakers reached the peak of their influence in the first decade of the twentieth century. They investigated governments, labor unions, and corporations. They explored the problems of child labor, immigrant ghettoes, prostitution, and family disorganization. They denounced the waste and destruction of natural resources, the subjugation of women, even occasionally the oppression of blacks.

Many reformers became committed to the idea of what was known as "social justice." A clear expression of that concern was the rise within American Protestantism of the "Social Gospel," the effort to make faith into a tool of social reform. The Salvation Army, which began in England

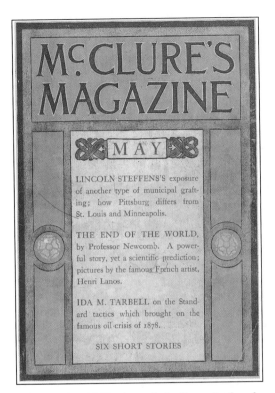

MCCLURE'S MAGAZINE, MAY 1903 *McClure's* was the leading outlet for a form of journalism known as "muckraking," which exposed social and economic scandals in the hope of promoting reform. This issue contains articles by two of the leading muckrakers, Lincoln Steffens and Ida Tarbell. *(Culver Pictures, Inc.)*

but soon spread to the United States, was a Christian social welfare organization with a vaguely military structure. By 1900, it had recruited 3,000 "officers" and 20,000 "privates" and was offering both material aid and spiritual service to the urban poor. In addition, many ministers, priests, and rabbis left traditional parish work to serve in the troubled cities. Charles Sheldon's *In His Steps* (1898), the story of a young minister who abandoned a comfortable post to work among the needy, sold more than 15 million copies. The engagement of religion with reform helped bring to progressivism a powerful moral impulse and a concern for the plight of some of society's most impoverished and degraded people.

The Settlement House Movement

One of the strongest elements of progressive thought was the belief that the environment shaped individual development. Ignorance, poverty, even criminality, progressives argued, were not the result of inherent moral or genetic failings or of the workings of providence. They were, rather, the effects of an unhealthy environment. To elevate the distressed, therefore, required an improvement of the conditions in which the distressed lived.

Nothing produced more distress, many reformers believed, than the crowded immigrant neighborhoods of American cities. One response to the problems of such communities, borrowed from England, was the set-
Hull House
tlement house. The most famous was Hull House, which opened in 1889 in Chicago as a result of the efforts of Jane Addams. It became a model for more than 400 similar institutions throughout the nation. Staffed by members of the educated middle class, settlement houses sought to help immigrant families adapt to the language and customs of their new country.

Central to the settlement houses were the efforts of educated women. Indeed, the movement became a training ground for many important female leaders of the twentieth century, among them Eleanor Roosevelt. The settlement houses also helped spawn another important institution of reform: the profession of social work—a profession in which women were to play an important role. The professional social worker combined a compassion for the poor with a commitment to the values of bureaucratic progressivism: scientific study, efficient organization, reliance on experts.

The Allure of Expertise

As the emergence of the social work profession suggests, progressives in-
Knowledge and Expertise Valued
volved in humanitarian efforts often placed high value on knowledge and expertise. That belief found expression in many ways, among them through the writings of a new group of scholars and intellectuals who envisioned a new civilization in which the expertise of scientists and engineers would be put into the service of the economy and society. Among the most influential of these theorists was the social scientist Thorstein Veblen. Harshly critical of the industrial tycoons of the late nineteenth century—the "leisure class," as he satirically described them in his first major work, *A Theory of the Leisure Class* (1899)—Veblen proposed instead a new economic system in which power would reside in the hands of highly trained engineers. Only they, he argued, could fully understand the "machine process" by which modern society must be governed.

In practical terms, the impulse toward expertise and organization helped produce the idea of scientific management, or "Taylorism" (see p. 462). It encouraged the development of modern mass-production techniques and, above all, the assembly line. It inspired a revolution in American education and the creation of a new area of inquiry—social science, the use of scientific techniques in the study of society and its institutions. It also helped create a movement toward organization among the expanding new group of middle-class professionals.

THE INFANT WELFARE SOCIETY, CHICAGO The Infant Welfare Society was one of many "helping" organizations in Chicago and other large cities—many of them closely tied to the settlement houses—that strove to help immigrants adapt to American life and create safe and healthy living conditions. Here, a volunteer helps an immigrant mother learn to bathe her baby sometime around 1910. *(Chicago Historical Society, ICHi–20216)*

The Professions

The late nineteenth century saw a dramatic expansion in the number of Americans engaged in administrative and professional tasks. Industries needed managers, technicians, and accountants as well as workers. Cities required commercial, medical, legal, and educational services. New technologies required scientists and engineers. By the turn of the century, the people performing these services had come to con-   *The New Middle Class* stitute a distinct social group—what some have called a new middle class.

By the early twentieth century, the millions of members of this new middle class were building organizations and establishing standards to secure their position in society. As one of their principal vehicles, they created the modern, organized professions. The idea of professionalism had been a frail one in America even as late as 1880. But as the demand for professional services increased, so did the pressures for reform.

Among the first to respond was the medical profession. Throughout the 1890s, doctors who considered themselves trained professionals began forming local associations and societies. In 1901, they reorganized the American Medical Association (AMA) into a national profes-   *American Medical Association* sional society. By 1920, nearly two-thirds of all

American doctors were members. The AMA quickly called for strict, scientific standards for admission to the practice of medicine. State and local governments responded by creating medical schools in their universities and by passing new laws that required the licensing of all physicians and that restricted licenses to those practitioners approved by the profession.

There was similar movement in other professions. By 1916, lawyers in all forty-eight states had established professional bar associations. Increasingly, aspiring lawyers found it necessary to enroll in graduate programs, and the nation's law schools accordingly expanded greatly. Businessmen supported the creation of schools of business administration and established their own national organizations: the National Association of Manufacturers in 1895 and the United States Chamber of Commerce in 1912. Farmers responded to the new order by forming, through the National Farm Bureau Federation, a network of agricultural organizations designed to spread scientific farming methods, teach sound marketing techniques, and lobby for the interests of their members.

Limiting Entry into the Professions
Among the chief purposes of the new professionalism was guarding entry into the professions. This was only partly an effort to defend the professions from the untrained and incompetent. The admission requirements also protected those already in the professions from excessive competition and lent prestige and status to the professional label. Some professions used their entrance requirements to exclude blacks, women, immigrants, and other "undesirables" from their ranks. Others used them simply to keep the numbers down, to ensure that demand for the services of existing members would remain high.

Women and the Professions

American women found themselves excluded from most of the emerging professions. But a substantial number of middle-class women—particularly those emerging from the new women's colleges and from the coeducational state universities—nevertheless entered professional careers.

A few women managed to establish themselves as physicians, lawyers, engineers, scientists, and corporate managers. Most, however, turned by necessity to those professions that society considered suitable for women.

Teaching and Social Work
Settlement houses and social work provided two professional outlets that were widely considered appropriate for women. The most important, however, was teaching. Indeed, in the late nineteenth century, more than two-thirds of all grammar-school teachers were women, and perhaps 90 percent of all professional women were teachers. For educated black women, in particular, teaching was often the only professional opportunity they could hope to find.

Women also dominated other professional activities. Nursing had become primarily a women's field around the time of the Civil War, when it was still considered a menial occupation, akin to domestic service. But by the early twentieth century, it too was adopting professional standards. Women also found opportunities as librarians. And many women entered academia—often studying at predominantly male institutions that permitted women to earn advanced degrees, among them the University of Chicago, MIT, and Columbia, and then finding professional opportunities in the new and expanding women's colleges.

The "women's professions" had much in common with other professions. But they also had distinctive qualities. Careers such as teaching, nursing, and library work were "helping" professions. Women's workplaces—schools, hospitals, and libraries—had a vaguely "domestic" or "feminine" image, which enabled men (and, indeed, most women) to reconcile the idea of female professional work with prevailing ideas about the proper role of women in society.

"Helping" Professions

WOMEN AND REFORM

The prominent role of women in reform movements is one of the most striking features of progressivism. Women became important reformers even though they could not vote in most states, seldom held office, and had footholds in only a few professions. But their relative insulation from political and professional life in some ways enhanced their ability to wield influence, for it enabled them to tie their causes to the idea of a nonpartisan, nurturing culture uncontaminated by economic or political interests.

The "New Woman"

The phenomenon of the "new woman" was a product of the social and economic changes of the era. By the end of the nineteenth century, almost all income-producing activity had moved out of the home and into the factory or the office. At the same time, many women were having fewer children, and their children were beginning school at earlier ages and spending more time there. For wives and mothers who did not work for wages, home and family were less all-consuming. Hence more and more women began looking for activities outside the home.

There were also more women who lived outside traditional families altogether. Approximately 10 percent of all American women in the last decades of the nineteenth century never married, and single women were among the most prominent female reformers of the time. Some of these women lived alone. Others lived with other women, often in long-term relationships known as "Boston marriages." The divorce rate also rose rapidly, from one divorce for every twenty-one marriages in 1880 to one in nine by 1916; women initiated the great majority of them.

"Boston Marriages"

Higher levels of education also contributed to the prominence of women in reform activities. The proliferation of women's colleges and of coeducational public universities in the late nineteenth century produced the first generation of women in which significant numbers had educations above the high-school level (see pp. 510–511). The new colleges also helped create female communities, within which women could find support for their ambitions and companionship for their activities.

The Clubwomen

In the vanguard of many progressive social reforms was a large network of women's clubs. The clubs began largely as cultural organizations to provide middle- and upper-class women with an outlet for their intellectual energies. In 1892, when women formed the General Federation of Women's Clubs to coordinate the activities of local organizations, there were more than 100,000 members in nearly 500 clubs. By 1917, there were over 1 million members.

Importance of Women's Club

By the early twentieth century, the clubs were becoming less concerned with cultural activities and more concerned with making a contribution to social reform. Much of what they did was uncontroversial: planting trees; supporting schools, libraries, and settlement houses; building hospitals and parks. But many women's clubs also supported such controversial measures as child labor laws, worker compensation, pure food and drug legislation, occupational safety, reforms in Indian policy, and—beginning in 1914—woman suffrage.

Black women occasionally joined clubs dominated by whites. But African Americans also formed clubs of their own, some of which affiliated with the General Federation, but more of which became part of the independent National Association of Colored Women. They modeled themselves on their white counterparts, but some black clubs took positions on issues of particular concern to blacks. Some crusaded against lynching and called for congressional legislation to make lynching a federal crime. Others protested aspects of segregation.

National Association of Colored Women

The women's club movement raised few overt challenges to prevailing assumptions about the proper role of women in society. But it did represent an important effort by women to extend their influence beyond the home and the family. The club movement allowed women to define a space for themselves in the public world without openly challenging the existing, male-dominated order.

Importance of the Club Movement

The importance of the club movement did not, however, lie simply in what it did for middle-class women. It lay also in what those women did for the working-class people they attempted to help. The women's club movement was an important force in winning passage of state (and ultimately federal) laws that regulated the conditions of woman and child labor, that established government inspection of workplaces, that regulated the food and drug industries, and that applied new standards to urban housing. In many of these efforts, the clubwomen formed alliances with other women's groups such as the Women's Trade Union League, founded in 1903 by female union members and upper-class reformers and committed to persuading women to join unions.

Woman Suffrage

The largest single reform movement of the progressive era, indeed one of the largest in American history, was the fight for woman suffrage. It was the culmination of many decades of struggle by women to obtain basic political rights. But it was also the product of forces peculiar to the early twentieth century.

It is sometimes difficult for today's Americans to understand why the suffrage (or right-to-vote) issue could have become the source of such enormous controversy in the early twentieth century. But at the time, suffrage seemed to many of its critics a very radical demand—in part because of the way some of its supporters promoted it. Throughout the late nineteenth century, many suffrage advocates presented their views in terms of "natural rights," arguing that women deserved the same rights as men—including, first and foremost, the right to vote. Elizabeth Cady Stanton, for example, wrote in 1892 of woman as "the arbiter of her own destiny . . . if we are to consider her as a citizen, as a member of a great nation, she must have the same rights as all other members." A woman's role as "mother, wife, sister, daughter" was "incidental" to her larger role as a part of society.

Radical Implications of Suffrage

This was an argument that boldly challenged the views of many men (and even many women) who believed that society required a distinctive female "sphere" in which women would serve first and foremost as wives and mothers. And so a powerful antisuffrage movement emerged. There were antisuffrage organizations, newspapers, and political crusades. Antisuffragists associated suffrage with divorce, promiscuity, and neglect of children. Throughout much of the late nineteenth century, they effectively blocked most efforts by women to gain the vote.

The suffrage movement began to overcome this opposition in the first years of the twentieth century. That was in part because suffragists were becoming better organized and more politically sophisticated than their opponents. Under the leadership of Anna Howard Shaw, a Boston social worker, and Carrie Chapman Catt, a journalist from Iowa, the National American Woman Suffrage Association grew from a membership of about 13,000 in 1893 to over 2 million in 1917.

NAWSA

But the movement also gained strength because many of its leaders began to justify suffrage in less threatening ways. Suffrage, some supporters began to argue, would allow women to bring their special and distinct virtues more widely to bear on society's problems. It was, they claimed, precisely because women occupied a distinct sphere—because as mothers and wives and homemakers they had special experiences and special sensitivities to bring to public life—that woman suffrage could make such an important contribution to politics. In particular, many suffragists argued that enfranchising women would help the temperance movement by giving its largest group of supporters a political voice. Some suffrage advocates claimed that once women had the vote, war would become a thing of the past, since women would—through their maternal instincts and their calming, peaceful influence—help curb the natural belligerence of men.

The principal triumphs of the suffrage movement began in 1910. That year, Washington became the first state in fourteen years to extend suffrage to women. California joined it a year later, and in 1912 four other western states did the same. In 1913, Illinois became the first state east of the Mississippi to embrace woman suffrage. And in 1917 and 1918, New York and Michigan—two of the biggest states in the Union—gave women the vote. By 1919, thirty-nine states had granted women the right to vote in at least some elections; fifteen had allowed them full participation. In 1920, finally, suffragists won ratification of the Nineteenth Amendment, which guaranteed political rights to women throughout the nation.

Nineteenth Amendment Ratified

To some feminists, however, the victory seemed incomplete. Alice Paul, the head of the militant National Woman's Party (founded in 1916), argued that the Nineteenth Amendment alone would not be sufficient to protect women's rights. Women needed more: a constitutional amendment that would provide clear, legal protection for their rights and would prohibit all discrimination on the basis of sex. But for many years Alice Paul's argument found limited favor even among many of the most important leaders of the recently triumphant suffrage crusade.

Alice Paul

THE ASSAULT ON THE PARTIES

Sooner or later, most progressive goals required the involvement of government. Only government, reformers agreed, could effectively counter the powerful private interests that threatened the nation. But American government at the dawn of the new century was, progressives believed, poorly adapted to meet their demands. Before progressives could reform society effectively, they would first have to reform government itself. In the beginning, at least, many progressives believed that such reform should start with an assault on the domination of government and politics by the political parties.

Early Attacks

Attacks on party dominance had been frequent in the late nineteenth century. Greenbackism and Populism, for example, had been efforts to break the hammerlock with which the Republicans and Democrats controlled public life. The Independent Republicans (or mugwumps) had attempted to challenge the grip of partisanship, and former mugwumps became important supporters of progressive political reform activity in the 1890s and later.

The early assaults enjoyed some success. In the 1880s and 1890s, for example, most states adopted the secret ballot. Prior to that, the political parties themselves had *Secret Ballot* printed ballots (or "tickets") with only the party's candidates listed, which they distributed to their supporters, who then simply went to the polls to deposit the tickets in the ballot box. The old system had made it possible for bosses to monitor the voting behavior of their constituents. The new ballot—printed by the government and distributed at the polls, where it was filled out and deposited in secret—helped chip away at the power of the parties over the voters.

By the late 1890s, critics of the parties were expanding their goals. Party rule could be broken, they believed, in one of two ways. It could be broken by increasing the power of the people, by permitting them to express their will directly at the polls. Or it could be broken by placing more power in the hands of nonpartisan, nonelective officials. Reformers promoted measures that moved along both those paths.

Municipal Reform

Many progressives believed the impact of party rule was most damaging in the cities. Municipal government, therefore, became the first target of those working for political reform. Muckraking journalists such as Lincoln Steffens were especially successful in arousing public outrage at corruption and incompetence in city politics.

The muckrakers struck a responsive chord among a powerful group of urban middle-class progressives, who set out to de- *Urban Machines Challenged* stroy the power of machines. They faced formidable opposition. In addition to challenging the powerful city bosses and their entrenched political organizations, they attacked a large group of special interests: saloon owners, brothel keepers, businessmen who had established lucrative relationships with the urban machines and viewed reform as a threat to their profits. Finally, there was the great constituency of urban working people, many of them recent immigrants, for whom the machines were a source of needed jobs and services. Gradually, however, the reformers gained in political strength, and in the first years of the twentieth century, they began to score some important victories.

An early and influential success came in Galveston, Texas, where the old city government proved completely unable to deal with the effects of a destructive tidal wave in 1900. Capitalizing on public dismay, reformers won approval of a new city charter that replaced the mayor and council with an elected, nonpartisan commission. In 1907, Des Moines, Iowa, adopted its own version of the commission plan, and other cities followed.

City-Manager Plan   Another approach to reform was the city-manager plan (first adopted in Staunton, Virginia, in 1908), by which elected officials hired an outside expert—often a professionally trained business manager or engineer—to take charge of the government. The city manager would presumably remain untainted by the corrupting influence of politics. By the end of the progressive era, almost 400, mostly smaller cities were operating under commissions, and another 45 employed city managers.

In other cities, reformers organized to challenge the municipal electoral process or to change the distribution of powers within the government. Some cities made the election of mayors nonpartisan or moved them to years when no presidential or congressional races were in progress (to reduce the influence of the large turnouts that party organizations produced on such occasions). Reformers tried to make city-council members run at large so as to limit the influence of ward leaders and district bosses. They tried to strengthen the power of the mayor at the expense of the city council, on the assumption that reformers were more likely to get a sympathetic mayor elected than to win control of the entire council.

Statehouse Progressivism

Other progressives turned to state government as an agent for reform. They looked with particular scorn on state legislatures, whose ill-paid, relatively undistinguished members were, they believed, generally incompetent, often corrupt, and almost always controlled by party bosses. Many reformers began looking for ways to circumvent the legislatures (and the party bosses who controlled them) by increasing the power of the electorate.

Two of the most important changes were innovations first proposed *Initiative and Referendum* by Populists in the 1890s: the initiative and the referendum. The initiative allowed reformers to circumvent state legislatures altogether by submitting new legislation directly to the voters in general elections. The referendum provided a method by which actions of the legislature could be returned to the electorate for approval. By 1918, more than twenty states had enacted one or both of these reforms.

The direct primary and the recall were, similarly, efforts to limit the power of parties and improve the quality of elected officials. The primary election was an attempt to take the selection of candidates away from the

ROBERT LA FOLLETTE CAMPAIGNING IN WISCONSIN After three terms as governor of Wisconsin, La Follette began a long career in the United States Senate in 1906, during which he worked uncompromisingly for advanced progressive reforms—so uncompromisingly, in fact, that he was often almost completely isolated. He entitled a chapter of his autobiography "Alone in the Senate." La Follette had a greater impact on his own state, whose politics he and his sons dominated for nearly forty years and where he was able to win passage of many reforms that the federal government resisted. *(State Historical Society of Wisconsin)*

bosses and give it to the people. (In the South, it was also a device for excluding African Americans from voting.) The recall gave voters the right to remove a public official from office through a special election, which could be called after a sufficient number of citizens had signed a petition. By 1915 every state in the nation had instituted primary elections for at least some offices. The recall encountered more strenuous opposition, but some states adopted it as well.

The most celebrated state-level reformer was Robert M. La Follette of Wisconsin. Elected governor in 1900, he helped turn his state into what reformers across the nation described as a "laboratory of progressivism." The Wisconsin progressives won approval of direct primaries, initiatives, and referendums. They regulated railroads and utilities. They passed laws to regulate the workplace and provide compensation for laborers injured on the job. They taxed inherited fortunes and nearly doubled state levies on railroads and other corporate interests.

Parties and Interest Groups

The reformers did not, of course, eliminate parties from American politi-cal life. But they did diminish the parties' centrality. Evidence of that came from, among other things, the decline in voter turnout. In the late nineteenth century, up to 81 percent of eligible voters routinely turned out for national elections. In the early twentieth century, the figure de-clined markedly. In the presidential election of 1900, 73 percent of the electorate voted. By 1912, the figure had dropped to about 59 percent. Never again did voter turnout reach as high as 70 percent.

Emergence of "Interest Groups" At the same time that parties were declining, other power centers were emerging to compete with them: what have become known as "interest groups": professional or-ganizations, trade associations representing particular businesses and in-dustries, labor organizations, farm lobbies, and many others. Social work-ers, the settlement house movement, women's clubs, and others learned to operate as interest groups to advance their demands. A new pattern of pol-itics, in which many individual interests organized to influence govern-ment directly rather than operating through party structures, was taking shape.

SOURCES OF PROGRESSIVE REFORM

Middle-class reformers, most of them from the East, dominated the pub-lic image and much of the substance of progressivism. But they were not alone in seeking to improve social conditions. Working-class Americans, African Americans, westerners, even party bosses also played crucial roles in advancing some of the important reforms of the era.

Labor, the Machine, and Reform

Although the American Federation of Labor, and its leader Samuel Gom-pers, remained largely aloof from many of the reform efforts of the time, some unions nevertheless played important roles in reform battles. In San Francisco, for example, workers in the Building Trades Council spear-headed the formation of the new Union Labor Party, committed to a pro-gram of reform almost indistinguishable from that of middle-class and elite progressives in the city. Between 1911 and 1913, in significant part because of the new party's efforts, California passed a child labor law, a workmen's compensation law, and a limitation on working hours for women. Union pressures contributed to the passage of similar laws in many other states as well.

One result of the assault on the parties was a change in the party or-ganizations themselves. Party bosses sometimes turned their machines into vehicles of social reform. One example was New York's Tammany

Hall, the nation's oldest and most notorious city machine. Its astute leader, Charles Francis Murphy, began in the early years of the century to fuse the techniques of boss rule with some of the concerns of social reformers. Tammany used its political power on behalf of legislation to improve working conditions and eliminate the worst abuses of the industrial economy.

In 1911, a terrible fire swept through the factory of the Triangle Shirtwaist Company in New York's Washington Square; 146 workers, most of them women, died. *Triangle Shirtwaist Fire* Many of them had been trapped inside the burning building because management had locked the emergency exits to prevent unauthorized absences. For the next three years, a state commission studied not only the background of the fire but the general condition of the industrial workplace. By 1914, the commission had issued a series of reports calling for major reforms in the conditions of modern labor. When its recommendations reached the New York legislature, its most effective supporters were not middle-class progressives but two Tammany Democrats from working-class backgrounds: Senator Robert F. Wagner and Assemblyman Alfred E. Smith. With the support of Murphy and the backing of other Tammany legislators, they steered through a series of pioneering labor laws that imposed strict regulations on factory owners and established effective mechanisms for enforcement.

Western Progressives

The American West produced some of the most notable progressive leaders of the time: Hiram Johnson of California, George Norris of Nebraska, William Borah of Idaho, and others—almost all of whom spent at least some of their political careers in the United States Senate. That was because for western states, the most important target of reform energies was the federal government, *Reforming the Federal Government* which exercised a kind of authority in the West that it had never possessed in the East.

Many of the most important issues to the future of the West required action above the state level. Disputes over water, for example, almost always involved rivers and streams that crossed state lines. More significant, perhaps, the federal government exercised enormous power over the lands and resources of the western states and provided substantial subsidies to the region in the form of land grants and support for railroad and water projects. Huge areas of the West remained (and still remain) public lands, controlled by Washington; and much of the growth of the West was (and continues to be) a result of federally funded dams and water projects.

Because so much authority in the region rested in federal bureaucracies that state and local governments could not control, political parties in most of the West were relatively weak. That was one reason why western states could move so quickly and decisively to embrace reforms that parties did

W. E. B. DU BOIS AT HIS DESK Although W. E. B. Du Bois, unlike Booker T. Washington, never developed a large popular following, he was the acknowledged leader of the black elite in the late nineteenth and early twentieth centuries. He was the first African American to earn a doctorate at Harvard University, and he published a number of distinguished works of history and sociology during his long career. He also served as editor of *The Crisis*, the newspaper of the NAACP (which he had helped to found). He died in 1963, at the age of ninety-five. *(Photographs and Prints Division, Schomburg Center for Research in Black Culture, The New York Public Library, Astor, Lenox, and Tilden Foundations)*

not like: the initiative, the referendum, the recall, direct primaries. It is also why aspiring politicians were much quicker to look to Washington as a place from which they could influence the future of their region.

African Americans and Reform

The question of race received serious attention from relatively few white progressives, except among those white southerners who believed that the construction of legalized segregation was a progressive reform. But among African Americans themselves, the progressive era produced some significant challenges to existing racial norms.

African Americans faced greater obstacles than any other group in challenging their own oppressed status and seeking reform. That was one reason why so many had embraced the message of Booker T. Washington in the late nineteenth century, to work for immediate self-improvement rather than long-range social change. By the turn of the century, however, a powerful challenge was emerging—to the philosophy of Washington and, more important, to the entire structure of race relations. The chief spokesman for

W. E. B. Du Bois

this new approach was W. E. B. Du Bois, a Harvard-trained sociologist and historian.

In *The Souls of Black Folk* (1903), Du Bois launched an open attack on Washington's "Atlanta Compromise," first presented in a speech in Atlanta, which had urged blacks to postpone efforts to achieve political equality and concentrate on self-improvement. Du Bois accused Washington of unnecessarily limiting the aspirations of his race. Rather than content themselves with education at the trade and agricultural schools, Du Bois advocated, talented blacks should accept nothing less than a full university education. They should aspire to the professions. They should, above all, fight for immediate progress on civil rights. In 1905, Du Bois and a group of his supporters met at Niagara Falls—on the Canadian side of the border because no hotel on the American side of the Falls would have them—and launched what became known as the Niagara Movement. Four years later, they joined with white progressives sympathetic to their cause to form the National Association for the Advancement of Colored People (NAACP). In the years that followed, the *NAACP Founded* new organization led the drive for equal rights, using as one of its principal weapons lawsuits in the federal courts.

CRUSADES FOR ORDER AND REFORM

Reformers directed many of their energies at the political process. But they also crusaded on behalf of what they considered moral issues. There were campaigns to eliminate alcohol from national life, to curb prostitution, to regulate divorce. There were efforts to restrict immigration and to curb the power of monopoly. There were crusades to resolve what many considered longstanding injustices, of which the most prominent was the campaign for woman suffrage. Proponents of each of those reforms believed that success would help regenerate society as a whole.

The Temperance Crusade

Many progressives considered the elimination of alcohol from American life a necessary step in restoring order to society. Workers in settlement houses and social agencies abhorred the effects of drinking on working-class families: scarce wages vanished as workers spent hours in saloons; drunkenness spawned violence, and occasionally murder. Women, in particular, saw alcohol as a source of some of the greatest problems of working-class wives and mothers, and hoped through temperance to reform abusive or irresponsible male behavior and thus improve women's lives. Employers complained that workers often missed time on the job because of drunkenness or, worse, came to the factory intoxicated and performed their tasks sloppily and dangerously. And political reformers, who looked on the saloon (correctly) as one of the central institutions of the machine,

PROGRESSIVISM

Until the early 1950s, most historians seemed to agree on the central characteristics of early-twentieth-century progressivism. It was just what many progressives themselves had said it was: a movement by the "people" to curb the power of "special interests." More specifically, it was a protest by an aroused citizenry against the excessive power of urban bosses, corporate moguls, and corrupt elected officials.

In 1951, George Mowry began the process of challenging these assumptions by examining progressives in California and describing them as a small, privileged elite of business and professional figures: people who considered themselves the natural leaders of society and who were trying to recover their fading influence from the new capitalist institutions that had displaced them. Progressivism was not, in other words, a popular, democratic movement; it was the effort of a displaced elite to restore its authority. Richard Hofstadter expanded on this idea in *The Age of Reform* (1955) by describing reformers as people afflicted by "status anxiety," fading elites suffering not from economic but from psychological discontent.

The Mowry-Hofstadter argument soon encountered a range of challenges. In 1963, Gabriel Kolko published his influential study *The Triumph of Conservatism*, in which he rejected both the older "democratic" view of progressivism and the newer "status-anxiety" view. Progressive reform, he argued, was not an effort to protect the people from the corporations; it was, rather, a vehicle through which corporate leaders used the government to protect themselves from competition.

A more moderate reinterpretation came from historians embracing what would later be called the "organizational" approach to twentieth-century American history. First Samuel Hays, in *The Response to Industrialism* (1957), and then Robert Wiebe, in *The Search for Order* (1967), portrayed progressivism as a broad effort by businessmen, professionals, and other middle-class people to bring order and efficiency to political and economic life. In the new industrial society, economic power was increasingly concentrated in large, national organizations, while social and political life remained centered primarily in local communities. Progressivism, Wiebe argued, was the effort of a "new middle class"—a class tied to the emerging national economy—to stabilize and enhance its position in society by bringing those two worlds together.

In the 1970s and 1980s, scholarship on progressivism moved in so many different directions that some historians came to despair of finding any consistent meaning in the term. Much of the new scholarship focused on discovering new groups among whom "progressive" ideas and efforts flourished. Historians found evidence of progressivism in the rising movement by consumers to define their interests; in the growth of reform movements among African Americans; in the changing nature of urban political machines; and in the political activism of working people and labor organizations.

Other scholars attempted to identify progressivism with broad changes in the structure and culture of politics. Richard McCormick, writing in 1981, argued that the crucial change in the "progressive era" was the decline of political parties and the corresponding rise of interest groups working for particular social and economic goals.

At the same time, many historians have focused on the role of women (and the vast network of voluntary associations they created in shaping and promoting progressive reform). Some progressive battles, such historians as Kathryn Sklar, Ruth Rosen, Elaine Tyler May, and Linda Gordon have argued, were part of an effort by women to protect their interests within the domestic sphere in the face of jarring challenges from the new industrial world. This protective urge drew women reformers to such issues as temperance, divorce, prostitution, and the regulation of female and child labor. Other women worked to expand their own roles in the public world, particularly through their support of suffrage. The gendered interests of women reformers are, many historians insist, critical to an understanding of progressivism.

The search for the "essence" of progressivism will undoubtedly continue. But the scholarship of recent decades suggests that the real answer to the nature of progressive reform may be a recognition of its enormous diversity.

(text continued from page 573)

saw an attack on drinking as part of an attack on the bosses. Out of such varied sentiments emerged the temperance movement.

Temperance had been a major reform movement before the Civil War, mobilizing large numbers of people in a crusade with strong religious overtones. Beginning in the 1870s, it experienced a major resurgence. As in the antebellum years, it was a movement led and supported primarily by women. In 1873, temperance advocates formed the Women's Christian Temperance Union (WCTU),   *WCTU* led after 1879 by Frances Willard. By 1911, it had 245,000 members and had become the largest single women's organization in American history to that point. In 1893, the Anti-Saloon League joined the temperance movement and, along with the WCTU, began to press for the legal abolition of saloons. Gradually, that demand grew to include the complete prohibition of the sale and manufacture of alcoholic beverages.

Pressure for prohibition grew steadily through the first decades of the new century. By 1916, nineteen states had passed prohibition laws. American entry into World War I, and the moral fervor it unleashed, provided the last push to the advocates of prohibition. In 1917, with the support of rural fundamentalists who opposed alcohol on moral and religious grounds, progressive advocates of prohibition steered through Congress a constitutional amendment embodying their demands. Two years later, after ratification by every state in the nation except Connecticut and Rhode Island (with large populations of Catholic immigrants opposed to prohibition), the   *Eighteenth Amendment Ratified* Eighteenth Amendment became law.

575

Immigration Restriction

Virtually all reformers agreed that the growing immigrant population had created social problems, but there was wide disagreement on how best to respond. Some progressives believed that helping the new residents adapt to American society was the proper approach. Others argued that the only solution was to limit the flow of new arrivals.

Growing Nativism   In the first decades of the century, the arguments of this second, more pessimistic, group gradually gained strength. New scholarly theories argued that the introduction of immigrants into American society was diluting the purity of the nation's racial stock. The spurious "science" of eugenics spread the belief that human inequalities were hereditary and that immigration was contributing to the multiplication of the unfit. A special federal commission of supposed experts, chaired by Senator William P. Dillingham of Vermont, issued an elaborate report filled with statistics and scholarly testimony. It argued that the newer immigrant groups—largely southern and eastern Europeans—had proved themselves less assimilable than earlier immigrants. Immigration, the report implied, should be restricted by nationality. Even many people who rejected racial arguments supported limiting immigration as a way to solve such urban problems as overcrowding, unemployment, strained social services, and social unrest.

The combination of these concerns gradually won for the nativists the support of some of the nation's leading public figures. Powerful opponents—employers who saw immigration as a source of cheap labor, immigrants themselves, and the immigrants' political representatives—managed to block the restriction movement for a time. But by the beginning of World War I the nativist tide was clearly rising.

The Dream of Socialism

At no time in the history of the United States to that point, and in few times after it, did radical critiques of the capitalist system attract more *Socialist Party of America*   support than in the period between 1900 and 1914. The Socialist Party of America grew during the progressive era into a force of considerable strength. In the election of 1900, it had attracted the support of fewer than 100,000 voters; in 1912, its durable leader and perennial presidential candidate, Eugene V. Debs, received nearly 1 million ballots. Strongest in urban immigrant communities (particularly among Germans and Jews), it attracted the loyalties, too, of a substantial number of Protestant farmers in the South and Midwest.

Virtually all socialists agreed on the need for basic structural changes in the economy, but they differed on the extent of those changes and the tactics necessary to achieve them. Some endorsed the radical goals of European Marxists (a complete end to capitalism and private property); others envisioned a more moderate reform that would allow small-scale private enterprise to survive. Militant groups within the party favored direct action. Most conspicuous was the radical labor union the Industrial Workers of the World *IWW* (IWW), whose members were known to their opponents as "Wobblies." Under the leadership of William ("Big Bill") Haywood, the IWW advocated a single union for all workers. The Wobblies were widely believed to have been responsible for the dynamiting of railroad lines and power stations and other acts of terror, although their use of violence was greatly exaggerated by their opponents.

More moderate socialists, who advocated peaceful change through political struggle, dominated the party. They emphasized a gradual education of the public to the need for change and patient efforts within the system to achieve it. But by the end of World War I, because the party had refused to support the war effort and because of a growing wave of anti-radicalism, socialism was in decline as a significant political force.

Decentralization and Regulation

Many reformers agreed with the socialists that the greatest threat to the nation's economy was excessive centralization of power and concentration of wealth, but they re- *Challenging Centralized Power* tained a faith in the possibilities of reform within a capitalist system. They argued that the federal government should ensure the survival of genuine economic competition. This viewpoint came to be identified particularly closely with Louis D. Brandeis, a brilliant lawyer and later a justice of the Supreme Court, who spoke and wrote widely (most notably in his 1913 book, *Other People's Money*) about the "curse of bigness."

Other progressives were less enthusiastic about the virtues of competition. More important to them was efficiency, which they believed economic concentration encouraged. Government, they argued, should not fight "bigness," but should guard against abuses of power by large institutions. It should distinguish between "good trusts" and "bad trusts." Since economic consolidation was destined to remain a permanent feature of American society, continuing oversight by a strong, modernized government, led by a strong president, was essential. One of the most important spokesmen for this emerging "nationalist" position was Herbert Croly, whose 1909 book, *The Promise* *Herbert Croly* *of American Life*, became an influential progressive document. One of those who came to endorse that position (although not fully until after 1910) was Theodore Roosevelt, who became for a time the most powerful symbol of the reform impulse at the national level.

CONCLUSION

A powerful surge of reform efforts emerged in the last years of the nineteenth century and the first years of the twentieth—reforms intended to deal with the vexing problems that the rise of the modern industrial economy had caused. American reformers at the time thought of themselves as "progressives." But neither then nor since has there ever been wide agreement on what the term "progressive" meant.

The reforms themselves were of a bewildering variety—efforts to improve the moral fabric of families and communities; efforts to make politics more efficient and less corrupt; efforts to tame or discipline the great industrial combinations of the time; efforts to empower some groups and restrict or control others. The ideas that lay behind these reforms were similarly various. "Progressivism" was a remarkably heterogeneous movement, united—if it was united at all—by the common belief among reformers that progress was indeed possible and that purposeful human intervention in the life of society and its economy was necessary. The reform crusades gained strength steadily from the 1880s onward, driven in large part by the energy and commitment of millions of women organized in clubs and other organizations. By the early years of the twentieth century, reform was beginning to transform the character of society and the nature of American politics.

FOR FURTHER REFERENCE

Richard Hofstadter, *The Age of Reform: From Bryan to FDR* (1955) is a classic, and now controversial, analysis of the partly psychological origins of the Populist and progressive movements. Robert Wiebe, *The Search for Order, 1877–1920* (1967) is an important organizational interpretation of the era. Gabriel Kolko makes a distinctly revisionist argument that business conservatism was at the heart of the progressive movement in *The Triumph of Conservatism* (1963). Alan Dawley, *Struggles for Justice: Social Responsibility and the Liberal State* (1991) is a sophisticated synthetic account of progressive movements and their ideas. John Milton Cooper, *The Pivotal Decades: The United States, 1900–1920* (1990) is a good narrative history of the period. Arthur S. Link and Richard L. McCormick, *Progressivism* (1983) is a brief interpretation. Daniel T. Rodgers, *Atlantic Crossings: Social Politics in a Progressive Age* (1998) is an important study of the passage of progressive ideas back and forth across the Atlantic. For powerful insights into pragmatism, an important philosophical underpinning to much reform, see Robert Westbrook, *John Dewey and American Democracy* (1991) and Louis Menand, *The Metaphysical Club: A Story of Ideas* (2001). Thomas L. Haskell, *The Emergence of Professional Social Science* (1977) is an important study of the social sciences and professionalism. Paul Starr, *The Social Transformation of American Medicine* (1982) is a pathbreaking study of the emergence of modern systems of health care. Morton J. Horwirtz, *The Transformation of American Law, 1870–1960: The Challenge to Legal Orthodoxy* (1992) is an important, controversial study of the way the legal world responded to economic and social change. Nancy Cott, *The Grounding of American Feminism* (1987) studies the shifting roles and beliefs of women. Kathryn Kish Sklar, *Florence Kelley and the Nation's Work: The Rise of Women's Political Culture, 1830–1900* (1995) examines the impact of female reformers on the progressive movement and the nation's political culture as a whole. Linda Gordon, *The Great Arizona Orphan Abduction* (1999) is the story of an early twentieth-century event that reveals the power of race, religion, and gender in dealing with immigrants. Paula Giddings, *When and Where I Enter: The Impact of Black Women on Race and Sex in America* (1984) is a good introduction to the intersection of gender and race. Glenda Gilmore, *Gender and Jim Crow: Women and the Politics of White Supremacy in North Carolina, 1896–1920* (1996) examines the role of gender in the construction of segregation. Louis Harlan, *Booker T. Washington: The Making of a Black Leader* (1956) and *Booker T. Washington: The Wizard of Tuskegee* (1983) are parts of an outstanding multivolume biography, as are David Levering Lewis, *W. E. B. Du Bois: Biography of a Race* (1993) and *W. E. B. Du Bois: The Fight for Equality and the American Century* (2000).

For quizzes, Internet resources, references to additional books and films, and more, consult this book's Online Learning Center site at www.mhhe.com/unfinishednation4.

THEODORE ROOSEVELT   This heroic portrait of Theodore Roosevelt is by the great American portraitist John Singer Sargent. It hangs today in the White House   *(John Singer Sargent/White House Historical Association)*

TIME LINE

1901	1902	1903	1904	1906	1908	
McKinley assassinated	Northern Securities antitrust case	Panamanian independence	Roosevelt Corollary	Hepburn Railroad Regulation Act	Taft elected president	
Theodore Roosevelt becomes president			Roosevelt elected president	Meat Inspection Act		

CHAPTER TWENTY-TWO

THE BATTLE FOR NATIONAL REFORM

Theodore Roosevelt and the Progressive Presidency
The Troubled Succession
Woodrow Wilson and the New Freedom
The "Big Stick": America and the World, 1901–1917

E fforts to reform the industrial economy encountered repeated frustrations at the state and local levels, so beginning early in the twentieth century, reformers began to look to the federal government. As at the state and local levels, however, the national government—mired in partisan politics—seemed poorly suited to serve as an agent of reform. Progressives attempted to make it more responsive to their demands. Some reformers, for example, urged an end to the system by which state legislatures elected the members of the United States Senate; they proposed instead a direct popular election, which they believed would force the Senate to react more directly to public demands. The Seventeenth Amendment, passed by Congress in 1912 and ratified by the states in 1913, provided for that change.

But even a reformed Congress, progressives believed, could not be expected to provide the kind of coherent leadership their agenda required. Congress was too clumsy, too divided, too tied to local, parochial interests. If the federal government was truly to fulfill its mission, most reformers agreed, it would require leadership from the presidency.

1909	1912	1913	1914	1915	1916	
Payne-Aldrich Tariff	Wilson elected president	16th Amendment (income tax)	Federal Trade Commission Act	U.S. troops in Haiti	U.S. troops in Mexico	
U.S. troops in Nicaragua		17th Amendment (direct election of U.S. senators)	Panama Canal opened			
		Federal Reserve Act				

THEODORE ROOSEVELT AND
THE PROGRESSIVE PRESIDENCY

෯෧

Roosevelt's Popularity To a generation of progressive reformers, Theodore Roosevelt was an idol. No president before and few after attracted such attention and devotion. Yet Roosevelt was also in many respects decidedly conservative. He earned his extraordinary popularity less because of the extent of his reforms than because of his ebullient public personality and because he invested the presidency with something of its modern status as the center of national political life.

The Accidental President

When President William McKinley suddenly died in September 1901, the victim of an assassination, Roosevelt (who had been elected vice president less than a year before) was only forty-two years old, the youngest man ever to assume the presidency. Already, however, he had achieved a reputation as something of a wild man. Mark Hanna, who had warned McKinley against selecting Roosevelt as his running mate, exclaimed, "Now look, that damned cowboy is president of the United States!" But Roosevelt as president never openly rebelled against the leaders of his party. He became, rather, a champion of cautious, moderate change.

Roosevelt's Vision of Federal Power Roosevelt envisioned the federal government not as the agent of any particular interest but as a mediator of the public good, with the president at its center. This attitude found expression in Roosevelt's policies toward the great industrial combinations. At the heart of Roosevelt's policy was his desire to win for government the power to investigate the activities of corporations and publicize the results. The pressure of educated public opinion, he believed, would alone eliminate most corporate abuses.

Roosevelt engaged in a few highly publicized efforts to break up combinations, among them a 1902 suit against a great new railroad combination in the Northwest, the Northern Securities Company. But he was not a trustbuster at heart, and his occasional use of antitrust law did not mark any serious effort to reverse the prevailing trend toward economic concentration.

A similar commitment to establishing the government as an impartial regulatory mechanism shaped Roosevelt's policy toward labor. In the past, federal intervention in industrial disputes had almost always meant action on behalf of employers. Roosevelt was no champion of unions, but he was willing to consider labor's position as well. When a bitter 1902 strike by the United Mine Workers against the anthracite coal industry dragged on long enough to endanger coal supplies for the coming winter, Roosevelt asked both the operators and the miners to accept impartial federal arbitration; and he threatened to dispatch federal troops to seize the mines when the owners refused. They soon relented. Arbitrators awarded the strikers a 10 percent wage increase and a nine-hour day.

Reform was not Roosevelt's main priority during his first years as president. He was too concerned with winning an election in his own right, which meant not antagonizing the conservative Republican Old Guard. By early 1904, Roosevelt had all but neutralized his opposition within the party. He won its presidential nomination with ease. And in the general election, where he faced a pallid conserva-   *Roosevelt Reelected* tive Democrat, Alton B. Parker, he captured over 57 percent of the popular vote.

The Square Deal

During the 1904 campaign, Roosevelt boasted that he had worked in the anthracite coal strike to provide everyone with a "square deal." In his second term, he set out to extend this square deal further. One of his first targets was the powerful railroad industry. The Interstate Commerce Act of 1887, establishing the Interstate Commerce Commission (ICC), had been an early effort to regulate the industry, but over the years the courts had sharply limited its influence. The Hepburn Railroad   *Hepburn Railroad* Regulation Act of 1906 sought to restore some reg-   *Regulation Act* ulatory authority to the government by giving the ICC authority to inspect the books of railroad companies.

Roosevelt also pressured Congress to enact the Pure Food and Drug Act, which restricted the sale of dangerous or ineffective medicines. When Upton Sinclair's powerful novel *The Jungle* appeared in 1906, featuring appalling descriptions of conditions in the meatpacking industry, Roosevelt insisted on passage of the Meat Inspection Act, which ultimately helped eliminate many diseases once transmitted in impure meat. Starting in 1907, he proposed even more stringent measures: an eight-hour day for workers, broader compensation for victims of industrial accidents, inheritance and income taxes, regulation of the stock market, and others. But conservative opposition blocked much of this agenda and was responsible for a widening gulf between the president and the conservative wing of his party.

Roosevelt and the Environment

Roosevelt's aggressive policies on behalf of conservation contributed to that gulf. Using executive powers, he restricted private development on millions of acres of undeveloped government land—most of it in the West—by adding them to the previously modest   *Conservation in the West* national forest system. When conservatives in Congress restricted his authority over public lands in 1907, Roosevelt and his chief forester, Gifford Pinchot, worked furiously to seize all the forests and many of the water power sites still in the public domain before the bill became law.

Roosevelt was the first president to take an active interest in the new and struggling American conservation movement, and his policies had a lasting effect on national environmental policies. Many people who considered themselves "conservationists" in his time promoted policies to protect land for carefully managed development. That was in part a result of the influence of Pinchot, the first director of the National Forest Service (which he had helped create), who supported rational and efficient human use of the wilderness. As a result, the most important legacy of Roosevelt's conservation policy was to establish the government's role as manager of the continuing development of the wilderness.

The Old Guard may have opposed Roosevelt's efforts to extend government control over vast new lands. But they eagerly supported another important aspect of Roosevelt's natural resource policy: public reclamation and irrigation projects. In 1902, the president backed the National Reclamation Act, which provided federal funds for the construction of dams, reservoirs, and canals in the West—projects that would open new lands for cultivation and, years later, provide cheap electric power.

Despite his sympathy with Pinchot's vision of conservation, Roosevelt also shared some of the concerns of the naturalists—those within the conservation movement committed to protecting the natural beauty of the land and the health of its wildlife from human intrusion. Early in his presidency, Roosevelt even spent four days camping in the Sierras with John
John Muir
Muir, the nation's leading preservationist and the founder of the Sierra Club. And he added significantly to the still-young National Park System, whose purpose was to protect public land from any exploitation or development at all.

The contending views of the early conservation movement came to a head beginning in 1906 in a sensational controversy over the Hetch Hetchy Valley in Yosemite National Park—a spectacular, high-walled valley highly popular with naturalists such as Muir and his fellow Sierra Club members. But many residents of San Francisco, worried about finding enough water to serve their growing population, saw Hetch Hetchy as an ideal place for a reservoir.

Preservation versus "Rational Use"
For over a decade, a battle raged between naturalists and the advocates of the dam, a battle that consumed the energies of John Muir for the rest of his life. To Pinchot, the issue was the practical one of whether "leaving this valley in a state of nature is greater than using it for the benefit of the city of San Francisco." Muir helped place a referendum question on the ballot in 1908, certain that the residents of the city would oppose the project "as soon as light is cast upon it." Instead, San Franciscans approved the dam by a huge margin. Construction of the dam finally began after World War I.

This setback for the naturalists was not, however, a total defeat. The fight against Hetch Hetchy helped mobilize a new coalition of people committed to preservation, not "rational use," of wilderness and made clear that the casual exploitation of natural wonders would no longer be unopposed.

BOYS IN THE MINES These young boys, covered in grime and no more than twelve years old, pose for the noted photographer Lewis Hine at the entrance to the coal mine in Pennsylvania where they worked—most likely as "breaker boys," crawling into newly blasted areas and breaking up the loose coal. The rugged conditions in the mines were one cause of the great strike of 1902, in which Theodore Roosevelt intervened. *(Lewis Hine/Corbis)*

Panic and Retirement

Despite the flurry of reforms Roosevelt was able to enact, the government still had relatively little control over the industrial economy. That became clear in 1907, when a serious recession began. Conservatives blamed Roosevelt's "mad" economic policies for the disaster. And while the president naturally (and correctly) disagreed, he nevertheless acted quickly to reassure business leaders that he would not interfere with their private recovery efforts.

The great financier J. P. Morgan helped construct a pool of the assets of several important New *J. P. Morgan*
York banks to prop up shaky financial institutions. The key to the arrangement, Morgan told the president, was the purchase by U.S. Steel of the shares of the Tennessee Coal and Iron Company, currently held by a threatened New York bank. He would, he insisted, need assurances that the purchase would not prompt antitrust action. Roosevelt informally agreed, and the Morgan plan proceeded.

Roosevelt loved being president, and many people assumed he would run for the office again in 1908 despite the longstanding tradition of presidents serving no more than two terms. But the Panic of 1907 and Roosevelt's reform efforts had so alienated conservatives in his own party that he

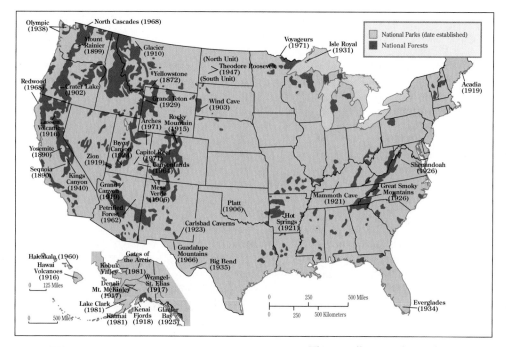

ESTABLISHMENT OF NATIONAL PARKS AND FORESTS This map illustrates the steady growth throughout the late nineteenth and twentieth centuries of the systems of national parks and national forests in the United States. Although Theodore Roosevelt is widely and correctly remembered as a great champion of national parks and forests, the greatest expansions of these systems occurred after his presidency. Note, for example, how many new areas were added in the 1920s. ◆ *What is the difference between national parks and national forests?*

might have had difficulty winning the Republican nomination for another term. In 1904, moreover, he had made a public promise to step down four years later. And so, after nearly eight energetic years in the White House, Theodore Roosevelt, fifty years old, retired from public life—briefly.

THE TROUBLED SUCCESSION

William Howard Taft William Howard Taft, who assumed the presidency in 1909, had been Theodore Roosevelt's most trusted lieutenant and his hand-picked successor; progressive reformers believed him to be one of their own. But Taft had also been a restrained and moderate jurist, a man with a punctilious regard for legal process; conservatives expected him to abandon Roosevelt's aggressive use of presidential powers. By seeming acceptable to almost everyone, Taft easily won election to the White House in 1908. He received his party's nomination virtually uncontested. His victory in the general election in November—over William Jennings Bryan, running for the Democrats for the third time—was a foregone conclusion.

Four years later, however, Taft would leave office the most decisively defeated president of the twentieth century. Taft's failure was a result in part of his failure to match Roosevelt's personal dynamism. (Contributing to Taft's image as a less than vigorous man was his enormous weight, which at times rose to 350 pounds.) More significant, however, was that having come into office as the darling of progressives and conservatives alike, he soon found that he could not please both groups. Gradually he found himself pleasing the conservatives and alienating the progressives.

Taft and the Progressives

Taft's first problem arose in the opening months of the new administration, when he called Congress into special session to lower protective tariff rates, an old progressive demand. But the president made no effort to overcome the opposition of the congressional Old Guard, arguing that it would violate the constitutional doctrine of separation of powers if he were to intervene in legislative matters. The result *Payne-Aldrich Tariff* was the feeble Payne-Aldrich Tariff, which reduced tariff rates scarcely at all.

A sensational controversy broke out late in 1909 that helped destroy Taft's popularity with reformers for good. Many progressives had been unhappy when Taft replaced Roosevelt's secretary of the interior, James R. Garfield, an aggressive conservationist, with Richard A. Ballinger, a more conservative corporate lawyer. Suspicion of Ballinger grew when he attempted to invalidate Roosevelt's removal of nearly 1 million acres of forests and mineral reserves from the public lands available for private development.

In the midst of this mounting concern, Louis Glavis, an Interior Department investigator, charged the new secretary with having once connived to turn over valuable public coal lands in Alaska to a private syndicate for personal profit. Glavis took the evidence to Gifford Pinchot, still head of the Forest Service and a critic of Ballinger's policies. Pinchot took the charges to the president. Taft investigated them and decided they were groundless. But Pinchot was not satisfied. He leaked the story to the press and asked Congress to investigate the scandal. The president discharged him for insubordination, and the congressional committee appointed to study the controversy, dominated by Old Guard Republicans, exonerated Ballinger. But progressives throughout *Pinchot-Ballinger Controversy* the country supported Pinchot. The controversy aroused as much public passion as any dispute of its time; and when it was over, Taft had alienated the supporters of Roosevelt completely and, it seemed, irrevocably.

The Return of Roosevelt

During most of these controversies, Theodore Roosevelt was far away: on a long hunting safari in Africa and an extended tour of Europe. To the American public, however, Roosevelt remained a formidable presence. His return to New York in the spring of 1910 was a major public event. Roosevelt insisted that he had no plans to reenter politics, but within a month he announced that he would embark on a national speaking tour before the end of the summer. Furious with Taft, he was becoming convinced that he alone was capable of reuniting the Republican Party.

The real signal of Roosevelt's decision to assume leadership of Republican reformers came in a speech he gave on September 1, 1910, in

Roosevelt's "New Nationalism"

Osawatomie, Kansas. In it he outlined a set of principles, which he labeled the "New Nationalism," that made clear he had moved a considerable way from the cautious reform conservatism of the first years of his presidency. He argued that social justice was possible only through the efforts of a strong federal government whose executive acted as the "steward of the public welfare." He supported graduated income and inheritance taxes, workers' compensation for industrial accidents, regulation of the labor of women and children, tariff revision, and firmer regulation of corporations.

Spreading Insurgency

The congressional elections of 1910 provided further evidence of how far the progressive revolt had spread. In primary elections, conservative Republicans suffered defeat after defeat. In the general election, the Democrats won control of the House of Representatives for the first time in sixteen years and gained strength in the Senate. But Roosevelt still denied any presidential ambitions and claimed that his real purpose was to pressure Taft to return to progressive policies. Two events, however, changed his mind. The first, on October 27, 1911, was the announcement by the administration of a suit against U.S. Steel, which charged, among other things, that the 1907 acquisition of the Tennessee Coal and Iron Company had been illegal. Roosevelt had approved that acquisition in the midst of the 1907 panic, and he was enraged by the implication that he had acted improperly.

Roosevelt was still reluctant to become a candidate for president, because Senator Robert La Follette, the great Wisconsin progressive, had been working since 1911 to secure the presidential nomination for himself. But La Follette's candidacy stumbled in February 1912 when, exhausted, and distraught over the illness of a daughter, he appeared to suffer a nervous breakdown during a speech in Philadelphia. Roosevelt announced his candidacy on February 22.

ROOSEVELT AT OSAWATOMIE Roosevelt's famous speech at Osawatomie, Kansas, in 1910 was the most radical of his career and openly marked his break with the Taft administration and the Republican leadership. *(Brown Brothers)*

T. R. versus Taft

For all practical purposes, the campaign for the Republican nomination had now become a battle between Roosevelt, the champion of the progressives, and Taft, the candidate of the conservatives. Roosevelt scored overwhelming victories in all thirteen presidential primaries. Taft, however, remained the choice of most party leaders.

The battle for the nomination at the Chicago convention revolved around an unusually large number of contested delegates: 254 in all. Roosevelt needed fewer than half the disputed seats to clinch the nomination. But the Republican National Committee, controlled by the Old Guard, awarded all but 19 of them to Taft. At a rally the night before the convention opened, Roosevelt addressed 5,000 cheering supporters and announced that if the party refused to seat his delegates, he would continue his own candidacy outside the party. "We stand at Armageddon," he told the roaring crowd, "and we battle for the Lord." The next day, he led his supporters out of the convention, and out of the party. The convention then nominated Taft on the first ballot.

Roosevelt summoned his supporters back to Chicago in August for another convention, this one to launch the new Progressive Party and nominate himself as its presidential candidate. Roosevelt approached the battle feeling, as he put it, "fit as a bull moose" (thus giving his new party an enduring nickname). But by

The "Bull Moose" Party

then, he was aware that his cause was virtually hopeless. That was partly because many of the insurgents who had supported him during the primaries refused to follow him out of the Republican Party. It was also because of the man the Democrats had nominated for president.

WOODROW WILSON AND THE NEW FREEDOM

The 1912 presidential contest was not simply one between conservatives and reformers. It was also one between two brands of progressivism that reflected two different views of America's future. And it was one that matched the two most important national leaders of the early twentieth century in unequal contest.

Woodrow Wilson

Reform sentiment had been gaining strength within the Democratic as well as the Republican Party in the first years of the century. At the 1912 Democratic Convention in Baltimore in June, Champ Clark, the conservative Speaker of the House, was unable to assemble the two-thirds majority necessary for nomination because of progressive opposition. Finally, on the forty-sixth ballot, Woodrow Wilson, the governor of New Jersey and the only genuinely progressive candidate in the race, emerged as the party's nominee.

Wilson had been a professor of political science at Princeton until 1902, when he was named president of the university. Elected governor of New Jersey in 1910, he demonstrated a commitment to reform. During his two years in the statehouse, he earned a national reputation for winning passage of progressive legislation. As a presidential candidate in 1912, Wilson presented a progressive program that came to *"New Freedom"* be called the "New Freedom." Wilson's New Freedom differed from Roosevelt's New Nationalism most clearly in its approach to economic policy and the trusts. Roosevelt believed in accepting economic concentration and using government to regulate and control it. Wilson seemed to side with those who (like Brandeis) believed that the proper response to monopoly was not to regulate it but to destroy it.

The 1912 presidential campaign was something of an anticlimax. William Howard Taft, resigned to defeat, barely campaigned at all. Roosevelt campaigned energetically (until a gunshot wound from a would-be assassin forced him to the sidelines during the last weeks before the election), but he failed to draw any significant numbers of Democratic progressives away from Wilson. In November, Roosevelt and Taft split the Republican vote; Wilson held onto most Democrats and won. He polled only a plurality of the popular vote: 42 percent, compared with 27 percent for Roosevelt, 23 percent for Taft, and 6 percent for the socialist Eugene Debs. But in the electoral college, Wilson won 435 of the 531 votes.

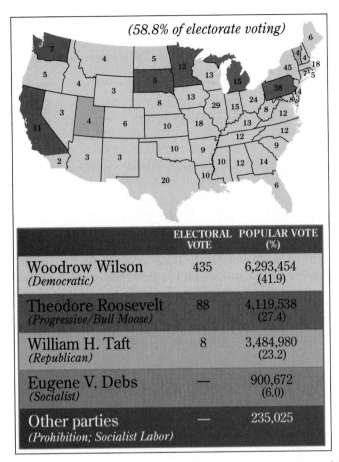

	ELECTORAL VOTE	POPULAR VOTE (%)
Woodrow Wilson (Democratic)	435	6,293,454 (41.9)
Theodore Roosevelt (Progressive/Bull Moose)	88	4,119,538 (27.4)
William H. Taft (Republican)	8	3,484,980 (23.2)
Eugene V. Debs (Socialist)	—	900,672 (6.0)
Other parties (Prohibition; Socialist Labor)	—	235,025

ELECTION OF 1912 The election of 1912 was one of the most unusual in American history because of the dramatic schism within the Republican party. Two Republican presidents— William Howard Taft, the incumbent, and Theodore Roosevelt, his predecessor—ran against each other in 1912, opening the way for a victory by the Democratic candidate Woodrow Wilson, who won with only about 42 percent of the popular vote. A fourth candidate, the socialist Eugene V. Debs, received a significant 6 percent of the vote. ◆ *What events caused the schism between Taft and Roosevelt?*

 For an interactive version of this map go to www.mhhe.com/unfinishednation4ch22maps

The Scholar as President

More than William Howard Taft, more even than Theodore Roosevelt, Wilson concentrated the powers of the executive branch in his own hands. He exerted firm control over his cabinet, and he delegated real authority only to those whose loyalty to him was beyond question. Perhaps the clearest indication of his style of leadership was the identity of his most powerful adviser: Colonel Edward M. House, an intelligent and ambitious Texan whose only claim to authority was his personal intimacy with the president.

In legislative matters, Wilson skillfully used his position as party leader to weld together a coalition that would support his program. Democratic majorities in both houses of Congress made his task easier. Wilson's first triumph as president was the fulfillment of an old Democratic (and progressive) goal: a substantial lowering of the protective tariff. The Underwood-Simmons Tariff, passed in a special session of Congress that Wilson summoned shortly after his inauguration, provided cuts substantial enough, progressives believed, to introduce real competition into American markets and thus to help break the power of trusts. To make up

Income Tax Adopted for the loss of revenue under the new tariff, Congress approved a graduated income tax. This first modern income tax imposed a 1 percent tax on individuals and corporations earning over $4,000, with rates ranging up to 6 percent on incomes over $500,000.

Wilson held Congress in session through the summer to work on a major reform of the American banking system: the Federal Reserve Act, which Congress passed and which the president signed on December 23, 1913. It created twelve regional banks, each to be owned and controlled by the individual banks of its district. The regional Federal Reserve banks would hold a certain percentage of the assets of their member banks in reserve; they would use those reserves to support loans to private banks at an interest (or "discount") rate that the Federal Reserve system would set; they would issue a new type of paper currency—Federal Reserve notes—that would become the nation's basic medium of trade and would be backed by the government. Most important, perhaps, they would be able to shift funds quickly to troubled areas—to meet increased demands for credit or to protect imperiled banks. Supervising and regulating the entire system was a national Federal Reserve Board, whose members were appointed by the president.

In 1914, turning to the central issue of his 1912 campaign, Wilson proposed two measures to deal with the problem of monopoly. There was a proposal to create a federal agency through which the government would help business police itself—a regulatory commission of the type Roosevelt had advocated in 1912. There were also proposals to strengthen the government's ability actually to break up trusts—a decentralizing approach more characteristic of Wilson's 1912 campaign. The two measures took shape as the Federal Trade Commission Act and the Clayton Antitrust Act. The Federal Trade Commission Act

Federal Trade Commission Act created a regulatory agency that would help businesses determine in advance whether their actions would be acceptable to the government. The agency would also have authority to launch prosecutions against "unfair trade practices," which the law did not define, and it would have wide power to investigate corporate behavior. The act, in short, increased the government's regulatory authority significantly. Wilson signed it happily. But he seemed to lose interest in the Clayton Antitrust Bill and did little to protect it from conservative assaults, which greatly weakened it. The vigorous legal pursuit of monopoly that Wilson had promised in 1912 never materialized.

Retreat and Advance

By the fall of 1914, Wilson believed that the program of the New Freedom was essentially complete. He refused to support the movement for national woman suffrage. Deferring to southern Democrats, he condoned the reimposition of segregation in the agencies of the federal government. When congressional progressives attempted to enlist his support for new reform legislation, he dismissed their proposals as unconstitutional or unnecessary.

The congressional elections of 1914, however, shattered the president's complacency. Democrats suffered major losses in the House of Representatives, and voters who in 1912 had supported the Progressive Party began returning to the Republicans. Wilson would not be able to rely on a divided opposition when he ran for reelection in 1916. By the end of 1915, therefore, Wilson had begun to support a second flurry of reforms. In January 1916, he appointed Louis Brandeis to the Supreme Court, making him not only the first Jew but the most advanced progressive to serve there. Later, he supported a measure to make it easier for farmers to receive credit and one creating a system of workers' compensation for federal employees.

In 1916, Wilson supported the Keating-Owen Act. The measure prohibited the shipment across state lines of goods produced by underage children, thus giving an expanded importance to the constitutional clause assigning Congress the task of regulating interstate commerce. (It would be some years before the Supreme Court would uphold this interpretation of the clause; the Court invalidated the Keating-Owen Act in 1918.) The president similarly supported measures that used federal taxing authority as a vehicle for legislating social change. After the Court struck down Keating-Owen, a new law attempted to achieve the same goal by imposing a heavy tax on the products of child labor. (The *Limiting Child Labor* Court later struck it down, too.) And the Smith-Lever Act of 1914 demonstrated another way in which the federal government could influence local behavior; it offered matching federal grants to states that agreed to support agricultural extension education.

THE "BIG STICK": AMERICA AND THE WORLD, 1901–1917

American foreign policy during the progressive years reflected many of the same impulses that were motivating domestic reform. But more than that, it reflected the nation's new sense of itself as a world power.

Roosevelt and "Civilization"

Theodore Roosevelt believed in the value and importance of using American power in the world (a conviction he once described by citing the proverb, "Speak softly, but carry a big stick"). But he had two different standards for using that power.

Roosevelt believed that an important distinction existed between the "civilized" and "uncivilized" nations of the world. "Civilized" nations, as he defined them, were predominantly white and Anglo-Saxon or Teutonic; "uncivilized" nations were generally nonwhite, Latin, or Slavic. But racism was only partly the basis of the distinction. Equally important was economic development. Civilized nations were, by Roosevelt's definition, producers of industrial goods; uncivilized nations were suppliers of raw materials and markets. There was, he believed, an economic relationship between the two parts that was vital to both of them. A civilized society, therefore, had the right and duty to intervene in the affairs of a "backward" nation to preserve order and stability—for the sake of both nations. That belief was one important reason for Roosevelt's early support of the development of American sea power. By 1906, the American navy had attained a size and strength surpassed only by that of Great Britain.

Justifying Intervention

Protecting the "Open Door" in Asia

In 1904 the Japanese staged a surprise attack on the Russian fleet at Port Arthur in southern Manchuria, a province of China that both Russia and Japan hoped to control. Roosevelt, hoping to prevent either nation from becoming dominant there, agreed to a Japanese request to mediate an end to the conflict. Russia, faring badly in the war, had no choice but to agree. At a peace conference in Portsmouth, New Hampshire, in 1905, Roosevelt extracted from the embattled Russians a recognition of Japan's territorial gains and from the Japanese an agreement to cease the fighting and expand no further. At the same time, he negotiated a secret agreement with the Japanese to ensure that the United States could continue to trade freely in the region. But in the years that followed, relations between the United States and Japan steadily deteriorated. Having destroyed the Russian fleet at Port Arthur, Japan now emerged as the preeminent naval power in the Pacific and soon began to exclude American trade from many of the territories it controlled. Roosevelt took no direct action against Japan, but to be sure the Japanese government recognized the power of the United States, he sent sixteen battleships of the new American navy (known as the "Great White Fleet" because the ships were temporarily painted white for the voyage) on an unprecedented journey around the world that included a call on Japan.

"Great White Fleet"

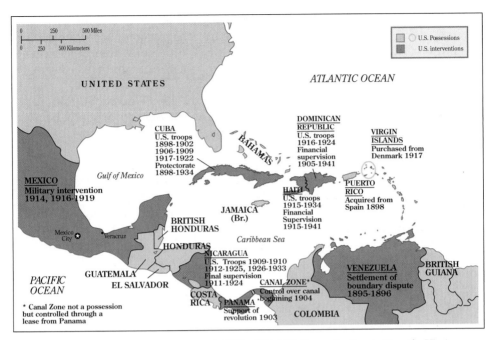

THE UNITED STATES AND LATIN AMERICA, 1895–1941 Except for Puerto Rico, the Virgin Islands, and the Canal Zone, the United States had no formal possessions in Latin America and the Caribbean in the late nineteenth century and the first half of the twentieth. But as this map reveals, the U.S. exercised considerable influence in these regions throughout this period—political and economic influence, augmented at times by military intervention. Note the particularly intrusive presence of the United States in the affairs of Cuba, Haiti, and the Dominican Republic—as well as the canal-related interventions in Colombia and Panama.

◆ *What were some of the most frequent reasons for American intervention in Latin America?*

 **For an interactive version of this map go to www.mhhe.com/unfinishednation4ch22maps**

The Iron-Fisted Neighbor

Roosevelt took a particular interest in events in Latin America. Unwilling to share trading rights, let alone military control, with any other nation, Roosevelt embarked on a series of ventures in the Caribbean and South America. He established a pattern of American intervention in the region that would long survive his presidency.

Crucial to Roosevelt's thinking was an incident early in his administration. In 1902, the government of Venezuela began to renege on debts to European bankers. Naval forces of Britain, Italy, and Germany blockaded the Venezuelan coast in response. Then German ships began to bombard a Venezuelan port amid rumors that Germany planned to establish a permanent base in the region. Roosevelt used the threat of American naval power to pressure the German navy to withdraw.

The incident helped persuade Roosevelt that European intrusions into Latin America could result not only from aggression but from instability or irresponsibility (such as defaulting on debts) within the Latin American nations themselves. As a result, in 1904 he announced what came to be known as the "Roosevelt Corollary" to the Monroe Doctrine. The United States, he claimed, had the right not only to oppose European intervention in the Western Hemisphere but also to intervene itself in the domestic affairs of its neighbors if those neighbors proved unable to maintain order and national sovereignty on their own.

"Roosevelt Corollary" Announced

The immediate motivation for the Roosevelt Corollary, and the first opportunity for using it, was a crisis in the Dominican Republic. A revolution had toppled its corrupt and bankrupt government in 1903, but the new regime proved no better able than the old to make good on the country's $22 million in debts to European nations. Using the rationale provided by the Roosevelt Corollary, Roosevelt established, in effect, an American receivership, assuming control of Dominican customs and distributing 45 percent of the revenues to the Dominicans and the rest to foreign creditors. This arrangement lasted, in one form or another, for more than three decades.

In 1902, the United States granted political independence to Cuba, but only after the new government had agreed to the so-called Platt Amendment (named after Senator Thomas Platt of Pennsylvania) to its constitution. The amendment gave the United States the right to prevent any foreign power from intruding into the new nation. In 1906, when domestic uprisings threatened the island's stability, American troops landed in Cuba, quelled the fighting, and remained there for three years.

Intervention in Cuba

The Panama Canal

The most celebrated accomplishment of Roosevelt's presidency was the construction of the Panama Canal, which linked the Atlantic and the Pacific by creating a channel through Central America. At first, Roosevelt and many others favored a route across Nicaragua, which would permit a sea-level canal requiring no locks. But they soon turned instead to the narrow Isthmus of Panama in Colombia, the site of an earlier, failed effort by a French company to construct a channel. Although the Panama route was not at sea level, it was shorter than the one in Nicaragua, and construction was already about 40 percent complete.

Roosevelt dispatched John Hay, his secretary of state, to negotiate an agreement with Colombian diplomats in Washington that would allow construction to begin without delay. Under heavy American pressure, the Colombian chargé d'affaires, Tomas Herrán, unwisely signed an agree-

OPENING THE PANAMA CANAL The great Miraflores locks of the Panama Canal open in October 1914 to admit the first ship to pass through the channel. The construction of the canal was one of the great engineering feats of the early twentieth century. But the heavy-handed political efforts of Theodore Roosevelt were at least equally important to its completion. *(Bettmann/Corbis)*

ment giving the United States perpetual rights to a six-mile-wide "canal zone" across Colombia; in return, the United States would pay Colombia $10 million and an annual rental of $250,000. The treaty produced outrage in the Colombian senate, which refused to ratify it. Colombia then sent a new representative to Washington with instructions to demand at least $20 million from the Americans plus a share of the payment to the French.

Roosevelt was furious and began to look for ways to circumvent the Colombian government. Philippe Bunau-Varilla, chief engineer of the French canal project, was a ready ally. In November 1903, he helped organize and finance a revolution *Panamanian Revolt* in Panama with the support of the United States. Roosevelt landed troops from the USS *Nashville* in Panama to "maintain order." Their presence prevented Colombian forces from suppressing the rebellion, and three days later Roosevelt recognized Panama as an independent nation. The new Panamanian government quickly agreed to the terms the Colombian senate had rejected. Work on the canal proceeded rapidly, and it opened in 1914.

Taft and "Dollar Diplomacy"

Like his predecessor, William Howard Taft worked to advance the nation's economic interests overseas. But he showed little interest in Roosevelt's larger vision of world stability. Taft's secretary of state, Philander C. Knox, worked aggressively to extend American investments into less-developed regions. Critics called his policies "Dollar Diplomacy."

Nicaragua Occupied　It was particularly visible in American policy in the Caribbean. When a revolution broke out in Nicaragua in 1909, the administration quickly sided with the insurgents and sent American troops into the country to seize the customs houses. As soon as peace was restored, Knox encouraged American bankers to offer substantial loans to the new government, thus increasing Washington's financial leverage over the country. When the new pro-American government faced an insurrection less than two years later, Taft again landed American troops in Nicaragua, this time to protect the existing regime. The troops remained there for more than a decade.

Diplomacy and Morality

Woodrow Wilson entered the presidency with relatively little interest or experience in international affairs. Yet he faced international challenges of a scope and gravity unmatched by those of any president before him. Although the greatest test of Wilsonian diplomacy did not occur until World War I, many of the qualities that he would bring to that ordeal were evident in his foreign policy from his first moments in office.

Having already seized control of the finances of the Dominican Republic in 1905, the United States established a military government there in 1916 when the Dominicans refused to accept a treaty that would have made the country a virtual American protectorate. The military occupation lasted eight years. In Haiti, Wilson landed the marines in 1915 to quell a revolution in the course of which a mob had murdered an unpopular president. American military forces remained in the country until 1934, and American officers drafted the new Haitian constitution adopted in 1918. When Wilson began to fear that the Danish West Indies might be about to fall into the hands of Germany, he bought the colony from Denmark and renamed it the Virgin Islands. Concerned about the possibility of European influence in Nicaragua, he signed a treaty with that country's government ensuring that no other nation would build a canal there and winning for the United States the right to intervene in Nicaragua's internal affairs to protect American interests. In all of these actions, Wilson was displaying an approach to Latin America very similar to the approaches of Roosevelt and Taft.

Intervention in Haiti and the Dominican Republic

But Wilson's view of America's role in the Western Hemisphere (and the world) was not entirely similar to the views of his predecessors. That became clear in his dealings with Mexico. For many years, under the friendly auspices of the corrupt dictator Porfirio Díaz, American businessmen had been establishing an enormous economic presence in Mexico. In 1910, however, Díaz had been overthrown by the popular leader Francisco Madero, who promised democratic reform but who also seemed hostile to American businesses in Mexico. The United States quietly encouraged a reactionary general, Victoriano Huerta, to depose Madero early in 1913, and the Taft administration, in its last weeks in office, prepared to recognize the new Huerta regime. Before it could *Recognition Withheld* do so, however, the new government murdered Madero, and Woodrow Wilson took office in Washington. The new president instantly announced that he would never recognize Huerta's "government of butchers."

The conflict dragged on for years. At first, Wilson hoped that simply by refusing to recognize Huerta he could help topple the regime and bring to power the opposing Constitutionalists, led by Venustiano Carranza. But when Huerta, with the support of American business interests, established a full military dictatorship in October 1913, the president became more assertive. In April 1914, a minor naval incident provided an excuse for open intervention. An officer in Huerta's army briefly arrested several American sailors from the U.S.S. *Dolphin* who had gone ashore in Tampico. The men were immediately released, but the American admiral demanded that the Huerta forces fire a twenty-one-gun salute to the American flag as a public display of penance. The Mexicans refused. Wilson used the trivial incident as a pretext for seizing the Mexican port of Veracruz.

Wilson had envisioned a bloodless action, but in a clash with Mexican troops in Veracruz, the *Veracruz Incident* Americans killed 126 of the defenders and suffered 19 casualties of their own. Now at the brink of war, Wilson began to look for a way out. His show of force, however, had helped strengthen the position of the Carranza faction, which captured Mexico City in August and forced Huerta to flee the country. At last, it seemed, the crisis might be over.

But Wilson was not yet satisfied. He reacted angrily when Carranza refused to accept American guidelines for the creation of a new government, and he briefly considered throwing his support to still another aspirant to leadership: Carranza's erstwhile lieutenant Pancho Villa. When Villa's military position deteriorated, however, Wilson abandoned him and finally, in October 1915, granted preliminary recognition to the Carranza government. By now, however, he had created yet another crisis. Villa, angry at what he considered an American betrayal, retaliated in January 1916 by taking sixteen American mining engineers from a train in northern Mexico and shooting them. Two months later, he led his soldiers across the border into Columbus, New Mexico, where they killed seventeen more Americans.

With the permission of the Carranza government, Wilson ordered General John J. Pershing to *Pershing Expedition*

PANCHO VILLA AND HIS TROOPS Pancho Villa (fourth from left) poses with some of the leaders of his army, whose members Americans came to consider bandits once they began staging raids across the U.S. border. He was a national hero in Mexico. *(Brown Brothers)*

lead an American expeditionary force across the Mexican border in pursuit of Villa. The American troops never found Villa, but they did engage in two ugly skirmishes with Carranza's army, in which forty Mexicans and twelve Americans died. Again, the United States and Mexico stood at the brink of war. But at the last minute, Wilson drew back. He quietly withdrew American troops from Mexico, and in March 1917, he at last granted formal recognition to the Carranza regime. By now, however, Wilson's attention was turning elsewhere—to the far greater international crisis engulfing the European continent and ultimately the United States as well.

CONCLUSION

Driven by the great surge of reform energies emerging throughout the United States, American national politics in the early twentieth century itself became an important battleground for progressives. The rise of national reform was a result of many things, but two in particular.

First, many reformers discovered that success required the engagement of the federal government in their efforts. Progressives themselves increasingly turned to Washington as a potential ally in their efforts. Second, two national leaders helped transform the federal government into a visible and muscular vehicle of reform. Theodore Roosevelt's eight years as president changed popular expectations of the office and launched a significant reform agenda. Woodrow Wilson, who defeated not only Roosevelt's ill-fated successor William Howard Taft in 1912, but also Roosevelt himself, running as a third-party challenger, became the most successful legislative president of the early twentieth century by winning passage of a broad and ambitious reform agenda of his own.

Roosevelt, Taft, and Wilson also contributed to a continuation, and indeed an expansion, of America's active role in international affairs, in part as an effort to abet the growth of American capitalism and in part as an attempt to impose American standards of morality and democracy on other parts of the world. Similar mixtures of ideals and self-interest would soon guide the United States into a great world war.

FOR FURTHER REFERENCE

John Milton Cooper, Jr., compares the lives and ideas of the progressive movement's leading national politicians in *The Warrior and the Priest: Woodrow Wilson and Theodore Roosevelt* (1983). John Morton Blum, *The Republican Roosevelt* (1954) is a long-popular brief study. Edmund Morris, *Theodore Rex* (2002) is a popular history of Roosevelt's presidency, and H. W. Brands, *TR* (1997) is a large biography. Donald E. Anderson, *William Howard Taft* (1973) is a useful account of this unhappy presidency. Arthur S. Link is Wilson's most important biographer and the author of *Woodrow Wilson*, 5 vols., (1947–1965). Kendrick A. Clements, *The Presidency of Woodrow Wilson* (1992) is a more recent study. Thomas K. McCraw, *Prophets of Regulation* (1984) is an excellent examination of important figures in the making of modern state capacity. Michael McGerr, *The Decline of Popular Politics* (1986) is a perceptive examination of the decline of public enthusiasm for parties in the North in the late nineteenth and early twentieth centuries. Samuel P. Hays, *The Gospel of Efficiency: The Progressive Conservation Movement, 1890–1920* (1962) makes a pioneering argument about the organizational imperatives behind the conservation movement and Stephen R. Fox, *The American Conservation Movement: John Muir and His Legacy* (1981) is another valuable study. John Opie, *Nature's Nation: An Environmental History of the United States* (1998) is an ambitious synthesis of environmental history. The effects of America's interventionist policies in Latin America are described in John Womack's arresting account of the revolution in *Mexico, Zapata and the Mexican Revolution* (1968). *Theodore Roosevelt*, by David Grubin (1997) is a fine biographical film. *The "Battle for Wilderness"* (1990) is a documentary film about the conservation movement and two of its rival leaders, Gifford Pinchot and John Muir.

For quizzes, Internet resources, references to additional books and films, and more, consult this book's Online Learning Center site at www.mhhe.com/unfinishednation4.

I WANT YOU
FOR U.S. ARMY
NEAREST RECRUITING STATION

AN APPEAL TO DUTY This most famous of all American war posters, by the artist James Montgomery Flagg, shows a fierce-looking Uncle Sam requesting, almost demanding, Americans to join the army to fight in World War I. With the nation very divided over the wisdom of entering the war, the Wilson administration believed it needed to persuade Americans not only to support the struggle but also—something unusual for Americans—to feel a sense of obligation to the government and its overseas commitments. *(The National Archives and Records Administration)*

TIME LINE

1914	1915	1916	1917
World War I begins	*Lusitania* torpedoed	Wilson reelected	German unrestricted submarine warfare
	Wilson supports preparedness		U.S. enters World War I
			Selective Service Act
			War Industries Board created

CHAPTER TWENTY-THREE

AMERICA AND THE GREAT WAR

The Road to War
"War Without Stint"
The Search for a New World Order
A Society in Turmoil

T he Great War, as it was known to a generation unaware that another, greater war would soon follow, began quietly in August 1914 when Austria-Hungary invaded the tiny Balkan nation of Serbia. Within weeks, however, it had grown into a conflagration engaging the armies of most of the major nations of Europe. Americans looked on with horror as the war became the most savage in history and as it dragged on, murderously and inconclusively, for two and a half years. But Americans also believed at first that the conflict had little to do with them. They were wrong. After nearly three years of attempting to affect the outcome of the conflict without becoming embroiled in it, the United States formally entered the war in April 1917.

THE ROAD TO WAR

By 1914, the European nations had created an unusually precarious international system. It careened into war very quickly on the basis of what most historians agree was a minor series of provocations.

1918	1919	1920	1927
Sedition Act	Senate rejects Treaty of Versailles	19th Amendment ratified	Sacco and Vanzetti executed
Wilson's Fourteen Points		Palmer Raids and Red Scare	
Armistice ends war	Race riots in Chicago and other cities		
Paris Peace Conference		Harding elected president	
	Steel strike and other labor actions		

The Collapse of the European Peace

The major powers of Europe were organized by 1914 in two great, competing alliances. The "Triple Entente," which during the war became known as the "Allies," linked Britain, France, and Russia. The "Triple Alliance," later called the "Central Powers," united Germany, the Austro-Hungarian Empire, and Italy, although Italy withdrew when war began and joined the Allies. The chief rivalry, however, was not between the two alliances but between the great powers that dominated them: Great Britain and Germany.

The Anglo-German rivalry was not the immediate cause of the war. The conflict emerged most directly out of a controversy involving nationalist movements within the Austro-Hungarian Empire. On June 28, 1914, the Archduke Franz Ferdinand, heir to the throne of the tottering empire, was assassinated while paying a state visit to Sarajevo. Sarajevo is the capital of Bosnia, then a province of Austria-Hungary, which Slavic nationalists wished to annex to neighboring Serbia; the archduke's assassin was a Serbian nationalist.

This local controversy quickly escalated through the workings of the system of alliances that the great powers had constructed. Germany supported Austria-Hungary's decision to launch a punitive assault on Serbia. The Serbians called on Russia to help with their defense. The Russians began mobilizing their army on July 30. By August 3, Germany had declared war on both Russia and France and had invaded Belgium. On

Mobilization for War   August 4, Great Britain—ostensibly to honor its alliance with France—declared war on Germany. Russia and the Austro-Hungarian Empire formally began hostilities on August 6. Within months, other smaller nations joined the fighting. By early 1915, virtually the entire European continent (and part of Asia) was embroiled in a major war.

Wilson's Neutrality

Wilson called on his fellow citizens in 1914 to remain "impartial in thought as well as deed." But that was impossible, for several reasons. For one thing, many Americans were not, in fact, genuinely impartial. Some

Sympathy with Britain   sympathized with the German cause; many more sympathized with Britain. Lurid reports of German atrocities in Belgium and France, skillfully exaggerated by British propagandists, strengthened the hostility of many Americans toward Germany.

Economic realities also made it impossible for the United States to deal with the belligerents on equal terms. The British had imposed a naval blockade on Germany to prevent munitions and supplies from reaching the enemy. As a neutral, the United States had the right, in theory, to trade with whomever it wished. A truly neutral response to the blockade would be either to defy it or to stop trading with Britain as well. But while the United States could survive an interruption of its relatively modest trade with Germany and its allies, it could not easily weather an embargo on its much more extensive trade with Britain and France. So America tacitly accepted the blockade of Germany and continued trading with Britain. By 1915, the United States had gradually transformed itself from a neutral power into the arsenal of the Allies.

The Germans, in the meantime, were resorting to a new and, in American eyes, barbaric tactic: submarine warfare. *Submarine Warfare* Unable to challenge British domination on the ocean's surface, the Germans announced early in 1915, enemy vessels would be sunk on sight. Months later, on May 7, 1915, a German submarine sank the British passenger liner *Lusitania* without warning, causing the deaths of 1,198 people, 128 of them Americans. The ship was carrying not only passengers but munitions; but most Americans considered the attack an unprovoked act on civilians.

Wilson angrily demanded that Germany promise not to repeat such outrages, and the Germans finally agreed to his demands. But early in 1916, in response to an announcement that the Allies were now arming merchant ships to sink submarines, Germany proclaimed that it would fire on such vessels without warning. A few weeks later, it attacked the unarmed French steamer *Sussex*, injuring several American passengers. Again, Wilson demanded that Germany abandon its "unlawful" tactics; again, the German government relented.

Preparedness versus Pacifism

Despite the president's increasing bellicosity in 1916, he was still far from ready to commit the United States to war. One obstacle was American domestic politics.

The question of whether America should make military and economic preparations for war provided a preliminary issue *Pacifists and Interventionists* over which pacifists and interventionists could debate. Wilson at first denounced the idea of an American military buildup as needless and provocative. In the fall of 1915, however, he endorsed an ambitious proposal by American military leaders for a large and rapid increase in the nation's armed forces.

Still, the peace faction wielded considerable political strength, as became clear at the Democratic Convention in the summer of 1916. The convention became almost hysterically enthusiastic when the keynote speaker punctuated his list of the president's diplomatic achievements with the chant, "What did we do? What did we do? . . . We didn't go to war! We didn't go to war!" That speech helped produce one of the most prominent slogans of Wilson's reelection campaign: "He kept us out of war." During the campaign, Wilson did nothing to discourage those who argued that the Republican candidate, the progressive New York governor

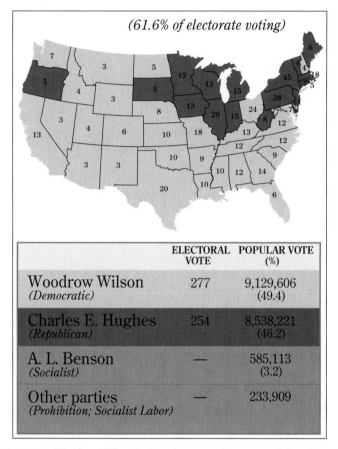

(61.6% of electorate voting)

	ELECTORAL VOTE	POPULAR VOTE (%)
Woodrow Wilson *(Democratic)*	277	9,129,606 (49.4)
Charles E. Hughes *(Republican)*	254	8,538,221 (46.2)
A. L. Benson *(Socialist)*	—	585,113 (3.2)
Other parties *(Prohibition; Socialist Labor)*	—	233,909

ELECTION OF 1916 Woodrow Wilson had good reason to be concerned about his re-election prospects in 1916. He had won only about 42 percent of the vote in 1912, and the Republican party—which had been divided four years earlier—was now reunited around the popular Charles Evans Hughes. In the end, Wilson won a narrow victory over Hughes with just under 50 percent of the vote and an even narrower margin in the electoral college. Note the striking regional character of his victory. ◆ *How did Wilson use the war in Europe to bolster his election prospects?*

Charles Evans Hughes, was more likely than he to lead the nation into war. Wilson ultimately won reelection by fewer than 600,000 popular votes and only 23 electoral votes.

A War for Democracy

Tensions between the United States and Germany remained high. But Wilson still required a justification for American intervention that would unite public opinion. In the end, he created that rationale himself. The United States, Wilson insisted, was committed to using the war as a vehicle for constructing a new world order, one based on the same progressive ideals that had motivated a generation of reform efforts in America. In a

MARCHING FOR VICTORY One of the great tasks facing the United States government as it entered World War I in 1917 was to generate popular support for a war that most Americans had been reluctant to enter. The effort to do so produced some alarming violations of civil liberties. It also encouraged an enormous number of parades, rallies, and other popular demonstrations of support for the war. Here, President Wilson marches in a Red Cross parade in Washington shortly after the declaration of war. *(Bettmann/Corbis)*

speech before a joint session of Congress in January 1917, he presented a plan for a postwar order in which the United States would help maintain peace through a permanent league of nations—a "peace without victory." These were, Wilson believed, goals worth fighting for if there was sufficient provocation.

"Peace without Victory"

In January, the military leaders of Germany decided on a dramatic gamble to achieve victory: a series of major assaults on the enemy's lines in France. At the same time, they would begin unrestricted submarine warfare (against American as well as Allied ships) to cut Britain off from vital supplies. Then, on February 25, the British gave Wilson an intercepted telegram sent by the German foreign minister, Arthur Zimmermann, to the government of Mexico. It proposed that in the event of war between Germany and the United States, the Mexicans should join with Germany against the Americans. In return, they would regain their "lost provinces" in the north when the war was over. Widely publicized by British propagandists and in the American press, the Zimmermann telegram inflamed public opinion. Wilson drew additional comfort from another event, in March 1917. A revolution in

Zimmermann Telegram

Russia toppled the reactionary czarist regime and replaced it with a new, republican government. The United States would now be spared the embarrassment of allying itself with a despotic monarchy.

On the rainy evening of April 2, two weeks after German submarines had torpedoed three American ships, Wilson appeared before a joint session of Congress and asked for a declaration of war. Even then, opposition remained. For four days, pacifists in Congress carried on their futile struggle. When the declaration of war finally passed on April 6, fifty representatives and six senators had voted against it.

"WAR WITHOUT STINT"

Armies on both sides in Europe were decimated and exhausted by the time of Woodrow Wilson's declaration of war. The Allies looked desperately to the United States for help in breaking the stalemate.

The Military Struggle

American intervention had its most immediate effect on the conflict at sea. By the spring of 1917, Great Britain was suffering such vast losses from attacks by German submarines that its ability to continue receiving vital supplies from across the Atlantic was in jeopardy. Within weeks of joining the war the United States had begun to alter the balance. A fleet of American destroyers aided the British navy in its assault on the U-boats. Other American warships escorted merchant vessels across the Atlantic. Americans also helped plant antisubmarine mines in the North Sea. The results were dramatic. Sinkings of Allied ships had totaled nearly 900,000 tons in the month of April 1917; by December, the figure had dropped to 350,000; by October 1918, it had declined to 112,000.

Many Americans had hoped that providing naval assistance alone would be enough to turn the tide in the war, but it quickly became clear that a major commitment of American ground forces would be necessary as well. Britain and France had few remaining reserves; and after the

Bolshevik Revolution

Bolshevik Revolution in November 1917, a new communist government, led by V. I. Lenin, negotiated a hasty and costly peace between Russia and the Central Powers, thus freeing German troops to fight on the western front.

But the United States did not have a large enough standing army to provide the necessary ground forces in 1917. Only a national draft could provide the needed men. Despite protests, Wilson won passage of the Selective Service Act in mid-May. The draft brought nearly 3 million men into the army.

The engagement of these forces in combat was brief but intense. Not until the spring of 1918 were significant numbers of American troops avail-

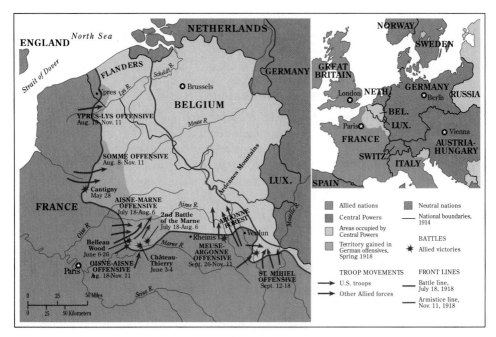

AMERICA IN WORLD WAR I: THE WESTERN FRONT, 1918 These maps show the principal battles in which the United States participated in the last year of World War I. The small map on the upper right helps locate the area of conflict within the larger European landscape. The larger map at left shows the long, snaking red line of the western front in France—stretching from the border between France and southwest Germany all the way to the northeast border between Belgium and France. Along that vast line, the two sides had been engaged in murderous, inconclusive warfare for over three years by the time the Americans arrived. Beginning in the spring and summer of 1918, bolstered by reinforcements from the United States, the Allies began to win a series of important victories that finally enabled them to begin pushing the Germans back. American troops, as this map makes clear, were decisive along the southern part of the front. ◆ *At what point did the Germans begin to consider putting an end to the war?*

For an interactive version of this map go to www.mhhe.com/unfinishednation4ch23maps

able for battle. Eight months later, the war was over. Under the command of General John J. Pershing, the American troops joined the existing Allied forces in turning back a series of new German assaults. In early June, they assisted the French in repelling a bitter German offensive at Château-Thierry, near Paris. Six weeks later, the American Expeditionary Force (AEF) helped turn away another assault, at Rheims, farther south. By July 18, the German advance had been halted. On September 26, an American fighting force of over 1 million soldiers advanced against the Germans in the Argonne Forest. By the end of October, the force had helped push the Germans back toward their own border and had cut the enemy's major supply lines to the front.

Faced with an invasion of their own country, German military leaders now began to seek an armistice. Pershing wanted to drive on into Germany itself; but other Allied leaders, after first insisting on terms that made the agreement (in their eyes at least) little different from a surrender, accepted the German proposal. On November 11, 1918, more than four years after it began, the Great War shuddered to a close.

The New Technology of Warfare

World War I was a proving ground for a range of military and other technologies. The trench warfare that characterized the conflict was necessary because of the enormous destructive power of newly improved machine guns and higher-powered artillery. It was no longer feasible to send troops out into an open field. The new weaponry would slaughter them in an instant. Trenches sheltered troops while allowing *Trench Warfare* limited, and usually inconclusive, fighting. But technology overtook the trenches, too, as mobile weapons—tanks and flamethrowers—proved capable of piercing entrenched positions. Most terrible of all, perhaps, new chemical weapons—poisonous mustard gas, which required troops to carry gas masks at all times—made it possible to attack entrenched soldiers without direct combat.

The new forms of technological warfare required elaborate maintenance. Faster machine guns required more ammunition. Motorized vehicles required fuel and spare parts and mechanics capable of servicing them. The logistical difficulties of providing so many supplies became a major factor in planning tactics and strategy. Once supplies were unloaded and stored, the process of repacking and moving them forward when troops broke through lines and advanced forward, was hopelessly time-consuming. Late in the war, when Allied armies were advancing toward Germany, they frequently had to stop for days at a time to wait for their equipment.

World War I was the first conflict in which airplanes played a significant role. The planes themselves were relatively simple and not very maneuverable; but anti-aircraft technology was not yet highly developed either, so their effectiveness was still considerable. Planes began to be constructed to serve various functions: bombers, fighters (planes that would engage in "dogfights" with other planes), and reconaissance aircraft.

The most "modern" part of the military during World War I was the navy. New battleships emerged that made use of new technologies such as turbine propulsion, hydraulic gun controls, electric light and power, wireless telegraphy, and advanced navigational aids. Submarines, which had made a brief appearance in the American Civil War, now became significant weapons (as the German U-boat campaign in 1915 and 1916 made clear). The new submarines were driven by diesel engines, which had the advantage of being more compact than steam engines and whose fuel was less explosive than that of gasoline engines.

The new technologies were to a large degree responsible for the most stunning and horrible characteristic of *Appalling Casualties* World War I—its appalling level of casualties. A

LIFE IN THE TRENCHES For most British, French, German, and ultimately American troops in France, the most debilitating part of World War I was the seeming endlessness of life in the trenches. Some young men lived in these cold, wet, muddy dugouts for months, even years, surrounded by filth, sharing their space with vermin, eating mostly rotten food. Occasional attacks to try to dislodge the enemy from its trenches usually ended in failure and became scenes of terrible slaughter. *(The National Archives and Records Administration)*

million men representing the British Empire (Britain, Canada, Australia, India, and others) died. France lost 1.7 million men; Germany 2 million; the former Austro-Hungarian Empire 1.5 million; Italy 460,000; and Russia 1.7 million. In Britain, one third of the men born between 1892 and 1895 died in the war. Similarly terrible percentages could be calculated for other warring nations. The United States, which entered the war near its end and became engaged only in the last successful offensives, suffered very light casualties in contrast—112,000 dead, half of them victims of influenza, not battle. But the American casualties were very high in the battles in which U.S. troops were centrally involved.

WARTIME TECHNOLOGY An American soldier mans one of the newly improved machine guns that became a staple of World War I combat, in a sandbagged bunker near the front in France. *(Bettmann/Corbis/Hutton-Deutsch Collection)*

Organizing the Economy for War

By the time the war ended, the federal government had appropriated $32 billion for expenses directly related to the conflict—a staggering sum at the time. The entire federal budget had seldom exceeded $1 billion before 1915, and the nation's entire gross national product had been only $35 billion as recently as 1910. To raise the money, the government relied on two devices. First, it launched a major drive to solicit loans from the American people by selling "Liberty Bonds" to the public. By 1920, the sale of bonds, accompanied by elaborate patriotic appeals, had produced $23 billion. At the same time, new taxes were bringing in an additional sum of nearly $10 billion—some from levies on the "excess profits" of corporations, much from new, steeply graduated income and inheritance taxes that ultimately rose as high as 70 percent in some brackets.

"Liberty Bonds"

An even greater challenge was organizing the economy to meet war needs. In 1916, Wilson established the Council of National Defense, composed of members of his cabinet, and the Civilian Advisory Commission, which set up local defense councils in every state and locality. But this early

WOMEN INDUSTRIAL WORKERS In World War II, such women were often called "Rosie the Riveter." Their presence in these previously all-male work environments was no less startling to Americans during World War I. These women are shown working with pneumatic hammers in the Midvale Steel and Ordnance factory in Philadelphia in 1918. *(The National Archives and Records Administration)*

administrative structure soon proved completely unworkable, and members of the Council of National Defense urged a more centralized approach. Instead of dividing the economy geographically, they proposed dividing it functionally by organizing a series of planning bodies, each to supervise a specific sector of the economy. Thus one agency would control transportation, another agriculture, another manufacturing. The administrative structure that slowly emerged from such proposals was dominated by a series of "war boards," one to oversee the railroads (led by Secretary of the Treasury William McAdoo), one to supervise fuel supplies (largely coal), another to handle food (a board that helped elevate to prominence the brilliant young engineer and business executive Herbert Hoover). The boards were not without weaknesses, but they generally succeeded in meeting essential war needs without paralyzing the domestic economy.

At the center of the effort to rationalize the economy was the War Industries Board (WIB), an *War Industries Board* agency created in July 1917 to coordinate government purchases of military supplies. Casually organized at first, it stumbled badly until March 1918, when Wilson restructured it and placed it under the control of the Wall Street financier Bernard Baruch. Baruch decided which factories would convert to the production of which war materials, and he set prices for the goods they produced. When materials were scarce, Baruch decided to whom they should go. When corporations were competing for government contracts, he chose among them.

Baruch viewed himself, openly and explicitly, as a partner of business; and within the WIB, businessmen themselves—the so-called dollar-a-year men, who took paid leave from their corporate jobs and worked for the government for a token salary—supervised the affairs of the private economy.

The National War Labor Board, established in April 1918, served as the final mediator of labor disputes. It pressured industry to grant important concessions to workers: an eight-hour day, the maintenance of minimal living standards, equal pay for women doing equal work, recognition of the right of unions to organize and bargain collectively. In return, it insisted that workers forgo strikes and that employers not engage in lockouts.

The Search for Social Unity

Government leaders were painfully aware that public sentiment about American involvement in the war was divided. Many believed that a crucial prerequisite for victory was uniting public opinion behind the war effort. The government approached that task in several ways.

The most conspicuous of its efforts was a vast propaganda campaign orchestrated by the Committee on Public Information (CPI), under the direction of the Denver journalist George Creel. The CPI supervised the distribution of over 75 million pieces of printed material and controlled much of the information available for newspapers and magazines. Creel encouraged journalists to exercise "self-censorship" when reporting war news, and most journalists complied by covering the war largely as the government wished. By 1918, however, government-distributed posters and films were offering lurid (and exaggerated) portrayals of the savagery of the Germans.

Committee on Public Information

The government also soon began efforts to suppress dissent. CPI-financed advertisements in magazines implored citizens to report to the authorities any evidence among their neighbors of disloyalty, pessimism, or yearning for peace. The Espionage Act of 1917 gave the government new tools with which to combat spying, sabotage, or obstruction of the war effort (crimes that were often broadly defined). More repressive were two measures of 1918: the Sabotage Act of April 20 and the Sedition Act of May 16. These bills expanded the meaning of the Espionage Act to make illegal any public expression of opposition to the war; in practice, they allowed officials to prosecute anyone who criticized the president or the government.

Espionage and Sedition Acts

The most frequent targets of the new legislation were anticapitalist groups such as the Socialist Party and the Industrial Workers of the World (IWW). Unlike their counterparts in Europe, American socialists had not dropped their opposition to the war after their country had decided to join it. Many Americans had favored the repression of socialists and radicals even before the war; the wartime policies now made it possible to move against them with full legal sanction. Eugene V. Debs, the humane leader of the Socialist Party and an opponent of the war, was sentenced to ten years in prison in 1918. (A pardon by President Warren G. Harding ultimately won his release in 1921.) Big Bill Haywood and members of the IWW were especially energetically prosecuted. Only by fleeing to the Soviet Union did Haywood avoid imprisonment. In all, more than 11,500 people were arrested in 1918 for the crime of criticizing the government or the war.

State and local governments, corporations, universities, and private citizens contributed as well to the climate of repression. A cluster of citizens' groups emerged to mobilize "respectable" *Suppressing Dissent* members of their communities to root out disloyalty. The greatest target of abuse was the German-American community. In the first years of the war in Europe, some had openly advocated American assistance to the Central Powers, and many had opposed United States intervention on behalf of the Allies. But while most German Americans supported the American war effort once it began, public opinion turned bitterly hostile. A campaign to purge society of all things German quickly gathered speed, at times assuming ludicrous forms. Performances of German music were frequently banned. German books were removed from the shelves of libraries. Courses in the German language were dropped from school curricula. Germans were routinely fired from jobs in war industries, lest they "sabotage" important tasks.

THE SEARCH FOR A NEW WORLD ORDER

Woodrow Wilson had led the nation into war promising a just and stable peace at its conclusion. Even before the armistice, he was preparing to lead the fight for what he considered a democratic postwar settlement—for a set of war aims resting on a vision of a new world order.

The Fourteen Points

On January 8, 1918, Wilson appeared before Congress to present the principles for which he claimed the nation was fighting. He grouped the war aims under fourteen headings, widely known as the Fourteen Points. They fell into three broad categories. First, Wilson's pro- *Wilson's International Vision* posals contained a series of eight specific recommendations for adjusting postwar boundaries and for establishing new nations to replace the defunct Austro-Hungarian and Ottoman Empires. Second, there was a set of five general principles to govern international conduct in the future: freedom of the seas, open covenants instead of secret treaties, reductions in armaments, free trade, and impartial mediation of colonial claims. Finally, there was a proposal for a "League of Nations" that would help implement these new principles and territorial adjustments and resolve future controversies.

Wilson's international vision ultimately came to enchant not only much of his own generation (in both America and Europe) but members of generations to come. It reflected his belief that the world was as capable of just and efficient government as were individual nations—that once the international community accepted certain basic principles of conduct, and once it constructed modern institutions to implement them, the human race could live in peace.

Allied Resistance   Despite Wilson's confidence, the leaders of the Allied powers were preparing to resist him even before the armistice was signed. Britain and France in particular were in no mood for a benign and generous peace. At the same time, Wilson was encountering problems at home. In 1918, with the war almost over, Wilson unwisely appealed to the American voters to support his peace plans by electing Democrats to Congress in the November elections. Days later, the Republicans captured majorities in both houses. Domestic economic troubles, more than international issues, had been the most important factor in the voting; but the results damaged his ability to claim broad popular support for his peace plans.

Wilson further antagonized the Republicans when he refused to appoint any important member of their party to the negotiating team that would represent the United States at the peace conference in Paris.

The Paris Peace Conference

Wilson arrived in Europe to a welcome such as few men in history have experienced. When he entered Paris on December 13, 1918, he was greeted, some claimed, by the largest crowd in the history of France. The peace conference itself, however, proved less satisfying.

Negotiating the Peace   The principal figures in the negotiations were the leaders of the victorious Allied nations: David Lloyd George, the prime minister of Great Britain; Georges Clemenceau, the president of France; Vittorio Orlando, the prime minister of Italy; and Wilson, who hoped to dominate them all.

From the beginning, the atmosphere of idealism Wilson had sought to create competed with a spirit of national self-interest. There was also a pervasive sense of unease about the unstable situation in eastern Europe and the threat of communism. Russia, whose new Bolshevik government was still fighting "White" counterrevolutionaries, was unrepresented in Paris; but the radical threat it seemed to pose to Western governments was never far from the minds of the delegates.

In this tense and often vindictive atmosphere, Wilson was unable to win approval of many of the broad principles he had espoused. He was also unable to prevent the other allies from imposing high reparations on the defeated Central Powers. Wilson did manage to win some important victories in Paris in setting boundaries and dealing with former colonies. But his most visible triumph, and the one of most importance to him, was the creation of a permanent international organization to oversee world affairs and prevent future wars. On January 25, 1919, the *The League of Nations* Allies voted to accept the "covenant" of the League of Nations.

The Ratification Battle

Wilson presented the Treaty of Versailles (which took its name from the former royal palace outside Paris where the final negotiating sessions had taken place) to the Senate on July 10, 1919. But members of the Senate had many objections to the treaty. Some—the so-called irreconcilables—opposed the agreement in principle. But many other opponents were principally concerned with constructing a winning issue for the Republicans in 1920. Most notable of these was Senator *Henry Cabot Lodge* Henry Cabot Lodge of Massachusetts, the powerful chairman of the Foreign Relations Committee, who loathed the president. He used every possible tactic to obstruct the treaty.

Public sentiment clearly favored ratification, so at first Lodge could do little more than play for time. Gradually, however, Lodge's general opposition to the treaty crystallized into a series of "reservations"—amendments to the League covenant further limiting American obligations to the organization. Wilson might still have won approval at this point if he had agreed to some relatively minor changes in the language of the treaty. But the president refused to yield. When he realized the Senate would not budge, he decided to appeal to the public.

He embarked on a grueling, cross-country speaking tour to arouse public support for the treaty. For more than three weeks, he traveled over 8,000 miles by train, speaking as often as four times a day, resting hardly at all. Finally, he reached the end of his strength. After speaking at Pueblo, Colorado, on September 25, 1919, he collapsed with severe headaches.

Canceling the rest of his itinerary, he rushed back to Washington, where, a few days later, he suffered a major stroke. For two weeks, he was close to death; for six weeks more, he was so seriously ill that he could conduct virtually no public business. His wife and his doctor formed an almost impenetrable barrier around him, shielding the president from any official pressures that might impede his recovery.

Wilson ultimately recovered enough to resume a limited official schedule, but he was essentially an invalid for the remaining eighteen months of his presidency. His condition only intensified what had already been his strong tendency to view public issues in moral terms and to resist any attempts at compromise. When the Foreign *League Membership Rejected* Relations Committee finally sent the treaty to the

Senate, recommending nearly fifty amendments and reservations, Wilson refused to consider any of them. The effort to win ratification failed.

In the aftermath of this defeat, Wilson became convinced that the 1920 national election would serve as a "solemn referendum" on the League. By now, however, public interest in the peace process had begun to fade.

A SOCIETY IN TURMOIL

Even during the Paris Peace Conference, many Americans were concerned less about international matters than about turbulent events at home. Some of this unease was a legacy of the almost hysterical social atmosphere of the war years; some of it was a response to issues that surfaced after the armistice.

The Unstable Economy

The war ended sooner than almost anyone had anticipated. Without warning, without planning, the nation lurched into the difficult task of economic reconversion. At first, the boom contin-

Postwar Recession

ued, but accompanied by raging inflation. Through most of 1919 and 1920, prices rose at an average of more than 15 percent a year. Finally, late in 1920, the economic bubble burst as inflation began killing the market for consumer goods. Between 1920 and 1921, the gross national product declined nearly 10 percent; 100,000 businesses went bankrupt; and nearly 5 million Americans lost their jobs.

Well before this severe recession began, there was a dramatic increase in labor unrest. The raging inflation of 1919 wiped out the modest wage gains workers had achieved during the war; many laborers were worried about job security as hundreds of thousands of veterans returned to the work force; arduous working conditions continued to be a source of discontent. Employers aggravated the resentment by using the end of the

Labor Unrest

war to rescind benefits they had been forced to concede to workers in 1917 and 1918—most notably recognition of unions. The year 1919, therefore, saw an unprecedented wave of strikes. In January, a walkout by shipyard workers in Seattle, Washington, evolved into a general strike that brought the entire city to a virtual standstill. In September, there was a strike by the Boston police force, which was demanding recognition of its union. Seattle had remained generally calm; but with its police off the job, Boston erupted in violence and looting.

These and other strikes aroused widespread middle-class hostility to the unions, a hostility that played a part in defeating the greatest strike of 1919: a steel strike that began in September, when 350,000 steelworkers in several midwestern cities demanded an eight-hour day and recognition of their union. The steel strike was long and bitter and climaxed in a riot in Gary, Indiana, in which eighteen strikers were killed. Steel executives managed to keep most plants running with nonunion labor, and public opinion was so hostile to the strikers that the AFL timidly repudiated them. By January, the strike—like most of the others in 1919—had collapsed.

The Demands of African Americans

The black men who had served in the armed forces during the war (367,000 of them) came home in 1919 and marched down the main streets of the industrial cities with other returning troops. And then (in New York and other cities) they marched again through the streets of black neighborhoods such as Harlem, led by jazz bands, cheered by thousands of African Americans, who believed that the glory of black heroism in the war would make it impossible for white society ever again to treat African Americans as less than equal citizens.

In truth, the fact that black soldiers had fought in the war had almost no impact at all on white attitudes. But it did have a profound effect on black attitudes: it accentuated African-American bitterness—and increased determination of blacks to fight for their rights. Nearly half a million migrated from the rural South to industrial cities (often enticed by northern "labor agents," who offered them free transportation) in search of the factory jobs the war was rapidly generating. This was the beginning of what became known as the "Great Migration." Within a few years, the na- *"Great Migration"* tion's racial demographics were transformed; suddenly there were large black communities crowding into northern cities, in some of which very few African Americans had lived in the past.

By 1919, however, the racial climate had become savage and murderous. In the South, there was a sudden increase in lynchings: more than seventy blacks, some of them war veterans, died at the hands of white mobs in 1919 alone. In the North, black factory workers faced widespread layoffs as returning white veterans displaced them from their jobs. And as whites became convinced that black workers with lower wage demands were hurting them economically, animosity grew rapidly.

Wartime riots in East St. Louis and elsewhere were a prelude to a summer of much worse racial violence in 1919. In Chicago, a black teenager swimming in Lake Michigan on a hot July day happened to drift toward a white beach. Whites on shore allegedly stoned him unconscious; he sank and drowned. Angry blacks gathered in crowds and marched into white neighborhoods to retaliate; whites formed even larger crowds and roamed into black neighborhoods. For more than a week, Chicago was virtually at war. In the end, 38 people died—15 whites and 23 blacks—and 537 were injured; over 1,000 people were left homeless. The Chicago *Chicago Race Riot* riot was the worst but not the only racial violence

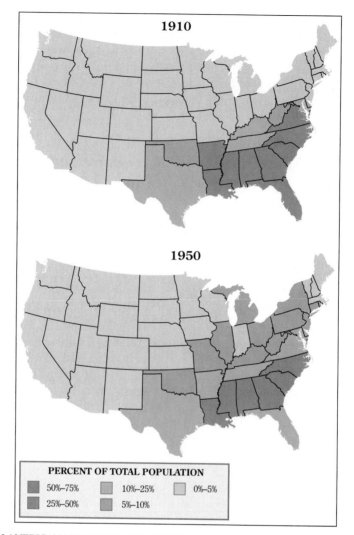

AFRICAN-AMERICAN MIGRATION, 1910–1950 Two great waves of migration produced a dramatic redistribution of the African-American population in the first half of the twentieth century—one around the time of World War I, the other during and after World War II. The map on the top shows the very heavy concentration of African Americans in the South as late as 1910. The map on the bottom shows both the tremendous increase of black populations in northern states by 1950, and the relative decline of black populations in parts of the South. Note in particular the changes in Mississippi and South Carolina. ◆ *Why did the wars produce such significant migration out of the South?*

during the so-called red summer of 1919; in all, 120 people died in such racial outbreaks in the space of little more than three months.

Racially motivated urban riots were not new. But the 1919 riots were different in one respect: they did not just involve white people attacking blacks; they also involved blacks fighting back. The NAACP signaled this change by urging blacks not just to demand government protection but also to defend themselves. The poet Claude McKay, one of the major figures of what would shortly be known as the Harlem Renaissance, wrote a poem after the Chicago riot called "If We Must Die":

> Like men we'll face the murderous cowardly pack.
> Pressed to the wall, dying, but fighting back.

At the same time, a black Jamaican, Marcus Garvey, began to attract a wide following in the United States with his ideology of black nationalism. Garvey encouraged African Americans to reject assimilation into white society and develop pride in their own race and culture. His Universal Negro Improvement *Universal Negro Improvement Association* Association (UNIA) launched a chain of black-owned grocery stores and pressed for the creation of other black businesses. Eventually, Garvey began urging his supporters to leave America and return to Africa, where they could create a new society of their own. In the 1920s, the Garvey movement experienced explosive growth for a time. It began to decline, however, after Garvey was indicted in 1923 on charges of business fraud. He was deported to Jamaica two years later. But the allure of black nationalism survived in black culture long after Garvey himself was gone.

The Red Scare

Much of the public considered the industrial warfare and the racial violence in 1919 a frightening *Popular Fears of Radicalism* omen of instability and radicalism. This was in part because other evidence emerging at the same time also seemed to suggest the existence of a radical menace. After the Russian Revolution of November 1917, communism was no longer simply a theory; it was now the basis of an important regime. Concerns about the communist threat grew in 1919 when the Soviet government announced the formation of the Communist International (or Comintern), whose purpose was to export revolution around the world.

In America, meanwhile, there was, in addition to the great number of imagined radicals, a modest number of real ones. These small groups of radicals were presumably responsible for a series of bombings in the spring of 1919 that produced great national alarm. In April, the post office intercepted several dozen parcels addressed to leading businessmen and politicians that were triggered to explode when opened. Two months later, eight bombs exploded in eight cities within minutes of one another, suggesting a nationwide conspiracy.

In response to these and other provocations, what became known as the Red Scare began. Nearly thirty states enacted new peacetime sedition laws imposing harsh penalties on those who promoted revolution. There were spontaneous acts of violence against supposed radicals in some communities, and more calculated efforts by universities and other institutions

SACCO AND VANZETTI The artist Ben Shahn painted this view of the anarchists Nicola Sacco and Bartolomeo Vanzetti, handcuffed together in a courtroom in 1927 waiting to hear if the appeal of their 1921 verdicts for murdering a Boston paymaster would succeed. It did not, and the two men were executed later that year. Just before his execution, Vanzetti said: "Never in our full life can we hope to do such work for tolerance, for man's understanding of man, as now we do by an accident. Our words—our lives—our pains—nothing! The taking of our lives—lives of a good shoemaker and a poor fish-peddler—all! That last moment belongs to us—that agony is our triumph." *(© Estate of Ben Shahn/Licensed by VAGA, New York, NY. Digital Image © The Museum of Modern Art/Licensed by SCALA/Art Resource, NY)*

to expel radicals from their midst. But the greatest contribution to the Red Scare came from the federal government. On New Year's Day, 1920, Attorney General A. Mitchell Palmer and his ambitious young assistant, J. Edgar Hoover, orchestrated a series of raids on alleged radical centers throughout the country and arrested more than 6,000 people. Most of those arrested were ultimately released, but about 500 who were not American citizens were summarily deported.

A. Mitchell Palmer

The ferocity of the Red Scare soon abated, but its effects lingered well into the 1920s. In May of 1920, two Italian immigrants, Nicola Sacco and Bartolomeo Vanzetti, were charged with the murder of a paymaster in Braintree, Massachusetts. The case against them was weak and suffused with nativist prejudices and fears; but because both men were confessed anarchists, they faced a widespread public presumption of guilt. They were convicted and sentenced to death. Over the next several years, public support for Sacco and Vanzetti

Sacco and Vanzetti

grew to formidable proportions. But on August 23, 1927, amid widespread protests around the world, Sacco and Vanzetti, still proclaiming their innocence, died in the electric chair.

The Retreat from Idealism

On August 26, 1920, the Nineteenth Amendment, guaranteeing women the right to vote, became part of the Constitution. To the woman suffrage movement, this was the culmination of nearly a century of struggle. To many progressives it seemed to promise new support for reform. Yet the passage of the Nineteenth Amendment marked not the beginning of an era of progressive reform but the end of one.

Economic problems, labor unrest, racial tensions, and the intensity of the antiradicalism they helped create—all combined in the years immediately following the war to produce a general sense of disillusionment. That became particularly apparent in the election of 1920. Woodrow Wilson wanted the campaign to be a referendum on the League of Nations, and the Democratic candidates, Governor James M. Cox of Ohio and Assistant Secretary of the Navy Franklin D. Roosevelt, dutifully tried to keep Wilson's ideals alive. The Republican presidential nominee, however, offered a different vision. He was Warren Gamaliel Harding, an obscure Ohio senator. Harding offered no ideals, only a vague promise of a return, as he later phrased it, to "normalcy." He won in a landslide. The Republican ticket received 61 percent of the popular vote and carried every state outside the South. The party made major gains in Congress as well. To many Americans it seemed that, for better or worse, a new era had begun.

Disillusionment and Reaction

CONCLUSION

For a time after the outbreak of war in Europe in 1914, most Americans—President Wilson among them—wanted nothing so much as to stay out of the conflict. Gradually, however, as the war dragged on and on and the tactics of Britain and Germany began to impinge on American trade and on freedom of the seas, the United States found itself drawn slowly into the conflict. In April 1917, finally, Congress agreed to the president's request that the United States enter the war as an ally of Britain.

American forces quickly broke the stalemate that had bogged the European forces down in years of inconclusive trench warfare. Within a few months of the arrival of substantial numbers of American troops in Europe, Germany agreed to an armistice and the war shuddered to a close. American casualties, although not inconsiderable, were negligible compared to the millions suffered by the European combatants.

The social experience of the war in the United States was, on the whole, dismaying to reformers. Although the war enhanced some reform efforts—most notably prohibition and woman suffrage—it also introduced an atmosphere of intolerance and repression into American life. The aftermath of the war was even more disheartening to progressives, both because of a brief but highly destabilizing recession and because of a wave of repression directed against labor, radicals, African Americans, and immigrants in 1919 and 1920.

At the same time, Woodrow Wilson's bold and idealistic dream of a peace based on the principles of democracy and justice suffered a painful death. The Treaty of Versailles, which he helped to draft, was itself far from what Wilson had hoped. It did, however, contain a provision for a League of Nations, which Wilson believed could transform the international order. But the League quickly became controversial in the United States; and despite strenuous efforts by the president—efforts that hastened his own physical collapse—the treaty was defeated in the Senate. In the aftermath of that traumatic battle, the American people turned away from Wilson and his ideals and prepared for a very different era.

FOR FURTHER REFERENCE

Ernest R. May, *The World War and American Isolation* (1959), is an authoritative account of America's slow and controversial entry into the Great War. Frank Freidel provides a sweeping account of the American soldier's battlefield experience during World War I in *Over There: The Story of America's First Great Overseas Crusade* (1964). David Kennedy, *Over Here: The First World War and American Society* (1980) is an important study of the domestic impact of the war. Robert D. Cuff, *The War Industries Board: Business-Government Relations During World War I* (1973) is a good account of mobilization for war in the United States. Ronald Schaffer, *America in the Great War: The Rise of the War Welfare State* (1991) examines the ways in which mobilization for war created new public benefits for various groups, including labor. Maureen Greenwald, *Women, War, and Work* (1980) describes the impact of World War I on women workers. John Keegan, *The First World War* (1998) is a superb military history. Thomas Knock, *To End All Wars: Woodrow Wilson and the Quest for a New World Order* (1992) is a valuable recent study of the battle for peace. Arno Mayer, *Wilson vs. Lenin* (1959) and *Politics and Diplomacy of Peacemaking: Containment and Counterrevolution* (1965) are important revisionist accounts of the peacemaking process. America's stormy debate over immigration and national identity before, during, and after World War I is best captured by John Higham, *Strangers in the Land: Patterns of American Nativism* (1955). William M. Tuttle, Jr., in *Race Riot: Chicago in the Red Summer of 1919* (1970) recounts the terrible riots of 1919 that showed America violently divided along racial and ideological lines. Paul L. Murphy, *World War I and the*

Origins of Civil Liberties (1979) shows how wartime efforts to quell dissent created new support for civil liberties. *The Great War—1918* (1997) is a documentary film chronicling the experiences of American soldiers in the closing battles of World War I through their letters and diaries.

For quizzes, Internet resources, references to additional books and films, and more, consult this book's Online Learning Center site at www.mhhe.com/unfinishednation4.

THE FLAPPER, 1927   The popular Condé Nast fashion magazine, *Vogue*, portrayed a fashionably dressed "flapper" on its cover in 1927. The short hair and the cap pulled down low over the forehead were both part of the flapper style. What had begin as a fashion among working-class women had by 1927 moved into stylish high society.   *(Georges Lepape/©Vogue, The Condé Nast Publications, Inc.)*

TIME LINE

1914-1920	1920	1922	1923
Great Migration of blacks to the North	Prohibition begins Harding elected president	Lewis's *Babbitt*	Harding dies; Coolidge becomes president Harding administration scandals revealed

CHAPTER TWENTY-FOUR

THE NEW ERA

The New Economy
The New Culture
A Conflict of Cultures
Republican Government

The 1920s are often remembered as an era of affluence, conservatism, and cultural frivolity. In reality, however, the decade was a time of significant, even dramatic social, economic, and political change. It was an era in which the American economy not only enjoyed spectacular growth but developed new forms of organization. It was a time in which American popular culture reshaped itself to reflect the increasingly urban, industrial, consumer-oriented society of the United States. And it was a decade in which American government experimented with new approaches to public policy. That was why contemporaries liked to refer to the 1920s as the "New Era"—an age in which America was becoming a modern nation.

At the same time, however, the decade saw the rise of a series of spirited and at times effective rebellions against the modern developments that were transforming American life. The intense cultural conflicts that characterized the 1920s were evidence of how much of American society remained unreconciled to the modernizing currents of the New Era.

1924	1925	1927	1928
National Origins Act passed	Fitzgerald's *The Great Gatsby*	Lindbergh's solo transatlantic flight	Hoover elected president
Coolidge elected president	Scopes trial	First sound motion picture, *The Jazz Singer*	
Ku Klux Klan membership peaks			

THE NEW ECONOMY

After the recession of 1921–1922, the United States began a long period of almost uninterrupted prosperity and economic expansion. Less visible at the time, but equally significant, was the survival (and even the growth) of inequalities and imbalances.

Technology, Organization, and Economic Growth

No one could deny the remarkable feats of the American economy in the 1920s. The nation's manufacturing output rose by more than 60 percent. Per capita income grew by a third. Inflation was negligible. A mild recession in 1923 interrupted the pattern of growth; but when it subsided early in 1924, the economy expanded with even greater vigor.

The economic boom was a result of many things, but one of the most important causes was technology. The automobile industry, as a result of the development of the assembly line and other innovations, now became one of the most important industries in the nation. It stimulated growth in other, related industries as well. Auto manufacturers purchased the products of steel, rubber, glass, and tool companies. Auto owners bought gasoline from the oil corporations. Road construction became an important industry. The increased mobility that the automobile made possible increased the demand for suburban housing, fueling a boom in the construction industry.

Rise of the Automobile Industry

Other new industries benefiting from technological innovations contributed as well to the economic growth. Radio began to become a popular technology. Early radio had been able to broadcast little beside pulses, which meant that radio communication could occur only through the Morse Code. But with the discovery of the theory of modulation, pioneered by the Canadian scientist Reginal Fessenden, it became possible to transmit speech and music. Many people built their own radio sets at home for very little money, benefiting from the discovery that inexpensive crystals could receive signals over long distances (but not very well over short ones). These "short wave" radios, which allowed individual owners to establish contact with each other, marked the beginning of what later became known as "ham radio." Once commercial broadcasting began, families flocked to buy more conventional radio sets, which could receive high-quality signals over short and medium distances. They were powered by vacuum tubes that were much more reliable than earlier models. By 1925, there were two million sets in American homes, and by the end of the 1920s almost every family had one.

Commercial aviation developed slowly in the 1920s, beginning with the use of planes to deliver

Commercial Aviation

mail. On the whole, airplanes remained curiosities and sources of entertainment. But technological advances—the development of the radial engine and the creation of pressurized cabins—were laying the groundwork for the great increase in commercial travel in the 1930s and beyond. Trains became faster and more efficient as well with the development of the diesel-electric engine. Electronics, home appliances, plastics and synthetic fibers such as nylon, aluminum, magnesium, oil, electric power, and other industries fueled by technological advances—all grew dramatically. Telephones continued to proliferate. By the late 1930s, there were approximately 25 million telephones in the United States, approximately one for every six people.

The seeds of future technological breakthroughs were also visible in the 1920s and 1930s. In both England and America, scientists and engineers were working to transform primitive calculating machines into devices capable of performing more complicated tasks. By the early 1930s, researchers at MIT, led by Vannevar Bush, had created an instrument capable of performing a variety of complicated tasks—the first analog computer. A few years later, Howard Aiken, with financial assistance from Harvard and MIT, built a much more complex computer with memory, capable of multiplying eleven-digit numbers in three seconds.

Genetic research had begun in Austria in the mid-nineteenth century through the work of Gregor Mendel, a Catholic monk who performed experiments on the hybridization of vegetables in the garden of his monastery. His findings attracted little attention during his lifetime, but in the early twentieth century they were discovered by several investigators and helped shape modern genetic research. Among the American pioneers was Thomas Hunt Morgan of Columbia University and later Cal Tech, whose experiments with fruit flies revealed how several genes could be transmitted together. He also revealed the way in which genes were arranged along the chromosome. His work helped open the path to understanding how genes could recombine—a critical discovery that led to more advanced experiments in hybridization and genetics.

Genetic Research

Large sectors of American business were accelerating their drive toward national organization and consolidation. Certain industries—notably those dependent on large-scale mass production, such as steel and automobiles—seemed naturally to move toward concentrating production in a few large firms. Others—industries less dependent on technology and less susceptible to great economies of scale—proved more resistant to consolidation.

Growing Industrial Consolidation

The strenuous efforts by industrialists throughout the economy to find ways to curb competition reflected a strong fear of overcapacity. Even in the booming 1920s, industrialists remembered how too-rapid expansion and overproduction had helped produce recessions in 1893, 1907, and 1920. The great, unrealized dream of the New Era was to find a way to stabilize the economy so that such collapses would never occur again.

THE STEAMFITTER Lewis Hine was among the first American photographers to recognize his craft as an art. In this carefully posed photograph from the mid-1920s, Hine made a point that many other artists were making in other media: The rise of the machine could serve human beings, but might also bend them to its own needs. *(Courtesy George Eastman House)*

Workers in an Age of Capital

Despite the remarkable economic growth, more than two-thirds of the American people in 1929 lived at no better than what one major study described as the "minimum comfort level." Half of those were at or below the level of "subsistence and poverty."

American labor experienced both the successes and the failures of the 1920s as much as any other group. On the one hand, most workers saw their standard of living rise during the decade. Some employers adopted paternal-

Welfare Capitalism

istic techniques that came to be known as "welfare capitalism." Henry Ford, for example, shortened the workweek, raised wages, and instituted paid vacations. By 1926, nearly 3 million industrial workers were eligible for at least modest pensions on retirement. When labor grievances surfaced despite these efforts, workers could voice them through the so-called company unions that were emerging in many industries—workers' councils and shop committees, organized by the corporations themselves. But welfare capitalism, in the end, gave workers no real control over their own fates. Company unions were feeble vehicles. And welfare capitalism survived only as long as industry prospered. After 1929, with the economy in crisis, the entire system collapsed.

Welfare capitalism affected only a relatively small number of workers in any case. Most laborers worked for employers interested primarily in keeping their labor costs low. Workers as a whole, therefore, received wage increases that were proportionately far below the growth of the economy as a whole. At the end of the decade, the average annual income of a worker remained below $1,500 a year, when $1,800 was considered necessary to maintain a minimally decent standard of living. Only by relying on the earnings of several family members at once could many working-class families make ends meet.

The New Era was a bleak time for labor organization, in part because many unions themselves were relatively conservative and failed to adapt to the realities of the modern economy. The American Federation of Labor (led by the cautious *Bleak Time for Labor* William Green) remained wedded to the concept of the craft union, in which workers were organized on the basis of particular skills. The AFL sought peaceful cooperation with employers. In the meantime, the number of unskilled industrial workers was rising rapidly. They received little attention from the craft unions.

But whatever the weaknesses of the unions, the strength of the corporations was the principal reason for the absence of effective labor organization in the 1920s. After the turmoil of 1919, corporate leaders worked hard to spread the doctrine that a crucial element of democratic capitalism was the protection of the "open shop" (a shop in which no worker could be required to join a union). The crusade for the open shop, euphemistically titled the "American Plan," became a pretext for a harsh cam- *"American Plan"* paign of union-busting. As a result, union membership fell from more than 5 million in 1920 to under 3 million in 1929.

Women and Minorities in the Work Force

A growing proportion of the work force consisted of women, who were concentrated in what have since become known as "pink-collar" jobs— low-paying service occupations. Large numbers of women worked as secretaries, salesclerks, and telephone operators and in other nonmanual service capacities. Because technically such positions were not industrial jobs, the AFL and other labor organizations were uninterested in organizing these workers. Similarly, the half-million African Americans who had migrated from the rural South into the cities during the Great Migration after 1914 had few opportunities for union representation. The skilled crafts represented in the AFL usually excluded blacks. Most blacks, however, worked in jobs in which the AFL took no interest at all—as janitors, dishwashers, garbage collectors, domestics, and other service capacities. A. Philip Randolph's Brotherhood of Sleeping Car Porters was one of the few important unions domi- *Brotherhood of Sleeping Car Porters* nated and led by African Americans.

In the West and the Southwest, the ranks of the unskilled included considerable numbers of Asians and Hispanics. In the wake of the Chinese

Exclusion Acts, Japanese immigrants increasingly took the place of the Chinese in menial jobs in California. They worked on railroads, construction sites, and farms and in many other low-paying workplaces. Some Japanese managed to escape the ranks of the unskilled by forming their own small businesses or setting themselves up as truck farmers; and many of the Issei (Japanese immigrants) and Nisei (their American-born children) enjoyed significant economic success—so much so that California passed laws in 1913 and 1920 to make it more difficult for them to buy land. Other Asians—most notably Filipinos—also swelled the unskilled work force and generated considerable hostility. Anti-Filipino riots in California beginning in 1929 helped produce legislation in 1934 virtually eliminating immigration from the Philippines.

Rising Mexican Immigration   Mexican immigrants formed a major part of the unskilled work force throughout the Southwest and California. Nearly half a million Mexicans entered the United States in the 1920s. Most lived in California, Texas, Arizona, and New Mexico; and by 1930, most lived in cities. Large Mexican barrios grew up in Los Angeles, El Paso, San Antonio, Denver, and many other cities and towns. Some of the residents found work locally in factories and shops; others traveled to mines or did migratory labor on farms but returned to the cities between jobs. Mexican workers, too, faced hostility and discrimination from the Anglo population of the region, but there were few efforts actually to exclude them. Employers in the relatively underpopulated West needed this ready pool of low-paid, unskilled, and unorganized workers.

Agricultural Technology and the Plight of the Farmer

Like industry, American agriculture in the 1920s was embracing new technologies. The number of tractors on American farms quadrupled during the 1920s, especially after they began to be powered by internal combustion engines (like automobiles) rather than by the cumbersome steam engines of the past. They helped to open 35 million new acres to cultivation. Increasingly sophisticated combines and harvesters were proliferating, helping to make it possible to produce more crops with fewer workers.

Agricultural researchers were already at work on other advances: the invention of hybrid corn (made possible by advances in genetic research), which became available to farmers in 1921 but was not grown in great quantities for a decade or more; and the creation of chemical fertilizers and pesticides, which also began to have limited use in the 1920s but which proliferated quickly in the 1930s and 1940s.

The new technologies greatly increased agricultural productivity, but the demand for agricultural goods was not rising as fast as production.

Declining Food Prices   The results were substantial surpluses, a disastrous decline in food prices, and a severe drop in farmers' income beginning early in the 1920s. More than 3 million people left

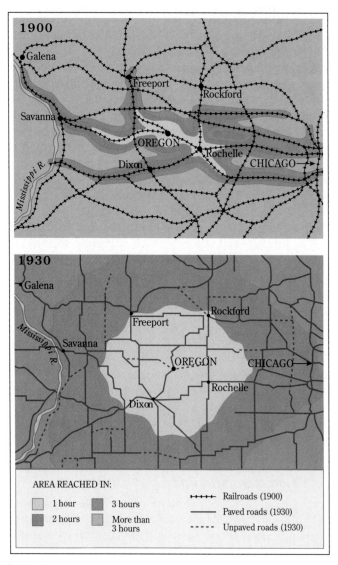

BREAKING DOWN RURAL ISOLATION: THE EXPANSION OF TRAVEL HORIZONS IN OREGON, ILLINOIS This map uses the small town of Oregon, Illinois—west of Chicago—to illustrate the way in which first railroads and then automobiles reduced the isolation of rural areas in the first decades of the twentieth century. The gold and purple areas of the two maps show the territory that residents of Oregon could reach within two hours. Note how small that area was in 1900 and how much larger it was in 1930, by which time an area of over a hundred square miles had become easily accessible to the town. Note, too, the significant network of paved roads in the region by 1930, few of which had existed in 1900. ◆ *Why did automobile travel do so much more than railroads to expand the travel horizons of small towns?*

 For an interactive version of this map go to www.mhhe.com/unfinishednation4ch24maps

agriculture altogether in the course of the decade. Of those who remained, many lost ownership of their lands and had to rent instead from banks or other landlords.

In response, some farmers began to demand relief in the form of government price supports. One price-raising scheme in particular came to dominate agrarian demands: the idea of "parity." Parity was a complicated formula for setting an adequate price for farm goods and ensuring that farmers would earn back at least their production costs no matter how the national or world agricultural market might fluctuate. Champions of parity urged high tariffs against foreign agricultural goods and a government commitment to buy surplus domestic crops at parity and sell them abroad.

McNary-Haugen Bill   The legislative expression of the demand for parity was the McNary-Haugen Bill, named after its two principal sponsors in Congress and introduced repeatedly between 1924 and 1928. In 1926 and again in 1928, Congress approved a bill requiring parity for grain, cotton, tobacco, and rice, but President Coolidge vetoed it both times.

THE NEW CULTURE

The urban and consumer-oriented culture of the 1920s helped Americans in all regions to live their lives and perceive their world in increasingly similar ways. That same culture exposed them to a new set of values. But different parts of American society experienced the new culture in very different ways.

Consumerism and Communications

Growing Consumer Culture   The United States of the 1920s was a consumer society. Many more people than ever before could buy items not just because of need but for convenience and pleasure. Middle-class families purchased electric refrigerators, washing machines, and vacuum cleaners. People wore wristwatches and smoked cigarettes. Women purchased cosmetics and mass-produced fashions. Above all, Americans bought automobiles. By the end of the decade, there were more than 30 million cars on American roads.

No group was more aware of the emergence of consumerism (or more responsible for creating it) than the advertising industry. In the 1920s, partly as a result of techniques pioneered by wartime propaganda, advertising came of age. Publicists no longer simply conveyed information; they sought to identify products with a particular lifestyle. They also encouraged the public to absorb the values of promotion and salesmanship and to admire those who were effective "boosters" and publicists. One of the most successful books of the 1920s was *The Man Nobody Knows*, by adver-

THE ELECTRIC REFRIGERATOR The development of new appliances for the home was an important part of the boom in the production and sale of consumer goods in the 1920s. Executives of the Delcom Light Company, a subsidiary of General Motors, pose here in front of the first Frigidaire electric refrigerator as it is readied for shipping from Dayton, Ohio, in 1921. *(Bettmann/Corbis)*

tising executive Bruce Barton. It portrayed Jesus Christ as not only a religious prophet but also a *Bruce Barton* "super salesman." Barton's message, a message in tune with the new spirit of the consumer culture, was that Jesus had been a man concerned with living a full and rewarding life in this world and that twentieth-century men and women should be concerned with doing the same.

The advertising industry could never have had the impact it did without the emergence of new vehicles of communication that made it possible to reach large audiences quickly and easily. Newspapers were being absorbed into national chains. Mass-circulation magazines attracted broad, national audiences. The movies were becoming an ever more popular and powerful form of mass communication; over 100 million people saw films in 1930, as compared with 40 million in 1922.

The most important communications vehicle, however, was radio. The first commercial radio sta- *Birth of Commercial Radio* tion in America, KDKA in Pittsburgh, began broadcasting in 1920, and the first national radio network, the National Broadcasting Company, was formed in 1927.

Psychology and Psychiatry

The increasing affluence and the growing consumerism of the 1920s produced new psychological challenges. The rise of anxiety and alienation as characteristic ailments of the consumer age coincided with the rise of new theories of psychology and psychiatry. Together these two phenomena helped entrench and expand important emerging fields in medicine and science.

Psychiatry had been spreading in the United States since the early twentieth century, driven in part by the growing awareness of the theories of Sigmund Freud and Carl Jung. Although Freud and Jung differed sharply on many points, they both helped legitimize the idea of exploring the unconscious as a way of discovering the roots of mental problems. Psychoanalysis, which Freud pioneered and Jung also advanced, began to attract American adherents as early as 1912 and spread significantly in the 1920s.

John B. Watson of Johns Hopkins University challenged the Freudian belief in introspection and the exploration of the unconscious. Instead, he argued that mental ailments, like physical ones, should be treated by observation and treatment of symptoms—of behavior.

Behavioralism

The point of therapy was to modify behavior—to discourage undesirable behavior and reinforce "acceptable" actions. Although many psychiatrists dismissed behavioralism and its associated therapies as treating symptoms rather than causes, it demonstrated significant success in treating such disorders as alcoholism, drug addiction, and phobias.

Although psychoanalysis and other forms of therapy could be performed by psychologists without medical training, the biggest growth in psychiatry was as a field of medicine. At first, medical psychiatrists worked mostly in mental institutions. But as mental hospitals evolved from places where patients came for treatment and then were discharged to places where chronically ill people (many of them aged) resided indefinitely, psychiatrists began to move into other venues—into conventional hospitals and most notably into private practice. Psychiatry began to expand its claims and to offer services not just to the mentally ill, but to otherwise stable individuals experiencing difficulties with everyday life. A new theory of "dynamic" psychiatry emerged early in the twentieth century; and by the 1920s, it had helped psychiatrists to offer therapy for ordinary anxieties, not just severe mental disturbance.

Psychology and psychiatry were, from the beginning, fields in which women played a much larger role than in most areas of medicine. That was in part because training in psychology was considered valuable for occupations in which women had been traditionally dominant—teaching, social work, nursing. Women who had medical training often found it easier to establish themselves in psychiatry than in other, more

Opportunities for Women

traditionally male-dominated areas of medicine.

Women in the New Era

College-educated women were no longer pioneers in the 1920s. There were now two and even three generations of graduates of women's or co-educational colleges and universities, and some were making their presence felt in professional areas that in the past women had rarely penetrated. The "new professional woman" was a vivid and widely publicized image in the 1920s. In reality, however, most employed women were non-professional, lower-class workers. Middle-class women, in the meantime, remained largely in the home.

Yet the 1920s constituted a new era for middle-class women nonetheless. In particular, the decade saw a redefinition of motherhood. Shortly after World War I, John B. *Motherhood Redefined* Watson and other behavioralist began to challenge the long-held assumption that women had an instinctive capacity for motherhood. Maternal affection was not, they claimed, sufficient preparation for child rearing. Instead, mothers should rely on the advice and assistance of experts and professionals: doctors, nurses, and trained educators.

For many middle-class women, these changes devalued what had been an important and consuming activity. Many attempted to compensate by devoting new attention to their roles as wives and companions. And many women now openly considered their sexual relationships with their husbands not simply as a means of procreation, as earlier generations had been taught to do, but as an important and pleasurable experience in its own right, as the culmination of romantic love.

One result was growing interest in birth control. The pioneer of the American birth-control movement, Margaret Sanger, began her career as a promoter of the di- *Margaret Sanger* aphragm and other birth-control devices out of a concern for working-class women; she believed that large families were among the major causes of poverty and distress in poor communities. By the 1920s, she was becoming more effective in persuading middle-class women to see the benefits of birth control. Nevertheless, some birth-control devices remained illegal in many states (and abortion remained illegal nearly everywhere).

Some women concluded that in the New Era it was no longer necessary to maintain a rigid, Victorian female "respectability." They could smoke, drink, dance, wear seductive clothes and makeup, and attend lively parties. Those assumptions became the basis of the "flapper"—the modern woman whose liberated *"Flappers"* lifestyle found expression in dress, hairstyle, speech, and behavior. The flapper lifestyle had a particular impact on lower-middle-class and working-class single women, who were flocking to new jobs in industry and the service sector. At night, such women flocked to clubs and dance halls in search of excitement and companionship.

Despite all the changes, most women remained highly dependent on men and relatively powerless when men exploited that dependence. The

National Woman's Party, under the leadership of Alice Paul, attempted to fight that powerlessness through its campaign for the Equal Rights Amendment, although it found little support in Congress. Responding to the suffrage victory, women organized the League of Women Voters and the women's auxiliaries of both the Democratic and Republican Parties. Female-dominated consumer groups grew rapidly and increased the range and energy of their efforts.

Women activists won a brief triumph in 1921 when they helped secure passage of the Sheppard-Towner Act, which provided federal funds to states to establish prenatal and child health-care programs. From the start, however, the Act produced controversy. Alice Paul and her supporters opposed the measure, complaining that it classified all women as mothers. More important, the American Medical Association fought Sheppard-Towner, warning that it would introduce untrained outsiders into the health-care field. In 1929, Congress terminated the program.

The Disenchanted

Many artists and intellectuals coming of age in the 1920s were experiencing a fundamental disenchantment with modern America. One result of this alienation was a series of savage critiques of *Modern Society Critiqued* modern society by a wide range of writers, some of whom were known as the "debunkers." Among them was the Baltimore journalist H. L. Mencken, who delighted in ridiculing religion, politics, the arts, even democracy itself. Sinclair Lewis published a series of savage novels—*Main Street* (1920), *Babbitt* (1922), *Arrowsmith* (1925), and others—in which he lashed out at one aspect of modern bourgeois society after another. Intellectuals of the 1920s claimed to reject the "success ethic" that they believed dominated American life. The novelist F. Scott Fitzgerald, for example, attacked the American obsession with material success in *The Great Gatsby* (1925). The roster of important American writers active in the 1920s may have no equal in any other period. It included Fitzgerald, Lewis, Ernest Hemingway, Thomas Wolfe, John Dos Passos, Ezra Pound, T. S. Eliot, Gertrude Stein, Edna Ferber, William Faulkner, and Eugene O'Neill.

It also included a remarkable group of black artists. In New York City, a new generation of African-American intellectuals created a flourishing artistic *"Harlem Renaissance"* life widely described as the "Harlem Renaissance." The Harlem poets, novelists, and artists drew heavily from their African roots in an effort to prove the richness of their own racial heritage. The poet Langston Hughes captured much of the spirit of the movement in a single sentence: "I am a Negro—and beautiful." Other black writers in Harlem and elsewhere—James Weldon Johnson, Countee Cullen, Zora Neale Hurston, Claude McKay, Alain Locke—as well as black artists and musicians helped to establish a thriving, and at times highly politicized, culture rooted in the historical legacy of their race.

A CONFLICT OF CULTURES

The modern, secular culture of the 1920s did not go unchallenged. It grew up alongside an older, more traditional culture, with which it continually and often bitterly competed.

Prohibition

When the prohibition of the sale and manufacture of alcohol went into effect in January 1920, it had the support of most members of the middle class and most of those who considered themselves progressives. Within a year, however, it had become clear that the "noble experiment," as its defenders called it, was not working well. Prohibition   *Failure of Prohibition*
did substantially reduce drinking in most parts of
the country. But it also produced conspicuous and growing violations. Before long, it was almost as easy to acquire illegal alcohol in many parts of the country as it had once been to acquire legal alcohol. And since an enormous, lucrative industry was now barred to legitimate businessmen, organized-crime figures took it over.

Many middle-class progressives who had originally supported prohibition soon soured on the experiment. But an enormous constituency of provincial, largely rural, Protestant Americans continued vehemently to defend it. To them, prohibition represented the effort of an older America to defend traditional notions of morality. Drinking, which they associated with the modern city and with Catholic immigrants, became a symbol of the new culture they believed was displacing them.

As the decade proceeded, opponents of prohi-   *"Wets" versus "Drys"*
bition (or "wets," as they came to be known) gained
steadily in influence. Not until 1933, however, when the Great Depression added weight to their appeals, were they finally able to effectively challenge the "drys" and win repeal of the Eighteenth Amendment.

Nativism and the Klan

The fear of immigrants that many prohibitionists expressed found other expressions as well. Agitation for a curb on foreign immigration to the United States had begun in the nineteenth century, and as with prohibition, it had gathered strength in the years before the war largely because of the support of middle-class progressives. In the years immediately following the war, when immigration began to be associated with radicalism, popular sentiment on behalf of restriction grew rapidly.

In 1921, Congress passed an emergency immigration act, establishing a quota system by which annual immigration from any country could not exceed 3 percent of the number of persons of that nationality who had been in the United States in 1910. The new law cut immigration from

800,000 to 300,000 in any single year, but the nativists remained unsatis-
National Origins Act of 1924 fied. The National Origins Act of 1924 banned immigration from east Asia entirely. It also reduced
the quota for Europeans from 3 to 2 percent. The quota would be based,
moreover, not on the 1910 census, but on the census of 1890, a year in
which there had been far fewer southern and eastern Europeans in the
country. What immigration there was, in other words, would heavily favor
northwestern Europeans. Five years later, a further restriction set a rigid
limit of 150,000 immigrants a year. In the years that followed, immigration officials seldom permitted even half that number actually to enter the
country.

To defenders of an older, more provincial America, the growth of
large communities of foreign peoples, alien in their speech, their habits,
and their values, came to seem a direct threat to their own embattled way
of life. Among other things, this provincial nativism helped instigate the
Rise of the New Klan rebirth of the Ku Klux Klan as a major force in
American society. The first Klan, founded during
Reconstruction, had died in the 1870s. But in 1915, a new group of white
southerners met on Stone Mountain near Atlanta and established a modern version of the society. Nativist passions had swelled in Georgia and
elsewhere in response to the case of Leo Frank, a Jewish factory manager
in Atlanta convicted in 1914 (on very flimsy evidence) of murdering a female employee; a mob stormed Frank's jail and lynched him. The pre-
miere (also in Atlanta) of D. W. Griffith's film *The Birth of a Nation*, which
glorified the early Klan, also helped inspire white southerners to join a
new one.

At first the new Klan, like the old, was largely concerned with intimi-
dating blacks. After World War I, however, concern about blacks gradually became secondary to concern about Catholics, Jews, and foreigners.
At that point, membership in the Klan expanded rapidly and dramatically,
not just in the small towns and rural areas of the South but in industrial
cities in the North and Midwest. By 1924, there were reportedly 4 million
members, including many women, organized in separate, parallel units,
and the largest state Klan was not in the South but in Indiana. Beginning
in 1925, a series of scandals involving the organization's leaders precipitated a slow but steady decline in the Klan's influence.

Most Klan units (or "klaverns") tried to present their members as pa-
triots and defenders of morality, and some did nothing more menacing
than stage occasional parades and rallies. Often, however, the Klan also
operated as a brutal, even violent, opponent of "alien" groups. Klansmen
systematically terrorized blacks, Jews, Catholics, and foreigners. At times,
they did so violently, through public whipping, tarring and feathering,
arson, and lynching. What the Klan feared, however, was not simply "foreign" or "racially impure" groups; it feared anyone who posed a challenge
to traditional values.

DARROW AND BRYAN IN DAYTON Although the Scopes trial was chiefly significant for the issues it raised, it attracted national attention in 1925 at least as much because of its two celebrated attorneys: Clarence Darrow, the best-known defense attorney in America and a personification of the modern, skeptical, secular intellect; and William Jennings Bryan, the great political leader who had become, in the last years of his life, an ardent defender of Christian fundamentalism. *(UPI/Corbis-Bettmann)*

Religious Fundamentalism

Fundamentalists and Modernists

Another cultural controversy of the 1920s was the result of a bitter conflict over the place of religion in contemporary society. By 1921, American Protestantism was already divided into two warring camps. On one side stood the modernists: mostly urban, middle-class people who were attempting to adapt religion to the teachings of modern science and to the realities of their modern, secular society. On the other side stood the fundamentalists: provincial, largely (although far from exclusively) rural men and women fighting to preserve traditional faith and to maintain the centrality of religion in American life. The fundamentalists insisted the Bible was to be interpreted literally. Above all, they opposed the teachings of Charles Darwin, whose theory of evolution had openly challenged the biblical story of the Creation.

By the mid-1920s, to the great alarm of modernists, fundamentalism was gaining political strength in some states with its demands for legislation to forbid the teaching of evolution in public schools. In Tennessee in March 1925, the legislature actually adopted a measure making it illegal for any public school teacher "to teach any theory that denies the story of the divine creation of man as taught in the Bible."

When the fledgling American Civil Liberties Union (ACLU) offered free counsel to any Tennessee educator willing to defy the law and become the defendant in a test case, a twenty-four-year-old biology teacher in the town of Dayton, John T. Scopes, agreed to have himself arrested. And when the ACLU decided to *Scopes Trial* send the famous attorney Clarence Darrow to defend Scopes, the aging William Jennings Bryan (now an important fundamentalist spokesman) announced that he would travel to Dayton to assist the prosecution. Journalists from across the country flocked to Tennessee to cover the trial. Scopes had, of course, clearly violated the law; and a verdict of guilty was a foregone conclusion, especially when the judge refused to permit "expert" testimony by evolution scholars. Scopes was fined $100, and the case was ultimately dismissed in a higher court because of a technicality. Nevertheless, Darrow scored an important victory for the modernists by calling Bryan himself to the stand to testify as an "expert on the Bible." In the course of the cross-examination, which was broadcast by radio to much of the nation, Darrow made Bryan's stubborn defense of biblical truths appear foolish and finally tricked Bryan into admitting the possibility that not all religious dogma was subject to only one interpretation.

The Scopes trial put fundamentalists on the defensive and discouraged many of them from participating openly in politics. But it did not resolve the conflict between fundamentalists and modernists. The issue continued to smolder for decades.

The Democrats' Ordeal

The anguish of provincial Americans attempting to defend an embattled way of life proved particularly troubling to the Democratic Party during the 1920s. More than the Republicans, the Demo-*Divided Democrats* crats consisted of a diverse coalition of interest groups, including prohibitionists, Klansmen, and fundamentalists on one side and Catholics, urban workers, and immigrants on the other.

At the 1924 Democratic National Convention in New York, a bitter conflict broke out over the platform when the party's urban wing attempted to win approval of planks calling for the repeal of prohibition and a denunciation of the Klan. Both planks narrowly failed. More serious was a deadlock in the balloting for a presidential candidate. Urban Democrats supported Alfred E. Smith, the Irish Catholic governor of New York; rural Democrats backed William McAdoo, Woodrow Wilson's Treasury secretary, who had skillfully positioned himself to win the support of southern and western delegates suspicious of modern urban life. For 103 ballots, the convention dragged on, until finally both Smith and McAdoo withdrew and the party settled on a compromise: the corporate lawyer John W. Davis.

Al Smith A similar schism plagued the Democrats again in 1928, when Al Smith finally secured his party's nomination for president. He was not, however, able to unite his divided party—in part because of widespread anti-Catholic sentiment, especially in the South. He was the first Democrat since the Civil War not to carry the entire South. Outside the South, he carried no states at all except Massachusetts and Rhode Island. Smith's opponent, and the victor in the presidential election, was a man who perhaps more than any other personified the modern, prosperous, middle-class society of the New Era: Herbert Hoover.

REPUBLICAN GOVERNMENT

For twelve years, beginning in 1921, both the presidency and the Congress rested in the hands of the Republican Party. For most of those years, the federal government enjoyed a warm and supportive relationship with the American business community. Yet the government of the New Era was more than the passive, pliant instrument that critics often described. It attempted to serve in many respects as an agent of economic change.

Harding and Coolidge

Nothing seemed more clearly to illustrate the unadventurous character of 1920s politics than the characters of the two men who served as president during most of the decade: Warren G. Harding and Calvin Coolidge.

Harding, who was elected to the presidency in 1920, was an undistinguished senator from Ohio. He had received the Republican presidential nomination as a result of an agreement among leaders of his party, who considered him, as one noted, a "good second-rater." Harding appointed capable men to the most important cabinet offices, and he attempted to stabilize the nation's troubled foreign policy. But he seemed baffled by his responsibilities, as if he recognized his *Warren Harding* own unfitness. "I am a man of limited talents from a small town," he reportedly told friends on one occasion. "I don't seem to grasp that I am President." Harding's intellectual limits were compounded by personal weaknesses: his penchant for gambling, illegal alcohol, and attractive women.

Harding lacked the strength to abandon the party hacks who had helped create his political success. One of them, Ohio party boss Harry Daugherty, he appointed attorney general. Another, New Mexico Senator Albert B. Fall, he made secretary of the interior. Members of the so-called Ohio Gang filled important offices throughout the administration. Unknown to the public, Daugherty, Fall, and others were engaged in fraud and corruption. The most spectacular scandal involved the rich naval oil reserves at Teapot Dome, Wyoming, and Elk Hills, *Teapot Dome Scandal* California. At the urging of Fall, Harding transferred control of those reserves from the Navy Department to the Interior Department. Fall then secretly leased them to two wealthy businessmen and received in return nearly half a million dollars in "loans" to ease his

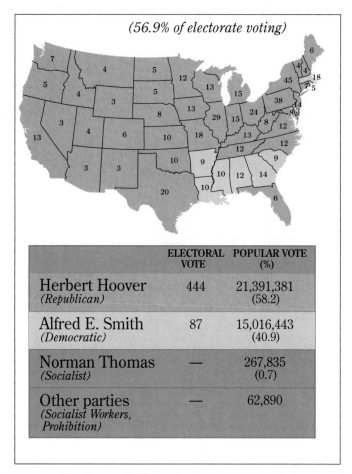

(56.9% of electorate voting)

	ELECTORAL VOTE	POPULAR VOTE (%)
Herbert Hoover *(Republican)*	444	21,391,381 (58.2)
Alfred E. Smith *(Democratic)*	87	15,016,443 (40.9)
Norman Thomas *(Socialist)*	—	267,835 (0.7)
Other parties *(Socialist Workers, Prohibition)*	—	62,890

ELECTION OF 1928 The election of 1928 was, by almost any measure, highly one-sided. Herbert Hoover won over 58 percent of the vote to Alfred Smith's 41. Smith carried only Massachusetts, Rhode Island, and some traditionally Democratic states in the South.

◆ *Why did Smith do so poorly even in traditionally Democratic areas of the country in 1928?*

For an interactive version of this map go to www.mhhe.com/unfinishednation4ch24maps

private financial troubles. Fall was ultimately convicted of bribery and sentenced to a year in prison; Harry Daugherty barely avoided a similar fate for his part in another scandal.

In the summer of 1923, only months before Senate investigations and press revelations brought the scandals to light, a tired and depressed Harding left Washington for a speaking tour in the West. In Seattle late in July, he suffered severe pain, which his doctors wrongly diagnosed as food poisoning. A few days later, in San Francisco, he died. He had suffered two major heart attacks.

In many ways, Calvin Coolidge, who succeeded Harding in the presidency, was utterly different from his predecessor. Where Harding was genial, garrulous, and debauched, Coolidge was dour, silent, even puritanical. In other ways, however, Harding and Coolidge were similar figures. Both took essentially passive approaches to their office.

Elected governor of Massachusetts in 1919, Coolidge had won national attention with his laconic response to the Boston police strike that year: "There is no right to strike against the public safety." That was enough to make him his party's vice presidential nominee in 1920. Three years later, after Harding's death, he took the oath of office from his father, a justice of the peace, by the light of a kerosene lamp.

Calvin Coolidge

If anything, Coolidge was even less active as president than Harding, partly as a result of his conviction that government should interfere as little as possible in the life of the nation. In 1924, he received his party's presidential nomination virtually unopposed. Running against John W. Davis, he won a comfortable victory: 54 percent of the popular vote and 382 of the 531 electoral votes. Coolidge probably could have won renomination and reelection in 1928. Instead, in characteristically laconic fashion, he walked into a press room one day and handed each reporter a slip of paper containing a single sentence: "I do not choose to run for president in 1928."

Government and Business

However passive the New Era presidents may have been, much of the federal government was working effectively and efficiently during the 1920s to adapt public policy to the widely accepted goal of the time: helping business and industry operate with maximum efficiency and productivity. The close relationship between the private sector and the federal government that had been forged during World War I continued. Secretary of the Treasury Andrew Mellon, a wealthy steel and aluminum tycoon, devoted himself to working for substantial reductions in taxes on corporate profits and personal incomes and inheritances. Largely because of his efforts, Congress cut them all by more than half. Mellon also worked closely with President Coolidge after 1924 on a series of measures to trim dramatically the already modest federal budget. The administration even managed to retire half the nation's World War I debt.

Sharp Tax Reductions

The most prominent member of the cabinet was Commerce Secretary Herbert Hoover. During his eight years in the Commerce Department, Hoover constantly encouraged voluntary cooperation in the private sector as the best avenue to stability. But the idea of voluntarism did not require that the government remain passive; on the contrary, public institutions, Hoover believed, had a duty to play an active role in creating the new, cooperative order. Above all, Hoover became the champion of the concept of business "associationalism"—a concept that envisioned the creation of national organizations of businessmen in particular industries. Through these trade associations, private entrepreneurs

"Associationalism"

could, Hoover believed, stabilize their industries and promote efficiency in production and marketing.

Some progressives derived encouragement from the election of Herbert Hoover to the presidency in 1928. Hoover easily defeated Al Smith, the Democratic candidate. And he entered office promising bold new efforts to solve the nation's remaining economic problems. But Hoover had few opportunities to prove himself. Less than a year after his inauguration, the nation plunged into the severest and most prolonged economic crisis in its history—a crisis that brought many of the optimistic assumptions of the New Era crashing down and launched the nation into a period of unprecedented social innovation and reform.

CONCLUSION

The remarkable prosperity of the 1920s shaped much of what exuberant contemporaries liked to call the "New Era." In the years after World War I, America built a vibrant and extensive national culture. Its middle class moved increasingly into the embrace of the growing consumer culture. Its politics reorganized itself around the needs of a booming, interdependent industrial economy—rejecting many of the reform crusades of the previous generation, but also creating new institutions to help promote economic growth and stability.

Beneath the glittering surface of the New Era, however, were great controversies and injustices. Although the prosperity of the 1920s was more widely spread than at any time in the nation's industrial history, more than half the population failed to achieve any real benefits from the growth. A new, optimistic, secular culture was attracting millions of urban, middle-class people. But many other Americans looked at it with alarm and fought against it with great fervor. The unprepossessing conservative presidents of the era suggested a time of stability, but in fact few eras in modern American history have seen so much political and cultural conflict.

The 1920s ended in a catastrophic economic crash that has colored the image of those years ever since. The crises of the 1930s should not obscure the real achievements of the New Era economy. Neither, however, should the prosperity of the 1920s obscure the inequity and instability in those years that helped produce the difficult years to come.

FOR FURTHER REFERENCE

Frederick Lewis Allen, *Only Yesterday* (1931) is a classic popular history of the 1920s. Michael Parrish, *Anxious Decades: America in Prosperity and Depression, 1920–1941* (1992) is a good recent survey. Ellis Hawley, *The Great War and the Search for a Mod-*

ern Order (1979) describes the effect of World War I on American ideas, culture, and society. William E. Leuchtenburg, *The Perils of Prosperity* (rev. ed. 1994) reveals the class divisions and culture dislocation that accompanied economic prosperity in the 1920s. David Brody, *Workers in Industrial America* (1980) includes important essays on welfare capitalism and other labor systems of the 1920s. T. J. Jackson Lears, *Fables of Abundance: A Cultural History of Advertising in America* (1994) and Roland Marchand, *Advertising the American Dream* (1985) are valuable inquiries into the role of advertising in the new consumer culture. James J. Flink, *The Car Culture* (1975) examines ways in which the automobile transformed American life. Susan Smulyan, *Selling Radio: The Commercialization of American Broadcasting, 1920–1934* (1994) chronicles the emergence of commercial radio. Robert Lynd and Helen Merrell Lynd, *Middletown* (1929) is a classic sociological study of how an American city encountered the consumer culture and economy of the 1920s. Ann Douglas, *Terrible Honesty: Mongrel Manhattan in the 1920s* (1995) examines the cultural and political history of the New Era in New York City. Lynn Dumenil, *The Modern Temper: America in the 1920s* (1995) examines the reactions of Americans to modern culture. George Chauncey, *Gay New York: Gender, Urban Culture, and the Making of the Gay Male World, 1890–1940* (1994) is an excellent work in a relatively new field of history. The decline of the feminist movement in the 1920s is explored in Nancy Cott, *The Grounding of American Feminism* (1987). Gary Gerstle, *American Crucible* (2000) is an important study of the changing role of race and ethnicity in defining American nationhood in the twentieth century. Andrew Gyory, *Closing the Gate: Race, Politics, and the Chinese Exclusion Act* (1998) examines an early chapter in immigration restriction. Nathan I. Huggins chronicles the cultural and political efflorescence of black Harlem during these years in *Harlem Renaissance* (1971), as does David Levering Lewis in *When Harlem Was in Vogue* (1981). George Marsden, *Fundamentalism and American Culture* (1980) is a good study of some of the religious battles that came to a head in the 1920s. Grant Wacker, *Heaven Below: Early Pentecostals and American Culture* (2001) examines the emergence of modern pentecostalism. Edward J. Larson, *Summer for the Gods: The Scopes Trial and America's Continuing Debate Over Science and Religion* (1997) is a valuable analysis of the Scopes Trial. Leonard Moore, *Citizen Klansmen: The Ku Klux Klan in Indiana, 1921–1928* (1991) is a challenging view of the Klan. Kathleen M. Blee, *Women and the Klan: Racism and Gender in the 1920s* (1991) recreates the female world of the Klan. David Burner, *The Politics of Provincialism* (1967) is a good study of the ordeal of the Democratic Party in the 1920s. Morton Keller, *Regulating a New Economy: Public Policy and Economic Change in America, 1900–1933* (1990) and *Regulating a New Society: Public Policy and Social Change in America, 1900–1933* (1994) are important studies of New Era public policy. *Coney Island* (1990) is a documentary film recreating the drama and fantasy of Coney Island. *That Rhythm, Those Blues* (1997) is a film documenting the one-night stands, makeshift housing, and poor transportation that were all a step toward the big time at the famed Apollo Theatre on Harlem's 125th Street. *Mr. Sears' Catalogue* (1997) is a film exploring how the Sears catalog became a symbol for the ambitions and dreams of a sprawling, fast developing America.

For quizzes, Internet resources, references to additional books and films, and more, consult this book's Online Learning Center site at www.mhhe.com/unfinishednation4.

DETAIL FROM *PRIVATE CAR* (1932), BY LECONTE STEWART
Thousands of men (and some women) left their homes during the Great
Depression and traveled from city to city looking for work, often hopping freight
trains for a free, if illegal, ride. *(Museum of Church History & Art, Salt Lake City, Utah)*

TIME LINE

1929	1930	1931	1932	
Stock market crash; Great Depression begins	Hawley-Smoot Tariff	Scottsboro defendants arrested	Reconstruction Finance Corporation established	
Agricultural Marketing Act	Drought begins in Dust Bowl		Bonus Army in Washington	
			Franklin D. Roosevelt elected president	

❧

CHAPTER TWENTY-FIVE

THE GREAT DEPRESSION

The Coming of the Depression
The American People in Hard Times
The Depression and American Culture
The Ordeal of Herbert Hoover

W e in America today," Herbert Hoover proclaimed in August 1928, "are nearer to the final triumph over poverty than ever before in the history of any land." Only fifteen months later, those words would return to haunt him, as the nation plunged into the severest and most prolonged economic depression in its history—a depression that continued in one form or another for a full decade, not only in the United States but throughout much of the world.

THE COMING OF THE DEPRESSION

❧

The sudden financial collapse in 1929 came as an especially severe shock because it followed so closely a period in which the New Era seemed to be performing another series of economic miracles—miracles that seemed especially evident in the remarkable performance of the stock market.

1934	1935	1936	1939	1940	
Southern Tenant Farmers Union organized	American Communist Party proclaims Popular Front	Mitchell's *Gone with the Wind*	Steinbeck's *The Grapes of Wrath*	Wright's *Native Son*	

Soaring Stock Market

In February 1928, stock prices began a steady ascent that continued, with only a few temporary lapses, for a year and a half. Between May 1928 and September 1929, the average price of stocks rose over 40 percent. Trading mushroomed from 2 or 3 million shares a day to over 5 million, and at times to as many as 10 or 12 million. There was, in short, a widespread speculative fever that grew steadily more intense, particularly once brokerage firms began encouraging the mania by offering absurdly easy credit to those buying stocks.

The Great Crash

"Black Tuesday"

In the autumn of 1929, the market began to fall apart. On October 29, "Black Tuesday," after a week of steadily rising instability, all efforts to save the market failed. Sixteen million shares of stock were traded; the industrial index dropped 43 points (or nearly 10 percent), wiping out all the gains of the previous year; stocks in many companies became virtually worthless. Within a month stocks had lost half their September value, and despite occasional, short-lived rallies, they continued to decline for several years after that.

Popular folklore has established the stock market crash as the beginning, and even the cause, of the Great Depression. But although October 1929 might have been the most visible early sign of the crisis, the Depression had earlier beginnings and more important causes.

Causes of the Depression

Economists, historians, and others have argued for decades about the causes of the Great Depression. But most agree on several things. They agree, first, that what is remarkable about the crisis is not that it occurred, but that it was so severe and that it lasted so long. Most observers agree, too, that a number of different factors account for the severity of the crisis.

Poor Economic Diversification

One of those factors was a lack of diversification in the American economy in the 1920s. Prosperity had depended excessively on a few basic industries, notably construction and automobiles. In the late 1920s, those industries began to decline. Expenditures on construction fell from $11 billion to under $9 billion between 1926 and 1929. Automobile sales fell by more than a third in the first nine months of 1929. Newer industries were emerging to take up the slack—among them petroleum, chemicals, electronics, and plastics—but had not yet developed enough strength to compensate for the decline in other sectors.

Uneven Distribution of Wealth

A second important factor was the maldistribution of purchasing power and, as a result, a weakness in consumer demand. As industrial and agricultural production increased, the proportion of the profits going to potential consumers was too small to create an adequate market for the goods the economy was producing. Even in 1929, after nearly a decade of economic growth, more than half the families in America lived on the edge of or below the minimum subsistence level.

A third major problem was the credit structure of the economy. Farmers were deeply in debt, and crop prices were too low to allow them to pay off what they owed. Small banks were in constant trouble as their customers defaulted on loans; large banks were in trouble, too. Although most American bankers were very conservative, some of the nation's biggest banks were investing recklessly in the stock market or making unwise loans. When the market crashed and the loans went bad, some banks failed and others made the crisis worse by contracting the already scarce credit and calling in loans that borrowers could not pay.

A fourth factor contributing to the Depression was America's position in international trade. Late in the 1920s, European demand for American goods began to decline. That was partly because European industry and agriculture were becoming more productive and partly because some European nations were having financial difficulties of their own. But it was also because the European economy was being destabilized by the international debt structure that had emerged in the aftermath of World War I.

The international debt structure, therefore, *International Debt Structure* was a fifth factor contributing to the Depression. When the war came to an end in 1918, all the European nations that had been allied with the United States owed large sums of money to American banks, sums much too large to be repaid out of their shattered economies. That was one reason why the Allies had insisted on reparation payments from Germany and Austria. Reparations, they believed, would provide them with a way to pay off their own debts. But Germany and Austria were no more able to pay the reparations than the Allies were able to pay their debts.

The American government refused to forgive or reduce the debts. Instead, American banks began making large loans to European governments, which used them to pay off their earlier loans. Thus debts (and reparations) were being paid only by piling up new and greater debts. At the same time, American protective tariffs were making it difficult for Europeans to sell their goods in American markets. Without any source of foreign exchange with which to repay their loans, they began to default. The collapse of the international credit structure was one of the reasons the Depression spread to Europe after 1931.

Progress of the Depression

The stock market crash of 1929 did not so much cause the Depression, then, as help trigger a chain of events that exposed larger weaknesses in the American economy. During the next three years, the crisis grew steadily worse.

CAUSES OF THE GREAT DEPRESSION

What were the causes of the Great Depression? Economists and historians have debated this question since the economic collapse began and still have not reached anything close to agreement on it. In the process, however, they have illustrated several very different theories about how a modern economy works.

During the Depression itself, different groups offered interpretations of the crisis that fit comfortably with their own self-interests. Some corporate leaders claimed that the Depression was the result of a lack of "business confidence," that businessmen were reluctant to invest because they feared government regulation and high taxes. The Hoover administration blamed international economic forces and sought, therefore, to stabilize world currencies and debt structures. New Dealers, determined to find a domestic solution to the crisis, argued that the Depression was a crisis of "underconsumption," that low wages and high prices had made it too difficult to buy the products of the industrial economy; and that a lack of demand had led to the economic collapse. Other groups offered equally self-serving explanations.

Scholars in the years since the Great Depression have also created interpretations that fit their view of how the economy works. One of the first important postwar interpretations came from the economists Milton Friedman and Anna Schwartz, in their *Monetary History of the United States* (1963). In a chapter entitled "The Great Contraction," they argued for what has become known as the "monetary" interpretation. The Depression, they claimed, was a result of a drastic contraction of the currency (a result of mistaken decisions by the Federal Reserve Board, which raised interest rates when it should have lowered them). These deflationary measures turned an ordinary recession into the Great Depression. The monetary argument fits comfortably with the ideas that Milton Friedman, in particular, has advocated for many years: that sound monetary policy is the best way to solve economic problems—as opposed to fiscal policies, such as taxation and spending.

A second, very different argument is known as the "spending" interpretation, an interpretation supported by many liberal, Keynesian economists. It is identified with, among others, the economist Peter Temin, and his book *Did Monetary Forces Cause the Great Depression?* (1976). Temin's answer to his own question is "no." The cause of the crisis was not monetary contraction (although the contraction made it worse), but a drop in investment and consumer spending, which preceded the decline in the money supply and helped to cause it. Here again, there are obvious political implications. If a decline in spending was the cause of the Depression, then the proper response was an effort to stimulate demand—raising government spending, increasing purchasing power, redistributing wealth. The New Deal never ended the Depression because it did not spend enough. World War II did end it because it pumped so much public money into the economy.

Another important explanation comes from the historian Michael Bernstein. In *The Great Depression* (1987) he avoids trying to explain why the economic downturn occurred and asks, instead, why it lasted so long. The reason the recession of 1929 became the Depression of the 1930s, he argues, was the timing of the collapse. The recession began as an ordinary cyclical downturn. Had it begun a few years earlier, the basic strength of the automobile and construction industries in the 1920s would have led to a reasonably speedy recovery. Had it begun a few years later, a group of newer, emerging industries would have helped produce a recovery in a reasonably short time. But the recession began in 1929, too late for the automobile and construction industries to help and too soon for emerging new industries—aviation, petrochemicals and plastics, aluminum, and others—to help, since they were still in their infancies.

The political implications of this argument are less obvious than those of some other interpretations. But one possible conclusion is that if economic growth depends on the successful development of new industries to replace declining ones, then the most sensible economic policy for government is to target investment and other policies toward the growth of new economic sectors. One of the reasons World War II was so important to the long-term recovery of the U.S. economy, Bernstein's argument suggests, was not just that it pumped money into the economy, but that much of that money contributed to developing new industries. This is, in other words, an explanation of the Depression that seems to support some of the economic ideas that became popular in the 1980s and 1990s calling for a more direct government role in stimulating the growth of new industries.

In the end, however, no single explanation of the Great Depression has ever seemed adequate to most scholars. The event, the economist Robert Lucas once argued, is simply "inexplicable" by any rational calculation. There is no one, wholly persuasive answer to the question of what caused it.

(text continued from page 651)

The most serious problem at first was the collapse of much of the banking system. Over 9,000 American banks either went bankrupt or closed their doors to avoid bankruptcy between 1930 and 1933. Partly as a result of these banking closures, the nation's money supply shrank by perhaps a third or more between 1930 and 1933. The declining money supply meant a decline in purchasing power, and thus deflation. Manufacturers and merchants began reducing prices, cutting back on production, and laying off workers. Some economists argue that a severe depression could have been avoided if the Federal Reserve system had acted responsibly. But late in 1931, in a misguided effort to build international confidence in the dollar, it raised interest rates, which contracted the money supply even further.

Banking Crisis

The American gross national product plummeted from over $104 billion in 1929 to $76.4 billion in 1932—a 25 percent decline in three years. By 1932, according to the relatively crude estimates of the time, 25 percent of the American work force was unemployed. (Some argue that the figure was even higher.) For the rest of the decade, unemployment averaged nearly 20 percent, never dropping below 15 percent. Up to another one-third of the work force was "underemployed"—experiencing major reductions in wages, hours, or both.

Plunging GNP

THE UNEMPLOYED, 1930 Thousands of unemployed men wait to be fed outside the Municipal Lodgers House in New York City. *(The Library of Congress)*

THE AMERICAN PEOPLE IN HARD TIMES

Someone asked the British economist John Maynard Keynes in the 1930s whether he was aware of any historical era comparable to the Great Depression. "Yes," Keynes replied. "It was called the Dark Ages, and it lasted 400 years." The Depression did not last 400 years. It did, however, bring unprecedented despair to the economies of the United States and much of the Western world.

Unemployment and Relief

In the industrial Northeast and Midwest, cities were becoming virtually paralyzed by unemployment. Cleveland, Ohio, for example, had an unemployment rate of 50 percent in 1932; Akron, 60 percent; Toledo, 80 percent. Unemployed workers walked through the streets day after day looking for jobs that did not exist. An increasing number of families were turning to state and local public relief systems, just to be able to eat. But those systems, which in the 1920s had served only a small number of indigents, were totally unequipped to handle the new demands being placed on them. In many cities, therefore, relief simply collapsed. Private charities attempted to supplement the public relief efforts, but the problem was far beyond their capabilities as well.

In rural areas conditions were in many ways worse. Farm income declined by 60 percent between 1929 and 1932. A third of all American farmers lost their land. In addition, a large area of agricultural settlement in the Great Plains was suffering from a catastrophic natural disaster: one of the worst droughts in the history of the nation. Beginning in 1930, the region, which came to be known as the "Dust Bowl" and which stretched north from Texas into *"Dust Bowl"* the Dakotas, experienced a steady decline in rainfall and an accompanying increase in heat. The drought continued for a decade, turning what had once been fertile farm regions into virtual deserts.

Many farmers, like many urban unemployed, left their homes in search of work. In the South, in particular, many dispossessed farmers—black and white—simply wandered from town to town, hoping to find jobs or handouts. Hundreds of thousands of families from the Dust Bowl (often known as "Okies," since many came from Oklahoma) traveled to California and other states, where they found conditions little better than those they had left. Many worked as agricultural migrants, traveling from farm to farm picking fruit and other crops at starvation wages.

African Americans and the Depression

Most African Americans had not shared very much in the prosperity of the previous decade. But they did share the hardships of the Great Depression.

As the Depression began, over half of all black Americans still lived in the South. Most were farm- *Soaring Black Unemployment* ers. The collapse of prices for cotton and other staple crops left some with no income at all. Many left the land altogether—either by choice or because they had been evicted by landlords who no longer found the sharecropping system profitable. Some migrated to southern cities. But there, unemployed whites believed they had first claim to what work there was, and some now began to take positions as janitors, street cleaners, and domestic servants, displacing the blacks who formerly occupied those jobs. By 1932, over half the blacks in the South were without employment.

Unsurprisingly, therefore, many black southerners—perhaps 400,000 in all—left the South in the 1930s and journeyed to the cities of the North. But conditions there were little better than those in the South. In New York, black unemployment was nearly 50 percent. In other cities, it was higher. Two million African Americans—half the total black population of the country—were on some form of relief by 1932.

Traditional patterns of segregation and disenfranchisement in the South survived the Depression largely unchallenged. But a few particularly notorious examples of racism did attract the attention of the nation.

The Great Depression began in the United States. But it did not end there. The American economy was the largest in the world, and its collapse sent shock waves across the globe. By 1931, the American depression had become a world depression, with important implications for the course of global history.

The origins of the worldwide depression lay in the pattern of debts that had emerged during and after World War I, when the United States loaned billions of dollars to European nations. In 1931, with American banks staggering and in many cases collapsing, large banks in New York began desperately calling in their loans from Germany and Austria. That precipitated the collapse of one of Austria's largest banks, which in turn created panic through much of central Europe. The economic collapse in Germany and Austria meant that those nations could not continue paying reparations to Britain and France (required by the Treaty of Versailles of 1919), which meant in turn that Britain and France could not continue paying off their loans to the United States. This spreading financial crisis was accompanied by a dramatic contraction of international trade, precipitated in part by the Hawley-Smoot Tariff in the United States, which established the highest import duties in history and stifled much global commerce. Depressed agricultural prices—a result of worldwide overproduction—also contributed to the downturn. By 1932, worldwide industrial production had declined by more than a third, and world trade had plummeted by nearly two thirds. By 1933, thirty million people in industrial nations were unemployed, five times the number of four years before.

But the Depression was not confined to industrial nations. Imperialism and industrialization had drawn almost all regions of the world into the international industrial economy. Colonies and nations in Africa, Asia, and South America—critically dependent on exporting raw materials and agricultural goods to industrial countries—experienced a collapse in demand for their products and thus rising levels of poverty and unemployment. Some nations—among them the Soviet Union and China—remained relatively unconnected to the global economy and suffered relatively little from the Great Depression. But in most parts of the world, the Depression caused tremendous social and economic hardship.

It also created political turmoil. Among the countries hardest hit by the Depression was Germany, where industrial production declined by 50 percent and unemployment reached 35 percent in the early 1930s. The desperate economic conditions there contributed greatly to the rise of the Nazi party and its leader Adolf Hitler, who became chancellor in 1933. Japan suffered greatly as well, dependent as it was on world trade to sustain its growing industrial economy and purchase essential commodities for its needs at home. And in Japan, as in Germany, economic troubles produced political turmoil and aided the rise of a new militaristic regime. In Italy, the fascist government of Benito Mussolini, which had first taken power in the 1920s, also saw militarization and territorial expansion as a way out of economic difficulties.

In other nations, governments sought solutions to the Depression through reform of their domestic economies. The most prominent example of that was the New Deal in the United States. But there were important experiments in other nations as well. Among the most common responses to the Depression around the world was substantial government investment in public works. In the United States, Britain, France, Germany, Italy, the Soviet Union, and other countries, there was substantial investment in roads, bridges, dams, public buildings, and other large projects. Another response was the expansion of government-funded relief for the unemployed. All the industrial countries of the world experimented with one or another form of relief, often borrowing ideas from one another in the process. And the Depression helped create new approaches to economics, in the face of the apparent failure of classical models of economic behavior to explain, or provide solutions to, the crisis. The great British economist John Maynard Keynes revolutionized economic thought in much of the world. His 1936 book *The General Theory of Employment, Interest, and Money*, despite its bland title, created a sensation by arguing that the Depression was a result not of declining production, but of inadequate consumer demand. Governments, he said, could stimulate their economies by increasing the money supply and creating investment—through a combination of lowering interest rates and public spending. Keynesianism, as Keynes's theories became known, began to have an impact in the United States in 1938, and in much of the rest of the world in subsequent years.

The Great Depression was an important turning point not only in American history, but in the history of the twentieth-century world. It transformed ideas of public policy and economics in many nations. It toppled old regimes and created new ones. And perhaps above all, it was a major factor—maybe the single most important factor—in the coming of World War II.

(text continued from page 655)

The most celebrated was the Scottsboro case. In March 1931, nine black teenagers were taken off a freight train in northern Alabama (in a small town near Scottsboro) and arrested for vagrancy and disorder. Later, two white women who had also been riding the train accused them of rape. In fact, there was overwhelming evidence, medical and otherwise, that the women had not been raped at all; they may have made their accusations out of fear of being arrested themselves. Nevertheless, an all-white jury in Alabama quickly convicted all nine of the "Scottsboro boys" (as they were known to both *"Scottsboro Boys"* friends and foes) and sentenced eight of them to death.

The Supreme Court overturned the convictions in 1932, and a series of new trials began. The International Labor Defense, an organization associated with the Communist Party, came to the aid of the accused youths and began to publicize the case. Although the white southern juries who sat on the case never acquitted any of the defendants, all of the accused eventually gained their freedom—although the last of the Scottsboro defendants did not leave prison until 1950.

BLACK MIGRANTS The Great Migration of blacks from the rural South into the cities had begun before World War I. But in the 1930s and 1940s the movement accelerated. Jacob Lawrence, an eminent African-American artist, created a series of paintings entitled, collectively, *The Migration of the Negro*, to illustrate this major event in the history of African Americans. *(Jacob Lawrence,* The Migration of the Negro Panel no. 57, *1940–41. Acquired 1942, The Phillips Collection, Washington, DC. Artwork Copyright 2002 Gwendolyn Knight Lawrence, courtesy of the Jacob and Gwendolyn Lawrence Foundation)*

Hispanics and Asians in Depression America

Similar patterns of discrimination confronted many Mexicans and Mexican Americans. The Hispanic population of the United States had been growing steadily since early in the century, largely in California and other areas of the Southwest through massive immigration from Mexico. Chicanos (as Mexican Americans are sometimes known) filled many of the same menial jobs there that blacks had traditionally filled in other regions. Some farmed small, marginal tracts; some became agricultural migrants. It had always been a precarious existence, and the Depression made things significantly worse. Unemployed whites in the Southwest demanded jobs held by Hispanics, jobs that whites had previously considered beneath them. Thus Mexican unemployment rose quickly to levels far higher than those for whites. Some officials arbitrarily removed Mexicans from relief rolls or simply rounded them up and transported them across the border. Perhaps half a million Chicanos left the United States for Mexico in the first years of the Depression.

Hispanic Resistance   There were, occasionally, signs of organized resistance by Mexican Americans themselves, most notably in California, where some formed a union of migrant farmworkers. But harsh repression by local growers and the public authorities allied with them prevented such organizations from having much impact. As a result, many Hispanics began to migrate to cities such as Los Angeles, where they lived in a poverty comparable to that of urban blacks in the South and Northeast.

For Asian Americans, too, the Depression rein- *Asians Marginalized* forced longstanding patterns of discrimination and economic marginalization. In California, where the largest Japanese-American and Chinese-American populations were, even educated Asians had always found it difficult, if not impossible, to move into mainstream professions. Japanese-American college graduates often found themselves working in family fruit stands. For those who found jobs in the industrial or service economy, employment was precarious; like blacks and Hispanics, Asians often lost jobs to white Americans desperate for work. Japanese farmworkers, like Chicano farmworkers, suffered from the increasing competition for even these low-paying jobs from white migrants from the Great Plains.

Chinese Americans fared no better. The overwhelming majority worked, as they had for many years, in Chinese-owned laundries and restaurants. Those who moved outside the Asian community could rarely find jobs above the entry level. Chinese women, for example, might find work as stock girls in department stores but almost never as salesclerks. Educated Chinese men and women could hope for virtually no professional opportunities outside the world of the Chinatowns.

Women and Families in the Great Depression

The economic crisis served in many ways to strengthen the widespread belief that a woman's proper place was in the home. Most men and many women believed that with employment so scarce, what work there was should go to men. There was a particularly strong belief that no woman whose husband was employed should accept a job. Indeed, from 1932 until 1937, it was illegal for more than one member of a family to hold a federal civil service job.

But the widespread assumption that married women, at least, should not work outside the home did not stop them from doing so. Both single and married women worked in the 1930s because they or their families needed the money. By the end of the Depression, 25 percent more women were working than had been doing so at the beginning. This occurred despite considerable obstacles. Professional opportu- *Growing Female Employment* nities for women declined because unemployed men began moving into professions that had previously been considered women's fields. Female industrial workers were more likely to be laid off or to experience wage reductions than their male counterparts. But white women also had certain advantages in the workplace. The nonprofessional jobs that women traditionally held—salesclerks, stenographers, and other service positions—were less likely to disappear than the predominantly male jobs in heavy industry.

Black women suffered massive unemployment, particularly in the South, because of a great reduction of domestic service jobs. As many as half of all black working women lost their jobs in the 1930s. Even so, at the end of the 1930s, 38 percent of black women were employed, as compared with 24 percent of white women. That was because black women—both married and unmarried—had always been more likely to work than white women, less out of preference than out of economic necessity.

The economic hardships of the Depression years placed great strains on American families. Middle-class families found themselves plunged suddenly into uncertainty, because of unemployment or the reduction of incomes among those who remained employed. Some working-class families had achieved a precarious prosperity in the 1920s but saw their gains disappear in the 1930s. Such circumstances caused many families to change the way they lived. Some women returned to sewing clothes for themselves and their families and to preserving their own food. Others engaged in home businesses such as taking in laundry or boarders. Many households expanded to take in relatives.

Declining Marriage and Birth Rates   But the Depression also worked to erode the strength of many family units. There was a decline in the divorce rate, but largely because divorce was now too expensive for some. More common was the informal breakup of families, particularly the desertion of families by unemployed men trying to escape the humiliation of being unable to earn a living. The marriage rate and the birth rate both declined for the first time since the early nineteenth century.

THE DEPRESSION AND AMERICAN CULTURE

The Great Depression was a traumatic experience for millions of Americans. Out of the crisis emerged probing criticisms of American life. But the Depression also produced powerful confirmations of more traditional values and reinforced many traditional goals. There was not one Depression culture, but many.

Depression Values

Prevailing Values Reinforced   Prosperity and industrial growth had done much to shape American values in the 1920s. Mainstream culture, at least, had celebrated affluence and consumerism. Many Americans assumed, therefore, that the experience of hard times would have profound effects on the nation's social values. In general, however, American social values seemed to change relatively little in response to the Depression. Instead, many people responded to hard times by redoubling their commitment to familiar ideas and goals.

No assumption would seem to have been more vulnerable to erosion during the Depression than the belief that anyone displaying sufficient talent and industry could become a success. And in some respects, the economic crisis did work to undermine the traditional "success ethic" in America. Many people began to look to government for assistance; many learned to blame corporate moguls and others for their distress. Yet the Depression did not destroy the success ethic.

The survival of the ideals of work and individual responsibility was evident in many ways, not least in the reactions of those most traumatized by the Depression: people who suddenly found themselves without employment. Some expressed anger and struck out at the economic system. Many, however, seemed to blame themselves. At the same time, millions responded eagerly to reassurances that they could, through their own efforts, restore themselves to prosperity and success. *Dale Carnegie* Dale Carnegie's *How to Win Friends and Influence People* (1936), a self-help manual preaching individual initiative, was one of the best-selling books of the decade.

Artists and Intellectuals in the Great Depression

Not all Americans, of course, responded to the crisis of the Depression so passively. Artists and intellectuals engaged in a broad effort to dramatize the problem of rural poverty. Among those involved in this venture was a group of documentary photographers, many of them employed by the federal Farm Security Administration in the late 1930s, who traveled through the South recording the nature of agricultural life. Men such as Walker Evans, Arthur Rothstein, Russell Lee, and Ben Shahn and women such as Margaret Bourke-White and Dorothea Lange produced memorable studies of farm families and their surroundings, studies designed to show the savage impact of a hostile environment on its victims. Many writers, similarly, devoted themselves to exposés of social injustice. Erskine Caldwell's *Tobacco Road* (1932), which later became a long-running play, was an exposé of poverty in the rural South. Richard Wright, a major African-American writer, exposed the plight of residents of the urban ghetto in novels such as *Native Son* (1940).

But the cultural products of the 1930s that attracted the widest popular audiences were those that diverted attention away from the Depression. And they came to Americans primarily through the two most powerful instruments of popular culture in the 1930s—radio and the movies.

Radio

Almost every American family had a radio in the *Radio's Mass Popularity* 1930s. In cities and towns, radio consoles were as familiar a part of the furnishing of parlors and kitchens as tables and chairs. Even in remote rural areas without access to electricity, many families purchased radios and hooked them up to car batteries when they wished to listen.

Listening to radio is generally considered a private experience—something people do alone, or with their families, in their homes. But in some communities, radio was often a community experience. Young people would place radios on their front porches and invite friends by to sit, talk, or dance. In poor urban neighborhoods, people would gather on a street or in a backyard to listen to sporting events or concerts. Within families, the radio often drew parents and children together to listen to favorite programs.

What did Americans hear on the radio? Although radio stations occasionally carried socially and politically provocative programs, the staple of broadcasting was escapism: comedies such as *Amos n' Andy* (with its humorous if demeaning picture of urban blacks); adventures such as *Superman, Dick Tracy,* and *The Lone Ranger;* and other entertainment programs.

Escapist Programming   Radio brought a new kind of comedy to a wide audience. Jack Benny, George Burns and Gracie Allen, and other masters of elaborately timed jokes and repartee began to develop broad followings. Soap operas were enormously popular as well, especially with women who were alone in the house during the day. (That was why they became known as soap operas; soap companies—whose advertising was targeted at women—generally sponsored them.)

Radio provided Americans with their first direct access to important public events, and radio news and sports divisions grew rapidly to meet the demand. Some of the most dramatic moments of the 1930s were a result of radio coverage of celebrated events: the World Series, the Academy Awards, political conventions. When the German dirigible the *Hindenburg* crashed in flames in Lakehurst, New Jersey, in 1937, it produced an enormous national reaction largely because of the live radio account by a broadcaster overcome with emotion who cried out, as he watched the terrible crash, "Oh the humanity! Oh the humanity!" The actor/director Orson Welles created another memorable event on Halloween night, 1938, when he broadcast a radio play about aliens whose spaceship landed in central New Jersey and who had set off toward New York armed with terrible weapons. The play took the form of a news broadcast, and it created panic among millions of people who believed for a while that the events it described were real.

The Movies

In the first years of the Depression, movie attendance dropped significantly. By the mid-1930s, however, most Americans had resumed their moviegoing habits to at least some extent in part because the movies (all of them now with sound, and by the end of the decade many of them in color) were becoming more appealing.

Hollywood's Self-Censorship   Hollywood continued to exercise tight control over its products in the 1930s through its resilient censor Will Hays, who ensured that most movies carried no sensational or controversial messages. The studio system—through which a few large movie companies exercised iron control over actors, writers, and directors—also worked to ensure that Hollywood films avoided controversy.

Neither the censor nor the studio system, however, could (or wished to) prevent films from exploring social questions altogether. A few films, such as King Vidor's *Our Daily Bread* (1932) and John Ford's adaptation of *The Grapes of Wrath* (1940), did explore political themes. Gangster movies such as *Little Caesar* (1930) and *The Public Enemy* (1931) portrayed a dark, gritty, violent world with which few Americans were familiar, but their desperate stories were popular nevertheless with those engaged in their own difficult struggles.

But the most effective presentation of a social message, even if a muted one, came from the brilliant Italian-born di- *Frank Capra* rector Frank Capra. Capra had a deep and some-what romanticized love for his adopted country, and he translated that love into a vaguely populistic admiration for ordinary people. He contrasted the decency of small-town America and the common man with what he considered the grasping opportunism of the city and the greedy capitalist marketplace. In *Mr. Deeds Goes to Town* (1936), a simple man from a small town inherits a large fortune, moves to the city, and—not liking the greed and dishonesty he finds there—gives the money away and moves back home. In *Mr. Smith Goes to Washington* (1939), a decent man from a western state is elected to the United States Senate, refuses to join in the self-interested politics of Washington, and dramatically exposes the corruption and selfishness of his colleagues. Capra's films, outstandingly popular in the 1930s, helped audiences find solace in a vision of an imagined American past—in the warmth and goodness of idealized small towns and the decency of ordinary people.

More often, however, the commercial films of the 1930s, like most radio programs, were deliberately and explicitly escapist: lavish musicals such as *Gold Diggers of 1933*, "screwball" comedies (such as Capra's *It Happened One Night*), or the many films of the Marx Brothers—films designed to divert audiences from their troubles and, often, indulge their fantasies about quick and easy wealth.

The 1930s saw the beginning of Walt Disney's *Walt Disney* long reign as the champion of animation and children's entertainment. After producing cartoon shorts for theaters in the late 1920s, many of them starring the newly created character of Mickey Mouse, Disney began to produce feature-length animated films, starting in 1937 with *Snow White*. Other enormously popular films of the 1930s were adaptations of popular novels: *The Wizard of Oz* and *Gone with the Wind*, both released in 1939.

Hollywood did little to challenge the conventions of popular culture on issues of gender and race. Women in movies were portrayed overwhelmingly as wives and mothers, or if not, as sexually attractive people engaged in elaborate flirtations with men. Mae West portrayed herself in a

A NIGHT AT THE OPERA The antic comedy of the Marx Brothers provided a popular and welcome escape from the rigors of the Great Depression. The Marx Brothers, shown here in a poster for one of their most famous films, effectively lampooned dilemmas that many Americans faced in their ceaseless, and usually unsuccessful, efforts to find an easy route to wealth and comfort. *(Everett Collection)*

series of successful films as an overtly sexual woman manipulating men through her attractiveness. Few films included important African-American characters. Most of the black men and women who did appear in movies were portrayed as servants or farmhands or entertainers.

Popular Literature and Journalism

The social and political strains of the Great Depression found voice much more successfully in print than they did on the airwaves or the screen. Much literature and journalism in the 1930s dealt directly or indirectly with the tremendous disillusionment, and the increasing radicalism, of the time.

Not all literature, of course, was challenging or controversial. The most popular books and magazines of the 1930s, in fact, were as escapist and romantic as the most popular radio shows and movies. Two of the best-selling novels of the decade were romantic sagas set in earlier eras: Margaret Mitchell's *Gone with the Wind* (1936) and Hervey Allen's *Anthony Adverse* (1933). Leading magazines focused more on fashions, stunts, scenery, and the arts than on the social conditions of the nation. The enormously popular new photographic journal *Life*, which began publication in 1936, had the largest readership of any publication in the United States (with the exception of the *Reader's Digest*). It devoted some attention to politics and to the economic conditions of the Depression, but it was best known for stunning photographs of sporting and theater events, natural landscapes, and impressive public projects. One of its most popular features was "*Life* Goes to a Party," which took the chatty social columns of daily newspapers and turned them into glossy photographic glimpses of the rich and famous.

Other Depression writing, however, was frankly and openly challenging to the dominant values of American popular culture. Some of the most significant literature offered corrosive portraits of the harshness and emptiness of American life: John Dos Passos's *U.S.A.* trilogy (1930–1936), which attacked what *John Dos Passos* he considered the materialistic madness of American culture; Nathanael West's *Miss Lonelyhearts* (1933), the story of an advice columnist overwhelmed by the sadness he encounters in the lives of those who consult him; Jack Conroy's *The Disinherited* (1933), a harsh portrait of the lives of coalminers; and James T. Farrell's *Studs Lonigan* (1932), a portrait of a lost, hardened working-class youth.

The Popular Front and the Left

In the later 1930s, much of the political literature adopted a more optimistic, although often no less radical, approach to society. This was in part a result of the rise of the Popular Front, a broad coalition of "antifascist" groups on the left, of which the most important was the American Communist Party. The party had long been a harsh and unrelenting critic of American capitalism and the government it claimed was controlled by it. But in 1935, under instructions from the Soviet Union, the party softened its attitude toward Franklin Roosevelt (whom Stalin now saw as a potential ally in the coming battle against Hitler) and formed loose alliances with many other "progressive" groups. The party began to praise the New Deal and John L. Lewis, a powerful (and strongly anticommunist) labor leader, and it adopted the slogan "Communism is twentieth-century Americanism." In its heyday, the Popular Front did much to enhance the reputation and influence of the Communist Party. It also helped mobilize writers, artists, and intellectuals behind a critical, democratic sensibility.

The importance to many American intellectuals of the Spanish Civil War of the mid-1930s was a good example of how the left helped give meaning and purpose to individual lives. The war in Spain pitted the fascists of Francisco Franco (who was receiving support from Hitler and Mussolini) against the existing republican government. It attracted a substantial group of young Americans—more than 3,000 in all—who formed the Abraham Lincoln Brigade and traveled to Spain to join in the fight against the fascists. The *Abraham Lincoln Brigade*

American Communist Party was instrumental in creating the Lincoln Brigade, and directed many of its activities.

The party was active as well in organizing the unemployed in the early 1930s and staged a hunger march in Washington, D.C., in 1931. Party members were among the most effective union organizers in some industries. And the party was virtually alone among political organizations in taking a firm stand in favor of racial justice; its active defense of the Scottsboro defendants was but one example of its efforts to ally itself with the aspirations of African Americans.

The American Communist Party was not, however, the open, patriotic organization it tried to appear. It was always under the close and rigid supervision of the Soviet Union. Most members obediently followed the "party line" (although there were many areas in which Communists were active for which there was no party line, areas in which members acted independently). The subordination of the party leadership to the Soviet Union was most clearly demonstrated in 1939, when Stalin signed a nonaggression pact with Nazi Germany. Moscow then sent orders to the American Communist Party to abandon the Popular Front and return to its old stance of harsh criticism of American liberals; and Communist Party leaders in the United States immediately obeyed—although thousands of disillusioned members left the party as a result.

The Socialist Party of America, under the leadership of Norman Thomas, also cited the economic crisis as evidence of the failure of capitalism and sought vigorously to win public support for its own political program. Among other things, it attempted to mobilize support among the rural poor. The Southern Tenant Farmers *Southern Tenant Farmers Union* Union, supported by the party and organized by a young socialist, H. L. Mitchell, attempted to create a biracial coalition of sharecroppers, tenant farmers, and others to demand economic reform. Neither the STFU nor the party itself, however, made any real progress toward establishing socialism as a major force in American politics.

Antiradicalism was a powerful force in the 1930s. Hostility toward the Communist Party, in particular, was intense at many levels of government. Congressional committees chaired by Hamilton Fish of New York and Martin Dies of Texas investigated communist influence wherever they could find (or imagine) it. White southerners tried to drive communist organizers out of the countryside, just as growers in California and elsewhere tried (unsuccessfully) to keep communists from organizing Mexican-American and other workers.

Even so, at few times before (and few since) in American history did being part of the left seem so respectable and even conventional among workers, intellectuals, and others. Thus the 1930s witnessed an impressive, if temporary, widening of the ideological range of mainstream art and politics. The New Deal, for example, sponsored artistic work through the Works Projects Administration that was frankly challenging to the capitalist norms of the 1920s. The filmmaker Pare Lorentz, with funding from New Deal agencies, made a series of powerful documentaries—*The Plow that Broke the Plains* (1936), *The River* (1937)—that combined a celebration of New Deal programs with a harsh critique of the exploitation of people and the environment that industrial capitalism had produced.

A less confrontational grappling with the social misery of the 1930s was a remarkable book by the novelist James Agee and the photographer Walker Evans, *Let Us Now Praise Famous Men* (1941). Agee and Walker had traveled to rural Al-   *Let Us Now Praise Famous Men* abama in the mid-1930s on an assignment from *Fortune* magazine to produce an article about sharecropping and rural poverty. The long, rambling, highly emotional text that Agee produced, accompanied by extraordinary photographs of three families of white southern sharecroppers, was too long and too unconventional for *Fortune*. But the book that eventually appeared is an enduring portrait of a distressed area of what Agee called "human existence," but also a passionate tribute to the strength and even nobility of the struggling people he had come to know.

Perhaps the most successful chronicler of social conditions in the 1930s was the novelist John Steinbeck, particularly in his celebrated novel *The Grapes of Wrath*, published in 1939. In   *The Grapes of Wrath* telling the story of the Joad family, migrants from the Dust Bowl to California who encounter an unending string of calamities and failures, he offered a harsh portrait of the exploitive features of agrarian life in the West, but also a tribute to the endurance of his main characters—and to the spirit of community they represent.

THE ORDEAL OF HERBERT HOOVER

Herbert Hoover began his presidency in March 1929 believing, like most Americans, that the nation faced a bright and prosperous future. For the first six months of his administration, he attempted to expand the policies he had advocated during his eight years as secretary of commerce. The economic crisis that began before the year was out forced the president to deal with a new set of problems, but for most of the rest of his term, he continued to rely on the principles that had always governed his public life.

The Hoover Program

Hoover's first response to the Depression was to attempt to restore public confidence in the economy. "The fundamental business of this country, that is, production and distribution of commodities," he said in 1930, "is on a sound and prosperous basis." He then summoned leaders of business, labor, and agriculture to the White House and urged them to adopt a program of

Failure of Voluntary Cooperation

voluntary cooperation for recovery. He implored businessmen not to cut production or lay off workers; he talked labor leaders into forgoing demands for higher wages or better hours. But by mid-1931, economic conditions had deteriorated so much that the structure of voluntary cooperation he had erected collapsed.

Hoover also attempted to use government spending as a tool for fighting the Depression. The president proposed to Congress an increase of $423 million—a significant sum by the standards of the time—in federal public works programs, and he exhorted state and local governments to fund public construction. But the spending was not nearly enough in the face of such devastating problems. And when economic conditions worsened, he became less willing to increase spending, worrying instead about keeping the budget balanced.

Agricultural Marketing Act

Even before the stock market crash, Hoover had begun to construct a program to assist the already troubled agricultural economy. In April 1929, he proposed the Agricultural Marketing Act, which established the first major government program to help farmers maintain prices. A federally sponsored Farm Board would make loans to national marketing cooperatives or establish corporations to buy surpluses and thus raise prices. At the same time, Hoover attempted to protect American farmers from international competition by raising agricultural tariffs. The Hawley-Smoot Tariff of 1930 contained increased protection on seventy-five farm products. But neither the Agricultural Marketing Act nor the Hawley-Smoot Tariff ultimately helped American farmers significantly.

By the spring of 1931, Herbert Hoover's political position had deteriorated considerably. In the 1930 congressional elections, Democrats won control of the House and made substantial inroads in the Senate. Many Americans held the president personally to blame for the crisis and began calling the shantytowns that unemployed people established on the outskirts of cities "Hoovervilles." Democrats urged the president to support more vigorous programs of relief and public spending. Hoover, instead, seized on a slight improvement in economic conditions early in 1931 as proof that his policies were working.

International Economic Collapse

The international financial panic of the spring of 1931 destroyed the illusion that the economic crisis was coming to an end. Throughout the 1920s, European nations had depended on loans from American banks to allow them to make payments on their debts. After 1929, when they could no longer get such loans, the financial fabric of several European nations began to unravel. In May 1931, the largest bank in Austria collapsed. Over the next several months, panic gripped the financial institutions of neighboring countries. The American economy rapidly declined to new lows.

By the time Congress convened in December 1931, conditions had grown so desperate that Hoover supported a series of measures designed to keep endangered banks afloat and protect homeowners from foreclosure on their mortgages. Most important was a bill passed in January 1932 establishing the Reconstruction Finance Corporation (RFC), a government agency whose purpose was to provide federal loans to troubled banks, railroads, and other businesses. Unlike some earlier Hoover programs, the RFC operated on a large scale. In 1932, it had a budget of $1.5 billion for public works alone.

Nevertheless, the new agency failed to deal directly or forcefully enough with the real problems *Failure of the RFC* of the economy to produce any significant recovery. The RFC lent funds only to financial institutions with sufficient collateral; much of its money went to large banks and corporations. At Hoover's insistence, it helped finance only those public works projects that promised ultimately to pay for themselves (toll bridges, public housing, and others). Above all, the RFC did not have enough money to make any real impact on the Depression, and it did not even spend all the money it had.

Popular Protest

For the first several years of the Depression, most Americans were either too stunned or too confused to raise any effective protest. By the middle of 1932, however, dissident voices began to be heard.

In the summer of 1932, a group of unhappy farm owners gathered in Des Moines, Iowa, to establish a new organization: *Farmers' Holiday Association* the Farmers' Holiday Association, which endorsed the withholding of farm products from the market—in effect a farmers' strike. The strike began in August in western Iowa, spread briefly to a few neighboring areas, and succeeded in blockading several markets, but in the end it dissolved in failure.

A more celebrated protest movement emerged from American veterans. In 1924, Congress had approved the payment of a $1,000 bonus to all those who had served in World War I, the money to be paid beginning in 1945. By 1932, however, many veterans were demanding that the bonus be paid immediately. Hoover, concerned about balancing the budget, rejected their appeal. In June, more than 20,000 veterans, members of the self-proclaimed Bonus Expeditionary Force, or "Bonus Army," marched into Washington, built crude camps around the city, and promised to stay until Congress approved legislation to pay the bonus. Some of the veterans departed in July, after Congress had voted down their proposal. Many, however, remained where they were.

Their continued presence in Washington embarrassed President Hoover. Finally, in mid-July, he ordered police to clear the marchers out of several abandoned federal buildings in which they had been staying. A few marchers threw rocks at the police, and someone opened fire; two veterans fell dead. Hoover called the incident evidence of uncontrolled violence and radicalism, and he ordered the United States Army to assist the police in clearing out the buildings.

CLEARING OUT THE BONUS MARCHERS In July 1932, President Hoover ordered the Washington, D.C. police to evict the Bonus Marchers from some of the public buildings and land they had been occupying. The result was a series of pitched battles (one of them visible here), in which both veterans and police sustained injuries. Such skirmishes persuaded Hoover to call out the army to finish the job. *(Bettmann/Corbis)*

Demise of the "Bonus Army" General Douglas MacArthur, the army chief of staff, carried out the mission himself and greatly exceeded the president's orders. He led the Third Cavalry, two infantry regiments, a machine-gun detachment, and six tanks down Pennsylvania Avenue in pursuit of the Bonus Army. The veterans fled in terror. MacArthur followed them across the Anacostia River, where he ordered the soldiers to burn their tent city to the ground. More than 100 marchers were injured.

The incident served as perhaps the final blow to Hoover's already battered political standing. The Great Engineer, the personification of the optimistic days of the 1920s, had become a symbol of the nation's failure to deal effectively with its startling reversal of fortune.

The Election of 1932

As the 1932 presidential election approached, few people doubted the outcome. The Republican Party dutifully renominated Herbert Hoover for a second term of office, but few delegates believed he could win. The Democrats, in the meantime, gathered jubilantly in Chicago to nominate the governor of New York, Franklin Delano Roosevelt.

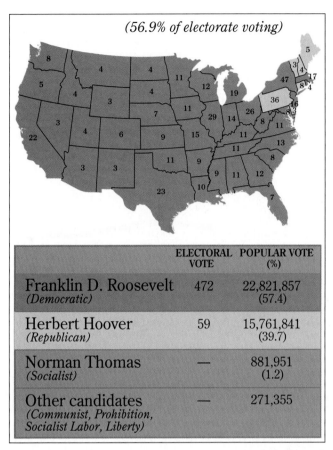

(56.9% of electorate voting)

	ELECTORAL VOTE	POPULAR VOTE (%)
Franklin D. Roosevelt *(Democratic)*	472	22,821,857 (57.4)
Herbert Hoover *(Republican)*	59	15,761,841 (39.7)
Norman Thomas *(Socialist)*	—	881,951 (1.2)
Other candidates *(Communist, Prohibition, Socialist Labor, Liberty)*	—	271,355

ELECTION OF 1932 Like the election of 1928, the election of 1932 was exceptionally one-sided. But this time, the landslide favored the Democratic candidate, Franklin Roosevelt, who overwhelmed Herbert Hoover in all regions of the country except New England. Roosevelt obviously benefited primarily from popular disillusionment with Hoover's response to the Great Depression. ◆ *But what characteristics of Roosevelt himself contributed to his victory?*

For an interactive version of this map go to www.mhhe.com/unfinishednation4ch25maps

Roosevelt had been a well-known figure in the party for many years already. A Hudson Valley aristocrat, a distant cousin of Theodore Roosevelt, and a handsome, charming young man, he progressed rapidly: from a seat in the New York State legislature to a position as assistant secretary of the navy under Woodrow Wilson during World War I to his party's vice presidential nomination in 1920 on the ill-fated ticket with James M. Cox. Less than a year later, he was stricken with polio. Although he never regained use of his legs (and could walk only by using crutches and braces), he built up sufficient physical strength to return to politics in 1928. When Al Smith received the Democratic nomination for president that year, Roosevelt was elected to succeed him as governor. In 1930, he easily won reelection.

Franklin Delano Roosevelt

Roosevelt worked no miracles in New York, but he did initiate enough positive programs of government assistance to be able to present himself as a more energetic and imaginative leader than Hoover. In national politics, he avoided divisive cultural issues and emphasized the economic grievances that most Democrats shared. He was able as a result to assemble a broad coalition within the party and win his party's nomination. In a dramatic break with tradition, he flew to Chicago to address the convention in person and accept the nomination. In the course of his acceptance speech, Roosevelt aroused the delegates with his ringing promise: "I pledge you, I pledge myself, to a new deal for the American people." Neither then nor in the subsequent campaign did Roosevelt give much indication of what that program would be. But Herbert Hoover's unpopularity virtually ensured Roosevelt's election.

FDR Elected

Roosevelt won by a landslide. He received 57.4 percent of the popular vote to Hoover's 39.7. In the electoral college, the result was even more overwhelming. Hoover carried Delaware, Pennsylvania, Connecticut, Vermont, New Hampshire, and Maine. Roosevelt won everything else. Democrats won majorities in both houses of Congress. It was a convincing mandate, but it was not yet clear what Roosevelt intended to do with it.

The "Interregnum"

The period between the election and the inauguration (which in the early 1930s lasted more than four months) was a season of growing economic crisis. Presidents-elect traditionally do not involve themselves directly in government. But in a series of brittle exchanges with Roosevelt, Hoover tried to exact from the president-elect a pledge to maintain policies of economic orthodoxy. Roosevelt genially refused.

Banking Collapse

In February, only a month before the inauguration, a new crisis developed when the collapse of the American banking system suddenly and rapidly accelerated. Depositors were withdrawing their money in panic; and one bank after another was closing its doors and declaring bankruptcy. Hoover again asked Roosevelt to give prompt public assurances that there would be no tinkering with the currency, no heavy borrowing, no unbalancing of the budget. Roosevelt again refused.

March 4, 1933, was, therefore, a day of both economic crisis and considerable personal bitterness. On that morning, Herbert Hoover rode glumly down Pennsylvania Avenue with a beaming, buoyant Franklin Roosevelt, who would shortly be sworn in as the thirty-second president of the United States.

THE CHANGING OF THE GUARD Long before the event actually occurred, Peter Arno of the
New Yorker magazine drew this image of Franklin D. Roosevelt and Herbert Hoover traveling
together to the Capitol for Roosevelt's inauguration. It predicted with remarkable accuracy the
mood of the uncomfortable ride—Hoover glum and uncommunicative, Roosevelt buoyant and
smiling. This was to have been the magazine's cover for the week of the inauguration, but after
an attempted assassination of the president-elect several weeks earlier in Florida (in which the
mayor of Chicago was killed), the editors decided to substitute a more subdued drawing.
(FDR & Hoover by Peter Arno, New Yorker, *1933. Franklin Delano Roosevelt Library)*

CONCLUSION
❧

The Great Depression changed many things in American life. It created unemployment on a scale never before experienced in the nation's history. It put enormous pressures on families, on communities, on state and local governments, and ultimately on Washington—which during the innovative but ultimately failed presidency of Herbert Hoover was unable to produce policies capable of dealing effectively with the crisis. In the nation's politics and culture, there were strong currents of radicalism and protest; and many middle-class Americans came to fear that a revolution might be approaching.

In reality, while the Great Depression shook much of American society and culture, it actually toppled very little. The capitalist system survived, damaged for a time but never truly threatened. The values of materialism and personal responsibility were shaken, but never overturned. The American people in the 1930s were more receptive than they had been in the 1920s to evocations of community, generosity, and the dignity of common people. They were more open to experiments in government and business and even private lives than they had been in earlier years. But for most Americans, belief in the "American way of life" remained strong throughout the long years of economic despair.

FOR FURTHER REFERENCE
❧

Donald Worster scathingly indicts agricultural capitalism for its destruction of the plains environment in *Dust Bowl: The Southern Plains in the 1930s* (1979). In *The Great Depression: Delayed Recovery and Economic Change in America, 1929–1939* (1987), Michael Bernstein argues that we should ask not so much why the economy crashed in 1929 but rather why the expected recovery from the crash was so slow. Richard Pells, *Radical Visions and American Dreams: Culture and Social Thought in the Depression Years* (1973) is an important survey of the cultural and intellectual history of the 1930s. Studs Terkel, *Hard Times* (1970) is an excellent oral history of the Depression. Susan Ware analyzes the effect of the Great Depression on women in *Holding Their Own: American Women in the 1930s* (1982). The Communist Party's most popular period in the United States is the subject of Harvey Klehr's *The Heyday of American Communism: The Depression Decade* (1984) and, from quite different viewpoints, Robin D. G. Kelley, *Hammer and Hoe: Alabama Communists During the Great Depression* (1990) and Michael Denning, *The Cultural Front: The Laboring of American Culture in the Twentieth Century* (1997). Joan Hoff Wilson, *Herbert Hoover: Forgotten Progressive* (1975) argues that

President Hoover was in many ways a surprisingly progressive thinker about the American social order.

The Great Depression (1993), a multipart film by Blackside Productions, is an eloquent picture of many aspects of the depression decade. *Union Maids* (1997) is a vivid film history of women organizing in the 1930s. *The Lemon Grove Incident* (1985) is a film providing a rare glimpse of Mexican-American civil rights activism over school integration in the early 1930s.

For quizzes, Internet resources, references to additional books and films, and more, consult this book's Online Learning Center site at www.mhhe.com/unfinishednation4.

WPA POSTER, 1930S The Works Progress Administration, which this striking poster celebrates, was the New Deal's most prominent experiment in work relief. In addition to providing jobs for unemployed farmers and industrial workers (as depicted here), it created programs to assist writers, artists, actors, and others. *(The Library of Congress)*

TIME LINE

1933	1934	1935	
"First New Deal" legislation	American Liberty League founded	Supreme Court invalidates NRA	
Prohibition ends	Long's Share-Our-Wealth Society established	"Second New Deal" legislation, including Social Security and Wagner Acts	
		Lewis breaks with AFL	

❧

CHAPTER TWENTY-SIX

THE NEW DEAL

Launching the New Deal
The New Deal in Transition
The New Deal in Disarray
Limits and Legacies of the New Deal

D uring his twelve years in office Franklin Roosevelt became more central to the life of the nation than any president had ever been. Most important, his administration constructed a series of programs that permanently altered the federal government and its relationship to society. By the end of the 1930s, the New Deal (as the Roosevelt administration was called) had not ended the Great Depression; only World War II did that. But it had created many of the broad outlines of the political world we know today.

LAUNCHING THE NEW DEAL

❧

Roosevelt's first task upon taking office was to alleviate the panic that was creating chaos in the financial system. He did so in part by force of personality and in part by very rapidly constructing an ambitious and diverse program of legislation.

	1936	1937	1938	1939	
	Supreme Court invalidates Agricultural Adjustment Act	Roosevelt's "Court-packing" plan	Fair Labor Standards Act	Marian Anderson sings at Lincoln Memorial	
	CIO established	Supreme Court upholds Wagner Act			
	Roosevelt reelected	Severe recession			
	Sit-down strikes				

Restoring Confidence

Much of Roosevelt's early success was a result of his ebullient personality. He was the first president to make regular use of the radio; and his friendly "fireside chats," during which he explained in simple terms his programs and plans to the people, helped build public confidence in the administration. But Roosevelt could not rely on image alone. On March 6, two days after taking office, he issued a proclamation closing all American banks for four days until Congress could meet in special session to consider

"Bank Holiday" Declared   banking reform legislation. So great was the panic about bank failures that the "bank holiday," as the president euphemistically described it, created a general sense of relief and hope.

Three days later, Roosevelt sent to Congress the Emergency Banking Act, a generally conservative bill designed primarily to protect the larger banks from being dragged down by the weakness of smaller ones. The bill provided for Treasury Department inspection of all banks before they would be allowed to reopen, for federal assistance to some troubled institutions, and for a thorough reorganization of those banks in the greatest difficulty. Congress passed the bill within a few hours of its introduction. Whatever else the new law accomplished, it helped dispel the panic.

Emergency Banking Act   Three-quarters of the banks in the Federal Reserve system reopened within the next three days, and $1 billion in hoarded currency and gold flowed back into them within a month. The immediate banking crisis was over.

On the morning after passage of the Emergency Banking Act, Roosevelt sent to Congress another measure—the Economy Act—designed to convince the public (and especially the business community) that the federal government was in safe, responsible hands. The act proposed to balance the federal budget by cutting the salaries of government employees and reducing pensions to veterans by as much as 15 percent. Like the banking bill, this one passed through Congress almost instantly. Later that spring, Roosevelt signed the Glass-Steagall Act of June 1933, which gave the government authority to curb irresponsible speculation by banks. More important, perhaps, it established the Federal Deposit Insurance Corporation, which guaranteed all bank deposits up to $2,500. In other words, even if a bank should fail, small depositors would be able to recover their money. (Later, in 1935, Congress passed another major banking act that transferred much of the authority once wielded by the regional Federal Reserve banks to the Federal Reserve Board in Washington.)

To restore confidence in the stock market, Congress passed the so-called Truth in Securities Act of 1933, requiring corporations issuing new securities to provide full and accurate information about them to the public.

Securities and Exchange Commission   Another act, of June 1934, established the Securities and Exchange Commission (SEC) to police the stock market. Roosevelt also signed a bill to legalize

THE RADIO PRESIDENT Franklin D. Roosevelt was the first American president to master the use of radio. Beginning in his first days in office, he regularly bypassed the newspapers (many of which were hostile to him) and communicated directly with the people through his famous "fireside chats." He is shown here speaking in 1938, urging communities to continue to provide work relief for the unemployed. *(Franklin Delano Roosevelt Library)*

the manufacture and sale of beer with a 3.2 percent alcohol content—an interim measure pending the repeal of prohibition, for which a constitutional amendment (the Twenty-first) was already in process. The amendment was ratified later in 1933.

Agricultural Adjustment

These initial actions were largely stopgaps, to buy time for more comprehensive programs. The first was the Agricultural Adjustment Act, which Congress passed in May 1933. Under the provisions of the act, producers of seven basic commodities (wheat, cotton, corn, hogs, rice, tobacco, and dairy products) would decide on production limits for their crops. The government, through the Agricultural Adjustment Administration (AAA), would then tell individual farmers how much they should produce and would pay them subsidies for leaving some of their land idle. A tax on food processing (for example, the milling of wheat) would provide the funds for the new payments. Farm prices were to be subsidized up to the point of parity.

The AAA helped bring about a rise in prices for farm commodities in the years after 1933. Gross farm income increased by half in the first three years of the New Deal, and the agricultural economy as a whole emerged from the 1930s much more stable and prosperous than it had been in many years. The AAA did, however, favor larger farmers over smaller ones. By distributing pay- *Large Farmers Favored* ments to landowners, not those who worked the land, the government did little to discourage planters who were reducing their acreage from evicting tenants and sharecroppers and firing field hands.

In January 1936, the Supreme Court struck down the crucial provisions of the Agricultural Adjustment Act, arguing that the government had no constitutional authority to require farmers to limit production. But within a few weeks the administration had secured passage of new legislation (the Soil Conservation and Domestic Allotment Act), which permitted the government to pay farmers to reduce production so as to "conserve soil," prevent erosion, and accomplish other secondary goals.

Farm Security Administration   The administration launched several efforts to assist poor farmers as well. The Resettlement Administration, established in 1935, and its successor, the Farm Security Administration, created in 1937, provided loans to help farmers cultivating submarginal soil to relocate to better lands. But the programs moved no more than a few thousand farmers. More effective was the Rural Electrification Administration, created in 1935, which worked to make electric power available for the first time to thousands of farmers through utility cooperatives.

Industrial Recovery

Ever since 1931, leaders of the United States Chamber of Commerce and many others had been urging the government to adopt an antideflation scheme that would permit trade associations to cooperate in stabilizing prices within their industries. Existing antitrust laws clearly forbade such practices, and Herbert Hoover had refused to endorse suspension of the laws. The Roosevelt administration was more receptive. In exchange for relaxing antitrust provisions, however, New Dealers insisted on other provisions. Business leaders would have to make important concessions to labor—recognize the workers' right to bargain collectively through unions—to ensure that the incomes of workers would rise along with prices. And to help create jobs and increase consumer buying power, the administration added a major program of public works spending. The result of these and many other impulses was the National Industrial Recovery Act, which Congress passed in June 1933.

National Recovery Administration Established   At its center was a new federal agency, the National Recovery Administration (NRA), under the direction of the flamboyant and energetic Hugh S. Johnson. Johnson called on every business establishment in the nation to accept a temporary "blanket code": a minimum wage of between 30 and 40 cents an hour, a maximum workweek of thirty-five to forty hours, and the abolition of child labor. At the same time, Johnson negotiated another, more specific set of codes with leaders of the nation's major industries. These industrial codes set floors below which no company would lower prices or wages in its search for a competitive advantage, and they included provisions for maintaining employment and production. He quickly won agreements from almost every major industry in the country.

SALUTING THE BLUE EAGLE Several thousand San Francisco schoolchildren assembled on a baseball field in 1933 to form the symbol of the National Recovery Administration: an eagle clutching a cogwheel (to symbolize industry) and a thunderbolt (to symbolize energy). This display is evidence of the widespread (if brief) popular enthusiasm the NRA produced. NRA administrators drew from their memories of World War I Liberty Loan drives and tried to establish the Blue Eagle as a symbol of patriotic commitment to recovery. *(Bettmann/Corbis)*

From the beginning, however, the NRA encountered serious difficulties. The codes themselves were hastily and often poorly written. Large producers consistently dominated the code-writing process and ensured that the new regulations would work to their advantage and to the disadvantage of smaller firms. And the codes at times did more than simply set floors under prices; they actively and artificially raised them—sometimes to levels higher than the market could sustain.

Other NRA goals did not progress as quickly as the efforts to raise prices. Section 7(a) of the National Industrial Recovery Act promised workers the right to form unions and engage in collective bargaining and encouraged many workers to join unions for the first time. But Section 7(a) contained no enforcement mechanisms. The Public Works Administration (PWA), established to administer the National Industrial Recovery Act's spending programs, only gradually allowed the $3.3 billion in public works funds to trickle out.

Section 7(a)

Perhaps the clearest evidence of the NRA's failure was that industrial production actually declined in the months after the agency's establishment despite the rise in prices that the codes had helped to create. By the spring of 1934, the NRA was besieged by criticism. That fall, Roosevelt pressured Johnson to resign

Failure of the NRA

and established a new board of directors to oversee the NRA. Then in 1935, the Supreme Court intervened.

In 1935, a case came before the Court involving alleged NRA code violations by the Schechter brothers, who operated a wholesale poultry business confined to Brooklyn, New York. The Court ruled unanimously that the Schechters were not engaged in interstate commerce (and thus not subject to federal regulation) and, further, that Congress had unconstitutionally delegated legislative power to the president to draft the NRA codes. The justices struck down the legislation establishing the agency. Roosevelt denounced the justices for their "horse-and-buggy" interpretation of the interstate commerce clause. He was rightly concerned, for the reasoning in the Schechter case threatened many other New Deal programs as well.

Regional Planning

The AAA and the NRA largely reflected the beliefs of New Dealers who favored economic planning but wanted private interests (farmers or business leaders) to dominate the planning process. Other reformers believed that the government itself should be the chief planning agent in the economy. Their most conspicuous success was an unprecedented experiment in

Tennessee Valley Authority   regional planning: the Tennessee Valley Authority (TVA).

Progressive reformers had agitated for years for public development of the nation's water resources as a source of cheap electric power. In particular, they had urged completion of a great dam at Muscle Shoals on the Tennessee River in Alabama—a dam begun during World War I but left unfinished when the war ended. But opposition from the utilities companies had been too powerful to overcome.

In 1932, however, one of the great utility empires—that of the electricity magnate Samuel Insull—collapsed spectacularly, amid widely publicized exposés of corruption. Hostility to the utilities soon grew so intense that the companies were no longer able to block the public power movement. The result was legislation supported by the president and enacted by Congress in May 1933 creating the Tennessee Valley Authority. The TVA was authorized to complete the dam at Muscle Shoals and build others in the region, and to generate and sell electricity from them to the public at reasonable rates. It was also intended to be an agent for a comprehensive redevelopment of the entire region: for encouraging the growth of local industries, for supervising a substantial program of reforestation, and for helping farmers improve productivity.

Opposition by conservatives ultimately blocked many of the ambitious social planning projects proposed by the more visionary TVA administra-

Benefits of the TVA   tors, but the Authority revitalized the region in numerous ways. It improved water transportation. It virtually eliminated flooding in the region. It provided electricity to thou-

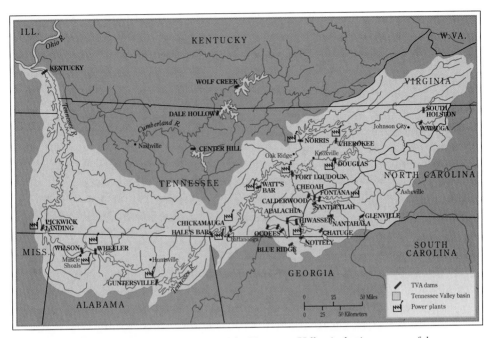

THE TENNESSEE VALLEY AUTHORITY The Tennessee Valley Authority was one of the largest experiments in government-funded public works and regional planning in American history to that point. The federal government had helped fund many projects in its history—canals, turnpikes, railroads, bridges, dams, and others. But never before had it undertaken a project of such great scope, and never before had it maintained such close control and ownership over the public works it helped create. This map illustrates the broad reach of the TVA within the Tennessee Valley region, which spanned seven states. TVA dams throughout the region helped control floods and also provided a source for hydroelectric power, which the government sold to consumers. Note the dam near Muscle Shoals, Alabama, in the bottom left of the map. It was begun during World War I, and efforts to revive it in the 1920s helped create the momentum that produced the TVA. ◆ *Why were progressives so eager to see the government enter the business of hydroelectric power in the 1920s?*

sands who had never before had it. Throughout the country, largely because of the "yardstick" provided by the TVA's cheap production of electricity, private power rates declined. Even so, the Tennessee Valley remained a generally impoverished region despite the TVA's efforts.

The Growth of Federal Relief

The Roosevelt administration did not consider relief to the unemployed its most important task, but it recognized the necessity of doing something to help impoverished Americans survive until the government could revive the economy to the point where relief might not be necessary. Among Roosevelt's first acts as president was the establishment of the Federal Emergency Relief Administration (FERA), which provided cash grants to states to prop up

FERA

bankrupt relief agencies. To administer the program, he chose the director of the New York State relief agency, Harry Hopkins. Both Hopkins and Roosevelt had misgivings about establishing a government "dole." They felt somewhat more comfortable with another form of government assistance: work relief. Thus when it became clear that the FERA grants were not enough, the administration established a second program: the Civil Works Administration (CWA). Between November 1933 and April 1934, it put more than 4 million people to work on temporary projects. Some of the projects were of lasting value, such as the construction of roads, schools, and parks; others were little more than make-work. To Hopkins, however, the important thing was pumping money into an economy badly in need of it and providing assistance to people with nowhere else to turn.

Civilian Conservation Corps   Roosevelt's favorite relief project was the Civilian Conservation Corps (CCC). The CCC created camps in national parks and forests and in other rural and wilderness settings. There young unemployed men from the cities worked in a semimilitary environment on such projects as planting trees, building reservoirs, developing parks, and improving agricultural irrigation.

Mortgage relief was a pressing need for millions of farm owners and homeowners. The Farm Credit Administration, which within two years refinanced one-fifth of all farm mortgages in the United States, was one response to that problem. The Frazier-Lemke Farm Bankruptcy Act of 1933 was another. It enabled some farmers to regain their land even after the foreclosure of their mortgages. Despite such efforts, however, 25 percent of all American farm owners had lost their land by 1934. Homeowners were similarly troubled, and in June 1933 the administration established the Home Owners' Loan Corporation, which by 1936 had refinanced the mortgages of more than 1 million householders. A year later, Congress established the Federal Housing Administration to insure mortgages for new construction and home repairs.

THE NEW DEAL IN TRANSITION

Seldom has an American president enjoyed such remarkable popularity as Franklin Roosevelt did during his first two years in office. But by early 1935, the New Deal found itself the target of fierce public criticism. In the spring of 1935, partly in response to these growing attacks, Roosevelt launched an ambitious new program of legislation that has often been called the "Second New Deal."

Critics of the New Deal

Some of the most strident attacks on the New Deal came from critics on the right. In August 1934, a group of the most fervent (and wealthiest) Roosevelt opponents, led by members of the Du Pont family, formed the

"AN ATTACK ON THE NEW DEAL" This cartoon by William Gropper appeared in *Vanity Fair* in 1935 to illustrate a long excerpt from an anti–New Deal editorial that had appeared a few weeks before in the Republican newspaper, the New York *Herald Tribune*. The cartoon echoes the newspaper's references to Jonathan Swift's famous satire, *Gulliver's Travels*. In this case, Gulliver is Uncle Sam, and the Lilliputians who tie him down with a thousand tiny cords are New Deal agencies and laws. "Here is a giant if there ever was one," the *Herald Tribune* wrote, "the most powerful nation the world has ever seen. It has the makings of good times, [but] it does not make them. Why? Because the Lilliputians of the New Deal will not let it. These busy little folk cannot bear the thought of letting the great giant, America, escape." *(Courtesy Vanity Fair © 1935 (renewed 1963, 1991) by The Condé Nast Publications, Inc.)*

American Liberty League, designed specifically to arouse public opposition to the New Deal's "dictatorial" policies and its supposed attacks on free enterprise. But the new organization was never able to expand its constituency much beyond the northern industrialists who had founded it.

American Liberty League Established

Roosevelt's critics on the far left also managed to produce alarm among some supporters of the administration, but like the conservatives, they proved to have only limited strength. The Communist Party, the Socialist Party, and other radical and semiradical organizations were at times harshly critical of the New Deal. But they too failed ever to attract genuine mass support.

More menacing to the New Deal than either the far right or the far left was a group of dissident political movements that defied easy ideological classification. Some gained substantial public support within particular states and regions. And three men succeeded in mobilizing genuinely national followings. Dr. Francis E. Townsend, an elderly California physician, rose from obscurity to lead a movement of more than 5 million members with his plan for federal pensions for the elderly. According to the Townsend Plan, all Americans over the age of sixty would receive monthly government pensions of $200, provided they retired (thus freeing jobs for younger, unemployed Americans) and spent the money in full each month (which would pump needed funds into the economy). By 1935, the Townsend Plan had attracted the support of many older men and women.

Dr. Francis Townsend

Father Charles E. Coughlin, a Catholic priest in the Detroit suburb of Royal Oak, Michigan, achieved even greater renown through his weekly sermons broadcast nationally over the radio. He proposed a series of monetary reforms—remonetization of silver, issuing of greenbacks, and nationalization of the banking system—that he insisted would restore prosperity and ensure economic justice. At first a warm supporter of Franklin Roosevelt, by late 1934 Coughlin had become disheartened by what he claimed was the president's failure to deal harshly enough with the "money powers." In the spring of 1935, he established his own political organization, the National Union for Social Justice.

Father Charles Coughlin

Most alarming of all to the administration was the growing national popularity of Senator Huey P. Long of Louisiana. Long had risen to power in his home state through his strident attacks on the banks, oil companies, and utilities and on the conservative political oligarchy allied with them. Elected governor in 1928, he launched an assault on his opponents so thorough and forceful that they were soon left with virtually no political power whatsoever. But he also maintained the overwhelming support of the Louisiana electorate, in part because of his flamboyant personality and in part because of his solid record of conventional progressive accomplishments: building roads, schools, and hospitals; revising the tax codes; distributing free textbooks; lowering utility rates. Barred by law from succeeding himself as governor, he ran in 1930 for a seat in the United States Senate and won easily.

Long, like Coughlin, supported Franklin Roosevelt for president in 1932. But within six months of Roosevelt's inauguration he had broken with the president. As an alternative to the New Deal, he advocated a drastic program of wealth redistribution, a program he ultimately named the Share-Our-Wealth Plan. The government, he claimed, could end the Depression easily by using the tax system to confiscate the surplus riches of the wealthiest men and women in America and distribute these surpluses to the rest of the population. That would, he claimed, allow the govern-

Long's Share-Our-Wealth Plan

ment to guarantee every family a minimum "homestead" of $5,000 and an annual wage of $2,500. In 1934, Long established his own national organization: the Share-Our-Wealth Society, which soon attracted a large following through much of the nation. A poll by the Democratic National Committee in the spring of 1935 disclosed that Long might attract more than 10 percent of the vote if he ran as a third-party candidate, possibly enough to tip a close election to the Republicans.

Members of the Roosevelt administration considered dissident movements—and the broad popular discontent they represented—a genuine threat to the president. An increasing number of advisers were warning Roosevelt that he would have to do something dramatic to counter their strength.

The "Second New Deal"

Roosevelt launched the so-called Second New Deal in the spring of 1935 in response both to the growing political pressures and to the continuing economic crisis. The new proposals represented, if not a new direction, at least a shift in the emphasis of New Deal policy. Perhaps the most conspicuous change was in the administration's attitude toward big business. Symbolically at least, the president was now willing to attack corporate interests openly. In March, for example, he proposed to Congress an act designed to break up the great utility holding companies. The Holding Company Act of 1935 was the *Holding Company Act* result, although furious lobbying by the utilities led to amendments that sharply limited its effects.

Equally alarming to affluent Americans was a series of tax reforms proposed by the president in 1935. Apparently designed to undercut the appeal of Huey Long's Share-Our-Wealth Plan, the Roosevelt proposals called for establishing the highest and most progressive peacetime tax rates in history—although the actual impact of these rates was limited.

The Supreme Court decision in 1935 to strike down the National Industrial Recovery Act also invalidated Section 7(a) of the act, which had guaranteed workers the right to organize and bargain collectively. A group of progressives in Congress led by Senator Robert E. Wagner of New York introduced what became the National Labor *National Labor Relations Board* Relations Act of 1935. The new law, popularly known as the Wagner Act, provided workers with a crucial enforcement mechanism missing from the 1933 law: the National Labor Relations Board (NLRB), which would have power to compel employers to recognize and bargain with legitimate unions. The president was not entirely happy with the bill, but he signed it anyway. That was in large part because American workers themselves had by 1935 become so important and vigorous a force that Roosevelt realized his own political future would depend in part on responding to their demands.

Labor Militancy

The emergence of a powerful trade union movement in the 1930s occurred partly in response to government efforts to enhance the power of unions, but it was also a result of the increased militancy of American workers and their leaders. During the 1920s, most workers had displayed relatively little militancy. In the 1930s, however, many of the factors that had impeded militancy vanished or grew weaker. Business leaders and industrialists lost (at least temporarily) the ability to control government policies. Equally important, new and more militant labor organizations emerged.

The American Federation of Labor remained committed to the idea of the craft union: organizing workers on the basis of their skills. But that concept had little to offer unskilled laborers, who now constituted the bulk of the industrial work force. During the 1930s, therefore, a newer concept of labor organization challenged the craft union ideal: industrial unionism. Advocates of this approach argued that all workers in a particular industry should be organized in a single union, regardless of what functions the workers performed. All autoworkers should be in a single automobile union; all steelworkers should be in a single steel union. United in this way, workers would greatly increase their power.

Leaders of the AFL craft unions for the most part opposed the new concept. But industrial unionism found a number of important advocates, most prominent among them John L. Lewis, the leader of the United Mine Workers. At first, Lewis and his allies attempted to work within the AFL, but friction between the new industrial organizations Lewis was promoting and the older craft unions grew rapidly. At the 1935 AFL convention, Lewis became embroiled in a series of angry confrontations with craft union leaders before finally walking out. A few weeks later, he created the Committee on Industrial Organization.

CIO Founded

When the AFL expelled the new committee and all the industrial unions it represented, Lewis renamed the committee the Congress of Industrial Organizations (CIO) and became its first president.

The CIO expanded the constituency of the labor movement. It was more receptive to women and to blacks than the AFL had been, in part because CIO organizing drives targeted previously unorganized industries (textiles, laundries, tobacco factories, and others) where women and minorities constituted much of the work force. The CIO was also more militant than the AFL. By the time of the 1936 schism, it was already engaged in major organizing battles in the automobile and steel industries.

Organizing Battles

Out of several competing auto unions, the United Auto Workers (UAW) was gradually emerging preeminent in the early and mid-1930s. But although it was gaining recruits, it was making little progress in winning recognition from the corporations. In December 1936, however, au-

toworkers employed a controversial and effective new technique for challenging corporate opposition: the sit-down strike.   *Sit-down Strike*
Employees in several General Motors plants in
Detroit simply sat down inside the plants, refusing either to work or to leave, thus preventing the company from using strikebreakers. The tactic spread to other locations, and by February 1937 strikers had occupied seventeen GM plants. The strikers ignored court orders and local police efforts to force them to vacate the buildings. When Michigan's governor refused to call up the National Guard to clear out the strikers, and when the federal government also refused to intervene on behalf of employers, General Motors relented. In February 1937 it became the first major manufacturer to recognize the UAW; other automobile companies soon did the same.

In the steel industry, the battle for unionization was less easily won. In 1936, the Steel Workers' Organizing Committee (SWOC; later the United Steelworkers of America) began a major organizing drive involving thousands of workers and frequent, at times bitter, strikes. In March 1937, to the surprise of almost everyone, United States Steel, the giant of the industry, recognized the union rather than risk a costly strike. But the smaller companies (known collectively as "Little Steel") were less accommodating. On Memorial Day 1937, a group of striking workers from Republic Steel gathered with their families for a picnic and demonstration in South Chicago. When they attempted to march peacefully (and legally) toward the steel plant, police opened fire on them. Ten demonstrators were killed; another ninety were wounded. Despite a public outcry   *"Memorial Day Massacre"*
against the "Memorial Day Massacre," the harsh
tactics of Little Steel companies succeeded. The 1937 strike failed.

But the victory of Little Steel was one of the last gasps of the kind of brutal strikebreaking that had proved so effective in the past. In 1937 alone, there were 4,720 strikes—over 80 percent of   *Rapid Union Growth*
them settled in favor of the unions. By the end of
the year, more than 8 million workers were members of unions recognized as official bargaining units by employers (as compared with 3 million in 1932). By 1941, that number had expanded to 10 million and included the workers of Little Steel, whose employers had finally recognized the SWOC.

Social Security

From the first moments of the New Deal, important members of the administration had been lobbying for a system of federally sponsored social insurance for the elderly and the unemployed. In 1935, Roosevelt gave public support to what became the Social Security Act, which Congress passed the same year. It established several distinct programs. For the elderly, there were two types of assistance. Those who were presently destitute could receive up to $15 a month in federal assistance. More important for the future, many Americans presently working were incorporated into a pension system, to which they and their employers would contribute through a payroll tax; it would provide them with an income on retirement. Pension payments would not begin until 1942 and even then would provide only $10 to $85 a month to recipients. And broad categories of workers (including domestic servants and agricultural laborers) were excluded from the program. But the act was a crucial first step in building the nation's most important social program for the elderly.

In addition, the Social Security Act created a system of unemployment insurance, which employers alone would finance. It also established a system of federal aid to people with disabilities and a program of aid to dependent children.

The framers of the Social Security Act wanted to create a system of "insurance," not "welfare." And the largest programs (old-age pensions and unemployment insurance) were in many ways similar to private insurance programs. But the act also provided considerable direct assistance based on need—to the elderly poor, to those with disabilities, to dependent children and their mothers. These groups were widely perceived to be small and genuinely unable to support themselves. But in later generations the programs for these groups would expand until they assumed dimensions that the planners of Social Security had not foreseen.

Need-based Direct Assistance

New Directions in Relief

Social Security was designed primarily to fulfill long-range goals. But millions of unemployed Americans had immediate needs. To help them, the Roosevelt administration established in 1935 the Works Progress Administration (WPA). Like the Civil Works Administration and other earlier efforts, the WPA established a system of work relief for the unemployed. But it was much bigger than the earlier agencies.

Harry Hopkins

Under the direction of Harry Hopkins, the WPA was responsible for building or renovating 110,000 public buildings and for constructing almost 600 airports, more than 500,000 miles of roads, and over 100,000 bridges. In the process, the WPA kept an average of 2.1 million workers employed and pumped needed money into the economy.

The WPA also displayed remarkable flexibility and imagination. The Federal Writers Project of the WPA, for example, gave unemployed writers a chance to do their work and receive a government salary. The Federal Arts Project, similarly, helped painters, sculptors, and others to continue their careers. The Federal Music Project and the Federal Theater Project oversaw the production of concerts and plays, creating work for unemployed musicians, actors, and directors. Other relief agencies emerged alongside the WPA. The National Youth Administration (NYA) provided work and scholarship assistance to high-school and college-age men and women. The Emergency Housing Division of the Public Works Administration began federal sponsorship of public housing.

WPA MURAL ART The Federal Arts Project of the Works Progress Administration commissioned an impressive series of public murals from the artists it employed. Many of these murals adorned post offices, libraries, and other public buildings constructed by the WPA. William Gropper, the same artist who drew the cartoon on p. 685, painted *Construction of the Dam*, a detail of which is seen here, is typical of much of the mural art of the 1930s in its celebration of the workingman. Workers are depicted in heroic poses, laboring in unison to complete a great public project. *(Detail,* Construction of the Dam *by William Gropper (Mural Study, Department of the Interior), c. 1937. Oil on canvas, overall: 27¼ × 87¼ inches. Smithsonian American Art Museum, Washington, DC/Art Resource, NY)*

The new welfare system dealt with men and women in very different ways. For men, the government concentrated mainly on work relief—on such programs as the CCC, the CWA, and the WPA. The principal government aid to women was not work relief but cash assistance—most notably through the Aid to Dependent Children program of Social Security, which was designed largely to assist single mothers. This disparity in treatment reflected a widespread assumption that men should constitute the bulk of the paid work force. In fact, millions of women were already employed by the 1930s.

The 1936 "Referendum"

By the middle of 1936—with the economy visibly reviving—there could be little doubt that Roosevelt would win a second term. The Republican Party nominated the moderate governor of Kansas, Alf M. Landon, who waged a generally pallid cam-

Alf Landon

paign. Roosevelt's dissident challengers now appeared powerless. One reason was the violent death of their most effective leader, Huey Long, who was assassinated in Louisiana in September 1935. Another reason was the ill-fated alliance among Father Coughlin, Dr. Townsend, and Gerald L. K. Smith (an intemperate henchman of Huey Long), who joined forces that summer to establish a new political movement—the Union Party, which nominated an undistinguished North Dakota congressman, William Lemke.

The result was the greatest landslide in American history to that point. Roosevelt polled just under 61 percent of the vote to Landon's 36 percent and carried every state except Maine and Vermont. The Democrats increased their already large majorities in both houses of Congress.

Electoral Realignment   The election results demonstrated the party realignment that the New Deal had produced. The Democrats now controlled a broad coalition of western and southern farmers, the urban working classes, the poor and unemployed, and the black communities of northern cities, as well as traditional progressives and committed new liberals—a coalition that constituted a substantial majority of the electorate. It would be decades before the Republican Party could again create a lasting majority coalition of its own.

THE NEW DEAL IN DISARRAY

Roosevelt emerged from the 1936 election at the zenith of his popularity. Within months, however, the New Deal was mired in serious new difficulties.

The Court Fight

The 1936 mandate, Franklin Roosevelt believed, made it possible for him to do something about the Supreme Court. No program of reform, he had become convinced, could long survive the conservative justices, who had already struck down the NRA and the AAA.

In February 1937, Roosevelt sent a surprise message to Capitol Hill proposing a general overhaul of the federal court system; included among the many provisions was one to add up to six new justices to the Supreme Court. The courts were "overworked," he claimed, and needed additional manpower and younger blood to enable them to cope with their increasing burdens. But Roosevelt's real purpose was to give himself the opportunity to appoint new, liberal justices and change the ideological balance of the Court.

Conservatives were outraged at the "Court-packing plan," and even *"Court-Packing Plan"*   many Roosevelt supporters were disturbed by what *Defeated*   they considered evidence of the president's hunger for power. Still, Roosevelt might well have persuaded Congress to approve at least a compromise measure had not the Supreme Court itself intervened. Of the nine justices, three reliably supported the New Deal, and four reliably opposed it. Of the remaining two, Chief Justice Charles Evans Hughes often sided with the progressives and Associate Justice Owen J. Roberts usually voted with the conservatives. On March 29, 1937, Roberts, Hughes, and the three progressive justices voted together to uphold a state minimum-wage law—in the case of *West Coast Hotel* v. *Parrish*—thus reversing a 5-to-4 decision of the previous year invalidating a similar law. Two weeks later, again by a 5-to-4 margin, the Court upheld the Wagner Act, and in May it validated the Social Security Act. Whatever the reasons for the decisions, the Court's newly moderate position made the Court-packing bill seem unnecessary. Congress ultimately defeated it.

On one level, Franklin Roosevelt had achieved a victory. The Court was no longer an obstacle to New Deal reforms. But the Court-packing episode did lasting political damage to the administration. From 1937 on, southern Democrats and other conservatives voted against Roosevelt's measures much more often than they had in the past.

Retrenchment and Recession

By the summer of 1937, the national income, which had dropped from $82 billion in 1929 to $40 billion in 1932, had risen to nearly $72 billion. Other economic indices showed similar advances. Roosevelt seized on these improvements as a justification for trying to balance the federal budget. Between January and August 1937, for example, he cut the WPA in half, laying off 1.5 million relief workers. A few weeks later, the fragile boom collapsed. The index of industrial production dropped from 117 in August 1937 to 76 in May 1938. Four million additional workers lost their jobs. Economic conditions were soon almost as bad as they had been in the bleak days of 1932–1933.

The recession of 1937, known to the president's critics as the "Roosevelt recession," was a result of many factors. But to many observers at the time (including, apparently, the president himself), it seemed to be a direct result of the administration's unwise decision to reduce spending. And so in April 1938, the president asked Congress for an emergency appropriation of $5 billion for public works and relief programs, and government funds soon began pouring into the economy once again. Within a few months, another tentative recovery seemed to be under way.

Sources of "Roosevelt Recession"

At about the same time, Roosevelt sent a stinging message to Congress, vehemently denouncing what he called an "unjustifiable concentration of economic power" and asking for the creation of a commission to examine that concentration with an eye to major reforms in the antitrust laws. In response, Congress established the Temporary National Economic Committee (TNEC), whose members included representatives of both houses of Congress and officials from several executive agencies. Later in 1938, the administration successfully supported one of its most ambitious pieces of labor legislation, the Fair Labor Standards Act, which for the first time established a national minimum wage and a forty-hour work week, and which also placed strict limits on child labor.

End of the New Deal   Despite these achievements, however, by the end of 1938 the New Deal had essentially come to an end. Congressional opposition now made it difficult for the president to enact any major new programs. But more important, perhaps, the threat of world crisis hung heavy in the political atmosphere, and Roosevelt was gradually growing more concerned with persuading a reluctant nation to prepare for war than with pursuing new avenues of reform.

LIMITS AND LEGACIES OF THE NEW DEAL

The New Deal made major changes in American government, some of them still controversial today. It also left important problems unaddressed.

African Americans and the New Deal

One group the New Deal did relatively little to assist was African Americans. The administration was not hostile to black aspirations. Eleanor Roosevelt spoke throughout the 1930s on behalf of racial justice and put continuing pressure on her husband and others in the federal government to ease discrimination against blacks. The president himself appointed a number of blacks to significant second-level positions in his administration, creating an informal network of officeholders that became known as the "Black Cabinet." Eleanor Roosevelt, Interior secretary Harold Ickes, and WPA director Harry Hopkins all made efforts to ensure that New Deal relief programs did not exclude blacks, and by 1935 an estimated 30 percent of all African Americans were receiving some form of government assistance. One result was a historic change in black electoral behavior. As late as 1932, most American blacks were voting Republican, as they had been doing since the Civil War. By 1936, more than 90 percent of them were voting Democratic.

Blacks supported Franklin Roosevelt, but they had few illusions that the New Deal represented a major turning point in American race relations. The president was, for example, never willing to risk losing the support of southern Democrats by supporting legislation to make lynching a federal crime or to ban the poll tax, one of the most potent tools by which white southerners kept blacks from voting.

Discrimination Reinforced   New Deal relief agencies did not challenge, and indeed reinforced, existing patterns of discrimination. The Civilian Conservation Corps established separate black

ELEANOR ROOSEVELT AND MARY MCLEOD BETHUNE Mrs. Roosevelt was a leading champion of racial equality within her husband's administration, and her commitment had an important impact on the behavior of the government even though she held no official post. She is seen here meeting in 1937 with Aubrey Williams, executive director of the National Youth Administration, and Mary McLeod Bethune, the agency's Director of Negro Affairs. *(UPI/Corbis-Bettmann)*

camps. The NRA codes tolerated paying blacks less than whites doing the same jobs. The WPA routinely relegated black and Hispanic workers to the least-skilled and lowest-paying jobs; when funding ebbed, African Americans, like women, were among the first to be dismissed.

The New Deal was not hostile to black Americans, and it made some contributions to their progress. But it refused to make the issue of race a significant part of its agenda.

The New Deal and the "Indian Problem"

New Deal policy toward the Indian tribes marked a significant break from the approach in the years before Roosevelt, largely because of the efforts of the extraordinary commissioner of Indian affairs in the 1930s, John Collier. Collier was greatly influenced by the work of twentieth-century anthropologists who advanced the idea of cultural relativism—the theory that every culture should be accepted and respected on its own terms.

Collier favored legislation that would, he hoped, reverse the pressures on Native Americans to assimilate and allow them to remain Indians. He effectively promoted legislation—which became *Indian Reorganization Act* the Indian Reorganization Act of 1934—to advance his goals. Among other things, it restored to the tribes the right to own land collectively and to elect tribal governments. In the thirteen years after passage of the 1934 bill, tribal land increased by nearly 4 million acres, and

Contemporaries of Franklin Roosevelt debated the impact of the New Deal with ferocious intensity: conservatives complaining of a menacing tyranny of the state, liberals celebrating the New Deal's progressive achievements, people on the left charging that the reforms of the 1930s were largely cosmetic and ignored the nation's fundamental problems. Although the conservative critique has found relatively little scholarly expression since Roosevelt's death, the liberal and left positions continued for many years to shape the way historians described the Roosevelt administration.

The dominant view from the beginning was an approving liberal interpretation, and its most important early voice was that of Arthur M. Schlesinger, Jr. He argued in the three volumes of *The Age of Roosevelt* (1957–1960) that the New Deal marked a continuation of the long struggle between public power and private interests, a struggle Roosevelt had moved to a new level. Workers, farmers, consumers and others now had much more protection than they had enjoyed in the past.

At almost the same time, however, other historians were offering more qualified assessments of the New Deal, although they remained securely within the liberal framework. Richard Hofstadter argued in 1955 that the New Deal gave American liberalism a "social-democratic tinge that had never before been present in American reform movements"; but that its highly pragmatic approach lacked a central, guiding philosophy. James MacGregor Burns argued in 1956 that Roosevelt failed to make full use of his potential as a leader and had accommodated himself unnecessarily to existing patterns of power.

William Leuchtenburg's *Franklin D. Roosevelt and the New Deal* (1963) was the first systematic "revisionist" interpretation. Leuchtenburg challenged the views of earlier scholars who had proclaimed the New Deal a "revolution" in social policy. Leuchtenburg could muster only enough enthusiasm to call it a "halfway revolution," one that helped some previously disadvantaged groups (most notably farmers and workers) but that did little or nothing for many others (blacks, sharecroppers, the urban poor).

Harsher criticisms soon emerged. Barton Bernstein in a 1968 essay concluded that the New Deal had saved capitalism, but at the expense of the least powerful. Ronald Radosh, Paul Conkin, and, more recently, Thomas Ferguson and Colin Gordon expanded on these criticisms; the New Deal, they contended, was part of the twentieth-century tradition of "corporate liberalism"—a tradition in which reform is closely wedded to the needs and interests of capitalism.

Most scholars in the 1980s and 1990s, however, seemed largely to have accepted the revised liberal view: that the New Deal was a significant (and most agree valuable) chapter in the history of reform, but one that worked within rigid, occasionally crippling limits. Much of the recent work on the New Deal, therefore, has focused on the constraints it faced. Some scholars (notably the sociologist Theda Skocpol) have emphasized the issue of "state capacity"—the absence of a government bureaucracy with sufficient strength and expertise to shape or administer many programs. James T. Patterson, Barry Karl, Mark Leff, and others have emphasized the political constraints the New Deal encountered—the conservative inhibitions about government that remained strong in Congress and among the public. Frank Freidel, Ellis Hawley, Herbert Stein, and many others point as well to the ideological constraints affecting Franklin Roosevelt and his supporters, the limits of their own understanding of their time. Alan Brinkley, in *The End of Reform* (1995), described an ideological shift within New Deal liberalism that marginalized older concerns about wealth and monopoly power.

The phrase "New Deal liberalism" has come in the postwar era to seem synonymous with modern ideas of aggressive federal management of the economy, elaborate welfare systems, a powerful bureaucracy, and large-scale government spending. But many historians of the New Deal would argue that the modern idea of New Deal liberalism bears only a limited relationship to the ideas that New Dealers themselves embraced.

(text continued from page 695)

Indian agricultural income increased dramatically (from under $2 million in 1934 to over $49 million in 1947). Even with the redistribution of lands under the 1934 act, however, Indians continued to possess, for the most part, only territory whites did not want—much of it arid, some of it desert. And as a group, they continued to constitute the poorest segment of the population.

Women and the New Deal

Symbolically, at least, the New Deal marked a breakthrough in the role of women in public life. Roosevelt appointed the first female member of the cabinet in the nation's history, Secretary of Labor Frances Perkins. He also named more than 100 other women to positions at lower levels of the federal bureaucracy. But the administration was concerned not so much about achieving gender equality as about obtaining special protections for women.

Frances Perkins

The New Deal generally supported the widespread belief that in hard times women should withdraw from the workplace to open up more jobs for men. Frances Perkins, for example, spoke out against what she called the "pin-money worker"—the married woman working to earn extra money for the household. New Deal relief agencies offered relatively little employment for women. The Social Security program excluded domestic servants, waitresses, and other predominantly female occupations.

As with African Americans, so also with women: The New Deal was not actively hostile to feminist aspirations, but it accepted prevailing cultural norms. There was not yet sufficient political pressure from women themselves to persuade the administration to do otherwise. Indeed, some of the most important supporters of policies that reinforced traditional gender roles (such as Social Security) were themselves women.

Prevailing Gender Norms Accepted

The New Deal and the West

One part of American society that did receive special attention from the New Deal was the American West. The West received more government funds per capita through relief programs than any other region.

The largest New Deal public works programs—the great dams and power stations—were mainly in the West, both because the best locations for such facilities were there and because the West had the most need for new sources of water and power. The Grand Coulee Dam on the Columbia River was the largest public works project in American history to that point, and it provided cheap electric power for much of the Northwest. Its construction, and the construction of other, smaller dams and water projects, created a basis for economic development in the region. Without this enormous public investment by the federal government, much of the economic growth that transformed the West after World War II would have been much more difficult, if not impossible, to achieve.

The New Deal, the Economy, and Politics

The most frequent criticisms of the New Deal involve its failure genuinely to revive or reform the American economy. New Dealers never fully recognized the value of government spending as a vehicle for recovery. The economic boom sparked by World War II, not the New Deal, finally ended the crisis. Nor did the New Deal substantially alter the distribution of power within American capitalism, and it had only a small impact on the distribution of wealth among the American people.

The New Deal's Economic Legacy

Nevertheless, the New Deal did have a number of important and lasting effects on both the behavior and the structure of the American economy. It helped elevate new groups—workers, farmers, and others—to positions from which they could at times effectively challenge the power of the corporations. It increased the regulatory functions of the federal government in ways that helped stabilize previously troubled areas of the economy: the stock market, the banking system, and others. And the administration helped establish the basis for new forms of federal fiscal policy, which in the postwar years would give the government tools for promoting and regulating economic growth.

American Welfare State Established

The New Deal also created the rudiments of the American welfare state, through its many relief programs and above all through the Social Security system. The conservative inhibitions New Dealers brought to this task ensured that the welfare system that ultimately emerged would be limited in its impact, would reinforce some traditional patterns of gender and racial discrimination, and would be expensive and cumbersome to administer. But for all its limits, the new system marked a historic break with the nation's traditional reluctance to offer any public assistance whatsoever to its neediest citizens.

Finally, the New Deal had a dramatic effect on the character of American politics. It took a weak and divided Democratic Party, which had been a minority force in American politics for many decades, and turned it into a mighty coalition that would dominate national party competition for more than thirty years. It turned the attention of many voters away from some of the cultural issues that had preoccupied them in the 1920s and awakened in them an interest in economic matters of direct importance to their lives.

CONCLUSION

From the time of Franklin Roosevelt's inauguration in 1933 to the beginning of World War II eight years later, the federal government engaged in a broad and diverse series of experiments designed to relieve the distress of unemployment and poverty; to reform the economy to prevent future crises; and to bring the Great Depression itself to an end. It had only partial success in all those efforts.

Unemployment and poverty remained high throughout the New Deal, although many federal programs provided assistance to millions of people who would otherwise have had none. The structure of the American economy remained essentially the same as it had been in earlier years, although there were by the end of the New Deal some important new regulatory agencies in Washington—and an important new role for organized labor. Nothing the New Deal did ended the Great Depression, but some of its policies kept it from getting worse—and some of them pointed the way toward more effective economic policies in the future.

Perhaps the most important legacy of the New Deal was to create a sense of possibilities among many Americans, to persuade them that the fortunes of individuals need not be left entirely to chance or to the workings of an unregulated market. Many Americans emerged from the 1930s convinced that individuals deserved some protections from the unpredictability and instability of the modern economy, and that the New Deal—for all its limitations—had demonstrated the value of enlisting government in the effort to provide those protections.

FOR FURTHER REFERENCE

William E. Leuchtenburg, *Franklin D. Roosevelt and the New Deal* (1963) is a classic short history of the New Deal. Anthony Badger, *The New Deal: The Depression Years* (1989) is another fine overview. David Kennedy, *Freedom from Fear: The American People in Depression and War, 1929–1945* (1999) is an important narrative history, a volume in the Oxford History of the United States. Geoffrey Ward, *Before the Trumpet: Young Franklin Roosevelt, 1882–1905* (1985) and *A First-Class Temperament: The Emergence of Franklin Roosevelt* (1989) are superb biographical accounts of the pre-presidential FDR. Frank Freidel, *Franklin D. Roosevelt: A Rendezvous with Destiny* (1990) is a one-volume biography by one of FDR's most important biographers. Blanche Wiesen Cook, *Eleanor Roosevelt 1884–1933* (1992) and *Eleanor Roosevelt, vol. 2, The Defining Years, 1933–1938* (1999) are the first two volumes of an important biography. Ellis Hawley, *The New Deal and the Problem of Monopoly* (1967) is a classic examination of the economic policies of the Roosevelt administration in its first five years. Colin Gordon, *New Deals: Business, Labor, and Politics in America, 1920–1935* (1994) is a challenging reinterpretation of the early New Deal years. The transformation of liberalism after 1937 is the subject of Alan Brinkley, *The End of Reform: New Deal Liberalism in Recession and War* (1995). G. Edward White, *The Constitution and the New Deal* (2000) examines the Roosevelt Administration's relationship with the judiciary. Linda Gordon, *Pitied but Not Entitled: Single Mothers and the History of Welfare* (1994) is a pioneering work on women as the recipients and also the authors of government welfare policies. The efforts of Chicago workers to protest and organize is the subject of Lizabeth Cohen, *Making a New Deal: Industrial Workers in Chicago, 1919–1939* (1990). Nelson Lichtenstein, *The Most Dangerous Man in Detroit: Walter Reuther and the Fate of American Labor* (1995) is a valuable study of one of the early leaders of the CIO. Richard Lowitt, *The New Deal and the West* (1984) pays particular attention to water policy and agriculture in the New Deal years. Jordan Schwarz, *The New Dealers: Power Politics in the Age of Roosevelt* (1993) examines the proponents of state-funded economic development of the South and West. Alan Brinkley, *Voices of Protest: Huey Long, Father Coughlin, and the Great Depression* (1982) examines some of the most powerful challenges to the New Deal. Bruce Shulman, *From Cotton Belt to Sunbelt* (1991) explores the New Deal's effort to transform the region Roosevelt and others considered the "nation's number one economic problem," the American South. Harvard Sitkoff, *A New Deal for Blacks* (1978) and Nancy J. Weiss, *Farewell to the Party of Lincoln: Black Politics in the Age of FDR* (1983) take contrasting positions on what the New Deal did for African Americans.

FDR (1994), a documentary by David Grubin, gives viewers a fine view of the private and public life of Franklin D. Roosevelt. One of the president's most vocal and powerful dissidents is featured in another film, by Ken Burns, *Huey Long* (1986). *The World of Tomorrow* (1984) is a provocative documentary on the 1939 World's Fair.

For quizzes, Internet resources, references to additional books and films, and more, consult this book's Online Learning Center site at www.mhhe.com/unfinishednation4.

"DEFENDING MADRID"   The Spanish Civil War, in which fascist forces led by Francisco Franco overturned the existing republican government, was an early signal to many Americans of the dangers of fascism and the threat to democracy. This 1938 Spanish war poster contains the words "Defending Madrid is Defending Catalonia," an effort by the government in Madrid to enlist the support of the surrounding regions in the defense of the capital against the fascists.   *(Hulton/Archives/Getty Images)*

TIME LINE

1924	1928	1931	1933	1937	
Dawes Plan	Kellogg-Briand Pact	Japan invades Manchuria	U.S. recognizes Soviet Union	Roosevelt's "quarantine" speech	
			Good Neighbor Policy		

᭜

CHAPTER TWENTY-SEVEN

THE GLOBAL CRISIS, 1921–1941

The Diplomacy of the New Era

Isolationism and Internationalism

From Neutrality to Intervention

Henry Cabot Lodge of Massachusetts, Republican chairman of the Senate Foreign Relations Committee, led the fight that defeated ratification of the Treaty of Versailles in 1919 and 1920. As a result, the United States declined to join the League of Nations; and American foreign policy embarked on an independent course that for the next two decades would attempt, but ultimately fail, to expand American influence and maintain international stability without committing the United States to any lasting relationships with other nations.

Lodge was not an isolationist. He believed the United States should exert its influence internationally. But he believed, too, that the United States should remain unfettered with obligations to anyone else. He said in 1919:

> We are a great moral asset of Christian civilization. . . . How did we get there? By our own efforts. Nobody led us, nobody guided us, nobody controlled us. . . . I would keep America as she has been— not isolated, not prevent her from joining other nations for . . . great purposes—but I wish her to be master of her own fate.

In the end, the limited American internationalism of the interwar years proved insufficient to protect the interests of the United States, to create global stability, or to keep the nation from becoming involved in the most catastrophic war in human history.

	1938	1939	1940	1941	
	Munich Conference	Nazi-Soviet nonaggression pact	Tripartite Pact	Lend-lease plan	
			America First Committee founded	Atlantic Charter	
		World War II begins		Japan attacks Pearl Harbor	
			Roosevelt reelected		
			Destroyers-for-bases deal	U.S. enters World War II	

THE DIPLOMACY OF THE NEW ERA

Critics of American foreign policy in the 1920s often described it with a single word: isolationism. But in reality, the United States played a more active role in world affairs in the 1920s than it had at almost any previous time in its history.

Replacing the League

By the time the Harding administration took office in 1921, American membership in the League of Nations was no longer a realistic possibility. But Secretary of State Charles Evans Hughes wanted to find something with which to replace the League as a guarantor of world peace and stability.

Charles Evans Hughes

The most important of such efforts was the Washington Conference of 1921—an attempt to prevent a destabilizing naval armaments race among the United States, Britain, and Japan. Hughes proposed a plan for dramatic reductions in the fleets of all three nations and a ten-year moratorium on the construction of large warships. To the surprise of almost everyone, the conference ultimately agreed to accept most of Hughes's terms. The Five-Power Pact of February 1922 established limits for total naval tonnage and a ratio of armaments among the signatories. For every 5 tons of American and British warships, Japan would maintain 3 and France and Italy 1.75 each.

When the French foreign minister, Aristide Briand, asked the United States in 1927 to join an alliance against Germany, Secretary of State Frank Kellogg (who had replaced Hughes in 1925) proposed instead a multilateral treaty outlawing war as an instrument of national policy. Fourteen nations signed the agreement in Paris on August 27, 1928, amid wide international acclaim. Forty-eight other nations later joined the Kellogg-Briand Pact. It contained no instruments of enforcement.

Kellogg-Briand Pact

Debts and Diplomacy

The first responsibility of diplomacy, Hughes, Kellogg, and others agreed, was to ensure that American overseas trade faced no obstacles. New financial arrangements to deal with international debts were central to that goal. The Allied powers of Europe were struggling to repay $11 billion in loans they had contracted with the United States during and shortly after the war. At the same time, Germany was attempting to pay the reparations levied by the Allies. The United States stepped in with a solution.

Charles G. Dawes, an American banker, negotiated an agreement in 1924 among France, Britain, Germany, and the United States under which American banks would provide enormous loans to the Germans, enabling them to meet

The Dawes Plan

A FORD PLANT IN RUSSIA The success of Henry Ford in creating affordable, mass-produced automobiles made him famous around the world, and particularly popular in the Soviet Union in the 1920s and early 1930s, as the communist regime strove to push the nation into the industrial future. Russians called the system of large-scale factory production "Fordism," and they welcomed assistance from the Ford Motor Company itself, which sent engineers and workers over to Russia to help build large automobile plants such as this one. *(UPI/Corbis-Bettmann)*

their reparations payments; in return, Britain and France would agree to reduce the amount of those payments. Under the Dawes Plan, the United States would lend money to Germany, which would use that money to pay reparations to France and England, which would in turn use those funds (as well as large loans they themselves were receiving from American banks) to repay war debts to the United States. The flow was able to continue only by virtue of the enormous debts Germany and the other European nations were acquiring to American banks and corporations. The American economic involvement in Europe continued to expand until the worldwide depression shattered the system in 1931.

The government assisted American economic expansion in Latin America even more aggressively. During the 1920s, American military forces *Economic Expansion in Latin America* maintained a presence in Nicaragua, Panama, and several other countries in the region, while United States investments in Latin America more than doubled. American banks were offering large loans to Latin American governments, just as they were in Europe; and just as in Europe, the Latin Americans were having difficulty earning the money to repay them in the face of the formidable United States tariff barrier.

Hoover and the World Crisis

By 1931, the world financial crisis that had begun in 1929 had produced a rising nationalism in Europe. It soon toppled some existing political leaders and replaced them with powerful, belligerent governments committed to expansion. An expansionist government in Japan created similar problems in Asia. Herbert Hoover confronted the beginning of a process that would ultimately lead to war.

In Latin America, Hoover tried to repair some of the damage earlier American policies had created. He made a ten-week good-will tour through the region before his inauguration. Once in office, he generally abstained from intervening in the internal affairs of neighboring nations and moved to withdraw American troops from Nicaragua and Haiti. He also announced a new policy: America would grant diplomatic recognition to any sitting government in the region without questioning the means it

Roosevelt Corollary Repudiated

had used to obtain power. He even repudiated the Roosevelt Corollary to the Monroe Doctrine by refusing to permit American intervention when several Latin American countries defaulted on debt obligations to the United States in October 1931.

In Europe, the administration enjoyed few successes. When Hoover's proposed moratorium on debts failed to attract broad support or produce financial stability, he refused to cancel all war debts to the United States as many economists advised him to do. Several European nations promptly went into default. Efforts to extend the 1921 limits on naval construction fell victim to French and British fears of German and Japanese militarism.

The ineffectiveness of American diplomacy in Europe was particularly troubling in light of the new governments on the Continent. Benito Mussolini's Fascist Party had been in control of Italy since the early 1920s and had become increasingly nationalistic and militaristic. Still more ominous was the growing power of the National Socialist (or Nazi) Party in Germany. By the late 1920s, the Weimar Republic, the nation's government since the end of World War I, had been largely discredited by, among other things, a ruinous inflation. Adolf Hitler, the leader of the Nazis, was growing rapidly in popular favor and would take power in 1933. Hitler believed in the genetic superiority of the Aryan (German) people and in extending German territory to provide *Lebensraum* (living space) for the German "master race." He also displayed a pathological anti-Semitism and a passionate militarism.

More immediately alarming to the Hoover administration was a major crisis in Asia—another early step toward World War II. The Japanese, suffering from an economic depression of their own, were concerned about the increasing power of the Soviet Union and about the insistence of the Chinese leader Chiang Kai-Shek on expanding his government's power in Manchuria, officially a part of China but over which the Japanese had maintained informal economic control since 1905. In 1931, Japan's military leaders staged what was, in effect, a coup in Tokyo. Weeks

Manchuria Invaded

later, they launched an invasion of northern Manchuria. They had conquered the region by the end of the year. Hoover permitted Secretary of State Henry Stimson to issue stern warnings to the Japanese but barred him from cooperating

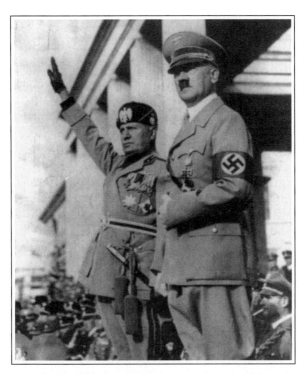

HITLER AND MUSSOLINI The German and Italian dictators, shown here reviewing troops together in Berlin in the mid-1930s, acted publicly as if they were equals. Privately, however, Hitler viewed Mussolini with contempt, and the Italian dictator complained frequently of being treated as a junior partner by his ally. *(Culver Pictures, Inc.)*

with the League of Nations to impose economic sanctions against them. Early in 1932, Japan moved further into China, attacking the city of Shanghai and killing thousands of civilians.

ISOLATIONISM AND INTERNATIONALISM

The administration of Franklin Roosevelt faced a dual challenge as it entered office in 1933. It had to deal with the worst economic crisis in the nation's history, and it had to deal as well with the effects of a decaying international structure.

Depression Diplomacy

Perhaps Roosevelt's sharpest break with the policies of his predecessor was on the question of American economic relations with Europe. Hoover had argued that only by resolving the question of war debts and reinforcing the gold standard could the American economy hope to recover. He had, therefore, agreed to participate in the World Economic Conference, to be held in London in June 1933, to attempt to resolve these issues. By the time the conference assembled, however, Roosevelt had already become convinced that the gold value of the dollar had to be allowed to fall in order for American goods to be able to compete in world markets. Shortly after the conference convened, he released what became known as the *FDR's "Bombshell Message"* "bombshell message," repudiating the orthodox views of most of the delegates and rejecting any agreement on currency stabilization. The conference quickly dissolved.

At the same time, Roosevelt abandoned the commitments of the Hoover administration to settle the issue of war debts through international agreement. In April 1934 he signed a bill that prohibited American banks from making loans to any nation in default on its debts. The legislation ended the old, circular system by which debt payments continued only by virtue of increasing American loans; within months, war-debt payments from every nation except Finland stopped for good.

Sixteen years after the Bolshevik Revolution of 1917, the American government still had not officially recognized the government of the Soviet Union. But a growing number of influential Americans were urging a *Soviet Union Recognized* change in policy—largely because the Soviet Union appeared to be a possible source of trade. The Russians, for their part, were hoping for American cooperation in containing Japan. In November 1933, the United States and the Soviet Union agreed to open formal diplomatic relations. Relations with the Soviet Union, however, soon soured once again. American trade failed to establish a foothold in Russia, disappointing hopes in the United States; and the American government did little to reassure the Soviets that it was interested in stopping Japanese expansion in Asia, dousing expectations in Russia. By the end of 1934, the Soviet Union and the United States were once again viewing each other with considerable mistrust.

The Roosevelt administration was also taking a new approach toward *"Good Neighbor Policy"* Latin America, an approach which became known as the "Good Neighbor Policy" and which expanded on the changes the Hoover administration had made. At an Inter-American Conference in Montevideo, Uruguay, in December 1933, Secretary of State Cordell Hull signed a formal convention declaring: "No state has the right to intervene in the internal or external affairs of another."

The Rise of Isolationism

With the international system of the 1920s now beyond repair, the United States faced a choice between more active efforts to stabilize the world *Sources of Isolationism* and more energetic attempts to isolate itself from it. Most Americans unhesitatingly chose the latter. Support for isolationism emerged from many quarters. Some Wilsonian internationalists had grown disillusioned with the League of Nations and its inability to stop Japanese aggression in Asia. Other Americans were listening to the argument that powerful business interests—Wall Street, munitions makers, and others—had tricked the United States into participating in World War I. An investigation by a Senate committee chaired by Senator Gerald Nye of North Dakota claimed to have produced evidence of exorbitant profiteering and tax evasion by many corporations during the war, and it suggested that bankers had pressured Wilson to intervene in the war so as to protect their loans abroad. (Few historians now lend much credence to these charges.)

Roosevelt continued to hope for at least a modest American role in maintaining world peace. In 1935, he proposed to the Senate a treaty to make the United States a member of the World Court—a largely symbolic gesture. Isolationists such as Father Coughlin and William Randolph Hearst aroused popular opposition to the agreement, and the Senate voted it down.

In the summer of 1935, Mussolini's Italy was preparing to invade Ethiopia. Fearing the invasion would provoke a new European war, American legislators began to design legal safeguards to prevent the United States from being dragged into the conflict. The *Neutrality Acts* result was the Neutrality Act of 1935. It established a mandatory arms embargo against both sides in any military conflict and directed the president to warn American citizens against traveling on the ships of warring nations. Thus, isolationists believed, the "protection of neutral rights" could not again become an excuse for American intervention in war. A 1937 law established the so-called cash-and-carry policy, by which warring nations could purchase only nonmilitary goods from the United States and could do so only by paying cash and shipping their purchases themselves.

Isolationist sentiment showed its strength again in 1936–1937 in response to the civil war in Spain. The Falangists of General Francisco Franco, a group much like the Italian fascists, revolted in July 1936 against the existing republican government. Hitler and Mussolini supported Franco, both vocally and with weapons and supplies. Some individual Americans traveled to Spain to assist the republican cause, but the United States government joined with Britain and France in an agreement to offer no assistance to either side.

In the summer of 1937, Japan intensified its six-year-old assault on Manchuria and attacked China's five northern provinces. Roosevelt responded in a speech in Chicago in October 1937. He warned of the dangers of the Japanese actions and argued that aggressors should be "quarantined" by the international community to prevent the contagion of war from spreading. He was deliberately vague about *"Quarantine" Speech* what such a "quarantine" would mean. Even so, public response to the speech was hostile, and Roosevelt drew back. On December 12, 1937, Japanese aviators bombed and sank the United States

Long before Pearl Harbor, well before war broke out in Europe in 1939, the first shots of what would become World War II had been fired in the Pacific in a conflict between Japan and China.

Having lived in almost complete isolation from the world until the nineteenth century, Japan had emerged from World War I as one of the world's great powers, with a proud and powerful military and growing global trade. But the Great Depression created severe economic problems for the Japanese; and as in other parts of the world, the crisis strengthened the political influence of highly nationalistic armed forces. Out of the military emerged dreams of a new Japanese empire in the Pacific. Such an empire would, its proponents believed, give the nation access to fuel, raw material, and markets for its industries, and land for its agricultural needs and its rapidly increasing population. Such an empire, they also argued, would free Asia from its exploitation by Europe and America and would create a "new world order based on moral principles."

During World War I, Japan had taken territory and economic concessions in China, and had created a particularly strong presence in the northern Chinese region of Manchuria. There, in September 1931, a group of militant young army officers seized on a railway explosion to justify a military campaign through which they conquered the entire province. Both the United States government and the League of Nations demanded that Japan evacuate Manchuria. The Japanese ignored them, and for the next six years consolidated their control over their new territory.

On July 7, 1937, Japan began a wider war when it attacked Chinese troops at the Marco Polo Bridge outside Beijing. Over the next few weeks, Japanese forces overran a large part of southern China, including most of the port cities, killing many Chinese solders and civilians in the process. Particularly notorious was the Japanese annihilation of many thousands of civilians in the city of Nanjing (the number has long been in dispute, but estimates range from 80,000 to over 300,000) in an event that became known in China and the West as the Nanjing Massacre. The Chinese government fled to the mountains. As in 1931, the United States and the League of Nations protested in vain.

The China that the Japanese had invaded was a nation in turmoil. It was engaged in a civil war of its own—between the so-called Kuomintang, a Nationalist party led by Chiang Kai-Shek, and the Chinese Communist Party, led by Mao Zedong; and this internal struggle weakened China's capacity to resist. But beginning in 1937, the two rivals agreed to an uneasy truce and began fighting the Japanese together, with some success—bogging the Japanese military down in a seemingly endless war and imposing great hardships on the Japanese people at home. The Japanese government and military, however, remained determined to continue the war against China, whatever the sacrifices.

One result of the costs of the war in China was a growing Japanese dependence on the United States for steel and oil to meet civilian and military needs. In July 1941, in an effort to pressure the Japanese to stop their expansion, the Roosevelt administration made it impossible for the Japanese to continue buying American oil. Japan now faced a choice between ending its war in China or finding other sources of fuel to keep its war effort (and its civilian economy) going.

They chose to extend the war beyond China in a search for oil. The best available sources were in the Dutch East Indies; but the only way to secure that European colony, they believed, would be to neutralize the increasingly hostile United States in Asia. Visionary military planners in Japan began advocating a daring move to immobilize the Americans in the Pacific before expanding the war elsewhere—with an attack on the American naval base at Pearl Harbor. The first blow of World War II in America, therefore, was the culmination of more than a decade of Japanese efforts to conquer China.

(text continued from page 709)

gunboat *Panay*, almost certainly deliberately, as it sailed the Yangtze River in China. But so reluctant was the Roosevelt administration to antagonize the isolationists that the United States eagerly seized on Japanese claims that the bombing had been an accident, accepted Japan's apologies, and overlooked the attack.

The Failure of Munich

In 1936, Hitler had moved the revived German army into the Rhineland, rearming an area that had been off-limits to German troops since World War I. In March 1938, German forces marched without opposition into Austria, and Hitler proclaimed a union (or *Anschluss*) between Austria, his native land, and Germany, his adopted one. Neither in America nor in most of Europe was there much more than a murmur of opposition.

The Austrian invasion, however, soon created another crisis. Germany had by now occupied territory surrounding three sides of western Czechoslovakia, a region Hitler dreamed of annexing. In September 1938, he demanded that Czechoslovakia cede him the Sudetenland, an area in which many ethnic Germans lived. Although Czechoslovakia was prepared to fight to stop Hitler, it needed assistance from other nations. But most Western governments, including the United States, were willing to pay almost any price to settle the crisis peacefully. On September 29, Hitler met with the leaders of France and Great Britain at Munich in an effort to resolve the crisis. The French and British agreed to accept the German demands in Czechoslovakia in return for Hitler's promise to expand no farther.

The Munich agreement, which Roosevelt applauded at the time, was the most prominent element of a policy that came to be known as "appeasement" and that came to be *"Appeasement"* identified (not altogether fairly) largely with British Prime Minister Neville Chamberlain. Whoever was to blame, the policy was a failure. In March 1939, Hitler occupied the remaining areas of Czechoslovakia, violating the Munich agreement unashamedly. And in April, he began issuing threats against Poland.

THE BLITZ, LONDON The German Luftwaffe terrorized London and other British cities in 1940–1941 and again late in the war by bombing civilian areas indiscriminately in an effort to break the spirit of the English people. The effort failed, and the fortitude of the British did much to arouse support for their cause in the United States. *(Brown Brothers)*

At that point, both Britain and France assured the Polish government that they would come to its assistance in case of an invasion; they even tried, too late, to draw the Soviet Union into a mutual defense agreement. But Stalin, who had not even been invited to the Munich Conference, had decided he could expect no protection from the West. He signed a nonaggression pact with Hitler in August 1939, freeing the Germans for the moment from the danger of a two-front war. Shortly after that, Hitler staged an incident on the Polish border to allow him to claim that Germany had been attacked, and on September 1, 1939, he launched a full-scale invasion of Poland. Britain and France, true to their pledges, declared war on Germany two days later. World War II had begun.

FROM NEUTRALITY TO INTERVENTION

"This nation will remain a neutral nation," the president declared shortly after the hostilities began in Europe, "but I cannot ask that every American remain neutral in thought as well." There was never any question that both he and the majority of the American people favored Britain, France, and the other Allied nations in the contest. The question was how much the United States was prepared to do to assist them.

Neutrality Tested

At the very least, Roosevelt believed, the United States should make armaments available to the Allied armies to help them counter the military advantage the large German munitions industry gave Hitler. In September 1939, he asked Congress to revise the Neutrality Acts and lift the arms embargo against any nation engaged in war. Congress maintained the prohibition on American ships entering war zones. But the 1939 law did permit belligerents to purchase arms on the same   *Cash-and-Carry* cash-and-carry basis that the earlier Neutrality Acts had established for the sale of nonmilitary materials.

After the German armies quickly subdued Poland, the war in Europe settled into a long, quiet lull that lasted through the winter and spring—a "phony war," some called it. But in the spring of 1940, Germany launched a massive invasion known as the "blitzkrieg," to the west—first attacking Denmark and Norway, sweeping next across the Netherlands and Belgium, and driving finally deep into the heart of France. On June 10, Mussolini invaded France from the south as Hitler was attacking from the north. On June 22, finally, France fell, and Nazi troops marched into Paris. A new French regime   *Fall of France* assembled in Vichy, largely controlled by the German occupiers; and in all Europe, only the shattered remnants of the British and French armies, rescued from the beaches of Dunkirk, remained to oppose the Axis forces.

On May 16, in the midst of the offensive, Roosevelt asked Congress for an additional $1 billion for defense and received it quickly. That was one day after Winston Churchill, the new British prime minister, had sent Roosevelt the first of many long lists of requests for armaments, without which, he insisted, England could not long survive. Some Americans (including the United States ambassador to London, Joseph P. Kennedy) argued that the British plight was already hopeless, that any aid to the English was a wasted effort. But the president was determined to make war materials available to Britain. He even circumvented the cash-and-carry provisions of the Neutrality Acts by giving England fifty American destroyers (most of them left over from World War I) in return for the right to build American bases on British territory in the Caribbean and he returned to the factories a number of new airplanes purchased by the American military so that the British could buy them instead.

Roosevelt was able to take such steps in part because of a major shift in American public opinion. By July 1940, more than 66 percent of the public (according to opinion polls) believed that Germany posed a direct threat to the United States. Congress was, therefore, more willing to permit expanded American assistance to the Allies. Congress was also becoming more concerned about the need for internal preparations for war, and in September it

Burke-Wadsworth Act   approved the Burke-Wadsworth Act, inaugurating the first peacetime military draft in American history.

But a powerful new isolationist lobby—the America First Committee, whose members included such prominent Americans as Charles Lindbergh and Senators Gerald Nye and Burton Wheeler—joined the debate over American policy toward the war. The lobby had at least the indirect support of a large proportion of the Republican Party. Through the summer and fall of 1940, the debate was complicated by a presidential campaign.

The Campaign of 1940

The biggest political question of 1940 was whether Franklin Roosevelt would break with tradition and run for an unprecedented third term. The president himself did not reveal his own wishes. But by refusing to withdraw from the contest, he made it impossible for any rival Democrat to establish a claim to the nomination. And when, just before the Democratic Convention in July, he let it be known that he would accept a "draft" from his party, the issue was virtually settled. The Democrats quickly renominated him and even reluctantly swallowed his choice for vice president: Agriculture secretary Henry A. Wallace, a man too liberal and too controversial for the taste of many party leaders.

The Republicans nominated for president a politically inexperienced Indiana businessman, Wendell Willkie, who benefited from a powerful grassroots movement. Both the candidate and the party platform took positions little different from Roosevelt's: they would keep the country out of war but would extend generous assistance to the Allies. But Willkie was an appealing figure and a vigorous campaigner, and he managed to evoke

FDR Reelected   more public enthusiasm than any Republican candidate in decades. But Roosevelt still won decisively. He received 55 percent of the popular vote to Willkie's 45 percent, and he won 449 electoral votes to Willkie's 82.

Neutrality Abandoned

In the last months of 1940, Roosevelt began to make subtle but profound changes in the American role in the war. Great Britain was virtually bankrupt and could no longer meet the cash-and-carry requirements imposed by the Neutrality Acts. The president, therefore, proposed a new system

"Lend-lease"   for supplying Britain: "lend-lease." It would allow the government not only to sell but also to lend or lease armaments to any nation deemed "pivotal to the defense of the United States." In other words, America could funnel weapons to England on the basis of no more than Britain's promise to return them when the war was over. Congress enacted the bill by wide margins.

Attacks by German submarines had made shipping lanes in the Atlantic extremely dangerous. The British navy was losing ships more rapidly than it could replace them and was finding it difficult to transport materials across the Atlantic from America. Roosevelt argued that the western Atlantic was a neutral zone and the responsibility of the American nations. By July 1941, therefore, American ships were patrolling the ocean as far east as Iceland.

At first Germany did little to challenge these obviously hostile American actions. By September 1941, however, the situation had changed. Nazi forces had invaded the Soviet Union in June of that year. When the Soviets did not surrender, as many had predicted they would, Roosevelt persuaded Congress to extend lend-lease privileges to them. Now American industry was providing vital assistance to Hitler's foes on two fronts, and the American navy was protecting the flow of those goods to Europe. In September, Nazi submarines began a concerted campaign against American vessels. Roosevelt ordered American ships to fire on German submarines "on sight." In October, Nazi submarines hit two American destroyers and sank one of them, the *Reuben James*, killing many American sailors. Congress now voted to allow the United States to arm its merchant vessels and to sail all the way into belligerent ports. The United States had, in effect, launched a naval war against Germany.

In August 1941, Roosevelt met with Churchill aboard a British vessel off the coast of Newfoundland. The president made no military commitments, but he did join with the prime minister in releasing a document that became known as the Atlantic Charter, in which the two nations set out "certain common principles" on which to base "a better future for the world." It called openly for "the final destruction of the Nazi tyranny" and for a new world order in which every nation controlled its own destiny. It was, in effect, a statement of war aims.

The Atlantic Charter

The Road to Pearl Harbor

Japan, in the meantime, extended its empire in the Pacific. In September 1940, the Japanese signed the Tripartite Pact, a loose defensive alliance with Germany and Italy (although in reality, the European Axis powers never developed a very strong relationship with Japan). In July 1941, Japanese troops moved into Indochina and seized the capital of Vietnam, a colony of France. The United States, having broken Japanese codes, knew Japan's next target was to be the oil-rich Dutch East Indies; and when Tokyo failed to respond to Roosevelt's stern warnings, the president froze all Japanese assets in the United States, severely limiting Japan's ability to purchase needed American supplies.

Japanese Assets Frozen

Tokyo now faced a choice. Either it would have to repair relations with the United States to restore the flow of supplies or it would have to find those supplies elsewhere, most notably by seizing British and Dutch possessions in the Pacific. In October, militants in Tokyo forced the moderate

PEARL HARBOR, DECEMBER 7, 1941 The destroyer U.S.S. *Shaw*, immobilized in a floating drydock in Pearl Harbor in December 1941, survived the first wave of Japanese bombers unscathed. But in the second attack, the Japanese scored a direct hit and produced this spectacular explosion, which blew off the ship's bow. Damage to the rest of the ship, however, was slight. Just a few months later the *Shaw* was fitted with a new bow and rejoined the fleet. *(U.S. Navy Photo)*

prime minister out of office and replaced him with the leader of the war party, General Hideki Tojo.

By late November, the State Department had given up on the possibility of a peaceful settlement. American intelligence, meanwhile, had decoded Japanese messages that made clear a Japanese attack was imminent. But Washington did not know where the attack would take place. Most officials continued to believe that the Japanese would move first not against American territory but against British or Dutch possessions to their south. A combination of confusion and miscalculation caused the government to overlook indications that Japan intended a direct attack on American forces.

At 7:55 A.M. on Sunday, December 7, 1941, a wave of Japanese
Pearl Harbor Attacked   bombers attacked the United States naval base at
Pearl Harbor in Hawaii. A second wave came an hour later. Within two hours, the United States lost 8 battleships, 3 cruisers, 4 other vessels, 188 airplanes, and several vital shore installations. More than 2,400 soldiers and sailors died, and another 1,000 were injured. The Japanese suffered only light losses.

American forces were now greatly diminished in the Pacific (although by a fortunate accident, no American aircraft carriers—the heart of the

Pacific fleet—had been at Pearl Harbor on December 7). Nevertheless, the raid on Hawaii unified the American people behind war. On December 8, after a stirring speech by the president, the Senate voted unanimously and the House voted 388 to 1 to approve a declaration of war against Japan. Three days later, Germany and Italy, Japan's European allies, declared war on the United States; on the same day, December 11, Congress reciprocated without a dissenting vote.

CONCLUSION

American foreign policy in the years after World War I attempted something that ultimately proved impossible. The United States was determined to be a major power in the world, to extend its trade broadly around the globe, and to influence other nations in ways Americans believed would be beneficial to their own, and the world's, interests. But the United States was also determined to do nothing that would limit its own freedom of action. It would not join the League of Nations. It would not join the World Court. It would not form alliances with other nations. It would operate powerfully—and alone.

But ominous forces were at work in the world that would gradually push the United States into greater engagement with other nations. The economic disarray that the Great Depression created all around the globe, the rise of totalitarian regimes, the expansionist ambitions of powerful new leaders: all worked to destroy the uneasy stability of the post–World War I international system. America's own interests, economic and otherwise, were now imperiled. And America's go-it-alone foreign policy seemed powerless to change the course of events.

Franklin Roosevelt tried throughout the later years of the 1930s to push the American people slowly into a greater involvement in international affairs. In particular, he tried to nudge the United States toward taking a more forceful stand against dictatorship and aggression. A powerful isolationist movement helped stymie him for a time, even after war broke out in Europe. Gradually, however, public opinion shifted toward support of the Allies (Britain, France, and the Soviet Union) and against the Axis (Germany, Italy, and Japan). The nation began to mobilize for war, to supply ships and munitions to Britain, even to engage in naval combat with German forces in the Atlantic. Finally, on December 7, 1941, the surprise Japanese attack on the American base at Pearl Harbor in Hawaii eliminated the last elements of uncertainty and drove the United States—now united behind the war effort—into the greatest and most terrible conflict in human history.

FOR FURTHER REFERENCE

Robert Dallek, *Franklin D. Roosevelt and American Foreign Policy, 1932–1945* (1979) is a comprehensive study of Roosevelt's foreign policy. Akira Iriye, *The Cambridge History of American Foreign Relations, vol. 3: The Globalizing of America, 1913–1945* (1993) is another important study. In *Inevitable Revolutions* (1983), Walter LaFeber recounts America's attempts to halt revolutionary movements throughout the world. James MacGregor Burns, *Roosevelt: the Soldier of Freedom* (1970) and Warren F. Kimball, *The Juggler: Franklin Roosevelt as Wartime Statesman* (1991) are two important studies of the president. Wayne S. Cole, *Charles A. Lindbergh and the Battle Against American Intervention in World War II* (1974) and *Roosevelt and the Isolationists, 1932–1945* (1983) examine prewar isolationism. A. Scott Berg, *Lindbergh* (1998) is an excellent biography of the aviation hero who became such a controversial figure in the 1930s. Charles DeBenedetti, *Origins of the Modern American Peace Movement, 1915–1929* (1978) and *The Peace Reform in American History* (1980) examine antiwar movements in American history, including prior to World War II. Joseph Lash's *Roosevelt and Churchill* (1976) explores the dynamic relationship between the two leaders of the United States and England. Akira Iriye, *The Origins of the Second World War in Asia and the Pacific* (1988) examines the conflict between China and Japan that preceded American intervention in the Pacific War. Gordon Prange, *At Dawn We Slept* (1981) examines the controversial attack on Pearl Harbor from both the Japanese and American sides.

For quizzes, Internet resources, references to additional books and films, and more, consult this book's Online Learning Center site at www.mhhe.com/unfinishednation4.

WORK TO WIN

"STEP ON 'EM" This government poster distributed during World War II suggests the dual character of the American war effort: on the one hand, a military assault on the Axis powers; on the other, the effort at home to expand the nation's industrial capacity and supply the war effort. American production was at least as important to the Allied victory in the war as the successes of American troops in the field. *(The National Archives and Records Administration)*

TIME LINE

	1942	1943	
	Battle of Midway	Americans capture Guadalcanal	
	Campaign in Northern Africa	Allied invasion of Italy	
	Japanese Americans interned	Soviet victory at Stalingrad	
	Manhattan Project begins		
	CORE founded		

CHAPTER TWENTY-EIGHT

AMERICA IN A WORLD AT WAR

War on Two Fronts
The American Economy in Wartime
Race and Gender in Wartime America
Anxiety and Affluence in Wartime Culture
The Defeat of the Axis

T he attack on Pearl Harbor had thrust the United States into the greatest and most terrible war in the history of humanity, a war that changed the world as profoundly as any event of the twentieth century, perhaps of any century. World War II also transformed the United States in profound, if not always readily visible, ways.

WAR ON TWO FRONTS

Whatever political disagreements and social tensions there may have been among the American people during World War II, there was striking unity of opinion about the conflict itself. But both unity and confidence faced severe tests in the first, troubled months of 1942.

	1944	1945	
	Allies invade Normandy	Roosevelt dies; Truman becomes president	
	Roosevelt reelected	Germany surrenders	
	Americans capture Philippines	U.S. drops atomic bombs on Hiroshima, Nagasaki	
		Japan surrenders	

Containing the Japanese

Ten hours after the strike at Pearl Harbor, Japanese airplanes attacked the American airfields at Manila in the Philippines, destroying much of America's remaining air power in the Pacific. Three days later Guam, an American possession, fell to Japan; Wake Island and Hong Kong followed. The great British fortress of Singapore in Malaya surrendered in February 1942, the Dutch East Indies in March, Burma in April. In the Philippines, exhausted Filipino and American troops gave up their defense of the islands on May 6.

Japanese Victories

American strategists planned two broad offensives to turn the tide against the Japanese. One, under the command of General Douglas MacArthur, would move north from Australia, through New Guinea, and eventually to the Philippines. The other, under Admiral Chester Nimitz, would move west from Hawaii toward major Japanese island outposts in the central Pacific. Ultimately, strategists predicted, the two offensives would come together to invade Japan itself.

Battle of Midway

The Allies achieved their first important victory in the Battle of the Coral Sea, just northwest of Australia, on May 7–8, 1942, when American forces turned back the previously unstoppable Japanese navy. A month later, there was an even more important turning point northwest of Hawaii. An enormous battle raged for four days, June 3–6, 1942, near the small American outpost at Midway Island, at the end of which the United States, despite great losses, was clearly victorious. The American navy destroyed four Japanese aircraft carriers and lost only one of its own; the action regained control of the central Pacific for the United States.

The Americans took the offensive for the first time several months later in the southern Solomon Islands, to the east of New Guinea. In August 1942, American forces assaulted three of the islands: Gavutu, Tulagi, and Guadalcanal. A struggle of terrible ferocity developed at Guadalcanal and continued for six months, inflicting heavy losses on both sides. In the end, however, the Japanese were forced to abandon the island—and with it their last chance of launching an effective offensive to the south. The Americans, with aid from the Australians and the New Zealanders, now began the slow, arduous process of moving toward the Philippines and Japan itself.

Holding Off the Germans

In the European war, the United States was fighting in cooperation with, among others, Britain and the exiled "Free French" forces in the west; and it was trying also to conciliate its new ally, the Soviet Union, which was now fighting Hitler in the east. The army chief of staff, General George C. Marshall, supported a plan for a major Allied invasion of France across the English Channel in the spring of 1943, and he placed a previously little-known general, Dwight D. Eisenhower, in charge of planning the operation. But the Soviet Union,

Dwight Eisenhower

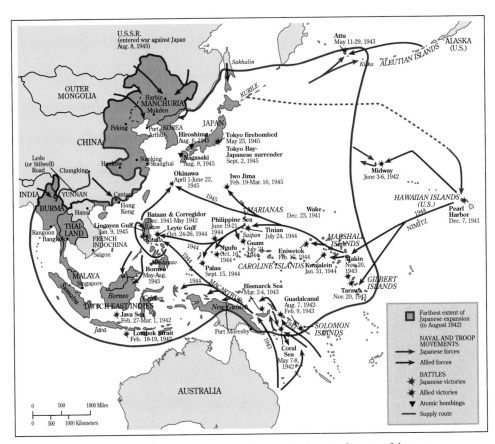

WORLD WAR II IN THE PACIFIC This map illustrates the changing fortunes of the two combatants in the Pacific phase of World War II. The long red line stretching from Burma around to Manchuria represents the eastern boundary of the vast areas of the Pacific that had fallen under Japanese control by the summer of 1942. The blue lines illustrate the advance of American forces back into the Pacific beginning in May 1942 and accelerating in 1943 and after, which drove the Japanese forces back. The American advance was a result of two separate offensives—one in the central Pacific, under the command of Chester Nimitz, which moved west from Hawaii; the other, under the command of Douglas MacArthur, which moved north from Australia. By the summer of 1945, American forces were approaching the Japanese mainland and were bombing Tokyo itself. The dropping of two American atomic bombs, on Hiroshima and Nagasaki, finally brought the war to an end. ◆ *Why did the Soviet Union enter the Pacific War in August 1945, as shown in the upper left corner of the map?*

which was absorbing the brunt of the German war effort, wanted the Allied invasion to begin at the earliest possible moment. The British, on the other hand, wanted first to launch a series of Allied offensives around the edges of the Nazi empire—in northern Africa and southern Europe—before undertaking the invasion of France.

Roosevelt ultimately decided to support the British plan—in part because he was eager to get American forces into combat quickly and knew that a cross-Channel invasion would take a long time to prepare. At the end of October 1942, the British opened a counteroffensive against General Erwin Rommel and the Nazi forces in North Africa that were threatening the Suez Canal. In a major battle at El Alamein, they forced the Germans to retreat from Egypt. On November 8, Anglo-American forces landed at Oran and Algiers in Algeria and at Casablanca in Morocco—areas under the Nazi-controlled French government at Vichy—and began moving east toward Rommel. The Germans threw the full weight of their forces in Africa against the inexperienced Americans and inflicted a serious defeat on them at the Kasserine Pass in Tunisia. General George S. Patton, however, regrouped the American troops and began an effective counteroffensive. With the help of Allied air and naval power and of British forces attacking from the east under Field Marshall Bernard Montgomery (the hero of El Alamein), the American offensive finally drove the last Germans from Africa in May 1943.

The North African campaign had tied up a large proportion of Allied resources. That was one reason why the planned May 1943 cross-Channel invasion of France had to be postponed, despite angry complaints from the Soviet Union. By now, however, the threat of a Soviet collapse seemed much diminished, for during the winter of 1942–1943, the Red Army had *Battle of Stalingrad* successfully held off a major German assault at Stalingrad in southern Russia. Hitler had committed such enormous forces to the battle, and had suffered such appalling losses, that he could not continue his eastern offensive.

The Soviet successes persuaded Roosevelt to agree, in a January 1943 meeting with Churchill in Casablanca, to a British plan for an Allied invasion of Sicily. Churchill argued that the operation *Italy Invaded* in Sicily might knock Italy out of the war and tie up German divisions that would otherwise be stationed in France. On the night of July 9, 1943, American and British armies landed in southeast Sicily; thirty-eight days later, they had conquered the island and were moving onto the Italian mainland. In the face of these setbacks, Mussolini's government collapsed and the dictator himself fled north toward Germany. (He was later captured by Italian insurgents and hanged.) Although Mussolini's successor, Pietro Badoglio, quickly committed Italy to the Allies, Germany moved eight divisions into the country and established a powerful defensive line south of Rome. The Allied offensive on the Italian peninsula, which began on September 3, 1943, soon bogged down. Not until May 1944 did the Allies break through the German defenses to resume their northward advance. On June 4, 1944, they captured Rome.

The invasion of Italy contributed to postponing the invasion of France by as much as a year, deeply embittering Stalin and giving the Soviets time to begin moving toward the countries of eastern Europe.

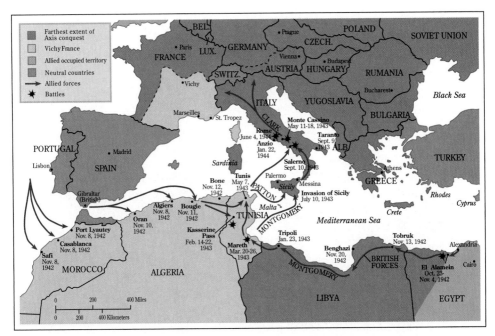

**WORLD WAR II IN NORTH AFRICA AND ITALY: THE ALLIED COUNTEROFFENSIVE,
1942–1943** This map shows the Anglo-American offensive in Europe that preceded the great
Normandy Invasion of 1944. Eight months after landing in North Africa, U.S. and British forces
established their first foothold in Europe when they landed in Sicily in July 1943. ◆ *Why did
Stalin have so little enthusiasm for the North African invasion?*

America and the Holocaust

In the midst of this intensive fighting, the leaders of the American government found themselves confronted with one of history's great tragedies:
the Nazi campaign to exterminate the Jews of Europe—the Holocaust. As
early as 1942, high officials in Washington had incontrovertible evidence
that Hitler's forces were rounding up Jews and others (including Poles,
homosexuals, and communists) from all over Europe, transporting them
to concentration camps in eastern Germany and Poland, and systematically murdering them. (The death toll would ultimately reach 6 million
Jews and at least 4 million others.) News of the atrocities was reaching the
public as well, and pressure began to build for an Allied effort to end the
killing or at least to rescue some of the surviving Jews.

The American government consistently resisted almost all such entreaties. Although by mid-1944 Allied bombers were flying missions
within a few miles of the most notorious death camp, at Auschwitz in
Poland, the War Department rejected as militarily unfeasible pleas that
the planes try to destroy the crematoria at the camp. American officials
also refused requests that the Allies try to destroy railroad lines leading to

THE *ST. LOUIS* Many people consider the fate of the German liner *St. Louis* to be a powerful symbol of the indifference of the United States and other nations to the fate of European Jews during the Holocaust, even though its forlorn journey preceded both the beginning of World War II and the beginning of systematic extermination of Jews by the Nazi regime. The *St. Louis* carried a group of over 900 Jews fleeing from Germany in 1939, carrying exit visas of dubious legality cynically sold to them by members of Hitler's Gestapo. It became a ship without a port as it sailed from country to country—Mexico, Paraguay, Argentina, Costa Rica, and Cuba—where its passengers were refused entry time and again. Most of the passengers were hoping for a haven in the United States, but the American State Department refused to allow the ship even to dock as it sailed up the American eastern seaboard. Eventually, the *St. Louis* returned to Europe and distributed its passengers among Britain, France, Holland, and Belgium (where this photograph was taken showing refugees smiling and waving as they prepared to disembark in Antwerp in June 1939). Less than a year later, all those nations except Britain fell under Nazi control. *(Bettmann/Corbis)*

the camp. And the United States resisted pleas that it admit large numbers of Jewish refugees attempting to escape Europe.

Moral Failure   After 1941, there was probably little American leaders could have done, other than defeat Germany in the war, to save most of Hitler's victims. But more forceful action by the United States (and Britain, which was even less amenable to Jewish requests for assistance) might well have saved at least some lives. That they did not take such action, it seems clear in retrospect, constituted a considerable moral failure. But policymakers justified their inaction by insisting that they needed to focus exclusively on the larger goal of winning the war. Any diversion of energy and attention to other purposes, they believed, would distract them from the overriding goal of victory.

THE AMERICAN ECONOMY IN WARTIME

Not since the Civil War had the United States been involved in so prolonged and consuming a military experience as World War II. American
armed forces engaged in combat around the globe for nearly four years.
American society, in the meantime, experienced changes that reached into
virtually every corner of the nation.

Prosperity and the Rights of Labor

World War II had its most profound impact on American domestic life by
ending the Great Depression. By the middle of 1941, the economic problems of the 1930s—unemployment, deflation, industrial sluggishness—had
virtually vanished before the great wave of wartime industrial expansion.

The most important agent of the new prosperity was government spending, which after 1939 was
Massive Government Spending
pumping more money into the economy each year than all the New Deal
relief agencies combined had done. In 1939, the federal budget had been
$9 billion; by 1945, it had risen to $100 billion. Largely as a result, the
gross national product soared: from $91 billion in 1939 to $166 billion in
1945. Personal incomes in some regions grew by as much as 100 percent
or more.

The impact of government spending was perhaps most dramatic in
the West. The West Coast, naturally, became the launching point for
most of the naval war against Japan, and the government created large
manufacturing facilities in California and elsewhere to serve the needs of
its military. Altogether, the government made almost $40 billion worth of
capital investments (factories, military and transportation facilities, highways, power plants) in the West during the war, more than in any other
region. By the end of the war, the Pacific Coast had become the center of
the growing American aircraft industry and an important center of the
shipbuilding industry. Los Angeles, formerly a medium-sized city notable
chiefly for its film industry, now became a major industrial center as well.

The war created a serious labor shortage. The armed forces took over
15 million men and women out of the civilian work force at the same time
that the demand for labor was rising rapidly. Nevertheless, the supply of
workers increased by almost 20 percent during the war—largely through
the employment of many people previously considered inappropriate for
the work force: the very young, the elderly, minorities, and, most important, several million women.

The war gave a substantial boost to union membership, which rose from about 10.5 million in 1941
Union Membership Boosted
to over 13 million in 1945. That was in part a result of a "maintenance-of-
membership" agreement with the government, which ensured that the

thousands of new workers pouring into unionized defense plants would be automatically enrolled in the unions. But the government also managed to win two important concessions from union leaders. One was the "no-strike" pledge, by which unions agreed not to stop production in wartime. Another was the so-called Little Steel formula, which set a 15 percent limit on wage increases.

Despite the no-strike pledge, there were nearly 15,000 work stoppages during the war, mostly wildcat strikes (strikes unauthorized by the union leadership). When the United Mine Workers defied the government by striking in May 1943, Congress reacted by passing, over Roosevelt's veto, the Smith-Connally Act (the War Labor Disputes Act), which required that unions wait thirty days before striking and which empowered the president to seize a struck war plant. In the meantime, public animosity toward labor rose rapidly, and many states passed laws to limit union power.

Stabilizing the Boom and Mobilizing Production

The fear of deflation, the central concern of the 1930s, gave way during the war to a fear of inflation, particularly after prices rose 25 percent in the two years before Pearl Harbor. Holding the line against inflation was the task of the Office of Price Administration *Office of Price Administration* (OPA), led first by Leon Henderson and then by Chester Bowles. The OPA was successful enough that inflation was a much less serious problem during World War II than it had been during World War I. Even so, the agency was never popular. Black-marketing and overcharging grew in proportions far beyond OPA policing capacity.

From 1941 to 1945, the federal government spent a total of $321 billion—twice as much as it had spent in the entire 150 years of its existence to that point, and ten times as much as the cost of World War I. The national debt rose from $49 billion in 1941 to $259 billion in 1945. The government borrowed about half the revenues it needed by selling $100 billion worth of bonds. Much of the rest it raised by radically increasing income-tax rates, through the Revenue Act of 1942. To simplify collection, Congress enacted a withholding system of payroll deductions in 1943.

In January 1942, the president responded to widespread criticism of earlier efforts to mobilize the economy for war by creating the War Production *War Production Board* Board (WPB), under the direction of former Sears Roebuck executive Donald Nelson. Throughout its troubled history, the WPB was never able to win complete control over military purchases; the army and navy often circumvented the board. It was never able to satisfy the complaints of small business, which charged (correctly) that most contracts were going to large corporations. Gradually, the president transferred much of the WPB's authority to a new office located within the White House: the Office of War Mobilization (OWM). But the OWM was only slightly more successful than the WPB.

Despite the administrative problems, however, the war economy managed to meet almost all of the nation's critical war needs. By the beginning of 1944, American factories were, in fact, producing more than the government needed. Their output was twice that of all the Axis countries combined.

Wartime Science and Technology

More than any previous American war, World War II was a watershed for technological and scientific innovation. That was partly because the American government poured substantial funds into research and development beginning in 1940. In that year the government created the National Defense Research Committee, headed by the MIT scientist Vannevar *National Defense Research Committee*
Bush, who had been a pioneer in the early development of the computer. (It later became the Office of Scientific Research and Development.) By the end of the war, the new agency had spent more that $100 million on research, more than four times the amount spent by the government on military research and development in the previous forty years.

In the first years of the war, all the technological advantages seemed to lie with the Germans and Japanese. Germany had made great advances in tanks and other mechanized armor in the 1930s, particularly during the Spanish Civil War, when it had helped arm Franco's fascist forces. It used its armor effectively during its blitzkrieg in Europe in 1940 and again in North Africa in 1942. German submarine technology was significantly advanced compared to British and American capabilities in 1940. Japan had developed extraordinary capacity in its naval-air technology. Its highly sophisticated fighter planes, launched from distant aircraft carriers, conducted the successful raid on Pearl Harbor in December 1941.

But Britain and America had advantages of their own. American techniques of mass production—the great automotive assembly lines in particular—were converted efficiently to military production in 1941 and 1942 and soon began producing airplanes, ships, tanks, and other armaments in much greater numbers than the Germans and Japanese could produce. Allied scientists and engineers moved quickly as well to improve Anglo-American aviation and naval technology, and particularly to improve the performance of submarines and tanks. By late 1942, Allied weaponry was at least as advanced, and coming to be more plentiful, than that of the enemy.

In addition, each technological innovation by the enemy produced a corresponding innovation to limit the damage of the new techniques. American and British physicists made rapid advances in improving radar and sonar—taking advantage of advances in radio technology in the 1920s and beyond—which *Sonar*
helped Allied naval forces decimate German U-boats in 1943 and effectively end their effectiveness in the naval war. Particularly important was

BOMBING AXIS FACTORIES The Boeing B-17 bomber was one of the great technological innovations of wartime aviation. It allowed Allied pilots to fly much further into enemy territory on bombing missions. Here, B-17s bomb factories in Austria in 1944. *(Archive Photos/American Stock/Getty Images)*

the creation in 1940 of "centimetric radar," whose narrow beams of short wavelength made radar more efficient and effective than ever before—as the British navy discovered in April 1941 when the instruments on one of its ships detected a surfaced submarine 10 miles away at night and, on another occasion, spotted a periscope at three-quarters of a mile range. With earlier technologies, both things would have been undetectable. This new radar could also be effectively miniaturized, which was critical to its use on airplanes and submarines in particular. These innovations put the Allies far in advance of Germany and Japan in radar technology. The Allies also learned early how to detect and disable German naval mines; and when the Germans tried to counter this progress by introducing an "acoustic" mine, which detonated when a ship came near it, not necessarily just on contact, the Allies developed acoustical countermeasures of their own, which transmitted sounds through the water to detonate mines before ships came near them.

Anglo-American antiaircraft technology—both on land and on sea—also improved, although never to the point where it could stop bombing raids altogether. Germany made substantial advances in the development of rocket technology in the early years of the war, and it managed to launch some rocket-propelled bombs (the V1s and V2s) across the English

Channel, aimed at London. The psychological effects of the rockets on the British people were considerable. But the Germans were never able to create a production technology capable of building enough such rockets to make a real difference in the balance of military power.

Beginning in 1942, British and American forces seized the advantage in the air war by producing new and powerful four-engine bombers in great numbers—among them the British Lancaster B1 and the American Boeing B17F, capable of flying a bomb load of *Long-range Bombing* 6,000 pounds for 1,300 miles, and capable of reaching 37,500 feet. Because they were able to fly higher and longer than the German equivalents, they were able to conduct extensive bombing missions over Germany (and later Japan) with much less danger of being shot down. But the success of the bombers rested heavily as well on new electronic devices capable of guiding their bombs to their targets. The Gee navigation system, which was also valuable to the navy, used electronic pulses to help pilots plot their exact location, something that in the past only a highly skilled navigator could do, and then only in good weather. In March 1942, eighty Allied bombers fitted with Gee systems staged a devastatingly effective bombing raid on German industrial and military installations in the Ruhr Valley. In the past, studies had shown that night-bombing raids were at best 30 percent accurate. The Gee system doubled the accuracy rate. Also effective was the Oboe system, a radio device that sent a sonic message to airplanes to tell them when they were within 20 yards of their targets, first introduced in December 1942.

The area in which the Allies had perhaps the greatest advantage was the gathering of intelligence, much of it through Britain's top-secret Ultra project. Some of the advantages the Allies enjoyed came from successful efforts to capture or steal German and Japanese intelligence devices. More important, however, were the efforts of cryptologists to *Importance of Code Breaking* puzzle out the enemy's systems, and advances in computer technology that helped the Allies decipher coded messages sent by the Japanese and the Germans. Much of Germany's coded communication made use of the so-called Enigma machine, which was effective because it constantly changed the coding systems it used. In the first months of the war, Polish intelligence had developed an electro-mechanical computer, which it called the "Bombe," which could decipher some Enigma messages. After the fall of Poland, British scientists, led by the brilliant computer pioneer Alan Turing, took the Bombe, which was too slow to keep up with the increasingly frequent changes of coding the Germans were using, and greatly improved it. On April 15, 1940, the new, improved, high-speed Bombe broke the coding of a series of German messages within hours (not days, as had previously been the case). A few weeks later, it began decrypting German messages at the rate of 1,000 a day, providing the British (and later the Americans) with a constant flow of information about enemy operations that continued—completely unknown to the Germans—until the end of the war. Later in the war, British scientists working for the intelligence services built the first real programmable, digital computer—the Colossus II, which became operational less than a week before the beginning of the Normandy invasion and which was able to decipher an enormous number of intercepted German messages almost instantly.

The United States also had some important intelligence break-throughs, including, in 1941, a dramatic success by the American Magic operation (the counterpart to the British Ultra) in breaking a Japanese coding system not unlike the German Enigma. The result was that Americans had access to intercepted information that, if properly interpreted, could have alerted them to the Japanese raid on Pearl Harbor in December 1941. But because such a raid had seemed entirely inconceivable to most American officials prior to its occurrence, those who received the information failed to understand or disseminate it in time.

RACE AND GENDER IN WARTIME AMERICA

In most ways, the war loosened traditional barriers that had restricted the lives of minorities and women. There was too much demand for fighting men, too much demand for labor, and too much fluidity and mobility in society for rigid, traditional barriers to survive intact.

African Americans and the War

A. Philip Randolph   In the summer of 1941, A. Philip Randolph, president of the Brotherhood of Sleeping Car Porters, an important union with a primarily black membership, began to insist that the government require companies receiving defense contracts to integrate their work forces. To mobilize support for the demand, Randolph planned a massive march on Washington. Roosevelt finally persuaded Randolph to cancel the march in return for a promise to establish what became the Fair Employment Practices Commission (FEPC) to investigate discrimination against African Americans in war industries.

Wartime Race Riots   The need for labor in war plants greatly increased the migration of African Americans from the rural areas of the South into industrial cities. The migration bettered the economic condition of many African Americans, but it also created urban tensions and occasionally violence. The most serious conflict occurred in Detroit in 1943, when racial friction in the city produced a major riot in which thirty-four people died, twenty-five of them black.

Despite such tensions, the leading black organizations redoubled their efforts during the war to challenge the system of segregation. The Congress of Racial Equality (CORE), organized in 1942, mobilized mass popular resistance to discrimination in a way that the older, more conservative organizations had never done. Randolph, Bayard Rustin, James Farmer, and other, younger African-American leaders helped organize sit-ins and demonstrations in segregated theaters and restaurants.

Pressure for change was also growing within the military. The armed forces maintained their traditional practice of limiting blacks to the most menial assignments, keeping them in segregated training camps and units, and barring them entirely from the Marine Corps and the Army Air Force. But there were signs of change. By the end of the war, the number of black servicemen had increased sevenfold, to 700,000; some training camps were being at least partially integrated; African Americans were being allowed to serve on ships with white sailors; and more black units were being sent into combat. The changes did not come easily. In some of the partially integrated army bases—Fort Dix, New Jersey, for example—riots occasionally broke out when black soldiers protested having to serve in segregated divisions.

Native Americans and the War

Approximately 25,000 Indians performed military service during World War II. Many Native Americans served in combat. Others (mostly Navajos) became "code-talkers," working in military communications and speaking their own language *Navajo "Code-Talkers"* (which enemy forces would be unlikely to understand) over the radio and the telephones. The war had important effects on the Indians who served in the military. It brought them into intimate contact (often for the first time) with white society, and it awakened among some of them a taste for the material benefits of life in capitalist America that they would retain after the war. Some never returned to the reservations, but chose to remain in the non-Indian world and assimilate to its ways.

The war had important effects, too, on those Native Americans who stayed on the reservations. Little war work reached the tribes. Government subsidies dwindled. Talented young people left the reservations to serve in the military or work in war production, creating manpower shortages in some tribes. The wartime emphasis on national unity undermined support for the revitalization of tribal autonomy that the Indian Reorganization Act of 1934 had launched. New pressures emerged to eliminate the reservation system and require the tribes to assimilate into white society—pressures so severe that John Collier, the energetic director of the Bureau of Indian Affairs who had done so much to promote the reinvigoration of the reservations, resigned in 1945.

Mexican-American War Workers

Large numbers of Mexican workers entered the United States during the war in response to labor shortages on the Pacific coast and in the Southwest. The American and Mexican governments agreed in 1942 to a program by which *braceros* *Braceros Program*

ZOOT-SUITER The baggy pants, the long, loose jacket, the big collar, the exaggerated watch chain, the slicked-back hair—all were features of the outfit known as the zoot suit, which was popular among young Mexican Americans in Los Angeles and elsewhere. The "zoot-suit riots" in Los Angeles in June 1943 were a product of the suspicion with which Anglos (in this case servicemen stationed nearby) looked at the culture of the Chicano communities that were growing rapidly throughout the Southwest. *(UPI/Corbis-Bettmann)*

(contract laborers) would be admitted to the United States for a limited time. Some worked as migrant farm laborers, but many Mexicans were able for the first time to find factory jobs. They formed the second-largest group of migrants (after African Americans) to U.S. cities in the 1940s. They were concentrated mainly in the West, but there were significant Mexican communities in Chicago, Detroit, and other industrial cities.

The sudden expansion of Mexican-American neighborhoods created tensions and occasionally conflict in some American cities. White residents of Los Angeles became alarmed at the activities of Mexican-American teenagers, many of whom were joining street gangs *(pachucos)*. The youths were particularly distinctive because of their style of dress. They wore long, loose jackets with padded shoulders, baggy pants tied at the ankles, long watch chains, broad-brimmed hats, and greased, ducktail hairstyles. The outfit was known as a "zoot suit." In June 1943, animosity toward the "zoot-suiters" produced a four-day riot in Los Angeles, during which white sailors stationed at a base in Long Beach invaded Mexican-American communities and attacked zoot-suiters (in response to alleged zoot-suiter attacks on servicemen). The police did little to restrain the sailors, who grabbed Hispanic teenagers, tore off and burned *"Zoot-Suit Riots"* their clothes, cut off their ducktails, and beat them. When Mexicans tried to fight back, the police moved in and arrested them. In the aftermath of the "zoot-suit riots," Los Angeles passed a law prohibiting the wearing of zoot suits.

The Internment of Japanese Americans

Although World War II, unlike World War I, produced little popular animosity toward Germans, it created considerable animosity toward the Japanese. After the attack on Pearl Harbor, government propaganda and popular culture combined to create an image of the Japanese as a devious, malign, and savage people.

Predictably, this racial animosity soon extended to Americans of Japanese descent. There were not many Japanese Americans in the United States—about 127,000, most of them concentrated in a few areas in California. About a third of them were unnaturalized, first-generation immigrants (Issei); two-thirds were naturalized or native-born citizens of the United States (Nisei). Because they generally kept to themselves and preserved traditional Japanese cultural patterns, it was easy for some to imagine that the Japanese Americans were engaged in conspiracies on behalf of their ancestral homeland. (There is no evidence that they actually were.)

In February 1942, in response to pressure from military officials and political leaders on the West Coast and recommendations from the War Department, the president authorized the army to "intern" the Japanese Americans. More than 100,000 people (Issei and Nisei alike) were rounded up, told to dispose of their property however they could (which often meant simply abandoning it), and taken to what the government *"Relocation Centers"* euphemistically called "relocation centers." In fact, they were facilities little different from prisons, many of them located in the western mountains and desert. Thus a group of innocent, hardworking people (many of them citizens of the United States) were forced to spend up to three years in grim, debilitating isolation, barred from lucrative employment, provided with only minimal medical care, and deprived of decent schools for their children. The Supreme Court upheld the evacuation in a 1944 decision; and although most of the Japanese Americans were released later that year, they were unable to win any significant compensation for their losses until Congress finally acted to redress the wrongs in the late 1980s.

Chinese Americans and the War

At the same time that the conflict with Japan undermined the position of Japanese Americans, the American alliance with China during World War II significantly enhanced both the legal and social status of Chinese Americans. In 1943, partly to improve relations with the government of China, Congress finally repealed the Chinese Exclusion Acts, which had barred almost all Chinese immigration since 1892. The new quota for Chinese immigrants was minuscule (105 a year), but a substantial number of Chinese women managed to gain entry into the country through other provisions covering war brides and fiancées. Over 4,000 Chinese women entered the United States in the first three years after the war. Permanent residents of the United States of Chinese descent were finally permitted to become citizens.

Declining Prejudice toward Chinese Americans   Racial animosity toward the Chinese did not disappear, but it did decline—in part because government propaganda and popular culture both began presenting positive images of the Chinese (partly to contrast them with the Japanese); in part because Chinese Americans (like African Americans and other previously marginal groups) began taking jobs in war plants and other booming areas suffering from labor shortages and hence moving out of the relatively isolated world of the Chinatowns. A higher proportion of Chinese Americans (22 percent of all adult males) were drafted than of any other national group, and the entire Chinese community in most cities worked hard and conspicuously for the war effort.

Women and Children in Wartime

The number of women in the work force increased by nearly 60 percent during the war, as many women took industrial jobs to replace male workers serving in the military. These wage-earning women were more likely to be married and were, on the whole, older than most of those who had entered the work force in the past.

Many factory owners continued to categorize jobs by gender, reserving the most lucrative positions for men. (Female work, like male work, was also categorized by race: black women were usually assigned more menial tasks, and paid at a lower rate, than their white counterparts.) But some women began now to take on heavy industrial jobs that had long *"Rosie the Riveter"*   been considered "men's work." The famous wartime image of "Rosie the Riveter" symbolized the new importance of the female industrial worker. Women joined unions in substantial numbers, and they helped erode at least some of the prejudice, including the prejudice against mothers working, that had previously kept many of them from paid employment.

Most women workers during the war, however, were employed not in factories but in service-sector jobs. Above all, they worked for the government, whose bureaucratic needs expanded dramatically alongside its mili-

U. S. ARMY
OFFICIAL POSTER

SOLDIERS *without guns*

WOMEN AT WAR Many American women enlisted in the army and navy women's corps during World War II, but an equally important contribution of women to the war effort was their work in factories and offices—often in jobs that would have been considered inappropriate for them in peacetime but that they were now encouraged to assume because of the absence of so many men. (*The Library of Congress*)

tary and industrial needs. Even within the military, which enlisted substantial numbers of women as WAACs (army) and WAVEs (navy), most female work was clerical. *WAACs and WAVEs*

Many mothers whose husbands were in the military had to combine working with caring for their children. The scarcity of child-care facilities or other community services meant that some women had no choice but to leave young children—often known as "latchkey children" or "eight-hour orphans"—at home alone (or sometimes locked in cars in factory parking lots) while they worked.

Perhaps in part because of the family dislocations the war produced, juvenile crime rose markedly in the war years. Young boys were arrested at rapidly increasing rates for car theft and other burglary, vandalism, and vagrancy. The arrest rate for prostitutes, many of whom were teenage girls, rose too, as did the incidence of venereal disease. For many children, however, the distinctive experience of the war years was not crime but work. More than a third of all teenagers between the ages of fourteen and eighteen were employed in the last years of the war, causing some reduction in high-school enrollments.

The return of prosperity helped increase the marriage rate and lower the age at which people married, but many marriages were unable to survive the pressures of wartime separation. The divorce rate rose rapidly. The rise in the birth rate that accompanied the increase in marriages was *Start of the "Baby Boom"* the first sign of what would become the great postwar "baby boom."

ANXIETY AND AFFLUENCE IN WARTIME CULTURE

The war created considerable anxiety in American lives. Families worried about loved ones at the front and, as the war continued, many mourned relatives who had died in combat. Women struggled to support families in the absence of husbands and fathers, who had been the principal breadwinners in peacetime. Businesses and communities struggled with shortages of goods and shortages of labor. People living on the two coasts, in particular, worried about enemy invasions and sabotage.

Consumerism Reborn But the abundance of the war years also created a striking buoyancy in American life. Suddenly people had money to spend again and—despite the many shortages—at least some things to spend it on. In fact, consumerism became, as it had in the 1920s, one of the most powerful forces in American culture and, for many, one of the features of American life that the war was being fought to defend.

Wartime Entertainment and Leisure

The book, theater, and movie industries did record business during the war. Audiences equal to about half the nation's population attended movies each week. Magazines, particularly pictorial ones such as *Life*, reached the peak of their popularity by providing pictures of and stories about the war. Radio ownership and listenership also increased, for the same reason.

Fuel rationing and rubber shortages limited travel by car, but many people traveled nevertheless—by train or bus, or to places relatively close to their homes. Resort hotels, casinos, and racetracks were jammed with customers. More often, however, people sought entertainment in their own communities. Dance halls were packed with young people drawn to the seductive music of bands; soldiers and sailors home on leave, or awaiting shipment abroad, were especially attracted to the dances and the big bands, which became to many of them a symbol of the life they were leaving and that they believed they were fighting to defend.

By far the most popular music in dance halls, and on radio, was the relatively new jazz form known as swing, which, like many other forms of popular music, had emerged from the African-American musical world. *Popularity of Swing*

During the heyday of swing, band leaders such as Benny Goodman, Duke Ellington, Tommy Dorsey, and Glenn Miller, were among the most recognized and popular figures in American popular culture, rivaling movie stars in their celebrity. Swing sold more records than any other kind of music. And it became one of the first forms of popular music to challenge racial taboos. Benny Goodman hired the black pianist Teddy Wilson to play with his band in 1935; other white bandleaders followed.

Women and Men in the Armed Services

For men at the front, the image of home was a powerful antidote to the rigors of wartime. They dreamed of music, food, movies, and other material comforts. Many also dreamed of women—wives and girlfriends, but also movie stars and others, who became the source of one of the most popular icons of the front: the pinup. Sailors pasted pinups inside their lockers. Infantrymen carried them (along with pictures of wives, mothers, and girlfriends) in their knapsacks. Fighter pilots gave their planes female names and painted bathing beauties on their nosecones.

For the servicemen who remained in America during the war, and for soldiers and sailors in cities far from home in particular, the company of friendly, "wholesome" women was, the military believed, critical to sustaining morale. The branches of the United Servicemen's Organization (known as USOs) recruited thousands of young women to serve as hostesses in their clubs. They were expected *Importance of USOs* to dress nicely, dance well, and chat happily with lonely men. Other women joined "dance brigades" and traveled by bus to military bases for social evenings with servicemen. They too were expected to be pretty, to dress attractively, and to interact comfortably with men they had never met before and would likely never see again. The "USO girls" and the members of the dance brigades were forbidden to have any contact with men except at parties at the clubs or during dances. Clearly such regulations were often violated. But while the military took elaborate measures to root out gay men and lesbians from their ranks—vigilantly searching for evidence of homosexuality and unceremoniously dismissing gay people with undesirable discharges—the services quietly tolerated illicit heterosexual relationships, which they believed were both natural and, for many men, necessary.

As during World War I, the armed services virtually took over many American colleges and universities. Emptied of male students and professors (and many females as well), who left to join the war effort, they turned themselves into training camps for military officers—helped by substantial funding from the federal government.

Retreat from Reform

Late in 1943, Franklin Roosevelt publicly suggested that "Dr. New Deal," as he called it, had served its purpose and should now give way to "Dr. Win-the-War." The statement reflected the president's own genuine shift in concern: victory was now more important than reform. But it reflected, too, the political reality that had emerged during the first two years of war.

Conservative Assault on the New Deal

The greatest assault on New Deal reforms came from conservatives in Congress, who seized on the war as an excuse to do what many had wanted to do in peacetime: dismantle many of the achievements of the New Deal. They were assisted by the end of mass unemployment, which decreased the need for such relief programs as the Civilian Conservation Corps and the Works Progress Administration (both of which Congress abolished). They were assisted, too, by their own increasing numbers. In the congressional elections of 1942, Republicans gained 47 seats in the House and 10 in the Senate.

Republicans approached the 1944 election determined to exploit what they believed was resentment of wartime regimentation and unhappiness with Democratic reform. They nominated as their candidate the young and vigorous governor of New York, Thomas E. Dewey. Roosevelt was unopposed within his party, but Democratic leaders pressured him to abandon Vice President Henry Wallace, an advanced New Dealer and hero of the CIO, and replace him with a more moderate figure. Roosevelt acquiesced in the selection of Senator Harry S. Truman of Missouri. He had won acclaim as chairman of the Senate War Investigating Committee (known as the Truman Committee), which compiled an impressive record uncovering waste and corruption in wartime production.

Roosevelt Reelected

The election revolved around domestic economic issues and, indirectly, the president's health. The president was, in fact, gravely ill, suffering from, among other things, advanced arteriosclerosis. But the campaign seemed momentarily to revive him. He made several strenuous public appearances late in October, which dispelled popular doubts about his health and ensured his reelection. He captured 53.5 percent of the popular vote to Dewey's 46 percent. He won 432 electoral votes to Dewey's 99. Democrats lost 1 seat in the Senate, gained 20 in the House, and maintained control of both.

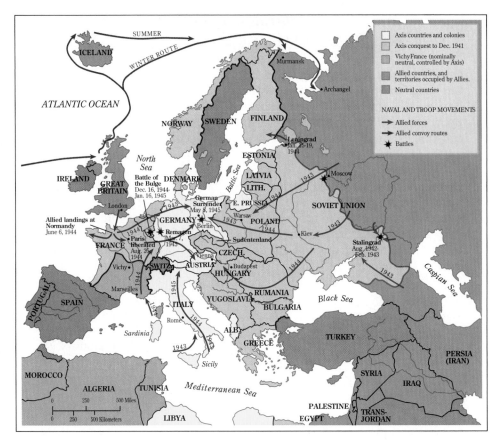

WORLD WAR II IN EUROPE: THE ALLIED COUNTEROFFENSIVE, 1943–1945 This map illustrates the final, climatic movements in the war in Europe—the two great offensives against Germany that began in 1943 and culminated in 1945. From the east, the armies of the Soviet Union, having halted the Germans at Stalingrad and Moscow, swept across eastern Europe toward Germany. From the west and the south, American, British, and other Allied forces moved toward Germany through Italy and—after the Normandy invasion in June 1944—through France. The two offensives met in Berlin in May 1945. Note, too, the northern routes that America and Britain used to supply the Soviet Union during the war. ◆ *What problems did the position of the Allied forces at the end of the war help to produce?*

For an interactive version of this map go to **www.mhhe.com/unfinishednation4ch28maps**

THE DEFEAT OF THE AXIS

By the middle of 1943, America and its allies had succeeded in stopping the Axis advance both in Europe and in the Pacific. In the next two years, the Allies themselves seized the offensive and launched a series of powerful drives that rapidly led the way to victory.

The Liberation of France

By early 1944, American and British bombers were attacking German industrial installations and other targets almost around the clock, drastically cutting production and impeding transportation. Especially devastating was the massive bombing of such German cities as Leipzig, Dresden, and Berlin. A February 1945 incendiary raid on Dresden created a great firestorm that destroyed three-fourths of the previously undamaged city and killed approximately 135,000 people, almost all civilians.

Invasion of France
An enormous offensive force had been gathering in England for two years before the spring of 1944: almost 3 million troops, and perhaps the greatest array of naval vessels and armaments ever assembled in one place. On the morning of June 6, 1944, this vast invasion force moved into action. The landing came not at the narrowest part of the English Channel, where the Germans had expected and prepared for it, but along sixty miles of the Cotentin Peninsula on the coast of Normandy. While airplanes and battleships offshore bombarded the Nazi defenses, 4,000 vessels landed troops and supplies on the beaches. (Three divisions of paratroopers had been dropped behind the German lines the night before.) Fighting was intense along the beach, but the superior manpower and equipment of the Allied forces gradually prevailed. Within a week, the German forces had been dislodged from virtually the entire Normandy coast.

For the next month, further progress remained slow. But in late July in the Battle of Saint-Lô, General Omar Bradley's First Army smashed through the German lines. George S. Patton's Third Army, spearheaded by heavy tank attacks, then moved through the hole Bradley had created and began a drive into the heart of France. On August 25, Free French forces arrived in Paris and liberated the city from four years of German occupation. By mid-September the Allied armies had driven the Germans almost entirely out of France and Belgium.

The great Allied drive came to a halt, however, at the Rhine River against a firm line of Nazi defenses. In mid-December, German forces struck in desperation along fifty miles of front in the Ardennes Forest. In
Battle of the Bulge
the Battle of the Bulge (named for a large bulge that appeared in the American lines as the Germans pressed forward), they drove fifty-five miles toward Antwerp before they were finally stopped at Bastogne. It was the last major battle on the western front.

While the western Allies were fighting their way through France, Soviet forces were sweeping westward into central Europe and the Balkans.
Germany Invaded
In late January 1945, the Russians launched a great offensive toward the Oder River, inside Germany. By early spring, they were ready to launch a final assault against Berlin. General Omar Bradley, in the meantime, was pushing toward the Rhine from the west. Early in March, his forces captured the city of Cologne, on the river's west bank. The next day, he discovered and seized an undamaged bridge over the river at Remagen; Allied troops were soon pouring

A VICTORY CELEBRATION IN SAN FRANCISCO Soldiers and sailors in San Francisco react jubilantly to the news that the war in Europe has ended. But the news they were celebrating was, in fact, one of the many false rumors of surrender circulating in the spring of 1945. The actual V-E Day occurred several weeks later. *(UPI/Corbis-Bettmann)*

across the Rhine. In the following weeks the British commander, Montgomery, with a million troops, pushed into Germany in the north while Bradley's army, sweeping through central Germany, completed the encirclement of 300,000 German soldiers in the Ruhr.

The German resistance was now broken on both fronts. American forces were moving eastward faster than they had anticipated and could have beaten the Russians to Berlin and Prague. The American and British high commands decided, instead, to halt the advance along the Elbe River in central Germany to await the Russians. That decision enabled the Soviets to occupy eastern Germany and Czechoslovakia.

On April 30, with Soviet forces on the outskirts of Berlin, Adolf Hitler killed himself in his bunker in the capital. And on May 8, 1945, the remaining German forces surrendered unconditionally.

The Pacific Offensive

In February 1944, American naval forces under Admiral Chester Nimitz won a series of victories in the Marshall Islands and cracked the outer perimeter of the Japanese Empire. Within a month, the navy had destroyed other vital Japanese bastions. American submarines, in the meantime, were decimating Japanese shipping and crippling Japan's domestic economy.

In mid-June 1944, an enormous American armada struck the heavily fortified Mariana Islands and, after some of the bloodiest operations of the war, captured Tinian, Guam, and Saipan, 1,350 miles from Tokyo. In September, American forces landed on the western Carolines. And on October 20, General MacArthur's troops landed on Leyte Island in the Philippines. The Japanese now employed virtually their entire fleet against the Allied invaders in three major encounters—which together constituted the decisive *Battle of Leyte Gulf* Battle of Leyte Gulf, the largest naval engagement in history. American forces held off the Japanese onslaught and sank four Japanese carriers, all but destroying Japan's capacity to continue a serious naval war. In February 1945, American marines seized the tiny volcanic island of Iwo Jima, only 750 miles from Tokyo, but only after the costliest battle in the history of the Marine Corps.

The battle for Okinawa, an island only 370 miles south of Japan, gave evidence of the strength of the Japanese resistance in these last desperate days. Week after week, the Japanese sent kamikaze (suicide) planes against American and British ships, sacrificing 3,500 of them while inflicting great damage. Japanese troops on shore launched desperate nighttime attacks on the American lines. The United States and its allies suffered nearly 50,000 casualties before finally capturing Okinawa in late June 1945. Over 100,000 Japanese died in the siege.

It seemed likely that the same kind of bitter fighting would await the Americans when they invaded Japan. But there were also some signs early in 1945 that such an invasion might not be necessary. The Japanese had *Tokyo Firebombed* almost no ships or planes left with which to fight. The firebombing of Tokyo in March, in which American bombers dropped napalm on the city and created a firestorm in which over 80,000 people died, further weakened the Japanese will to resist. Moderate Japanese leaders, who had long since concluded the war was lost, were looking for ways to bring the fighting to an end, although they continued to face powerful opposition from military leaders. Whether the moderates could ultimately have prevailed is a question about which historians and others continue to disagree. In any case, their efforts became superfluous in August 1945, when the United States made use of a terrible new weapon it had been developing throughout the war.

The Manhattan Project and Atomic Warfare

Reports had reached the United States in 1939 that Nazi scientists had taken the first step toward the creation of an atomic bomb, a weapon more powerful than any ever previously devised. The United States and Britain immediately began a race to develop the weapon before the Germans did.

The search for the new weapon emerged from theories developed by atomic physicists, beginning early in the century, and particularly from

There has been continuing disagreement since 1945 among historians—and among many others—about how to explain and evaluate President Truman's decision to use the atomic bomb in the war against Japan.

Truman himself, both at the time and in his 1955 memoirs, and many of his contemporaries insisted that the decision was a simple and straightforward one. The alternative to using atomic weapons, he claimed, was an American invasion of mainland Japan that might have cost as many as a million lives. That view has received considerable support from historians. Herbert Feis argued in *The Atomic Bomb and the End of World War II* (1966) that Truman made his decision on purely military grounds—to ensure a speedy American victory. David McCullough, the author of an enormously popular biography of Truman published in 1992, also accepted Truman's own account of his actions largely uncritically, as did Alonzo L. Hamby in *Man of the People* (1995), an important scholarly study of Truman. "One consideration weighed most heavily on Truman," Hamby concluded. "The longer the war lasted, the more Americans killed."

Others have strongly disagreed. As early as 1948, a British physicist, P. M. S. Blackett, wrote in *Fear, War, and the Bomb* that the destruction of Hiroshima and Nagasaki was "not so much the last military act of the second World War as the first major operation of the cold diplomatic war with Russia." The most important critic of Truman's decision is the historian Gar Alperovitz, the author of two influential books on the subject: *Atomic Diplomacy: Hiroshima and Potsdam* (1965) and *The Decision to Use the Atomic Bomb* (1995). Alperovitz dismissed the argument that the bomb was used to shorten the war and save lives. Japan was likely to have surrendered soon even if the bomb had not been used, he claimed. Instead, he argued, the United States used the bomb less to influence Japan than to intimidate the Soviet Union, "to make Russia more manageable in Europe."

John W. Dower's *War Without Mercy* (1986) contributed, by implication at least, to another controversial explanation of the American decision: racism. The Japanese, many Americans came to believe during the war, were almost a subhuman species. Even many of Truman's harshest critics, however, note that it is, as Alperovitz has written, "all but impossible to find specific evidence that racism was an important factor in the decision to attack Hiroshima and Nagasaki."

The debate over the decision to drop the atomic bomb is an unusually emotional one, and it has inspired bitter professional and personal attacks on advocates of almost every position. It illustrates clearly how history has often been, and remains, a powerful force in the way societies define themselves.

some of the founding ideas of modern science developed by Albert Einstein. Einstein's famous theory of relativity had revealed the relationships between mass and energy. More precisely, he had argued that, in theory at least, matter could be converted into a tremendous force of energy. Einstein himself, who was by then living in the United States, warned Franklin Roosevelt that the Germans were developing atomic weapons and that the United States must begin trying to do the same. The effort to build atomic weapons centered on the use of uranium, whose atomic structure made possible the creation of a nuclear chain reaction. A nuclear chain reaction occurs when the atomic nuclei in radioactive matter are split (a process known as nuclear fission) by neutrons. Each fission creates new neutrons that produce fissions in additional atoms at an ever increasing and self-sustaining pace.

Atomic Fission

The construction of atomic weapons had become feasible by the 1940s because of the discovery of the radioactivity of uranium in the 1930s by Enrico Fermi in Italy. In 1939, the great Danish physicist Niels Bohr, sent news of German experiments in radioactivity to the United States, where experiments began in many places. In 1940, scientists at Columbia University began chain-reaction experiments with uranium and produced persuasive evidence of the feasibility of using uranium as fuel for a weapon. The Columbia experiments stalled in 1941, and the work moved to Berkeley and the University of Chicago, where Enrico Fermi (who had emigrated to the United States in 1938) achieved the first controlled fission chain reaction in December 1942.

By then, the army had taken control of the research and appointed General Leslie Groves to reorganize the project—which soon became known as the Manhattan Project, because it was devised in the Manhattan Engineer District Office of the Army Corps of Engineers. Over the next three years, the government secretly poured nearly $2 billion into the Manhattan Project—a massive scientific and technological effort conducted at hidden laboratories in Oak Ridge, Tennessee; Los Alamos, New Mexico; Hanford, Washington; and other sites. Scientists in Oak Ridge, who were charged with finding a way to create a nuclear chain reaction that could be feasibly replicated within the confined space of a bomb, began experimenting with plutonium—a derivative of uranium first discovered by scientists at Berkeley. Plutonium proved capable of providing a practical fuel for the weapon. Scientists in Los Alamos, under the direction of J. Robert Oppenheimer, were charged with the construction of the actual atomic bomb.

J. Robert Oppenheimer

By 1944, the government was secretly funneling over $1 billion a year to the Manhattan Project, and despite many unforeseen problems, the scientists pushed ahead much faster than anyone had predicted. Even so, the war in Europe ended before they were ready to test the first weapon. Just before dawn on July 16, 1945, in the desert near Alamogordo, New Mexico, the scientists gathered to witness the first atomic explosion in history: the detonation of a plutonium-fueled bomb that scientists had named Trinity. The explosion—a blinding flash of light, probably brighter than any ever seen on earth, followed by a huge, billowing mushroom cloud—created a vast crater in the barren desert.

News of the explosion reached President Harry S. Truman (who had taken office in April on the death of Roosevelt) in Potsdam, Germany, where he was attending a conference of Allied leaders. He issued an ultimatum to the Japanese (signed jointly by the British) demanding that they

HIROSHIMA Long after the city was destroyed by the first atomic bomb ever used in warfare, Hiroshima remained a ghostly landscape—an incongruous backdrop for a Japanese couple strolling along the street. *(UPI/Corbis-Bettmann)*

surrender by August 3 or face utter devastation. When the Japanese failed to meet the deadline, Truman ordered the air force to use the new atomic weapons against Japan.

Controversy has continued for decades over whether Truman's decision to use the bomb was *Persistent Controversy* justified and what his motives were. Some have argued that the atomic attack was unnecessary—that had the United States agreed to the survival of the emperor (which it ultimately did agree to in any case), or had it waited only a few more weeks, the Japanese would have surrendered. Others argue that nothing less than the atomic bombs could have persuaded the Japanese to surrender without a costly American invasion.

The nation's military and political leaders, however, seemed little concerned about such matters. Truman, who had not even known of the existence of the Manhattan Project until he became president, was, apparently, making what he believed to be a simple military decision. A weapon was available that would end the war quickly; he could see no reason not to use it.

On August 6, 1945, an American B-29, the *Enola Gay*, dropped an atomic weapon on the Japanese industrial center at Hiroshima. With a single bomb, the United States *Hiroshima Destroyed* completely incinerated a four-square-mile area at the center of the previously undamaged city. More than 80,000 civilians died, according to later American estimates. Many more suffered the crippling effects of radioactive fallout or passed those effects on to their children in the form of birth defects.

The Japanese government, stunned by the attack, was at first unable to agree on a response. Two days later, on August 8, the Soviet Union declared war on Japan. And the following day, another American plane dropped another atomic weapon—this time on the city of Nagasaki—inflicting 100,000 deaths and horrible damage on yet another unfortunate community. Finally, the emperor intervened to break the stalemate in the cabinet, and on August 14 the government announced that it was ready to give up. On September 2, 1945, on board the American battleship *Missouri*, anchored in Tokyo Bay, Japanese officials signed the articles of surrender.

Surrender of Japan

The greatest war in the history of mankind had come to an end, and the United States had emerged from it not only victorious but in a position of unprecedented power, influence, and prestige. It was a victory, however, that few could greet with unambiguous joy. Fourteen million combatants had died in the struggle. Many more civilians had perished. The United States had suffered only light casualties in comparison with some other nations (and particularly in comparison with Russia and Germany), but the cost had still been high: 322,000 dead, another 800,000 injured. And the world continued to face an uncertain future, menaced by the threat of nuclear warfare and by an emerging antagonism between the world's two strongest nations—the United States and the Soviet Union—that would darken the peace for many decades to come.

CONCLUSION

The United States played a critical, indeed decisive, role in the war against Germany and Italy; and it defeated Imperial Japan in the Pacific largely alone. But America's contributions to and sacrifices in the war paled next to those of its most important allies. Britain, France, and above all the Soviet Union paid a staggering price—in lives, treasure, and social unity—that had no counterpart in the United States. Most American citizens experienced a booming prosperity and only modest privations during the four years of American involvement in the conflict. There were, of course, jarring social changes during the war that even prosperity could not entirely offset: shortages, restrictions, regulations, family dislocations, and perhaps most of all the absence of millions of men, and considerable numbers of women, who went overseas to fight.

American fighting men and women, of course, had very different experiences from those of the people who remained at home. They endured tremendous hardships, substantial casualties, and great loneliness. They fought effectively and bravely. They helped liberate North Africa and Italy from German occupation. And in June 1944, finally, they joined British, French, and other forces in a great and successful invasion of France, which led less than a year later to the destruction of the Nazi regime and the end of the European war. In the Pacific, they turned back the Japanese offensive through a series of difficult naval and land battles. Ultimately, however, it was not the American army and navy that brought the war against Japan to a close. It was the unleashing of the most destructive weapon mankind had ever created—the atomic bomb—on the people of Japan that finally persuaded the leaders of that nation to surrender.

FOR FURTHER REFERENCE

John Morton Blum, *V Was for Victory: Politics and American Culture During World War II* (1976) and Richard Polenberg, *War and Society* (1972) are important studies of the home front during World War II. David Kennedy, *Freedom from Fear: The American People in Depression and War, 1929–1945* (1999) is an important narrative of both the American military experience in the war and the war's impact on American politics and society. Alan Brinkley, *The End of Reform: New Deal Liberalism in Recession and War* (1995) examines the impact of the war on liberal ideology and political economy. Doris Kearns Goodwin, *No Ordinary Time: Franklin and Eleanor Roosevelt: The Home Front in World War II* (1994) is an engaging portrait of the Roosevelts during the war. Susan Hartmann examines the transformation in women's work and family roles during and after the war in *The Homefront and Beyond: American Women in the 1940s* (1982). Richard M. Dalfiume, *Desegregation of the U.S. Armed Forces: Fighting on Two Fronts, 1939–1953* (1969) discusses race relations in the military during World War II and beyond. Barbara Dianne Savage, *Broadcasting Freedom: Radio, War, and the Politics of Race, 1938–1948* (1999) reveals the role of African-American radio in tying the war to the struggle for black freedom. Maurice Isserman, *Which Side Were You On? The American Communist Party During World War II* (1982) portrays the dramatic shifts in Communist Party strategy and status during the war. John W. Dower, *War Without Mercy: Race and Power in the Pacific War* (1986) examines the intense racism that shaped both sides of the war between the United States and Japan. Peter Irons, *Justice at War* (1983) and Roger Daniels, *Concentration Camps USA: Japanese-Americans and World War II* (1981) examine the internment of Japanese Americans. John Keegan, *Six Armies in Normandy: From D-Day to the Liberation of Paris, June 6–August 25, 1944* (1982) is a superb account of the Normandy Invasion. David S. Wyman, *The Abandonment of the Jews: America and the Holocaust, 1941–1945* (1984) is sharply critical of American policy toward the victims of the Holocaust. Richard Rhodes, *The Making of the Atomic Bomb* (1987) is an excellent account of one of the great scientific projects of the twentieth century. Gar Alperovitz, *The Decision to Use the Atomic Bomb and the Architecture of an American Myth* (1995) is an exhaustive and highly critical study of why the United States used atomic weapons in 1945. A sharply different view is visible in Herbert Feis, *The Atomic Bomb and the End of World War II* (1966). John Hersey's *Hiroshima* (1946) reconstructs in minute detail the terrifying experience of the American atomic bomb attack on that Japanese city.

For quizzes, Internet resources, references to additional books and films, and more, consult this book's Online Learning Center site at www.mhhe.com/unfinishednation4.

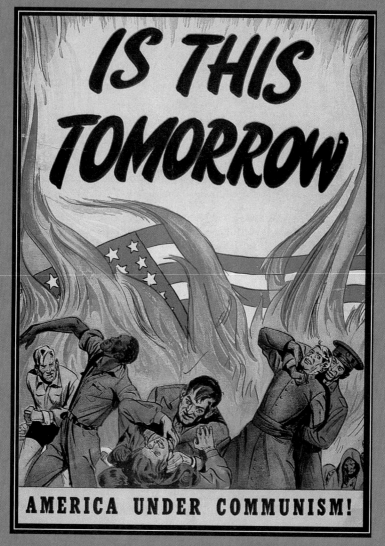

THE AMERICAN NIGHTMARE Nightmarish visions of what life would be like under communism were staples of American anticommunist propaganda in the early years of the Cold War. This is the cover of a comic book widely distributed beginning in 1947 by Christian groups concerned about inadequate popular awareness of the threat. *(Michael Barson Collection)*

TIME LINE

1945	1946	1947	1948
Yalta and Potsdam Conferences	Atomic Energy Commission established	Truman Doctrine	Berlin blockade
United Nations founded	Iran crisis	Marshall Plan proposed	Truman elected president
		National Security Act	Hiss case begins
		Taft-Hartley Act	

◆

CHAPTER TWENTY-NINE

THE COLD WAR

Origins of the Cold War
The Collapse of the Peace
America after the War
The Korean War
The Crusade against Subversion

E ven before World War II ended, there were signs of tension between the United States and the Soviet Union. Once the hostilities were over, those tensions quickly grew to create what became known as the "Cold War"—a tense and dangerous rivalry between the two former allies that would cast its shadow over international affairs and American domestic life for decades.

ORIGINS OF THE COLD WAR

◆

No issue in twentieth-century American history has aroused more debate than the question of the origins of the Cold War. Some have claimed that Soviet duplicity and expansionism created the international tensions, others that American provocations and global ambitions were at least equally to blame.

1949	1950	1951	1952
NATO established	NSC-68	Truman fires MacArthur	American occupation of Japan ends
Soviet Union explodes A-bomb	Korean War begins		Eisenhower elected president
Mao victorious in China	McCarthy's anticommunism campaign begins		

Sources of Soviet-American Tension

At the heart of the rivalry between the United States and the Soviet Union in the 1940s was a fundamental difference in the ways the great powers envisioned the postwar world. One vision, first openly outlined in the Atlantic Charter in 1941, was of a world in which nations abandoned their traditional beliefs in military alliances and spheres of influence and governed their relations with one another through democratic processes, with an international organization serving as the arbiter of disputes and the protector of every nation's right of self-determination. That vision ap-

America's Postwar Vision pealed to many Americans, including Franklin Roosevelt.

The other vision was that of the Soviet Union and to some extent of Great Britain. Both Stalin and Churchill had signed the Atlantic Charter. But Britain had always been uneasy about the implications of the self-determination ideal for its own enormous empire. And the Soviet Union was determined to create a secure sphere for itself in Central and Eastern Europe as protection against possible future aggression from the West. Both Churchill and Stalin, therefore, tended to envision a postwar structure in which the great powers would control areas of strategic interest to them, in which something vaguely similar to the traditional European balance of power would reemerge. Gradually, the differences between these two positions would turn the peacemaking process into a form of warfare.

Wartime Diplomacy

Serious strains had already begun to develop in the alliance with the Soviet Union in January 1943, when Roosevelt and Churchill met in Casablanca, Morocco, to discuss Allied strategy. The two leaders could not accept Stalin's most important demand—the immediate opening of a second front in western Europe. But they tried to reassure Stalin by announcing that they would accept nothing less than the unconditional surrender of the Axis powers, thus indicating that they would not negotiate a separate peace with Hitler and leave the Soviets to fight on alone.

In November 1943, Roosevelt and Churchill traveled to Teheran, Iran, for their first meeting with Stalin. By now, however, Roosevelt's most effective bargaining tool—Stalin's need for American assistance in his struggle against Germany—had been largely removed. The German advance against Russia had been halted; Soviet forces were now launching their own westward offensive. Nevertheless, the

Teheran Conference Teheran Conference seemed in most respects a success. Roosevelt and Stalin established a cordial personal relationship. Stalin agreed to an American request that the Soviet Union enter the war in the Pacific soon after the end of hostilities in Europe. Roosevelt, in turn, promised that an Anglo-American second front would be established within six months.

YALTA, 1945 Churchill *(left)* and Stalin *(right)* were shocked at the physical appearance of Franklin Roosevelt *(center)* when he arrived for their critical meeting at Yalta. Roosevelt had enough energy to perform capably at the conference, but he was in fact gravely ill. Two months later, not long after he gave Congress what turned out to be an unrealistically optimistic report of the prospects for postwar peace, he died. *(Bettmann/Corbis)*

On other matters, however, the origins of future disagreements were already visible. Most important was the question of the future of Poland. Roosevelt and Churchill were willing to agree to a movement of the Soviet border westward, allowing Stalin to annex some historically Polish territory. But on the nature of the postwar government in the portion of Poland that would remain independent, there were sharp differences. Roosevelt and Churchill supported the claims of the Polish government-in-exile that had been functioning in London since 1940; Stalin wished to install another, pro-communist exiled government that had spent the war in Lublin, in the Soviet Union. The three leaders left the Teheran Conference with the issue unresolved.

Yalta

More than a year later, in February 1945, Roosevelt joined Churchill and Stalin for a great peace conference in the Soviet city of Yalta. In return for Stalin's renewed promise to enter the Pacific war, Roosevelt agreed that the Soviet Union should receive some of the territory in the Pacific that Russia had lost in the 1904 Russo-Japanese War.

The negotiators also agreed to a plan for a new international organization, a plan that had been *United Nations Established* hammered out the previous summer at a conference in Washington, D.C. The new United Nations would contain a General Assembly, in which every member would be represented, and a Security Council, with permanent representatives of the five major powers (the United States, Britain,

France, the Soviet Union, and China), each of which would have veto power. The Security Council would also have temporary delegates from several other nations. These agreements became the basis of the United Nations charter, drafted at a conference of fifty nations beginning April 25, 1945, in San Francisco. The United States Senate ratified the charter in July by a vote of 80 to 2.

On other issues, however, the Yalta Conference produced no real accord. Basic disagreement remained about the postwar Polish government. Stalin, whose armies now occupied Poland, had already installed a government composed of the pro-communist "Lublin"

Disagreements over Poland Poles. Roosevelt and Churchill insisted that the pro-Western "London" Poles must be allowed a place in the Warsaw regime. Roosevelt envisioned a government based on free, democratic elections—which both he and Stalin recognized the pro-Western forces would win. Stalin agreed only to a vague compromise by which an unspecified number of pro-Western Poles would be granted a place in the government. He reluctantly consented to hold "free and unfettered elections" in Poland on an unspecified future date. They did not take place for more than forty years.

Nor was there agreement about the future of Germany. Roosevelt seemed to want a reconstructed and reunited Germany. Stalin wanted to impose heavy reparations on Germany and to ensure a permanent dismemberment of the nation. The final agreement was, like the Polish accord, vague and unstable. The decision on reparations would be referred to a future commission. The United States, Great Britain, France, and the Soviet Union would each control its own "zone of occupation" in Germany—the zones to be determined by the position of troops at the end of the war. Berlin, the German capital, was already well inside the Soviet zone, but because of its symbolic importance it would itself be divided into four sectors, one for each nation to occupy. At an unspecified date, Germany would be reunited. As for the rest of Europe, the conference produced a murky accord on the establishment of governments "broadly representative of all democratic elements" and "responsible to the will of the people."

Problems of the Yalta Accords The Yalta accords, in other words, were less a settlement of postwar issues than a set of loose principles that sidestepped the most difficult questions. Roosevelt, Churchill, and Stalin returned home from the conference each apparently convinced that he had signed an important agreement. But the Soviet interpretation of the accords differed so sharply from the Anglo-American interpretation that the illusion endured only briefly. In the weeks following the Yalta Conference, Roosevelt watched with growing alarm as the Soviet Union moved systematically to establish pro-communist governments in one Central or Eastern European nation after another and as Stalin refused to make the changes in Poland that the president believed he had promised. Still believing the differences could be settled, Roosevelt left Washington early in the spring for a vacation at his retreat in Warm Springs, Georgia. There, on April 12, 1945, he suffered a sudden, massive stroke and died.

THE COLLAPSE OF THE PEACE

Harry S. Truman, who succeeded Roosevelt in the presidency, had almost no familiarity with international issues. Nor did he share Roosevelt's apparent faith in the flexibility of the Soviet Union. Truman sided instead with those in the government (and there were many) who considered the Soviet Union fundamentally untrustworthy and viewed Stalin himself with suspicion and even loathing.

The Failure of Potsdam

Truman had been in office only a few days before he decided to "get tough" with the Soviet Union. Stalin had made what the new president considered solemn agreements with the United States at Yalta. The United States should insist that the Soviets honor them. Truman met on April 23 with Soviet Foreign Minister Molotov and sharply chastised him for violations of the Yalta accords.

In fact, Truman had little leverage with which to compel the Soviet Union to carry out its agreements. Russian forces already occupied Poland and much of the rest of Central and Eastern Europe. Germany was already divided among the conquering nations. The United States was still engaged in a war in the Pacific and was neither able nor willing to enter into a second conflict in Europe. Truman insisted that the United States should be able to get "85 percent" of what it wanted, but *Limited American Leverage* he was ultimately forced to settle for much less.

He conceded first on Poland. When Stalin made a few minor concessions to the pro-Western exiles, Truman recognized the Warsaw government, hoping that noncommunist forces might gradually expand their influence there. Until the 1980s, they did not. To settle other questions, Truman met in July at Potsdam, in Russian-occupied Germany, with Churchill (who, after elections in Britain in the midst of the talks, was replaced as prime minister by Clement Attlee) and Stalin. Truman reluctantly accepted the adjustments of the Polish-German border that Stalin had long demanded; he refused, however, to permit the Russians to claim any reparations from the American, French, and British zones of Germany. This stance effectively confirmed that Germany would remain divided. The western zones ultimately united into one nation, friendly to the United States, and the Russian zone survived as another nation, with a pro-Soviet, communist government.

The China Problem

American hopes for an open, peaceful world "policed" by the great powers required a strong, independent China. But those hopes faced a major, perhaps insurmountable obstacle: the Chinese government of Chiang Kai-shek. Chiang was generally friendly to the United States, but his government was corrupt and incompetent with feeble popular support. Ever since 1927, the nationalist government he headed had been engaged in a bitter rivalry with the communist armies of Mao Zedong. By 1945, Mao was in control of one-fourth of the population.

Chiang Kai-shek

Some Americans urged the government to try to find a "third force" to support as an alternative to either Chiang or Mao. Truman, however, decided reluctantly that he had no choice but to continue supporting Chiang. For the next several years the United States continued to pump money and weapons to Chiang, even as it was becoming clear that the cause was lost. But Truman was not prepared to intervene militarily to save the nationalist regime.

Instead, the American government was beginning to consider an alternative to China as the strong, pro-Western force in Asia: a revived Japan. Abandoning the strict occupation policies of the first years after the war (when General Douglas MacArthur had governed the nation), the United States lifted all restrictions on industrial development and encouraged rapid economic growth in Japan. The vision of an open, united world was giving way in Asia, as it was in Europe, to an acceptance of a divided world with a strong, pro-American sphere of influence.

Japan Restored

The Containment Doctrine

By the end of 1945, a new American foreign policy was slowly emerging. It became known as containment. Rather than attempting to create a unified, "open" world, the United States and its allies would work to "contain" the threat of further Soviet expansion.

The new doctrine emerged in part as a response to events in Europe in 1946. In Turkey, Stalin was trying to win control over the vital sea lanes to the Mediterranean. In Greece, communist forces were threatening the pro-Western government; the British had announced they could no longer provide assistance. Faced with these challenges, Truman decided to enunciate a firm new policy. In doing so, he drew from the ideas of the influential American diplomat George F. Kennan, who had warned not long after the war that in the Soviet Union the United States faced "a political force committed fanatically to the belief that with the U.S. there can be no permanent modus vivendi," and that the only answer was "a long-term, patient but firm and vigilant containment of Russian expansive tendencies." On March 12, 1947, Truman appeared before Congress and used

Kennan's warnings as the basis of what became known as the Truman Doctrine. "I believe," he argued, "that it must be the policy of the United States to support free peoples who are resisting attempted subjugation by armed minorities or by outside pressures." In the same speech he requested $400 million—for aid to Greece and Turkey. Congress quickly approved the measure.

Truman Doctrine

The American commitment ultimately helped ease Soviet pressure on Turkey and helped the Greek government defeat the communist insurgents. More important, it established a basis for American foreign policy that would survive for more than thirty years.

The Marshall Plan

An integral part of the containment policy was a proposal to aid in the economic reconstruction of Western Europe. There were many motives: humanitarian concern for the European people; a fear that Europe would remain an economic drain on the United States if it could not quickly rebuild and begin to feed itself; a desire for a strong European market for American goods. But above all, American policymakers believed that unless something could be done to strengthen the shaky pro-American governments in Western Europe, those governments might fall under the control of rapidly growing domestic communist parties.

In June 1947, Secretary of State George C. Marshall announced a plan to provide economic assistance to all European nations (including the Soviet Union) that would join in drafting a program for recovery. Although Russia and its Eastern satellites quickly and predictably rejected the plan, sixteen Western European nations eagerly participated. Whatever domestic opposition there was in the United States largely vanished after a sudden coup in Czechoslovakia in February 1948 that established a Soviet-dominated communist government there. In April, Congress approved the creation of the Economic Cooperation Administration, the agency that would administer the Marshall Plan, as it became known. Over the next three years, the Marshall Plan channeled over $12 billion of American aid into Europe, helping to spark a substantial economic revival. By the end of 1950, European industrial production had risen 64 percent, communist strength in the member nations had declined, and opportunities for American trade had revived.

Rebuilding Europe

Mobilization at Home

In 1948, at the president's request, Congress approved a new military draft and revived the Selective Service System. In the meantime, the United States, having failed to reach agreement with the Soviet Union on international control of nuclear weapons, redoubled its own efforts in atomic research, elevating nuclear weaponry to a central place in its military arsenal. The Atomic Energy Commission, established in 1946, became the supervisory body charged with overseeing all nuclear research, civilian and military alike. And in 1950, the Truman administration approved the development of the new hydrogen bomb, a nuclear weapon far more powerful than the bombs the United States had used in 1945.

The National Security Act of 1947   The National Security Act of 1947 reshaped the nation's major military and diplomatic institutions. A new Department of Defense would oversee all branches of the armed services, combining functions previously performed separately by the War and Navy departments. A National Security Council (NSC), operating out of the White House, would govern foreign and military policy. A Central Intelligence Agency (CIA) would replace the wartime Office of Strategic Services and would be responsible for collecting information through both open and covert methods; as the Cold War continued, the CIA would also engage secretly in political and military operations on behalf of American goals. The National Security Act, in other words, gave the president expanded powers with which to pursue the nation's international goals.

The Road to NATO

The United States was also moving to strengthen the military capabilities of Western Europe. Convinced that a reconstructed Germany was essential to the hopes of the West, Truman reached an agreement with England and France to merge the three western zones of occupation into a new West German republic (which would include the American, British, and French sectors of Berlin, even though that city lay within the Soviet zone). Stalin responded quickly. On June 24, 1948, he imposed a tight blockade around the western sectors of Berlin. If Germany was to be officially divided, he was implying, then the country's Western government would have to abandon its outpost in the heart of the Soviet-controlled eastern zone. Truman refused to do so. Unwilling to risk war through a military challenge to the blockade, *Berlin Airlift* he ordered a massive airlift to supply the city with food, fuel, and other needed goods. The airlift continued for more than ten months, transporting nearly 2.5 million tons of material, keeping a city of 2 million people alive. In the spring of 1949, Stalin lifted the now ineffective blockade. And in October, the division of Germany into two nations—the Federal Republic in the west and the Democratic Republic in the East—became official.

The crisis in Berlin accelerated the consolidation of what was already in effect an alliance among the United States and the countries of Western Europe. On April 4, 1949, twelve nations signed an agreement establishing the North Atlantic Treaty Organization (NATO) and declaring that an armed attack against one member would be considered an attack against all. The NATO countries would, moreover, maintain a standing military force in Europe to defend against what many believed was the threat of a

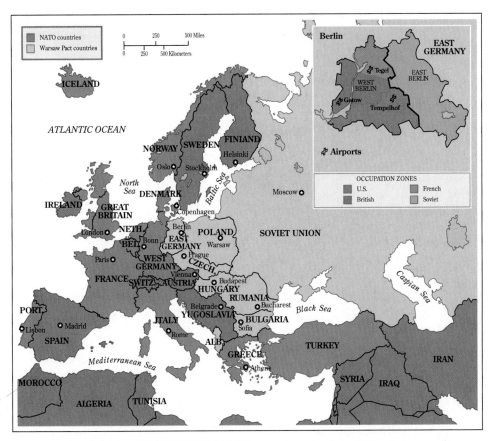

DIVIDED EUROPE AFTER WORLD WAR II This map shows the sharp division that emerged in Europe after World War II between the area under the control of the Soviet Union, and the area allied with the United States. In the east, Soviet control or influence extended into all the nations shaded gold—including the eastern half of Germany. In the west and south, the green-shaded nations were allied with the United States as members of the North Atlantic Treaty Organization (NATO). The countries shaded brown were aligned with neither of the two superpowers. The small map in the upper right shows the division of Berlin among the various occupying powers at the end of the war. Eventually, the American, British, and French sectors were combined to create West Berlin, a city governed by West Germany but entirely surrounded by communist East Germany. ◆ *How did the West prevent East Germany from absorbing West Berlin?*

Soviet invasion. The formation of NATO eventually spurred the Soviet Union to create an alliance of its own with the communist governments in Eastern Europe—an alliance formalized in 1955 by the Warsaw Pact.

Reevaluating Cold War Policy

In September 1949, the Soviet Union successfully exploded its first atomic weapon, years earlier than predicted, an event that shocked and frightened many Americans. So did the collapse of Chiang Kai-shek's nationalist government in China, which occurred with startling speed in the last months

For more than a decade after the beginning of the Cold War, few historians saw any reason to challenge the official American interpretation of its origins. The breakdown of relations between the United States and the Soviet Union was, most agreed, a direct result of Soviet expansionism and of Stalin's violation of the wartime agreements forged at Yalta and Potsdam. The Soviet imposition of communist regimes in Eastern Europe was part of a larger ideological design to spread communism throughout the world. American policy was the logical and necessary response: a firm commitment to oppose Soviet expansionism and to keep American forces in a continual state of readiness.

Disillusionment with the official justifications for the Cold War began to find expression even in the late 1950s, when anticommunist sentiment in America remained strong and pervasive. William Appleman Williams's *The Tragedy of American Diplomacy* (1959) insisted that the Cold War was simply the most recent version of a consistent American effort in the twentieth century to preserve an "open door" for American trade in world markets. The confrontation with the Soviet Union, he argued, was less a response to Soviet aggressive designs than an expression of the American belief in the necessity of capitalist expansion.

As the Vietnam War grew larger and more unpopular in the 1960s, the scholarly critique of the Cold War quickly gained intensity. Walter LaFeber's *America, Russia, and the Cold War,* first published in 1967, maintained that America's supposedly idealistic internationalism at the close of the war was in reality an effort to ensure a postwar order shaped in the American image—with every nation open to American influence (and to American trade). That was why the United States was so apt to misinterpret Soviet policy, much of which reflected a perfectly reasonable commitment to ensure the security of the Soviet Union itself, as part of a larger aggressive design.

The revisionist interpretations of the Cold War ultimately produced a reaction of their own: what has come to be known as "postrevisionist" scholarship. The most important works in this school have attempted to strike a balance between orthodoxy and revisionism and to identify areas of blame and patterns of misconceptions on both sides of the conflict. An important early statement of this approach was John Lewis Gaddis, *The United States and the Cold War, 1941–1947* (1972), which argued that "neither side can bear sole responsibility for the onset of the Cold War." Both sides had limited options, given their own political constraints and their own preconceptions. Other postrevisionist works—by Thomas G. Paterson, Melvyn Leffler, William Taubman, and others—have elaborated on ways in which the United States and the Soviet Union acted in response to genuine, if not necessarily accurate, beliefs about the intentions of the other. "The United States and the Soviet Union were doomed to be antagonists," Ernest May wrote in 1984. "There probably was never any real possibility that the post-1945 relationship could be anything but hostility verging on conflict."

The collapse of Soviet communism and the dissolution of the Soviet empire has begun to stimulate new interpretations of the Cold War and (by facilitating the opening of Soviet archives) to cast new light on many contested issues. For the moment, however, the dominant scholarly view is one that de-emphasizes the question of who is to blame and emphasizes the ways in which both sides learned to manage a conflict that neither could easily have avoided.

HARRY AND BESS TRUMAN AT HOME Senator Harry Truman and his wife Bess pose for photographers in the kitchen of their Washington apartment, suggesting the "common man" image that Truman retained throughout his public life. The picture was taken shortly before the 1944 Democratic National Convention, which would nominate Truman for vice president. Less than a year later, the Trumans would be living in the White House. *(UPI/Corbis-Bettmann)*

(text continued from page 759)

of 1949. Chiang fled with his political allies and the remnants of his army to the offshore island of Formosa (Taiwan), and the entire Chinese mainland came under the control of a communist government that many Americans believed to be an extension of the Soviet Union. The United States refused to recognize the new communist regime.

In this atmosphere of escalating crisis, Truman called for a thorough review of American foreign policy. The result was a National Security Council report, issued in 1950 and commonly known as NSC-68, which outlined a shift in the American position. The first state- *Containment Expanded* ments of the containment doctrine—the writings of George Kennan, the Truman Doctrine speech—had made at least some distinctions between areas of vital interest to the United States and areas of less importance to the nation's foreign policy and called on America to share the burden of containment with its allies. But the April 1950 document argued that the United States could no longer rely on other nations to take the initiative in resisting communism. It must move on its own to stop communist expansion virtually anywhere it occurred, regardless of the intrinsic strategic or economic value of the lands in question. Among other things, the report called for a major expansion of American military power, with a defense budget almost four times the previously projected figure.

AMERICA AFTER THE WAR

The crises overseas were not the only frustrations the American people encountered after the war. The nation also faced serious, if short-lived, economic difficulties in adapting to the peace. And it suffered from an exceptionally heated political climate that produced a new wave of insecurity and repression.

The Problems of Reconversion

Despite widespread predictions that the end of the war would return America to depression conditions, economic growth continued after 1945. Pent-up consumer demand from workers who had accumulated substantial savings during the war helped spur the boom. So did a $6 billion tax cut. The Servicemen's Readjustment Act of 1944, *GI Bill* better known as the GI Bill of Rights, provided housing, education, and job training subsidies to veterans and increased spending even further.

This flood of consumer demand contributed to more than two years of serious inflation, during which prices rose at rates of 14 to 15 percent annually. Compounding the economic difficulties was a sharp rise in labor unrest. By the end of 1945, there had been major strikes in the automobile, electrical, and steel industries. In April 1946, John L. Lewis led the United Mine Workers out on strike, shutting down the coal fields for forty days. Truman finally forced coal production *Inflation and Labor Unrest* to resume by ordering government seizure of the mines. But in the process, he pressured mine owners to grant the union most of its demands. Almost simultaneously, the nation's railroads suffered a total shutdown—the first in the nation's history—as two major unions walked out on strike. By threatening to use the army to run the trains, Truman pressured the strikers back to work after only a few days.

Reconversion was particularly difficult for the millions of women and minorities who had entered the work force during the war. With veterans returning home and looking for jobs in the industrial economy, employers tended to push women, African Americans, Hispanics, and others out of the plants to make room for white males. Some of the war workers, particularly women, left the work force voluntarily, out of a desire to return to their former domestic lives. But as many as 80 percent of women workers, and virtually all black and Hispanic males, wanted to continue working. The postwar inflation, the pressure to meet the growing expectations of a high-consumption society, the rising divorce rate (which left many women responsible for their own economic well-being)—all combined to create a high demand for paid employment among women. As they found themselves excluded from industrial jobs, therefore, women workers moved increasingly into other areas of the economy (above all, the service sector).

The Fair Deal Rejected

Days after the Japanese surrender, Truman submitted to Congress a twenty-one-point domestic program outlining what he later named the "Fair Deal." It called for expansion of Social Security benefits, the raising of the legal minimum wage from 40 to 65 cents an hour, a program to ensure full employment through aggressive use of federal spending and investment, a permanent Fair Employment Practices Act, public housing and slum clearance, long-range environmental and public works planning, and government promotion of scientific research. Weeks later he added other proposals: federal aid to education, government health insurance and prepaid medical care, funding for the St. Lawrence Seaway, and nationalization of atomic energy.

But most of Truman's programs fell victim to the same public and congressional conservatism that had crippled the last years of the New Deal. Indeed, that conservatism seemed to be intensifying, as the November 1946 congressional elections suggested. Using the simple but devastating slogan "Had Enough?" the Republican Party won control of both houses of Congress. The new Republican Congress quickly moved to reduce government spending and chip away at New Deal reforms. Its most notable action was its assault on the Wagner Act of 1935, in the form of the Labor-Management Relations Act of 1947, better known as the Taft-Hartley Act. It made illegal the closed shop (a workplace in which no one can be hired without first being a member of a union). And although it continued to permit the creation of union shops (in which workers must join a union after being hired), it permitted states to pass "right-to-work" laws prohibiting even that. The Taft-Hartley Act also empow- *Taft-Hartley Act* ered the president to call for a ten-week "cooling-off" period before a strike by issuing an injunction against any work stoppage that endangered national safety or health. Outraged workers and union leaders denounced the measure as a "slave labor bill." Truman vetoed it. But both houses easily overruled him the same day. The Taft-Hartley Act did not destroy the labor movement. But it did damage weaker unions in relatively lightly organized industries such as chemicals and textiles, and it made much more difficult the organizing of workers who had never been union members at all, especially in the South and the West.

The Election of 1948

Truman and his advisers believed that the American public was not ready to abandon the achievements of the New Deal, despite the 1946 election results. As they planned their strategy for the 1948 campaign, therefore, they placed their hopes in an appeal to enduring Democratic loyalties.

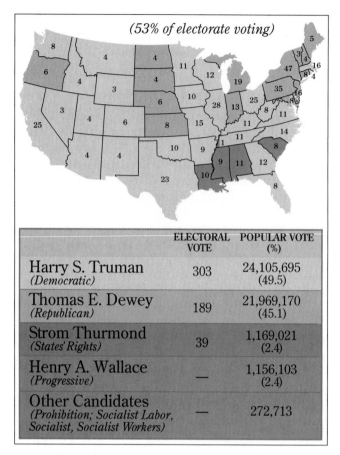

	ELECTORAL VOTE	POPULAR VOTE (%)
Harry S. Truman *(Democratic)*	303	24,105,695 (49.5)
Thomas E. Dewey *(Republican)*	189	21,969,170 (45.1)
Strom Thurmond *(States' Rights)*	39	1,169,021 (2.4)
Henry A. Wallace *(Progressive)*	—	1,156,103 (2.4)
Other Candidates *(Prohibition; Socialist Labor, Socialist, Socialist Workers)*	—	272,713

ELECTION OF 1948 Despite the widespread expectation that the Republican candidate, Thomas Dewey, would easily defeat Truman in 1948, the president in fact won a substantial re-election victory that year. This map shows the broad geographic reach of Truman's victory. Dewey swept most of the Northeast, but Truman dominated almost everywhere else. Strom Thurmond, the States' Rights candidate, carried four states in the South. ◆ *What had prompted Thurmond to desert the Democratic Party and run for president on his own?*

For an interactive version of this map go to www.mhhe.com/unfinishednation4ch29maps

Throughout 1948, Truman proposed one reform measure after another (including, on February 2, the first major civil rights bill of the century). To no one's surprise, Congress ignored or defeated them all, but the president was building campaign issues for the fall.

There remained, however, the problem of Truman's personal unpopularity—the assumption among much of the electorate that he

Divided Democratic Party

lacked stature and that his administration was weak and inept—and the deep divisions within the Democratic Party. At the Democratic Convention that summer, two factions abandoned the party altogether. Southern conservatives were angered by Truman's proposed civil rights bill and by the approval at the convention of a civil rights plank in the platform (engineered by Hubert Humphrey, the reform mayor of Minneapolis). They walked out and formed the States' Rights (or "Dixiecrat") Party, with Governor Strom Thurmond of South Carolina as its nominee. At the same time, some members of the party's left wing joined the new Progressive Party, whose candidate was Henry A. Wallace. Wallace supporters objected to what they considered the slow and ineffective domestic policies of the Truman administration, but they resented even more the president's confrontational stance toward the Soviet Union.

Many Democratic liberals who were unhappy with Truman were unwilling to leave the party. The Americans for Democratic Action (ADA), a coalition of anticommunist liberals, tried to entice Dwight D. Eisenhower, the *Americans for Democratic Action* popular war hero, to contest the nomination. Only after Eisenhower had refused did liberals concede the nomination to Truman. The Republicans, in the meantime, once again nominated Governor Thomas E. Dewey of New York. Austere, dignified, and competent, he seemed to offer an unbeatable alternative to the president.

Only Truman, it seemed, believed he could win. As the campaign gathered momentum, he became ever more aggressive, turning the fire away from himself and toward Dewey and the "do-nothing, good-for-nothing" Republican Congress, which was, he told the voters, responsible for fueling inflation and abandoning workers and common people. To dramatize his point, he called Congress into special session in July to give it a chance, he said, to enact the liberal measures the Republicans had recently written into their platform. Congress met for two weeks and, predictably, did almost nothing.

On election night, to the surprise of almost everyone, he won a narrow but decisive and dra- *Truman's Stunning Victory* matic victory: 49.5 percent of the popular vote to Dewey's 45.1 percent (with the two splinter parties dividing the small remainder evenly between them), and an electoral margin of 303 to 189. Democrats, in the meantime, had regained both houses of Congress by substantial margins.

The Fair Deal Revived

Despite the Democratic victories, the Eighty-first Congress was little more hospitable to Truman's Fair Deal reform than its Republican predecessor had been. Truman did win some important victories, to be sure. Congress raised the legal minimum wage from 40 cents to 75 cents an hour. It approved an important expansion of the Social Security system, increasing benefits by 75 percent and extending them to 10 million additional people. And it passed the National Housing Act of 1949, which provided for the construction of 810,000 units of low-income housing accompanied by long-term rent subsidies.

But on other issues—national health insurance and aid to education among them—Truman made little progress. Nor was he able to persuade Congress to accept the civil rights legislation he proposed in 1949, legislation that would have made lynching a federal crime, provided federal protection of black voting rights, abolished the poll tax, and established a new Fair Employment Practices Commission to curb discrimination in hiring. Southern Democrats filibustered to kill the bill.

Truman did proceed on his own to battle several forms of racial discrimination. He ordered an end to discrimination in the hiring of government employees. He began to dismantle segregation within the armed forces. And he allowed the Justice Department to become actively involved in court battles against discriminatory statutes. The Supreme Court, in the meantime, signaled its own growing awareness of the issue by ruling, in

Renewed Federal Commitment to Civil Rights

Shelley v. *Kraemer* (1948), that the courts could not be used to enforce private "covenants" meant to bar blacks from residential neighborhoods.

The Nuclear Age

Looming over the political, economic, and diplomatic struggles of the postwar years was the image of the great and terrible mushroom clouds that had risen over Alamogordo in July 1945 and over the ruined Japanese cities of Hiroshima and Nagasaki that atomic weapons had destroyed. Americans greeted the introduction of these terrible new instruments of destruction with fear and awe, but also with expectation. Postwar culture was torn between a dark image of the nuclear war that many Americans feared would be a result of the rivalry with the Soviet Union, and the bright image of a dazzling technological future that atomic power might help to produce.

The fear of nuclear weapons appeared widely in popular culture, but it was often disguised. The late 1940s and early 1950s were the heyday of

Film Noir

the *film noir,* a kind of filmmaking that had originated in France and had been named for the dark lighting that was characteristic of the genre. American *film noir* portrayed the loneliness of individuals in an impersonal world—a staple of American culture for many decades—but also suggested the menacing character of the age, the looming possibility of vast destruction. Sometimes, films and television programs addressed nuclear fear explicitly—for example, the celebrated television show of the 1950s and early 1960s, *The Twilight Zone,* which featured dramatic portrayals of the aftermath of nuclear war; or postwar comic books, which depicted powerful superheroes saving the world from destruction.

Such images resonated with the public because awareness of nuclear weapons was increasingly built into their daily lives. Schools and office buildings had regular air raid drills, to prepare people for the possibility of nuclear attack. Radio stations regularly tested the emergency broadcast systems, which stood in readiness for war. Fallout shelters sprang up in public buildings and private homes, stocked with water and canned goods, to protect citizens in case of war. America was a nation filled with anxiety.

And yet at the same time, the United States was also an exuberant nation, dazzled by its own prosperity and excited by the technological innovations that were transforming the world. Among those innovations was nuclear power. The same scientific knowledge that could destroy the world, many believed, might also lead it into a dazzling future. The *New York Times*, only days after Hiroshima, expressed its own rosy view of the nuclear future:

> The atomic bomb was perfected for war, but the knowledge which made it possible came out of . . . the deathless yearning to know and to use the gifts of nature for the common good. . . . This new knowledge . . . can bring to this earth not death but life, not tyranny and cruelty, but a divine freedom.

That kind of optimism soon became widespread. The "secret of the atom," many Americans soon predicted, would bring "prosperity and a more complete life." A public opinion poll late in 1948 revealed that approximately two-thirds of those who had an opinion on the subject believed that, "in the long run," atomic energy would "do more good than harm." Nuclear power plants *Atomic Optimism* began to spring up in many areas of the country, welcomed as the source of cheap and unlimited electricity, their potential dangers scarcely even discussed by those who celebrated their creation.

THE KOREAN WAR

On June 24, 1950, the armies of communist North Korea swept across their southern border and invaded the pro-Western half of the Korean peninsula to the south. Within days, they had occupied much of South Korea, including Seoul, its capital. Almost immediately, the United States committed itself to the conflict.

The Divided Peninsula

When World War II ended, both the United States and the Soviet Union had troops in Korea fighting the Japanese; neither army was willing to leave. Instead, they divided the nation, supposedly temporarily, along the 38TH parallel. The Russians finally departed in 1949, leaving behind a communist government in the north with a strong, Soviet-equipped army. The Americans left a few months later, handing control to the pro-Western government of Syngman Rhee, who was anticommunist but only nominally democratic. He had a relatively *Syngman Rhee* small military, which he used primarily to suppress internal opposition.

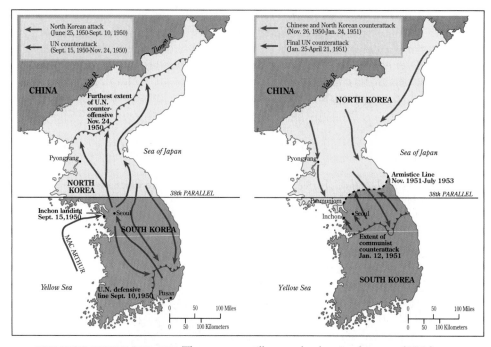

THE KOREAN WAR, 1950–1953 These two maps illustrate the changing fortunes of UN forces (which were mostly American) in Korea during the 1950–1953 war. The map at the left shows the extent of the North Korean invasion of the South in 1950; communist forces for a time controlled all of Korea except a small area around Pusan in the southeast. On September 15, 1950, UN troops under Douglas MacArthur landed in force at Inchon and soon drove the North Koreans back across the border. MacArthur then pursued the North Koreans well into their own territory. The map at right shows the very different circumstances once the Chinese entered the war in November 1950. Chinese forces drove the UN army back below the 38th parallel and, briefly, deep into South Korea, below Seoul. The UN troops fought back to the prewar border between North and South Korea late in 1951, but the war then bogged down into a stalemate that continued for a year and a half. ◆ *What impact did the Korean War have on American politics in the early 1950s?*

The relative weakness of the south offered a strong temptation to nationalists in the North Korean government who wanted to reunite the country. The temptation grew stronger when the American government implied that it did not consider South Korea within its own "defense perimeter." The Soviets may not have approved the invasion in advance, but they supported the offensive once it began.

Almost immediately on June 27, 1950, the president ordered limited American military assistance to South Korea, and on the same day he appealed to the United Nations to intervene. The Soviet Union was boycotting the Security Council at the time (to protest the council's refusal to recognize the new communist government of China) and was thus unable to exercise its veto power. As a result, American delegates were able to win UN agreement to a resolution calling for international assistance to the Rhee government. On June 30, the United States ordered its own ground

WINTER IN KOREA, 1950 An American soldier trudges to the crest of an icy and embattled ridge during the bitter fighting in North Korea between American divisions and Chinese communist forces, who had entered the war as the United Nations forces approached the Korean-Chinese border. *(The National Archives and Records Administration)*

forces into Korea, and Truman appointed General Douglas MacArthur to command the UN operations there. (Several other nations provided assistance and troops, but the "UN" armies were, in fact, overwhelmingly American.)

After a surprise American invasion at Inchon in September had routed the North Korean forces *Inchon* from the south and sent them fleeing back across the 38TH parallel, Truman gave MacArthur permission to pursue the communists into their own territory. The president's aim was to create "a unified, independent and democratic Korea." He was moving beyond simple containment and envisioning a rollback of communist power.

From Invasion to Stalemate

For several weeks, MacArthur's invasion of North Korea proceeded smoothly. On October 19, the capital, Pyongyang, fell to the UN forces. Victory seemed near—until the Chinese government, alarmed by the movement of American forces toward its border, intervened. By November 4,

China Intervenes

eight divisions of the Chinese army had entered the war. The UN offensive stalled and then collapsed. Through December 1950, outnumbered American forces fought a bitter, losing battle against the Chinese divisions. Within weeks, communist forces had pushed the Americans back below the 38TH parallel once again and had recaptured the South Korean capital of Seoul. By mid-January 1951 the rout had ceased; and by March the UN armies had managed to regain much of the territory they had recently lost, taking back Seoul and pushing the communists north of the 38TH parallel for the second time. With that, the war degenerated into a protracted stalemate.

From the start, Truman had been determined to avoid a direct conflict with China, which he feared might lead to a new world war. Once China entered the war, he began seeking a negotiated solution to the struggle. But General MacArthur had ideas of his own. The United States was really fighting the Chinese, MacArthur argued. It should, therefore, attack China itself, if not through an actual invasion, then at least by bombing communist forces massing north of the Chinese border. In March 1951, he indicated his unhappiness in a public letter to House Republican leader Joseph W. Martin that concluded: "There is no substitute for victory." His position had wide popular support. The release of the Martin letter struck the president as intolerable insubordination. On April 11, 1951, he relieved MacArthur of his command.

Sixty-nine percent of the American people supported MacArthur, a Gallup poll reported. When the general returned to the United States later in 1951, he was greeted with wild enthusiasm.

Truman-MacArthur Controversy

Public criticism of Truman finally abated somewhat when a number of prominent military figures, including General Omar Bradley, publicly supported the president's decision. But substantial hostility toward Truman remained. In the meantime, the Korean stalemate continued. Negotiations between the opposing forces began at Panmunjom in July 1951, but the talks—and the war—dragged on until 1953.

Limited Mobilization

Just as the war in Korea produced only a limited American military commitment abroad, so it created only a limited economic mobilization at home.

Truman set up the Office of Defense Mobilization to fight inflation by holding down prices and discouraging high union wage demands. When these cautious regulatory efforts failed, the president took more drastic action. Railroad workers walked off the job in 1951, and Truman, who considered the workers' demands inflationary, ordered the government to seize control of the railroads. In 1952, during a nationwide steel strike, Truman seized the steel mills, citing his powers as commander in chief. But in a 6-to-3 decision, the Supreme Court ruled that the president had exceeded his authority, and Truman was forced to relent.

The Korean War gave a significant boost to economic growth by pumping new government funds into the economy at a point when many believed it was about to decline. But the war had other, less welcome effects. It came at a time of rising insecurity about America's position in the world and intensified anxiety about communism. As the long stalemate continued, producing 140,000 American dead and wounded, frustration turned to anger. The United States, which had recently won the greatest war in *Rising Insecurity and Frustration* history, seemed unable to conclude what many Americans considered a minor border skirmish in a small country. Many began to believe that something must be deeply wrong—not only in Korea but within the United States as well. Such fears contributed to the rise of the second major campaign of the century against domestic communism.

THE CRUSADE AGAINST SUBVERSION

Why did the American people develop a growing fear of internal communist subversion—a fear that by the early 1950s had reached the point of near hysteria? There are many possible answers, but no single definitive explanation.

One factor was obvious. Communism was not an imagined enemy. It had tangible shape, in Josef Stalin and the Soviet Union. Adding to the concern were the Korean stalemate, the "loss" of China, the Soviet development of an atomic bomb. Searching for someone to blame, many were attracted to the idea of a communist conspiracy within American borders. But there were other factors as well, rooted in events in American domestic politics.

HUAC and Alger Hiss

Much of the anticommunist furor emerged out of the search by the Republican Party for an issue with which to attack the Democrats, and out of the efforts of the Democrats to take that issue away from them. Beginning in 1947, the House Un-American Activities Committee (HUAC) held widely publicized investigations to prove that, under Democratic rule, the government had tolerated (if not actually encouraged) communist subversion. The committee turned first to the movie industry, arguing that communists had infiltrated Hollywood and tainted American films with propaganda. Writers and producers, some of them former communists, were called to testify; and when some of them ("the Hollywood Ten") refused *The "Hollywood Ten"* to answer questions about their own political beliefs and those of their colleagues, they were sent to jail for contempt. Others were barred from employment in the industry when Hollywood, attempting to protect its public image, adopted a "blacklist" of those of "suspicious loyalty."

ALGER HISS No single figure did more to polarize opinion about the dangers of domestic communism than Alger Hiss, the once-respected diplomat accused in 1948 of having been a spy in the 1930s for the Soviet Union and later convicted of perjury for testifying falsely before a congressional committee. *(UPI/Corbis-Bettmann)*

More alarming to the public was HUAC's investigation into charges of disloyalty leveled against a former high-ranking member of the State Department: Alger Hiss. In 1948, Whittaker Chambers, a former communist agent, now a conservative editor at *Time* magazine, told the committee that Hiss had passed classified State Department documents to him in 1937 and 1938. When Hiss sued him for slander, Chambers produced microfilms of the documents (called the "pumpkin papers," because Chambers had kept them hidden in a pumpkin in his vegetable garden). Hiss could not be tried for espionage because of the statute of limitations (which protects individuals from prosecution for most crimes after seven years have passed). But largely because of the relentless efforts of Richard M. Nixon, a freshman Republican congressman from California and a member of HUAC, Hiss was convicted of perjury and served several years in prison. The Hiss case not only discredited a prominent young diplomat; it cast suspicion on a generation of liberal Democrats. It also transformed Nixon into a national figure and helped him win a seat in the United States Senate in 1950.

The Federal Loyalty Program and the Rosenberg Case

Partly to protect itself against Republican attacks, partly to encourage support for the president's foreign policy initiatives, the Truman administration in 1947 initiated a widely publicized program to review the "loyalty" of federal employees. By 1951, more than 2,000 government employees had resigned under pressure and 212 had been dismissed.

The employee loyalty program became a signal throughout the executive branch to launch a major assault on subversion. The attorney general established a widely cited list of supposedly subversive organizations. The director of the Federal Bureau of Investigation (FBI), J. Edgar Hoover, investigated and harassed alleged radicals. In 1950, Congress passed the McCarran Internal Security Act, which, among other restrictions on "subversive" activity, required that all communist organizations register with the government and publish their records. Truman vetoed the bill. Congress easily overrode his veto.

McCarran Internal Security Act

The successful Soviet detonation of an atomic bomb in 1949, earlier than generally expected, suggested to some people that there had been a conspiracy to pass American atomic secrets to the Russians. In 1950, Klaus Fuchs, a young British scientist, seemed to confirm those fears when he testified that he had delivered to the Russians details of the manufacture of the bomb. The case ultimately moved to an obscure New York couple, Julius and Ethel Rosenberg, members of the Communist Party. The government claimed the Rosenbergs had received secret information from Ethel's brother, a machinist on the Manhattan Project in New Mexico, and had passed it on to the Soviet Union through other agents (including Fuchs). The Rosenbergs were convicted and, on April 5, 1951, sentenced to death. After two years of appeals and public protests, they died in the electric chair on June 19, 1953.

All these factors—the HUAC investigations, the Hiss trial, the loyalty investigations, the McCarran Act, the Rosenberg case—combined with other concerns by the early 1950s to create a fear of communist subversion that seemed to grip the entire country. State and local governments, the judiciary, schools and universities, labor unions—all sought to purge themselves of real or imagined subversives. It was a climate that made possible the rise of an extraordinary public figure.

Growing Fear of Subversion

McCarthyism

Joseph McCarthy was an undistinguished, first-term Republican senator from Wisconsin when, in February 1950, in the midst of a speech in Wheeling, West Virginia, he lifted up a sheet of paper and claimed to "hold in my hand" a list of 205 known communists currently working in the American State Department. No person of comparable stature had ever made so bold a charge against the federal government; and in the months to come, as McCarthy repeated and expanded on his accusations, he emerged as the nation's most prominent leader of the crusade against domestic subversion.

Within weeks of his charges against the State Department, McCarthy was leveling accusations at other agencies. After 1952, with the Republicans in control of the Senate and McCarthy the chairman of a special subcommittee, he conducted highly publicized investigations of alleged subversion in many areas of the government. McCarthy never produced conclusive evidence that any federal employee was a communist. But a growing constituency adored him nevertheless for *McCarthy's Soaring Popularity* his coarse, "fearless" assaults on a government establishment that many considered arrogant, effete, even traitorous. Republicans, in particular, rallied to his claims that the Democrats had been responsible for "twenty years of treason" and that only a change of parties could rid the country of subversion. McCarthy, in short, provided his followers with an issue into which they could channel a wide range of resentments: fear of communism, animosity toward the country's "eastern establishment," and frustrated partisan ambitions. For a time, McCarthy intimidated all but a few people from opposing him. Even the highly popular Dwight D. Eisenhower, running for president in 1952, did not speak out against him, although he disliked McCarthy's tactics and was outraged at, among other things, McCarthy's attacks on General George Marshall.

The Republican Revival

Public frustration over the stalemate in Korea and popular fears of internal subversion combined to make 1952 a bad year for the Democratic Party. Truman, now deeply unpopular, withdrew from the presidential contest. The party united instead behind Governor Adlai E. Stevenson of Illinois. Stevenson's dignity, wit, and eloquence made him a beloved figure to many liberals and intellectuals. But those same qualities seemed only to fuel Republican charges that Stevenson lacked the strength or the will to combat communism sufficiently.

Stevenson's greatest problem, however, was the Republican candidate opposing him. Rejecting the efforts of conservatives to nominate Robert Taft or Douglas MacArthur, the Republicans turned to a man who had no previous identification with the party: General Dwight D. Eisenhower—military hero, commander of NATO, president of Columbia University in New York—who won nomination on the first ballot. He chose as his running mate the young California senator who had gained national prominence through his crusade against Alger Hiss: Richard M. Nixon.

In the fall campaign, Eisenhower attracted support through his geniality and his statesmanlike pledges to settle the Korean conflict. Nixon (after surviving early accusations of financial improprieties, which he effectively neutralized in a famous television address, the "Checkers speech") exploited the issue of domestic anticommunism by attacking the Democrats for "cowardice" and "appeasement." The response at the polls was overwhelming. Eisenhower won both a popular and an electoral landslide: 55 percent of the popular vote to Stevenson's 44 percent, 442 electoral votes to Stevenson's 89. Republicans gained control of both houses of Congress for the first time since 1946.

Eisenhower Elected

CONCLUSION

Even during World War II itself, when the United States and the Soviet Union were allies, it was evident to leaders in both nations that America and Russia had quite different visions of what the postwar world should look like. Very quickly after the war ended, the once fruitful relationship between the world's two greatest powers quickly soured. Americans came to believe that the Soviet Union was an expansionist tyranny little different from Hitler's Germany. Soviets came to believe that the United States was trying to protect its own dominance in the world by encircling the Soviet Union. The result of these tensions was what became known by the end of the 1940s as the Cold War.

In the early years of the Cold War, the United States constructed a series of policies designed to prevent both war and Soviet aggression. It helped rebuild the shattered nations of Western Europe with substantial economic aid through the Marshall Plan, to stabilize those nations and prevent them from becoming communist. America embraced a new foreign policy—known as containment—that committed it to an effort to keep the Soviet Union from expanding its influence further into the world. The United States and Western Europe formed a strong and enduring alliance, NATO, to defend Europe against possible Soviet advances.

In 1950, however, the armed forces of communist North Korea launched an invasion of the noncommunist South; and to most Americans the conflict quickly came to be seen as a test of American resolve in the Cold War. The Korean War was long, costly, and unpopular, with many military setbacks and frustrations. In the end, however, the United States—working through the United Nations—managed to drive the North Koreans out of the south and stabilize the original division of the peninsula.

The Korean War hardened American foreign policy into a much more rigidly anticommunist form. It undermined the Truman administration, and the Democratic Party, and helped strengthen conservatives and Republicans. It greatly strengthened an already powerful crusade against communists, and those believed to be communists, within the United States—a crusade often known as McCarthyism, because of the notoriety of Senator Joseph McCarthy of Wisconsin, the most celebrated leader of the effort.

America after World War II was indisputably the wealthiest and most powerful nation in the world. But in the harsh climate of the Cold War, neither wealth nor power could dispel deep anxieties and bitter divisions.

FOR FURTHER REFERENCE

Two books by John Lewis Gaddis, *Strategies of Containment* (1982) and *The United States and the Origins of the Cold War, 1941–1947* (1972) provide a sound introduction to Cold War history. Walter LaFeber, *America, Russia, and the Cold War, 1945–1967* (7th ed. 1993) is a classic survey of American-Soviet relations. Melvyn P. Leffler, *A Preponderance of Power: National Security, the Truman Administration, and the Cold War* (1992) is a superb, densely researched history of the policies of the 1940s. Warren I. Cohen, *The Cambridge History of American Foreign Relations, Vol. 4: America in the Age of Soviet Power, 1945–1991* (1991) is a good general history. Michael Hogan, *The Marshall Plan* (1987) is a provocative interpretation of one of the pillars of the early containment doctrine. David McCullough, *Truman* (1992) is an elegant popular biography, while Alonzo Hamby, *Man of the People: A Life of Harry S. Truman* (1995) is a fine scholarly one. Bruce Cumings, *The Origins of the Korean War* (1980) is an important study of America's first armed conflict of the Cold War. Ellen Schrecker, *Many Are the Crimes: McCarthyism in America* (1998) is an important interpretation of McCarthyism, and David Oshinsky, *A Conspiracy So Immense: The World of Joe McCarthy* (1983) is a fine biography. Richard Fried, *Nightmare in Red* (1990) is a good, short overview of the Red Scare. Frances Stonor Saunders, *The Cultural Cold War* (2000) is a provocative and controversial study. Richard Pells, *The Liberal Mind in a Conservative Age: American Intellectuals in the 1940s and 1950s* (1985) is a valuable overview of postwar intellectual life. Mary L. Dudziak, *Cold War Civil Rights: Race and the Image of American Democracy* (2000) examines the connection between Cold War fervor and civil rights. *The Spy in the Sky* (1996) is a documentary film that tells the story of a team of engineers and pilots racing to design, perfect, and deploy the high-flying U2 spy plane in the 1950s. *Truman* (1997) is an excellent documentary about the 33rd president.

For quizzes, Internet resources, references to additional books and films, and more, consult this book's Online Learning Center site at www.mhhe.com/unfinishednation4.

THE NEW TELEVISION SET Norman Rockwell was one of the best-known American illustrators of the 1930s, 1940s, and 1950s—the creator of countless covers for the popular magazine the *Saturday Evening Post* and of some of the most beloved images of his era. In the 1930s and 1940s, most of his pictures evoked life in small-town America. By the late 1940s, however, he was beginning to portray as well the rise of the new suburban and consumer culture—as this 1949 illustration suggests. The new television antenna rises against the sky almost as if to compete with the older church steeple in the background. (The New Television Set *by Norman Rockwell. Los Angeles County Museum of Art. Gift of Mrs. Ned Crowell. Printed by permission of the Norman Rockwell Family Trust. © 1949 The Norman Rockwell Family Trust*)

TIME LINE

1947	1952	1953	1954	1955	1956
Levittown construction begins	Eisenhower elected	Korean War ends	*Brown* v. *Board of Education*	Montgomery bus boycott	Federal Highway Act
			Army-McCarthy hearings		Eisenhower reelected
					Suez crisis

THE AFFLUENT SOCIETY

The Economic "Miracle"
The Explosion of Science and Technology
People of Plenty
The Other America
The Rise of the Civil Rights Movement
Eisenhower Republicanism
Eisenhower, Dulles, and the Cold War

I f America experienced a golden age in the 1950s and early 1960s, as many Americans believed at the time and many continue to believe today, it was largely a result of two developments. One was a booming national prosperity, which profoundly altered the social, economic, and even physical landscape of the United States. The other was the continuing struggle against communism, a struggle that created considerable anxiety but that also encouraged Americans to look even more approvingly at their own society. But if these powerful forces created a widespread sense of national purpose and self-satisfaction, they also helped blind many Americans to serious problems plaguing large groups of the population.

THE ECONOMIC "MIRACLE"

Perhaps the most striking feature of American society in the 1950s and early 1960s was the booming economic growth that made even the heady 1920s seem pale by comparison. It was a better-balanced and more widely distributed prosperity than that of thirty years earlier. It was not, however, as universal as some Americans liked to believe.

Booming Economic Growth

1957	1959	1960	1961	1969	
Sputnik launched	Castro seizes power in Cuba	U-2 incident	First American in space	Americans land on moon	
Kerouac's *On the Road*					
Little Rock desegregation crisis					

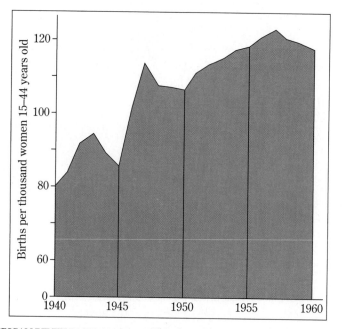

THE AMERICAN BIRTH RATE, 1940–1960 This chart shows how the American birth rate grew rapidly during and after World War II (after a long period of decline in the 1930s) to produce what became known as the "baby boom." At the peak of the baby boom, during the 1950s, the nation's population grew by 20 percent. ◆ *What impact did the baby boom have on the nation's economy?*

Economic Growth

By 1949, despite the continuing problems of postwar reconversion, an economic expansion had begun that would continue with only brief interruptions for almost twenty years. Between 1945 and 1960, the gross national product grew by 250 percent, from $200 billion to over $500 billion. Unemployment remained at about 5 percent or lower throughout the 1950s and early 1960s. Inflation, in the meantime, hovered around 3 percent a year or less.

Government Spending   The causes of this growth were varied. Government spending, which had ended the Depression in the 1940s, continued to stimulate growth through public funding of schools, housing, veterans' benefits, welfare, interstate highways, and above all military spending. Economic growth was at its peak during the first half of the 1950s, when military spending was highest because of the Korean War.

The national birth rate reversed a long pattern of decline with the so-called baby boom, which had begun during the war and peaked in 1957. The nation's population rose almost 20 percent in the decade, from 150 million in 1950 to 179 million in 1960. The baby boom meant increased consumer demand and expanding economic growth.

The rapid expansion of suburbs—whose population grew 47 percent in the 1950s—helped stimulate growth in several important sectors of the economy. The number of privately owned cars more than doubled in a decade. Demand for new homes helped sustain a vigorous housing industry. The construction of roads stimulated the economy as well. *Suburban Expansion*

These and other forces helped the American economy to grow nearly ten times as fast as the population in the thirty years after the war. And while that growth was far from equally distributed, it affected most of society. The average American in 1960 had over 20 percent more purchasing power than in 1945, and more than twice as much as during the prosperous 1920s. The American people had achieved the highest standard of living of any society in the history of the world.

The Rise of the Modern West

No region of the country experienced more dramatic changes as a result of the new economic growth than the American West. Its population expanded dramatically; its cities boomed; its industrial economy flourished. By the 1960s, some parts of the West were among the most important (and populous) industrial and cultural centers of the nation in their own right.

As during World War II, much of the growth of the West was a result of federal spending and investment—on the dams, power stations, highways, and other infrastructure projects that made economic development possible; and on the military contracts that continued to flow disproportionately to factories in California and Texas, many of them built with government funds during the war. But other factors played a role as well. The growing number of automobiles created new demands for petroleum and contributed to the rapid growth of oil fields in Texas and Colorado and of the metropolitan centers serving them: Houston, Dallas, and Denver. State governments in the West invested heavily in their universities. The University of Texas and University of California systems, in particular, became among the nation's largest and best; as centers of research, they helped attract technology-intensive industries to the region. Climate also contributed. Southern California, Nevada, and Arizona, in particular, attracted many migrants from the East because of their warm, dry climates. The growth of Los Angeles after World War II was a remarkable phenomenon: more than 10 percent of all new businesses in the United States between 1945 and 1950 began in Los Angeles. Its population rose by over 50 percent between 1940 and 1960. *Government-Induced Growth*

Capital and Labor

Corporations enjoying booming growth were reluctant to allow strikes to interfere with their operations; and since the most important labor unions were now so large and entrenched that they could not easily be suppressed

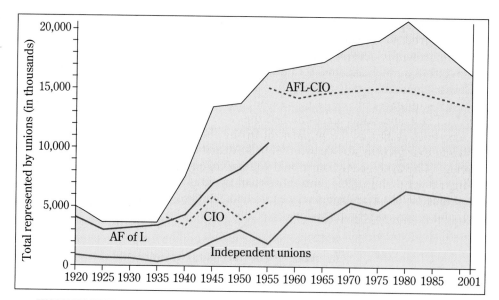

WORKERS REPRESENTED BY UNIONS, 1920–2001 This chart shows the number of workers represented by unions over an eighty-year period. Note the dramatic rise in the unionized work force during the 1930s and 1940s, the slower but still significant rise in the 1960s and 1970s, and the steady decline that began in the 1980s. The chart, in fact, understates the decline of unionized labor in the postwar era, since it shows union membership in absolute numbers and not as a percentage of the rapidly growing work force. Measured in that way, even a consistent number of union members would represent a relative decline for unions.
◆ *Why did unions cease recruiting new members successfully in the 1970s, and why did they begin actually losing members in the 1980s?*

or intimidated, leaders of large businesses made important concessions to them. By the mid-1950s, factory wages in all industries had risen substantially, to an average of $80 per week. In December 1955, the American Federation of Labor and the Congress of Industrial Organizations ended their twenty-year rivalry and merged to create the AFL-CIO, under the leadership of George Meany.

But success also bred stagnation and corruption in some union bureaucracies. In 1957, the powerful Teamsters Union became the subject of a congressional investigation, and its president, David Beck, was charged with the misappropriation of union funds. Beck ultimately

Jimmy Hoffa   stepped down to be replaced by Jimmy Hoffa, whom government investigators pursued for nearly a decade before finally winning a conviction against him in 1967. The United Mine Workers, similarly, became tainted by violence and charges of corruption.

THE EXPLOSION OF SCIENCE
AND TECHNOLOGY

In 1961, *Time* magazine selected as its "man of the year" not a specific person but "the American Scientist." The choice was an indication of the widespread fascination with which Americans in the age of atomic weapons viewed science and technology.

Medical Breakthroughs

The twentieth century saw more progress in the development of medical science than had occurred in all the centuries before it. A very large proportion of that progress occurred during and after World War II. Particularly important was the development of new antibacterial drugs capable of fighting infections that in the past had been all but untreatable.

The development of antibiotics had its origins in the discoveries of Louis Pasteur and Jules-Francois Joubert. Working in France in the 1870s, they produced the first conclusive evidence that virulent bacterial infections could be defeated by other, more ordinary bacteria. Using their discoveries, the English physician Joseph Lister revealed the value of antiseptic solutions to prevent infection during surgery.

Development of Antibacterial Drugs

But the practical use of antibacterial agents to combat disease did not begin until many decades later. In the 1930s, scientists in Germany, France, and England demonstrated the power of so-called sulfa drugs— drugs derived from an antibacterial agent known as sulfanilamide—which could be used effectively to treat streptococcal blood infections. New sulfa drugs were soon being developed at an astonishing rate, and were frequently improved, with dramatic results in treating what had once been a major cause of death.

In 1928, in the meantime, Alexander Fleming, an English medical researcher, accidentally discovered the antibacterial properties of an organism that he named penicillin. There was little progress in using penicillin to treat human illness, however, until a group of researchers at Oxford University, directed by Howard Florey and Ernest Chain, learned how to produce stable, potent penicillin in sizable enough quantities to make it a practical weapon against bacterial disease. The first human trials of the new drug, in 1941, were dramatically successful, but progress toward the mass availability of penicillin was stalled in England because of World War II. American laboratories took the next crucial steps in developing methods for the mass production and commercial distribution of penicillin, which became widely available to doctors and hospitals around the world by

Penicillin

1948. Since then, a wide range of new antibiotics of highly specific character have been developed so that bacterial infections are now among the most successfully treated of all human illnesses.

There was also dramatic progress in immunization—the development of vaccines that can protect humans from contracting both bacterial and viral diseases. The first great triumph was the development of the small-pox vaccine by the English researcher Edward Jenner in the late eighteenth century. A vaccine effective against typhoid was developed by an English bacteriologist, Almorth Wright, in 1897, and was in wide use by World War I. Vaccination against tetanus became widespread just before and during World War II. Medical scientists also developed a vaccine, BCG, against another major killer, tuberculosis, in the 1920s; but controversy over its safety stalled its adoption, especially in the United States, for many years. It was not widely used in the United States until after World War II, when it largely eliminated tuberculosis until a limited recurrence began in the 1990s.

Viruses are much more difficult to prevent and treat than bacterial infections, and progress toward vaccines against viral infections—except for smallpox—was relatively slow. Not until the 1930s, when scientists discovered how to grow viruses in laboratories in tissue cultures, could researchers study them with any real effectiveness. Gradually, they discovered how to produce forms of a virus capable of triggering antibodies in vaccinated people that would protect them from contracting disease. An effective vaccine against yellow fever was developed in the late 1930s, and one against influenza—one of the great killers of the first half of the twentieth century—appeared in 1945.

A particularly dramatic postwar triumph was the development of a *Salk Vaccine* vaccine against polio. In 1954, the American scientist Jonas Salk introduced an effective vaccine against the disease that had killed and crippled thousands of children and adults (among them Franklin Roosevelt). It was provided free to the public by the federal government beginning in 1955. After 1960, an oral vaccine developed by Albert Sabin—usually administered in a sugar cube—made widespread vaccination even easier. By the early 1960s, these vaccines had virtually eliminated polio from American life and from much of the rest of the world.

As a result of these and many other medical advances, both infant mortality and the death rate among young children declined significantly in the first twenty-five years after the war (although not by as much as in Western Europe). Average life expectancy in that same period rose by five years, to seventy-one.

Pesticides

Scientists were also developing new kinds of chemical pesticides, which they hoped would protect crops from destruction by insects and protect humans from such insect-carried diseases as typhus and malaria. Perhaps

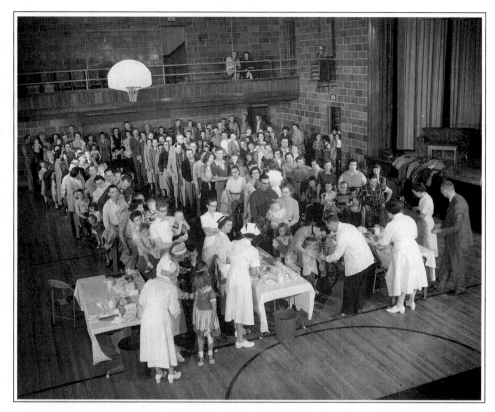

THE SALK VACCINE Dr. Jonas Salk, a medical researcher at the University of Pittsburgh, developed in the mid-1950s the first vaccine that proved effective in preventing polio. In its aftermath, scenes similar to this one—a mass inoculation of families in a school gymnasium in Kansas—repeated themselves all over the country. A few years later, Dr. Albert Sabin of the University of Cincinnati created a vaccine that could be administered more easily, through sugar cubes. *(March of Dimes Birth Defects Foundation)*

the most famous of the new pesticides was dichlorodiphenyl-trichloroethane, generally known as DDT, a compound discovered in 1939 by a Swiss chemist named Paul Muller. He had discovered that although DDT seemed harmless to human beings and other mammals, it was extremely toxic to insects. American scientists learned of Muller's discovery in 1942, just as the army was grappling with the insect-borne tropical diseases—especially malaria and typhus—that threatened American soldiers.

DDT was first used on a large scale in Italy in 1943–1944 during a typhus outbreak, which it quickly helped end. Soon it was being sprayed in mosquito-infested areas of Pacific islands where American troops were fighting the Japanese. The incidence of malaria dropped precipitously. DDT quickly gained a reputation as a miraculous tool for controlling insects, and it undoubtedly saved thousands of lives. Only later did it become evident that DDT had long-term toxic effects on animals and humans.

Postwar Electronic Research

The 1940s and 1950s saw dramatic new developments in electronic technology. Researchers in the 1940s produced the first commercially viable televisions and created a technology that made it possible to broadcast programming over large areas. In the late 1950s, scientists at RCA's David Sarnoff Laboratories in New Jersey developed the technology for color television, which first became widely available in the early 1960s.

Television

In 1948 Bell Labs, the research arm of AT&T, produced the first transistor, a solid-state device capable of amplifying electrical signals, which was much smaller and more efficient than the cumbersome vacuum tubes that had powered most electronic equipment in the past. Transistors made possible the miniaturization of many devices (radios, televisions, audio equipment, hearing aids) and were also important in aviation, weaponry, and satellites. They contributed as well to another major breakthrough in electronics: the development of integrated circuitry in the late 1950s. Integrated circuits combined a number of once-separate electronic elements (transistors, resistors, diodes, and others) and embedded them into a single, microscopically small device. They made it possible to create increasingly complex electronic devices requiring complicated circuitry that would have been impractical to produce through other means. Most of all, integrated circuits helped advance the development of the computer.

Integrated Circuits Invented

Postwar Computer Technology

Prior to the 1950s, computers had been constructed mainly to perform complicated mathematical tasks, such as those required to break military codes. In the 1950s, they began to perform commercial functions for the first time.

The first significant computer of the 1950s was the Universal Automatic Computer (or UNIVAC), which was developed initially for the U.S. Bureau of the Census by the Remington Rand Company. It was the first computer able to handle both alphabetical and numerical information easily. It used tape storage and could perform calculations and other functions much faster than its predecessor, the ENIAC. Searching for a larger market than the census for their very expensive new device, Remington Rand arranged to use a UNIVAC to predict the results of the 1952 election for CBS television news. It would, they believed, produce valuable publicity for the machine. Analyzing early voting results, the UNIVAC accurately predicted an enormous landslide victory for Eisenhower over Stevenson. Few Americans had ever heard of a computer before that night, and the UNIVAC's television debut became, therefore, a critical breakthrough in public awareness of computer technology.

Remington Rand had limited success in marketing the UNIVAC, but in the mid-1950s the International Business Machines Company (IBM) introduced its first major *IBM* data-processing computers and began to find a wide market for them among businesses in the United States and abroad. These early successes, combined with the enormous amount of money IBM invested in research and development, made the company the worldwide leader in computers for many years.

Bombs, Rockets, and Missiles

In 1952, the United States successfully detonated the first hydrogen bomb. (The Soviet Union tested its first H-bomb a year later.) Unlike the plutonium and uranium bombs developed during World War II, the hydrogen bomb derives its power not from fission *Nuclear Fusion* (the splitting of atoms) but fusion (the joining together of lighter atomic elements with heavier ones). It is capable of producing explosions of vastly greater power than the earlier fission bombs.

The development of the hydrogen bomb gave considerable impetus to a stalled scientific project in both the United States and the Soviet Union: the effort to develop unmanned rockets and missiles capable of traveling the new weapons—not suitable for delivery by airplanes—to their targets. Both nations began to put tremendous resources into their development. The United States benefited from the emigration to America of some of the German scientists who had helped develop rocketry for Germany during World War II.

In the United States, early missile research was conducted almost entirely by the Air Force, and there were significant early successes in developing rockets capable of traveling several hundred miles. But American and Soviet leaders were both struggling to build longer-range missiles that could cross oceans and continents—intercontinental ballistic missiles, or ICBMs, capable of traveling through space to distant targets. American scientists experimented in *ICBMs* the 1950s first with the Atlas and then the Titan ICBM. There were some early successes, but there were also many setbacks, particularly because of the difficulty of massing sufficient, stable fuel to provide the tremendous power needed to launch missiles beyond the atmosphere. By 1958, scientists had created a solid fuel to replace the volatile liquid fuels of the early missiles; and they had also produced miniaturized guidance systems capable of ensuring that missiles could travel to reasonably precise destinations. Within a few years, a new generation of missile, known as the Minuteman, became the basis of the American atomic weapons arsenal. It was capable of traveling several thousand miles. American scientists also developed a nuclear missile capable of being carried and fired by submarines— the Polaris, which is launched from below the surface of the ocean by compressed air and fires its engines only once it is above the surface. A Polaris was first successfully fired from underwater in 1960.

The Space Program

The American space program eventually developed a rationale of its own. In the beginning, however, it was a byproduct of the rivalry with the Soviet Union. Its origins can perhaps be traced most directly to a dramatic event in 1957, when the Soviet Union announced that it had launched an earth-orbiting satellite—*Sputnik*—into outer space.

Sputnik

The United States had yet to perform any similar feats, and the American government (and much of American society) reacted to the announcement with alarm. Federal policy began encouraging (and funding) strenuous efforts to improve scientific education in the schools, to create more research laboratories, and, above all, to speed the development of America's own exploration of outer space. The United States launched its own first satellite, *Explorer I*, in January 1958.

The centerpiece of space exploration, however, soon became the manned space program, established in 1958 along with a new agency, the National Aeronautics and Space Administration (NASA). The first American space pilots, or "astronauts," quickly became the nation's most revered heroes. On May 5, 1961, Alan Shepard became the first American launched into space. But his short, suborbital flight came several months after a Soviet "cosmonaut," Yuri Gagarin, had made a flight in which he had actually orbited the earth. On February 2, 1962, John Glenn (later a United States senator) became the first American to orbit the globe. NASA later introduced the Gemini program, whose spacecraft could carry two astronauts at once.

Apollo

Mercury and Gemini were followed by the Apollo program, whose purpose was to land men on the moon. It had some catastrophic setbacks, most notably a fire in January 1967 that killed three astronauts during a training session. But on July 20, 1969, Neil Armstrong, Edwin Aldrin, and Michael Collins successfully traveled in a space capsule into orbit around the moon. Armstrong and Aldrin then detached a smaller craft from the capsule, landed on the surface of the moon, and became the first men to walk on a body other than earth. Six more lunar missions followed, the last in 1972.

Eventually, the space program became a relatively modest effort to make travel in near-space easier and more practical through the development of the "space shuttle," an airplane-like device launched by a missile but capable both of navigating in space and landing on earth much like a conventional aircraft. The first space shuttle was successfully launched in 1982. The explosion of one shuttle, *Challenger*, in January 1986 shortly after takeoff, killing all seven astronauts, stalled the program for two years. But missions resumed in the late 1980s. The space shuttle has been used to launch and repair communications satellites, to insert the Hubble

Space Telescope into orbit in 1990 (and later to repair its flawed lens), and to service the orbiting Spacelab.

PEOPLE OF PLENTY

Among the most striking social developments of the immediate postwar era was the rapid extension of a middle-class lifestyle and outlook to an expanding portion of the population. The historian David Potter published an influential examination of "economic abundance and American character" in 1954. He called it *People of Plenty*. For the American middle class in the 1950s, at least, it seemed an appropriate label.

The Consumer Culture

At the center of middle-class culture in the 1950s was a growing absorption with consumer goods. That was a result of increased prosperity, of the in-

Growing Focus on Consumer Goods

creasing variety and availability of products, and of the adeptness of advertisers in creating a demand for those products. It was also a result of the growth of consumer credit, which increased by 800 percent between 1945 and 1957 through the development of credit cards, revolving charge accounts, and easy-payment plans. Prosperity fueled such longtime consumer crazes as the automobile, and Detroit responded to the boom with ever-flashier styling and accessories. Consumers also responded eagerly to the development of such new products as dishwashers, garbage disposals, television, hi-fis, and stereos.

Because consumer goods were so often marketed (and advertised) nationally, the 1950s were notable for the rapid spread of great national consumer crazes. For example, children, adolescents, and even some adults became entranced in the late 1950s with the hula hoop—a large plastic ring kept spinning around the waist. The popularity of the Walt Disney-produced children's television show *The Mickey Mouse Club* created a national demand for related products such as Mickey Mouse watches and hats. It also helped produce the stunning success of Disneyland, an amusement park near Los Angeles that re-created many of the characters and events of Disney entertainment programs.

The Suburban Nation

A third of the nation's population lived in suburbs by 1960. The growth of suburbs was a result not only of increased affluence but of important innovations in home building, which made single-family houses affordable to millions of new people. The most famous of the suburban developers, William Levitt, came to symbolize

William Levitt

LEVITTOWN BEFORE THE TREES A section of the Levittown on Long Island in New York, photographed in July 1948, a few months after the first families moved in. The Levitt family pioneered techniques in constructing mass-produced housing that made possible the proliferation of similar inexpensive suburbs in many areas of the country. *(Culver Pictures, Inc.)*

the new suburban growth with his use of mass-production techniques to construct large housing developments, the first of which was on Long Island, near New York City. The houses sold for under $10,000. Many other relatively inexpensive suburban developments soon began appearing throughout the country.

Why did so many Americans want to move to the suburbs? One reason was the enormous importance postwar Americans placed on family life after five years of war. Suburbs provided families with larger homes than they could find (or afford) in the cities, and thus made it easier to raise larger numbers of children. They provided privacy. They also provided a sense of security from the noise and dangers of urban living. They offered space for the new consumer goods—the appliances, cars, boats, outdoor furniture, and other products that many middle-class Americans craved.

Another factor motivating white Americans to move to the suburbs was race. Most suburbs were restricted to white *Segregated Suburbs* inhabitants—both because relatively few African Americans could afford to live in them and because formal and informal barriers kept even prosperous blacks out of all but a few. In an era when the black population of most cities was rapidly growing, many white families fled to the suburbs to escape the integration of urban neighborhoods and schools.

The Suburban Family

For professional men (who tended to work in the city, at some distance from their homes), suburban life generally meant a rigid division between their working and personal worlds. For many middle-class women, it meant an increased isolation from the workplace. Many middle-class husbands considered it demeaning for their wives to be employed. And many women themselves shied away from the workplace when they could afford to, in part because of prevailing ideas about motherhood (popularized by such widely consulted books as Dr. Benjamin Spock's *Baby and Child Care*, first published in 1946) that advised women to stay at home with their children.

Traditional Gender Norms Reinforced

Some women, however, had to balance these pressures against other, contradictory ones. As expectations of material comfort rose, many middle-class families needed a second income to maintain the standard of living they desired. As a result, the number of married women working outside the home actually increased in the postwar years. By 1960, nearly a third of all married women were part of the paid work force.

The Birth of Television

Television was the result of a series of scientific and technological discoveries, but its impact was largely social and cultural. It quickly became perhaps the most powerful medium of mass communication in history. Experiments in broadcasting pictures (along with sound) had begun as early as the 1920s, but commercial television began only shortly after World War II. Its growth was phenomenally rapid. In 1946, there were only 17,000 sets in the country; by 1957, there were 40 million television sets in use—almost as many sets as there were families. More people had television sets, according to one report, than had refrigerators.

Growing Popularity of Television

The television industry emerged directly out of the radio industry, and all three of the major networks—the National Broadcasting Company, the Columbia Broadcasting System, and the American Broadcasting Company—had started as radio companies. Like radio, the television business was driven by advertising. The need to attract advertisers determined most programming decisions; and in the early days of television, sponsors often played a direct role in determining the content of the programs they chose to sponsor. Many early television shows bore the names of the corporations that were paying for them: the GE Television Theater, the Chrysler Playhouse, the Camel News Caravan, and others. Some daytime serials (known as "soap operas," because their sponsors were almost always companies making household goods targeted at women) were actually written and produced by Procter & Gamble and other companies.

By the late 1950s, television news had replaced newspapers, magazines, and radios as the nation's most important vehicle of information.

Television advertising helped create a vast market for new fashions and products. Televised athletic events gradually made college and professional sports one of the most important sources of entertainment (and one of the biggest businesses) in America. Television entertainment programming—almost all of it controlled by the three national networks and their corporate sponsors—replaced movies and radio as the principal source of diversion for American families.

Much of the programming of the 1950s and early 1960s created a common image of American life—an image that was predominantly white, middle class, and suburban, and that was epitomized by the popular situation comedies, which showed families in which, as the title of one of the most popular put it, *Father Knows Best*, and in which most women were mothers and housewives striving to serve their children and please their husbands.

Social Conflict Accentuated   Yet television also, inadvertently, created conditions that could accentuate social conflict. Even those unable to share in the affluence of the era could, through television, acquire a vivid picture of how the rest of their society lived. Thus at the same time that television was celebrating the white middle class, it was also contributing to the sense of alienation and powerlessness among groups excluded from the world it portrayed. And television news conveyed with unprecedented power the social upheavals that gradually spread beginning in the late 1950s.

Travel, Outdoor Recreation, and Environmentalism

Although the idea of a paid vacation for American workers, and the connection of that idea with travel, had entered American culture beginning in the 1920s, it was not until the postwar years that vacation travel became truly widespread among middle-income Americans. The construction of the interstate highway system contributed dramatically to the growth of travel. So did the increasing affluence of workers. Even in the 1950s, there was a healthy market for vacation vehicles—trailers and small vans—that some families used while traveling, and that market grew steadily larger in subsequent decades. But the urge to travel was also an expression of some of the same impulses that produced the move to suburbs: a desire to escape the crowding and stress of densely populated areas and find a place where it was possible to experience the natural world.

Nowhere was this surge in travel and recreation more visible than in the nation's national parks, which experienced the beginnings of what became a long-term surge in attendance in the 1950s. People who traveled to national parks did so for many reasons—some to hike and camp; some to fish and hunt (activities that themselves grew dramatically in the 1950s and spawned a large number of clubs), some simply to look in awe at the landscape. But whatever their motives, most visitors came in search of an experience in the wilderness. The importance of that search became clear in the early 1950s in the first of many battles over development of wilderness areas: the fight to preserve Echo Park.

Echo Park is a spectacular valley in the Dinosaur National Monument, on the border between Utah and Colorado, near the southern border of Wyoming. In the early 1950s, the federal government's Bureau of Reclamation—which had been created early in the century to encourage irrigation, develop electric power, and increase water supplies—proposed building a dam across the Green River, which runs through Echo Valley, so as to create a lake for recreation and a source of hydroelectric power. The American environmental movement had been relatively quiet since its searing defeat early in the century in its effort to stop a similar dam in the Hetch Hetchy valley at Yosemite National Park. (See p. 584.) But the Echo Park proposal helped rouse it from its slumber.

In 1950, Bernard DeVoto—a well-known writer and a great champion of the American West—published an essay in *The Saturday Evening Post* entitled "Shall We Let Them Ruin Our National Parks?" It had a sensational impact, arousing opposition to the Echo Valley dam from many areas of the country. The Sierra Club, relatively obscure in previous decades, now sprang into ac- *Sierra Club Reborn* tion; the controversy helped elevate a new and aggressive leader, David Brower, who eventually transformed the Club into the nation's leading environmental organization. By the mid-1950s, a large coalition of environmentalists, naturalists, and wilderness vacationers had mobilized in opposition to the dam, and in 1956 Congress—bowing to public pressure—blocked the project and preserved Echo Park in its natural state. The controversy was a major victory for those who wished to preserve the sanctity of the national parks, and it was an important spur to the dawning environmental consciousness that would become so important a decade and more later.

Organized Society and Its Detractors

Large-scale organizations and bureaucracies increased their influence over American life in the postwar era, as they had been doing for many decades before. White-collar workers came to outnumber blue-collar laborers for the first time, and an increasing proportion of them worked in corporate settings with rigid hierarchical structures. Industrial workers also confronted large bureaucracies both in the workplace and in their own unions.

The debilitating impact of bureaucratic life on the individual became one of the central themes of popular and scholarly debate. William H. Whyte, Jr., produced one of the most widely discussed books of the decade: *The Organization Man* (1956), which at- *The Organization Man* tempted to describe the special mentality of the worker in a large, bureaucratic setting. Self-reliance, Whyte claimed, was losing place to the ability to "get along" and "work as a team" as the most valuable trait in the modern character. The sociologist David Riesman made similar observations in *The Lonely Crowd* (1950), in which he argued that the traditional "inner-directed man," who judged himself on the basis of his own values and the esteem of his family, was giving way to a new "other-directed man," more concerned with winning the approval of the larger organization or community.

Novelists, too, expressed misgivings in their work about the impersonality of modern society. Saul Bellow produced a series of novels—*The Adventures of Augie March* (1953), *Seize the Day* (1956), *Herzog* (1964), and many others—that chronicled the difficulties American Jewish men had in finding fulfillment in modern urban America. J. D. Salinger wrote in *The Catcher in the Rye* (1951) of a prep-school student, Holden Caulfield, who was unable to find any area of society—school, family, friends, city—in which he could feel secure or committed.

The Beats and the Restless Culture of Youth

The most derisive critics of bureaucracy, and of middle-class society generally, were a group of young poets, writers, and artists known as the "beats" (or, by disapproving critics, as "beatniks"). They wrote harsh critiques of what they considered the sterility and conformity of American life, the meaninglessness of American politics, and the banality of popular culture. Allen Ginsberg's dark, bitter poem *Howl*

Howl

(1955) decried the "Robot apartments! invincible suburbs! skeleton treasuries! blind capitals! demonic industries!" of modern life. Jack Kerouac produced the most popular document of the Beat Generation in his novel *On the Road* (1957), an account of a cross-country automobile trip that depicted the rootless, iconoclastic lifestyle of Kerouac and his friends.

The beats were the most visible evidence of a widespread restiveness among young Americans in the 1950s. Youths in the 1950s never staged rebellions as widespread or as bitter as those of the 1960s, but their restlessness was visible nevertheless. The phenomenon

"Juvenile Delinquency"

of "juvenile delinquency" attracted tremendous public attention, and in both politics and popular culture there were dire warnings about the growing criminality of American youth. The 1955 film *Blackboard Jungle*, for example, was a frightening depiction of crime and violence in city schools. Scholarly studies, presidential commissions, and journalistic exposés all contributed to the sense of alarm about the spread of delinquency—although in fact youth crime did not dramatically increase in the 1950s.

Many young people began to wear clothes and adopt hairstyles that mimicked popular images of juvenile criminal gangs. The culture of alienation that the beats so vividly represented had counterparts even in ordinary middle-class behavior: teenage rebelliousness toward parents, youthful fascination with fast cars and motorcycles, increasing sexual activity, assisted by the greater availability of birth-control devices. The popularity of James Dean, in such movies as *Rebel Without a Cause* (1955), *East of Eden* (1955), and *Giant* (1956), was a particularly vivid sign of youth culture in the 1950s. Both in the roles he played (moody, alienated teenagers and young men with a streak of self-destructive violence) and in the way he lived his own life (he died in 1955, at the age of 24, in an automobile accident), Dean became an icon of the unfocused rebelliousness of American youth in his time.

Rock 'n' Roll

One of the most important cultural developments for American youth in the 1950s was the enormous popularity of rock 'n' roll—and of the greatest early rock star, Elvis Presley. Presley became a symbol of a youthful determination to push at the *Elvis Presley* borders of the conventional and acceptable. Presley's sultry good looks, his self-conscious effort to dress in the vaguely rebellious style of urban gangs (motorcycle jackets and slicked-back hair, even though Presley himself was a product of the rural South), and, most of all, the open sexuality of his music and his public performances—all made him wildly popular among young Americans in the 1950s. His first great hit, "Heartbreak Hotel," established him as a national phenomenon in 1956, and he remained a powerful figure in American popular culture until—and indeed beyond—his death in 1977.

Presley's music, like that of many early white rock musicians, drew heavily from black rhythm and blues traditions. Sam Phillips, a record promoter who had recorded some of the important black rhythm and blues musicians of his time *Rock 'n' Roll's Black Origins* (among them B. B. King), reportedly said in the early 1950s: "If I could find a white man with a Negro sound, I could make a billion dollars." Soon after that, he found Presley. But there were others as well—among them Buddy Holly and Bill Haley (whose 1955 song "Rock Around the Clock"—used in the film *Blackboard Jungle*—served to announce the arrival of rock 'n' roll to millions of young people)—who were closely connected to African-American musical traditions. Rock drew from other sources too: from country western music (another strong influence on Presley), from gospel music, even from jazz.

The 1950s also produced growth in the popularity of African-American bands and singers among both black and white audiences. Chuck Berry, Little Richard, B. B. King, Chubby Checker, the Temptations, and others— many of them recorded by the black producer Berry Gordy, the founder and president of Motown Records in Detroit—never rivaled Presley in their popularity among white youths but did develop significant multiracial audiences of their own.

The rapid rise of rock owed a great deal to innovations in radio and television programming. By the 1950s, radio stations no longer felt obliged to

ELVIS IN CONCERT Elvis Presley ended his career performing before wealthy audiences in Las Vegas, wearing garish sequined suits. But in the early years of his career, as this concert in the late 1950s suggests, both he and his fans were younger—and the connection between them was immediate and intense. *(Bettmann/Corbis)*

present mostly live programming—especially once television took over many of the entertainment functions radio had once performed. Instead, many radio stations devoted themselves almost entirely to playing recorded music. Early in the 1950s, a new breed of radio announcers, known as "disk jockeys," began to create programming aimed specifically at young fans of rock music; and when those programs became wildly successful, other stations followed suit. *American Bandstand*, which began airing in 1957, was a televised showcase for rock 'n' roll hits in which a live audience danced to recorded music. The program helped spread the popularity of rock—and made its host, Dick Clark, one of the best-known figures among young Americans.

Radio and television were important to the recording industry, of course, because they encour- *Rapidly Growing Record Sales* aged the sale of records, which was increasing rapidly in the mid- and late 1950s, especially in the inexpensive and popular 45 rpm format—small disks that contained one song on each side. Also important were juke boxes, which played individual songs on 45s and which proliferated in soda fountains, diners, bars, and almost every other place where young people were likely to congregate. Sales of records increased from $182 million to $521 million between 1954 and 1960. So eager were record promoters to get their songs on the air that they routinely made secret payments to station owners and disk jockeys to encourage them to showcase their artists. These payments, which became known as "payola," produced a briefly sensational series of scandals when they were exposed in the late 1950s and early 1960s.

THE OTHER AMERICA

It was relatively easy for white, middle-class Americans in the 1950s to believe that the world they knew—a world of economic growth, personal affluence, and cultural homogeneity—was the world virtually all Americans knew, that the values and assumptions they shared were ones that most other Americans shared, too. But such beliefs were false. Large groups of Americans remained outside the circle of abundance and shared neither in the affluence of the middle class nor in many of its values.

On the Margins of the Affluent Society

In 1962, the socialist writer Michael Harrington published a celebrated book called *The Other* *Michael Harrington* *America.* In it, he chronicled the continuing existence of poverty in the United States.

The great economic expansion of the postwar years reduced poverty dramatically but did not eliminate it. In 1960, at any given moment, more than a fifth of all American families (over 30 million people) continued to live below what the government defined as the poverty line (down from a third of all families fifteen years before). Many millions more lived just above the official poverty line, but with incomes that gave them little comfort and no security.

Most of the poor—up to 80 percent—experienced poverty intermittently and temporarily. But approximately 20 percent of the poor were people for whom poverty was a continuous reality from which there was no easy escape. That included approximately half the nation's elderly and a significant proportion of African Americans and Hispanics. Native Americans constituted the single poorest group in the country.

Persistent Poverty　　　　This "hard-core" poverty rebuked the assumptions of those who argued that economic growth would eventually lead everyone into prosperity—that, as many claimed, "a rising tide lifts all boats." It was a poverty that the growing prosperity of the postwar era seemed to affect hardly at all, a poverty, as Harrington observed, that appeared "impervious to hope."

Rural Poverty

Among those on the margins of the affluent society were many rural Americans. In 1948, farmers had received 8.9 percent of the national income; in 1956, they received only 4.1 percent. In part, this decline reflected the steadily shrinking farm population; in 1956 alone, nearly 10 percent of the rural population moved into or was absorbed by cities. But it also reflected declining farm prices. Because of enormous surpluses in basic staples, prices fell 33 percent in those years, even though national income as a whole rose 50 percent at the same time.

Sharecroppers and tenant farmers (most of them African American) continued to live at or below subsistence levels throughout the rural South—in part because of the mechanization of cotton picking beginning in 1944, in part because of the development of synthetic fibers that reduced demand for cotton generally. (Two-thirds of the cotton acreage of the South went out of production between 1930 and 1960.) Migrant farmworkers, a group concentrated especially in the West and Southwest and containing many Mexican-American and Asian-American workers, lived in similarly dire circumstances. In rural areas without much commercial agriculture—such as the Appalachian region in the East, where the decline of the coal economy reduced the one significant source of support for the region—whole communities lived in desperate poverty, increasingly cut off from the market economy. All these groups were vulnerable to malnutrition and even starvation.

The Inner Cities

As prospering white families moved from cities to suburbs in vast numbers, more and more inner-city neighborhoods became repositories for the poor, "ghettoes" from which there was no easy escape. The growth of these neighborhoods owed much to a vast migration of African Americans out of the countryside and into industrial cities. Not all these black migrants were poor, and many found in the city some of the same routes to economic progress that many whites were finding. But African Americans were substantially more likely to live in poverty than most other groups, in part because of the persistence of patterns of discrimination that denied them any real opportunities.

"Ghettoes"

More than 3 million black men and women moved from the South to northern cities between 1940 and 1960. Chicago, Detroit, Cleveland, New York, and other eastern and midwestern industrial cities experienced a major expansion of their black populations—both in absolute numbers and, even more, as a percentage of the whole, since so many whites were leaving at the same time.

Similar migrations from Mexico and Puerto Rico expanded poor Hispanic neighborhoods in many American cities at the same time. Between 1940 and 1960, nearly a million Puerto Ricans moved into American cities (the largest group to New York). Mexican workers crossed the border into Texas and California and swelled the already substantial Latino communities of such cities as San Antonio, Houston, San Diego, and Los Angeles (which by 1960 had the largest Mexican-American population of any city, approximately 500,000 people).

Inner cities were filling up with poor minority residents at the same time that the unskilled industrial jobs they were seeking were diminishing. Employers were moving factories and mills from old industrial cities to new locations in rural areas, smaller cities, and even abroad—places where the cost of labor or of other things were lower. Even in the factories that remained, automation was reducing the number of unskilled jobs. The economic opportunities that had helped earlier immigrant groups to rise up from poverty were unavailable to many of the postwar migrants. Racial discrimination in hiring, education, and housing doomed many members of these communities to continuing, and in some cases increasing, poverty.

Declining Opportunities for Unskilled Workers

THE RISE OF THE CIVIL RIGHTS MOVEMENT

After decades of skirmishes, an open battle began in the 1950s against racial segregation and discrimination, a battle that would prove to be one of the longest and most difficult social struggles of the century. White Americans played an important role in the civil rights movement. But pressure from African Americans themselves was the crucial element in raising the issue of race to prominence.

The Brown Decision and "Massive Resistance"

On May 17, 1954, the Supreme Court announced its decision in the case of *Brown* v. *Board of Education of Topeka*. In considering the legal segregation of a Kansas public school system, the Court rejected its own 1896 *Plessy* v. *Ferguson* decision, which had ruled that communities could provide African Americans with separate facilities as long as the facilities were equal to those of whites.

Plessy v. Ferguson Overturned

LITTLE ROCK An African-American student passes by jeering whites in Arkansas on her way to Central High School in Little Rock, newly integrated by federal court order. The black students later admitted that they had been terrified during the first difficult weeks of integration. But in public, most of them acted with remarkable calm and dignity. *(UPI/Corbis-Bettman)*

The *Brown* decision unequivocally declared the segregation of public schools on the basis of race to be unconstitutional. The justices argued that school segregation inflicted unacceptable damage on those it affected, regardless of the relative quality of the separate schools. Chief Justice Earl Warren explained the unanimous opinion of his colleagues: "We conclude that in the field of public education the doctrine of 'separate but equal' has no place. Separate educational facilities are inherently unequal." The following year, the Court issued another decision (known as *Brown II*) to provide rules for implementing the 1954 order. It ruled that communities must work to desegregate their schools "with all deliberate speed," but it set no timetable and left specific decisions up to lower courts.

In some communities, for example, Washington, D.C., compliance came relatively quickly and quietly. More often, however, strong local opposition (what came to be known in the South as "massive resistance") produced long delays and bitter conflicts. More than 100 southern members of Congress signed a "manifesto" in 1956 denouncing the *Brown* decision and urging their constituents to defy it. Southern governors, mayors, local school boards, and nongovernmental pressure groups (including hundreds of White Citizens' Councils) all worked to obstruct desegregation. By the fall of 1957, only 684 of 3,000 affected school districts in the South had even begun to desegregate their schools.

The Eisenhower administration was not eager to join the battle over desegregation. But in September 1957, it faced a case of direct state defiance of federal authority and felt compelled to act. Federal courts had ordered the desegregation of Central High School in Little Rock, Arkansas. An angry white mob tried to block implementation of the order by blockading *Little Rock's Central High School* the entrances to the school, and Governor Orval Faubus refused to do anything to stop the obstruction. President Eisenhower finally responded by sending federal troops to Little Rock to keep the peace and ensure that the court orders would be obeyed. Only then did Central High School admit its first black students.

The Expanding Movement

The *Brown* decision helped spark a growing number of popular challenges to other forms of segregation in the South. On December 1, 1955, Rosa Parks, an African-American woman, was arrested in Montgomery, Alabama, when she refused *Rosa Parks* to give up her seat on a Montgomery bus to a white passenger (as required by the Jim Crow laws that regulated race relations in the city and throughout most of the South). The arrest of this admired woman and local civil-rights leader produced outrage in the city's African-American community, which organized a boycott of the bus system to demand an end to segregated seating.

The boycott was almost completely effective. It put economic pressure not only on the bus company but on many Montgomery merchants, because the bus boycotters found it difficult to get to downtown stores and shopped instead in their own neighborhoods. Even so, the boycott might well have failed had it not been for a Supreme Court decision late in 1956, inspired in part by the protest, that declared segregation in public transportation to be illegal. The buses in Montgomery abandoned their discriminatory seating policies, and the boycott came to a close.

Among the most important accomplishments of the Montgomery boycott were the legitimization of a new form of racial protest and the elevation to prominence of a new figure in the movement for civil rights. The man chosen to lead the boycott movement once it was launched was a local Baptist pastor, Martin Luther King, Jr., the son of a prominent Atlanta minister, a powerful orator, and *Martin Luther King, Jr.*

a gifted leader. King's approach to black protest was based on the doctrine of nonviolence—that is, of nonviolent resistance to injustice even in the face of direct attack. And he produced an approach to racial struggle that captured the moral high ground for his supporters. For the next thirteen years—as leader of the Southern Christian Leadership Conference (SCLC), an interracial group he founded shortly after the bus boycott—he was the most influential and most widely admired black leader in the country. The popular movement he came to represent soon spread throughout the South and throughout the country.

Causes of the Civil Rights Movement

Several factors contributed to the rise of African-American protest in these years. The legacy of World War II was one of the most important. Millions of black men and women had served in the military or worked in war plants during the war and had derived from the experience a broader view of the world, and of their place in it, than they had been able to develop in their relatively isolated lives prior to the 1940s.

Another factor was the growth of an urban black middle class, which had been developing for decades but which began to flourish after the war. Much of the impetus for the civil rights movement came *Growing Urban Black* from the leaders of urban black communities— *Middle Class* ministers, educators, professionals—and much of it came as well from students at black colleges and universities, which had expanded significantly in the previous decades. Men and women with education and a stake in society were often more aware of the obstacles to their advancement than poorer and more oppressed people. And urban African Americans had considerably more freedom to associate with one another and to develop independent institutions than did rural blacks, who were often under the very direct supervision of white landowners.

Television and other forms of popular culture were another factor in the rising consciousness of racism among African Americans. More than any previous generation, postwar blacks had constant, vivid reminders of how the white majority lived—of the world from which they were effectively excluded. Television also conveyed the activities of demonstrators to a national audience, ensuring that activism in one community would inspire similar protests in others.

Other forces were mobilizing many white Americans to support the movement once it began. One was the Cold War, which made racial injustice an embarrassment to Americans trying to pres- *Political Mobilization* ent their nation as a model to the world. Another *of Northern Blacks* was the political mobilization of northern blacks, who were now a substantial voting bloc within the Democratic Party; politicians from northern industrial states could not ignore their views. Labor unions with substantial black memberships also played an important part in supporting (and funding) the civil rights movement.

This great and largely spontaneous social movement emerged, in short, out of an unpredictable combination of broad social changes and specific local grievances. Whatever its causes, it quickly took on a momentum that, by the early 1960s, had made it one of the most powerful forces in America.

EISENHOWER REPUBLICANISM

Dwight D. Eisenhower was the least experienced politician to serve in the White House in the twentieth century. He was also among the most popular and politically successful presidents of the postwar era. At home, he pursued essentially moderate policies, avoiding most new initiatives but accepting the work of earlier reformers. Abroad, he continued and even intensified American commitments to oppose communism but brought to some of those commitments a measure of restraint that his successors did not always match.

"What Was Good for . . . General Motors"

The first Republican administration in twenty years staffed itself with men drawn from the same quarter as those who had staffed Republican administrations in the 1920s: the business community. But by the 1950s, many business leaders had acquired a social and political outlook very different from that of their predecessors of earlier decades. Above all, many of the nation's leading business executives and financiers had reconciled themselves to at least the broad outlines of the Keynesian welfare state the New Deal had launched. Indeed, some corporate leaders had come to see it as something that actually benefited them—by helping maintain social order, by increasing mass purchasing power, and by stabilizing labor relations.

Keynesian Welfare State Accepted

To his cabinet, Eisenhower appointed wealthy corporate lawyers and business executives who were not apologetic about their backgrounds. Charles Wilson, president of General Motors, assured senators considering his nomination for secretary of defense that he foresaw no conflict of interest because he was certain that "what was good for our country was good for General Motors, and vice versa."

Eisenhower's consistent inclination was to limit federal activities and encourage private enterprise. He supported the private rather than public development of natural resources. To the chagrin of farmers, he lowered federal support for farm prices. He also removed the last limited wage and price controls maintained by the Truman administration. He opposed the creation of new social service programs such as national health insurance. He strove constantly to reduce federal expenditures (even during the recession

Eisenhower's Fiscal Conservatism

of 1958) and balance the budget. He ended 1960, his last full year in office, with a $1 billion budget surplus.

The Survival of the Welfare State

The president took few new initiatives in domestic policy, but he resisted pressure from the right wing of his party to dismantle those welfare policies of the New Deal that had survived the conservative assaults of the war years and after. Indeed, during his term, he agreed to extend the Social Security system to an additional 10 million people and unemployment compensation to an additional 4 million, and he agreed to increase the minimum hourly wage from 75 cents to $1. One of the most significant legislative accomplishments of the Eisenhower administration was the Federal Highway Act of 1956, which authorized $25 billion for a ten-year project that built over 40,000 miles of interstate highways—the largest public works project in American history. The program was to be funded through a highway "trust fund," whose revenues would come from new taxes on the purchase of fuel, automobiles, trucks, and tires.

Federal Highway Act of 1956

In 1956, Eisenhower ran for a second term, even though he had suffered a serious heart attack the previous year. With Adlai Stevenson opposing him once again, he won by another, even greater landslide, receiving nearly 57 percent of the popular vote and 457 electoral votes to Stevenson's 73. Democrats retained the control of both houses of Congress they had won back in 1954. In 1958—during a serious recession—they increased that control by substantial margins.

The Decline of McCarthyism

The Eisenhower administration did little in its first years in office to discourage the anticommunist furor that had gripped the nation. By 1954, however, the crusade against subversion was beginning to produce significant popular opposition. The clearest signal of that change was the political demise of Senator Joseph McCarthy.

During the first year of the Eisenhower administration, McCarthy continued to operate with impunity. But in January 1954 he attacked Secretary of the Army Robert Stevens and the armed services in general. At that point, the administration and influential members of Congress organized a special investigation of the charges, which became known as the Army-McCarthy hearings. They were among the first congressional hearings to be nationally televised. Watching McCarthy in action—bullying witnesses, hurling groundless (and often cruel) accusations, evading issues—much of the public began to see him as a villain, and even a buffoon. In December 1954, the Senate voted 67 to 22 to condemn him for "conduct unbecoming a senator." Three years later, he died—a victim, apparently, of complications arising from alcoholism.

Army-McCarthy Hearings

THE ARMY-MCCARTHY HEARINGS Senator Joseph McCarthy uses a map to show the supposed distribution of communists throughout the United States during the televised 1954 Senate hearings to mediate the dispute between McCarthy and the U.S. Army. Joseph Welch, chief counsel for the army, remains conspicuously unimpressed. *(UPI/Corbis-Bettmann)*

EISENHOWER, DULLES, AND THE COLD WAR

The threat of nuclear war with the Soviet Union created a sense of high anxiety in international relations in the 1950s. But the nuclear threat also encouraged both superpowers to edge away from direct confrontations. The attention of both the United States and the Soviet Union began to turn instead to the rapidly escalating instability in the nations of the Third World.

Dulles and "Massive Retaliation"

Eisenhower's secretary of state, and (except for the president himself) the dominant figure in the nation's foreign policy in the 1950s, was John Foster Dulles, an aristocratic corporate lawyer with a stern moral revulsion to communism. He entered office denouncing the containment policies of the Truman years as excessively passive, arguing that the United States should pursue an active program of "liberation," which would lead to a "rollback" of communist expansion. Once in power, however, he had to defer to the more moderate views of the president himself.

The most prominent of Dulles's innovations was the policy of "massive retaliation," which he announced early in 1954. The United States would, he explained, respond to communist threats to its allies not by using conventional forces in local conflicts (a policy that had led to so much frustration in Korea) but by relying on "the deterrent of massive retaliatory power" (by which he clearly meant nuclear weapons). In part, the new doctrines reflected Dulles's inclination for tense confrontations, an

"Brinksmanship" approach he once defined as "brinksmanship"— pushing the Soviet Union to the brink of war in order to exact concessions. But the real force behind the massive-retaliation policy was economics. With pressure growing both in and out of government for a reduction in American military expenditures, an increasing reliance on atomic weapons seemed to promise, as some advocates put it, "more bang for the buck."

France, America, and Vietnam

On July 27, 1953, negotiators at Panmunjom finally signed an agreement ending the hostilities in Korea. Each antagonist was to withdraw its troops a mile and a half from the existing battle line, which ran roughly along the 38th parallel, the prewar border between North and South Korea. A conference in Geneva was to consider means by which to reunite the nation peacefully—although in fact that 1954 meeting produced no agreement and left the cease-fire line as the apparently permanent border between the two countries.

Almost simultaneously, however, the United States was being drawn into a long, bitter struggle in Southeast Asia. Ever since 1945, France had been attempting to restore its authority over Vietnam, its one-time colony, which it had been forced to abandon to the Japanese toward the end of World War II. Opposing the French, however, were the powerful

Ho Chi Minh nationalist forces of Ho Chi Minh, determined to win independence for their nation. Ho had hoped for American support in 1945, on the basis of the anticolonial rhetoric of the Atlantic Charter and Franklin Roosevelt's speeches, and also because he had received support from American intelligence forces during World War II while he was fighting the Japanese. He was, however, not only a committed nationalist but a committed communist. The Truman administration ignored him and supported the French, one of America's most important Cold War allies.

By 1954, Ho was receiving aid from communist China and the Soviet Union. America, in the meantime, had been paying most of the costs of France's ineffective military campaign in Vietnam since 1950. Early in 1954, 12,000 French troops became surrounded in a disastrous siege at

Dien Bien Phu the village of Dien Bien Phu. Only American intervention, it was clear, could prevent the total collapse of the French military effort. Yet despite the urgings of Secretary of State Dulles, Vice President Nixon, and others, Eisenhower refused to permit direct American military intervention in Vietnam, claiming that neither Congress nor America's other allies would support such action.

Without American aid, the French defense of Dien Bien Phu finally collapsed on May 7, 1954, and France quickly agreed to a settlement of the conflict at the same international conference in Geneva that summer that was considering the Korean settlement. The Geneva accords on Vietnam of July 1954, to which the United States was not a direct party, established a supposedly temporary division of Vietnam along the 17TH parallel. The north would be governed by Ho Chi Minh, the south by a pro-Western regime. Democratic elections would be the basis for uniting the nation in 1956. The agreement marked the end of the French commitment to Vietnam and the beginning of an expanded American presence there. The United States helped establish a pro-American government in the south, headed by Ngo Dinh Diem, a member of his country's Roman Catholic minority. Diem refused to permit the 1956 elections, which he knew he would lose. He felt secure in his refusal because the United States had promised to provide him with ample military assistance against any attack from the north.

Cold War Crises

American foreign policy in the 1950s was challenged by both real and imagined crises in far-flung areas of the world. Among them were a series of crises in the Middle East, a region in which the United States had been little involved until after World War II.

On May 14, 1948, after years of Zionist efforts and a decision by the new United Nations, the nation of Israel proclaimed its independence. President Truman recognized the new Jewish homeland the next day. But the creation of Israel, while it resolved some conflicts, created others. Palestinian Arabs, unwilling to accept being displaced from what they considered their own country, joined with Israel's Arab neighbors and fought determinedly against the new state in 1948—the first of several Arab-Israeli wars.

Israel Recognized

Committed as the American government was to Israel, it was also concerned about the stability and friendliness of the Arab regimes in the oil-rich Middle East, in which American petroleum companies had major investments. Thus the United States reacted with alarm as it watched Mohammed Mossadegh, the nationalist prime minister of Iran, begin to resist the presence of western corporations in his nation in the early 1950s. In 1953, the American CIA joined forces with conservative Iranian military leaders to engineer a coup that drove Mossadegh from office. To replace him, the CIA helped elevate the young Shah of Iran, Mohammed Reza Pahlevi, from his position as token constitutional monarch to that of virtually absolute ruler. The Shah remained closely tied to the United States for the next twenty-five years.

American policy was less effective in dealing with the nationalist government of Egypt, under the leadership of General Gamal Abdel Nasser, which began to develop a trade relationship with the Soviet Union in the early 1950s. In 1956, to punish Nasser for his friendliness toward the communists, Dulles withdrew American offers to assist in building the great Aswan Dam across the Nile. A week later, Nasser retaliated by seizing control of the Suez Canal

Gamal Abdel Nasser

from the British, saying that he would use the income from it to build the dam himself.

On October 29, 1956, Israeli forces attacked Egypt. The next day the British and French landed troops in the Suez to drive the Egyptians from the canal. Dulles and Eisenhower feared that the Suez crisis would drive the Arab states toward the Soviet Union and precipitate a new world war. By refusing to support the invasion, and by joining in a United Nations denunciation of it, the United States helped pressure the French and British to withdraw and helped persuade Israel to agree to a truce with Egypt.

Cold War concerns affected American relations in Latin America as well. In 1954, the Eisenhower administration ordered the CIA to help topple the new, leftist government of Jacobo Arbenz Guzmán in Guatemala, a regime that Dulles (responding to the entreaties of the United Fruit Company, a major investor in Guatemala fearful of Arbenz) argued was potentially communist.

Jacobo Arbenz Guzmán Overthrown

No nation in the region had been more closely tied to America than Cuba. Its leader, Fulgencio Batista, had ruled as a military dictator since 1952, when with American assistance he had toppled a more moderate government. Cuba's relatively prosperous economy had become a virtual fiefdom of American corporations, which controlled almost all the island's natural resources and had cornered over half the vital sugar crop. American organized-crime syndicates controlled much of Havana's lucrative hotel and nightlife business. In 1957, a popular movement of resistance to the Batista regime began to gather strength under the leadership of Fidel Castro. On January 1, 1959, with Batista having fled to exile in Spain, Castro marched into Havana and established a new government.

Castro soon began implementing drastic policies of land reform and expropriating foreign-owned businesses and resources. When Castro began accepting assistance from the Soviet Union in 1960, the United States cut back the "quota" by which Cuba could export sugar to America at a favored price. Early in 1961, as one of its last acts, the Eisenhower administration severed diplomatic relations with Castro. Isolated by the United States, Castro soon cemented an alliance with the Soviet Union.

Growing Conflict with Cuba

Europe and the Soviet Union

Although the problems of the Third World were moving slowly toward the center of American foreign policy, the direct relationship with the Soviet Union and the effort to resist communist expansion in Europe remained the principal concerns of the Eisenhower administration. Relations between the Soviet Union and the West soured further in 1956 in response to the Hungarian Revolution. Hungarian dissidents had launched a popular uprising in November to demand democratic reforms.

Before the month was out, Soviet tanks and troops entered Budapest to crush the uprising and restore an orthodox, pro-Soviet regime.

The U-2 Crisis

In November 1958, Nikita Khrushchev, who had become Soviet premier and Communist Party chief earlier that year, renewed the demands of his predecessors that the NATO powers abandon West Berlin. When the United States and its allies predictably refused, Khrushchev suggested that he and Eisenhower discuss the issue personally, both in visits to each other's countries and at a summit meeting in Paris in 1960. The United States agreed. Khrushchev's 1959 visit to America produced a cool but polite public response. Plans proceeded for the summit conference and for Eisenhower's visit to Moscow shortly thereafter. Only days before the scheduled beginning of the Paris meeting, however, the Soviet Union announced that it had shot down an American U-2, a high-altitude spy plane, over Russian territory. Its pilot, Francis Gary Powers, was in captivity. Khrushchev lashed out angrily at the American incursion into Soviet air space, breaking up the Paris summit almost before it could begin and withdrawing his invitation to Eisenhower to visit the Soviet Union.

After eight years in office, Eisenhower had failed to eliminate, and in some respects had actually increased, the tensions between the United States and the Soviet Union. Yet Eisenhower had brought to the Cold War his own sense of the limits of American power. He had resisted military intervention in Vietnam. And he had placed a measure of restraint on those who urged the creation of an enormous American military establishment. In his farewell address in January 1961, he warned of the "unwarranted influence" of a vast "military-industrial complex." His caution, in both domestic and international affairs, stood in marked contrast to the attitudes of his successors, who argued that the United States must act more boldly and aggressively on behalf of its goals at home and abroad.

"Military-Industrial Complex"

CONCLUSION

The booming economic growth of the 1950s—and the anxiety over the Cold War that formed a backdrop to it—shaped the politics and the culture of the decade. For most Americans, the 1950s were years of increasing personal prosperity. Sales of private homes increased dramatically; suburbs grew precipitously; young families had children at an astounding rate—creating what came to be known as the postwar "baby boom." After the end of the divisive Korean War, the nation's politics entered a period of relative calm, symbolized by the genial presence in the White House of

Dwight D. Eisenhower, who provided moderate and undemanding leadership through most of the decade.

The nation's culture, too, helped create a broad sense of stability and calm. Television, which emerged in the 1950s as the most powerful medium of mass culture, presented largely uncontroversial programming dominated by middle-class images and traditional values. Movies, theater, popular magazines, and newspapers all contributed to a broad sense of well-being.

But the 1950s were not, in the end, as calm and contented as the politics and popular culture of the time suggested. A powerful youth culture emerged in these years that displayed a considerable level of restiveness and even disillusionment. African Americans began to escalate their protests against segregation and inequality. The continuing existence of widespread poverty among large groups of Americans attracted increasing attention as the decade progressed. These pulsing anxieties, combined with frustration over the continuing tensions of the Cold War, produced by the late 1950s a growing sense of impatience with the calm, placid public culture of the time. That was one reason for the growing desire for action and innovation as the 1960s began.

FOR FURTHER REFERENCE

James T. Patterson, *Grand Expectations: Postwar America, 1945–1974* (1996), a volume in the Oxford History of the United States, is an important general history of the postwar era. John P. Diggins, *The Proud Decades: America in War and Peace, 1941–1960* (1989) and Godfrey Hodgson, *America in Our Time* (1976) are other important surveys. Kenneth T. Jackson, *The Crabgrass Frontier: The Suburbanization of the United States* (1985) is a classic history of a major social movement. Joshua B. Freeman, *Working-Class New York: Life and Labor Since World War II* (2000) is an important study of postwar labor. Eric Barnouw, *Tube of Plenty* (1982) and Karal Ann Marling, *As Seen on TV: The Visual Culture of Everyday Life in the 1950s* (1995) are good studies of the new medium. Elaine Tyler May, *Homeward Bound: American Families in the Cold War* (1988) is a challenging cultural history. Paul Boyer, *By the Bomb's Early Light: American Thought and Culture at the Dawn of the Atomic Age* (1985) examines the impact of the atomic bomb on American social thought. Stephen Ambrose, *Eisenhower the President* (1984) is a good biography and Fred Greenstein, *The Hidden-Hand Presidency* (1982) is a challenge to earlier, dismissive views of Eisenhower's leadership style. Taylor Branch, *Parting the Waters: America in the King Years, 1954–1963* (1988) and *Pillar of Fire: America in the King Years, 1963–1965* (1998) are superb narratives of the early years of the civil rights movement. Richard Kluger, *Simple Justice* (1975) is a classic narrative history of the *Brown* decision and James T. Patterson, *Brown v. Board of Edu-*

cation: A Civil Rights Milestone and Its Troubled Legacy (2001) is an important recent examination. John Egerton, *Speak Now Against the Day: The Generation Before the Civil Rights Movement in the South* (1994) is a history of struggles over white supremacy in the first years after World War II.

The stunning effect of the first Soviet satellite launch in 1957 is vividly portrayed in the documentary film *The Satellite Sky* (1990). *Eisenhower* (1993) is an extensive film portrait, offering a fresh reassessment of his legacy. *An Age of Conformity* (1991) is a film portraying domestic life in the 1940s and 1950s.

For quizzes, Internet resources, references to additional books and films, and more, consult this book's Online Learning Center site at www.mhhe.com/unfinishednation4.

KHE SANH, VIETNAM, 1968 A beleaguered American soldier shows his exhaustion during the 76-day siege of the American marine base at Khe Sanh, which began shortly before the 1968 Tet offensive in Vietnam. American forces sustained record casualties in the fierce fighting at Khe Sanh; the Vietnamese communist forces suffered far more. *(Robert Ellison/Black Star)*

TIME LINE

1960	1961	1962	1963
Kennedy elected president	Freedom rides	Cuban missile crisis	March on Washington
	Bay of Pigs		Kennedy assassinated; Johnson becomes president
	Berlin Wall erected		Civil rights demonstrations in Birmingham

☙

CHAPTER THIRTY-ONE

THE ORDEAL OF LIBERALISM

Expanding the Liberal State
The Battle for Racial Equality
"Flexible Response" and the Cold War
The Agony of Vietnam
The Traumas of 1968

B y the late 1950s, a growing restlessness was becoming visible beneath the apparently placid surface of American society. Ultimately, that restlessness would make the 1960s one of the most turbulent and divisive eras of the twentieth century. But at first, it contributed to a bold and confident effort by political leaders to attack social and international problems within the framework of conventional liberal politics.

EXPANDING THE LIBERAL STATE

☙

Those who yearned for a more active government in the late 1950s and who accused the Eisenhower administration of allowing the nation to "drift" hoped for vigorous new leadership. The two men who served in the White House through most of the 1960s—John Kennedy and Lyndon Johnson—seemed for a time to be the embodiment of these liberal hopes.

1964	1965	1967	1968	
Johnson launches war on poverty	Malcolm X assassinated	Antiwar movement grows	Tet offensive	
Civil Rights Act	Voting Rights Act	Racial violence in Detroit	Martin Luther King, Jr. assassinated	
Gulf of Tonkin Resolution	U.S. troops in Vietnam		Robert Kennedy assassinated	
Johnson elected president	Racial violence in Watts		Nixon elected president	

(64% of electorate voting)

	ELECTORAL VOTE	POPULAR VOTE (%)
John F. Kennedy *(Democratic)*	303	34,227,096 (49.9)
Richard M. Nixon *(Republican)*	219	34,108,546 (49.6)
Harry F. Byrd *(Dixiecrat)*	15	501,643 (0.7)
Other candidates *(Prohibition; Socialist Labor; Constitution; Socialist Workers; National States Rights)*	—	197,029

THE ELECTION OF 1960 The election of 1960 was, in the popular vote at least, one of the closest in American history. John Kennedy's margin over Richard Nixon was less than one-third of one percent of the total national vote, but greater in the electoral college. Note the distribution of electoral strength of the two candidates. Kennedy was strong in the industrial northeast and the largest industrial states of the Midwest, and he retained at least a portion of his party's traditional strength in the South and Southwest. But Nixon made significant inroads into the upper South, carried Florida, and swept most of the Plains and Mountain states. ◆ *What was the significance of this distribution of strength to the future of the two parties?*

For an interactive version of this map go to www.mhhe.com/unfinishednation4ch31maps

John Kennedy

The campaign of 1960 produced two young candidates who claimed to offer the nation active leadership. The Republican nomination went almost uncontested to Vice President Richard Nixon, who promised moderate reform. The Democrats, in the meantime, emerged from a spirited primary campaign united, somewhat uneasily, behind John Fitzgerald Kennedy, an attractive and articulate senator from Massachusetts who had narrowly missed being the party's vice presidential candidate in 1956.

JOHN KENNEDY The new president and his wife, Jacqueline, attend one of the five balls in Washington marking Kennedy's inauguration in 1961. *(Paul Schutzer, Life Magazine, © 1961 Time Warner, Inc./Getty Images)*

John Kennedy was the son of the wealthy, powerful, and highly controversial Joseph P. Kennedy, former American ambassador to Britain. He premised his campaign, he said, "on the single assumption that the American people are uneasy at the present drift in our national course." But his appealing public image was at least as important as his political positions in attracting popular support.

Kennedy Elected

He overcame doubts about his youth (he turned forty-three in 1960) and religion (he was Catholic) to win with a tiny plurality of the popular vote (49.9 percent to Nixon's 49.6 percent) and only a slightly more comfortable electoral majority (303 to 219).

The "New Frontier" Kennedy had campaigned promising a set of domestic reforms he described as the "New Frontier."
But his thin popular mandate and a Congress dominated by a coalition of
Republicans and conservative Democrats frustrated many of his hopes.
Kennedy did manage to win approval of tariff reductions his administration
had negotiated, and he began to build a legislative agenda that he hoped he
might eventually see enacted—including a call for a significant tax cut to
promote economic growth.

More than any other president of the century (except perhaps the two
Roosevelts and, later, Ronald Reagan), Kennedy made his own personality
an integral part of his presidency and a central focus of national attention.
Nothing illustrated that more clearly than the popular reaction to the
tragedy of November 22, 1963. Kennedy had traveled to Texas with his
wife and Vice President Lyndon Johnson for a series of political appearances. While the presidential motorcade rode slowly through the streets
of Dallas, shots rang out. Two bullets struck the president—one in the
throat, the other in the head. He was sped to a nearby hospital, where
minutes later he was pronounced dead. Lee Harvey Oswald, a confused
and embittered Marxist, was arrested for the crime later that day, and then
mysteriously murdered by a Dallas nightclub owner, Jack Ruby, two days
later as he was being moved from one jail to another. Most Americans at
the time accepted the conclusions of a federal commission, chaired by
Chief Justice Earl Warren, appointed by President Johnson to investigate
the assassination. The commission found that both Oswald and Ruby had
acted alone, that there was no larger conspiracy. In later years, however,
many Americans came to believe that the Warren Commission report had
ignored evidence of a wider conspiracy behind the murders. Controversy
over the truth about the assassination continues today.

Lyndon Johnson

The Kennedy assassination was a national trauma—a defining event for
almost everyone old enough to be aware of it. At the time, however, much
of the nation took comfort in the personality and performance of
Kennedy's successor in the White House, Lyndon Baines Johnson. Johnson was a native of the poor "hill country" of west Texas and had risen to
become majority leader of the U.S. Senate by dint of extraordinary, even
obsessive effort and ambition. Having failed to win the Democratic nomination for president in 1960, he surprised many who knew him by agreeing to accept the second position on the ticket with Kennedy. The events
in Dallas thrust him into the White House.

Johnson's rough-edged, even crude personality could hardly have been
more different from Kennedy's. But like Kennedy, Johnson was a man
who believed in the active use of power. Between 1963 and 1966, he compiled the most impressive legislative record of any president since
Franklin Roosevelt. He was aided by the tidal wave of emotion that fol-

lowed the death of President Kennedy, which helped win support for many New Frontier proposals. But Johnson also constructed a remarkable reform program of his own, one that he ultimately labeled the "Great Society." And he won approval *"Great Society"* of much of it through the same sort of skillful lobbying in Congress that had made him an effective majority leader.

Johnson's first year in office was, by necessity, dominated by the campaign for reelection. There was little doubt that he would win—particularly after the Republican Party nominated the very conservative Senator Barry Goldwater of Arizona. In the November 1964 election, the president received a larger plurality, over 61 percent, than any candidate before or since. Goldwater managed to carry only his home state of Arizona and five states in the Deep South. Record Democratic majorities in both houses of Congress, many of whose members had been swept into office only because of the margin of Johnson's victory, ensured that the president would be able to fulfill many of his goals.

The Assault on Poverty

For the first time since the 1930s, the federal government took steps in the 1960s to create important new social welfare programs. The most important of these, perhaps, *Medicare and Medicaid* was Medicare: a program to provide federal aid to the elderly for medical expenses. Its enactment in 1965 came at the end of a bitter, twenty-year debate between those who believed in the concept of national health assistance and those who denounced it as "socialized medicine." But Medicare pacified many critics. For one thing, it avoided the stigma of "welfare" by making Medicare benefits available to all elderly Americans, regardless of need (just as Social Security had done with pensions). That created a large middle-class constituency for the program. The program also defused the opposition of the medical community by allowing doctors serving Medicare patients to practice privately and (at first) to charge their normal fees; Medicare simply shifted responsibility for paying those fees from the patient to the government. In 1966, Johnson steered to passage the Medicaid program, which extended federal medical assistance to welfare recipients and other indigent people of all ages.

Medicare and Medicaid were early steps in a much larger assault on poverty—one that Kennedy had been planning in the last months of his life and that Johnson launched only weeks after taking office. The centerpiece of this "war on poverty," as Johnson called it, was the Office of Economic Opportunity (OEO), which created an array of new educational, employment, housing, and health-care programs. But the OEO was controversial from the start, in part because of its commitment to the idea of "Community Action."

Community Action was an effort to involve members of poor communities themselves in the planning and administration of the programs designed to help them. The Community Action programs provided jobs for many poor people and gave them valuable experience in administrative and political work. But despite its achievements, the Community Action approach proved impossible to sustain, both because of administrative failures and because the apparent excesses of a few agencies damaged the popular image of the Community Action programs, and indeed the war on poverty, as a whole.

Failure of the OEO   The OEO spent nearly $3 billion during its first two years of existence, and it helped reduce poverty in some areas. But it fell far short of eliminating poverty altogether. That was in part because of the weaknesses of the programs themselves and in part because funding for them, inadequate from the beginning, dwindled as the years passed and a costly war in Southeast Asia became the nation's first priority.

Cities, Schools, and Immigration

Closely tied to the antipoverty program were federal efforts to promote the revitalization of decaying cities and to strengthen the nation's schools. The Housing Act of 1961 offered $4.9 billion in federal grants to cities for the preservation of open spaces, the development of mass-transit systems, and the subsidization of middle-income housing. In 1966, Johnson established a new cabinet agency, the Department of Housing and Urban Development (whose first secretary, Robert Weaver, was the first African American ever to serve in the cabinet). Johnson also inaugurated the Model Cities program, which offered federal subsidies for urban redevelopment pilot programs.

Federal Aid to Education   Kennedy had fought for federal aid to public education, but he had failed to overcome two important obstacles: Many Americans feared that aid to education was the first step toward federal control of the schools, and Catholics insisted that federal assistance must extend to parochial as well as public schools. Johnson managed to circumvent both objections with the Elementary and Secondary Education Act of 1965 and a series of subsequent measures. The bills extended aid to both private and parochial schools and based the aid on the economic conditions of the students, not on the needs of the schools themselves.

Immigration Act of 1965   The Johnson administration also supported the Immigration Act of 1965, one of the most important pieces of legislation of the 1960s. The law maintained a strict limit on the number of newcomers admitted to the country each year (170,000), but it eliminated the "national origins" system established in the 1920s, which gave preference to immigrants from northern Europe over those from other parts of the world. It continued to restrict immigration from some parts of Latin America, but it allowed people from all parts of Europe, Asia, and Africa to enter the United States on an equal basis. By the early 1970s, the character of American immigration had changed dramatically, with members of new national groups—and particularly large groups of Asians—entering the United States and changing the character of the American population.

Legacies of the Great Society

Taken together, the Great Society reforms meant a significant increase in federal spending. For a time, rising tax revenues from the growing economy nearly compensated for the new expenditures. In 1964, Johnson managed to win passage of the $11.5 billion tax cut that Kennedy had first proposed in 1962 to promote economic growth. The cut increased the federal deficit, but substantial economic growth over the next several years made up for much of the revenue initially lost. As Great Society programs began to multiply, however, and particularly as they began to compete with the escalating costs of America's military ventures, the federal budget rapidly outpaced increases in revenues. In 1961, the federal government had spent $94.4 billion. By 1970, that sum had risen to $196.6 billion.

The high costs of the Great Society programs, the failures of many of them, and the inability of the government to find the revenues to pay for them contributed to a growing disillusionment in later years with the idea of federal efforts to solve social problems. But the Great Society, despite *Achievements of the Great Society* many failures, was also responsible for some significant achievements. It significantly reduced hunger in America. It made medical care available to millions of elderly and poor people who would otherwise have had great difficulty affording it. It contributed to the greatest reduction in poverty in American history. In 1959, according to the most widely accepted estimates, 21 percent of the American people lived below the officially established poverty line. By 1969, only 12 percent remained below that line. Much of that progress was a result of economic growth, but some of it was a result of Great Society programs.

THE BATTLE FOR RACIAL EQUALITY

The nation's most important domestic initiative in the 1960s was the effort to provide justice and equality to African Americans. It was the most difficult commitment, the one that produced the severest strains on American society. But it was one that could not be avoided. African Americans were themselves ensuring that the nation would have to deal with the problem of race.

Expanding Protests

John Kennedy was sympathetic to the cause of racial justice, but he was hardly a committed crusader. Like presidents before him, he feared alienating southern Democratic voters and powerful southern Democrats in Congress. His administration hoped to contain the racial problem by expanding enforcement of existing laws and supporting litigation to overturn existing segregation statutes.

But the pressure for change was growing uncontainable even before Kennedy took office. In February 1960, black college students in Greensboro, North Carolina, staged a sit-in at a segregated Woolworth's lunch counter; and in the following months, such demonstrations spread throughout the South, forcing many merchants to integrate their facilities. In the fall of 1960, some of those who had participated in the sit-ins *SNCC* formed the Student Nonviolent Coordinating Committee (SNCC)—a student branch of Martin Luther King, Jr.'s Southern Christian Leadership Council; SNCC worked to keep the spirit of resistance alive.

In 1961, an interracial group of students, working with the Congress *"Freedom Rides"* of Racial Equality (CORE), began what they called "freedom rides." Traveling by bus throughout the South, they tried to force the desegregation of bus stations. They were met in some places with such savage violence on the part of whites that the president finally dispatched federal marshals to help keep the peace and ordered the integration of all bus and train stations.

Events in the Deep South in 1963 helped bring the growing movement to something of a climax. In April, Martin Luther King, Jr., helped launch a series of nonviolent demonstrations in Birmingham, Alabama. Police Commissioner Eugene "Bull" Connor personally supervised a brutal effort to break up the peaceful marches, arresting hundreds of demonstrators and using attack dogs, tear gas, electric cattle prods, and fire hoses—at times even against small children—in full view of television cameras. Two months later, Governor George Wallace stood in the doorway of a building at the University of Alabama to prevent the court-ordered enrollment of several black students. Only after the arrival of federal marshals did he give way. The same night, NAACP official Medgar Evers was murdered in Mississippi. And in September, a bombing of a black church in Birmingham killed four African-American children.

A National Commitment

The events in Alabama and Mississippi were a warning to the president that he could no longer avoid the issue of race. In an important television address the night of the University of Alabama confrontation, Kennedy spoke eloquently of the "moral issue" facing the nation. Days later, he introduced new legislative proposals prohibiting segregation in "public ac-

THE MARCH ON WASHINGTON, 1963 Martin Luther King, Jr., waves to the vast crowd spreading out from the Lincoln Memorial shortly after delivering his famous "I Have a Dream" speech—the centerpiece of the March on Washington. Initially envisioned as a broad and militant protest against discrimination, it became in the end a moderate, interracial demonstration of support for the civil rights bill President Kennedy had recently proposed to Congress, which passed in 1964. *(UPI/Corbis-Bettmann)*

commodations" (stores, restaurants, theaters, hotels), barring discrimination in employment, and increasing the power of the government to file suits on behalf of school integration.

To generate support for the legislation, and to dramatize the power of the growing movement, more than 200,000 demonstrators marched down the Mall in Washington, D.C., in August 1963 and gathered before the Lincoln Memorial for the *March on Washington* largest civil rights demonstration in the nation's history. Martin Luther King, Jr., in one of the greatest speeches of his distinguished oratorical career, aroused the crowd with a litany of images prefaced again and again by the phrase "I have a dream."

The assassination of President Kennedy three months later gave new impetus to the battle for civil rights legislation. The ambitious measure that Kennedy had proposed in June 1963 was stalled in the Senate after having passed through the House of Representatives with relative ease. Early in 1964, after Johnson had applied both public and private pressure, supporters of the measure finally mustered the two-thirds majority necessary to end a filibuster by southern senators; and the Senate passed the most important civil rights bill of the twentieth century.

The Battle for Voting Rights

Having won a significant victory in one area, the civil rights movement shifted its focus to another: voting rights. During the summer of 1964, thousands of civil rights workers, black and white, northern and southern, spread out through the South, but primarily into Mississippi, to work on behalf of black voter registration and participation. The campaign was known as "Freedom Summer," and it produced a violent response from some southern whites. Three of the first freedom workers to arrive in the South—two whites, Andrew Goodman and Michael Schwerner, and one black, James Chaney—were murdered. Local law enforcement officials were involved in the crime.

"Freedom Summer"

The "Freedom Summer" also produced the Mississippi Freedom Democratic Party (MFDP), an integrated alternative to the regular state party organization. Under the leadership of Fannie Lou Hamer and others, the MFDP challenged the regular party's right to its seats at the Democratic National Convention that summer. President Johnson, with King's help, managed to broker a compromise by which members of the MFDP could be seated as observers, with promises of party reforms later on, while the regular party retained its official standing. Many MFDP members rejected the agreement and left the convention embittered.

A year later, in March 1965, King helped organize a major demonstration in Selma, Alabama, to press for the right of blacks to register to vote. Selma sheriff Jim Clark led local police in a brutal attack on the demonstrators, which was televised nationally. Two northern whites participating in the Selma march were murdered in the course of the effort there. The widespread national outrage that followed the events in Alabama helped push Lyndon Johnson to propose and win passage of the Civil Rights Act of 1965, better known as the Voting Rights Act, which provided federal protection to African Americans attempting to exercise their right to vote. But important as such gains were, they failed to satisfy the rapidly rising expectations of American blacks as the focus of the movement began to move from political to economic issues.

Voting Rights Act Approved

The Changing Movement

By 1966, 69 percent of American blacks were living in metropolitan areas and 45 percent were living outside the South. Although the economic condition of most Americans was improving, in many poor urban black communities things were getting significantly worse. More than half of all nonwhite Americans lived in poverty at the beginning of the 1960s.

By the mid-1960s, therefore, the issue of race was moving out of the South and into the rest of the nation and beyond the issue of formal, legal segregation to an attack on the informal practices that often sustained discrimination. That carried the fight into northern cities, which had no Jim Crow laws but much segregation. Many African-American leaders (and their white supporters) soon began demanding that the battle against job discrimination move to a new level. They argued that the only way for employers to prove that they were not discriminating against African Americans was for them to demonstrate that they were hiring minorities. If necessary, they should adopt positive measures to recruit minorities. Lyndon Johnson gave his sup- *"Affirmative Action"* port to the concept of "affirmative action" in 1965. Over the next decade, affirmative action guidelines gradually extended to virtually all institutions doing business with or receiving funds from the federal government (including schools and universities)—and to many others as well.

A symbol of the movement's new direction, and of the problems it would cause, was a major campaign in the summer of 1966 in Chicago, in which King played a prominent role. Organizers of the Chicago campaign hoped to direct national attention to housing and employment discrimination in northern industrial cities. But the Chicago campaign evoked vicious and at times violent opposition from white residents of that city and failed to attract wide attention or support in the way events in the South had done.

Urban Violence

Well before the Chicago campaign, the problem of urban poverty had thrust itself into national prominence when riots broke out in black neighborhoods in major cities. There were a few scattered disturbances in the summer of 1964, most notably in New York City's Harlem. The most serious race riot since the end of World War II occurred the following summer in the Watts *Riots* section of Los Angeles. In the midst of a traffic arrest, a white police officer struck a protesting black bystander with his club. The incident triggered a storm of anger and a week of violence. Thirty-four people died during the uprising, which was eventually quelled by the National Guard. In the summer of 1966, there were forty-three additional outbreaks, the most serious of them in Chicago and Cleveland. And in the summer of 1967, there were eight major disorders, including the largest of them all—a racial clash in Detroit in which forty-three people died.

Televised reports of the violence alarmed millions of Americans and created both a new sense of urgency and a growing sense of doubt among some whites who had embraced the cause of racial justice only a few years before. A special Commission on Civil Disorders, created by the president in response to the riots, issued a celebrated report in the spring of 1968 recommending massive spending to eliminate the abysmal conditions of the ghettoes. To many white Americans, however, the lesson of the riots was the need for stern measures to stop violence and lawlessness.

Black Power

Disillusioned with the ideal of peaceful change through cooperation with whites, an increasing number of African Americans were turning to a new

Racial Distinctiveness Emphasized

approach to the racial issue: the philosophy of "black power." Black power meant many different things. But in all its forms, it suggested a shift away from the goal of assimilation and toward increased awareness of racial distinctiveness.

Perhaps the most enduring impact of the black-power ideology was a social and psychological one: instilling racial pride in African Americans. But black power took political forms as well, and it created a deep schism within the civil rights movement. Traditional black organizations that emphasized cooperation with sympathetic whites—groups such as the NAACP, the Urban League, and King's Southern Christian Leadership Conference— now faced competition from more radical groups. The Student Nonviolent Coordinating Committee and the Congress of Racial Equality had both begun as relatively moderate, interracial organizations. By the mid-1960s, however, these and other groups were calling for more radical and occasionally even violent action against the racism of white society and were openly rejecting the approaches of older, more established black leaders.

Black Panthers

The most radical expressions of the black-power idea came from such revolutionary organizations as the Black Panthers, based in Oakland, California, and the separatist group, the Nation of Islam, which denounced whites as "devils" and appealed to blacks to embrace the Islamic faith and work for complete racial separation. The most celebrated of the Black Muslims, as whites often termed them, was Malcolm Little, who had adopted the name Malcolm X ("X" to denote his lost African surname). He died in 1965 when black gunmen, presumably under orders from rivals within the Nation of Islam, assassinated him. But he remained a major figure in many black communities long after his death—as important to and revered by as many African Americans as Martin Luther King, Jr.

"FLEXIBLE RESPONSE" AND THE COLD WAR

In international affairs as much as in domestic reform, the optimistic liberalism of the Kennedy and Johnson administrations dictated a more active and aggressive approach to dealing with the nation's problems than that of the 1950s.

Diversifying Foreign Policy

The Kennedy administration entered office convinced that the United States needed to be able to counter communist aggression in more flexible ways than the atomic-weapons-oriented defense strategy of the Eisenhower years permitted. In particular, Kennedy was unsatisfied with the nation's ability to meet communist threats in "emerging areas" of the Third World—the areas in which, Kennedy believed, the real struggle against communism would be waged in the future. He gave enthusiastic support to the expansion of the Special Forces (or "Green Berets," as they were soon known)—soldiers trained specifically to fight guerrilla conflicts and other limited wars.

Kennedy also favored expanding American influence through peaceful means. To repair the badly deteriorating relation-   *"Alliance for Progress"*
ship with Latin America, he proposed an "Alliance
for Progress": a series of projects for peaceful development and stabilization of the nations of that region. Kennedy also inaugurated the Agency for International Development (AID) to coordinate foreign aid. And he established what became one of his most popular innovations: the Peace Corps, which sent young American volunteers abroad to work in developing areas.

Among the first foreign policy ventures of the Kennedy administration was a disastrous assault on the Castro government in Cuba. The Eisenhower administration had started the project; and by the time Kennedy took office, the CIA had been working for months to train a small army of anti-Castro Cuban exiles in Central   *Bay of Pigs*
America. On April 17, 1961, with the approval of
the new president, 2,000 of the armed exiles landed at the Bay of Pigs in Cuba, expecting first American air support and then a spontaneous uprising by the Cuban people on their behalf. They received neither. At the last minute, as it became clear that things were going badly, Kennedy withdrew the air support, fearful of involving the United States too directly in the invasion. The expected uprising did not occur. Instead, well-armed Castro forces easily crushed the invaders, and within two days the entire mission had collapsed.

Confrontations with the Soviet Union

In the grim aftermath of the Bay of Pigs, Kennedy traveled to Vienna in June 1961 for his first meeting with Soviet Premier Nikita Khrushchev. Their frosty exchange of views did little to reduce tensions between the two nations—nor did Khrushchev's veiled threat of war unless the United States ceased to support a noncommunist West Berlin in the heart of East Germany.

Khrushchev was particularly unhappy about the mass exodus of residents of East Germany to the West through the easily traversed border in the center of Berlin. But he ultimately found a method short of war to stop it. Before dawn on August 13, 1961, the East German government, complying with directives from Moscow, constructed a wall between East and West Berlin. Guards fired on those who continued to try to escape. For nearly thirty years, the Berlin Wall served as the most potent physical symbol of the conflict between the communist and noncommunist worlds.

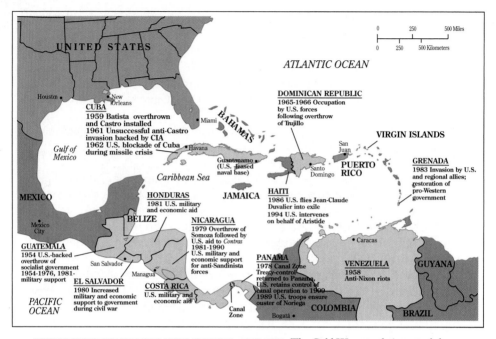

THE UNITED STATES IN LATIN AMERICA, 1954–2001 The Cold War greatly increased the readiness of the United States to intervene in the affairs of its Latin American neighbors. This map presents the many times and ways in which Washington ordered interventions in Central America, the Caribbean, and the northern nations of South America. During much of this period, the interventions were driven by Cold War concerns—by fears that communists might take over nations near the United States as they had taken over Cuba in the early 1960s. ◆ *What other interests motivated the U.S. to exert influence in Latin America, even after the end of the Cold War?*

The rising tensions culminated the following October in the most dangerous and dramatic crisis of the Cold War. During the summer of 1962, *Cuban Missile Crisis* American intelligence agencies had become aware of the arrival of a new wave of Soviet technicians and equipment in Cuba and of military construction in progress. On October 14, aerial reconnaissance photos produced clear evidence that the Soviets were constructing sites on the island for offensive nuclear weapons. To the Soviets, placing missiles in Cuba probably seemed a reasonable—and relatively inexpensive—way to counter the presence of American missiles in Turkey (and a way to deter any future American invasion of Cuba). But to Kennedy and most other Americans, the missile sites represented an act of aggression by the Soviets toward the United States. Almost immediately, the president decided that the weapons could not be allowed to remain. On October 22, he ordered a naval and air blockade around Cuba, a "quarantine" against all offensive weapons. Preparations were under way for an American air attack on the missile sites when, late in the evening of October 26, Kennedy received a message from Khrushchev implying that the Soviet Union would remove the missile bases in exchange for an American pledge not to invade Cuba. Ignoring other, tougher Soviet messages, the president agreed. The crisis soon ended.

Johnson and the World

Lyndon Johnson entered the presidency with little prior experience in international affairs. He was eager, therefore, not only to continue the policies of his predecessor but to prove quickly that he too was a strong and forceful leader.

An internal rebellion in the Dominican Repub-
lic gave him an early opportunity to do so. A 1961 *Intervention in the Dominican Republic*
assassination had toppled the repressive dictator-
ship of General Rafael Trujillo, and for the next four years various factions in the country had struggled for dominance. In the spring of 1965, a conservative regime began to collapse in the face of a revolt by a broad range of groups on behalf of the left-wing nationalist Juan Bosch. Arguing (without any evidence) that Bosch planned to establish a pro-Castro, communist regime, Johnson dispatched 30,000 American troops to quell the disorder. Only after a conservative candidate defeated Bosch in a 1966 election were the forces withdrawn.

From Johnson's first moments in office, however, his foreign policy was almost totally dominated by the bitter civil war in Vietnam and by the expanding involvement of the United States there.

THE AGONY OF VIETNAM

George Kennan, who helped devise the containment doctrine in the name of which America went to war in Vietnam, once called the conflict "the most disastrous of all America's undertakings over the whole 200 years of its history." In retrospect, few would now wholly disagree. Yet at first, the conflict in Vietnam seemed simply one more Third World struggle on the periphery of the Cold War.

America and Diem

Having thrown its support to the new leader of South Vietnam, Ngo Dinh Diem, in the aftermath of the 1954 Geneva accords, and having supported Diem in his refusal to hold the elections in 1956 that the accords had required, the United States found itself drawn steadily deeper into the unstable politics of this fractious new nation.

Although Diem was an aristocratic Catholic *Growing Support for Diem*
from central Vietnam, an outsider in the south, he
was also a nationalist, uncontaminated by collaboration with the French. And he was, for a time, apparently successful. With the help of the American

THE WAR IN VIETNAM AND INDOCHINA, 1964–1975 Much of the Vietnam War was fought in small engagements in widely scattered areas and did not conform to traditional notions of combat. But as this map shows, there were traditional battles and invasions and supply routes as well. The red arrows in the middle of the map show the general path of the Ho Chi Minh Trail, the main supply route by which North Vietnam supplied its troops and allies in the South. The blue arrow in southern South Vietnam indicates the point at which American troops invaded Cambodia in 1970. ◆ *What is there in the geography of Indochina, as presented on this map, that helps to explain the great difficulty the American military had in securing South Vietnam against communist attacks?*

CIA, Diem waged an effective campaign against some of the powerful religious sects and the South Vietnamese mafia, which had challenged the authority of the central government. As a result, the United States came to regard Diem as a powerful and impressive alternative to Ho Chi Minh. America poured military and economic aid into South Vietnam.

Diem's early successes in suppressing the sects in Vietnam led him in 1959 to begin a similar campaign to eliminate the supporters of Ho Chi Minh, the Vietminh, who had stayed behind in the south after the partition. That campaign persuaded Ho to resume the armed struggle for national unification. In 1959, the Vietminh cadres in the south created the National Liberation Front (NLF), known to many Americans as the Viet Cong—an organization closely allied with the North Vietnamese government. In 1960, under orders from Hanoi, and with both material and manpower support from North Vietnam, the NLF began military operations in the south. This marked the beginning of what Americans know as the Vietnam War.

By 1961, NLF forces had established effective control over many areas of the countryside. Diem was also by now losing the support of many other groups in South Vietnam, including his own military. In 1963, the Diem regime precipitated a major crisis by trying to discipline and repress the South Vietnamese Buddhists in an effort to make Catholicism the dominant religion of the country. The Buddhists staged enormous antigovernment demonstrations, during which several monks doused themselves with gasoline, sat cross-legged in the streets of downtown Saigon, and set themselves on fire—in view of photographers and television cameras.

American officials pressured Diem to reform his now tottering government, but the president made no significant concessions. As a result, in the fall of 1963, Kennedy gave his approval to a plot by a group of South Vietnamese generals to topple Diem. In early November 1963, the generals staged the coup, assassinated Diem along with his brother and principal adviser, Ngo Dinh Nhu   *Diem Assassinated* (killings the United States had not wanted or expected), and established the first of a series of new governments, which were, for over three years, even less stable than the one they had overthrown. A few weeks after the coup, John Kennedy too was dead.

From Aid to Intervention

Lyndon Johnson, therefore, inherited what was already a substantial American commitment to the survival of an anticommunist South Vietnam. During his first months in office, he expanded the American involvement in Vietnam only slightly, sending an additional 5,000 military advisers there and preparing to send 5,000 more. Then, early in August 1964, the president announced that American destroyers on patrol in international waters in the Gulf of Tonkin had been attacked by North Vietnamese torpedo boats. Later information raised serious doubts as to whether the administration reported the attacks accurately. At the time, however, virtually no one questioned Johnson's portrayal of the incident as a serious act of aggression. By a vote of 416 to 0 in the House and 88 to 2 in the Senate, Congress hurriedly passed the Gulf of Tonkin Resolution, which authorized the president to "take all   *Gulf of Tonkin Resolution* necessary measures" to protect American forces and "prevent further aggression" in Southeast Asia. The resolution became, in Johnson's view at least, an open-ended legal authorization for escalation of the conflict.

With the South Vietnamese leadership still in disarray and the communist military pressure on the south growing stronger, more and more of the burden of opposition to the Viet Cong fell on the United States. In February 1965, after communist forces attacked an American military base at Pleiku, Johnson ordered American bombings of the north, in an attempt to destroy the depots and transportation lines responsible for the flow of North Vietnamese soldiers and supplies into South Vietnam. The bombing continued intermittently until 1972. A month later, in March 1965, two battalions of American marines landed at Da Nang in South Vietnam. There were now more than 100,000 American troops in Vietnam.

Four months later, the president announced that American soldiers would now begin playing an active role in the conflict. By the end of the year, there were more than 180,000 American combat troops in Vietnam; in 1966, that number doubled; and by the end of 1967, there were over 500,000 American soldiers there. In the meantime, the air war intensified. By the spring of 1966, more than 4,000 Americans had been killed.

The Quagmire

"Attrition" Strategy

Central to the American war effort in Vietnam was the strategy known to the military as "attrition," one premised on the belief that the United States could inflict more damage on the enemy than the enemy could absorb. But the attrition strategy failed because the North Vietnamese were willing to commit many more soldiers and resources to the conflict than the United States had predicted.

It failed, too, because the United States was wrong in expecting its bombing of the north to eliminate the communists' war-making capacity. North Vietnam was not a modern industrial society, and it had relatively few of the sort of targets against which bombing is effective. The North Vietnamese also responded to the bombing with great ingenuity: creating a network of underground tunnels, shops, and factories; securing substantial aid from the Soviet Union and China; and continually moving the Ho Chi Minh Trail to make it elusive to American bombers. Far from breaking the north's resolve, the bombing seemed actually to strengthen popular commitment to the war.

"Pacification"

Another important part of the American strategy was the "pacification" program, whose purpose was to push the Viet Cong from particular regions and then "pacify" those regions by winning the "hearts and minds" of the people. Routing the Viet Cong was often possible, but the subsequent pacification was more difficult. Gradually, the pacification program gave way to a more heavy-handed relocation strategy, through which American troops uprooted villagers from their homes, sent them fleeing to refugee camps or into the cities (producing by 1967 more than 3 million refugees), and then destroyed the vacated villages and surrounding countryside.

As the war dragged on and victory remained elusive, some American officers and officials began to urge the president to expand the military efforts. But the Johnson administration resisted—in part because it was beginning to encounter obstacles and frustrations at home.

The War at Home

Few Americans, and even fewer influential ones, had protested the American involvement in Vietnam as late as the end of 1965. But as the war dragged on inconclusively, political support for it began to erode.

By the end of 1967, American students opposed to the war had become a significant political *Growing Antiwar Movement* force. Enormous peace marches in New York, Washington, D.C., and other cities drew broad public attention to the antiwar movement. In the meantime, a growing number of journalists, particularly reporters who had spent time in Vietnam, helped sustain the movement with their frank revelations about the brutality and apparent futility of the war.

Senator J. William Fulbright of Arkansas, chairman of the Senate Foreign Relations Committee, also turned against the war and in January 1966 began to stage highly publicized and occasionally televised congressional hearings to air criticisms of it. Other members of Congress joined Fulbright in opposing Johnson's policies—including, in 1967, Robert F. Kennedy, brother of the slain president, now a senator from New York. Even within the administration, the consensus seemed to be crumbling. Robert McNamara, who had done much to help extend the American involvement in Vietnam, quietly left the government, disillusioned, in 1968. His successor as secretary of defense, Clark Clifford, became a quiet but powerful voice within the administration on behalf of a cautious scaling down of the commitment.

In the meantime, Johnson's commitment to fighting the war while continuing his Great Society reforms helped cause *War-induced Inflation* a rise in inflation, from the 2 percent level it had occupied through most of the early 1960s to 3 percent in 1967, 4 percent in 1968, and 6 percent in 1969. In August 1967, Johnson asked Congress for a tax increase to avoid even more ruinous inflation. In return, congressional conservatives demanded and received a $6 billion reduction in the funding for Great Society programs.

THE TRAUMAS OF 1968

By the end of 1967, the twin crises of the war in Vietnam and the deteriorating racial situation at home had produced great social and political tensions. In the course of 1968, those tensions burst to the surface and seemed to threaten national chaos.

THE VIETNAM COMMITMENT

The debate over why the United States became involved in the conflict in Vietnam (which is only one of many debates about the meaning of the war) has centered on two different, if related, questions. One is an effort to assess the broad objectives Americans believed they were pursuing in Vietnam. The other is an effort to explain how and why policymakers made the specific decisions that led the United States to a military commitment in Indochina.

Scholars and writers such as Norman Podhoretz, Guenter Lewy, and R. B. Smith, echoing elements of the official government explanation of American intervention in the war in the 1960s, have argued that the communist aggression in Vietnam was part of a Chinese and Soviet design to spread revolution throughout Asia. America, therefore, was not only protecting Vietnam, although that was an important part of its mission; it was also defending the rest of Asia, which would soon be threatened by communism if Vietnam fell. The intervention in Vietnam was a rational and even necessary expression of America's legitimate security interests and its belief in democracy.

Most scholars, however, have been more skeptical. Historians on the left argue that America's intervention in Vietnam was a form of imperialism—part of a larger effort by the United States after World War II to impose a particular political and economic order on the world. "The Vietnam War," Gabriel Kolko wrote in 1985, "was for the United States the culmination of its frustrating postwar effort to merge its arms and politics to halt and reverse the emergence of states and social systems opposed to the international order Washington sought to establish." Others argued that the United States fought in Vietnam to serve the American economic interests that had a stake in the region or in the arms production the war stimulated. More moderate critics blame the Vietnam intervention on the myopia of a foreign policy elite unwilling to question its own unreflective commitment to containing communism everywhere and unable to distinguish between international aggression and domestic insurgency.

Those who have looked less at the nation's broad objectives than at the workings of the policymaking process have also produced competing explanations. David Halberstam's *The Best and the Brightest* (1972) argued that

> policymakers deluded themselves into thinking they could achieve their goals in Vietnam by ignoring, suppressing, or dismissing information that should have suggested that they were wrong; because of arrogance or ideological rigidity, they simply refused to consider that victory was beyond their grasp.

Larry Berman, writing in 1982, offered a somewhat different view. Neither Johnson nor his advisers were unaware of the obstacles to success in Vietnam. Almost everyone suspected that victory would be difficult, even impossible, to attain. The president was not misled or misinformed. But Johnson committed troops to the war anyway, because he feared that allowing Vietnam to fall would ruin him politically and destroy his hopes for building his "Great Society" at home. Leslie Gelb and Richard Betts made a related argument in 1979. Vietnam, they claimed, was the logical, perhaps inevitable result of a political and bureaucratic order shaped by the ideology of the Cold War. However costly the intervention in Vietnam, policymakers concluded, the costs of not intervening and allowing South Vietnam to fall always seemed higher. The war escalated in the 1960s not because American aims changed but because the situation in Vietnam deteriorated to the point where nothing short of intervention would prevent defeat. Only when the national and international political situation itself shifted in the late 1960s and early 1970s—only when it became clear that the political costs of staying in Vietnam were higher than the political costs of getting out—was it possible for the United States to begin disengaging.

(text continued from page 831)

The Tet Offensive

On January 31, 1968, the first day of the Vietnamese New Year (Tet), communist forces launched an enormous, concerted attack on American strongholds throughout South Vietnam. A few cities, most notably Hue, fell temporarily to the communists. But what made the Tet offensive so shocking to the American people, who saw vivid reports of it on television, was the sight of communist forces in the heart of Saigon, setting off bombs, shooting down South Vietnamese officials and troops, and holding down fortified areas (including, briefly, the grounds of the American embassy). The Tet offensive also suggested to the American public something of the brutality of the fighting in Vietnam. In the midst of the fighting, television cameras recorded the sight of a South Vietnamese officer shooting a captured and defenseless young Viet Cong soldier in the head in the streets of Saigon.

American forces soon dislodged the Viet Cong from most of the positions they had seized. The Tet offensive inflicted *Political Defeat* enormous casualties on the communists and permanently depleted the ranks of the NLF, forcing North Vietnamese troops to take on a much larger share of the subsequent fighting. But all that had little impact on American opinion. Tet may have been a military victory for the United States, but it was a political defeat for the administration.

In the following weeks, opposition to the war grew substantially. Leading newspapers and magazines, television commentators, and mainstream politicians began taking public stands against the conflict. Public opposition to the war almost doubled. And Johnson's personal popularity rating had slid to 35 percent, the lowest of any president since Harry Truman.

The Political Challenge

Beginning in the summer of 1967, dissident Democrats tried to mobilize support behind an antiwar candidate who would challenge Lyndon Johnson in the 1968 primaries. When Robert Kennedy turned them down, they recruited Senator Eugene McCarthy of Minnesota. A brilliantly orchestrated campaign *Eugene McCarthy*

JOHNSON AND HUMPHREY, MARCH 27, 1968 Four days before announcing he would not run for reelection, a grim and tired Lyndon Johnson, accompanied by Vice President Hubert Humphrey, receives a briefing on the military situation in Vietnam. *(Bettmann/Corbis)*

by young volunteers in the New Hampshire primary produced a startling showing by McCarthy in March; he nearly defeated the president.

A few days later, Robert Kennedy entered the campaign, embittering many McCarthy supporters but bringing his own substantial strength among minorities, poor people, and workers to the antiwar cause. Polls showed the president trailing badly in the next scheduled primary, in Wisconsin. On March 31, 1968, Johnson went on television to announce a limited halt in the bombing of North Vietnam—his first major concession to the antiwar forces—and, much more surprising, his withdrawal from the presidential contest.

Robert Kennedy quickly established himself as the champion of the Democratic primaries, winning one election after another. In the meantime, however, Vice President Hubert Humphrey, with the support of President Johnson, entered the contest and began to attract the support of party leaders and of the many delegations that were selected not by popular primaries but by state party organizations. He soon appeared to be the front-runner in the race.

The King Assassination

On April 4, Martin Luther King, Jr., who had traveled to Memphis, Tennessee, to lend his support to striking black sanitation workers in the city, *James Earl Ray* was shot and killed while standing on the balcony of his motel. The assassin, James Earl Ray, who was captured two months later in London, had no apparent motive. Subsequent evidence suggested that he had been hired by others to do the killing, but he himself never revealed the identity of his employers.

King's tragic death produced a great outpouring of grief. Among African Americans, it also produced anger. In the days after the assassination, major riots broke out in more than sixty American cities. Forty-three people died.

The Kennedy Assassination and Chicago

Late in the night of June 6, Robert Kennedy appeared in the ballroom of a Los Angeles hotel to acknowledge his victory in that day's California primary. As he left the ballroom after his victory statement, Sirhan Sirhan, a young Palestinian apparently enraged by pro-Israeli remarks Kennedy had recently made, emerged from a crowd and shot him in the head. Early the next morning, Kennedy died. The shock of this second tragedy in two months cast a pall over the remainder of the presidential campaign.

When the Democrats finally gathered in Chicago in August, for a convention in which Hubert Humphrey was now the only real contender, even the most optimistic observers were predicting turbulence. *Democratic National Convention* Inside the hall, delegates bitterly debated an antiwar plank in the party platform that both Kennedy and McCarthy supporters favored. Miles away, in a downtown park, thousands of antiwar protesters were staging demonstrations. On the third night of the convention, as the delegates were beginning their balloting on the now virtually inevitable nomination of Hubert Humphrey, demonstrators and police clashed in a bloody riot in the streets of Chicago. Hundreds of protesters were injured as police attempted to disperse them with tear gas and billy clubs. Aware that the violence was being televised to the nation, the demonstrators taunted the authorities with the chant, "The whole world is watching!" And Hubert Humphrey, who had spent years dreaming of becoming his party's candidate for president, received a nomination that night which appeared at the time to be almost worthless.

The Conservative Response

The turbulent events of 1968 persuaded some observers that American society was in the throes of revolutionary change. In fact, however, the response of most Americans to the turmoil was a conservative one.

The most visible sign of the conservative backlash was the surprising success of the campaign of George Wallace for the presidency. Wallace had established himself in *George Wallace* 1963 as one of the leading spokesmen for the defense of segregation when, as governor of Alabama, he had attempted to block the admission of black students to the University of Alabama. In 1968, he became a

The year 1968 was one of the most turbulent in the postwar history of the United States. Much of what made it so traumatic were specifically American events—the growing controversy over the war in Vietnam, the assassinations of Martin Luther King, Jr. and Robert Kennedy, racial unrest across the nation's cities, student protests on campuses throughout America. But the turmoil of 1968 was not confined to the United States. There were tremendous upheavals in many parts of the globe that year.

The most common form of turbulence around the world in 1968 was student unrest. In France, in May 1968, there was a student uprising that far exceeded in size and ferocity anything that occurred in the United States. It attracted the support of French workers and briefly paralyzed Paris and other cities. It contributed to the downfall of the government of Charles de Gaulle a year later. In England, Ireland, Germany, Italy, the Netherlands, Mexico, Canada, Japan, and South Korea, students and other young people demonstrated in great numbers, and at times with some violence, against governments and universities and other structures of authority. Elsewhere, 1968 created more widespread protest, as in Czechoslovakia, where hundreds of thousands of citizens took to the streets in support of what became known as "Prague spring"—a demand for greater democracy and a repudiation of many of the oppressive rules and structures imposed on the nation by its Soviet-dominated communist regimes—until Russian tanks rolled into the city to crush the uprising.

Both at the time and since, many people have tried to explain why so much instability emerged in so many nations at the same time. One factor that contributed to the worldwide turbulence of 1968 was simple numbers. The postwar baby boom had created a very large age cohort in many nations, and by the late 1960s it was coming of age. In the industrial west, the sheer size of the new generation produced a tripling of the number of people attending colleges and universities in fewer than twenty years, and a heightened sense of the power of youth. The long period of postwar prosperity and relative peace in which this generation had grown up contributed to heightened expectations of what the world should offer them—and a greater level of impatience than previous generations had demonstrated with the obstacles that stood in the way of their hopes. A new global youth culture emerged that was in many ways at odds with the dominant culture of older generations. It valued nonconformity, personal freedom, and even rebellion.

A second force contributing to the widespread turbulence of 1968 was the power of global media. Satellite communication introduced in the early 1960s made it possible to transmit live news instantly across the world. Videotape technology and the creation of lightweight portable television cameras enabled media organizations to respond to events much more quickly and flexibly than in the past. The audience for these televised images was by now global and enormous, particularly in industrial nations but even in the poorest areas of the world. Protests in one country were suddenly capable of inspiring protests in others. Demonstrators in Paris, for example, spoke openly of how campus protests in the United States in 1968—for example, the student uprising at Columbia University in New York the previous month—had helped motivate French students to rise up as well. Just as American students were protesting against what they considered the antiquated, paternalistic features of their universities, French students demanded an end to the rigid, autocratic character of their own academic world.

In most parts of the world, the 1968 uprisings came and went without fundamentally altering the institutions and systems they were attacking. But many changes came in the wake of these protests. Universities around the globe undertook significant reforms. Religious observance in mainstream churches and synagogues in the West declined dramatically after 1968. New concepts of personal freedom gained legitimacy, helping to inspire new social movements in the years that followed—among them the dramatic growth of feminism in many parts of the world. The events of 1968 did not produce a revolution, in the United States or in most of the rest of the world, but it did help launch a period of dramatic social, cultural, and political change that affected the peoples of many nations.

(text continued from page 835)

third-party candidate for president, basing his campaign on a host of conservative grievances. He denounced the forced busing of students, the proliferation of government regulations and social programs, and the permissiveness of authorities toward crime, race riots, and antiwar demonstrations. There was never any serious chance that Wallace would win the election, but his standing in the polls rose at times to over 20 percent.

A more effective effort to mobilize the conservative middle in favor of order and stability was under way within the Republican Party. Richard Nixon, whose political ca-

Nixon Elected

reer had seemed at an end after his losses in the presidential race of 1960 and a California gubernatorial campaign two years later, reemerged as the spokesman for what he sometimes called the "silent majority." By offering a vision of stability, law and order, government retrenchment, and "peace with honor" in Vietnam, he easily captured the nomination of his party for the presidency. And despite a last-minute surge by Humphrey, he hung on to eke out a victory almost as narrow as his defeat in 1960. He received 43.4 percent of the popular vote to Humphrey's 42.7 percent (a margin of only about 500,000 votes), and 301 electoral votes to Humphrey's 191. George Wallace, who like most third-party candidates faded in the last weeks of the campaign, still managed to poll 13.5 percent of the popular vote and to carry five southern states with a total of 46 electoral ballots. Nixon had hardly won a decisive personal mandate. But the election made clear that a majority of the American electorate was more interested in restoring stability than in promoting social change.

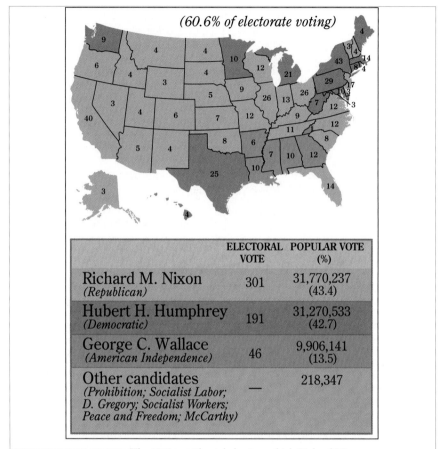

(60.6% of electorate voting)

	ELECTORAL VOTE	POPULAR VOTE (%)
Richard M. Nixon *(Republican)*	301	31,770,237 (43.4)
Hubert H. Humphrey *(Democratic)*	191	31,270,533 (42.7)
George C. Wallace *(American Independence)*	46	9,906,141 (13.5)
Other candidates *(Prohibition; Socialist Labor; D. Gregory; Socialist Workers; Peace and Freedom; McCarthy)*	—	218,347

THE ELECTION OF 1968 The 1968 presidential election, which Richard Nixon won, was almost as close as the election of 1960, which he lost. Nixon might have won a more substantial victory had it not been for the independent candidacy of Governor George C. Wallace, who attracted many of the same conservative voters to whom Nixon appealed. ◆ *How does the distribution of Democratic and Republican strength in this election compare to that in 1960?*

For an interactive version of this map go to www.mhhe.com/unfinishednation4ch31maps

CONCLUSION

Perhaps no decade of the twentieth century created more powerful and enduring images in America than the 1960s. It began with the election—and then the traumatic assassination—of an attractive and energetic young president, John Kennedy, who captured the imagination of millions and seemed to symbolize the rising idealism of the time. It produced a dramatic period of political innovation, christened the Great Society by President Lyndon Johnson, which greatly expanded the size and functions of the federal government and its responsibility for the welfare of the nation's citizens. It saw the emergence of a sustained and enormously powerful civil rights movement that won a series of important legal victories, including two civil rights acts that dismantled the Jim Crow system constructed in the late nineteenth and early twentieth centuries.

The very spirit of dynamism and optimism that made the early 1960s so productive also helped bring to the surface problems and grievances that had no easy solutions. The civil rights movement awakened expectations of social and economic equality that laws alone could not provide and that remained in many respects unfulfilled. The peaceful, interracial crusade of the early 1960s gradually turned into a much more militant, confrontational, and increasingly separatist movement toward the decade's end. The idealism among white youths that began the 1960s, and played an important role in the political success of John Kennedy, evolved into an angry rebellion against many aspects of American culture and politics and produced a large upsurge of student protest that rocked the nation at the decade's end. Perhaps most of all, a small and largely unnoticed Cold War commitment to defend South Vietnam against communist aggression from the north led to a large and disastrous American military commitment that destroyed the presidency of Lyndon Johnson, shook the faith of millions in their leaders and their political system, sent thousands of young men to their deaths, and showed no signs of producing a victory. A decade that began with high hopes and soaring ideals ended with ugly and at times violent division, and deep disillusionment.

FOR FURTHER REFERENCE
ॐ

Allen J. Matusow, *The Unraveling of America: A History of Liberalism in the 1960s* (1984) is a provocative history of this turbulent decade. David Farber, *The Age of Great Dreams: America in the 1960s* (1994) is an intelligent and lively general history. Arthur M. Schlesinger, Jr., *A Thousand Days* (1965) is a celebrated and celebratory memoir of the Kennedy years. Garry Wills, *The Kennedy Imprisonment* (1982) is an important demystification. Robert Dallek, *Lone Star Rising: Lyndon Johnson and His Times, 1908–1960* (1991) and *Flawed Giant: Lyndon B. Johnson, 1960–1973* (1998) are an important biography. Rick Perlstein, *Before the Storm: Barry Goldwater and the Unmaking of the American Consensus* (2001) is an excellent biography of the first postwar hero of the right, and Matthew Dallek, *The Right Moment: Ronald Reagan's First Victory and the Decisive Turning Point in American Politics* (2000) is a good study of the rise of Reagan in the 1960s. Robert Weisbrot, *Freedom Bound: A History of America's Civil Rights Movement* (1990) is a good synthetic history of the movement. John Dittmer, *Local People: The Struggle for Civil Rights in Mississippi* (1994) is an important study of the grass-roots origins of the movement. William Chafe, *Civilities and Civil Rights: Greensboro, North Carolina, and the Black Struggle for Freedom* (1980) is an excellent study of the southern civil rights movement and the white reaction to it. Taylor Branch,

Parting the Waters: America in the King Years, 1959–1963 (1988) and *Pillar of Fire: America in the King Years, 1963–1965* (1998) are good narrative histories of the movement. Nicholas Lemann, *The Promised Land: The Great Black Migration and How it Changed America* (1991) is a challenging study of the postwar African-American migration to northern cities and of the Great Society's response to it. Graham T. Allison, *The Essence of Decision: Explaining the Cuban Missile Crisis* (1971) is an important interpretation of the greatest crisis of the Cold War. Ernest R. May and Philip D. Zelikow, *The Kennedy Tapes: Inside the White House during the Cuban Missile Crisis* (1997) provides the annotated transcripts of the taped meetings of Kennedy's inner circle during the crisis. Robert D. Schulzinger, *A Time for War: The United States and Vietnam, 1945–1975* (1997) is a good general history of the war. Neil Sheehan, *A Bright Shining Lie: John Paul Vann and America in Vietnam* (1988) is a compelling picture of the war as experienced by a significant military figure of the 1960s. Frederik Logevall, *Choosing War: The Lost Chance for Peace and the Escalation of War in Vietnam* (1999); David Kaiser, *American Tragedy: Kennedy, Johnson, and the Origins of Vietnam* (2000); A. J. Langguth, *Our Vietnam/Nuoc Viet Ta: A History of the War, 1954–1975* (2000); and James Mann, *A Grand Delusion: America's Descent into Vietnam* (2001) are important recent studies. Christian J. Appy, *Working-Class War: American Combat Soldiers and Vietnam* (1993) examines the class basis of the army that fought in Vietnam. Larry Berman, *Planning a Tragedy* (1982) and *Lyndon Johnson's War* (1989); Leslie Gelb and Richard Betts, *The Irony of Vietnam: The System Worked* (1979); and David Halberstam, *The Best and the Brightest* (1972) are important interpretations of the American decision to intervene and stay in Vietnam, Dan T. Carter, *The Politics of Rage: George Wallace, The Origins of the New Conservatism, and the Transformation of American Politics* (1995) is a good study of the career of George Wallace. David Farber, *Chicago '68* (1988) examines the turbulent Democratic Convention and, through it, the passions that shaped a traumatic year in recent American history.

Berkeley in the Sixties (1990) is a documentary film portraying the tumultuous student politics at the University of California, Berkeley, and through them larger themes of the decade. *Eyes on the Prize: The American Civil Rights Struggle, 1954–1965* (1986–1987) is a six-part film series by Blackside Productions on the history of the civil rights movement. *Malcolm X: Make it Plain* (1994) is the definitive film biography of Malcolm X. *The Kennedys* (1992) is a film presentation on the lives of President John F. Kennedy and various members of his powerful family. *LBJ* (1991), a film by David Grubin, is a biographical treatment of President Lyndon Johnson. *America's War on Poverty* (1995) is a five-part series on the Kennedy and Johnson administrations' most dramatic welfare initiative.

For quizzes, Internet resources, references to additional books and films, and more, consult this book's Online Learning Center site at www.mhhe.com/unfinishednation4.

"TODAY'S TEENAGERS" The coming of age of the "baby-boom" generation, and the rise of youthful activism, led *Time* magazine to devote a 1965 cover story to "Today's Teen-Agers." As notable as the choice of subject was the choice of artist for the cover image: Andy Warhol, the great pop artist whose serial portraits of both famous and unknown people helped define his era. Warhol's work was instrumental in breaking down barriers between serious art and popular culture, both in its subject matter (celebrities, commercial products) and in its techniques, which drew heavily from commercial art. This series of silk-screened photographs made use of one of his trademark media. *(TIME Magazine, copyright TIME, Inc./Getty Images)*

TIME LINE

1963	1964	1966	1968	1969	1970
Friedan's *The Feminine Mystique*	Free Speech Movement begins	National Organization for Women formed	Turmoil in universities	Antiwar movement's Vietnam "moratoriums"	Cambodian incursion
				Rock concert in Woodstock, NY	

CHAPTER THIRTY-TWO

THE CRISIS OF AUTHORITY

The Youth Culture
The Mobilization of Minorities
The New Feminism
Environmentalism in a Turbulent Society
Nixon, Kissinger, and the War
Nixon, Kissinger, and the World
Politics and Economics in the Nixon Years
The Watergate Crisis

T he election of Richard Nixon in 1968 was the result of more than the unpopularity of Lyndon Johnson and the war. It was the result, too, of a broad popular reaction against what many Americans considered a dangerous assault on the foundations of their society and culture. In Richard Nixon such Americans found a man who seemed perfectly to match their mood. Himself a product of a hardworking, middle-class family, he projected an image of stern dedication to traditional values. Yet the presidency of Richard Nixon, far from returning calm and stability to American politics, coincided with, and helped to produce, more years of crisis.

THE YOUTH CULTURE

Perhaps most alarming to many conservatives in the 1960s and 1970s was a pattern of social and cultural protest by younger Americans, who were giving vent to two related impulses. One was the impulse, emerging from the political left, to create a great new community of "the people," which

1971	1972	1973	1974	1975	
Nixon imposes wage-price controls	Nixon visits China	U.S. withdraws from Vietnam	Nixon resigns; Ford becomes president	South Vietnam falls	
	SALT I	Arab oil embargo			
	"Christmas bombing" of North Vietnam	Agnew resigns			
	Watergate burglary	Supreme Court decides *Roe* v. *Wade*			
	Nixon reelected				

would rise up to break the power of elites and force the nation to end the war, pursue racial and economic justice, and transform its political life.

Personal "Liberation"   The other, at least equally powerful impulse was the vision of personal "liberation." It found expression in part through the efforts of many groups—African Americans, Indians, Hispanics, women, gay people, and others—to define and assert themselves and make demands on the larger society. It also found expression through the efforts of individuals to create a new culture—one that would allow them to escape from what some considered the dehumanizing pressures of the modern "technocracy."

The New Left

Among the products of the racial crisis and the war in Vietnam was a radicalization of many American students, who in the course of the 1960s formed what became known as the New Left. In 1962, a group of students (most of them white) gathered in Michigan to form an organization to give

SDS   voice to their demands: Students for a Democratic Society (SDS). Their declaration of beliefs, the Port Huron Statement, expressed their disillusionment with the society they had inherited and their determination to build a new politics. In the following years, SDS became the leading organization of student radicalism.

Campus Unrest   Since most members of the New Left were students, much of their radicalism centered for a time on issues related to the modern university. A 1964 dispute at the University of California at Berkeley over the rights of students to engage in political activities on campus—the Free Speech Movement—was the first outburst of what was to be nearly a decade of campus turmoil. The antiwar movement greatly inflamed and expanded the challenge to the universities; and beginning in 1968, campus demonstrations, riots, and building seizures became almost commonplace. At Columbia University in New York, students seized the offices of the president and others and occupied them for several days until local police forcibly ejected them. Over the next several years, hardly any major university was immune to some level of disruption. Small groups of especially dogmatic radicals—among them the "Weathermen," an offshoot of SDS—were responsible for a few cases of arson and bombing that destroyed campus buildings and claimed several lives.

Not many people ever accepted the radical political philosophy of the New Left. But many supported the position of SDS and other groups on particular issues, and above all on the Vietnam War. Between 1967 and 1969, student activists organized some of the largest political demonstrations in American history to protest the war.

Opposition to the Draft   A related issue that helped fuel the antiwar movement was opposition to the military draft.

THE WAR AT HOME Demonstrators gather on the Mall in Washington in the fall of 1967 for one of the first of the great antiwar demonstrations of the late 1960s. Over time, the antiwar movement helped erode the national consensus on the conflict in Vietnam. But the principal basis for opposing the war was never the moral or economic arguments of the left; it was simply the frustration among many Americans of seeing a war continuing too long and too inconclusively. *(Leif Skoogfors/Woodfin Camp & Associates)*

The gradual abolition of many traditional deferments—for graduate students, teachers, husbands, fathers, and others—swelled the ranks of those faced with conscription (and thus likely to oppose it). Many draft-age Americans simply refused induction, accepting what were occasionally long terms in jail as a result. Thousands of others fled to Canada, Sweden, and elsewhere (where they were joined by deserters from the armed forces) to escape conscription.

The Counterculture

Closely related to the New Left was a new youth culture openly scornful of the values and conventions of middle-class society. The most visible characteristic of the counterculture, as it became known, was a change in personal styles. As if to display their contempt for conventional standards, young Americans flaunted long hair, shabby or flamboyant clothing, and a rebellious disdain for traditional speech and decorum. Also important to the counterculture were drugs: marijuana smoking—which after 1966 became almost as common a youthful diversion as beer drinking had once been—and the use of other, more potent hallucinogens, such as LSD. There was also a new, more permissive view of sex.

Like the New Left, with which it in many ways overlapped, the counterculture challenged the structure of modern American society, attacking what it claimed were its banality, its hollowness, its artificiality, its isolation from nature. The most committed adherents of the counterculture— the hippies, who came to dominate the Haight-Ashbury neighborhood of San Francisco and other places, and the social dropouts, many of whom retreated to rural communes—rejected modern society altogether and attempted to find refuge in a simpler, more "natural" existence. But even

Commitment to Personal Fulfillment

those whose commitment to the counterculture was less intense shared a commitment to the idea of personal fulfillment through rejecting the inhibitions and conventions of middle-class culture and giving fuller expression to personal instinct and desire.

The counterculture was only an exaggerated expression of impulses that were coursing through the larger society. Long hair and freakish clothing became the badge not only of hippies and radicals but of an entire generation. The use of marijuana, the freer attitudes toward sex, the iconoclastic (and often obscene) language—all spread far beyond the realm of the true devotees of the counterculture.

One of the most pervasive elements of the new youth society was one that even the least radical members of the generation embraced: rock music. Its growing influence in the 1960s was a result in part of the phenomenal popularity of the Beatles, the English group whose first visit to the United States in 1964 created a remarkable sensation. For a time, most rock musicians—like most popular musicians before them—concentrated largely on uncontroversial romantic themes. By the late 1960s, however, rock had begun to reflect many of the new iconoclastic values of its time. The Beatles, for example, abandoned their once simple and seemingly innocent style for a new, experimental, even mystical approach that reflected the growing popular fascination with drugs and Eastern religions. Other groups, such as the Rolling Stones, turned even more openly to themes of anger, frustration, and rebelliousness. Many popular musicians used their music to express explicit political radicalism as well—especially some of the leading folk singers of the era, such as Bob Dylan and Joan Baez. Rock's driving rhythms, its undisguised sensuality, its often harsh and angry

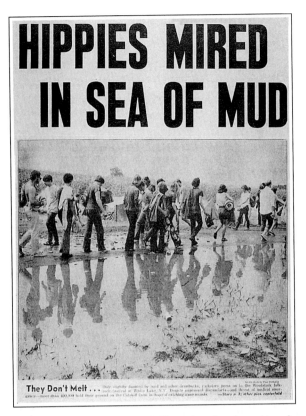

REPORTING WOODSTOCK The *New York Daily News*, whose largely working-class readership was not notably sympathetic toward the young people at Woodstock, ran this slightly derisive front-page story on the concert as heavy rains turned the concert site into a sea of mud. ["They Don't Melt," the caption said.] *(©New York Daily News, L.P. Reprinted with Permission. Archive Photos/Blank Archive/Getty Images)*

tone—all made it an appropriate vehicle for expressing the themes of the social and political unrest of the late 1960s.

A powerful symbol of the fusion of rock music and the counterculture was the great music festival at Woodstock, New York, in the summer of 1969, where 400,000 people gath- *Woodstock* ered on a farm for nearly a week. Despite heavy rain, mud, inadequate facilities, and impossible crowding, the crowd remained peaceful and harmonious. Champions of the counterculture spoke rhapsodically at the time of how Woodstock represented the birth of a new youth culture, the "Woodstock nation." Four months later, however, another great rock concert—at the Altamont racetrack near San Francisco, featuring the Rolling Stones and attended by 300,000 people—exposed a darker side of the youth culture. Altamont became a brutal and violent event at which four people died, several accidentally or from drug overdoses, but one because of injuries received at the hands of members of the Hell's Angels motorcycle gang, who were serving as security guards at the concert and who brutally beat and stabbed a number of people.

THE MOBILIZATION OF MINORITIES

The growth of African-American protest encouraged other minorities to assert themselves and demand redress of their grievances. For Indians, Hispanic Americans, gay men and lesbians, and others, the late 1960s and 1970s were a time of growing self-expression and political activism.

Seeds of Indian Militancy

Few minorities had deeper or more justifiable grievances against the prevailing culture than did American Indians—or Native Americans, as they began defiantly to call themselves in the 1960s. Indians were the least prosperous, least healthy, and least stable group in the nation. And while African Americans attracted the attention (for good or for ill) of many whites, Indians for years had remained largely ignored.

For much of the postwar era, federal policy toward the tribes had been shaped by a determination to incorporate Indians into mainstream American society whether Indians wanted to assimilate or not. Two laws passed in 1953 established the basis of a new policy, which became known *"Termination"* as "termination." Through termination, the federal government withdrew all official recognition of the tribes as legal entities, administratively separate from state governments, and made them subject to the same local jurisdictions as white residents. At the same time, the government encouraged Indians to assimilate into the white world and worked to funnel Native Americans into cities, where, presumably, they would adapt themselves to the larger society and lose their cultural distinctiveness.

Despite some individual successes, the new policies were a disastrous failure on the whole. Indians themselves fought so bitterly against them that in 1958 the Eisenhower administration barred further "terminations" without the consent of the affected tribes. In the meantime, the struggle against termination mobilized a new generation of Indian militants and breathed life into the principal Native American organization, the National Congress of American Indians, which had been created in 1944.

The Democratic administrations of the 1960s made no effort to revive termination. Instead, they made modest efforts to restore at least some degree of tribal autonomy. The funneling of OEO money to tribal organizations through the Community Action program was one prominent example. In the meantime, the tribes themselves were beginning to fight for self-determination. The new militancy benefited from the rapid increase in the Indian population, which was growing much faster than that of the rest of the nation (nearly doubling between 1950 and 1970 to a total of about 800,000).

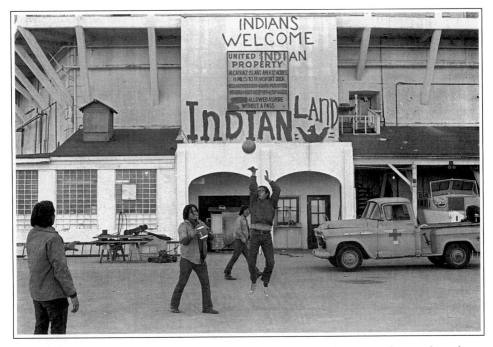

THE OCCUPATION OF ALCATRAZ Alcatraz is an island in San Francisco Bay that once housed a large federal prison that by the late 1960s had been abandoned. In 1969, a group of Indian activists occupied the island and claimed it as Indian land—precipitating a long standoff with authorities. *(AP/Wide World Photos)*

The Indian Civil Rights Movement

In 1961, more than 400 members of 67 tribes gathered in Chicago and issued the Declaration of Indian Purpose, which stressed the "right to choose our own way of life" and the "responsibility of preserving our precious heritage." The meeting was only one example of a growing Indian self-consciousness. The National Indian Youth Council, created in the aftermath of the 1961 Chicago meeting, promoted the idea of Indian nationalism and intertribal unity. In 1968, a group of young, militant Indians established the American Indian Movement (AIM), which drew support from urban areas and reservations alike.

The new activism produced results. In 1968, *AIM*
Congress passed the Indian Civil Rights Act, which guaranteed reservation Indians many of the protections accorded other citizens by the Bill of Rights, but which also recognized the legitimacy of tribal laws within the reservations. But leaders of AIM and other insurgent groups were not satisfied. In 1968, Indian fishermen, citing old treaty rights, clashed with Washington State officials on the Columbia River and in Puget Sound. The following year, members of several tribes occupied the abandoned federal prison on Alcatraz Island in San Francisco Bay, claiming the site "by right of discovery."

In response to the growing pressure, the Nixon administration appointed Louis Bruce, a Mohawk-Sioux, to the position of commissioner of Indian affairs in 1969; and in 1970 the president promised both increased tribal self-determination and an increase in federal aid. But the protests continued. In November 1972, nearly a thousand demonstrators, most of them Lakota Sioux, forcibly occupied the building of the Bureau of Indian Affairs in Washington for six days. In February 1973, members of AIM
Wounded Knee Occupied   seized and occupied the town of Wounded Knee, South Dakota, the site of the 1890 massacre of Sioux by federal troops, for two months, demanding radical changes in the administration of the reservation and insisting that the government honor its long-forgotten treaty obligations.

The Indian civil rights movement, like other civil rights movements of the same time, fell far short of winning full justice and equality for Native Americans. But it helped the tribes win a series of new legal rights and protections that, together, gave them a stronger position than they had enjoyed at any previous time in the twentieth century.

Latino Activism

The fastest-growing minority group in the United States in the 1970s was Latinos, or Hispanic Americans. Large numbers of Mexicans had entered the country during World War II in response to the wartime labor shortage, and many had remained in the cities of the Southwest and the Pacific Coast. By 1960, Los Angeles had a bigger Mexican population than any place except Mexico City.
Growing Latino Population   But the greatest expansion in the Hispanic population of the United States was yet to come. In 1960, the census reported slightly more than 3 million Latinos living in the United States. By 1970, that number had grown to 9 million and by 2000 to 35 million. Hispanics constituted more than a third of all legal immigrants to the United States after 1960. There was also an uncounted but very large number of illegal Latino immigrants in those years (estimates ranged from 7 million to 12 million).

Large numbers of Puerto Ricans (who were entitled to American citizenship by birth) migrated to eastern urban areas, particularly New York, where they formed one of the poorest communities in the city. South Florida's substantial Cuban population began with a wave of middle-class refugees fleeing the Castro regime in the early 1960s. These first Cuban migrants quickly established themselves as a successful and highly assimilated part of Miami's middle class. In 1980, a second, much poorer wave of Cuban immigrants—the so-called Marielietos, named for the port from which they left Cuba—arrived in Florida when Castro temporarily relaxed exit restrictions. Later in the 1980s, large numbers of immigrants (both legal and illegal) began to arrive from Central and South America—from Guatemala, Nicaragua, El Salvador, Peru, and other countries.

Like African Americans and Indians, many Latinos responded to the highly charged climate of the 1960s by strengthening their ethnic identification and by organizing for political and economic power. Affluent Hispanics in Miami filled influential positions in the professions and local government; in the Southwest, Latino voters elected Mexican Americans to seats in Congress and to governorships. A Mexican-American political organization, La Raza Unida, exercised influence in southern California and elsewhere in the Southwest in the 1970s and beyond. One of the most visible efforts to organize Hispanics occurred in California, where an Arizona-born farmworker of Mexican descent, César Chávez, created an effective union of itinerant farmworkers: the United Farm Workers (UFW), a largely Mexican organization.

United Farm Workers

For most Hispanics, however, the path to economic and political power was more difficult. Mexican Americans and others were slow to develop political influence in proportion to their numbers. In the meantime, Hispanics formed one of the poorest segments of the United States population.

Gay Liberation

The last important liberation movement to emerge in the 1960s was the effort by gay men and lesbians to win political and economic rights and social acceptance. Homosexuality has been a generally unacknowledged reality throughout American history. Nonheterosexual men and women were forced for generations either to suppress their sexual preferences, to exercise them surreptitiously, or to live within isolated and often persecuted communities. But by the late 1960s, the liberating impulses that had affected other groups helped mobilize gay men and lesbians to fight for their own rights.

On June 27, 1969, police officers raided the Stonewall Inn, a gay nightclub in New York City's Greenwich Village, and began arresting patrons simply for frequenting the place. The raid was not unusual, but the response was. Gay onlookers taunted the police and then attacked them. Someone started a blaze in the Stonewall Inn itself, almost trapping the policemen inside. Rioting continued throughout Greenwich Village (the center of New York's gay community) through much of the night.

The "Stonewall Riot" marked the beginning of the gay liberation movement—one of the most con-

"Stonewall Riot"

troversial challenges to traditional values and assumptions of its time. New organizations—among them the Gay Liberation Front, founded in New York in 1969—sprang up around the country. Public discussion and media coverage of homosexuality, long subject to an unofficial taboo, quickly and dramatically increased. Gay activists had some success in challenging the longstanding assumption that homosexuality was aberrant behavior; many argued that no sexual preference was any more normal than another.

Most of all, however, the gay liberation movement transformed the outlook of many gay men and lesbians themselves. It helped them to "come out," to express their preferences openly and unapologetically, and to demand from society a recognition that gay relationships could be as significant and worthy of respect as heterosexual ones. By the early 1980s, the gay liberation movement had made remarkable strides. Even the ravages of the AIDS epidemic, which, in the beginning at least, affected the gay community more disastrously than it affected any other group, failed to halt the growth of gay liberation. In many ways, it strengthened it.

By the early 1990s, gay men and lesbians were achieving many of the same milestones that other oppressed minorities had attained in earlier decades. Openly gay politicians won election to public office. Universities established gay and lesbian studies programs. Laws prohibiting discrimination on the basis of sexual preference made slow, halting progress at the state and local levels. But gay liberation produced a powerful backlash as well, as became evident in 1993 when President Bill Clinton's effort to end the ban on gay men and lesbians serving in the military met a storm of criticism from members of Congress and within the military itself. At the same time, voters in some cities and states were approving referendum questions on their ballots outlawing civil rights protections for gay men and lesbians. And antigay violence continued periodically in communities around the country.

Backlash against Gay Liberation

THE NEW FEMINISM

Women constitute over 50 percent of the United States population. But during the 1960s and 1970s, many women began to identify with minority groups as they renewed demands for a liberation of their own.

The Rebirth

Betty Friedan

The 1963 publication of Betty Friedan's *The Feminine Mystique* is often cited as the first event of contemporary women's liberation. Friedan, who had been a writer for women's magazines in the 1950s, traveled around the country interviewing the women who had graduated with her from Smith College in 1947. Most of these women were living out the dream that postwar American society had created for them: they were affluent wives and mothers living in comfortable suburbs. And yet many of them were deeply frustrated and unhappy, with no outlets for their intelligence, talent, and education. Friedan's book did not so much cause the revival of feminism as help give voice to a movement that was already stirring.

By the time *The Feminine Mystique* appeared, John Kennedy had established the President's Commission on the Status of Women, which

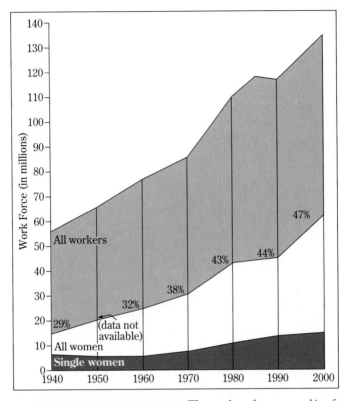

WOMEN IN THE PAID WORK FORCE, 1940–2000 The number of women working for wages steadily expanded from 1940 on, to the point that in 2000, they constituted just under half the total work force. ◆ *What role did this growing participation in the paid work force have on the rise of feminism in the 1960s and beyond?*

brought national attention to sexual discrimination. Also in 1963, the Kennedy administration helped win passage of the Equal Pay Act, which barred the pervasive practice of paying women less than men for the same work. A year later, Congress incorporated into the Civil Rights Act of 1964 an amendment—Title VII—that extended to women many of the same legal protections against discrimination that were being extended to African Americans and other minorities.

In 1966, Friedan joined with other feminists to create the National Organization for Women (NOW), which was to become the nation's largest and most influential feminist organization. NOW responded to the complaints of the women Friedan's book had examined—affluent suburbanites with no outlet for their interests—by demanding greater educational opportunities for women and denouncing the domestic ideal and the traditional concept of marriage. But the heart of the movement, at least in the beginning, was an effort to address the needs of women in the workplace.

Women's Liberation

By the late 1960s, new and more radical feminist demands were also at-tracting a large following, especially among younger, white, educated women. Many of them drew inspiration from the New Left and the coun-terculture. Some were involved in the civil rights movement, others in the antiwar crusade. Many had found that even within those movements, they faced discrimination and exclusion and were subordinated to male leaders.

Increasing Radicalism   In its most radical form, the new feminism re-jected the whole notion of marriage, family, and even heterosexual relationships (a vehicle, some women claimed, of male domination). Not many women, not even many feminists, embraced such extremes. But by the early 1970s large numbers of women were coming to see themselves as an exploited group banding together against oppression and developing a culture of their own. In cities and towns across the coun-try, feminists opened women's bookstores, bars, and coffee shops. They founded feminist newspapers and magazines. They created women's health clinics, centers to assist victims of rape and abuse, day-care centers, and, particularly after 1973, abortion clinics.

Expanding Achievements

By the early 1970s, the public and private achievements of the women's movement were already substantial. In 1971, the government extended its affirmative action guidelines to include women—linking sexism with racism as an officially acknowledged social problem. Women made rapid progress, in the meantime, in their efforts to move into the economic and political mainstream. The nation's major all-male educational institutions began to open their doors to women. (Princeton and Yale did so in 1969, and most others soon did the same.)

Women were also becoming an important force in business and the professions. Nearly half of all married women held jobs by the mid-1970s, and almost 90 percent of all women with college *Economic Success* degrees worked. The two-career family, in which both the husband and the wife maintained active professional lives, be-came a widely accepted middle-class norm. (It had been common within the working class for decades.) There were also important symbolic changes, such as the refusal of many women to adopt their husbands' names when they married and the use of the term "Ms." in place of "Mrs." or "Miss" to signal the irrelevance of a woman's marital status in the pro-fessional world.

By the mid-1980s, women were serving in both houses of Congress, on the Supreme Court, in numerous federal cabinet positions, as governors of several states, and in many other political positions. In 1981, Ronald Rea-gan named the first female Supreme Court justice, Sandra Day O'Connor; in 1993, Bill Clinton named the second, Ruth Bader Ginsburg. In 1984, the Democratic Party chose a woman, Representative Geraldine Ferraro of

New York, as its vice presidential candidate. In academia, women were expanding their presence in traditional scholarly fields; they were also creating new fields—women's and gender studies, which in the 1980s and 1990s were among the fastest-growing areas of American scholarship.

In 1972, Congress approved the Equal Rights Amendment (ERA) to the Constitution and sent it *Failure of the ERA* to the states. For a while ratification seemed almost certain. By the late 1970s, however, the momentum behind the amendment had died because of a rising chorus of objections to it from people (including many antifeminist women) who feared that it would disrupt traditional social patterns. In 1982, the amendment finally died when the ten years allotted for ratification expired.

The Abortion Issue

A major focus of American feminism since the 1920s has been the effort by women to win greater control of their own sexual and reproductive lives. In its least controversial form, this impulse helped produce an increasing awareness beginning in the 1970s of the problems of rape, sexual abuse, and wife beating. The dissemination of contraceptives and birth-control information became far more widespread and much less controversial than it had been earlier in the century. A related issue, however, stimulated as much popular passion as any question of its time: abortion.

Abortion had once been legal in much of the United States, but by the beginning of the twentieth century it was banned by statute in most of the country and remained so into the 1960s (although many abortions continued to be performed quietly, and often dangerously, out of sight of the law). The women's movement created strong new pressures on behalf of the legalization of abortion. Several states had abandoned restrictions on abortion by the end of the 1960s. And in 1973, the Supreme Court's decision in *Roe* v. *Wade*, based on a new theory of a *Roe v. Wade* constitutional "right to privacy" first recognized by the Court only a few years earlier, invalidated all laws prohibiting abortion during the "first trimester"—the first three months of pregnancy. But even then, the issue was far from settled.

ENVIRONMENTALISM IN A TURBULENT SOCIETY

Like feminism, environmentalism entered the 1960s with a long history and relatively little public support. Also like feminism, environmentalism both profited from and transcended the turbulence of the era and emerged by the 1970s as a powerful and enduring force in American life. The rise of this new movement was in part a result of the environmental degradation in advanced industrial society of the late twentieth century. It was a result, too, of the growth of the science of ecology, which provided environmentalists with new and powerful arguments. And it was a product as well of other social movements that rejected aspects of the modern, industrial, consumer society and called for a return to a more natural existence.

The New Science of Ecology

New Rationale for Environmentalism

Until the mid-twentieth century, most people who considered themselves environmentalists (or, to use the more traditional term, conservationists) based their commitment on aesthetic or moral grounds. They wanted to preserve nature because it was too beautiful to despoil, or because it was a mark of divinity on the world, or because it permitted humans a spiritual experience that would otherwise be unavailable to them. In the course of the twentieth century, however, scientists in the United States and other nations began to create a new rationale for environmentalism. They called it ecology.

Ecology is the science of the inter-relatedness of the natural world. Such problems as air and water pollution, the destruction of forests, the extinction of species, and toxic wastes are not, ecology teaches, separate, isolated problems. All elements of the earth's environment are intimately and delicately linked. Damaging any one of those elements, therefore, risks damaging all the others.

Aldo Leopold

Among the early contributions to popular knowledge of ecology was the work of the writer and naturalist Aldo Leopold. During a career in forest management, Leopold sought to apply the new scientific findings on ecology to his interactions with the natural world. And in 1949, he published a classic of environmental literature, *The Sand County Almanac*, in which he argued that humans had a responsibility to understand and maintain the balance of nature, that they should behave in the natural world according to a code that he called the "land ethic." By then, the science of ecology was spreading widely in the scientific community. Among the findings of ecologists were such now-common ideas as the "food chain," the "ecosystem," "biodiversity," and "endangered species." Rachel Carson's sensational 1962 book, *Silent Spring*, which revealed the dangers of pesticides, was based solidly on the ideas of ecologists and did at least as much as Leopold's work to introduce those ideas to a larger public.

Between 1945 and 1960, the number of professional ecologists in the United States grew threefold, and that number doubled again between 1960 and 1970. Funded by government agencies, by universities, by foundations, and eventually even by some corporations, ecological science gradually established itself as a significant field. By century's end, there were programs in and departments of ecological science in major universities throughout the United States and in many other nations.

Much more than other scientists, however, ecologists tend to fuse their commitment to research and testing with a commitment to publicizing their work and working for responsible public action to deal with environmental crises. Many ecologists argue that environmental problems must be addressed energetically even if firm scientific proof is not yet available to sustain their diagnosis of the problem. To wait for absolute proof, they insist, would be to invite irreversible damage to the environment.

Environmental Advocacy

The emergence or re-emergence of environmental organizations committed to public action and political lobbying in the 1960s and 1970s was among the most important developments in the growth of an environmental

Re-emergence of Environmental Organizations

movement. Among the most important environmental organizations were the Wilderness Society, the Sierra Club, the National Audubon Society, the Nature Conservancy, the National Wildlife Federation, and the National Parks and Conservation Association. All of these organizations predated the rise of modern ecological science, but all of them entered the last decades of the twentieth century re-energized and committed to the new concepts of environmentalism. They found allies among other not-for-profit organizations that had no previous experience with environmentalism but now chose to join the battle—among them such groups as the American Civil Liberties Union, the League of Women Voters, the National Council of Churches, and even the AFL-CIO.

Out of these organizations emerged a new generation of professional environmental activists able to contribute to the legal and political battles of the movement. Scientists provided the necessary data. Lawyers fought battles with government agencies and in the courts. Lobbyists used traditional techniques of political persuasion with legislators and other officials—knowing that corporations and other opponents of environmental efforts would be doing the same in opposition to their goals. Perhaps most of all, these organizations learned how to mobilize public opinion on their behalf—an effort much aided by the rise of a popular movement beginning in the early 1970s.

Environmental Degradation

Many other forces contributed as well in the 1960s and 1970s to create what became the environmental movement. Lady Bird Johnson, the wife of the president, helped raise public awareness of the landscape with her energetic "beautification" campaign in the mid-1960s—a campaign unconnected to any ecological concepts, but one that reflected a growing popular dismay at the despoliation of the landscape by rapid economic growth. Members of the counterculture contributed to environmental awareness with their romanticization of the natural world and their repudiation of the "technocracy."

But perhaps the greatest force behind environmentalism was the condition of the environment itself. By the 1960s, the damage to the natural world from the dramatic economic growth of the postwar era was becoming impossible to ignore. Water pollution—which *Water Pollution* had been a problem in some areas of the country for many decades—was becoming so widespread that almost every major city was dealing with the unpleasant sight and odor, as well as the very real health risks, of polluted rivers and lakes. In Cleveland, Ohio, for example, the Cuyahoga River actually burst into flame from time to time from the petroleum waste being dumped into it; the city declared the river an official fire hazard.

Perhaps more alarming was the growing awareness that the air itself was becoming unhealthy, that toxic fumes from factories and power plants and, most of all, automobiles were poisoning the atmosphere. Weather forecasts and official atmospheric information began to refer to "smog" levels—using a relatively new word formed from a combination of smoke and fog. In some large cities—Los Angeles and Denver among them—smog became an almost perpetual fact of life, rising steadily through the day, blotting out the sun, and creating respiratory difficulties for many citizens. In 1969, an oil-well platform off Santa Barbara, California had a blowout that spewed hundreds of thousands of gallons of crude oil into the ocean just off the popular beaches of an affluent city. This oil spill had a tremendous impact on the environmental consciousness of millions of Americans. Another, much larger spill—indeed, the largest in American history—occurred off the *Exxon Valdez* coast of Alaska in 1989 when the giant tanker *Exxon Valdez* hit a reef in Prince William Sound. The damage it caused to the nearby shoreline, and to the wildlife that inhabited it, also greatly increased environmental consciousness.

Environmentalists brought to public attention some longer-term dangers of unchecked industrial development: the rapid depletion of oil and other irreplaceable fossil fuels; the destruction of lakes and forests as a result of "acid rain" (rainfall polluted by chemical contaminants); the rapid destruction of vast rain forests, in Brazil and elsewhere, which limited the earth's capacity to replenish its oxygen supply; the depletion of the ozone layer as a result of the release of chlorofluorocarbons into the atmosphere, which threatened to limit the earth's protection from dangerous ultraviolet rays from the sun; and global warming, which—if unchecked—would create dramatic changes in the earth's climate and would threaten existing cities and settlements in coastal areas all over the world by causing a rise in ocean levels. Many of these claims became—and remain—controversial. But most environmentalists—and many others—came to believe that while much remained to be learned about all of these developments, the problems were real and deserving of immediate attention.

Earth Day and Beyond

On April 22, 1970, people all over the United States participated in the first "Earth Day." Originally proposed by Wisconsin Senator Gaylord Nelson as a series of teach-ins on college campuses, Earth Day gradually took on a much larger life. Carefully managed by people who wanted to avoid associations with the radical left, it had an unthreatening quality that made it appealing to many people for whom antiwar demonstrations and civil-rights rallies seemed somehow threatening. According to some estimates, over 20 million Americans joined in some part of the Earth Day observances, which may have made it the largest single demonstration in the nation's history.

The cautious, centrist character of Earth Day and related efforts to popularize environmentalism helped create a movement that was less divisive than other, more controversial causes. Gradually, environmentalism became more than simply a series of demonstrations and protests. It became part of the consciousness of the vast majority of Americans—absorbed into popular culture, built into primary and secondary education, endorsed by almost all politicians (even if many of them actually opposed some environmental goals).

It also became part of the fabric of public policy. In 1970, Congress passed and President Nixon signed the National Environmental Protection Act, which created a new agency—the Environmental Protection Agency—to enforce *EPA Established* antipollution standards on businesses and consumers. The Clean Air Act, also passed in 1970, and the Clean Water Act, passed in 1972, added additional tools to the government's arsenal of weapons against environmental degradation. The actions of the federal government—and of state and local governments that soon followed its lead—had a measurable, even at times dramatic, impact on many kinds of pollution. Many lakes and rivers that had long been serious environmental hazards became markedly cleaner; restrictions on auto emissions and other air pollutants substantially improved air quality in many cities; industries found it much more difficult to dump toxic wastes in unsafe ways.

But the enlistment of the government behind many of the goals of environmentalists did not put an end to the movement. Different administrations displayed varying levels of support for environmental goals, and advocacy groups remained ready to spring into action to force them to change their positions. And of course new environmental problems continued to emerge even as older ones sometimes found solutions. Environmentalism was simultaneously a movement, a set of public policies, and a broad national ideal—and it was the combination of all those aspects that made it such a continually powerful force in American life.

NIXON, KISSINGER, AND THE WAR

Richard Nixon assumed office in 1969 committed not only to restoring stability at home but to creating a new and more stable order in the world. Central to Nixon's hopes for international stability was a resolution of the stalemate in Vietnam. Yet the new president felt no freer than his predecessor to abandon the American commitment there.

Vietnamization

Despite Nixon's own deep interest in international affairs, he brought with him into government a man who at times seemed to overshadow the president himself in the conduct of diplomacy: Henry Kissinger, a Harvard professor whom Nixon appointed as his special assistant for national security affairs. Kissinger quickly established dominance over Secretary of State William Rogers and Secretary of Defense Melvin Laird, who were both more experienced in public life. Together, Nixon and Kissinger set out to find an acceptable solution to the stalemate in Vietnam.

Henry Kissinger

The new Vietnam policy moved along several fronts. One was the move to "Vietnamize" the conflict—that is, train and equip the South Vietnamese military to assume the burden of combat in place of American forces. In the fall of 1969, Nixon announced the withdrawal of 60,000 American ground troops from Vietnam. By the fall of 1972, relatively few American soldiers remained in Indochina. From a peak of more than 540,000 in 1969, the number had dwindled to about 60,000.

Vietnamization (and the decreased draft calls it produced) did help quiet domestic opposition to the war for a time. It did nothing, however, to break the stalemate in the negotiations with the North Vietnamese in Paris. The new administration decided that new military pressures would be necessary to do that.

Escalation

By the end of 1969, Nixon and Kissinger had decided that the most effective way to tip the military balance in America's favor was to destroy the bases in Cambodia and Laos from which the American military believed the North Vietnamese were launching many of their attacks. Very early in his presidency, Nixon secretly ordered the air force to begin bombing Cambodian and Laotian territory to destroy the enemy sanctuaries. On April 30, Nixon went on television to announce that he was ordering American ground troops across the border into Cambodia to clean out the bases that the enemy had been using for its attacks on South Vietnam.

Literally overnight, the Cambodian invasion restored the dwindling antiwar movement to vigorous life. The first days of May saw the most widespread and vocal antiwar demonstrations ever. A mood of crisis was already mounting when, on May 4, four college students were killed and nine others injured after *Kent State* members of the National Guard opened fire on antiwar demonstrators at Kent State University in Ohio. Ten days later, police killed two African-American students at Jackson State University in Mississippi during a demonstration there.

The clamor against the war spread into the government and the press. Congress angrily repealed the Gulf of Tonkin Resolution in December. Then, in June 1971, first the *New York Times* and later other newspapers began publishing excerpts from a secret study of the war prepared by the Defense Department during the Johnson adminis- *Pentagon Papers* tration. The so-called Pentagon Papers, leaked to the press by former Defense official Daniel Ellsberg, provided evidence the government had been dishonest, both in reporting the military progress of the war and in explaining its own motives for American involvement. The administration went to court to suppress the documents, but the Supreme Court ruled that the press had the right to publish them.

Morale and discipline among American troops in Vietnam were rapidly deteriorating. The 1971 trial and conviction of Lieutenant William Calley, who was charged with overseeing a massacre of more than 100 unarmed South Vietnamese civilians in 1968 near the village of My Lai, attracted wide public attention to the dehumanizing impact of the war on those who fought it—and to the terrible consequences that dehumanization imposed on the Vietnamese people. Less publicized were other, more widespread problems among American troops in Vietnam: desertion, drug addiction, racial bias, refusal to obey orders, even the killing of unpopular officers by enlisted men.

By 1971, nearly two-thirds of those interviewed in public opinion polls were urging American withdrawal from Vietnam. President Nixon, however, believed that a defeat in Vietnam would cause unacceptable damage to the nation's (and his own) credibility. The FBI, the CIA, the White House itself, and other federal agencies increased their efforts to discredit and harass antiwar and radical groups, often through illegal means.

In Indochina, meanwhile, the fighting raged on. American bombing in Vietnam and Cambodia increased. In March 1972, the North Vietnamese mounted their biggest offensive since 1968 (the so- *Easter Offensive* called Easter offensive). American and South Vietnamese forces managed to halt the communist advance, but it was clear that without American support the South Vietnamese would not have succeeded. At the same time, Nixon ordered American planes to bomb targets near Hanoi, the capital of North Vietnam, and Haiphong, its principal port, and called for the mining of seven North Vietnamese harbors.

"Peace with Honor"

As the 1972 presidential election approached, the administration stepped up its effort to produce a breakthrough in negotiations with the North Vietnamese. In April 1972, the president dropped his longtime insistence on the removal of North Vietnamese troops from the south before any American withdrawal. Meanwhile, Henry Kissinger met privately in Paris with the North Vietnamese foreign secretary, Le Duc Tho, to work out terms for a cease-fire. On October 26, only days before the presidential election, Kissinger announced that "peace is at hand."

Several weeks later (after the election), negotiations broke down once again. Although both the American and the North Vietnamese governments were ready to accept the Kissinger-Tho plan for a cease-fire, President Nguyen Van Thieu of South Vietnam balked, still insisting on a full withdrawal of North Vietnamese forces from the south. Kissinger tried to win additional concessions from the communists to meet Thieu's objections, but on December 16 talks broke off.

The next day, December 17, American B-52s began the heaviest and most destructive air raids of the entire war on Hanoi, Haiphong, and other North Vietnamese targets. Civilian casualties were high, and fifteen American B–52s were shot down by the North Vietnamese; in the entire war to that point, the United States had lost only one of the giant *"Christmas Bombing"* bombers. On December 30, Nixon terminated the "Christmas bombing." The United States and the North Vietnamese returned to the conference table; and on January 27, 1973, they signed an "agreement on ending the war and restoring peace in Vietnam." Nixon claimed that the Christmas bombing had forced the North Vietnamese to relent. At least equally important, however, was the enormous American pressure on Thieu to accept the cease-fire.

The terms of the Paris accords were little different from those Kissinger and Tho had accepted in principle a few months before. There would be an immediate cease-fire. The North Vietnamese would release several hundred American prisoners of war. The Thieu regime would survive for the moment, but North Vietnamese forces already in the south would remain there. An undefined committee would work out a permanent settlement.

Defeat in Indochina

American forces were hardly out of Indochina before the Paris accords began to collapse. In March 1975, finally, the North Vietnamese launched a full-scale offensive against the now greatly weakened forces of the south. Thieu appealed to Washington for assistance. The president (now Gerald Ford) appealed to Congress for additional funding; Congress refused. *Fall of Saigon* Late in April 1975, communist forces marched into Saigon, shortly after officials of the Thieu regime and the staff of the American embassy had fled the country in humiliating

THE EVACUATION OF SAIGON A harried U.S. official struggles to keep panicking Vietnamese from boarding an already overburdened helicopter on the roof of the American embassy in Saigon. The hurried evacuation of Americans took place only hours before the arrival of North Vietnamese troops, signaling the final defeat of South Vietnam. (*AP/Wide World Photos*)

disarray. The communist forces quickly occupied the capital, renamed it Ho Chi Minh City, and began the process of reuniting Vietnam under the harsh rule of Hanoi. At about the same time, the Lon Nol regime in Cambodia fell to the murderous forces of the Khmer Rouge—whose brutal policies led to the death of more than a third of the country's people over the next several years.

Such were the dismal results of more than a decade of direct American military involvement in Vietnam. More than 1.2 million Vietnamese soldiers had died in combat, along with countless civilians throughout the region. A beautiful land had been ravaged, its agrarian economy left in ruins; until an economic revival began in the early 1990s, Vietnam remained one of the poorest and most politically oppressive nations in the world. The United States had paid a heavy price as well. The war had cost the nation almost $150 billion in direct costs and much more indirectly. It had resulted in the deaths of over 57,000 young Americans and the injury of 300,000 more. And the nation had suffered a blow to its confidence and self-esteem from which it would not soon recover.

NIXON, KISSINGER, AND THE WORLD

The continuing war in Vietnam provided an unhappy backdrop to what Nixon considered his larger mission in world affairs: the construction of a new international order. The president had become convinced that the

Nixon's Multipolar Vision old assumptions of a "bipolar" world—in which the United States and the Soviet Union were the only real great powers—were now obsolete. America must adapt to the new "multipolar" international structure, in which China, Japan, and Western Europe were becoming major, independent forces.

The China Initiative and Soviet-American Détente

For more than twenty years, ever since the fall of Chiang Kai-shek in 1949, the United States had treated China, the most populous nation on earth, as if it did not exist. Instead, America recognized the regime-in-exile on the small island of Taiwan as the legitimate government of mainland China. Nixon and Kissinger wanted to forge a new relationship with the Chinese communists—in part to strengthen them as a counterbalance to the Soviet Union. The Chinese, for their part, were eager to end China's own isolation from the international arena.

In July 1971, Nixon sent Henry Kissinger on a secret mission to Beijing. When Kissinger returned, the president made the startling announcement that he would visit China himself within the next few months. That fall, with American approval, the United Nations admitted the communist government of China and expelled the representatives of the Taiwan regime. Finally, in February 1972, Nixon paid a formal visit to China and, in a single stroke, erased much of the deep animosity between the United States and the Chinese communists. Nixon did not yet formally recognize the communist regime, but in 1972 the United States and China began low-level diplomatic relations.

The initiatives in China coincided with an effort by the Nixon administration to improve relations with the Soviet Union, an initiative known by the French word détente. In 1971, American and Soviet diplomats produced the first Strategic Arms Limitation Treaty (SALT I),

DÉTENTE AT HIGH TIDE The visit of Soviet premier Leonid Brezhnev to Washington in 1973 was a high-water mark in the search for détente between the two nations. Here, Brezhnev and Nixon share friendly words on the White House balcony. *(J. P. Laffont/Sygma/Corbis)*

which froze the arsenals of some nuclear missiles (ICBMs) on both sides at present levels. In May of that year, the president traveled to Moscow to sign the agreement. The next year, the Soviet premier, Leonid Brezhnev, visited Washington.

Dealing with the Third World

The policies of rapprochement with communist China and détente with the Soviet Union reflected Nixon's and Kissinger's belief in the importance of stable relationships among the great powers. But the so-called Third World remained the most volatile and dangerous source of international tension.

The Nixon-Kissinger policy toward the Third World was to maintain the status quo without involving the United States too deeply in local disputes. In 1969 and 1970, the president described what became known as the Nixon Doctrine, by which the United States would *Nixon Doctrine* "participate in the defense and development of allies and friends" but would leave the "basic responsibility" for the future of those "friends" to the nations themselves. In practice, the Nixon Doctrine meant a declining American interest in contributing to Third World development; a growing contempt for the United Nations, where underdeveloped nations were gaining influence through their sheer numbers; and increasing support to authoritarian regimes attempting to withstand radical challenges from within.

In 1970, for example, the CIA poured substantial funds into Chile to help support the established government against a communist challenge. When the Marxist candidate for president,

Allende Overthrown

Salvador Allende, came to power through an open election despite American efforts, the United States began funneling more money to opposition forces in Chile to help destabilize the new government. In 1973, a military junta seized power from Allende, who was subsequently murdered. The United States developed a friendly relationship with the new, repressive military government of General Augusto Pinochet.

In the Middle East, conditions grew more volatile in the aftermath of the 1967 war, in which Israel had occupied substantial new territories, dislodging many Palestinian Arabs from their homes. The refugees were a source of considerable instability in Jordan, Lebanon, and the other surrounding countries into which they moved. In October 1973, on the Jewish high holy day of Yom Kippur, Egyptian and Syrian forces attacked Israel. For ten days, the Israelis struggled to recover from the surprise attack; finally, they launched an effective counteroffensive against Egyptian forces in the Sinai. At that point, the United States intervened, placing heavy pressure on Israel to accept a cease-fire rather than press its advantage.

The imposed settlement of the Yom Kippur War demonstrated the growing dependence of the United States and its

Arab Oil Embargo

allies on Arab oil. A brief but painful embargo by the Arab governments on the sale of oil to America in 1973 provided an ominous warning of the costs of losing access to the region's resources.

A larger lesson of 1973 was that the nations of the Third World could no longer be expected to act as passive, cooperative "client states." And the United States could not depend on cheap, easy access to raw materials as it had in the past.

POLITICS AND ECONOMICS
IN THE NIXON YEARS

Nixon ran for president in 1968 promising a return to more conservative social and economic policies and a restoration of law and order. Once in office, however, his domestic policies sometimes continued and even expanded the liberal initiatives of the previous two administrations.

Domestic Initiatives

Many of Nixon's domestic policies were a response to what he believed to be the demands of his constituency—conservative, middle-class people, the "silent majority" who he believed wanted to re- *Nixon's "Silent Majority"* duce federal interference in local affairs. He tried, unsuccessfully, to persuade Congress to pass legislation prohibiting school desegregation through the use of forced busing. He forbade the Department of Health, Education, and Welfare to cut off federal funds from school districts that had failed to comply with court orders to integrate. At the same time, he began to reduce or dismantle many of the social programs of the Great Society and the New Frontier. In 1973, he abolished the Office of Economic Opportunity, the centerpiece of the antipoverty program of the Johnson years.

Yet Nixon's domestic policies had progressive and creative elements as well. He signed legislation creating the Environmental Protection Agency and establishing the most stringent environmental regulations in the nation's history. He ordered the first affirmative action program for workers on federally funded projects. One of the administration's boldest efforts was an attempt to overhaul the nation's welfare system. Nixon proposed replacing the existing system with what he called the Family Assistance Plan (FAP). It would in effect have created a guaranteed annual income for all Americans: $1,600 in federal grants, which could be supplemented by outside earnings up to $4,000. The FAP won approval in the House in 1970, but the bill failed in the Senate. Nixon also became the first president since Truman to propose a plan for national health insurance, which likewise made no progress in Congress.

From the Warren Court to the Nixon Court

Of all the liberal institutions that aroused the enmity of the conservative "silent majority" in the 1950s and 1960s, none evoked more anger and bitterness than the Supreme Court under Chief Justice Earl Warren. Not only did the Warren Court's rulings on racial matters disrupt traditional social patterns in both the North and the South, but its staunch defense of civil liberties directly contributed, in the eyes of *Civil Liberties Expanded* many Americans, to the increase in crime, disorder, and moral decay. In *Engel* v. *Vitale* (1962), the Court ruled that prayers in public schools were unconstitutional, sparking outrage among religious fundamentalists and others. In *Roth* v. *United States* (1957), the Court sharply limited the authority of local governments to curb pornography. In a series of other decisions, the Court greatly strengthened the civil rights of criminal defendants and, many Americans believed, greatly weakened the power of law enforcement officials to do their jobs. For example, in *Gideon* v. *Wainwright* (1963), the Court ruled that every felony defendant was entitled to a lawyer regardless of his or her ability to pay. In *Escobedo* v.

Illinois (1964), it ruled that a defendant must be allowed access to a lawyer before questioning by police. In *Miranda* v. *Arizona* (1966), the Court confirmed the obligation of authorities to inform a criminal suspect of his or her rights. By 1968, the Warren Court had become the target of Americans of all kinds who felt the balance of power in the United States had shifted too far toward the poor, the dispossessed, and the criminal at the expense of the middle class.

Nixon promised to give the Court a more conservative cast. When Chief Justice Earl Warren retired early in 1969, Nixon replaced him with a federal appeals court judge of known conservative leanings, Warren Burger. At about the same time, Associate Justice Abe Fortas resigned his seat after the disclosure of a series of alleged financial improprieties. To replace him, Nixon named Clement F. Haynsworth, a respected federal circuit court judge from South Carolina. But Haynsworth came under fire from Senate liberals, black organizations, and labor unions for his conservative record on civil rights. The Senate rejected him. Nixon's next choice was G. Harrold Carswell, a judge of the Florida federal appeals court of little distinction. The Senate rejected his nomination, too.

Nixon angrily denounced the votes. But he was careful thereafter to choose men of standing within the legal community to fill vacancies on the Supreme Court: Harry Blackmun, a moderate jurist from Minnesota; Lewis F. Powell, Jr., a respected lawyer from Virginia; and William Rehnquist, a member of the Nixon Justice Department.

The new Court, however, fell short of what the president and many conservatives had expected. Rather than retreating from its commitment to social reform, the Court in many areas actually moved further toward it. In *Swann* v. *Charlotte-Mecklenburg Board of Education* (1971), it ruled in favor of the use of forced busing to achieve racial balance in schools. Not even the intense and occasionally violent opposition of local communities as diverse as Boston and Louisville, Kentucky, was able to weaken the judicial commitment to integration. In *Furman* v. *Georgia* (1972), the Court overturned existing capital punishment statutes and established strict new guidelines for such laws in the future. In *Roe* v. *Wade* (1973), one of the most controversial decisions in the Court's modern history, it struck down laws forbidding abortions.

In other decisions, however, the Burger Court did demonstrate a more conservative temperament than the Warren Court had shown. Although the justices approved busing as a tool for achieving integration, *Milliken v. Bradley* they rejected, in *Milliken* v. *Bradley* (1974), a plan to transfer students across municipal lines (in this case, between Detroit and its suburbs) to achieve racial balance. While the Court upheld the principle of affirmative action in its celebrated 1978 decision in *Bakke* v. *Board of Regents of California*, it established restrictive new guidelines for such programs in the future. In *Stone* v. *Powell* (1976), the Court agreed to certain limits on the right of a defendant to appeal a state conviction to the federal judiciary.

The Election of 1972

Nixon entered the presidential race in 1972 with a substantial reserve of strength. His energetic reelection committee had collected enormous sums of money to support the campaign. The president himself used the powers of incumbency to strengthen his political standing in strategic areas. And Nixon's foreign policy successes, especially his trip to China, increased his stature in the eyes of the nation.

Nixon was most fortunate in 1972, however, in his opposition. George Wallace, partly at Nixon's urging, entered the Democratic primaries and helped divide the party until a would-be assassin shot the Alabama governor during a rally at a Maryland shopping center in May. Paralyzed from the waist down, Wallace was unable to continue campaigning. In the meantime, the most liberal factions of the party were succeeding in establishing their candidate, Senator George S. McGovern of South *George McGovern* Dakota, as the front-runner for the nomination. An outspoken critic of the war and a forceful advocate of advanced liberal positions on many social and economic issues, McGovern profited greatly from party reforms (which he himself had helped to draft) that gave increased influence to women, minorities, and young people in the selection of the Democratic ticket. But in the process, the McGovern campaign came to be associated with aspects of the turbulent 1960s that many middle-class Americans were eager to reject.

On election day, Nixon won reelection by one of the largest margins in history: 60.7 percent of the popular vote compared with 37.5 percent for McGovern, and an electoral margin of 520 to 17. The Democratic candidate had carried only Massachusetts and the District of Columbia. But serious problems, some beyond the president's control and some of his own making, were already lurking in the wings.

The Troubled Economy

Although it was political scandal that would ultimately destroy the Nixon presidency, the most important issue of the early 1970s was the beginning of a long-term transformation of the American economy. For three decades, that economy had been the envy of the world. In fact, however, America's prosperity rested in part on several artificial conditions that were rapidly disappearing by the late 1960s.

The most immediate change was the end of the nation's easy access to cheap raw materials, a change that became a major cause of the serious inflation that plagued the economy through much of the 1970s. For many years, the Organization of Petroleum Exporting *OPEC* Countries (OPEC) had operated as an informal bargaining unit for the sale of oil by Third World nations but had seldom managed to exercise any real strength. But in the early 1970s, OPEC began to assert itself, to use its oil both as an economic tool and as a political weapon. In 1973, in the midst of the Yom Kippur War, Arab members of OPEC announced that they would no longer ship petroleum to nations supporting Israel—that is, to the United States and its allies in Western Europe. At about the same time, the OPEC nations agreed to raise their prices 500 percent (from $3 to $15 a barrel). These twin shocks produced momentary economic chaos in the West. The United States suffered its first fuel shortage since World War II. And although the crisis eased a few months later, the price of energy continued to skyrocket.

The energy crisis eventually subsided, but another, longer-term change in the American economy was the transformation of the nation's manufacturing sector. Ever since World War II, American industry had
Growing Foreign Competition enjoyed relatively little competition from the rest of the world. By the end of the 1960s, however, both Western Europe and Japan had recovered from the damage their manufacturing sectors had absorbed during World War II; by the early 1970s, they were providing stiff competition to American firms in the sale of automobiles, steel, and many other products both in world markets and within the United States. Some American corporations failed. Others restructured themselves to become more competitive again in world markets. In the process, they closed many older plants and eliminated hundreds of thousands of once-lucrative manufacturing jobs. The high-wage, high-employment industrial economy that had been a central fact of American life since the 1940s was gradually disappearing.

The Nixon Response

Nixon's initial answer to these mounting economic problems was a conventional anti-inflationary one. He reduced spending and raised taxes, producing a modest budget surplus in 1969. But when those policies proved difficult to sustain, Nixon turned increasingly to control of the currency. Placing conservative economists at the head of the Federal Reserve Board, he ensured sharply higher interest rates and a contraction of the money supply. Even so, the cost of living rose a cumulative 15 percent during Nixon's first two and a half years in office. Economic growth, in the meantime, declined. The United States was encountering a new dilemma: "stagflation," a combination of rising prices and general economic stagnation.

In the summer of 1971, Nixon imposed a ninety-day freeze on all wages and prices at their existing levels. Then, in November, he launched Phase II of his economic plan: mandatory guidelines for some wage and price increases, to be administered by a federal agency. Inflation subsided temporarily, but the recession continued. Fearful that the recession would
Rising Inflation be more damaging than inflation in an election year, the administration reversed itself late in 1971: interest rates were allowed to drop sharply, and government spending increased—producing the largest budget deficit since World War II. The

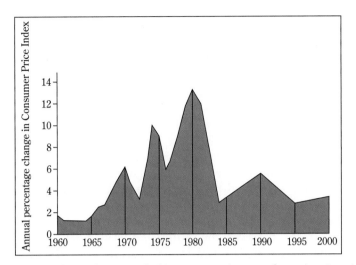

INFLATION, 1960–2000 Inflation was the biggest economic worry of most Americans in the 1970s and early 1980s, and this chart shows why. Having remained very low through the early 1960s, inflation rose slowly in the second half of the decade and then dramatically in the mid- and late 1970s, before beginning a sharp and reasonably steady decline in the early 1980s.
◆ *What caused the great spike in inflation in the 1970s?*

new tactics helped revive the economy in the short term, but inflation rose substantially. In 1973, prices rose 9 percent; in 1974, after the Arab oil embargo and the OPEC price increases, they rose 12 percent—the highest rate since shortly after World War II. The new energy crisis, in the meantime, was quickly becoming a national preoccupation. But while Nixon talked often about the need to achieve "energy independence," he offered few concrete proposals.

THE WATERGATE CRISIS

Although economic problems greatly concerned the American people in the 1970s, another stunning development almost entirely preoccupied the nation beginning early in 1973: the fall of Richard Nixon. The president's demise was a result in part of his own personality. But the larger explanation for the crisis lay in Nixon's view of American society and the world, and of his own role in both. The president believed the United States faced grave dangers from the radicals and dissidents who were challenging his policies. He came increasingly to consider any challenge to his policies a threat to "national security," thus creating a climate in which he and those who served him could justify almost any tactics to stifle dissent and undermine opposition.

CHAPTER THIRTY-TWO

The Scandals

Early on the morning of June 17, 1972, police arrested five men who had broken into the offices of the Democratic National Committee in the Watergate office building in Washington, D.C. Two others were seized a short time later and charged with supervising the break-in. When reporters for the *Washington Post* began researching the backgrounds of the culprits, they discovered that among those involved in the burglary were former employees of the Committee for the Re-Election of the President (CRP). One of them had worked in the White House itself. They had, moreover, been paid for the break-in from a secret fund of the reelection committee, a fund controlled by, among others, members of the White House staff.

Public interest in the disclosures grew slowly in the last months of 1972. Early in 1973, however, the Watergate burglars went on trial; and under prodding from federal judge John J. Sirica, one of the defendants, James W. McCord, agreed to cooperate both with the grand jury and with a special Senate investigating committee recently established under Senator Sam J. Ervin of North Carolina. McCord's testimony opened a floodgate of confessions, and for months a parade of White House and campaign officials exposed one illegality after another. Foremost among them was a member of the inner circle of the White House, John Dean, counsel to the president, who leveled allegations against Nixon himself.

Two different sets of scandals emerged from the investigations. One was a general pattern of abuses of power involving both the White House and the Nixon campaign committee, which included, but was not limited to, the Watergate break-in. The other scandal, and the one that became the major focus of public attention for nearly two years, was the way in which the administration tried to manage the investigations of the Watergate break-in

Watergate "Cover-up"

and other abuses—a pattern of behavior that became known as the "cover-up." There was never any conclusive evidence that the president had planned or approved the burglary in advance. But there was mounting evidence that he had been involved in illegal efforts to obstruct investigations of the episode.

Nixon accepted the departure of members of his administration implicated in the scandals. But the president continued to insist on his own innocence. There the matter might have rested had it not been for the

Watergate Tapes

disclosure during the Senate hearings of a White House taping system that had recorded virtually every conversation in the president's office during the period in question. All those investigating the scandals sought access to the tapes; Nixon, pleading "executive privilege," refused to release them. A special prosecutor appointed by the president to handle the Watergate cases, Harvard law professor Archibald Cox, took Nixon to court in October 1973 in an effort to force him to relinquish the recordings. Nixon, now clearly growing desperate, fired Cox and suffered the humiliation of watching both Attorney General Elliot Richardson and his deputy resign in protest. This "Saturday night massacre" made the president's predicament much worse. Not only did public pressure force him to appoint a new special prosecutor, Texas attorney Leon Jaworski, who proved just as determined as Cox to subpoena the tapes; but the episode precipitated an investigation by the House of Representatives into the possibility of impeachment.

The Fall of Richard Nixon

Nixon's situation deteriorated further in the following months. Late in 1973, Vice President Spiro Agnew became embroiled in a scandal of his own when evidence surfaced that he had accepted bribes and kickbacks while serving as governor of Maryland and even as vice president. In return for a Justice Department agreement not to press the case, Agnew pleaded no contest to a lesser charge of income-tax evasion and resigned from the government. With the controversial Agnew no longer in line to succeed to the presidency, the prospect of removing Nixon from the White House became less worrisome to his opponents. The new vice president (the first appointed under the terms of the Twenty-fifth Amendment, which had been adopted in 1967) was House Minority Leader Gerald Ford, an amiable and popular Michigan congressman.

The impeachment investigation quickly gathered momentum. In April 1974, in an effort to head off further subpoenas of the tapes, the president released transcripts of a number of relevant conversations, claiming that they proved his innocence. Investigators and much of the public felt otherwise. Even these edited tapes seemed to suggest Nixon's complicity in the cover-up. In July, the crisis reached a climax. First the Supreme Court ruled unanimously, in *United States* v. *Richard M. Nixon*, that the president must relinquish the tapes to Special Prosecutor Jaworski. Days later, the House Judiciary Committee voted to recommend three articles of impeachment.

United States v. Richard Nixon

Even without additional evidence, Nixon might well have been impeached by the full House and convicted by the Senate. Early in August, however, he provided at last the "smoking gun"—the concrete proof of his guilt— that his defenders had long contended was missing from the case against him. Among the tapes that the Supreme Court compelled Nixon to relinquish were several that offered apparently incontrovertible evidence of his involvement in the Watergate cover-up. Only three days after the burglary, the recordings disclosed, the president had ordered the FBI to stop investigating the break-in. Impeachment and conviction now seemed inevitable.

For several days, Nixon brooded in the White House, on the verge, some claimed, of a breakdown. Finally, on August 8, 1974, he announced his resignation—the first president in American history ever to do so. At noon the next day, while Nixon and his family were flying west to their home in California, Gerald Ford took the oath of office as president.

Resignation

WATERGATE

Thirty years after Watergate—the most famous political scandal in American history—historians and others continue to argue about its causes and significance. Their interpretations tend to fall into several broad categories.

One argument emphasizes the evolution of the institution of the presidency over time and sees Watergate as the result of a much larger pattern of presidential usurpations of power that stretched back at least several decades. Arthur Schlesinger, Jr., helped develop this argument in his 1973 book _The Imperial Presidency_, which argued that the belief of a succession of presidents in the urgency of the Cold War, and in their duty to take whatever measures might be necessary to combat it, led them gradually to usurp more and more power from Congress, from the courts, and from the public. Gradually, presidents began to look for ways to circumvent constraints not just in foreign policy, but in domestic matters as well. Nixon's actions in the Watergate crisis were, in other words, a culmination of this long and steady expansion of covert presidential power. Jonathan Schell, in _The Time of Illusion_ (1975), offered a variation of this argument, tying the crisis of the presidency to the pressure that nuclear weapons placed on presidents to protect the nation's—and their own "credibility."

A second explanation of Watergate emphasizes the difficult social and political environment of the late 1960s and early 1970s. Nixon entered office, according to this view, facing an unprecedentedly radical opposition that would stop at nothing to discredit the war and destroy his authority. He found himself, therefore, drawn into taking similarly desperate measures of his own to defend himself from these extraordinary challenges. Nixon made this argument himself in his 1975 memoirs:

> This epidemic of unprecedented domestic terrorism . . . prompted our efforts to discover the best means by which to deal with this new phenomenon of highly organized and highly skilled revolutionaries dedicated to the violent destruction of our democratic system.

The historian Herbert Parmet echoed parts of this argument in _Richard Nixon and His America_ (1990). Stephen Ambrose offered a more muted version of the same view in _Richard Nixon_ (1989).

Most of those who have written about Watergate, however, search for the explanation not in institutional or social forces, but in the personalities of the people involved, and most notably in the personality of Richard Nixon. Even many of those who have developed structural explanations (Schlesinger, Schell, and Ambrose, for example) return eventually to Nixon himself as the most important explanation for Watergate. Others begin there, perhaps most notably Stanley I. Kutler, in _The Wars of Watergate_ (1990) and, more recently, _Abuse of Power_ (1997), in which he presents extensive excerpts from conversations about Watergate taped in the Nixon White House. Kutler emphasizes Nixon's lifelong resort to vicious political tactics and his longstanding belief that he was a special target of unscrupulous enemies and had to "get" them before they got him. Watergate was rooted, Kutler argues, "in the personality and history of Nixon himself." A "corrosive hatred," he claims, "decisively shaped Nixon's own behavior, his career, and eventually his historical standing."

Many Americans expressed relief and exhilaration that, as the new president put it, "our long national nightmare is over." But the wave of good feeling could not obscure the deeper and more lasting damage of the Watergate crisis. In a society in which distrust of leaders and institutions of authority was already widespread, the fall of Richard Nixon confirmed for many Americans their most cynical assumptions about the character of American public life.

CONCLUSION

The victory of Richard Nixon in the 1968 presidential election represented a popular repudiation of turbulence and radicalism. It was a call for a restoration of order and stability. But order and stability were not the dominant characteristics of Nixon's troubled years in office. Nixon entered office, rather, when the forces of the left and the counterculture were approaching the peak of their influence. American culture and society in the late 1960s and early 1970s were shaped decisively by, and were deeply divided over, the challenges by young people to the norms by which most Americans had lived. They were also the years in which a host of new liberation movements joined the drive for racial equality, and when, above all, women mobilized effectively and powerfully to demand changes in the way their society treated gender differences.

Nixon had run for office attacking the failure of his predecessor to end the war in Vietnam. But for four years under his presidency, the war—and the protests against it—continued and even in some respects escalated. The division of opinion over the war was as deep as any of the many other divisions in national life. It continued to poison the nation's politics and social fabric until the American role in the conflict finally shuddered to a close in 1973.

But much of the controversy and division in the 1970s was a product of the Nixon presidency itself. Nixon was in many ways a dynamic and even visionary leader, who proposed (but rarely succeeded in enacting) some important domestic reforms and who made important changes in American foreign policy, most notably making overtures to communist China and forging détente with the Soviet Union. He was also, however, a devious, secretive, and embittered man whose White House became engaged in a series of covert activities—many of them connected with the president's reelection campaign in 1972—that produced the most dramatic political scandal in American history. Watergate, as it was called, preoccupied much of the nation for nearly two years beginning in 1972; and ultimately, in the summer of 1974, the scandal forced Richard Nixon—who had been reelected to office only two years before by one of the largest majorities in modern history—to become the first president in American history to resign.

FOR FURTHER REFERENCE

John Morton Blum, *Years of Discord: American Politics and Society, 1961–1974* (1991) is a good overview. James Miller, *"Democracy in the Streets": From Port Huron to the Siege of Chicago* (1987) is a perceptive history of the New Left through its leading organization, SDS. Kristin Luker, *Abortion and the Politics of Motherhood* (1984) is an excellent account of this central battle over the nature of feminism. Daniel Horowitz, *Betty Friedan and the Making of "The Feminine Mystique"* (1998) is a fine study of a major figure in the feminist movement. Margaret Cruikshank, *The Rise of a Gay and Lesbian Liberation Movement* (1992) recounts another important struggle of the 1960s and beyond. David Allyn, *Make Love Not War: The Sexual Revolution: An Unfettered History* (2000) and Beth Bailey, *Sex in the Heartland* (1999) are studies of a major social change. Ronald Takaki, *Strangers from a Distant Shore: A History of Asian Americans* (1989) examines the growing Asian community in postwar America. Stephen Ambrose, *Nixon: The Triumph of a Politician, 1962–1972* (1989), and *Nixon, Ruin and Recovery, 1973–1990* (1992) provide a thorough chronicle of this important presidency. Joan Hoff, *Nixon Reconsidered* (1994) is a more sympathetic account of Nixon's presidency before Watergate. Stanley I. Kutler, *The Wars of Watergate* (1990) is a scholarly study of the great scandal, and Jonathan Schell, *The Time of Illusion* (1975) is a perceptive contemporary account. Marilyn Young, *The Vietnam Wars, 1945–1990* (1991) provides, among other things, a full account of the last years of American involvement in Vietnam and of the conflicts in the region that followed the American withdrawal. Larry Berman, *No Peace, No Honor: Nixon, Kissinger, and Betrayal in Vietnam* (2001) is a study of the end of the war.

Chicago 1968 (1995) is a complex and riveting film portrait of the dramatic events around the Democratic National Convention of 1968. The three-part film series *America in 1968* (1979) examines the political, cultural, and international events of that pivotal year. *Nixon* (1990) is a three-hour film biography of one of the most powerful and controversial figures in modern American history. *Watergate* (1994) is a documentary film on the unmaking of the Nixon presidency, including recent interviews with major participants. *In the Spirit of Crazy Horse* (1990) relates the history of the Lakota Indians on the centennial of the Wounded Knee massacre. *Chicano! History of the Mexican-American Civil Rights Movement* (1996) is a four-part series on the Mexican-American movement from 1967.

For quizzes, Internet resources, references to additional books and films, and more, consult this book's Online Learning Center site at www.mhhe.com/unfinishednation4.

DEMONSTRATING AGAINST BILINGUALISM Among the many divisive issues that sparked controversy in the 1970s and 1980s, and helped fuel the rise of a powerful conservative movement, was the growing number of residents of the United States for whom English was a second language. In California and a few other states educators responded by introducing "bilingualism" into the public school system, to ensure that students whose command of English was poor could receive instruction in their own language—usually Spanish since the largest number of immigrants in the Southwest came from Mexico. Hostility to bilingualism grew rapidly among mostly conservative Americans, who feared that the movement would not stop in the schools. This woman demonstrates in favor of one of the prized causes of the right—the campaign to make English the "official" language of the United States. *(Nathan Benn/Corbis)*

TIME LINE

1974	1976	1977	1978-1979	1980	1981	1982	1983
"Stagflation" Ford pardons Nixon	Carter elected president	Panama Canal treaties signed	Camp David accords	U.S. boycotts Moscow Olympics	American hostages in Iran released	Severe recession	U.S. invades Grenada
		Apple introduces first personal computer	American hostages in Iran	Reagan elected president	Reagan wins tax and budget cuts		
			Soviet Union invades Afghanistan		U.S. military buildup begins		
			U.S. and China restore relations		AIDS first reported in U.S.		
			Three Mile Island nuclear accident				

CHAPTER THIRTY-THREE

FROM "THE AGE OF LIMITS" TO THE AGE OF REAGAN

Politics and Diplomacy after Watergate
The Rise of the New American Right
The "Reagan Revolution"
America and the Waning of the Cold War

T he frustrations of the early 1970s—the defeat in Vietnam, the Watergate crisis, the decay of the American economy—inflicted damaging blows to the confident, optimistic nationalism that had characterized so much of the postwar era. Some Americans responded to these problems by announcing the arrival of an "age of limits," in which America would have to learn to live with increasingly constricted expectations. By the end of the decade, however, another response to the challenges was gaining strength—one that combined a conservative retreat from some of the heady visions of the 1960s with a reinforced commitment to the idea of economic growth, international power, and American virtue.

1984	1985	1986	1987	1988	1989	1990	1991	1992
Reagan reelected	Reagan and Gorbachev meet	U.S. bombs Libya	Gorbachev visits U.S.	Bush elected president	Berlin Wall dismantled	Iraq invades Kuwait	Collapse of Soviet regime	Los Angeles race riots
	Crack cocaine appears in U.S. cities	Iran-contra scandal revealed	Stock market falls		Communist regimes collapse		Persian Gulf War	Clinton elected president
					U.S. troops in Panama			
					Human Genome Project launched			

POLITICS AND DIPLOMACY
AFTER WATERGATE

In the aftermath of Richard Nixon's ignominious departure from office, many wondered whether faith in the presidency, and in the government as a whole, could easily be restored. The administrations of the two presidents who succeeded Nixon did little to answer those questions.

The Ford Custodianship

Gerald Ford inherited the presidency under unenviable circumstances. He had to try to rebuild confidence in government in the wake of the Watergate scandals. And he had to try to restore prosperity in the face of major economic difficulties.

The new president's effort to establish himself as a symbol of political integrity suffered a setback only a month after he took office, when he granted Richard Nixon "a full, free, and absolute pardon" for any crimes he may have committed during his presidency. The pardon caused a decline in Ford's popularity from which he never fully recovered. Nevertheless, most Americans considered him a decent man; his honesty and amiability did much to reduce the bitterness and acrimony of the Watergate years.

Nixon Pardoned

The Ford administration enjoyed less success in its effort to solve the problems of the economy. In his efforts to curb inflation, the president called for largely ineffective voluntary efforts. After supporting high interest rates, opposing increased federal spending (through liberal use of his veto power), and resisting pressures for a tax reduction, Ford had to deal with a serious recession in 1974 and 1975. Central to the economic problems was the continuing energy crisis. In the aftermath of the Arab oil embargo of 1973, the OPEC cartel raised the price of oil—by 400 percent in 1974 alone—one of the principal reasons why inflation reached 11 percent in 1976.

Economic Problems

Ford retained Henry Kissinger as secretary of state and continued the general policies of the Nixon years. Late in 1974, Ford met with Leonid Brezhnev at Vladivostok in Siberia and signed an arms control accord that was to serve as the basis for SALT II, thus achieving a goal the Nixon administration had long sought. Meanwhile, in the Middle East, Henry Kissinger helped produce a new accord by which Israel agreed to return large portions of the occupied Sinai to Egypt, and the two nations pledged not to resolve future differences by force.

1976 Election

As the 1976 presidential election approached, Ford's policies were coming under attack from both the right and the left. In the Republican primary campaign, Ford faced a powerful challenge from former California governor Ronald Reagan, leader of the party's conservative wing, who spoke for many on the right who opposed any agreements with communists. The president only barely survived the assault to win his party's nomination. The Democrats, in the meantime,

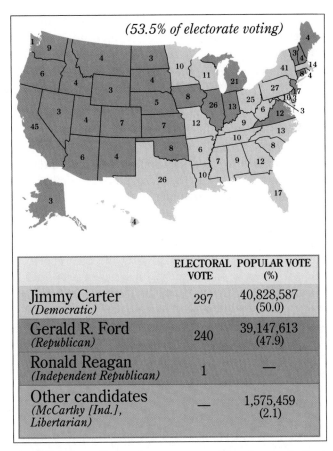

	ELECTORAL VOTE	POPULAR VOTE (%)
Jimmy Carter *(Democratic)*	297	40,828,587 (50.0)
Gerald R. Ford *(Republican)*	240	39,147,613 (47.9)
Ronald Reagan *(Independent Republican)*	1	—
Other candidates *(McCarthy [Ind.], Libertarian)*	—	1,575,459 (2.1)

THE ELECTION OF 1976 Jimmy Carter, a former governor of Georgia, swept the South in the 1976 election and carried enough of the industrial states of the Northeast and Midwest to win a narrow victory over President Gerald R. Ford. His showing indicated the importance to the Democratic Party of having a candidate capable of attracting support in the South, which was becoming increasingly Republican by the 1970s. ◆ *What drove so many southerners into the Republican Party?*

were gradually uniting behind a new and, before 1976, almost entirely un-known candidate: Jimmy Carter, a former governor of Georgia who ap-pealed to the general unhappiness with Washington by offering honesty, piety, and an outsider's skepticism of the federal government. Unhappiness with the economy and a general disenchantment with Ford enabled the De-mocrat to win a narrow victory. Carter received 50 percent of the popular vote to Ford's 47.9 percent and 297 electoral votes to Ford's 240.

The Trials of Jimmy Carter

Like Ford, Jimmy Carter assumed the presidency at a moment when the nation faced problems of staggering complexity and difficulty. But Carter seemed at times to make his predicament worse by a style of leadership that many considered self-righteous and inflexible.

Carter devoted much of his time to the problems of energy and the economy. Entering office in the midst of a recession, he moved first to reduce unemployment by raising public spending and cutting federal taxes. *Soaring Inflation* Unemployment declined, but inflation soared— mostly because of the continuing, sharp increases in energy prices by OPEC. During Carter's last two years in office, retail prices rose at well over a 10 percent annual rate. Like Nixon and Ford before him, Carter responded with a combination of tight money and calls for voluntary restraint. The conservative economists he appointed to head the Federal Reserve Board, determined to stop inflation, helped push interest rates to the highest levels in American history; at times, they exceeded 20 percent.

In the summer of 1979, instability in the Middle East produced a second major fuel shortage in the United States. In the midst of the crisis, OPEC announced another major price increase. Faced with increasing pressure to act, Carter retreated to Camp David, the presidential retreat in the Maryland mountains. Ten days later, he emerged to deliver a remarkable television address. It included a series of proposals for resolving the energy crisis. But it was most notable for Carter's bleak assessment of the national condition and his claim that there was a "crisis of confidence" that had struck "at the very heart and soul of our national will." The address became known as the "malaise" speech (although Carter himself had never used that word), and it helped fuel charges that the president was trying to blame his own problems on the American people. Carter's sudden firing of several members of his cabinet a few days later deepened his political problems.

Human Rights and National Interests

Among Jimmy Carter's most frequent campaign promises was a pledge to build a new basis for American foreign policy, one in which the defense of "human rights" would replace the pursuit of "selfish interests." Carter spoke out sharply and often about violations of human rights in many countries (including, most prominently, the Soviet Union). But the Carter administration also focused on several more traditional concerns. Carter completed negotiations begun several years earlier on a pair of treaties to *Panama Canal Treaty* turn over control of the Panama Canal to the government of Panama. After an acrimonious debate, the Senate ratified the treaties by 68 to 32, only one vote more than the necessary two-thirds majority.

Carter's greatest success was in arranging a peace treaty between Egypt and Israel. Middle East negotiations had seemed hopelessly stalled when Egyptian president Anwar Sadat accepted an invitation in November 1977 from Prime Minister Menachem Begin to visit Israel. In Tel Aviv, he announced that Egypt was now willing to accept the state of Israel as a legitimate political entity.

When talks between Israeli and Egyptian negotiators stalled, Carter invited Sadat and Begin to a summit conference at Camp David in September

FORGING THE CAMP DAVID ACCORDS Probably the greatest achievement of Jimmy Carter's generally frustrating presidency was his success in guiding Israel and Egypt toward a peaceful settlement of their longstanding grievances. While hosting Israeli Prime Minister Menachem Begin *(right)* and Egyptian president Anwar Sadat *(left)* at his Camp David retreat in September 1978, he helped the two leaders reach a historic agreement. *(UPI/Corbis-Bettmann)*

1978, and persuaded them to remain there for two weeks while he and others helped mediate the disputes between them. On September 17, Carter escorted the two leaders into the White House to announce agreement on a "framework" for an Egyptian-Israeli peace treaty. On March 26, 1979, Begin and Sadat returned together to the White House to sign a formal peace treaty between their two nations known as the Camp David Accords.

Camp David Accords

In the meantime, Carter continued trying to improve relations with China and the Soviet Union. He responded eagerly to the overtures of Deng Xiaoping, the new Chinese leader who was attempting to open his nation to the outside world. On December 15, 1978, Washington and Beijing announced the resumption of formal diplomatic relations. A few months later, Carter traveled to Vienna to meet with the aging and ailing Brezhnev to finish drafting the new SALT II arms control agreement, which set limits on the number of long-range missiles, bombers, and nuclear warheads on each side. Almost immediately, however, SALT II met with fierce conservative opposition in the United States.

The Year of the Hostages

Ever since the early 1950s, the United States had provided political support and, more recently, massive military assistance to the government of the Shah of Iran, hoping to make his nation a bulwark against Soviet expansion in the Middle East. By 1979, however, the Shah was in deep trouble with his own people. Many Iranians resented the repressive, authoritarian tactics through which the Shah had maintained his autocratic rule. At the same time, Islamic clergy (and much of the fiercely religious populace) opposed his efforts to modernize and westernize Iranian society. The combination of resentments produced a powerful revolutionary movement. In January 1979, the Shah fled the country.

Ayatollah Ruhollah Khomeini

By late 1979, power in Iran resided with a zealous religious leader, the Ayatollah Ruhollah Khomeini, who was fiercely anti-western and anti-American. In late October 1979, the deposed Shah arrived in New York to be treated for cancer. Days later, on November 4, an armed mob invaded the American embassy in Teheran, seized the diplomats and military personnel inside, and demanded the return of the Shah to Iran in exchange for their freedom. Fifty-three Americans remained hostages in the embassy for over a year.

Afghanistan Invaded

Only weeks after the hostage seizure, on December 27, 1979, Soviet troops invaded Afghanistan, the mountainous Islamic nation lying between the USSR and Iran. The Soviet Union had in fact been a power in Afghanistan for years, and the dominant force since April 1978. But while some observers claimed that the Soviet invasion was a Russian attempt to secure the status quo, Carter claimed it was a Russian "stepping stone to their possible control over much of the world's oil supplies" and the "gravest threat to world peace since World War II." Carter angrily imposed a series of economic sanctions on the Russians, canceled American participation in the 1980 summer Olympic Games in Moscow, and announced the withdrawal of SALT II from Senate consideration.

THE RISE OF THE NEW AMERICAN RIGHT

The jarring social and economic changes in American life in the 1960s and 1970s disillusioned many liberals, perplexed the already weakened left, and provided the right with its most important opportunity in generations to seize a position of authority in American life.

The Sunbelt and Its Politics

The most widely discussed demographic phenomenon of the 1970s was the rise of what became known as the "Sunbelt"—a term created to describe a collection of regions that emerged together in the postwar era to become the most dynamically growing parts of the country. The Sunbelt included the Southeast (particularly Florida), the Southwest (particularly Texas), and above all, California, which became the nation's most populous state in 1964, and continued to grow dramatically in the years that followed. By 1980, the population of the Sunbelt had risen to exceed that of the older industrial regions of the North and the East.

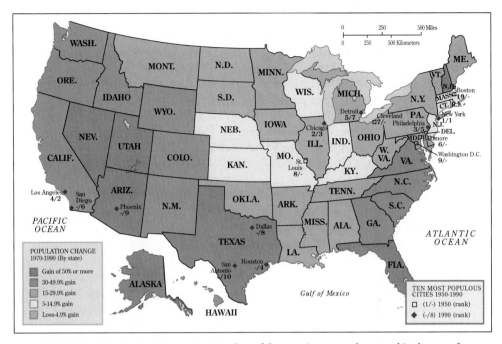

GROWTH OF THE SUNBELT, 1970–1990 One of the most important demographic changes of the last decades of the twentieth century was the shift of population out of traditional population centers in the Northeast and Midwest and toward the states of the so-called "Sunbelt"—most notably the Southwest and the Pacific coast. This map gives a dramatic illustration of the changing concentration of population between 1970 and 1990. The pale green states are those that lost population, while the purple and dark green states are those that made very significant gains (30 percent or more). ◆ *What was the impact of this population shift on the politics of the 1980s?*

The rise of the Sunbelt helped produce a change in the political climate. The strong populist traditions in the South and the West helped produce a strong opposition to the growth of government and a resentment of the proliferating regulations and restrictions that the liberal state was producing. Many of those regulations and restrictions—environmental laws, land-use restrictions, even the fifty-five-mile-per-hour speed limit created during the energy crisis to force motorists to conserve fuel—affected the West more than any other region. White southerners equated the federal government's effort to change racial norms in the region with what they believed was the tyranny of Reconstruction.

Growing Opposition to Government Regulation

The so-called Sagebrush Rebellion, which emerged in parts of the West in the late 1970s, mobilized conservative opposition to environmental laws and restrictions on development. It also sought to portray the West (which had benefited substantially from federal investment) as a victim of government control. Its members complained about the very large amounts of land the federal government owned in many western states and demanded that the land be opened for development.

Sagebrush Rebellion

Suburbanization also fueled the rise of the right. Not all suburbs bred conservative politics, of course; but the most militantly conservative communities in America—among them Orange County in southern California—were mostly suburbs. Many suburbs insulated their residents from contact with different groups—through the relative homogeneity of the population, through the transferring of retail and even work space into suburban office parks and shopping malls. The seemingly tranquil life of the suburb reinforced the conservative view that other parts of the nation—cities in particular—were abandoning the values and norms that society required.

Religious Revivalism

In the 1960s, organized religion had experienced a conspicuous decline. But in the 1970s the United States experienced the beginning of a major religious revival. Some of the new religious enthusiasm found expression in the rise of various cults and pseudo-faiths: the Church of Scientology; the Unification Church of the Reverend Sun Myung Moon; even the tragic People's Temple, whose members committed mass suicide in their jungle retreat in Guyana in 1978. But the most important impulse of the religious revival was the growth of evangelical Christianity.

Surging Evangelicalism   Evangelicals have in common a belief in personal conversion (being "born again") through direct communication with God. Evangelical religion had been the dominant form of Christianity in America through much of its history, and a substantial subculture since the late nineteenth century. In its modern form, it became increasingly visible during the early 1950s, when evangelicals such as Billy Graham and Pentecostals such as Oral Roberts began to attract huge national (and international) followings for their energetic revivalism.

By the late 1970s, evangelical Christians were becoming more visible and more assertive. More than 70 million Americans now described themselves as "born-again" Christians—men and women who had established a "direct personal relationship with Jesus." Christian evangelicals owned their own newspapers, magazines, radio stations, and television networks. They operated their own schools and universities. And one of them ultimately occupied the White House itself—Jimmy Carter, who during the 1976 campaign had talked proudly of his own "conversion experience" and who continued openly to proclaim his "born-again" Christian faith during his years in office.

For Jimmy Carter and for some others, evangelical Christianity had formed the basis for a commitment to racial and economic justice and world peace. For many evangelicals, however, the message of the new religion was very different—but no less political. In the 1970s, some Christian evangelicals became active on the political and cultural right. They were alarmed by what they considered the spread of immorality and disorder in American life; and they were concerned about the way a secular culture was intruding into their communities and schools and families. Many evangelical men and women feared the growth of feminism and the threat they believed it posed to the traditional family, and they resented the way in which government policies advanced the goals of the women's movement. Particularly alarming to them were Supreme Court decisions eliminating all religious observance from schools and, later, the decision guaranteeing women the right to an abortion.

By the late 1970s, the "Christian right" had become a powerful political force. Jerry Falwell, a fundamentalist minister in Virginia with a substantial television audience, launched a highly visible movement he called the Moral Majority. The Pentecostal minister Pat Robertson began a political movement of his own and, in the 1990s, launched an organization known as the Christian Coalition. These and other organizations of the Christian right opposed federal interference in local affairs; denounced abortion, divorce, feminism, and homosexuality; defended unrestricted free enterprise; and supported a strong American posture in the world. Some denied the scientific doctrine of evolution and instead urged the teaching in schools of the biblical story of the Creation. Their goal was a new era in which Christian values once again dominated American life.

Christian Coalition

The Emergence of the New Right

Evangelical Christians were an important part, but only a part, of what became known as the new right—a diverse but powerful movement that enjoyed rapid growth in the 1970s and early 1980s. It had begun to take shape after the 1964 election, in which Barry Goldwater had suffered his shattering defeat. Energetic organizers responded to that disaster by building a new and powerful set of right-wing institutions to help conservatives campaign more effectively in the future. Beginning in the 1970s, largely because of these organizational advances, conservatives found themselves almost always better funded and organized than their opponents. By the late 1970s, there were right-wing think tanks, consulting firms, lobbyists, foundations, and scholarly centers.

Barry Goldwater

Another factor in the revival of the right was the emergence of a credible right-wing leadership in the late 1960s and early 1970s in the person of Ronald Reagan. Once a moderately successful actor, he had moved into politics in the early 1960s and in 1964 delivered a memorable television speech on behalf of Goldwater. After Goldwater's defeat, he worked quickly to seize the leadership of the conservative wing of the party. In 1966, with the support of a group of wealthy conservatives, he won the first of two terms as governor of California.

The presidency of Gerald Ford also played an important role in the rise of the right. Ford, probably without realizing it, touched on some of the right's rawest nerves. He appointed as vice president Nelson Rockefeller, the liberal Republican governor of New York and an heir to one of America's great fortunes; many conservatives had been demonizing Rockefeller and his family for more than twenty years. Ford proposed an amnesty program for draft resisters, embraced and even extended the hated Nixon-Kissinger policies of détente, presided over the fall of Vietnam, and agreed to cede the Panama Canal to Panama. When Reagan challenged Ford in the 1976 Republican primaries, the president survived, barely, only by dumping Nelson Rockefeller from the ticket and agreeing to a platform largely written by conservatives.

The Tax Revolt

At least equally important to the success of the new right was a new and potent conservative issue: the tax revolt. It had its public beginnings in 1978, when Howard Jarvis, a conservative activist in California, launched the first successful major citizens' tax revolt in California with Proposition 13, a referendum question on the state ballot rolling back property tax rates. Similar antitax movements soon began in other states and eventually spread to national politics.

Proposition 13

In Proposition 13 and similar initiatives, members of the right succeeded in separating the issue of taxes from the issue of what taxes supported. Instead of attacking popular programs such as Social Security, they attacked taxes themselves and argued that much of the money government raised through taxes was wasted. Virtually no one liked to pay taxes, and as the economy grew weaker and the relative burden of paying taxes grew heavier, that resentment naturally rose.

The Campaign of 1980

By the time of the crises in Iran and Afghanistan, Jimmy Carter was in desperate political trouble—his standing in popularity polls lower than that of any president in history. Senator Edward Kennedy, younger brother of John and Robert Kennedy, challenged him in the primaries. And while Carter managed to withstand the confrontation with Kennedy and win his party's nomination, Carter's campaign aroused little popular enthusiasm as he prepared to face a powerful challenge.

Challenge from Kennedy

The Republican Party, in the meantime, had rallied enthusiastically behind the man who, four years earlier, had nearly stolen the nomination from Gerald Ford. Ronald Reagan was a sharp critic of the excesses of the federal government. He linked his campaign to the spreading tax revolt by promising substantial tax cuts. He also championed a restoration of American "strength" and "pride" in the world.

1980 Election

On election day 1980, the anniversary of the seizure of the hostages in Iran, Reagan swept to victory, winning 51 percent of the vote to 41 percent for Jimmy Carter,

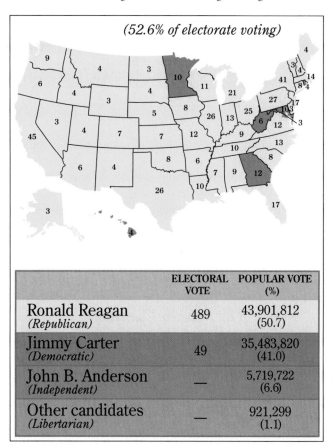

(52.6% of electorate voting)

	ELECTORAL VOTE	POPULAR VOTE (%)
Ronald Reagan *(Republican)*	489	43,901,812 (50.7)
Jimmy Carter *(Democratic)*	49	35,483,820 (41.0)
John B. Anderson *(Independent)*	—	5,719,722 (6.6)
Other candidates *(Libertarian)*	—	921,299 (1.1)

THE ELECTION OF 1980 Although Ronald Reagan won only slightly more than half of the popular vote in the 1980 presidential election, his electoral majority was overwhelming—a reflection to a large degree of the deep unpopularity of President Jimmy Carter in 1980. ◆ *What had made Carter so unpopular?*

For an interactive version of this map go to www.mhhe.com/unfinishednation4ch33maps

and 7 percent for John Anderson—a moderate Republican congressman from Illinois who had mounted an independent campaign. The Republican Party won control of the Senate for the first time since 1952; and although the Democrats retained a modest majority in the House, the lower chamber too seemed firmly in the hands of conservatives.

On the day of Reagan's inauguration, the American hostages in Iran were released after their 444-day ordeal. The government of Iran, desperate for funds to support its floundering war against neighboring Iraq, had ordered the hostages freed in return for a release of billions in Iranian assets that the Carter administration had frozen in American banks. Americans welcomed the hostages home with demonstrations of joy and patriotism not seen since the end of World War II. But while the celebration in

1945 had marked a great American triumph, the euphoria in 1981 marked something quite different—a troubled nation grasping for reassurance. Ronald Reagan set out to provide it.

THE "REAGAN REVOLUTION"

Ronald Reagan assumed the presidency in January 1981 promising a change in government more fundamental than any since the New Deal of fifty years before. While his eight years in office produced a significant shift in public policy, they brought nothing so fundamental as many of his supporters had hoped or his opponents had feared. But Reagan succeeded brilliantly in making his own engaging personality the central fact of American politics in the 1980s. He also benefited from the power of the diverse coalition that had united behind him.

The Reagan Coalition

The Reagan coalition included a relatively small but highly influential group of wealthy Americans firmly committed to capitalism and to unfettered economic growth. They believed that the market offers the best solutions to most problems, and they shared a deep hostility to most (although not all) government interference in markets. Central to this group's agenda in the 1980s was opposition to what it considered the "redistributive" politics of the federal government (and especially its highly progressive tax structure) and hostility to the rise of what they believed were "antibusiness" government regulations. Reagan courted these free-market conservatives carefully and effectively, and in the end it was their interests his administration most effectively served.

Free-Market Conservatives

A second element of the Reagan coalition was a small but influential group of intellectuals commonly known as "neo-conservatives," who gave to the right something it had not had in many years—a firm base among "opinion leaders," people with access to the most influential public forums for ideas. Many of these people had once been liberals and, before that, socialists. But during the turmoil of the 1960s, they had become alarmed by what they considered a dangerous and destructive radicalism. Neo-conservatives were sympathetic to the complaints and demands of capitalists, but their principal concern was to reassert legitimate authority and reaffirm Western democratic, anticommunist values and commitments. They considered themselves engaged in a battle to "win back the culture"—from the crass, radical ideas that had polluted it.

"Neo-Conservatives"

RONALD AND NANCY REAGAN The president and the first lady greet guests at a White House social event. Nancy Reagan was most visible in her efforts to make the White House, and her husband's presidency, seem more glamorous than those of most recent administrations. But she also played an important, if quiet, policy role in the administration. *(Dirck Halstead/Getty Images)*

These groups formed an uneasy alliance with what became known as the "new right." The new right shared a fundamental distrust of the "eastern establishment": a suspicion of its motives and goals; a sense that it exercised a dangerous, secret power in American life. These populist conservatives expressed the kinds of concerns that outsiders, non-elites, have traditionally voiced in American society: an opposition to centralized power and influence, a fear of living in a world where distant, hostile forces are controlling society and threatening individual freedom and community autonomy. It was a testament to Ronald Reagan's political skills and personal charm that he was able to generate enthusiastic support from these populist conservatives while at the same time appealing to more elite conservative groups whose concerns were in many ways antithetical to those of the new right.

Reagan in the White House

Even many people who disagreed with Reagan's policies found themselves

Reagan's Personal Appeal

drawn to his attractive and carefully honed public image. He turned seventy a few weeks after taking office and was the oldest man ever to serve as president. But through most of his presidency, he appeared to be vigorous, resilient, even youthful. When he was wounded in an assassination attempt in 1981, he joked with doctors on his way into surgery and appeared to bounce back from the ordeal with remarkable speed. Even when things went wrong, as they often did, the blame seldom seemed to attach to Reagan himself (inspiring some Democrats to begin referring to him as the "Teflon president").

Reagan was not much involved in the day-to-day affairs of running the government; he surrounded himself with tough, energetic administrators who insulated him from many of the pressures of the office and who apparently relied on him largely for general guidance, not specific decisions. At times, the president revealed a startling ignorance about the nature of his own policies or the actions of his subordinates. But Reagan did make active use of his office to generate public support for his administration's programs.

"Supply-Side" Economics

Reagan's 1980 campaign for the presidency had promised to restore the economy to health by a bold experiment that became known as "supply-side"

Reaganomics

economics or, to some, "Reaganomics." Supply-side economics operated from the assumption that the woes of the American economy were in large part a result of excessive taxation, which left inadequate capital available to investors to stimulate growth. The solution, therefore, was to reduce taxes, with particularly generous benefits to corporations and wealthy individuals, in order to encourage new investments.

In its first months in office, the new administration hastily assembled a legislative program based on the supply-side idea. It proposed $40 billion in budget reductions and managed to win congressional approval of

Tax Cuts

almost all of them. In addition, the president proposed a bold three-year, 30 percent reduction on both individual and corporate tax rates. In the summer of 1981, Congress passed it too, after lowering the reductions to 25 percent. Reagan was successful because he had a disciplined Republican majority in the Senate, and because the Democratic majority in the House was weak and riddled with defectors.

Men and women whom Reagan appointed fanned out through the executive branch of government committed to reducing the role of government in American economic life. "Deregulation," an idea many Democrats had begun to embrace in the Carter years, became almost a religion in the Reagan administration. Secretary of the Interior James Watt had been a major figure in the Sagebrush Rebellion, a movement among western conservatives to fight federal environmental regulations, which they believed had a particularly devastating effect on their region's economy. Watt opened up public lands and water to development. The Environmental Protection Agency (before its directors were indicted for corruption) relaxed or entirely eliminated enforcement of major environmental laws and regulations.

By early 1982, however, the nation had sunk into the most severe recession since the 1930s. The Reagan economic program was not directly to blame for the problems, but neither did it offer a quick solution to them. In 1982 unemployment reached 11 percent, its highest level in over forty years. But before the recession could do great damage to Reagan, the economy recovered more rapidly and impressively *Economic Recovery* than almost anyone had expected. By late 1983, unemployment had fallen to 8.2 percent, and it declined steadily for several years after that. The gross national product had grown 3.6 percent in a year, the largest increase since the mid-1970s. Inflation had fallen below 5 percent. The economy continued to grow, and both inflation and unemployment remained low through most of the decade.

The recovery was a result of many things. The years of tight money policies by the Federal Reserve Board had helped lower inflation; perhaps equally important, the Board had lowered interest rates early in 1983 in response to the recession. A worldwide "energy glut" and the virtual collapse of the OPEC cartel had produced at least a temporary end to the inflationary pressures of spiraling fuel costs. And staggering federal budget deficits were pumping billions of dollars into the flagging economy. As a result, consumer spending and business investment both increased. The stock market rose up from its doldrums of the 1970s and began a sustained and historic boom. In August 1982, the Dow Jones Industrial Average stood at 777. Five years later it had passed 2,000. Despite a frightening crash in the fall of 1987, the market continued to grow for more than another decade: in early 2000, the Dow Jones average briefly passed 11,000.

The Fiscal Crisis

The economic revival did little at first to reduce the staggering, and to many Americans alarming, federal budget deficits *Growing Budget Deficits* (the gap between revenue and spending in a single year) or to slow the growth in the national debt (the debt the nation accumulates over time as a result of its annual deficits). By the mid-1980s, this growing fiscal crisis had become one of the central issues in American politics. Having entered office promising a balanced budget within four years, Reagan presided over record budget deficits and accumulated more debt in his eight years in office than the American government had accumulated in

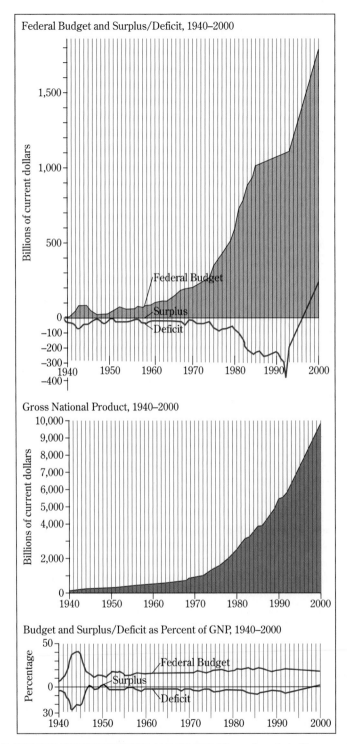

FEDERAL BUDGET SURPLUS/DEFICIT, 1940 TO 2000 These charts help illustrate why the pattern of federal deficits seemed so alarming to Americans in the 1980s, and also why those deficits proved much less damaging to the economy than many predicted. ◆ *What factors contributed to the increasing deficits of the 1980s? How were those deficits eliminated in the 1990s?*

its entire previous history. Before the 1980s, the highest single-year budget deficit in American history had been $66 billion (in 1976). Throughout the 1980s, the annual budget deficit consistently exceeded $100 billion (and in 1991 peaked at $268 billion). The national debt rose from $907 billion in 1980 to nearly $3.5 trillion by 1991.

The enormous deficits had many causes. The budget suffered from enormous increases in the costs of "entitlement" programs (especially Social Security and Medicare), a result of the aging of the population and dramatic increases in the cost of health care. The 1981 tax cuts, the largest in American history, also contributed to the deficit. The massive increase in military spending on which the Reagan administration insisted added much more to the federal budget than its cuts in domestic spending removed.

In the face of these deficits, the administration proposed further cuts in "discretionary" domestic spending, which included many programs aimed at the poorest (and politically weakest) Americans. By the end of Reagan's third year in office, funding for domestic programs had been cut nearly as far as Congress (and, apparently, the public) was willing to tolerate, and still no end to the rising deficit was in sight. By the late 1980s, many fiscal conservatives were calling for a constitutional amendment mandating a balanced budget—a provision the president himself claimed to support. But Congress never approved the amendment.

Reagan and the World

Relations with the Soviet Union, which had been steadily deteriorating in the last years of the Carter administration, grew still chillier in the first years of the Reagan presidency. The president spoke harshly of the Soviet regime (which he once called the "evil empire"), accusing it of sponsoring world terrorism and declaring that any armaments negotiations must be linked to negotiations on Soviet behavior in other areas. Although the president had long denounced the SALT II arms control treaty as unfavorable to the United States, he continued to honor its provisions. But the Reagan administration at first made little progress toward arms control in other areas. In fact, the president proposed the most ambitious (and potentially most expensive) new military program in many years: the Strategic Defense Initiative (SDI), widely known as "Star Wars" (after the *"Star Wars"* popular movie of that name). Reagan claimed that SDI, through the use of lasers and satellites, could provide an effective shield against incoming missiles and thus make nuclear war obsolete. The Soviet Union claimed that the new program would elevate the arms race to new and more dangerous levels (a complaint many domestic critics of SDI shared) and insisted that any arms control agreement begin with an American abandonment of SDI.

The escalation of Cold War tensions and the slowing of arms control initiatives helped produce an important popular movement in Europe and the United States calling for an end to nuclear weapons buildups. In America, the principal goal of the movement was a "nuclear freeze," an agreement between the two superpowers not to expand their atomic arsenals. In what many believed was the largest mass demonstration in American history, nearly a million people rallied in New York City's Central Park in 1982 to support the freeze. Perhaps partly in response to this growing pressure, the administration began tentative efforts to revive arms control negotiations in 1983.

Reagan Doctrine

It also created a new policy, which became known as the Reagan Doctrine, to help groups resisting communism in the Third World. The most conspicuous examples of the new activism came in Latin America. In October 1982, the administration sent American soldiers and marines into the tiny Caribbean island of Grenada to oust an anti-American Marxist regime that showed signs of forging a relationship with Moscow. In El Salvador, whose government was fighting left-wing revolutionaries, the administation provided increased military and economic assistance. In neighboring Nicaragua, a pro-American dictatorship had fallen to the revolutionary "Sandinistas" in 1979; the new government had grown increasingly anti-American (and increasingly Marxist) throughout the early 1980s. The Reagan administration supported the so-called contras, an antigovernment guerrilla movement fighting (without great success) to topple the Sandinista regime.

In other parts of the world, the administration's tough rhetoric seemed to hide an instinctive restraint. In June 1982, the Israeli army launched an invasion of Lebanon in an effort to drive guerrillas of the Palestinian Liberation Organization from the country. An American peacekeeping force entered Beirut to supervise the evacuation of PLO forces from Lebanon. American marines then remained in the city, apparently to protect the fragile Lebanese government. Now identified with one faction in the struggle, Americans became the targets in 1983 of a terrorist bombing of a U.S. military barracks in Beirut that left 241 marines dead. Rather than become more deeply involved in the Lebanese struggle, Reagan withdrew American forces.

Terrorism

The disaster in Lebanon was an example of the changing character of Third World struggles: an increasing reliance on terrorism by otherwise powerless groups to advance their political aims. A series of terrorist acts in the 1980s—attacks on airplanes, cruise ships, commercial and diplomatic posts; the seizing of American and other Western hostages—alarmed and frightened much of the Western world. The Reagan administration spoke bravely about its resolve to punish terrorism; and at one point in 1986, the president ordered American planes to bomb sites in Tripoli, the capital of Libya, whose controversial leader Muammar al-Qaddafi was widely believed to be a leading sponsor of terrorism. In general, however, American leaders had little success in identifying or controlling terrorists.

The Election of 1984

Reagan approached the campaign of 1984 at the head of a united Republican Party firmly committed to his candidacy. The Democrats nominated former vice president Walter Mondale, the early frontrunner, who fought off challenges from Senator Gary Hart of Colorado and the magnetic Jesse Jackson, who had established himself as the nation's most prominent spokesman for minorities and the poor. Mondale brought momentary excitement to the Democratic campaign by selecting a woman, Representative Geraldine Ferraro of New York, to be his running mate and the first female candidate ever to appear on a national ticket.

Reagan's triumphant campaign scarcely took note of his opponents and spoke instead of what he *Reagan Reelected* claimed was the remarkable revival of American fortunes and spirits under his leadership. His victory in 1984 was decisive. He won approximately 59 percent of the vote, and carried every state but Mondale's native Minnesota and the District of Columbia. But Reagan was much stronger than his party. Democrats gained a seat in the Senate and maintained only slightly reduced control of the House of Representatives.

To many Reagan supporters, the 1984 election seemed to be the dawn of a new conservative era. But almost no one anticipated the revolutionary changes that would change the world, and America's place in it, within a very few years. The election of 1984, therefore, was not so much the first of a new era as the last of an old one. It was the final campaign of the Cold War.

AMERICA AND THE WANING OF THE COLD WAR

Many factors contributed to the collapse of the Soviet empire. The long, stalemated war in Afghanistan proved at least as disastrous to the Soviet Union as the Vietnam War had been to America. The government in Moscow had failed to address a long-term economic decline in the Soviet republics and the Eastern-bloc nations. Restiveness with the heavy-handed policies of communist police states was growing throughout much of the Soviet empire. But the most visible factor at the time was the emergence of Mikhail Gorbachev, *Mikhail Gorbachev* who succeeded to the leadership of the Soviet Union in 1985 and, to the surprise of almost everyone (probably including himself), very quickly became the most revolutionary figure in world politics in at least four decades.

SMASHING THE WALL Once it became clear in November 1989 that the East German government was no longer defending the wall that had divided Berlin for nearly thirty years, Germans on both sides of the divide swarmed over it in celebration. Here, a West German takes a sledgehammer to the already battered wall as East German border guards passively look on. *(Reuters/Corbis-Bettmann)*

The Fall of the Soviet Union

Glasnost and Perestroika Gorbachev quickly transformed Soviet politics with two dramatic new initiatives. The first he called *glasnost* (openness): the dismantling of many of the repressive mechanisms that had been conspicuous features of Soviet life for over half a century. The other policy Gorbachev called *perestroika* (reform): an effort to restructure the rigid and unproductive Soviet economy by introducing, among other things, such elements of capitalism as private ownership and the profit motive. He also began to transform Soviet foreign policy.

The severe economic problems at home evidently convinced Gorbachev that the Soviet Union could no longer sustain its extended commitments around the world. As early as 1987, he began reducing Soviet influence in Eastern Europe. And in 1989, in the space of a few months, every communist state in Europe—Poland, Hungary, Czechoslovakia, Bulgaria, Romania, East Germany, Yugoslavia, and Albania—either overthrew its government or forced it to transform itself into an essentially noncommunist (and in some cases, actively anticommunist) regime.

In May 1989, students in China launched a mass movement calling for greater democratization. But in June, hard-line leaders seized control of the government and sent military forces to crush the uprising. The result was a bloody massacre on June 3, 1989, in Tiananmen Square in Beijing, in which an unknown number of demonstrators died. The assault crushed the democracy movement and restored hard-liners to power. It did not, however, stop China's efforts to modernize and even westernize its economy.

Tiananmen Square

But China was an exception to a widespread movement toward democratization. Early in 1990, the government of South Africa, long an international pariah for its rigid enforcement of "apartheid" (a system designed to protect white supremacy), began a cautious retreat from its traditional policies. Among other things, it legalized the chief black party in the nation, the African National Congress (ANC), which had been banned for decades, and released from prison the leader of the ANC, Nelson Mandela, who had been in jail for twenty-seven years. Over the next several years, the South African government repealed its apartheid laws. And in 1994, there were national elections in which all South Africans could participate. As a result, Nelson Mandela became the first black president of South Africa.

In 1991, communism began to collapse in the Soviet Union itself. An unsuccessful coup by hard-line Soviet leaders on August 19 precipitated a dramatic unraveling of communist power. Within days, the coup itself collapsed in the face of resistance from the public and crucial elements within the military. Mikhail Gorbachev returned to power, but it soon became evident that the legitimacy of both the Communist Party and the central Soviet government had been fatally injured. By the end of August, many of the republics of the Soviet Union had declared independence; the Soviet government was clearly powerless to stop the fragmentation. Gorbachev himself finally resigned as leader of the now virtually powerless Communist Party and Soviet government, and the Soviet Union ceased to exist.

Collapse of the USSR

The last years of the Reagan administration coincided with the first years of the Gorbachev regime; and while Reagan was skeptical of Gorbachev at first, he gradually became convinced that the Soviet leader was sincere in his desire for reform. At a summit meeting with Reagan in Reykjavik, Iceland, in 1986, Gorbachev proposed reducing the nuclear arsenals of both sides by 50 percent or more, although continuing disputes over Reagan's commitment to the SDI program prevented agreements. But in 1988, the two superpowers signed a treaty eliminating American and Soviet intermediate-range nuclear forces (INF) from Europe—the most significant arms control agreement of the nuclear age. At about the same time, Gorbachev ended the Soviet Union's long and frustrating military involvement in Afghanistan.

The Fading of the Reagan Revolution

For a time, the dramatic changes around the world and Reagan's personal popularity deflected attention from a series of scandals that might well have destroyed another administration. There were revelations of illegality, corruption, and ethical lapses in the Environmental Protection Agency, the CIA, the Department of Defense, the Department of Labor, the Department of Justice, and the Department of Housing and Urban

Savings and Loan Crisis

Development. A more serious scandal emerged within the savings and loan industry, which the Reagan administration had helped deregulate in the early 1980s. By the end of the decade the industry was in chaos, and the government was forced to step in to prevent a complete collapse. The cost of the debacle to the public eventually ran to more than half a trillion dollars.

But the most politically damaging scandal of the Reagan years came to light in November 1986, when the White House conceded that it had sold weapons to the revolutionary government of Iran as part of a largely unsuccessful effort to secure the release of several Americans being held hostage by radical Islamic groups in the Middle East. Even more damaging was the revelation that some of the money from the arms deal with Iran had been covertly and illegally funneled into a fund to aid the contras in Nicaragua.

In the months that followed, aggressive reporting and a series of congressional hearings exposed a widespread pattern of covert activities orchestrated by the White House and dedicated to advancing the administration's foreign policy aims through secret and at times illegal means. The principal figure in this covert world appeared at first to be an obscure

Oliver North

marine lieutenant colonel assigned to the staff of the National Security Council, Oliver North. But gradually it became clear that North was acting in concert with other, more powerful figures in the administration. The Iran-contra scandal, as it became known, did serious damage to the Reagan presidency—even though the investigations were never able decisively to tie the president himself to the most serious violations of the law.

The Election of 1988

The fraying of the Reagan administration helped the Democrats regain control of the United States Senate in 1986 and fueled hopes in the party for a presidential victory in 1988. Michael Dukakis, a three-term governor of Massachusetts, eventually captured the nomination, even though he was a dry, even dull campaigner. But Vice President George Bush, the largely unopposed Republican candidate, had also failed to spark any real public enthusiasm. He entered the last months of the campaign well behind Dukakis.

Bush's Negative Campaign

Beginning at the Republican Convention, however, Bush staged a remarkable turnaround by making his campaign a long, relentless attack on Dukakis, tying him to all

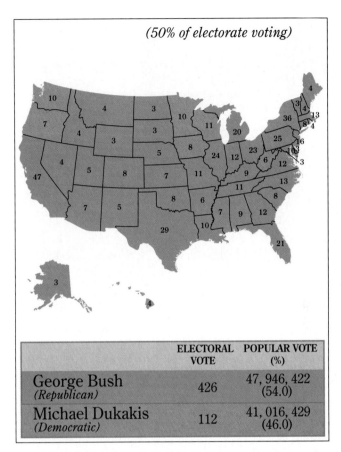

(50% of electorate voting)

	ELECTORAL VOTE	POPULAR VOTE (%)
George Bush *(Republican)*	426	47, 946, 422 (54.0)
Michael Dukakis *(Democratic)*	112	41, 016, 429 (46.0)

THE ELECTION OF 1988 Democrats had high hopes going into the election of 1988, but Vice President George Bush won a decisive victory over Michael Dukakis, who did only slightly better than Walter Mondale had done four years earlier. ◆ *What made it so difficult for a Democrat to challenge the Republicans in 1988 after eight years of a Republican administration?*

the unpopular social and cultural stances Americans had come to identify with "liberals." Bush won a substantial victory in November: 54 percent of the popular vote to Dukakis's 46 percent, and 426 electoral votes to Dukakis's 112. But Bush carried few Republicans into office with him; the Democrats retained secure majorities in both houses of Congress.

The Bush Presidency

The Bush presidency was notable for the dramatic developments in international affairs with which it coincided and at times helped to advance, and for the absence of important initiatives or ideas on domestic issues.

The broad popularity Bush enjoyed during his first three years in office was partly a result of his subdued, unthreatening public image. But it was primarily because of the wonder and excitement with which Americans

GORBACHEV AND BUSH When Bush became president in 1989, the Cold War with the Soviet Union—although much less intense than it had been several years earlier—was still in progress. By the time he left office in 1993, the Cold War was over; the once "captive nations" of eastern Europe were free of Soviet domination; and the Soviet Union itself had unravelled and dissolved. Much of the impetus for these changes originated with the last Soviet leader, Mikhail Gorbachev, whose efforts at reform unleashed forces he ultimately could not control. But before he lost power, he negotiated a series of historic agreements with the United States—some of them through summit meetings such as this one in Washington in 1990. *(Archive/Ron Sachs/Consolidated News Pictures/Getty Images)*

viewed the dramatic events in the rest of the world. Bush moved cautiously at first in dealing with the changes in the Soviet Union. But like Reagan, he eventually cooperated with Gorbachev and reached a series of significant agreements with the Soviet Union in its waning years. In the three years after the INF agreement in 1988, the United States and the Soviet Union moved rapidly toward even more far-reaching arms reduction agreements.

Arms Reduction

On domestic issues, the Bush administration was less successful—partly because the president himself seemed to have little interest in promoting a domestic agenda and partly because he faced serious obstacles. His administration inherited a staggering burden of debt and a federal deficit that had been out of control for nearly a decade. Any domestic agenda that required significant federal spending was, therefore, incompatible with the president's pledge to reduce the deficit and his 1988 campaign promise of "no new taxes." Bush was constantly concerned about the right wing of his own party and, in his eagerness to ingratiate himself with it, took divisive positions on such cultural issues as abortion and affirmative action that damaged his ability to work with the Democratic Congress.

Despite this political stalemate, Congress and the White House managed on occasion to agree on significant measures. In 1990, the president bowed to congressional pressure and agreed to a significant tax increase as part of a multiyear "budget package" designed to reduce the deficit—thus violating his own 1988 campaign pledge of "no new taxes."

But the most serious domestic problem facing the Bush administration was one for which neither the president nor Congress had any answer: a recession that began *1990 Recession* late in 1990 and became more serious in 1991 and 1992. Because of the enormous level of debt that corporations (and individuals) had accumulated in the 1980s, the recession caused an unusual number of bankruptcies. It also produced fear and frustration among middle- and working-class Americans.

The Gulf War

The events of 1989–1991 had left the United States in the unanticipated position of being the only real superpower in the world. The Bush administration, therefore, had to consider what to do with America's formidable political and military power in a world in which the major justification for that power—the Soviet threat—was now gone.

The events of 1989–1991 suggested two possible answers, both of which had some effect on policy. One was that the United States would reduce its military strength dramatically and concentrate its energies and resources on pressing domestic problems. There was, in fact, considerable movement in that direction both in Congress and within the administration. The other was that America would continue to use its power actively, not to fight communism but to defend its regional and economic interests. In 1989, that led the administration to order an invasion of Panama, which overthrew the unpopular military leader Manuel Noriega (under indictment in the United States for drug trafficking) and replaced him with an elected, pro-American regime. And in 1990, that same impulse drew the United States into the turbulent politics of the Middle East.

On August 2, 1990, the armed forces of Iraq invaded and quickly overwhelmed their small, oil-rich neighbor, the emirate of Kuwait. Saddam Hussein, the militaris- *Saddam Hussein* tic leader of Iraq, soon announced that he was annexing Kuwait. After some initial indecision, the Bush administration agreed to lead other nations in a campaign to force Iraq out of Kuwait—through the pressure of economic sanctions if possible, through military force if necessary. Within a few weeks, Bush had persuaded virtually every important government in the world, including the Soviet Union and almost all the Arab and Islamic states, to join in a United Nations–sanctioned trade embargo of Iraq.

At the same time, the United States and its allies (including the British, French, Egyptians, and Saudis) began deploying a massive military force along the border between Kuwait and Saudi Arabia, a force that ultimately reached 690,000 troops (425,000 of them American). And on January 16, American and allied air forces began a massive bombardment of Iraqi troops in Kuwait and of military and industrial installations in Iraq itself.

The allied bombing continued for six weeks. On February 23, allied *General Norman Schwartzkopf* (primarily American) forces under the command of General Norman Schwarzkopf began a major ground offensive—not primarily against the heavily entrenched Iraqi forces along the Kuwait border, as expected, but to the north of them into Iraq itself. The allied armies encountered almost no resistance and suffered only light casualties (141 fatalities). Estimates of Iraqi deaths in the war were 100,000 or more. On February 28, Iraq announced its acceptance of allied terms for a cease-fire, and the brief Persian Gulf War came to an end.

The quick and (for America) relatively painless victory over Iraq was highly popular in the United States. But the tyrannical regime of Saddam Hussein survived, in a weakened form but showing few signs of retreat from its militaristic ambitions.

The Election of 1992

President Bush's popularity reached a record high in the immediate aftermath of the Gulf War. But the glow of that victory faded quickly as the recession worsened in late 1991, and as the administration failed to produce any effective policies for combating it.

Because the early maneuvering for the 1992 presidential election occurred when President Bush's popularity remained high, many leading Democrats declined to run. That gave Bill Clinton, the young five-term governor of Arkansas, an opportunity to emerge early as the front-runner, as a result of a skillful campaign that emphasized broad economic issues instead of the racial and cultural questions that had so divided the Democrats in the past. Clinton survived a bruising primary campaign and a series of damaging personal controversies to win his party's nomination. And George Bush withstood an embarrassing primary challenge from the conservative journalist Pat Buchanan to become the Republican nominee again.

Ross Perot Complicating the campaign was the emergence of Ross Perot, a blunt, forthright Texas billionaire who became an independent candidate by tapping popular resentment of the federal bureaucracy and by promising tough, uncompromising leadership to deal with the fiscal crisis and other problems of government. At several moments in the spring, Perot led both Bush and Clinton in public opinion polls. In July, as he began to face hostile scrutiny from the media, he abruptly withdrew from the race. But early in October, he reentered and soon regained much (although never all) of his early support.

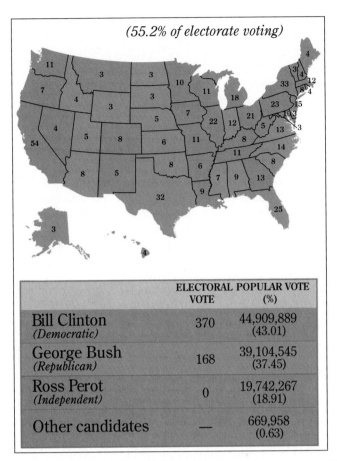

(55.2% of electorate voting)

	ELECTORAL VOTE	POPULAR VOTE (%)
Bill Clinton *(Democratic)*	370	44,909,889 (43.01)
George Bush *(Republican)*	168	39,104,545 (37.45)
Ross Perot *(Independent)*	0	19,742,267 (18.91)
Other candidates	—	669,958 (0.63)

THE ELECTION OF 1992 For the first time since 1976, a Democrat captured the White House in the 1992 election. And although the third party candidacy of Ross Perot deprived Bill Clinton of an absolute majority, he nevertheless defeated George Bush by a decisive margin in both the popular and electoral vote. ◆ *What factors had eroded President Bush's once-broad popularity by 1992? What explained the strong showing of Ross Perot?*

For an interactive version of this map go to www.mhhe.com/unfinishednation4ch33maps

After a campaign in which the economy and the president's unpopularity were the principal issues, Clinton won a clear, but hardly overwhelming, victory over Bush   *Clinton Elected* and Perot. He received 43 percent of the vote in the three-way race, to the president's 38 percent and Perot's 19 percent (the best showing for a third-party or independent candidate since Theodore Roosevelt in 1912). Clinton won 370 electoral votes to Bush's 168; Perot won none. Democrats retained control of both houses of Congress.

CONCLUSION

America in the late 1970s was, by the standards of its own recent history, an unusually troubled nation: numbed by the Watergate scandals, the fall of Vietnam, and perhaps most of all the nation's increasing economic difficulties. The unhappy presidencies of Gerald Ford and Jimmy Carter provided little relief from these accumulating problems and anxieties. Indeed, in the last year of the Carter presidency, the nation's prospects seemed particularly grim in light of severe economic problems, a traumatic seizure of American hostages in Iran, and a Soviet invasion of Afghanistan.

In the midst of these problems, American conservatives were slowly and steadily preparing for an impressive revival. A coalition of disparate but impassioned groups on the right—including a large movement known as the "new right" with vaguely populist impulses—gained strength from the nation's troubles and from their own success in winning support for a broad-ranging revolt against taxes. Their efforts culminated in the election of 1980, when Ronald Reagan became the most conservative man in at least sixty years to be elected president of the United States.

Reagan's first term was a dramatic contrast to the troubled presidencies that had preceded it. He won substantial victories in Congress (cutting taxes, reducing spending on domestic programs, building up the military). Perhaps equally important, he made his own engaging personality one of the central political forces in national life. Easily reelected in 1984, he seemed to have solidified the conservative grip on national political life. In his second term, a series of scandals and misadventures—and the president's own declining energy—limited the administration's effectiveness. Nevertheless, Reagan's personal popularity remained high, and the economy continued to prosper—factors that helped his vice president, George H. W. Bush, to succeed him in 1989.

Bush's presidency was defined not by domestic initiatives, as Reagan's had been—and the perception of its disengagement with the nation's growing economic problems contributed to Bush's defeat in 1992. But a colossal historic event often overshadowed domestic concerns during Bush's term in office: the collapse of the Soviet Union and the fall of communist regimes all over Europe and in other parts of the world. The United States was to some degree a dazzled observer of this process. But the end of the Cold War also propelled the United States into the possession of unchallenged global pre-eminence—and drew it increasingly into the role of international arbiter and peacemaker. The Gulf War of 1991 was only the most dramatic example of the new global role the United States would now increasingly assume.

FOR FURTHER REFERENCE

Bruce J. Schulman, *The Seventies: The Great Shift in American Culture, Society, and Politics* (2001) is a good general history of the period. James M. Cannon, *Time and Chance: Gerald Ford's Appointment with History* (1994) is a journalist's account of the Ford presidency. Charles O. Jones, *The Trusteeship Presidency: Jimmy Carter and the United States Congress* (1988) looks at Carter's frustrations in domestic policy, and Gaddis Smith, *Morality, Reason, and Power* (1986) examines his foreign policy. Steven Gillon, *The Democrats' Dilemma: Walter Mondale and the Liberal Legacy* (1992) is a good discussion of the travails of the Democrats in the 1970s. Jerome L. Himmelstein, *To the Right: The Transformation of American Conservatism* (1990) and Godfrey Hodgson, *The World Turned Upside Down: A History of the Conservative Ascendancy in America* (1996) are good introductions to the subject. Lisa McGirr, *Suburban Warriors: The Origins of the New American Right* (2001) is an excellent grass-roots study. E. J. Dionne, *Why Americans Hate Politics* (1991) is a perceptive discussion of the political discontents of the 1980s and early 1990s. Garry Wills, *Reagan's America* (1987) is an interesting, critical interpretation. Lou Cannon, *President Reagan: The Role of a Lifetime* (1990) and Haynes Johnson, *Sleepwalking Through History* (1991) are accounts by journalists who covered the Reagan White House. Frances Fitzgerald, *Way Out There in the Blue: Reagan, Star Wars, and the End of the Cold War* (2000) is a fine history of the Reagan presidency, and its foreign policy in particular. Hedrick Smith, *The Power Game* (1988) is a sweeping portrait of the culture of political Washington during the Reagan years. John Lewis Gaddis, *The United States and the End of the Cold War* (1992) and *We Now Know: Rethinking Cold War History* (1997) examine the transformation of the world order after 1989. Thomas Crothers, *In the Name of Democracy: U.S. Foreign Policy toward Latin America in the Reagan Years* (1991) examines a controversial area of Reagan's international record, including aspects of the Iran-Contra scandal. Herbert Parmet, *George Bush: The Life of a Lone Star Yankee* (1997) is the first major scholarly study of the 41st president.

The Conservative Resurgence (1991) is a documentary film examining the growing conservative trend in American politics during the late 1970s and the 1980s.

For quizzes, Internet resources, references to additional books and films, and more, consult this book's Online Learning Center site at www.mhhe.com/unfinishednation4.

SEPTEMBER 11, 2001 One great American symbol, the Statue of Liberty, stands against a sky filled with the thick smoke from the destruction of another American symbol, New York City's World Trade Center towers, a few hours after terrorists crashed two planes into them. *(Daniel Hatshizer/AP/Wide World Photos)*

TIME LINE

1993	1994	1995	1996	1997	
North American Free Trade Agreement ratified	Health care reform fails	Government shutdown	Welfare reform passed	Microsoft antitrust suit begins	
	Republicans capture Congress	Crime rates decline	Clinton reelected	Balanced budget agreement	
		O. J. Simpson trial			

THE AGE OF GLOBALIZATION

A Resurgence of Partisanship
The Economic Boom
Science and Technology in the New Economy
A Changing Society
A Contested Culture
The Perils of Globalization

t 8:45 A.M. on the bright, sunny morning of September 11, 2001, as tens of thousands of workers were beginning a day's work in lower Manhattan, a commercial airliner crashed into the side of one of the two towers of the World Trade Center, the tallest buildings in New York, and exploded in flame. Less than half an hour later, as thousands of workers fled the burning building, another commercial airliner rammed into the companion tower, creating a second fireball. Little more than an hour after that, both towers—their steel girders buckling in response to the tremendous heat—collapsed. One of New York's (and America's) most famous symbols fell to the ground. At about the same time, in Washington, another commercial airliner crashed into a side of the Pentagon—the headquarters of the nation's military—turning part of the building's facade into rubble. And several hundred miles away, still another airplane crashed in a field not far from Pittsburgh, after passengers apparently seized the cockpit and prevented the hijackers from taking the plane to its unknown target.

These four almost simultaneous catastrophes were the result of a single orchestrated plan to bring terrorism—for years the bane of such nations as Israel, Lebanon, Turkey, Italy, Germany, Britain, and Ireland—into the United States, which had previously had relatively little recent experience of it. The people who organized the attack on America were

1998	1999	2000	2001	2002
Lewinsky scandal breaks	Clinton acquitted by Senate	George W. Bush wins contested election	Terrorists destroy World Trade Center and attack Pentagon	Corporate scandals contribute to economic downturn
Democrats gain in congressional elections			U.S. defeats Taliban regime in Afghanistan	
Clinton impeached by House				

Islamic radicals, engaged in what they considered a holy war against "infidels" in the United States. Similarly committed Middle Eastern terrorists had previously attacked American targets overseas—military barracks, a naval vessel, embassies, and consulates—and had tried and failed to organize other episodes of terror within the United States.

The events of September 11 and their aftermath produced significant and perhaps longlasting changes in American life. They also seemed to bring to a close an extraordinary period in modern American history—a time of heady prosperity, bitter partisanship, cultural frivolity and excess, and tremendous social and economic change. And yet there was also at least one great continuity between the world of the 1990s and the world that seemed to begin on September 11, 2001. The United States in the last years of the twentieth century and the first years of the twenty-first, more than at any other time in its history, was becoming more and more deeply entwined in a new age of globalism—an age that combined great promise with great peril.

A RESURGENCE OF PARTISANSHIP

Bill Clinton

Bill Clinton entered office in January 1993 as the first Democratic president since Jimmy Carter, and the first self-proclaimed activist president since Lyndon Johnson. He had a domestic agenda more ambitious than that of any president since the 1960s. But Clinton also had significant political weaknesses. Having won the votes of well under half the electorate, he enjoyed no powerful mandate. Democratic majorities in Congress were frail. The Republican leadership in Congress was highly adversarial and it opposed the president with unusual unanimity on many issues. The president's tendency toward reckless personal behavior gave his many enemies repeated opportunities to discredit him. The Clinton years, therefore, became a time of unusually intense and bitter partisan struggles.

Launching the Clinton Presidency

The new administration compounded its problems with a series of missteps and misfortunes in its first months. The president's effort to end the longtime ban on gay men and women serving in the military met with ferocious resistance, and he was forced to settle for a pallid compromise. Several of his early appointments became so controversial he had to withdraw them. A longtime friend of the president, Vince Foster, serving in the office of the White House counsel, committed suicide in the summer of 1993. His death helped spark an escalating inquiry into some banking and real estate ventures involving the president and his wife in the early 1980s, which became known as the Whitewater affair. An independent counsel began examining these issues in 1993.

Despite its many problems, the Clinton administration could boast of some significant achievements in its first year. The president narrowly won approval of a budget that marked a significant turn away from the policies of the Reagan-Bush years. It included a substantial tax increase on the wealthiest Americans, a significant reduction in many areas of government spending, and a major expansion of tax credits to low-income working people, designed to help lift many struggling families out of poverty.

Clinton was a committed advocate of free trade. After a long and difficult battle against, among others, Ross Perot, the AFL-CIO, and many Democrats in Congress, he won approval of the North American Free Trade Agreement (or NAFTA), which eliminated *NAFTA* most trade barriers among the United States, Canada, and Mexico. Later he won approval of other far-reaching trade agreements negotiated in the General Agreement on Trade and Tarriffs (or GATT).

The president's most important and ambitious initiative was a major reform of the nation's health-care system. Early in 1993, he appointed a task force chaired by his wife, Hillary Rodham Clinton, which proposed a sweeping reform designed to guarantee coverage to every American and hold down the costs of medical care. The Clinton plan relied heavily on existing institutions, most notably private insurance companies; and some critics from the left complained that the new system would be too closely tied to an undependable market. But the most substantial opposition came from the right, from those who believed the reform would transfer too much power to the government; and that well-funded opposition doomed the plan. In September 1994, Congress abandoned the health-care reform effort.

The foreign policy of the Clinton administration was at first cautious and even tentative. That was particularly clear in the administration's handling of one of the most troubling international questions of the early 1990s. Yugoslavia, a nation created after World War I out of a group of small Balkan countries, dissolved again into several different nations in the wake of the collapse of its communist govern- *Bosnia* ment in 1989. Bosnia was among the new nations, and it quickly became embroiled in a bloody civil war between its two major ethnic groups: one Muslim, the other Serbian and Christian backed by the neighboring Serbian republic. All efforts by the other European nations and the United States to negotiate an end to the struggle failed until 1995, when the American negotiator Richard Holbrooke finally brought the warring parties together and crafted an agreement to partition Bosnia.

BREAKING PRECEDENT Bill Clinton broke with precedent in 1993 when he appointed his wife, Hillary Rodham Clinton, to head a task force on health care reform. The prominent role of the first lady in the Clinton administration surprised many Americans, pleasing some and angering others. The Clintons are shown here with Vice President Al Gore, as the first lady talks about health care. Hillary Clinton broke precedent again in 2000 when she was elected to the United States Senate from New York. *(Wally McNamee/Corbis)*

The Republican Resurgence

The trials of the Clinton administration, and the failure of health-care reform in particular, proved enormously damaging to the Democratic Party as it faced the congressional elections of 1994. For the first time in over forty years, Republicans gained control of both houses of Congress.

Throughout 1995, the Republican Congress worked at a sometimes feverish pace to construct one of the most ambitious and even radical legislative programs in modern times. They proposed a series of measures to transfer important powers from the federal government to the states. They proposed dramatic reductions in federal spending, including a major restructuring of the once-sacrosanct Medicare program, to reduce costs. They attempted to scale back a wide range of federal regulatory functions.

President Clinton responded to the 1994 election results by proclaiming that "the era of big government is over" and by shifting his own agenda conspicuously to the center—announcing his own plan to cut taxes and balance the budget. But because the legislative politics of 1995 was becoming part of the presidential politics of 1996, compromise between the president and Congress became very difficult. In November 1995 and again in January

1996, the federal government literally shut down for several days because the president and Congress could not agree on a budget. Republican leaders refused to pass a "continuing resolution" (to allow government operations to continue during negotiations) in hopes of pressuring the president to agree to their terms. That proved to be an epic political blunder. Public opinion turned quickly and powerfully against the Republican leadership, and against much of its agenda. Newt Gingrich, the controversial Republican Speaker of the House, quickly became one of the most unpopular political leaders in the nation, while President Clinton slowly improved his standing in the polls.

The Election of 1996

By the time the 1996 presidential campaign began in earnest, President Clinton—who had seemed so disastrously wounded after the 1994 elections—was in a commanding position to win reelection. Unopposed for the Democratic nomination, he faced a Republican opponent—Senator Robert Dole of Kansas—who inspired little enthusiasm even within his own party. Clinton's revival was in part a result *Clinton's Renewed Popularity* of his adroitness in taking centrist positions that undermined the Republicans on one issue after another, and in championing traditional Democratic issues—such as raising the minimum wage—that were broadly popular. Clinton benefited even more from the disastrous errors by congressional Republicans in 1995 and early 1996. But his greatest strength came from the remarkable success of the American economy and the marked reduction in the federal deficit that had occurred during his presidency. Like Reagan in 1984, he could campaign as the champion of peace, prosperity, and national well-being.

As the election approached, both Democrats and Republicans grew uneasy about the failure of the 104th Congress to pass any significant measures. In a flurry of activity in the spring and summer of 1996, the Congress passed several important bills. The most dramatic of them was a welfare reform bill, which President Clinton somewhat uneasily signed, that ended the fifty-year federal guarantee of assistance to families with dependent children and turned most of the responsibility for allocating federal welfare funds (now greatly reduced) to the states. Most of all, it shifted the bulk of welfare benefits away from those without jobs and toward support for low-wage workers. A strong economy in the first few years after the bill passed helped many former welfare recipients move into the paid workforce.

Clinton's buoyant campaign flagged slightly in the last weeks before the election in the face of allegations of improper or illegal fund-raising techniques by the Democrats. But the president *Clinton Reelected* nevertheless won a substantial victory. He received just over 49 percent of the popular vote to Dole's 41 percent; Ross Perot, running now as the candidate of what he called the Reform Party, generated much less enthusiasm than he had in 1992 but still received over 8 percent of the vote. Clinton won 379 electoral votes to Dole's 159; Perot

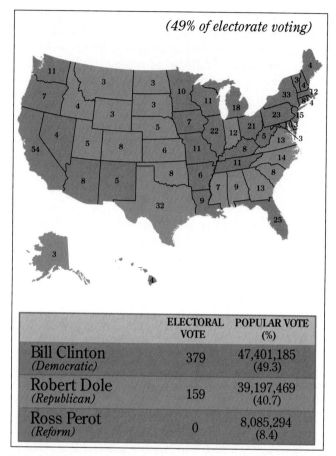

(49% of electorate voting)

	ELECTORAL VOTE	POPULAR VOTE (%)
Bill Clinton *(Democratic)*	379	47,401,185 (49.3)
Robert Dole *(Republican)*	159	39,197,469 (40.7)
Ross Perot *(Reform)*	0	8,085,294 (8.4)

THE ELECTION OF 1996 Rose Perot did much less well in 1996 than he had in 1992, and President Clinton came much closer than he had four years earlier to winning a majority of the popular vote. Once again, Clinton defeated his Republican opponent, this time Robert Dole, by a decisive margin in both the popular and electoral vote. After the 1994 Republican landslide in the congressional elections, Bill Clinton had seemed permanently weakened. ◆ *What explains his political revival?*

For an interactive version of this map go to www.mhhe.com/unfinishednation4ch34maps

again won none. But the president's victory did not have much effect on other Democrats, who made only modest gains over their disastrous showing in 1994 and failed to regain either house of Congress.

Clinton Triumphant and Embattled

Bill Clinton was the first Democratic president to win two terms as president since Franklin Roosevelt, and he began his second administration with what appeared to be serene confidence. Facing a somewhat chastened but still hostile Republican Congress, he proposed a relatively modest domestic agenda. He also negotiated effectively with the Republican leadership on a plan for a balanced budget, which passed with much fanfare late in 1997. By the end of 1998, the federal budget was generating its first surplus in thirty years. The president finished his fifth year in office more popular than he had ever been before.

That popularity would be important to him in the turbulent year that followed, when the most serious crisis of his presidency suddenly erupted. Clinton had been bedeviled by scandals almost from his first weeks in office. Among his problems was a civil suit for sexual harassment filed against the president by a former state employee in *Paula Jones* Arkansas, Paula Jones, who charged that Clinton, while governor, had made unwanted sexual advances toward her.

In early 1998, inquiries associated with the Paula Jones case led to charges that the president had had a sexual relationship with a young White House intern, Monica Lewinsky; that he *Monica Lewinsky* had lied about it in his deposition before Jones's attorneys; and that he had encouraged Lewinsky to do the same. Those revelations produced a new investigation by the independent counsel in the Whitewater case, Kenneth Starr, a former judge and official in the Reagan Justice Department.

Starr had been investigating the Whitewater matter for nearly four years without any significant results. But he suddenly resurfaced as a major threat to the president with a vigorous effort to prove that the president had lied under oath and had advised others to lie as well. Clinton forcefully denied the charges, and the public strongly backed him. His popularity soared to record levels—a 79 percent approval rating in one poll, and it remained over sixty percent throughout the year that followed. In the meantime, a federal judge dismissed the Paula Jones case, which had launched the scandal.

But the scandal revived again with great force in August 1998, when Lewinsky struck a deal with the independent counsel and testified about her relationship with Clinton. Starr then subpoenaed Clinton himself, who—faced with the prospect of speaking to a grand jury—finally admitted that he and Lewinsky had had what he called an "improper relationship." A few weeks later, Starr submitted a lengthy and at times salacious report to Congress on the results of his investigation, recommending that Congress impeach the president.

The prospect of impeachment became an issue in the 1998 congressional elections. Democrats believed that the public's strong opposition to impeachment would damage the Republicans, and they turned out to be right. The Republicans lost ten seats in the House, cutting their already thin majority to five, and gained no seats in the Senate.

Impeachment, Acquittal, and Resurgence

Despite the polls and the election results, House leaders resisted all calls for compromise or dismissal of the charges. On December 19, 1998, the House, voting on strictly partisan lines, narrowly *Clinton Acquitted* approved two counts of impeachment: lying to the grand jury and obstructing justice. The matter then moved to the Senate, where a trial of the president—the first since the trial of Andrew Johnson in 1868—began in early January. The Senate trial continued for several weeks without generating any significant public support. It ended with a decisive acquittal of the president. Neither of the charges attracted even a majority of the votes, let alone the two-thirds necessary for conviction.

The investigation into the president's sexual behavior, and the political battle that followed it, illustrated two significant changes in the character of American public life in the 1990s. One was the expanding role of scandal in American politics, driven by an increasingly sensationalist media culture, the legal device of independent counsels, and the intensely adversarial quality of partisan politics. The other was the blurring of the distinction between public and private behavior, which made almost every facet of a politician's life a target of inquiry and exposure.

The last two years of the Clinton presidency were relatively quiet ones domestically. The president had no real hope of major domestic achievements in the face of a hostile Republican Congress. Overseas, however, he was more active than he had ever been before. Beginning in 1998, the United States found itself once again in conflict with Iraqi president Saddam Hussein, who balked at the agreements he had signed at the end of the Gulf War and refused to permit international inspectors to examine military sites in his country. Clinton responded by ordering a series of American bombing strikes at military targets in Iraq.

In 1999, the president faced another crisis in the Balkans. This time, the *Serbia Bombed* conflict involved a province of Serbian-dominated Yugoslavia—Kosovo—most of whose residents were Albanian Muslims. A savage civil war erupted there in 1998 between Kosovo nationalists and Serbians. Numerous reports of Serbian atrocities against the Kosovans, and an enormous refugee crisis spurred by Yugoslavian military action in the province, slowly roused world opinion. In May 1999, NATO forces—dominated and led by the United States—began a major bombing campaign against the Serbians, which after little more than a week led the leader of Yugoslavia, Slobodan Milosevic, to agree to a cease-fire. Serbian troops withdrew from Kosovo entirely, replaced by NATO peacekeeping forces. A precarious peace returned to the region.

Clinton finished his eight years in office with his popularity higher than it had been when he had begun. Indeed, public approval of Clinton's presidency—a presidency marked by astonishing prosperity and general world stability as well as persistent scandal—was consistently among the highest of any postwar president.

The Election of 2000

The 2000 presidential election was one of the most extraordinary in American history—not because of the campaign that preceded it, but because of the sensational controversy over its results, which preoccupied the nation for more than five weeks after the actual voting.

ELECTION NIGHT, 2000 The electronic billboard in New York City's Times Square, showing network coverage of the presidential contest, reports George Bush the winner of the 2000 presidential race late on election night. A few hours later, the networks retracted their projections because of continuing uncertainty over the results in Florida. Five weeks later, and then only because of the controversial intervention of the Supreme Court, Bush finally emerged the victor. *(Chris Hondros/Newsmakers)*

George W. Bush—son of the former president and a second-term governor of Texas—rode his famous name and his enormous campaign war chest to overcome a powerful challenge from Senator John McCain of Arizona, a maverick reformer. Vice President Al Gore, an even more prohibitive favorite in the Democratic race, easily beat back a challenge from former Senator Bill Bradley of New Jersey.

Both men ran cautious, centrist campaigns, making much of their relatively modest differences over how to use the large budget surpluses forecast for the years ahead. Although polls showed an exceptionally tight race right up to the end, no one anticipated how close the election would be. In the congressional races, Republicans maintained control of the House of Representatives by a scant five seats, while the Senate split evenly between Democrats and Republicans. (Among the victors in the Senate races was

First Lady Hillary Rodham Clinton, who won a highly publicized race in New York.) In the presidential race, Gore won the national popular vote by the thin margin of about 540,000 votes out of about 100 million cast (or .5%). But on election night, both candidates remained short of the 270 electoral votes needed for victory because no one could determine who had actually won Florida.

Florida Disputed

After a mandatory recount over the next two days, Bush led Gore in the state by fewer than 300 votes. (Ralph Nader, the presidential candidate of the new Green Party, had done poorly nationally but nevertheless drew over 90,000 votes in Florida, which almost certainly denied Gore what would otherwise have been a comfortable victory there.) The technology of voting soon became central to the dispute. In a number of Florida counties, including some of the most heavily Democratic ones, votes were cast by punch-card ballots, which were then counted by machines. But punch cards are notoriously inaccurate, and many voters failed to punch out the appropriate holes adequately, leaving the machines unable to read them. In heavily Democratic Palm Beach County, where the ballot was especially poorly designed, thousands of confused voters punched the wrong hole, or punched two holes when they were supposed to punch one. The Gore campaign asked for hand recounts of punch-card ballots in three critical counties.

Katherine Harris

The Bush campaign immediately struck back in court and through the Republican Secretary of State, Katherine Harris, who had worked actively on the Bush campaign. As the official responsible for certifying elections in the state, she refused to authorize the recounts and declined to extend a deadline for making an official certification. But the Florida Supreme Court voted unanimously to require Harris to permit the hand recounts and to accept the results after the deadline. Such recounts proceeded in two of those counties, but in the third and largest (Dade County, which includes Miami) the local election board—for complicated reasons, which may have included intimidation by Republican demonstrators in the municipal building—abruptly called off the recount, claiming they could not finish in time.

When the new, court-ordered deadline arrived, Harris quickly certified Bush the winner in Florida by a little more than 500 votes. The Gore campaign immediately contested the results in court, asking for the Dade County recount to be reopened. Again they prevailed in the Florida Supreme Court, which ordered hand recounts of all previously uncounted ballots in all Florida counties.

In the meantime, the Bush campaign appealed desperately to the United States Supreme Court to stop the recounts. To the surprise of most observers, the Court issued a stay on Saturday, December 9 (by a vote of 5-4), and late on Tuesday, the Court issued one of the most unusual and controversial decisions in its history. Voting 5-4 again, dividing sharply along party and ideological lines, the conservative majority overruled the Florida Supreme Court's order for a recount, insisted that any

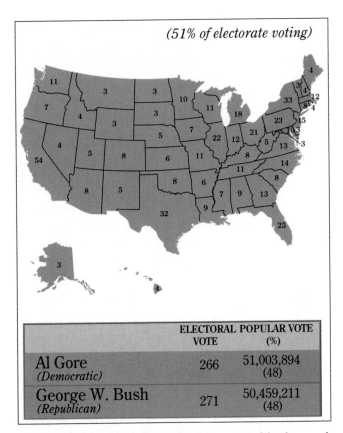

(51% of electorate voting)

	ELECTORAL VOTE	POPULAR VOTE (%)
Al Gore (*Democratic*)	266	51,003,894 (48)
George W. Bush (*Republican*)	271	50,459,211 (48)

THE ELECTION OF 2000 The 2000 presidential election was one of the closest and most controversial in American history. It also starkly revealed a new pattern of party strength, which had been developing over the previous decade. Democrats swept the Northeast and most of the industrial Midwest and carried all the states of the Pacific Coast. Republicans swept the South, the Plains States, and the Mountain States (with the exception of New Mexico) and held onto a few traditional Republican strongholds in the Midwest. Compare this map to earlier elections, and in particular the election of 1896, and ask how the pattern of party support changed over the course of the twentieth century.

revised recount order be completed by December 12 (an obviously impossible demand, since the Court issued its ruling late at night on the 12th), and argued that the standards for evaluating punch-card ballots were too arbitrary and unfair to withstand constitutional scrutiny. The four-member minority bitterly protested the majority's reasoning, and the majority itself appeared deeply divided on some crucial issues. But divided or not, the Court had decided the election. The next day, Gore gave a brief and conciliatory concession speech. Bush then delivered a subdued acknowledgment of one of the most controversial victories in the history of American presidential elections.

The Supreme Court's Divisive Ruling

The Second Bush Presidency

George W. Bush assumed the presidency in January 2001 burdened both by the controversies surrounding his election and the widespread perception, even among some of his own supporters, that he was ill-prepared for the office. His first eight months in the White House were notable for some important legislative successes but also for little progress in winning over the 52 percent of the electorate that had voted against him.

Bush's principal campaign promise had been that he would use the predicted budget surplus to finance a massive tax reduction. *Bush's Tax Cuts* By relying on his own party's control of both houses of Congress (Republicans controlled the 50-50 Senate because the Republican vice president, Richard Cheney, broke all ties), he narrowly won passage of the largest tax cut in American history—$1.35 trillion. But a few weeks later, the administration—and the Republican party—suffered a stunning setback when Senator James Jeffords of Vermont, a moderate Republican unhappy with the conservative policies of both the administration and the Republican leadership in Congress, declared himself an independent and announced he would vote with the Democrats to organize the Senate. Suddenly, Bush's legislative road became much less promising, and over the next several months most of the bills he had proposed made little progress.

In the 2002 midterm elections, however, the Republicans regained control of the Senate (replacing the Democrats' narrow 51–49 margin with a 51–49 division in their favor) and retained a slim majority in the House of Representatives. That enabled the administration and the Republican leadership to move much more aggressively, and with much greater chance of success, to pursue its ambitious agenda.

Having campaigned as a moderate adept at building coalitions across party lines, Bush spent his first two years as president governing as a staunch conservative, allied with the most determinedly right-wing figures in his party. The administration proposed nothing less than a radical shift in both domestic and foreign policy. Domestically, it sought a series of enormous reductions, and even eliminations, of taxes—especially for wealthy Americans, whom conservatives believed were best suited to promote economic growth through investment. It also sought to reduce government regulation of and interference in the market. Internationally, it proposed a dramatically new foreign policy, which asserted the United States to launch "preemptive" wars to eliminate regimes it considered hostile or dangerous and which committed the nation to working toward a world in which all nations embraced America's commitment to free and open markets.

THE ECONOMIC BOOM

The last twenty years of the twentieth century saw remarkable changes in American life—some of them a result of the end of the Cold War, some of them a result of the changing character of the American population and a rapidly evolving culture. But most of these changes were at least in part a product of the dramatic transformation of the American economy.

From "Stagflation" to Growth

The roots of the economic growth of the 1980s and 1990s lay in part in the troubled years of the 1970s. In the face of the sluggish growth and persistent inflation of those years, many American corporations began making important changes in the way they ran their businesses—changes that contributed both to the prosperity of the last decades of the twentieth century, and the growing inequality that accompanied it. Businesses invested heavily in new technology. Corporations began to consider mergers with other companies, *Corporate Restructuring* to provide a more diversified basis for growth. Many enterprises created more energy-efficient plants and offices. Perhaps most of all, American businesses sought to reduce their labor costs, which were among the highest in the world and which many believed had made the United States uncompetitive against economies that relied on low-wage workers.

Businesses cut labor costs in many ways. Non-union companies became more successful in staving off unionization drives. Companies already unionized won important concessions from their unions on wages and benefits in exchange for preserving jobs. Some companies moved their operations to areas of the country where unions were weak and wages low. And many companies moved much of their production out of the United States entirely, to such nations as Mexico and China where there were large available labor pools willing to work for much less than American workers earned.

At least as important as the restructuring of existing businesses was the emergence of powerful new sectors of the economy—most notably what became known as the "technology industries." The growth of digital technologies made *"Technology Industries"* possible an enormous range of new products and services that quickly became central to American economic life: computers, the Internet, cellular phones, digital music, video cameras, personal digital assistants, and many others. The technology industries employed hundreds of thousands of people, created new consumer needs and appetites, and even spawned their own stock exchange—the NASDAQ—which enjoyed an enormous boom in the late 1990s.

For these and many other reasons, the American economy experienced astonishing growth in the last decades of the twentieth century. The Gross National Product (the total of goods and services produced by the United States) rose from *Surging GNP* $2.7 trillion in 1980 to over $9.8 trillion in 2000, quadrupling in twenty years. Inflation was low throughout these decades, never rising above 3 percent in any year and for a while in the late 1990s dropping below 2 percent. Stock prices soared to unprecedented levels, and with few interruptions, from the mid-1980s to the end of the century. The Dow Jones Industrial Average, the most common index of stock performance, stood at 1,000 in late 1980. Late in 1999, it passed 11,000. Economic growth was particularly dramatic in the last years of the 1990s. In 1997 and 1998, annual growth rates reached five percent for the first time since the 1960s. Most impressive of all was the longevity of the boom. From 1994 to 2000, the economy recorded growth—at times very substantial growth—in every year, indeed in every quarter, something that had never before happened so continuously in peacetime since modern economic measurements began. Except for the relatively brief recession of 1992–1993, the period of dramatic growth actually extended unbroken from late 1983.

Downturn

The most powerful single figure in the American economy—Alan Greenspan, chairman of the Federal Board—warned in 1999 of the "irrational exuberance" with which Americans were pursuing profits in the stock market. The market justified his concern when, in April 2001, there was a sudden and disastrous collapse of the booming technology sector of the economy, which had seen particular growth in the stock values of companies doing business on the Internet. Investors decided that they had greatly overestimated the short-term profitability of Internet-based business. The result was a dramatic sell-off of technology stocks.

The bursting of the "tech bubble" did not have immediate effects on the rest of the market. But in the first months of 2001, the market as a
Plummeting Stock Market whole began a long slide down from its historic highs of 1999 and 2000. That slide continued for more than a year, so that by the summer of 2002 the Dow Jones Industrial Average—the most commonly cited index of stock values—had lost almost 40 percent of its value. Having once soared above 11,000, it fell for a time in July 2002 below 7,000.

In the fall of 2001, the economy as a whole slipped into a recession. And although there was a weak recovery in early 2002, many factors continued to depress growth and to threaten long-term economic sluggishness. Among them was a series of major corporate failures that revealed not just weakness, but corruption and dishonesty, at the heart of the business world. The revelations of corruption began in December 2001 when the Enron Corporation, an energy-trading company based in Houston that had claimed to be the seventh-largest company in America and the world's largest energy merchant, declared bankruptcy. A model to many managers of bold innovation, it conceded that it had vastly inflated its declared earnings through unorthodox and perhaps illegal accounting methods.

Corporate Scandals The Enron collapse was only the first of a series of corporate scandals that attracted both media and popular attention and did grave damage to public confidence in corporate leadership. One major company after another admitted that their reported earnings greatly exaggerated their real income. Major accounting firms—most notably Arthur Andersen, the Enron accountant—came under intense public and legal scrutiny for failing to give reliable accounts of the corporate finances they were supposed to monitor. And the aggressive innovation that had been so lionized in corporate America in the late nineties suddenly projected a different image—recklessness, occasional lawlessness, and (in the words of Alan Greenspan) "infectious greed."

The Two-Tiered Economy

Although the American economy in the late twentieth century revived triumphantly from the sluggishness of the 1970s and early 1980s, the benefits of the new economy were less widely shared than those of earlier boom times. The increasing abundance created enormous new wealth that enriched those talented, or lucky, enough to profit from the areas of booming growth. The rewards for education increased enormously. In 1995, the average annual income of a person with less than a high-school education was $14,000. A college graduate's average salary was $37,000, and the average salary of someone with an advanced degree was $56,700—four times the level of those who did not graduate from high school. Between 1980 and the mid-1990s, the average family incomes of the wealthiest 20 percent of the population grew by nearly 20 percent (to over $100,000 a year); the average family income of the next 20 percent of the population grew by more than 8 percent. Incomes remained flat for most of the remaining 60 percent of the public, and actually declined for many in the bottom 20 percent.

Poverty in America had declined steadily and at times dramatically in the years after World War II, so that by the end of the 1970s the percentage of people living in poverty had declined to 12 percent (from about 20 percent in preceding decades). But the decline in poverty did not continue. In the 1980s, the poverty rate rose again, at *Rising Poverty Rates* times as high as 18 percent. By the late 1990s, it had dropped to under 13 percent again, but that was about the same as it had been twenty years before.

Globalization

The great prosperity of the 1950s and 1960s had rested on, among other things, the relative insulation of the United States from the pressures of international competition. As late as 1970, international trade still played a relatively small role in the American economy as a whole, which thrived on the basis of the huge domestic market in North America.

By the end of the 1970s, however, the world had intruded on the American economy in profound ways. Exports rose from just under $43 billion in 1970 to over $789 billion in 2000. Imports rose even more dramatically: from just over $40 billion in 1970 to over $1.2 trillion in 2000. Most American products, in other words, now faced foreign competition inside the

Mounting Foreign Competition United States. America had made 76 percent of the world's automobiles in 1950 and 48 percent in 1960. By 2000 the American share was only 21.5 percent. The first American trade imbalance in the postwar era occurred in 1971; only twice since then, in 1973 and 1975, has the balance been favorable.

Costs and Benefits of Globalization Globalization brought many benefits for the American consumer: new and more varied products, and lower prices for many of them. Most economists, and most national leaders, welcomed the process and worked to encourage it through lowering trade barriers. The North American Free Trade Agreement (NAFTA) and the General Agreement on Trade and Tariffs (GATT) were the boldest of a long series of treaties designed to lower trade barriers stretching back to the 1960s. But globalization had many costs as well. It was particularly hard on industrial workers, who saw industrial jobs disappear as American companies lost market share to foreign competitors and as American companies began exporting work—building plants in Mexico, Asia, and other lower-wage countries to avoid having to pay the high wages workers had won in America.

SCIENCE AND TECHNOLOGY IN THE NEW ECONOMY

The "new economy" that emerged in the last decades of the twentieth century was driven by, and in turn helped to drive, dramatic new scientific and technological discoveries. Much as in the late nineteenth century when technological innovations transformed both society and the economy, so in the late twentieth century, new technologies had profound effects on the way Americans—and peoples throughout the world—lived.

The Personal Computer

The Computer Revolution The most visible element of the technological revolution to most Americans was the dramatic growth in the use of computers in almost every area of life. By the early 1990s, most Americans were doing their banking by computer. Most retail transactions were conducted by computerized credit mechanisms. Most businesses, schools, and other institutions were using computerized record-keeping. Many areas of manufacturing were revolutionized by computer-driven product design and factory robotics. Scientific and technological research in almost all areas was transformed by computerized methods.

Among the most significant innovations was the development of the microprocessor, first introduced in 1971 by Intel, which represented a notable advance in the technology of integrated circuitry. A microprocessor miniaturized the central processing unit of a computer, making it possible for a small machine to perform calculations that in the past only very large machines could do. Considerable technological innovation was needed before the microprocessor could actually become the basis of what was first known as a "minicomputer" and then a personal computer. But in 1977, Apple launched its Apple II personal computer, the first such machine to be widely available to the public. Several years later, IBM entered the personal computer market with the first "PC." IBM had engaged a small software development company, Microsoft, to design an operating system for their new computer. Microsoft produced a program known as MS-DOS (DOS for "disk operating system"). No PC could operate without it. The PC, and its software, made its debut in August 1981 and immediately became enormously successful. Three years later, Apple introduced its Macintosh computer, which marked another major innovation in computer technology, among other things because its software—very different from DOS—was more graphical and much easier to use than that of the PC. But Apple could not match IBM's marketing power, and by the mid-1980s the PC had clearly established its dominance in the booming personal computer market—a dominance enhanced by the introduction of a new software package to replace DOS in 1985: Windows, also developed by Microsoft, which borrowed many concepts (most notably the Graphical User Interface, or GUI) from the Apple operating system. IBM, however, was not in the end the principal beneficiary of the dominance of its own system, as other companies began marketing their own IBM-compatible personal computers, usually at a lower price than IBMs, and seizing most of the market.

The computer revolution created thousands of new, lucrative businesses: computer manufacturers themselves (IBM, Apple, Compaq, Dell, Gateway, Sun, Digital, and many others); makers of the tiny silicon chips that ran the computers (most notably Intel); and makers of software—chief among them Microsoft, *Microsoft* the most powerful new corporation to arise in American life in generations. In the 1990s, Microsoft had a virtual monopoly on the operating systems for most personal computers in the world. It had also moved into new areas: creating other kinds of software (word processing, spreadsheets, databases, communications, personal finance, and many others) and producing software and content for the Internet. In 1997, after many abortive efforts, the Justice Department filed a series of antitrust suits against the giant corporation—a suit that in 2000 produced a strong ruling against the corporation that was later partly overturned by an appeals court.

But if Microsoft was the most conspicuous success story of the computer age, it was only one of many. Whole regions—the so-called Silicon Valley in northern California; areas around Boston, Austin, Texas, and Seattle, Washington; areas in downtown New York City—became centers of booming economic activity servicing the new computer age.

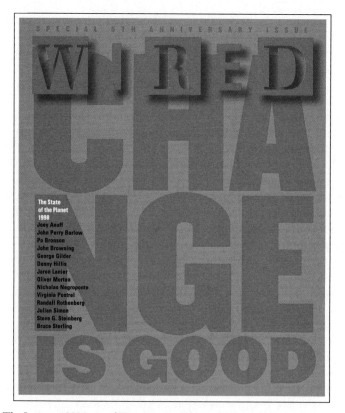

WIRED 6.01 The January 1998 issue of *Wired*, a magazine aimed at young, hip, computer-literate readers, expressed the optimistic, even visionary approach to the possibilities of new electronic technologies that was characteristic of many computer and Internet enthusiasts in the 1990s. *Wired*, which began publication in 1992, was careful to differentiate itself from the slick, commercial computer magazines that were principally interested in trumpeting new products. It tried, instead, to capture the simultaneously skeptical and the progressive spirit of a generation to whom technology seemed to define much of the future. *(Designer, John Plunkett; Writer, Louis Rossetto. Copyright © 2002 by the Condé Nast Publications, Inc. All rights reserved.)*

The Internet

Out of the computer revolution emerged another dramatic source of information and communication: the Internet—a vast, geographically far-flung network of computers that allows people connected to the network to communicate with others all over the world. It had its beginning in 1963, in the U.S. government's Advanced Research Projects Agency (ARPA), which funneled federal funds into scientific research projects. In the early 1960s, J. C. R. Licklider, the head of ARPA's Information Processing Technique Office, launched a program to link together computers over large distances. It was known as the Arpanet. *Arpanet* For several years, the Arpanet served mainly as a way for people to make use of what were then relatively scarce computer facilities without having to go to the site of the computer. Gradually, however, both the size and the uses of the network expanded.

This expansion was facilitated in part by two important new technologies. One was a system developed in the early 1960s at the RAND Corporation in the United States and the National Physical Laboratory in England. It was known as "store-and-forward packet switching," and it made possible the transmission of large quantities of data between computers without directly wiring the computers together. There could be a central communications backbone through which messages and information could be routed to individual computers, much as the telegraph and telephone system used centralized carriers that eventually branched off into local connections. The other technological breakthrough was the development of computer software that would allow individual computers to handle the traffic over the network—what became known as the Interface Message Processor.

By 1971, twenty-three computers were linked together in the Arpanet, which served mostly research labs and universities. Gradually, interest in the system began to spread, and with it the number of computers connected to it. By the end of 2001, there were over 650 million computers in use in the world, and over 180 million in the United States, the great majority of them personal computers. The great majority of them had connections to the Internet. In the early 1980s, the Defense Department, an early partner in the development of the Arpanet, withdrew from the project for security reasons. The network, soon renamed the Internet, was then free to develop independently. It did so rapidly, especially after the invention of technologies that made possible electronic mail (or e-mail) and the emergence of the personal computer, which vastly increased the number of potential users of the Internet. In 1984, fewer than a thousand host computers connected to the Internet. A decade later, there were over 6 million. And in 2001, an estimated 400 million people around the world were using the Internet, including 130 million in the United States.

The Internet

As the amount of information on the Internet unexpectedly proliferated, without any central direction, new forms of software emerged to make it possible for individual users to navigate through the vast number of Internet sites. In 1989, a laboratory in Geneva introduced the World Wide Web, which helped establish an orderly system for both the distribution and retrieval of electronic information.

The Internet revolutionized many areas of life. E-mail replaced conventional mail, telephone calls, and even face-to-face conversation for millions of people. Newspapers, magazines, and other publications began to publish on the Internet. It became a powerful marketing tool, through which people can purchase items as small as books and as large as automobiles. It is a site for vast amounts of documentary material for researchers, reporters, students and others. And it is, finally, a highly democratic medium—through which virtually anyone with access to a personal computer can establish a website and present information in a form that is available to virtually anyone in the world who chooses to look at it. New technologies that make it easier to transmit moving images over the Internet—and new forms of "broadband" access that give more users high-speed connections to the Web—promise to expand greatly the functions that the Internet can perform.

Breakthroughs in Genetics

Aided in part by computer technology, there was explosive growth in the late twentieth century of another area of scientific research: genetics. Early discoveries in genetics by Gregor Mendel, Thomas Hunt Morgan, and others laid the groundwork for more dramatic breakthroughs—the

DNA discovery of DNA by the British scientists Oswald Avery, Colin MacLeod, and Maclyn McCarty in 1944; and in 1953, the dramatic discovery by the American biochemist James Watson and the British biophysicist Francis Crick of the double-helix structure of DNA, and thus of the key to identifying genetic codes. From these discoveries emerged the new science—and ultimately the new industry—of genetic engineering, through which new medical treatments and new techniques for hybridization of plants and animals have already become possible.

Little by little, scientists began to identify specific genes in humans and other living things that determine particular traits, and to learn how to alter or reproduce them. But the identification of genes was painfully slow; and in 1989, the federal government appropriated $3 billion to fund the National Center for the Human Genome, to accelerate the mapping

Human Genome Project of human genes. The Human Genome Project set out to identify all of the more than 100,000 genes by 2005. But new technologies for research, and competition from other projects (some of them funded by pharmaceutical companies) drove the project forward faster than expected. In 1998, the genome project announced that it would finish its work in 2003. In the meantime, in 2000, other researchers produced a list of all the genes in the human body, even if their relationship to one another remained unmapped.

In 1997, scientists in Scotland announced that they had cloned a sheep—which they named Dolly—using a cell from an adult ewe; in other words, the genetic structure of the newborn Dolly was identical to that of the sheep from which the cell was taken. The DNA structure of an individual, scientists have discovered, is as unique and as identifiable as a fingerprint. DNA testing, therefore, makes it possible to identify individuals through their blood, semen, skin, or even hair. It played a major role first in the O. J. Simpson trial in 1995 and then in the 1998 investigation into President Clinton's relationship with Monica Lewinsky. Also in 1998, DNA testing appeared to establish with certainty that Thomas Jefferson had fathered a child with his slave Sally Hemings, by finding genetic similarities between descendants of both, thus resolving a political and scholarly dispute stretching back nearly 200 years. Genetic research has already spawned important new areas of medical treatment—and has helped the relatively new biotechnology industry to grow into one of the nation's most important economic sectors.

But genetic research was also the source of great controversy. Some critics feared genetic research on religious grounds, seeing it as an interference with God's plan. Others used moral arguments and expressed fears that it would allow parents, for example, to choose what kinds of children they would have. And a particularly *Ethical Issues* heated controversy emerged over one of the most promising areas of medical research, which involved the use of stem cells, genetic material obtained in large part from undeveloped fetuses—mostly fetuses created by couples attempting in vitro fertilization. (*In vitro fertilization* is the process by which couples unable to conceive a child have a fetus conceived outside the womb using their eggs and sperm and then implanted in the mother.) Anti-abortion advocates denounced the research, claiming that it exploited (and endangered) unborn children. Supporters of stem-cell research—which showed promising signs of offering cures for Parkinson's disease, Alzheimer's disease, ALS, and other previously uncurable illnesses—argued that the stem cells they used came from fetuses that would otherwise be discarded, since in vitro fertilization always produces many more fetuses than can be used. The controversy over stem-cell research became an issue in the 2000 campaign. George W. Bush, once president, kept his promise to anti-abortion advocates and in the summer of 2001 issued a ruling barring the use of federal funds to support research using any stem cells that scientists were not already using at the time of his decision.

A CHANGING SOCIETY

The changes in the economy were only one of many factors producing major changes in the character of American society. By the end of the twentieth century, the American population was growing larger, older, and more racially and geographically diverse.

The Graying of America

One of the most important, if often unnoticed, features of American life in the late twentieth century was the aging of the American population. After decades of steady *Growing Elderly Population* growth, the nation's birth rate began to decline in the 1970s and remained low through the 1980s and 1990s. In 1970, there were 18.4 births for every 1,000 people in the population. By 1996, the rate had dropped to 14.8 births. The declining birth rate and a significant rise in life expectancy produced a substantial increase in the proportion of elderly citizens. Almost 13 percent of the population was more than sixty-five years old in 2000, as compared with 8 percent in 1970.

The aging of the population was a cause of the increasing costliness of Social Security pensions. It meant rapidly increasing health costs, both for the federal Medicare system and for private hospitals and insurance companies. It also ensured that the elderly, who already formed one of the most powerful interest groups in America, would remain politically formidable well into the twenty-first century.

It also had important implications for the nature of the work force in the twenty-first century. In the last twenty years of the twentieth century, the number of people aged 25–54 in the native-born work force in the United States grew by over 26 million. In the first ten years of the twenty-first century, the number of workers in that age group will not grow at all. That will put increasing pressure on the economy to employ more older workers. It will also create a greater demand for immigrant workers.

New Patterns of Immigration and Ethnicity

Surging Immigration The nation's immigration quotas expanded significantly in the last decades of the twentieth century, allowing more newcomers to enter the United States legally than at any point since the beginning of the twentieth century. In 2000, over 28 million Americans—over 10 percent of the total population—consisted of immigrants (people born outside the United States).

The Immigration Reform Act of 1965 (see p. 818–819) had eliminated quotas based on national origin; from then on, newcomers from regions other than Latin America (who were governed by different laws) were generally admitted on a first-come, first-served basis. In 1965, 90 percent of the immigrants to the United States came from Europe. By the mid-1980s, only 10 percent of the new arrivals were Europeans, although that figure rose slightly in the 1990s as emigrants from Russia and eastern Europe—now free to leave their countries—came in increasing numbers. The extent and character of the new immigration was causing a dramatic change in the composition of the American population. By the end of the twentieth century, people of white European background constituted under 80 percent of the population (as opposed to 90 percent a half-century before).

Latino Immigrants Particularly important to the new immigration were two groups: Latinos (people from Spanish-speaking nations, particularly Mexico) and Asians. Both experienced enormous, indeed unprecedented, growth after 1965. People from Latin America constituted more than a third of the total number of legal immigrants to the United States in every year after 1965—and a much larger proportion of the total number of illegal immigrants. Mexico alone accounted for over one-fourth of all the immigrants living in the United States in 2000.

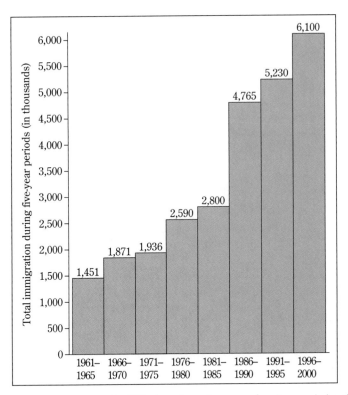

TOTAL IMMIGRATION, 1961–2000 This chart shows the tremendous increase in immigration to the United States in the decades since the Immigration Reform Act of 1965. The immigration of the 1980s and 1990s was the highest since the late nineteenth century.

In the 1980 census, 6 percent of the population (about 14 million) was listed as being of Hispanic origin. By 1997, census figures showed an increase to 11 percent—or 29 million people.

In the 1980s and 1990s, Asian immigrants arrived in even greater numbers than Latinos, constituting more than 40 percent of the total of legal newcomers. They swelled the already substantial Chinese and Japanese communities in California and elsewhere. And they created substantial new communities of immigrants from Vietnam, Thailand, Cambodia, Laos, the Philippines, Korea, and India. By 2000, there were more than 10 million Asian Americans in the United States (4 percent of the population), more than twice the number of fifteen years before.

The Black Middle Class

For the black middle class, which by the end of the twentieth century constituted over half of the African-American population of America, progress was remarkable in the more than thirty years after the high point of the

Remarkable Black Economic Progress

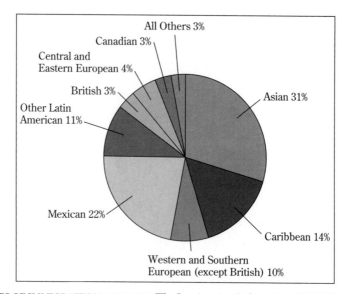

SOURCES OF IMMIGRATION, 1960–1990 The Immigration Reform Act of 1965 lifted the national quotas imposed on immigration policy in 1924 and opened immigration to large areas of the world that had previously been restricted. In 1965, 90 percent of the immigrants to the United States came from Europe. As this chart shows, by 1990 almost the reverse was true. Over 80 percent of all immigrants came from non-European sources. ◆ *What impact did this new immigration have on American politics?*

civil rights movement. Disparities between black and white professionals did not vanish, but they diminished substantially. African-American families moved into more affluent urban and suburban communities. African Americans made up 12 percent of the college population in the 1990s (up from 5 percent twenty-five years earlier). The percentage of black high-school graduates going on to college was virtually the same as that of white high-school graduates by the end of the twentieth century (although a far smaller proportion of blacks than whites managed to complete high school). And African Americans were making rapid strides in many professions from which, a generation earlier, they had been barred or within which they had been segregated. Middle-class blacks, in other words, had realized great gains from the legislation of the 1960s, from the changing national mood on race, from the creation of controversial affirmative action programs, and from their own strenuous efforts.

Poor and Working-Class African Americans

But the rise of the black middle class also accentuated (and perhaps even contributed to) the increasingly desperate plight of other African Americans, whom the economic growth and the liberal programs of the 1960s and beyond had never reached. These impoverished people—sometimes described as the "underclass"—made up as much as a third of the nation's

black population. As more successful African
Americans moved out of the inner cities, the poor
Black "Underclass"
were left virtually alone in their decaying neighborhoods. Fewer than half
of young inner-city blacks finished high school; more than 60 percent
were unemployed. The black family structure suffered as well from the
dislocations of urban poverty. There was a radical increase in the number
of single-parent, female-headed black households. In 1970, 59 percent of
all black children under 18 lived with both their parents (already down
from 70 percent a decade earlier). In 2000, only 38 percent of African-
American children lived in such households, while 75 percent of white
children did.

Nonwhites were disadvantaged by many factors in the changing social
and economic climate of the 1980s and 1990s. Among them was a growing
public and political impatience with affirmative action and other programs
designed to advance their fortunes. They suffered as well from a steady decline in the number of unskilled jobs in the economy; the departure of
businesses from their neighborhoods; the absence of adequate transportation to areas where jobs were more plentiful; and failing schools that did
not prepare them adequately for employment. And they suffered, in many
cases, from a sense of futility and despair, born of years of entrapment in
brutal urban ghettoes.

The anger and despair such conditions were creating among inner-city
residents was expressed at times artistically, as in some aspects of the most
popular new black musical form of the 1980s and 1990s, rap. The frustration became visible even more graphically in the summer of 1992 in Los
Angeles. The previous year, a bystander had videotaped several Los Angeles police officers beating an apparently helpless black man, Rodney King,
whom they had captured after an auto chase. Broadcast repeatedly around
the country, the tape evoked outrage among whites and blacks alike. But an
all-white jury in a suburban community just outside Los Angeles acquitted
the officers when they were tried for assault. Black residents of South Central Los Angeles, one of the poorest communities in
the city, erupted in anger—precipitating one of the
Los Angeles Riots
largest racial disturbances of the twentieth century. There was widespread
looting and arson. More than fifty people died.

What Americans had long called "race relations," the way in which
white and black Americans viewed each other, grew increasingly sour in
these difficult years. Nowhere was this mutual suspicion more evident
than in the celebrated trial of the former football
star O. J. Simpson, who was accused of murdering
Simpson Trial
his former wife and a young man in Los Angeles in 1994. The long and
costly "O. J. trial" was an enormous media sensation for over a year.
Throughout the proceedings, opinions about Simpson's guilt broke down
strikingly along racial lines. A vast majority of whites believed that he was
guilty, and a significant majority of blacks believed he was innocent. Simpson's acquittal in the fall of 1995, after a trial in which the defense tried to

"IGNORANCE = FEAR" The artist Keith Haring (whose work was inspired in large part by urban graffiti) created this striking poster in 1989, the year before he himself died of AIDS, to generate support for the battle against the disease. "ACT UP," the organization that distributed it, was among the most militant groups in demanding more rapid efforts to search for a cure. *(Silence=Death, Ignorance=Fear, 1989 © The Estate of Keith Haring)*

portray him as a victim of police racism, caused celebrations in many black communities and a quiet disgust among many whites.

Modern Plagues: Drugs and AIDS

America in the 1980s and 1990s was ravaged by two new and deadly epidemics. One was a dramatic increase in drug use, which penetrated nearly every community in the nation. The enormous demand for illegal drugs, and particularly for "crack" cocaine, spawned what was in effect a multibillion-dollar industry; and those reaping the enormous profits of the trade fought strenuously and often savagely to protect their positions. Political figures of both parties spoke heatedly about the need for a "war on drugs"; but government efforts to stop drug imports and reduce demand had little effect. Drug use declined significantly among middle-class people beginning in the late 1980s, but the epidemic showed no signs of abating in the poor urban neighborhoods where it was doing the most severe damage.

The drug epidemic was closely related to another scourge of the 1980s and 1990s: the epidemic spread of a new and lethal disease first documented *AIDS Epidemic* in 1981 and soon named AIDS (acquired immune deficiency syndrome). AIDS is the product of the HIV virus, which is transmitted by the exchange of bodily fluids (blood or semen). The virus gradually destroys the body's immune system and makes its victims highly vulnerable to a number of diseases (particularly to various forms of cancer and pneumonia) to which they would otherwise have a natural resistance. Those infected with the virus (i.e., HIV positive) can live for a long time without developing AIDS, but in the first years of the disease, those who became ill were virtually certain to die. The first American victims of AIDS (and for years the group among whom cases remained the most numerous) were homosexual men. But by the late 1980s, as the gay community began to take preventive measures, the most rapid increase in the spread of the disease occurred among heterosexuals, many of them intravenous drug users, who spread the virus by sharing contaminated hypodermic needles. In 2000, U.S. government agencies estimated that about 780,000 Americans were infected with the HIV virus and that another 427,000 had already died from the disease. But the United States represented only a tiny proportion of the worldwide total of people afflicted with AIDS, an estimated 36.1 million people at the end of 2000. Seventy percent (over 25 million) of those cases were concentrated in Africa. Governments and private groups, in the meantime, began promoting AIDS awareness in increasingly visible and graphic ways—urging young people, in particular, to avoid "unsafe sex" through abstinence or the use of latex condoms. The success of that effort in the United States was suggested by the drop in new cases from 70,000 in 1995 to approximately 40,000 in 2000.

In the mid-1990s, AIDS researchers, after years of frustration, began discovering effective treatments for the disease. By taking a combination of powerful drugs on a rigorous schedule, among them a group known as protease inhibitors, even people with relatively advanced cases of AIDS experienced dramatic improvement. The new drugs gave promise for the first time of dramatically extending the lives of people with AIDS, perhaps to normal life spans. The drugs were not a cure for AIDS; people who stopped taking them experienced a rapid return of the disease. And the effectiveness of the drugs varied from person to person. In addition, the drugs were very expensive and difficult to administer; poorer AIDS patients often could not obtain access to them, and they remained very scarce in Africa and other less affluent parts of the world where the epidemic was rampant. Nevertheless, the new medications restored hundreds of thousands of desperately ill people to health and gave them realistic hopes of long and relatively normal lives.

The Decline in Crime

One of the most striking social developments of the late 1990s was a dramatic reduction in crime rates across most of the United States. The rising incidence of violent crime had been one of the most disturbing facts of American life for two generations—and a central fact of national politics since at least the 1960s. But beginning in the early-1990s, crime began to fall—in many cities, quite dramatically. The government's crime index—which measures the incidence of seven serious crimes—fell by 19.5 percent between 1992 and 2000, with some of the most dramatic reductions occurring in murder and other violent crimes.

Prosperity and declining unemployment were certainly factors. So were new, sophisticated police techniques that *New Police Techniques* helped deter many crimes and that led to the arrest of many criminals who would previously have escaped capture. New incarceration policies—longer, tougher sentences and fewer paroles and early releases for violent criminals—led to a radical increase in the prison population and, consequently, a reduction in the number of criminals at liberty to commit crimes.

A CONTESTED CULTURE

Few things created more controversy and anxiety in the 1980s and 1990s than the battles over the character of American culture.

Battles over Feminism and Abortion

Among the principal goals of the New Right as it became more powerful and assertive in the 1980s and 1990s, and as it focused on cultural changes it did not like, was to challenge feminism and its achievements. Leaders of the New Right had campaigned successfully against the proposed Equal Rights Amendment to the Constitution. And they played a central role in the most divisive issue of the late 1980s and 1990s: the controversy over abortion rights.

For those who favored allowing women to choose to terminate unwanted pregnancies, the Supreme Court's decision in *Roe* v. *Wade* (1973) had seemed to settle the question. By the 1980s, abortion was the most commonly performed surgical procedure in the country. But at the same time, opposition to abortion was creating a powerful grassroots movement. The right-to-life movement, as it called it- *Right-to-Life Movement* self, found its most fervent supporters among Catholics; and indeed, the Catholic Church itself lent its institutional authority to the battle against legalized abortion. Religious doctrine also motivated the anti-abortion stance of Mormons, fundamentalist Christians, and other groups. The opposition of some other anti-abortion activists had less to do with religion than with their commitment to traditional notions of family and gender relations. To them, abortion was a particularly offensive part of a much larger assault by feminists on the role of women as wives and mothers. It was also, many foes contended, a form of murder. Fetuses, they claimed, were human beings who had a "right to life" from the moment of conception.

In the 1970s, Congress and many state legislatures began barring the use of public funds to pay for abortions, thus making them inaccessible for many poor women. The Reagan and both Bush administrations imposed further restrictions on federal funding and even on the right of doctors in federally funded clinics to give patients any information on abortion. Extremists in the right-to-life movement began picketing, occupying, and at times bombing abortion clinics. Several anti-abortion activists murdered doctors who performed abortions.

The changing composition of the Supreme Court in the 1980s and early 1990s (when five new conservative justices were named by Presidents Reagan and Bush) renewed the right-to-life movement's hopes for a reversal of *Roe* v. *Wade*. In *Webster* v. *Reproductive Health Services* (1989), the Court upheld a Missouri law that forbade any institution receiving state funds from performing abortions, whether or not those funds were used to finance the abortions. But the Court stopped short of overturning its 1973 decision.

Through much of the 1970s and 1980s, defenders of abortion had remained confident that *Roe* v. *Wade* protected their right to choose abortion and that the anti-abortion movement was unlikely to prevail. But the changing judicial climate of the late 1980s mobilized defenders of abortion as never before. They called themselves the "pro-choice" movement, because they were defending not so much abortion itself as every woman's right to choose whether and when to bear a child. It quickly became clear that the pro-choice movement was in many parts of the country at least as strong as, and in some areas much stronger than, the right-to-life movement, and it contributed substantially to the election and reelection of Bill Clinton. But abortion rights remained highly vulnerable, given the intensity of feeling among those who opposed them. Clinton's successor, George W. Bush, openly opposed abortion.

Other efforts by feminists to protect and expand the rights of women continued. Women's organizations and many individual women worked strenuously in the 1980s and 1990s to improve access to child care for poor women, and to win the right to caregiver leaves for parents, which a law passed by Congress and signed by President Clinton in 1993 helped secure. They also worked to raise awareness of sexual harassment in the workplace, with considerable success. Colleges, universities, the military, government agencies, even many corporations established strict new standards of behavior for their employees in dealing with members of the opposite sex and created grievance procedures for those who believed they had been harassed.

Women's Rights Expanded

Both the achievements and the limits of their progress on this issue were evident in the sensational controversy in 1991 over Judge Clarence Thomas, President Bush's nominee for a seat on the Supreme Court. Late in the confirmation proceedings, accusations of sexual harassment from Anita Hill, a law professor and former employee of Thomas, became public. Hill's testimony before the Senate Judiciary Committee dramatically polarized both the Senate and the nation. Feminists and others

Anita Hill and Clarence Thomas

tended to believe the accusations and hailed the accuser for drawing national attention to the issue of harassment; but many Americans (and most members of the virtually all-male Senate) apparently did not believe her. Thomas was ultimately confirmed by a narrow margin.

The Changing Left and the Growth of Environmentalism

The New Left of the 1960s and early 1970s did not disappear after the end of the war in Vietnam, but it faded rapidly. Yet a left of sorts did survive, giving evidence in the process of how greatly the nation's political climate had changed. Where 1960s activists had rallied to protest racism, poverty, and war, their counterparts in the 1980s and 1990s more often worked to organize communities to fight for local concerns. A great resurgence of grassroots organizing in many parts of the country was, in part, testament to the legacy of the New Left. Most of all, activists in the 1980s and 1990s organized to stop the proliferation of nuclear weapons and power plants, to save the wilderness, to protect endangered species, to limit reckless economic development, and to otherwise protect the environment.

The environmental movement, which had grown so dramatically in the late 1960s and early 1970s, continued to expand in the last decades of the twentieth century. Several highly visible environmental catastrophes in those years greatly increased their commitment. Among them were a major oil spill off Santa Barbara, California, in 1969; the discovery of large deposits of improperly disposed toxic waste in the residential community of Love Canal in upstate New York in 1978; a frightening accident at the nuclear power plant on Three Mile Island, Pennsylvania in 1979; and the largest oil spill in American history in Alaska in 1989.

In the decades after the first Earth Day, environmental issues gained increasing attention and support. Environmentalists helped block the construction of roads, airports, and other projects (in-

Global Warming

cluding American development of the supersonic transport airplane, or SST) that they claimed would be ecologically dangerous, taking advantage of new legislation protecting endangered species and environmentally fragile regions. By the end of the 1970s, many scientists were warning that the release of certain industrial pollutants (most notably chlorofluorocarbons) into the atmosphere was depleting the ozone layer of the earth's atmosphere, which protects the globe from the sun's most dangerous rays. They warned, too, of the related danger of global warming, a rise in the earth's temperature as a result of emissions from the burning of fossil fuels (coal and oil). These problems—and such others as the pollution of the oceans and the destruction of rain forests—required international solutions, which were much more difficult to produce. In 1997, representatives of the major industrial nations met in Kyoto, Japan and agreed to a broad treaty banning certain emissions into the atmosphere as a step toward reversing global warming. But in March

2001, under pressure from business leaders, the second Bush administration rejected the treaty.

The concern for the environment, the opposition to nuclear power, the resistance to economic development—all were reflections of a more fundamental characteristic of the post-Vietnam left. In a sharp break from the nation's long commitment to growth and progress, many dissidents argued that only by limiting growth and curbing traditional forms of progress could society hope to survive. Such arguments evoked strong opposition from conservatives and others, who ridiculed the no-growth ideology as an expression of defeatism and despair.

The Fragmentation of Mass Culture

One of the most powerful cultural trends throughout much of the twentieth century was the growing power and the increasing standardization of mass culture. The institutions of the media—news, entertainment, advertising, and others—grew steadily more influential. Almost without exception, they also strove to attract the largest possible audience or market. In doing so, they attempted to standardize their products so that they would be familiar and accessible to everyone. The drive toward standardization was reinforced by the philosophy of the advertising industry to promote most products for the largest possible audience.

Beginning in the 1970s, and accelerating in the 1980s and 1990s, the character of mass culture changed in some important ways. There was, of course, continued standardization in many areas. McDonald's, Burger King, and other fast-food chains became the most widely known restaurants in America (and indeed the world). Huge retail chains—Kmart, Bradlees, Wal-Mart, Barnes & Noble, Blockbuster, the Gap, and others—dominated retail sales in *Growing Cultural Segmentation* many communities. The most popular Hollywood films attracted larger audiences than ever before; and the most powerful media companies—most notably, Disney—produced merchandise that made their film and television characters familiar to almost everyone in the world. But there was also a very different trend at work at the same time: a tendency in both retailing and entertainment to appeal less to mass markets and more to specific segments of the market.

This segmentation was first visible in new ideas about advertising that became powerful in the 1970s, ideas known as "targeting." Instead of finding promotional techniques to appeal to everyone, advertisers sought to identify a product with a particular "segment" of the market (men, women, young people, old people, health-conscious people, the rich, people of modest means, children) and create advertisements designed to appeal to it. As if in response, the television networks began to produce programming that focused on particular segments of the audience. Some programs were aimed at women, some at African Americans, some at affluent, urban middle-class viewers, some at more rural and provincial people. Fewer and fewer programs had a truly "mass" audience; more and more aimed at a particular group within that audience.

Even more important was the rapid proliferation of media outlets. As late as the 1970s, American television audiences overwhelmingly watched programs on the three major networks: NBC, CBS, and ABC. In the 1980s, that began to change. One reason was the proliferation of videocassette recorders (VCRs), which were in well over 75 percent of all homes by 2000. Instead of watching network television, viewers could now rent or buy videotapes and watch movies or other programming of their own choosing—available in enormous variety at thousands of video stores all across the country. In the late 1990s, VCRs began to give way to digital video disk players (DVDs), which spread rapidly and seemed likely eventually to displace VCRs altogether. Another reason was the increasing availability of cable and satellite television, which allowed homes to receive many more channels than ever before. The percent of television viewers watching the major networks declined steadily in the 1980s. New networks (among them Fox and Warner Brothers), along with specialized sports, movies, shopping, music, weather, and other channels, began to compete with the traditional leaders, distributing their programming over a combination of broadcast and cable channels. And many people turned away from television altogether and began to explore the powerful new medium of the Internet, with its huge variety of sites tailored to almost every conceivable interest and taste.

New Consumer Technologies

As audiences fragmented among many different stations and media, the phenomenon of the national "shared experience" declined as well. Network news, once the most important source for the vast majority of information, experienced a dramatic decline in viewership. Young people found their own media world in MTV and other cable stations that focused on rock music and other elements of youth culture. Hollywood continued to turn out hugely expensive "blockbusters" in a search for a mass audience. But some filmgoers turned instead to smaller independent films, which targeted particular segments of the population.

The "Culture Wars"

Few issues attracted more attention in the 1990s than the battle over what became known as "multiculturalism." Multiculturalism meant different things to different people, but at its core it was an effort to legitimize the cultural pluralism of the rapidly diversifying American population. That meant acknowledging that "American culture," which had long been defined primarily by white males of European descent, also included other traditions: female, African American, Native American, and increasingly in the late twentieth century, Hispanic, Asian, and Middle Eastern. Particular acri-

"Multiculturalism"

mony emerged out of efforts by some revisionists to portray traditional Western culture as inherently racist and imperialistic. Many critics of multiculturalism complained of a tyranny of "political correctness," by which feminists, cultural radicals, and others introduced a new form of intolerance to public discourse in the name of defending the rights of women and minorities.

The controversies surrounding multiculturalism and "political correctness" were illustrations of a painful change in the character of American society. Traditional patterns of authority faced challenges from women, minorities, and others. The liberal belief in tolerance and assimilation was fraying in the face of the growing cultural separatism of some ethnic and racial groups. But multiculturalism, in many of its forms, was also a way of broadening the definition of American culture to include all the nation's diverse peoples. It was often an expression of confidence in society's ability to tolerate and understand its many differences.

THE PERILS OF GLOBALIZATION

The celebration of the beginning of a new millennium on January 1, 2000 was a notable moment not just because of the dramatic change in the calendar. It was significant above all as a global event—a shared and for the most part joyous experience that united the world in its exuberance. Television viewers around the world followed the dawn of the new century from Australia, through Asia, Africa, and Europe, and on into the Americas. Never had the world seemed more united. But if the millennium celebrations suggested the bright promise of globalization, other events at the dawn of the new century suggested its dark perils.

Opposing the "New World Order"

In the United States and other industrial nations, opposition to globalization—or to what President George H. W. Bush once called "the new world order"—took several forms. To many Americans on both the left and the right, the nation's increasingly interventionist foreign policy was deeply troubling. Critics on the left charged that the United States was using military action to advance its economic interests, most notably in the 1991 Gulf War. Critics on the right claimed that the nation was allowing itself to be swayed by the interests of other nations; they opposed such supposedly humanitarian interventions as the 1993 invasion of Somalia and the American interventions in the Balkans in the late 1990s—both because they insisted no vital American interests were at stake and because they feared that the United States was ceding its sovereignty in these actions to international organizations.

But the most impassioned opposition to globalization in the West came from an array of groups that challenged the claim that the "new world order" was economically beneficial. Labor unions insisted that the rapid expansion of free-trade agreements led to the export of jobs from advanced nations to less developed ones. Other groups attacked working conditions in new manufacturing countries on humanitarian grounds, arguing that the global economy was creating new classes of "slave laborers." Environmentalists argued that globalization, in exporting industry to low-wage countries, also exported industrial pollution and toxic waste into nations that had no effective laws to control them. And still others opposed global economic arrangements on the grounds that they enriched and empowered large multinational corporations and threatened the freedom and autonomy of individuals and communities.

Intervention Criticized   The varied opponents of globalization may have had different reasons for their hostility, but they agreed on the targets of their discontent: not just free-trade agreements, but also the multinational institutions that policed and advanced the global economy. Among them were the World Trade Organization, which monitored the enforcement of the GATT treaties of the 1990s; the International Monetary Fund, which controlled international credit and exchange rates; and the World Bank, which made money available for development projects in many countries. In November 1999, when the leaders of the seven leading industrial nations (as well as the leader of Russia) gathered for their annual meeting in Seattle, Washington, tens of thousands of protestors—most of them peaceful, but some of them violent—clashed with police, smashed store windows, and all but paralyzed the city. A few months later a smaller but still substantial demonstration disrupted meetings of the IMF and the World Bank in Washington. And in July 2001, at a meeting of the same leaders in Genoa, Italy, thousands of demonstrators clashed violently with police in a melee that left one protester dead and several hundred injured. In the days that followed, the number of protesters in Genoa rose to an esti-

Antiglobalization Protests   mated 50,000. The participants in the meeting responded to the demonstrations by pledging $1.2 billion to fight the AIDS epidemic in developing countries, and also by deciding to hold their next meeting at a remote resort in Canada.

Defending Orthodoxy

Outside the industrialized West, many people resented the way the world economy had left them in poverty and had, in their view, exploited and oppressed them. In some parts of the nonindustrialized world—and particularly in some of the Islamic nations of the Middle East—the increasing reach of globalization created additional concerns, less rooted in economics than in religion and culture.

The Iranian Revolution of 1979, in which orthodox Muslims ousted a despotic government whose leaders had embraced many aspects of modern western culture, was one of the first large and visible manifestations of a phenomenon that would eventually reach across the Islamic world and threaten the stability of the globe. In one Islamic nation after another, waves of fundamentalist orthodoxy (known as "Islamism") emerged to defend traditional culture against incursions from the West. The new fundamentalism met considerable resistance within much of Islam—from established governments, from affluent middle classes that had made their peace with the modern industrial world, from women who feared the anti-feminist agenda of many of these movements. But it emerged nevertheless as a powerful force—and in a few nations, among them Iran after 1979 and Afghanistan in the late 1990s—the dominant force.

Among some particularly militant fundamentalists, the battle to preserve orthodoxy came to be defined as a battle against the West generally and the United States in particular. Resentment of the West was rooted in the incursion of new and, *Resentment of the West* in their view, threatening cultural norms into traditional societies. It was rooted as well in resentment of the support western nations gave to corrupt and tyrannical regimes in some Islamic countries, and in opposition to western (and particularly American) military incursions into the region. The continuing struggle between Palestinians and Israelis—a struggle defined in the eyes of many Muslims by American support for Israel—added further to their contempt.

One product of this combination of resentments was individuals and groups committed to using violence to fight the influence of the West. No fundamentalist movement had any advanced military capabilities. Militants resorted instead to isolated incidents of violence and mayhem, designed to disrupt societies and governments and to create fear among their peoples. Such tactics became known to the world as terrorism.

The Rise of Terrorism

The term "terrorism" was used first during the French Revolution in the 1790s to describe the actions of the radical Jacobins against the French government. The word continued to be used intermittently throughout the nineteenth and early twentieth centuries to describe the use of violence as a form of intimidation against peoples and governments. But the widespread understanding of terrorism as an important fact of modern life is largely a product of the second half of the twentieth century.

Acts of what are now known as terrorism have occurred in many parts of the world. Irish revolu- *Origins of Terrorism* tionaries engaged in terrorism regularly against the English through much of the twentieth century. Jews used it in Palestine against the British before the creation of Israel, and Palestinians have used it frequently against Jews in Israel—particularly in the last several decades. Revolutionary groups in Italy, Germany, Japan, and France have engaged in terrorist acts intermittently over the last thirty years.

The United States, too, has experienced terrorism for many years, much of it against American targets abroad. These included bombing of the Marine barracks in Beirut in 1983, the explosion that brought down an American airliner over Lockerbie, Scotland in 1988, the bombing of American embassies in 1998, the assault on the U.S. naval vessel *Cole* in 2000, and other events around the world. Terrorist incidents were relatively rare, but not unknown, within the United States itself prior to September 11, 2001. Militants on the American left performed various acts of terror in the 1960s and early 1970s. In February, 1993, a bomb exploded in the parking garage of the World Trade Center in New York killing six people and causing serious, but not irreparable, structural damage to the towers. Several men connected with militant Islamic organizations were convicted of the crime. In April 1995, a van containing explosives blew up in front of a federal building in Oklahoma City, killing 168 people. Timothy McVeigh, a former Marine who had become part of a militant anti-government movement on the right, was convicted of the crime and eventually executed in 2001.

Most Americans, however, considered terrorism a problem that mainly plagued other nations. Few thought very much about it as an important concern in their own country. One of the many results of the terrible events of September 11, 2001 was to jolt the American people out of complacency and alert them to the presence of continuing danger. That awareness increased in the weeks after September 11. New security measures began to change the way in which Americans traveled. New government regulations began to alter immigration policies and to affect the character of international banking. Warnings of possible new terrorist attacks created widespread tension and uneasiness. A puzzling and frightening epidemic of anthrax—a potent bacterial agent that can cause illness and death if not properly treated—began in the weeks after September 11 and spread through the mail to media outlets, members of Congress, and random others.

In the meantime, the United States government launched what President Bush called a "war against terrorism."
"War against Terrorism"
The attacks on the World Trade Center and the Pentagon, government intelligence indicated, had been planned and orchestrated by Middle Eastern agents of a powerful terrorist network known as Al Qaeda. Its leader, Osama Bin Laden—until 2001 little known outside the Arab world—quickly became one of the best known and most notorious figures in the world. Fighting a shadowy terrorist network spread out among many nations of the world was a very difficult task, and the administration made clear from the beginning that the battle would be waged in many ways, not just militarily. But the first visible act of the war against terrorism was, in fact, a military one. Convinced that the militant "Taliban" government of Afghanistan had sheltered and supported Bin Laden and his organization, the United States began a sustained campaign of bombing against the regime and sent in small

numbers of ground troops to help a resistance organization overthrow the Afghan government. The Taliban soon fled in disarray, and with it most of the Al Qaeda forces they had sheltered. How many survived the American onslaught remained unknown for some time, as did the fate of Osama Bin Laden himself.

In early 2002, President Bush spoke to Con- *"Axis of Evil"* gress of an "axis of evil" in the world, which included North Korea, Iran, and Iraq. By the end of 2002, the Bush administration was talking openly of invading Iraq and was amassing troops and weapons in the region, to topple the regime of Saddam Hussein, the enemy of the first Bush administration a decade before. But it was also being drawn, reluctantly, into the turbulent politics of the Middle East, as violence between Israelis and Palestinians escalated. Palestinian "suicide bombers"terrorized the Israeli people. The hard-line Israeli prime minister, Ariel Sharon, sent troops and tanks into Palestinian areas of the West Bank. American leaders seemed torn between their desire to stop the violence and their reluctance to criticize Sharon for combating terrorism.

While the American military built up a presence in the Gulf, the Bush administration made a strenuous but unsuccessful effort to attract broad international support for the proposed war against Hussein and Iraq. The United Nations voted in the fall of 2002 to demand a resumption of inspections of Iraqi weapons—mandated by the settlement of the 1991 Gulf War and ignored by Hussein for the previous several years; and early in 2003, the new inspections began in earnest. Although the Iraqi government disclosed, and even destroyed, some forbidden weapons, the Bush administration insisted that they were not complying adequately with the UN requirements and that only a "regime change" (that is, the ouster of Hussein) would be sufficient *War in Iraq* evidence of disarmament. One by one, many of America's traditional allies in Europe and the Middle East turned against the American policy, insisting that the United States was moving too rapidly toward war. France, Germany, Russia, and China all opposed a UN Security Council resolution in support of war in Iraq; the Bush administration ultimately abandoned the effort to secure it. Large antiwar demonstrations occurred across much of the world, including within the United States. Anti-American sentiment intensified in Europe, the Middle East, and elsewhere. In the end, only Britain among America's principal allies supported the American effort in Iraq.

By mid-March 2003, the American military build-up in the Gulf was nearing completion, and President Bush gave Hussein 48 hours to leave the country so as to avert a war. Hussein rejected that demand and on the evening of March 19, American missiles struck Baghdad for the first time since 1991. The next day American and British troops began moving into the Iraqi desert, and the second American war against Iraq in twelve years had begun.

CHAPTER THIRTY-FOUR

A New Era?

In the immediate aftermath of September 11, 2001, many Americans came to believe that they had entered a new era in their history. The instability that had plagued so much of the rest of the world for years seemed suddenly to have arrived in the United States, shattering long-standing assumptions about safety and security and opening a period of uncertainty and fear. The prospects for the future were clouded further by a significant weakening of the economy that was already well advanced before September 11 and that the events of that day helped to increase.

America United   But fear and uncertainty were not the only results of the September 11 disasters. The reaction to the catastrophe—in New York, in Washington, and in much of the rest of the country—exposed a side of American life and culture that had always existed but that had not always been visible during the booming, self-indulgent years of the 1980s and 1990s. Americans responded to the tragedies with countless acts of courage and generosity, large and small, and with a sense of national unity and commitment that seemed, at least for a time, to resemble the unity and commitment at the beginning of World War II. The displays of courage began with the heroism of firefighters and rescue workers in New York City, who unhesitatingly plunged into the burning towers of the World Trade Center in an effort to save the people inside. Over 300 such workers died when the towers collapsed. In the weeks after the disaster, New York was flooded with volunteers—welders, metal workers, police, firefighters, medical personnel, and many others—who flocked to the city from around the country and the world to assist with rescue and recovery. Charitable donations to help the victims of the disasters exceeded $1 billion, the largest amount ever raised for a single purpose in such a short time in American history. Open and unembarrassed displays of patriotism and national pride—things that many Americans had once scorned—suddenly became fashionable again. Faith in government and its leaders, in decline for decades, suddenly (if not necessarily permanently) surged.

Alongside the many changes that occurred in American life and culture in the months after the attacks, many things remained constant. Most Americans continued to pursue their lives more or less as they always had. Most national institutions continued to function normally. The economy, despite its temporary weakness, remained the strongest, most diverse, and most productive in the world. The nation's traditional strengths—and its traditional problems—remained.

"Nothing has changed. . . . Everything has changed," wrote one prominent journalist in the weeks after September 11. In fact, no one could reliably predict whether the catastrophe would prove to be a fundamental turning point in the course of American and world history, or simply another in the countless changes and adjustments, great and small, that have characterized the nation's experience for centuries.

CONCLUSION

꧁꧂

Americans entered the twenty-first century afflicted with many anxieties, doubts, and resentments. Faith in the nation's institutions—most notably, government—was at its lowest point in many decades. Confidence in the nation's leaders had dramatically eroded in the wake of the tawdry scandals and vicious partisanship of the Clinton years and the dispiriting controversy over the results of the 2000 election. Ugly battles over differing standards of morality and different cultural styles disturbed many communities. Vague resentments over the increasingly unequal patterns of income and wealth in the new economy, which few Americans seemed able to translate into a coherent economic agenda, increased the nation's unease.

But the United States at the end of the century was, despite its many problems, a remarkably successful society. It had made dramatic strides in improving the lives of its citizens and in dealing with many of its social problems since the end of World War II. It entered the new century with the strongest economy in the world; with violent crime—one of its most corrosive problems for more than a generation—in a marked decline; and with its power and stature in the world unrivaled.

The traumatic events of September 11, 2001 changed many aspects of American life, not least the nation's sense of its isolation, and insulation, from the problems of the rest of the world. But both the many longstanding problems and the many longstanding strengths of the United States survived the attacks. It seemed safe to predict that the American people would go forward into their suddenly uncertain future not simply burdened by difficult problems, but also armed with great wealth, great power, and perhaps most of all with the extraordinary energy and resilience that has allowed the nation—throughout its long and often turbulent history—to endure, to flourish, and to strive continually for a better future.

FOR FURTHER REFERENCE

꧁꧂

John Lewis Gaddis, *The United States and the End of the Cold War* (1992) and *We Now Know: Rethinking Cold War History* (1997) are early examinations of the transformation of the world order. E. J. Dionne, *Why Americans Hate Politics* (1991) is a perceptive discussion of the political discontents of the 1980s and early 1990s. Thomas Byrne Edsall and Mary D. Edsall, *Chain Reaction: The Impact of Race, Rights, and Taxes on American Politics* (1991) is an alternative interpretation of the changes in American politics, focusing primarily on the impact of race. David Maraniss, *First in His Class: A Biography of Bill Clinton* (1995) traces Clinton's pre-presidential career. Theda Skocpol,

Boomerang: Clinton's Health Security Effort and the Turn against Government in U.S. Politics (1996) is an account of one of the major setbacks of Clinton's first term. Jeffrey Toobin, *A Vast Conspiracy* (1999) is an account of the scandals that rocked the Clinton presidency. Toobin is also the author of an important account of the disputed 2000 presidential election, *Too Close to Call* (2001). Haynes Johnson, *The Best of Times: America in the Clinton Years* (2001) is an account of the politics and culture of the 1990s. David Halberstam, *War in a Time of Peace: Bush, Clinton, and the Generals* (2001) examines the foreign policy and military ventures of the Bush and Clinton years. Michael A. Bernstein and David E. Adler, *Understanding American Economic Decline* (1994) is an important collection of essays on the changes in the American economy since the 1970s. *Computer: A History of the Information Machine* by Martin Campbell-Kelly and William Aspray (1996) is an introduction to the development of one of the critical technologies of the late twentieth century, and Janet Abbate, *Inventing the Internet* (1999) examines the emergence of the powerful new vehicle of communication. Randy Shilts, *And the Band Played On: Politics, People, and the AIDS Epidemic* (1987) is a provocative discussion of the early years of AIDS in America. Andrew Hacker, *Two Nations: Black and White, Separate, Hostile, Unequal* (1992) and Michael Katz, *The Undeserving Poor: From the War on Poverty to the War on Welfare* (1989) are two contrasting arguments about the nature of African-American life and inner-city poverty. William Julius Wilson, *The Truly Disadvantaged* (1987) and *When Work Disappears* (1996) are important studies of the inner-city poor from one of America's leading sociologists. David A. Hollinger, *Postethnic America: Beyond Multiculturalism* (1995) is an intelligent and spirited comment on the debates over multiculturalism.

For quizzes, Internet resources, references to additional books and films, and more, consult this book's Online Learning Center site at www.mhhe.com/unfinishednation4.

APPENDICES

❧

Documents and Tables

THE UNITED STATES

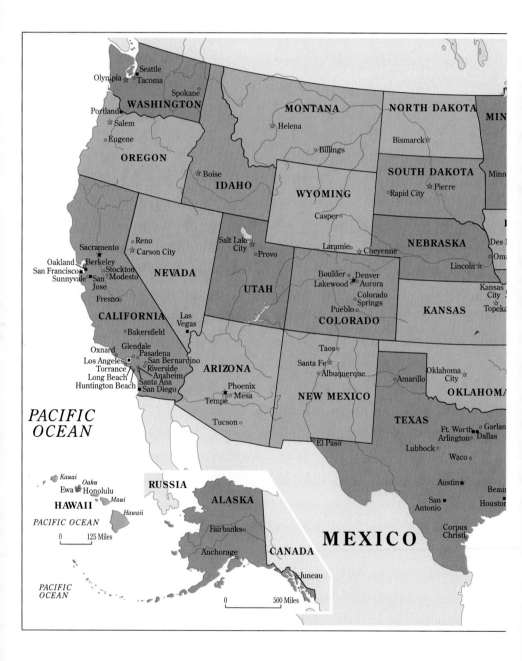

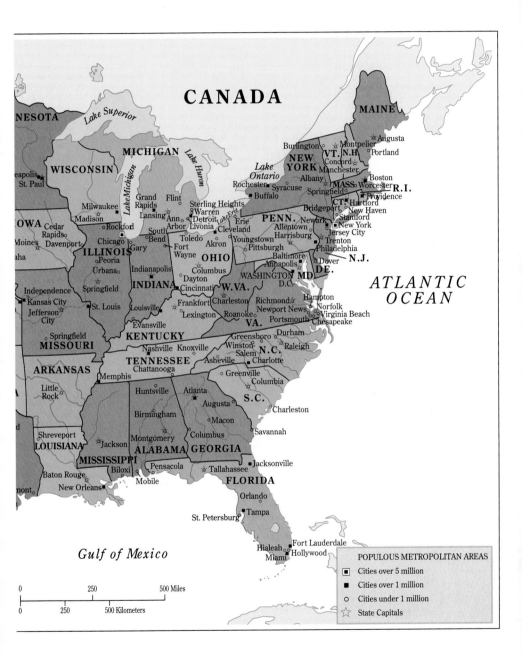

POPULOUS METROPOLITAN AREAS

- Cities over 5 million
- Cities over 1 million
- Cities under 1 million
- State Capitals

UNITED STATES TERRITORIAL EXPANSION, 1783–1898

United States Territorial Expansion, 1783–1898

(1859) Date of statehood
The United States in 1783
Louisiana Purchase, 1803

West Florida annexation, 1810, 1813
Florida: East Florida cession by Spain, 1819
Texas Annexation, 1845

Oregon Country, 1846
Mexican Cession, 1848
Gadsden Purchase, 1853

—— 1819 Treaty with Spain defined border of Oregon and Louisiana
- - - Texas boundary claimed by U.S., 1845–1848

ARCTIC OCEAN

GREENLAND
(Denmark)

ALASKA
(1959)
Purchased from Russia
1867

Hudson Bay

CANADA

United States claim
ceded to Britain 1846

Ceded by Britain 1818

Disputed by United States
and Britain 1783–1842

PACIFIC OCEAN

ME.
(1820)

WASH.
(1889)

British claim
ceded 1846

MONT.
(1889)

N.D.
(1889)

VT.
(1791)

N.H. (1788)

ORE.
(1859)

IDAHO
(1890)

S.D.
(1889)

MINN.
(1858)

WIS.
(1848)

MICH.
(1837)

N.Y.
(1788)

MASS. (1788)
R.I. (1790)
CONN. (1788)

WYO.
(1890)

IOWA
(1846)

PA.
(1787)

N.J. (1787)

NEV.
(1864)

NEB.
(1867)

ILL.
(1818)

IND.
(1816)

OHIO
(1803)

DEL. (1787)

UTAH
(1896)

COLO.
(1876)

KAN.
(1861)

MO.
(1821)

W.VA.
(1863)

VA.
(1788)

MD. (1788)

CALIF.
(1850)

KY.
(1792)

N.C.
(1789)

0   400 Miles
0   400 Kilometers

ARIZ.
(1912)

N.M.
(1912)

OKLA.
(1907)

ARK.
(1836)

TENN.
(1796)

S.C.
(1788)

ATLANTIC OCEAN

TEXAS
(1845)

MISS.
(1817)

ALA.
(1819)

GA.
(1788)

HAWAII
(1959)
PACIFIC
OCEAN
HAWAIIAN ISLANDS
Annexed 1898

MEXICO

LA.
(1812)

Annexed 1810

Annexed 1813

FLA.
(1845)

BAHAMAS

Gulf of Mexico

PUERTO RICO
(1898)

CUBA

THE DECLARATION OF INDEPENDENCE

In Congress, July 4, 1776,

The Unanimous Declaration of the Thirteen United States of America

When, in the course of human events, it becomes necessary for one people to dissolve the political bands which have connected them with another, and to assume, among the powers of the earth, the separate and equal station to which the laws of nature and of nature's God entitle them, a decent respect to the opinions of mankind requires that they should declare the causes which impel them to the separation.

We hold these truths to be self-evident, that all men are created equal; that they are endowed by their Creator with certain unalienable rights; that among these, are life, liberty, and the pursuit of happiness. That, to secure these rights, governments are instituted among men, deriving their just powers from the consent of the governed; that, whenever any form of government becomes destructive of these ends, it is the right of the people to alter or to abolish it, and to institute a new government, laying its foundation on such principles, and organizing its powers in such form, as to them shall seem most likely to effect their safety and happiness. Prudence, indeed, will dictate that governments long established, should not be changed for light and transient causes; and, accordingly, all experience hath shown, that mankind are more disposed to suffer, while evils are sufferable, than to right themselves by abolishing the forms to which they are accustomed. But, when a long train of abuses and usurpations, pursuing invariably the same object, evinces a design to reduce them under absolute despotism, it is their right, it is their duty, to throw off such government and to provide new guards for their future security. Such has been the patient sufferance of these colonies, and such is now the necessity which constrains them to alter their former systems of government. The history of the present King of Great Britain is a history of repeated injuries and usurpations, all having, in direct object, the establishment of an absolute tyranny over these States. To prove this, let facts be submitted to a candid world:

He has refused his assent to laws the most wholesome and necessary for the public good.

He has forbidden his governors to pass laws of immediate and pressing importance, unless suspended in their operation till his assent should be obtained; and, when so suspended, he has utterly neglected to attend to them.

He has refused to pass other laws for the accommodation of large districts of people, unless those people would relinquish the right of representation in the legislature; a right inestimable to them, and formidable to tyrants only.

He has called together legislative bodies at places unusual, uncomfortable, and distant from the depository of their public records, for the sole purpose of fatiguing them into compliance with his measures.

He has dissolved representative houses repeatedly for opposing, with manly firmness, his invasions on the rights of the people.

He has refused, for a long time after such dissolutions, to cause others to be elected; whereby the legislative powers, incapable of annihilation, have returned to the people at large for their exercise; the state remaining, in the meantime, exposed to all the danger of invasion from without, and compulsions within.

He has endeavored to prevent the population of these States; for that purpose, obstructing the laws for naturalization of foreigners, refusing to pass others to encourage their migration hither, and raising the conditions of new appropriations of lands.

He has obstructed the administration of justice, by refusing his assent to laws for establishing judiciary powers.

He has made judges dependent on his will alone, for the tenure of their offices, and the amount and payment of their salaries.

He has erected a multitude of new offices, and sent hither swarms of officers to harass our people, and eat out their substance.

He has kept among us, in time of peace, standing armies, without the consent of our legislatures.

He has affected to render the military independent of, and superior to, the civil power.

He has combined, with others, to subject us to a jurisdiction foreign to our Constitution, and unacknowledged by our laws; giving his assent to their acts of pretended legislation:

For quartering large bodies of armed troops among us:

For protecting them by a mock trial, from punishment, for any murders which they should commit on the inhabitants of these States:

For cutting off our trade with all parts of the world:

For imposing taxes on us without our consent:

For depriving us, in many cases, of the benefit of trial by jury:

For transporting us beyond seas to be tried for pretended offences:

For abolishing the free system of English laws in a neighboring province, establishing therein an arbitrary government, and enlarging its boundaries, so as to render it at once an example and fit instrument for introducing the same absolute rule into these colonies:

For taking away our charters, abolishing our most valuable laws, and altering, fundamentally, the powers of our governments:

For suspending our own legislatures, and declaring themselves invested with power to legislate for us in all cases whatsoever.

He has abdicated government here, by declaring us out of his protection, and waging war against us.

He has plundered our seas, ravaged our coasts, burnt our towns, and destroyed the lives of our people.

He is, at this time, transporting large armies of foreign mercenaries to complete the works of death, desolation, and tyranny, already begun, with circumstances of cruelty and perfidy scarcely paralleled in the most barbarous ages, and totally unworthy the head of a civilized nation.

He has constrained our fellow citizens, taken captive on the high seas, to bear arms against their country, to become the executioners of their friends, and brethren, or to fall themselves by their hands.

He has excited domestic insurrections amongst us, and has endeavored to bring on the inhabitants of our frontiers, the merciless Indian savages, whose known rule of warfare is an undistinguished destruction of all ages, sexes, and conditions.

In every stage of these oppressions, we have petitioned for redress, in the most humble terms; our repeated petitions have been answered only by repeated injury. A prince, whose character is thus marked by every act which may define a tyrant, is unfit to be the ruler of a free people.

Nor have we been wanting in attention to our British brethren. We have warned them, from time to time, of attempts made by their legislature to extend an unwarrantable jurisdiction over us. We have reminded them of the circumstances of our emigration and settlement here. We have appealed to their native justice and magnanimity, and we have conjured them, by the ties of our common kindred, to disavow these usurpations, which would inevitably interrupt our connections and correspondence. They, too, have been deaf to the voice of justice and consanguinity. We must, therefore, acquiesce in the necessity which denounces our separation, and hold them as we hold the rest of mankind, enemies in war, in peace, friends.

We, therefore, the representatives of the United States of America, in general Congress assembled, appealing to the Supreme Judge of the world for the rectitude of our intentions, do, in the name, and by the authority of the good people of these colonies, solemnly publish and declare, that these united colonies are, and of right ought to be, free and independent states: that they are absolved from all allegiance to the British Crown, and that all political connection between them and the state of Great Britain is, and ought to be, totally dissolved; and that, as free and independent states, they have full power to levy war, conclude peace, contract alliances, establish commerce, and to do all other acts and things which independent states may of right do. And, for the support of this declaration, with a firm reliance on the protection of Divine Providence, we mutually pledge to each other our lives, our fortunes, and our sacred honor.

The foregoing Declaration was, by order of Congress, engrossed, and signed by the following members:

John Hancock

New Hampshire
Josiah Bartlett
William Whipple
Matthew Thornton

Connecticut
Roger Sherman
Samuel Huntington
William Williams
Oliver Wolcott

New York
William Floyd
Philip Livingston
Francis Lewis
Lewis Morris

New Jersey
Richard Stockton
John Witherspoon
Francis Hopkinson
John Hart
Abraham Clark

Massachusetts Bay
Samuel Adams
John Adams
Robert Treat Paine
Elbridge Gerry

Pennsylvania
Robert Morris
Benjamin Rush
Benjamin Franklin
John Morton
George Clymer
James Smith
George Taylor
James Wilson
George Ross

Delaware
Caesar Rodney
George Read
Thomas M'Kean

Maryland
Samuel Chase
William Paca
Thomas Stone
Charles Carroll,
   of Carrollton

Rhode Island
Stephen Hopkins
William Ellery

Virginia
George Wythe
Richard Henry Lee
Thomas Jefferson
Benjamin Harrison
Thomas Nelson, Jr.
Francis Lightfoot Lee
Carter Braxton

North Carolina
William Hooper
Joseph Hewes
John Penn

South Carolina
Edward Rutledge
Thomas Heyward, Jr.
Thomas Lynch, Jr.
Arthur Middleton

Georgia
Button Gwinnett
Lyman Hall
George Walton

Resolved, That copies of the Declaration be sent to the several assemblies, conventions, and committees, or councils of safety, and to the several commanding officers of the continental troops; that it be proclaimed in each of the United States, at the head of the army.

THE CONSTITUTION OF THE UNITED STATES[1]

We the People of the United States, in Order to form a more perfect Union, establish Justice, insure domestic Tranquility, provide for the common defence, promote the general Welfare, and secure the Blessings of Liberty to ourselves and our Posterity, do ordain and establish this CONSTITUTION for the United States of America.

Article I

Section 1.
All legislative Powers herein granted shall be vested in a Congress of the United States, which shall consist of a Senate and House of Representatives.

Section 2.
The House of Representatives shall be composed of Members chosen every second Year by the People of the several States, and the Electors in each State shall have the Qualifications requisite for Electors of the most numerous Branch of the State Legislature.

No Person shall be a Representative who shall not have attained to the Age of twenty-five Years, and been seven Years a Citizen of the United States, and who shall not, when elected, be an Inhabitant of that State in which he shall be chosen.

[Representatives and direct Taxes[2] shall be apportioned among the several States which may be included within this Union, according to their respective Numbers, which shall be determined by adding to the whole Number of free Persons, including those bound to Service for a Term of Years, and excluding Indians not taxed, three fifths of all other Persons.][3] The actual Enumeration shall be made within three Years after the first Meeting of the Congress of the United States, and within every subsequent Term of ten Years, in such Manner as they shall by Law direct. The Number of Representatives shall not exceed one for every thirty Thousand, but each State shall have at Least one Representative; and until such enumeration shall be made, the State of New Hampshire shall be entitled to chuse three, Massachusetts eight, Rhode-Island and Providence Plantations one, Connecticut five, New York six, New Jersey four, Pennsylvania eight, Delaware one, Maryland six, Virginia ten, North Carolina five, South Carolina five, and Georgia three.

When vacancies happen in the Representation from any State, the Executive Authority thereof shall issue Writs of Election to fill such Vacancies.

The House of Representatives shall chuse their Speaker and other Officers; and shall have the sole Power of Impeachment.

---

[1]This version, which follows the original Constitution in capitalization and spelling, was published by the United States Department of the Interior, Office of Education, in 1935.
[2]Altered by the Sixteenth Amendment.
[3]Negated by the Fourteenth Amendment.

Section 3.

The Senate of the United States shall be composed of two Senators from each State, chosen by the Legislature thereof, for six Years; and each Senator shall have one Vote.

Immediately after they shall be assembled in Consequence of the first Election, they shall be divided as equally as may be into three Classes. The Seats of the Senators of the first Class shall be vacated at the Expiration of the second Year, of the second Class at the Expiration of the fourth Year, and of the third Class at the Expiration of the sixth Year, so that one-third may be chosen every second Year; and if Vacancies happen by Resignation, or otherwise, during the Recess of the Legislature of any State, the Executive thereof may make temporary Appointments until the next Meeting of the Legislature, which shall then fill such Vacancies.

No Person shall be a Senator who shall not have attained to the Age of thirty Years, and been nine Years a Citizen of the United States, and who shall not, when elected, be an Inhabitant of that State for which he shall be chosen.

The Vice President of the United States shall be President of the Senate, but shall have no vote, unless they be equally divided.

The Senate shall chuse their other Officers, and also a President pro tempore, in the absence of the Vice President, or when he shall exercise the Office of President of the United States.

The Senate shall have the sole Power to try all Impeachments. When sitting for that purpose they shall be on Oath or Affirmation. When the President of the United States is tried, the Chief Justice shall preside: And no person shall be convicted without the Concurrence of two thirds of the Members present.

Judgment in Cases of Impeachment shall not extend further than to removal from Office, and disqualification to hold and enjoy any Office of honor, Trust, or Profit under the United States: but the Party convicted shall nevertheless be liable and subject to Indictment, Trial, Judgment, and Punishment, according to Law.

Section 4.

The Times, Places and Manner of holding Elections for Senators and Representatives, shall be prescribed in each State by the Legislature thereof; but the Congress may at any time by Law make or alter such Regulations, except as to the Places of Chusing Senators.

The Congress shall assemble at least once in every Year, and such Meeting shall be on the first Monday in December, unless they shall by Law appoint a different Day.

Section 5.

Each House shall be the Judge of the Elections, Returns and Qualifications of its own Members, and a Majority of each shall constitute a Quorum to do Business; but a smaller number may adjourn from day to day, and may be authorized to compel the Attendance of absent Members, in such Manner, and under such Penalties, as each House may provide.

Each House may determine the Rules of its Proceedings, punish its Members for disorderly Behaviour, and, with the Concurrence of two thirds, expel a Member.

Each House shall keep a Journal of its Proceedings, and from time to time publish the same, excepting such Parts as may in their Judgment require Secrecy; and the Yeas and Nays of the Members of either House on any question shall, at the Desire of one fifth of those Present, be entered on the Journal.

Neither House, during the Session of Congress, shall, without the Consent of the other, adjourn for more than three days, nor to any other Place than that in which the two Houses shall be sitting.

Section 6.
The Senators and Representatives shall receive a Compensation for their Services, to be ascertained by Law, and paid out of the Treasury of the United States. They shall in all Cases, except Treason, Felony, and Breach of the Peace, be privileged from Arrest during their Attendance at the Session of their respective Houses, and in going to and returning from the same; and for any Speech or Debate in either House, they shall not be questioned in any other Place.

No Senator or Representative shall, during the Time for which he was elected, be appointed to any civil Office under the Authority of the United States, which shall have been created, or the Emoluments whereof shall have been increased, during such time; and no Person holding any Office under the United States shall be a Member of either House during his continuance in Office.

Section 7.
All Bills for raising Revenue shall originate in the House of Representatives; but the Senate may propose or concur with Amendments as on other bills.

Every Bill which shall have passed the House of Representatives and the Senate, shall, before it become a Law, be presented to the President of the United States; If he approve he shall sign it, but if not he shall return it, with his Objections, to that House in which it shall have originated, who shall enter the Objections at large on their Journal, and proceed to reconsider it. If after such Reconsideration two thirds of that House shall agree to pass the bill, it shall be sent, together with the objections, to the other House, by which it shall likewise be reconsidered, and if approved by two thirds of that House, it shall become a Law. But in all such Cases the Votes of both Houses shall be determined by Yeas and Nays, and the Names of the Persons voting for and against the Bill shall be entered on the Journal of each House respectively. If any Bill shall not be returned by the President within ten Days (Sundays excepted) after it shall have been presented to him, the Same shall be a Law, in like Manner as if he had signed it, unless the Congress by their Adjournment prevent its Return, in which Case it shall not be a Law.

Every Order, Resolution, or Vote to which the Concurrence of the Senate and House of Representatives may be necessary (except on a question of Adjournment) shall be presented to the President of the United States; and before the Same shall take Effect, shall be approved by him, or being disapproved by him, shall be repassed by two thirds of the Senate and House of Representatives, according to the Rules and Limitations prescribed in the Case of a Bill.

Section 8.
The Congress shall have Power To lay and collect Taxes, Duties, Imposts and Excises, to pay the Debts and provide for the common Defence and general Welfare of the United States; but all Duties, Imposts and Excises shall be uniform throughout the United States;

To borrow money on the credit of the United States;

To regulate Commerce with foreign Nations, and among the several States, and with the Indian Tribes;

To establish an uniform rule of Naturalization, and uniform Laws on the subject of Bankruptcies throughout the United States;

To coin Money, regulate the Value thereof, and of foreign Coin, and fix the Standard of Weights and Measures;

To provide for the Punishment of counterfeiting the Securities and current Coin of the United States;

To establish Post Offices and post Roads;

To promote the Progress of Science and useful Arts, by securing for limited Times to Authors and Inventors the exclusive Right to their respective Writings and Discoveries;

To constitute Tribunals inferior to the Supreme Court;

To define and punish Piracies and Felonies committed on the high Seas, and Offenses against the Law of Nations;

To declare War, grant Letters of Marque and Reprisal, and make Rules concerning Captures on Land and Water;

To raise and support Armies, but no Appropriation of Money to that Use shall be for a longer Term than two Years;

To provide and maintain a Navy;

To make Rules for the Government and Regulation of the land and naval forces;

To provide for calling forth the Militia to execute the Laws of the Union, suppress Insurrections and repel Invasions;

To provide for organizing, arming, and disciplining the Militia, and for governing such Part of them as may be employed in the Service of the United States, reserving to the States respectively, the Appointment of the Officers, and the Authority of training the Militia according to the discipline prescribed by Congress;

To exercise exclusive Legislation in all Cases whatsoever, over such District (not exceeding ten Miles square) as may, by Cession of particular States, and the acceptance of Congress, become the Seat of the Government of the United States, and to exercise like Authority over all Places purchased by the Consent of the Legislature of the State in which the Same shall be, for the Erection of Forts, Magazines, Arsenals, Dock-yards, and other needful Buildings;—And

To make all Laws which shall be necessary and proper for carrying into Execution the foregoing Powers, and all other Powers vested by this Constitution in the Government of the United States, or in any Department or Officer thereof.

Section 9.

The Migration or Importation of such Persons as any of the States now existing shall think proper to admit, shall not be prohibited by the Congress prior to the Year one thousand eight hundred and eight, but a tax or duty may be imposed on such Importation, not exceeding ten dollars for each Person.

The privilege of the Writ of Habeas Corpus shall not be suspended, unless when in Cases of Rebellion or Invasion the public Safety may require it.

No bill of Attainder or ex post facto Law shall be passed.

No capitation, or other direct, Tax shall be laid unless in Proportion to the Census or Enumeration herein before directed to be taken.

No Tax or Duty shall be laid on Articles exported from any State.

No Preference shall be given by any Regulation of Commerce or Revenue to the Ports of one State over those of another: nor shall Vessels bound to, or from, one State, be obliged to enter, clear, or pay Duties in another.

No Money shall be drawn from the Treasury, but in Consequence of Appropriations made by Law; and a regular Statement and Account of the Receipts and Expenditures of all public Money shall be published from time to time.

No Title of Nobility shall be granted by the United States: And no Person holding any Office of Profit or Trust under them, shall, without the Consent of the Congress, accept of any present, Emolument, Office, or Title, of any kind whatever, from any King, Prince, or foreign State.

Section 10.

No State shall enter into any Treaty, Alliance, or Confederation; grant Letters of Marque and Reprisal; coin Money; emit Bills of Credit; make any Thing but gold and silver Coin a Tender in Payment of Debts; pass any Bill of Attainder, ex post facto Law, or Law impairing the Obligation of Contracts, or grant any Title of Nobility.

No State shall, without the Consent of the Congress, lay any Imposts or Duties on Imports or Exports, except what may be absolutely necessary for executing its inspection Laws; and the net Produce of all Duties and Imposts, laid by any State on Imports or Exports, shall be for the use of the Treasury of the United States; and all such Laws shall be subject to the Revision and Control of the Congress.

No state shall, without the Consent of Congress, lay any duty of Tonnage, keep Troops, or Ships of War in time of Peace, enter into any Agreement or Compact with another State, or with a foreign Power, or engage in War, unless actually invaded, or in such imminent Danger as will not admit of delay.

Article II

Section 1.

The executive Power shall be vested in a President of the United States of America. He shall hold his Office during the Term of four years, and, together with the Vice President, chosen for the same Term, be elected, as follows:

Each State shall appoint, in such Manner as the Legislature thereof may direct, a Number of Electors, equal to the whole Number of Senators and Representatives to which the State may be entitled in the Congress: but no Senator or Representative, or Person holding an Office of Trust or Profit under the United States, shall be appointed an Elector.

[The Electors shall meet in their respective States, and vote by Ballot for two persons, of whom one at least shall not be an Inhabitant of the same State with themselves. And they shall make a List of all the Persons voted for, and of the Number of Votes for each; which List they shall sign and certify, and transmit sealed to the Seat of the Government of the United States, directed to the President of the Senate. The President of the Senate shall, in the Presence of the Senate and House of Representatives, open all the Certificates, and the Votes shall then be counted. The Person having the greatest Number of Votes shall be the President, if such Number be a Majority of the whole Number of Electors appointed; and if there be more than one who have such Majority, and have an equal Number of Votes, then the House of Representatives shall immediately chuse by Ballot one of them for President; and if no Person have a Majority, then from the five highest on the List the said House shall in like Manner chuse the President. But in chusing the President, the Votes shall be taken by States, the Representation from each

State having one Vote; a quorum for this Purpose shall consist of a Member or Members from two-thirds of the States, and a Majority of all the States shall be necessary to a Choice. In every Case, after the Choice of the President, the Person having the greatest Number of Votes of the Electors shall be the Vice President. But if there should remain two or more who have equal votes, the Senate shall chuse from them by Ballot the Vice President.][4]

The Congress may determine the Time of chusing the Electors, and the Day on which they shall give their Votes; which Day shall be the same throughout the United States.

No person except a natural-born Citizen, or a Citizen of the United States, at the time of the Adoption of this Constitution, shall be eligible to the Office of President; neither shall any Person be eligible to that Office who shall not have attained to the Age of thirty-five years, and been fourteen Years a Resident within the United States.

In Case of the Removal of the President from Office, or of his Death, Resignation, or Inability to discharge the Powers and Duties of the said Office, the same shall devolve on the Vice President, and the Congress may by Law provide for the Case of Removal, Death, Resignation, or Inability, both of the President and Vice President, declaring what Officer shall then act as President, and such Officer shall act accordingly, until the disability be removed, or a President shall be elected.

The President shall, at stated Times, receive for his Services a Compensation, which shall neither be increased nor diminished during the Period for which he shall have been elected, and he shall not receive within that Period any other Emolument from the United States, or any of them.

Before he enter on the execution of his Office, he shall take the following Oath or Affirmation:—"I do solemnly swear (or affirm) that I will faithfully execute the Office of President of the United States, and will, to the best of my Ability, preserve, protect, and defend the Constitution of the United States."

Section 2.
The President shall be Commander in Chief of the Army and Navy of the United States, and of the Militia of the several States, when called into the actual Service of the United States; he may require the Opinion, in writing, of the principal Officer in each of the executive Departments, upon any subject relating to the Duties of their respective Offices, and he shall have Power to Grant Reprieves and Pardons for Offenses against the United States, except in Cases of Impeachment.

He shall have Power, by and with the Advice and Consent of the Senate, to make Treaties, provided two-thirds of the Senators present concur; and he shall nominate, and by and with the Advice and Consent of the Senate, shall appoint Ambassadors, other public Ministers and Consuls, Judges of the supreme Court, and all other Officers of the United States, whose Appointments are not herein otherwise provided for, and which shall be established by Law: but the Congress may by Law vest the Appointment of such inferior Officers, as they think proper, in the President alone, in the Courts of Law, or in the Heads of Departments.

The President shall have Power to fill up all Vacancies that may happen during the Recess of the Senate, by granting Commissions which shall expire at the End of their next Session.

[4]Revised by the Twelfth Amendment.

Section 3.
He shall from time to time give to the Congress Information of the State of the Union, and recommend to their Consideration such Measures as he shall judge necessary and expedient; he may, on extraordinary occasions, convene both Houses, or either of them, and in Case of Disagreement between them, with respect to the Time of Adjournment, he may adjourn them to such Time as he shall think proper; he shall receive Ambassadors and other public Ministers; he shall take care that the Laws be faithfully executed, and shall Commission all the Officers of the United States.

Section 4.
The President, Vice President and all civil Officers of the United States, shall be removed from Office on Impeachment for, and Conviction of, Treason, Bribery, or other high Crimes and Misdemeanors.

Article III

Section 1.
The judicial Power of the United States, shall be vested in one supreme Court, and in such inferior Courts as the Congress may from time to time ordain and establish. The Judges, both of the supreme and inferior Courts, shall hold their Offices during good Behaviour, and shall, at stated Times, receive for their Services, a Compensation, which shall not be diminished during their Continuance in Office.

Section 2.
The judicial Power shall extend to all Cases, in Law and Equity, arising under this Constitution, the Laws of the United States, and Treaties made, or which shall be made, under their Authority;—to all Cases affecting ambassadors, other public ministers and consuls;—to all cases of admiralty and maritime Jurisdiction;—to Controversies to which the United States shall be a Party;—to Controversies between two or more States;—between a State and Citizens of another State;[5]— between Citizens of different States—between Citizens of the same State claiming Lands under Grants of different States, and between a State, or the Citizens thereof, and foreign States, Citizens, or Subjects.

In all Cases affecting Ambassadors, other public Ministers and Consuls, and those in which a State shall be Party, the supreme Court shall have original Jurisdiction. In all the other Cases before mentioned, the supreme Court shall have appellate Jurisdiction, both as to Law and Fact, with such Exceptions, and under such Regulations as the Congress shall make.

The trial of all Crimes, except in Cases of Impeachment, shall be by Jury; and such Trial shall be held in the State where the said Crimes shall have been committed; but when not committed within any State, the Trial shall be at such Place or Places as the Congress may by Law have directed.

Section 3.
Treason against the United States, shall consist only in levying War against them, or in adhering to their Enemies, giving them Aid and Comfort. No Person shall be convicted of Treason unless on the Testimony of two Witnesses to the same overt Act, or on Confession in open Court.

[5]Qualified by the Eleventh Amendment.

The Congress shall have power to declare the Punishment of Treason, but no Attainder of Treason shall work Corruption of Blood, or Forfeiture except during the Life of the Person attained.

Article IV

Section 1.
Full Faith and Credit shall be given in each State to the public Acts, Records, and judicial Proceedings of every other State. And the Congress may by general Laws prescribe the Manner in which such Acts, Records and Proceedings shall be proved, and the Effect thereof.

Section 2.
The Citizens of each State shall be entitled to all Privileges and Immunities of Citizens in the several States.

A Person charged in any State with Treason, Felony, or other Crime, who shall flee from Justice, and be found in another State, shall on demand of the executive Authority of the State from which he fled, be delivered up, to be removed to the State having Jurisdiction of the crime.

No Person held to Service or Labour in one State, under the Laws thereof, escaping into another, shall, in Consequence of any Law or Regulation therein, be discharged from such Service or Labour, but shall be delivered up on Claim of the Party to whom such Service or Labour may be due.

Section 3.
New States may be admitted by the Congress into this Union; but no new State shall be formed or erected within the Jurisdiction of any other State; nor any State be formed by the Junction of two or more States, or parts of States, without the Consent of the Legislatures of the States concerned as well as of the Congress.

The Congress shall have Power to dispose of and make all needful Rules and Regulations respecting the Territory or other Property belonging to the United States; and nothing in this Constitution shall be so construed as to Prejudice any Claims of the United States, or of any particular State.

Section 4.
The United States shall guarantee to every State in this Union a Republican Form of Government, and shall protect each of them against Invasion; and on Application of the Legislature, or of the Executive (when the Legislature cannot be convened) against domestic Violence.

Article V

The Congress, whenever two-thirds of both Houses shall deem it necessary, shall propose Amendments to this Constitution, or, on the Application of the Legislatures of two-thirds of the several States, shall call a Convention for proposing Amendments, which, in either Case, shall be valid to all Intents and Purposes, as part of this Constitution, when ratified by the Legislatures of three-fourths of the several States, or by Conventions in three-fourths thereof, as the one or the other Mode of Ratification may be proposed by the Congress; Provided that no Amendment which may be made prior to the Year One thousand eight hundred and eight shall in any Manner affect the first and fourth Clauses in the Ninth Section of the first Article; and that no State, without its Consent, shall be deprived of its equal Suffrage in the Senate.

Article VI

All Debts contracted and Engagements entered into, before the Adoption of this Constitution, shall be as valid against the United States under this Constitution, as under the Confederation.

This Constitution, and the Laws of the United States which shall be made in Pursuance thereof; and all Treaties made, or which shall be made, under the Authority of the United States, shall be the supreme Law of the Land; and the Judges in every State shall be bound thereby, any Thing in the Constitution or Laws of any State to the Contrary notwithstanding.

The Senators and Representatives before mentioned, and the Members of the several State Legislatures, and all executive and judicial Officers, both of the United States and of the several States, shall be bound by Oath or Affirmation to support this Constitution; but no religious Tests shall ever be required as a qualification to any Office or public Trust under the United States.

Article VII

The Ratification of the Conventions of nine States shall be sufficient for the Establishment of this Constitution between the States so ratifying the same.

Done in Convention by the Unanimous Consent of the States present the Seventeenth Day of September in the Year of our Lord one thousand seven hundred and Eighty seven, and of the Independence of the United States of America the Twelfth. In Witness whereof We have hereunto subscribed our Names.[6]

George Washington
President and deputy from Virginia

New Hampshire
John Langdon
Nicholas Gilman

Massachusetts
Nathaniel Gorham
Rufus King

Connecticut
William Samuel Johnson
Roger Sherman

New York
Alexander Hamilton

New Jersey
William Livingston
David Brearley
William Paterson
Jonathan Dayton

Pennsylvania
Benjamin Franklin
Thomas Mifflin
Robert Morris
George Clymer
Thomas FitzSimons
Jared Ingersoll
James Wilson
Gouverneur Morris

Delaware
George Read
Gunning Bedford, Jr.
John Dickinson
Richard Bassett
Jacob Broom

Maryland
James McHenry
Daniel of
St. Thomas Jenifer
Daniel Carroll

Virginia
John Blair
James Madison, Jr.

North Carolina
William Blount
Richard Dobbs
Spaight
Hugh Williamson

South Carolina
John Rutledge
Charles Cotesworth
Pinckney
Charles Pinckney
Pierce Butler

Georgia
William Few
Abraham Baldwin

---

[6]These are the full names of the signers, which in some cases are not the signatures on the document.

Articles in Addition to, and Amendment of, the Constitution of the United States of America, Proposed by Congress, and Ratified by the Legislatures of the Several States, Pursuant to the Fifth Article of the Original Constitution.[7]

[Article I]

Congress shall make no law respecting an establishment of religion, or prohibiting the free exercise thereof; or abridging the freedom of speech, or of the press; or the right of the people peaceably to assemble, and to petition the Government for a redress of grievances.

[Article II]

A well regulated Militia, being necessary to the security of a free State, the right of the people to keep and bear Arms shall not be infringed.

[Article III]

No Soldier shall, in time of peace, be quartered in any house, without the consent of the Owner, nor in time of war, but in a manner to be prescribed by law.

[Article IV]

The right of the people to be secure in their persons, houses, papers, and effects, against unreasonable searches and seizures, shall not be violated, and no Warrants shall issue, but upon probable cause, supported by Oath or affirmation, and particularly describing the place to be searched, and the persons or things to be seized.

[Article V]

No person shall be held to answer for a capital or otherwise infamous crime, unless on a presentment or indictment of a Grand Jury, except in cases arising in the land or naval forces, or in the Militia, when in actual service in time of War or public danger; nor shall any person be subject for the same offence to be twice put in jeopardy of life or limb; nor shall be compelled in any criminal case to be a witness against himself, nor be deprived of life, liberty, or property, without due process of law; nor shall private property be taken for public use, without just compensation.

[Article VI]

In all criminal prosecutions, the accused shall enjoy the right to a speedy and public trial, by an impartial jury of the State and district wherein the crime shall have been committed, which district shall have been previously ascertained by law, and to be informed of the nature and cause of the accusation; to be confronted with the witnesses against him; to have compulsory process for obtaining witnesses in his favour, and to have the Assistance of Counsel for his defense.

[Article VII]

In suits at common law, where the value in controversy shall exceed twenty dollars, the right of trial by jury shall be preserved, and no fact tried by a jury, shall be otherwise reexamined in any Court of the United States, than according to the rules of the common law.

---

[7]This heading appears only in the joint resolution submitting the first ten amendments.

[Article VIII]

Excessive bail shall not be required, nor excessive fines imposed, nor cruel and unusual punishments inflicted.

[Article IX]

The enumeration of the Constitution, of certain rights, shall not be construed to deny or disparage others retained by the people.

[Article X]

The powers not delegated to the United States by the Constitution, nor prohibited by it to the States, are reserved to the States respectively, or to the people.
[Amendments I–X, in force 1791.]

[Amendment XI][8]

The Judicial power of the United States shall not be construed to extend to any suit in law or equity, commenced or prosecuted against one of the United States by Citizens of another State, or by Citizens or Subjects of any Foreign State.

[Amendment XII][9]

The Electors shall meet in their respective States and vote by ballot for President and Vice-President, one of whom, at least, shall not be an inhabitant of the same State with themselves; they shall name in their ballots the person voted for as President, and in distinct ballots the person voted for as Vice-President, and they shall make distinct lists of all persons voted for as President, and of all persons voted for as Vice-President, and of the number of votes for each, which lists they shall sign and certify, and transmit sealed to the seat of the government of the United States, directed to the President of the Senate;—The President of the Senate shall, in the presence of the Senate and House of Representatives, open all the certificates and the votes shall then be counted;—The person having the greatest number of votes for President, shall be the President, if such number be a majority of the whole number of Electors appointed; and if no person have such majority, then from the persons having the highest numbers not exceeding three on the list of those voted for as President, the House of Representatives shall choose immediately, by ballot, the President. But in choosing the President, the votes shall be taken by states, the representation from each state having one vote; a quorum for this purpose shall consist of a member or members from two-thirds of the states, and a majority of all the states shall be necessary to a choice. And if the House of Representatives shall not choose a President whenever the right of choice shall devolve upon them, before the fourth day of March next following, then the Vice-President shall act as President, as in the case of the death or other constitutional disability of the President.—The person having the greatest number of votes as Vice-President, shall be the Vice-President, if such number be a majority of the whole number of Electors appointed, and if no person have a majority, then from the two highest numbers on the list, the Senate shall choose the Vice-President; a quorum for the purpose shall consist of two-thirds of the whole number of Senators, and a majority of the whole number shall be necessary to a choice. But no person constitutionally ineligible to the office of President shall be eligible to that of Vice-President of the United States.

[8]Adopted in 1798.
[9]Adopted in 1804.

[Amendment XIII][10]

Section 1.

Neither slavery nor involuntary servitude, except as a punishment for crime whereof the party shall have been duly convicted, shall exist within the United States, or any place subject to their jurisdiction.

Section 2.

Congress shall have power to enforce this article by appropriate legislation.

[Amendment XIV][11]

Section 1.

All persons born or naturalized in the United States, and subject to the jurisdiction thereof, are citizens of the United States and of the State wherein they reside. No State shall make or enforce any law which shall abridge the privileges or immunities of citizens of the United States; nor shall any State deprive any person of life, liberty, or property, without due process of law; nor deny to any person within its jurisdiction the equal protection of the laws.

Section 2.

Representatives shall be apportioned among the several States according to their respective numbers, counting the whole number of persons in each State, excluding Indians not taxed. But when the right to vote at any election for the choice of electors for President and Vice-President of the United States, Representatives in Congress, the Executive and Judicial officers of a State, or the members of the Legislature thereof, is denied to any of the male inhabitants of such State, being twenty-one years of age, and citizens of the United States, or in any way abridged, except for participation in rebellion, or other crime, the basis of representation therein shall be reduced in the proportion which the number of such male citizens shall bear to the whole number of male citizens twenty-one years of age in such State.

Section 3.

No person shall be a Senator or Representative in Congress, or elector of President and Vice-President, or hold any office, civil or military, under the United States, or under any State, who, having previously taken an oath, as a member of Congress, or as an officer of the United States, or as a member of any State legislature, or as an executive or judicial officer of any State, to support the Constitution of the United States, shall have engaged in insurrection or rebellion against the same, or given aid or comfort to the enemies thereof. But Congress may by a vote of two-thirds of each House, remove such disability.

Section 4.

The validity of the public debt of the United States, authorized by law, including debts incurred for payment of pensions and bounties for services in suppressing insurrection or rebellion, shall not be questioned. But neither the United States

[10]Adopted in 1865.
[11]Adopted in 1868.

nor any State shall assume or pay any debts or obligation incurred in aid of insurrection or rebellion against the United States, or any claim for the loss or emancipation of any slave; but all such debts, obligations, and claims shall be held illegal
and void.

Section 5.
The Congress shall have the power to enforce, by appropriate legislation, the provisions of this article.

[Amendment XV][12]

Section 1.
The right of citizens of the United States to vote shall not be denied or abridged
by the United States or by any State on account of race, color, or previous condition of servitude—

Section 2.
The Congress shall have power to enforce this article by appropriate legislation.

[Amendment XVI][13]

The Congress shall have power to lay and collect taxes on incomes, from whatever source derived, without apportionment among the several States, and without regard to any census or enumeration.

[Amendment XVII][14]

The Senate of the United States shall be composed of two Senators from each
State, elected by the people thereof, for six years; and each Senator shall have one
vote. The electors in each State shall have the qualifications requisite for electors
of the most numerous branch of the State legislatures.

When vacancies happen in the representation of any State in the Senate, the
executive authority of such State shall issue writs of election to fill such vacancies:
Provided, That the legislature of any State may empower the executive thereof to
make temporary appointments until the people fill the vacancies by election as the
legislature may direct.

This amendment shall not be so construed as to affect the election or term of
any Senator chosen before it becomes valid as part of the Constitution.

[Amendment XVIII][15]

Section 1.
After one year from the ratification of this article the manufacture, sale, or transportation of intoxicating liquors within, the importation thereof into, or the ex-
portation thereof from the United States and all territory subject to the jurisdiction thereof for beverage purposes is hereby prohibited.

[12]Adopted in 1870.
[13]Adopted in 1913.
[14]Adopted in 1913.
[15]Adopted in 1918.

Section 2.

The Congress and the several States shall have concurrent power to enforce this article by appropriate legislation.

Section 3.

This article shall be inoperative unless it shall have been ratified as an amendment to the Constitution by the legislatures of the several States, as provided in the Constitution, within seven years from the date of the submission hereof to the States by the Congress.

[Amendment XIX][16]

The right of citizens of the United States to vote shall not be denied or abridged by the United States or by any State on account of sex.

Congress shall have power to enforce this article by appropriate legislation.

[Amendment XX][17]

Section 1.

The terms of the President and Vice-President shall end at noon on the 20th day of January, and the terms of Senators and Representatives at noon on the 3d day of January, of the years in which such terms would have ended if this article had not been ratified; and the terms of their successors shall then begin.

Section 2.

The Congress shall assemble at least once in every year, and such meeting shall begin at noon on the 3d day of January, unless they shall by law appoint a different day.

Section 3.

If, at the time fixed for the beginning of the term of the President, the President elect shall have died, the Vice-President elect shall become President. If a President shall not have been chosen before the time fixed for the beginning of his term or if the President elect shall have failed to qualify, then the Vice-President elect shall act as President until a President shall have qualified; and the Congress may by law provide for the case wherein neither a President elect nor a Vice-President elect shall have qualified, declaring who shall then act as President, or the manner in which one who is to act shall be selected, and such person shall act accordingly until a President or Vice-President shall have qualified.

Section 4.

The Congress may by law provide for the case of the death of any of the persons from whom the House of Representatives may choose a President whenever the right of choice shall have devolved upon them, and for the case of the death of any of the persons from whom the Senate may choose a Vice-President whenever the right of choice shall have devolved upon them.

Section 5.

Sections 1 and 2 shall take effect on the 15th day of October following the ratification of this article.

[16]Adopted in 1920.
[17]Adopted in 1933.

Section 6.
This article shall be inoperative unless it shall have been ratified as an amendment to the Constitution by the legislatures of three-fourths of the several States within seven years from the date of its submission.

[Amendment XXI][18]

Section 1.
The eighteenth article of amendment to the Constitution of the United States is hereby repealed.

Section 2.
The transportation or importation into any State, Territory, or possession of the United States for delivery or use therein of intoxicating liquors, in violation of the laws thereof, is hereby prohibited.

Section 3.
This article shall be inoperative unless it shall have been ratified as an amendment to the Constitution by conventions in the several States, as provided in the Constitution, within seven years from the date of the submission hereof to the States by the Congress.

[Amendment XXII][19]

No person shall be elected to the office of the President more than twice, and no person who has held the office of President, or acted as President, for more than two years of a term to which some other person was elected President shall be elected to the office of the President more than once.

But this Article shall not apply to any person holding the office of President when this Article was proposed by the Congress, and shall not prevent any person who may be holding the office of President, or acting as President, during the term within which this Article becomes operative from holding the office of President or acting as President during the remainder of such term.

This article shall be inoperative unless it shall have been ratified as an amendment to the Constitution by the legislatures of three-fourths of the several states within seven years from the date of its submission to the states by the Congress.

[Amendment XXIII][20]

Section 1.
The District constituting the seat of Government of the United States shall appoint in such manner as the Congress may direct:

A number of electors of President and Vice-President equal to the whole number of Senators and Representatives in Congress to which the District would be entitled if it were a State, but in no event more than the least populous State; they shall be in addition to those appointed by the States, but they shall be considered,

[18]Adopted in 1933.
[19]Adopted in 1961.
[20]Adopted in 1961.

for the purposes of the election of President and Vice-President, to be electors appointed by a State; and they shall meet in the District and perform such duties as provided by the twelfth article of amendment.

Section 2.
The Congress shall have power to enforce this article by appropriate legislation.

[Amendment XXIV][21]

Section 1.
The right of citizens of the United States to vote in any primary or other election for President or Vice President, for electors for President or Vice President, or for Senator or Representative in Congress, shall not be denied or abridged by the United States or any state by reason of failure to pay any poll tax or other tax.

Section 2.
The Congress shall have the power to enforce this article by appropriate legislation.

[Amendment XXV][22]

Section 1.
In case of the removal of the President from office or of his death or resignation, the Vice President shall become President.

Section 2.
Whenever there is a vacancy in the office of the Vice President, the President shall nominate a Vice President who shall take office upon confirmation by a majority vote of both Houses of Congress.

Section 3.
Whenever the President transmits to the President Pro Tempore of the Senate and the Speaker of the House of Representatives his written declaration that he is unable to discharge the powers and duties of his office, and until he transmits to them a written declaration to the contrary, such powers and duties shall be discharged by the Vice President as Acting President.

Section 4.
Whenever the Vice President and a majority of either the principal officers of the executive departments or of such other body as Congress may by law provide, transmit to the President Pro Tempore of the Senate and the Speaker of the House of Representatives their written declaration that the President is unable to discharge the powers and duties of his office, the Vice President shall immediately assume the powers and duties of the office as Acting President.

[21]Adopted in 1964.
[22]Adopted in 1967.

Thereafter, when the President transmits to the President Pro Tempore of the Senate and the Speaker of the House of Representatives his written declaration that no inability exists, he shall resume the powers and duties of his office unless the Vice President and a majority of either the principal officers of the executive departments or of such other body as Congress may by law provide, transmit within four days to the President Pro Tempore of the Senate and the Speaker of the House of Representatives their written declaration that the President is unable to discharge the powers and duties of his office. Thereupon Congress shall decide the issue, assembling within forty-eight hours for that purpose if not in session. If the Congress, within twenty-one days after receipt of the latter written declaration, or, if Congress is not in session, within twenty-one days after Congress is required to assemble, determines by two-thirds vote of both Houses that the President is unable to discharge the powers and duties of his office, the Vice President shall continue to discharge the same as Acting President; otherwise, the President shall resume the powers and duties of his office.

[Amendment XXVI][23]

Section 1.
The right of citizens of the United States, who are eighteen years of age or older, to vote shall not be denied or abridged by the United States or by any State on account of age.

Section 2.
The Congress shall have power to enforce this article by appropriate legislation.

[Amendment XXVII][24]

No law varying the compensation for the services of the Senators and Representatives shall take effect until an election of Representatives shall have intervened.

[23]Adopted in 1971.
[24]Adopted in 1992.

PRESIDENTIAL ELECTIONS

Year	Candidates	Parties	Popular Vote	Percentage of Popular Vote	Electoral Vote	Percentage of Voter Participation
1789	GEORGE WASHINGTON (VA.)*				69	
	John Adams				34	
	Others				35	
1792	GEORGE WASHINGTON (VA.)				132	
	John Adams				77	
	George Clinton				50	
	Others				5	
1796	JOHN ADAMS (MASS.)	Federalist			71	
	Thomas Jefferson	Democratic Republican			68	
	Thomas Pinckney	Federalist			59	
	Aaron Burr	Dem.-Rep.			30	
	Others				48	
1800	THOMAS JEFFERSON (VA.)	Dem.-Rep.			73	
	Aaron Burr	Dem.-Rep.			73	
	John Adams	Federalist			65	
	C. C. Pinckney	Federalist			64	
	John Jay	Federalist			1	
1804	THOMAS JEFFERSON (VA.)	Dem.-Rep.			162	
	C. C. Pinckney	Federalist			14	
1808	JAMES MADISON (VA.)	Dem.-Rep.			122	
	C. C. Pinckney	Federalist			47	
	George Clinton	Dem.-Rep.			6	

Year	Candidates	Parties	Popular Vote	Percentage of Popular Vote	Electoral Vote	Percentage of Voter Participation
1812	**JAMES MADISON (VA.)**	Dem.-Rep.			128	
	De Witt Clinton	Federalist			89	
1816	**JAMES MONROE (VA.)**	Dem.-Rep.			183	
	Rufus King	Federalist			34	
1820	**JAMES MONROE (VA.)**	Dem.-Rep.			231	
	John Quincy Adams	Dem.-Rep.			1	
1824	**JOHN Q. ADAMS (MASS.)**	Dem.-Rep.	108,740	30.5	84	26.9
	Andrew Jackson	Dem.-Rep.	153,544	43.1	99	
	William H. Crawford	Dem.-Rep.	46,618	13.1	41	
	Henry Clay	Dem.-Rep.	47,136	13.2	37	
1828	**ANDREW JACKSON (TENN.)**	Democratic	647,286	56.0	178	57.6
	John Quincy Adams	National Republican	508,064	44.0	83	
1832	**ANDREW JACKSON (TENN.)**	Democratic	687,502	55.0	219	55.4
	Henry Clay	National Republican	530,189	42.4	49	
	John Floyd	Independent			11	
	William Wirt	Anti-Mason	33,108	2.6	7	
1836	**MARTIN VAN BUREN (N.Y.)**	Democratic	765,483	50.9	170	57.8
	W. H. Harrison	Whig			73	
	Hugh L. White	Whig	739,795	49.1	26	
	Daniel Webster	Whig			14	
	W. P. Magnum	Independent			11	
1840	**WILLIAM H. HARRISON (OHIO)**	Whig	1,274,624	53.1	234	80.2
	Martin Van Buren	Democratic	1,127,781	46.9	60	
	J. G. Birney	Liberty	7,069		—	

*State of residence at time of election.

(continued)

Year	Candidates	Parties	Popular Vote	Percentage of Popular Vote	Electoral Vote	Percentage of Voter Participation
1844	JAMES K. POLK (TENN.)	Democratic	1,338,464	49.6	170	78.9
	Henry Clay	Whig	1,300,097	48.1	105	
	J. G. Birney	Liberty	62,300	2.3	—	
1848	ZACHARY TAYLOR (LA.)	Whig	1,360,967	47.4	163	72.7
	Lewis Cass	Democratic	1,222,342	42.5	127	
	Martin Van Buren	Free-Soil	291,263	10.1	—	
1852	FRANKLIN PIERCE (N.H.)	Democratic	1,601,117	50.9	254	69.6
	Winfield Scott	Whig	1,385,453	44.1	42	
	John P. Hale	Free-Soil	155,825	5.0	—	
1856	JAMES BUCHANAN (PA.)	Democratic	1,832,955	45.3	174	78.9
	John C. Frémont	Republican	1,339,932	33.1	114	
	Millard Fillmore	American	871,731	21.6	8	
1860	ABRAHAM LINCOLN (ILL.)	Republican	1,865,593	39.8	180	81.2
	Stephen A. Douglas	Democratic	1,382,713	29.5	12	
	John C. Breckinridge	Democratic	848,356	18.1	72	
	John Bell	Union	592,906	12.6	39	
1864	ABRAHAM LINCOLN (ILL.)	Republican	2,213,655	55.0	212	73.8
	George B. McClellan	Democratic	1,805,237	45.0	21	
1868	ULYSSES S. GRANT (ILL.)	Republican	3,012,833	52.7	214	78.1
	Horatio Seymour	Democratic	2,703,249	47.3	80	
1872	ULYSSES S. GRANT (ILL.)	Republican	3,597,132	55.6	286	71.3
	Horace Greeley	Democratic; Liberal Republican	2,834,125	43.9	66	

Year	Candidate	Party	Popular Vote	%	Electoral Vote	Voter Participation
1876	**RUTHERFORD B. HAYES (OHIO)**	Republican	4,036,298	48.0	185	81.8
	Samuel J. Tilden	Democratic	4,300,590	51.0	184	
1880	**JAMES A. GARFIELD (OHIO)**	Republican	4,454,416	48.5	214	79.4
	Winfield S. Hancock	Democratic	4,444,952	48.1	155	
1884	**GROVER CLEVELAND (N.Y.)**	Democratic	4,874,986	48.5	219	77.5
	James G. Blaine	Republican	4,851,981	48.2	182	
1888	**BENJAMIN HARRISON (IND.)**	Republican	5,439,853	47.9	233	79.3
	Grover Cleveland	Democratic	5,540,309	48.6	168	
1892	**GROVER CLEVELAND (N.Y.)**	Democratic	5,556,918	46.1	277	74.7
	Benjamin Harrison	Republican	5,176,108	43.0	145	
	James B. Weaver	People's	1,041,028	8.5	22	
1896	**WILLIAM MCKINLEY (OHIO)**	Republican	7,104,779	51.1	271	79.3
	William J. Bryan	Democratic People's	6,502,925	47.7	176	
1900	**WILLIAM MCKINLEY (OHIO)**	Republican	7,207,923	51.7	292	73.2
	William J. Bryan	Dem.-Populist	6,358,133	45.5	155	
1904	**THEODORE ROOSEVELT (N.Y.)**	Republican	7,623,486	57.9	336	65.2
	Alton B. Parker	Democratic	5,077,911	37.6	140	
	Eugene V. Debs	Socialist	402,283	3.0	—	
1908	**WILLIAM H. TAFT (OHIO)**	Republican	7,678,908	51.6	321	65.4
	William J. Bryan	Democratic	6,409,104	43.1	162	
	Eugene V. Debs	Socialist	420,793	2.8	—	
1912	**WOODROW WILSON (N.J.)**	Democratic	6,293,454	41.9	435	58.8
	Theodore Roosevelt	Progressive	4,119,538	27.4	88	
	William H. Taft	Republican	3,484,980	23.2	8	
	Eugene V. Debs	Socialist	900,672	6.0	—	

(continued)

Year	Candidates	Parties	Popular Vote	Percentage of Popular Vote	Electoral Vote	Percentage of Voter Participation
1916	**WOODROW WILSON (N.J.)**	Democratic	9,129,606	49.4	277	61.6
	Charles E. Hughes	Republican	8,538,221	46.2	254	
	A. L. Benson	Socialist	585,113	3.2	—	
1920	**WARREN G. HARDING (OHIO)**	Republican	16,152,200	60.4	404	49.2
	James M. Cox	Democratic	9,147,353	34.2	127	
	Eugene V. Debs	Socialist	919,799	3.4	—	
1924	**CALVIN COOLIDGE (MASS.)**	Republican	15,725,016	54.0	382	48.9
	John W. Davis	Democratic	8,386,503	28.8	136	
	Robert M. LaFollette	Progressive	4,822,856	16.6	13	
1928	**HERBERT HOOVER (CALIF.)**	Republican	21,391,381	58.2	444	56.9
	Alfred E. Smith	Democratic	15,016,443	40.9	87	
	Norman Thomas	Socialist	267,835	0.7	—	
1932	**FRANKLIN D. ROOSEVELT (N.Y.)**	Democratic	22,821,857	57.4	472	56.9
	Herbert Hoover	Republican	15,761,841	39.7	59	
	Norman Thomas	Socialist	881,951	2.2	—	
1936	**FRANKLIN D. ROOSEVELT (N.Y.)**	Democratic	27,751,597	60.8	523	61.0
	Alfred M. Landon	Republican	16,679,583	36.5	8	
	William Lemke	Union	882,479	1.9	—	
1940	**FRANKLIN D. ROOSEVELT (N.Y.)**	Democratic	27,244,160	54.8	449	62.5
	Wendell L. Willkie	Republican	22,305,198	44.8	82	
1944	**FRANKLIN D. ROOSEVELT (N.Y.)**	Democratic	25,602,504	53.5	432	55.9
	Thomas E. Dewey	Republican	22,006,285	46.0	99	

Year	Candidate	Party	Popular Vote	%	Electoral Vote	% Voter Participation
1948	**HARRY S. TRUMAN (MO.)**	Democratic	24,105,695	49.5	304	53.0
	Thomas E. Dewey	Republican	21,969,170	45.1	189	
	J. Strom Thurmond	State-Rights Democratic	1,169,021	2.4	38	
	Henry A. Wallace	Progressive	1,156,103	2.4	—	
1952	**DWIGHT D. EISENHOWER (N.Y.)**	Republican	33,936,252	55.1	442	63.3
	Adlai E. Stevenson	Democratic	27,314,992	44.4	89	
1956	**DWIGHT D. EISENHOWER (N.Y.)**	Republican	35,575,420	57.6	457	60.6
	Adlai E. Stevenson	Democratic	26,033,066	42.1	73	
	Other	—			1	
1960	**JOHN F. KENNEDY (MASS.)**	Democratic	34,227,096	49.9	303	62.8
	Richard M. Nixon	Republican	34,108,546	49.6	219	
	Other	—			15	
1964	**LYNDON B. JOHNSON (TEX.)**	Democratic	43,126,506	61.1	486	61.7
	Barry M. Goldwater	Republican	27,176,799	38.5	52	
1968	**RICHARD M. NIXON (N.Y.)**	Republican	31,770,237	43.4	301	60.6
	Hubert H. Humphrey	Democratic	31,270,533	42.7	191	
	George Wallace	American Independent	9,906,141	13.5	46	
1972	**RICHARD M. NIXON (N.Y.)**	Republican	47,169,911	60.7	520	55.2
	George S. McGovern	Democratic	29,170,383	37.5	17	
	Other	—			1	
1976	**JIMMY CARTER (GA.)**	Democratic	40,828,587	50.0	297	53.5
	Gerald R. Ford	Republican	39,147,613	47.9	241	
	Other	—	1,575,459	2.1	—	

(continued)

Year	Candidates	Parties	Popular Vote	Percentage of Popular Vote	Electoral Vote	Percentage of Voter Participation
1980	RONALD REAGAN (CALIF.)	Republican	43,901,812	50.7	489	52.6
	Jimmy Carter	Democratic	35,483,820	41.0	49	
	John B. Anderson	Independent	5,719,722	6.6	—	
	Ed Clark	Libertarian	921,188	1.1	—	
1984	RONALD REAGAN (CALIF.)	Republican	54,455,075	59.0	525	53.3
	Walter Mondale	Democratic	37,577,185	41.0	13	
1988	GEORGE BUSH (TEX.)	Republican	47,946,422	54.0	426	50.2
	Michael S. Dukakis	Democratic	41,016,429	46.0	112	
1992	WILLIAM J. CLINTON (ARK.)	Democratic	43,728,375	43.0	370	55.0
	George Bush	Republican	38,167,416	38.0	168	
	Ross Perot	Independent	19,237,247	19.0	0	
1996	WILLIAM J. CLINTON (ARK.)	Democratic	47,401,185	49.3	379	49.0
	Robert Dole	Republican	39,197,469	40.7	159	
	Ross Perot	Reform	8,085,294	8.4	—	
2000	GEORGE W. BUSH (TEXAS)	Republican	50,459,211	47.89	271	51.0
	Albert Gore, Jr.	Democratic	51,003,894	48.41	266	
	Ralph Nader	Green	2,834,410	2.69	—	

POPULATION OF THE UNITED STATES, 1790–2000

Year	Population	Percent Increase	Population per Square Mile	Percent Urban/ Rural	Percent White/ Nonwhite	Median Age
1790	3,929,214		4.5	5.1/94.9	80.7/19.3	NA
1800	5,308,483	35.1	6.1	6.1/93.9	81.1/18.9	NA
1810	7,239,881	36.4	4.3	7.3/92.7	81.0/19.0	NA
1820	9,638,453	33.1	5.5	7.2/92.8	81.6/18.4	16.7
1830	12,866,020	33.5	7.4	8.8/91.2	81.9/18.1	17.2
1840	17,069,453	32.7	9.8	10.8/89.2	83.2/16.8	17.8
1850	23,191,876	35.9	7.9	15.3/84.7	84.3/15.7	18.9
1860	31,443,321	35.6	10.6	19.8/80.2	85.6/14.4	19.4
1870	39,818,449	26.6	13.4	25.7/74.3	86.2/13.8	20.2
1880	50,155,783	26.0	16.9	28.2/71.8	86.5/13.5	20.9
1890	62,947,714	25.5	21.2	35.1/64.9	87.5/12.5	22.0
1900	75,994,575	20.7	25.6	39.6/60.4	87.9/12.1	22.9
1910	91,972,266	21.0	31.0	45.6/54.4	88.9/11.1	24.1
1920	105,710,620	14.9	35.6	51.2/48.8	89.7/10.3	25.3
1930	122,775,046	16.1	41.2	56.1/43.9	89.8/10.2	26.4
1940	131,669,275	7.2	44.2	56.5/43.5	89.8/10.2	29.0
1950	150,697,361	14.5	50.7	64.0/36.0	89.5/10.5	30.2
1960	179,323,175	18.5	50.6	69.9/30.1	88.6/11.4	29.5
1970	203,302,031	13.4	57.4	73.5/26.5	87.6/12.4	28.0
1980	226,545,805	11.4	64.0	73.7/26.3	86.0/14.0	30.0
1990	248,709,873	9.9	70.3	77.5/22.5	80.3/19.7	32.9
2000	281,421,906	13.0	79.6	NA/NA	83.0/17.0	35.3

NA = Not available.

EMPLOYMENT, 1870–2000

Year	Number of Workers (in millions)	Male/Female Employment Ratio	Percentage of Workers in Unions
1870	12.5	85/15	—
1880	17.4	85/15	—
1890	23.3	83/17	—
1900	29.1	82/18	3
1910	38.2	79/21	6
1920	41.6	79/21	12
1930	48.8	78/22	7
1940	53.0	76/24	27
1950	59.6	72/28	25
1960	69.9	68/32	26
1970	82.1	63/37	25
1980	108.5	58/42	23
1985	108.9	57/43	19
1990	118.8	55/45	16
2000	134.3	53/47	13.5

PRODUCTION, TRADE, AND FEDERAL SPENDING/DEBT, 1790–2000

Year	Gross National Product (GNP) (in billions $)	Balance of Trade (in millions $)	Federal Budget (in billions $)	Federal Surplus/ Deficit (in billions $)	Federal Debt (in billions $)
1790	—	-3	.004	+0.00015	.076
1800	—	-20	.011	+0.0006	.083
1810	—	-18	.008	+0.0012	.053
1820	—	-4	.018	-0.0004	.091
1830	—	+3	.015	+0.100	.049
1840	—	+25	.024	-0.005	.004
1850	—	-26	.040	+0.004	.064
1860	—	-38	.063	-0.01	.065
1870	7.4	-11	.310	+0.10	2.4
1880	11.2	+92	.268	+0.07	2.1
1890	13.1	+87	.318	+0.09	1.2
1900	18.7	+569	.521	+0.05	1.2
1910	35.3	+273	.694	-0.02	1.1
1920	91.5	+2,880	6.357	+0.3	24.3
1930	90.7	+513	3.320	+0.7	16.3
1940	100.0	-3,403	9.6	-2.7	43.0
1950	286.5	+1,691	43.1	-2.2	257.4
1960	506.5	+4,556	92.2	+0.3	286.3
1970	992.7	+2,511	196.6	+2.8	371.0
1980	2,631.7	+24,088	579.6	-59.5	914.3
1985	4,087.7	-148,480	946.3	-212.3	1,827.5
1990	5,764.9	-101,012	1,251.8	-220.5	4,064.6
2000	9,860.8	-369.7	1,789.6	+237.0	5,674.2

Index

Note: Page numbers followed by the letter *"i"* refer to illustrations and by the letter *"m"* refer to maps.

Abortion controversy, 855, 887, 929, 936–938
Abraham Lincoln Brigade, 665–666
Abuse of Power (Kutler, 1997), 874
ACT UP (AIDS organization), 935*i*
Adams, Charles Francis, Jr., 558
Addams, Jane, 560
Adding machines, 458
Advanced Research Projects Agency (ARPA), 926
Adventures of Augie March, The (Bellow, 1953), 794
Adventures of Huckleberry Finn, The (Twain, 1885), 442–443
Adventures of Tom Sawyer, The (Twain, 1876), 442
Advertising
    consumerism in 1920s, 634–635
    mass culture of 1980s and 1990s, 940
    and television in 1950s, 791–792
Affirmative action, 823, 854, 867, 868, 933
Affluent society (1950s-1960s)
    civil rights movement, 799–803
    class and distribution of wealth, 797–799
    economy, 779–782
    science and technology, 783–789
    society and culture, 789–797
Afghanistan, 884, 897, 899, 943, 945
AFL; *see* American Federation of Labor
AFL-CIO (American Federation of Labor-Congress of Industrial Organizations)
    environmentalism, 857
    formation of, 782
    North American Free Trade Agreement, 911
Africa
    AIDS epidemic, 935, 936
    British imperialism, 539
African Americans; *see also* Civil rights; Great Migrations; Race; Segregation
    late nineteenth century
        migration from South to Northern cities, 484
        New South, 422–426
        Populism, 525
        progressivism and reform movements, 572–573
        Spanish-American War, 544
        vaudeville, 501
        women and teaching as profession, 562
        women's clubs, 564
    Reconstruction era
        Black Codes, 403, 405
        concepts of freedom, 398
        economic status, 411
        education, 409–410
        family, 412
        Fifteenth Amendment and voting rights, 406
        Fourteenth Amendment and citizenship, 405
        important moments, 396*i*
        land ownership and tenancy, 410
        legacy of, 404, 418–419
        legacy of Reconstruction, 397
        politics of South during, 408, 415
    twentieth century
        American Communist Party, 666
        black power movement, 824
        demographic shift in 1960s, 822–823
        education in late 1900s, 932
        Great Depression, 655, 657, 660
        Harlem Renaissance, 638
        jazz and swing music, 739
        middle class in 1990s, 931–932
        migrations from South to northern cities, 619, 620*m*, 655, 658, 732
        New Deal, 694–695
        poor and working-class, in 1990s, 932–933
        popular music in 1950s, 795
        work force in 1920s, 631
        World War I and postwar period, 619–621
        World War II, 732–733
African National Congress (ANC), 899
Age of Reform, The (Hofstadter, 1955), 524, 574
Age of Roosevelt, The (Schlesinger, 1957-1960), 696
Agee, James, 667
Agency for International Development (AID), 825
Agnew, Spiro, 873
Agrarian revolt, 522–526
Agricultural Adjustment Act (1933), 679–680
Agricultural Marketing Act (1929), 668
Agriculture; *see also* Farmers; Rural life
    child labor, 474
    Far West in late 1800s, 450–454
    Great Depression, 655, 679–680
    land-grant institutions and, 509
    pesticides in 1950s, 784–785
    productivity and prices in 1920s, 632, 634
    Reconstruction in South, 410–411
    tenancy and sharecropping, 410, 421–422
Aguinaldo, Emilio, 550, 551
Aid to Dependent Children program, 691
AIDS epidemic, 852, 934–935, 943
Aiken, Howard, 629
Air Force, African Americans and, 733
Airplanes
    advances in 1920s, 628–629
    invention of, 461
    World War I, 610
    World War II, 730*i*, 731
Alabama
    civil rights movement, 801, 820, 822
    post-Reconstruction ruling class, 419
Alabama claims, 415
Alamagordo, New Mexico, and first atomic explosion, 746
Alaska, 414, 858, 938
Alcott, Louisa May, 504
Aldrich, Nelson W., 521
Aldrin, Edwin, 788
Alger, Horatio, 468–469
Allen, Gracie, 662

Churchill, Winston
  Cold War, 752
  World War II, 713, 715, 724, 752–753
  Yalta Conference, 753–755
Cities
  African-American poverty in late 1900s and, 932
  civil rights movement in mid-1960s, 822–823
  migrations from South to northern cities, 619,
    620*m*, 655, 658*i*, 799
  poverty in 1950s and early 1960s, 798–799
  progressivism and municipal reform, 567–568
  unemployment in Great Depression, 654
City beautiful movement, 490
City manager plan, 568
Civil rights; *see also* Segregation; Voting rights
  battle for racial equality in 1960s, 819–824
  rise of movement in 1950s, 799–803
  Truman and, 764, 765, 766
Civil Rights Act (1866), 405
Civil Rights Act (1964), 853
Civil Rights Act (Voting Rights Act, 1965), 822
Civil service system, 518, 519
Civil Works Administration (CWA), 684
Civilian Advisory Commission, 612
Civilian Conservation Corps (CCC), 684, 694–695, 740
Clark, Champ, 590
Clark, Dick, 796
Clark, Jim, 822
Clark, William, 438
Class; *see also* Middle class; Working class
  affluent society of 1950s, 797–799
  entertainment in cities of late 1800s, 500
  high culture of urban age, 505–511
Clayton Antitrust Act, 592
Clean Air Act (1970), 859
Clean Water Act (1972), 859
Clemenceau, Georges, 616
Cleveland, Grover
  conservatism and political crisis of 1890s, 526
  election of 1884, 519–520
  election of 1892, 521
  gold standard, 529–530
  Pullman Strike, 478
  Spanish-American War, 543
  Venezuela, 536–537
Cleveland, Ohio, 823, 858
Clifford, Clark, 831
Climate
  global warming, 858, 939
  growth of West in 1950s, 781
Clinton, Bill
  abortion controversy, 938
  domestic policies, 911, 938
  election of 1992, 904–905
  election of 1996, 913–914
  foreign policy, 911, 916
  impeachment, 915–916
  military and homosexuality, 852, 910
  personal scandals, 915, 928
  Supreme Court, 854
Clinton, Hillary Rodham, 911, 912*i*, 918
Cloning, and genetic research, 928–929
Clothing
  and consumer culture, 499
  ready-made, 497
Cochise, 448
"Code-talkers", 733
Cody, Buffalo Bill, 442

Cold War
  civil rights movement, 802
  collapse of postwar peace, 755–759, 761–762
  Eisenhower administration and foreign policy,
    803–809
  historical debate about, 760
  Kennedy and Johnson administrations, 824–827
  origins of, 751–755
  waning of, 897–899
Cole (ship), 944
Colfax, Schuyler, 413
College Equal Suffrage League of Northern
    California, 556*i*
Colleges and universities
  black, 410, 422, 424*i*
  military, 554
  Morrill Act and land-grant, 509
  professional schools, 562
  sports in late 1800s, 500, 501
  women in 1970s–1990s, 854, 855
  women in late 1800s, 510–511, 563, 564
  World War II, 740
Collier, John, 695, 733
Collins, Michael, 788
Colorado
  mining boom, 437–438
  statehood, 436
Columbia Broadcasting System (CBS), 791, 940
Columbia University, and student unrest, 844
Columbian Exposition (Chicago, 1893), 490
Comic books, 766
Command of the Army Act (1867), 406
Commerce, agriculture in Far West, 452–453;
    see also Trade
Commission on Civil Disorders, 823
Committee for the Re-Election of the President
    (CRP), 872
Committee on Public Information (CPI), 614
Communications; *see also* Media, mass; Newspapers;
    Radio; Telegraph; Television
  consumerism in 1920s, 635
  technological growth in late 1800s, 458
  technology of mass, 504–505
Communism; *see also* China; Cold War; Communist
    International; Communist Party (China);
    Communist Party (U.S.); Soviet Union
  crusade against subversion in 1950s, 771–775, 804
  Red Scare of 1919, 621–623
Communist International (Comintern), 621
Communist Party (China), 710
Communist Party (U.S.), 665, 666, 685
Community Action programs, 817–818, 848
Compaq, 925
Computers
  early developments, 629
  personal, and growth of market in 1980s and
    1990s, 924–927
  postwar developments in, 786–787
  World War II, 731
Comstock, Henry, 438
Comstock Lode, 438
Coney Island, New York, 503–504
Congress of Industrial Organizations (CIO), 688, 782;
    see also AFL-CIO
Congress of Racial Equality (CORE), 732, 820, 824
Conkin, Paul, 696
Conkling, Roscoe, 518
Connor, Eugene "Bull", 820

Friedman, Milton, 652
Frontier and Far West
  concept of, 429, 442–443, 444–445
  historical debate on, 444–445
Fuchs, Klaus, 773
Fulbright, J. William, 831
Fundamentalism, religious, 507, 641–642, 942–943
Furman v. *Georgia* (1972), 868

Gaddis, John Lewis, 760
Gagarin, Yuri, 788
Gangs, 734–735
Gap (clothing chain), 939
Garfield, James, 518
Garfield, James R., 587
Garland, Hamlin, 454
Garvey, Marcus, 621
Gast, John, 428*i*
Gateway, 926
Gay Liberation Front, 851
Gelb, Leslie, 832
General Agreement on Trade and Tariffs (GATT), 911, 924, 942
General Electric, 461–462
General Federation of Women's Clubs, 564
General Motors, 462, 689, 803
General Theory of Employment, Interest, and Money, The (Keynes, 1936), 657
Genetics, 629, 632, 928–929
Geneva accords (1954), 806–807, 827
Genoa, Italy, 942
George, David Lloyd, 616
George, Henry, 470
Germ theory, 510
German-Americans, and World War I, 615
Germany; *see also* Berlin
  division of, 758
  Fascism and rise of Hitler in 1930s, 706
  global depression, 656
  international debt in 1920s, 704–705
  Munich agreement, 711–712
  World War I, 604–605, 606, 607, 608, 609, 611
  World War II, 712*i*, 714–715, 717, 722–724, 729–732, 742–743, 744
  Yalta Conference, 754
Geronimo, 448, 449*i*
Gestapo, 726
Ghost Dance, 449
GI Bill, 762
Giant (1956), 795
Gideon v. *Wainwright* (1963), 867
Gingrich, Newt, 913
Ginsberg, Allen, 794
Ginsburg, Ruth Bader, 854
Glasnost, 898
Glass-Steagall Act (1933), 678
Glavis, Louis, 587
Glenn, John, 788
Glidden, Joseph H., 451
Global warming, 858, 938
Globalization
  economic, 923–924, 941
  perils of, 941–947
Gold Diggers of 1933 (film, 1933), 663
Gold rush, 432
Gold standard, 528–530, 532
Goldwater, Barry, 817, 887
Gompers, Samuel, 476, 570

Gone with the Wind (film, 1939), 663
Gone with the Wind (Mitchell, 1936), 664
Good Neighbor Policy, 708
Goodman, Andrew, 822
Goodman, Benny, 739
Goodwyn, Lawrence, 524
Gorbachev, Mikhail, 897–898, 899, 902
Gordon, Colin, 696
Gordon, Linda, 575
Gordy, Berry, 795
Gore, Al, 912*i*, 917–919
Gospel of Wealth, The (Carnegie, 1901), 468
Government, federal
  Clinton administration and shutdown of, 912–913
  liberal state of 1960s, 813–819
  New Deal and government planning, 682–683
  renewal of faith in, after September 11, 2001 terrorist attacks, 946
  Republican control in 1920s, 643–646
  Theodore Roosevelt administration, 582
  tribal policy, 443, 445–446
  weakness in late 1800s, 517
Government, state
  New South, 419
  progressivism and reform of, 568–569
  Reconstruction and, 401, 403, 406, 407*m*
  statehood in Far West, 436
Grady, Henry, 420
Graham, Billy, 886
Grand Coulee Dam, 698
Grangers, 521, 522
Grant, Ulysses S.
  election of 1868, 412–413
  election of 1872, 413
  Reconstruction, 406, 412–415
  and scandal, 413–414
Grapes of Wrath, The (film, 1940), 663
Grapes of Wrath, The (Steinbeck, 1939), 667
Great Britain
  Alabama claims, 415
  Atlantic Charter opposition, 752
  expansion of empire in 19th century, 538–539
  Munich agreement, 711–712
  Suez crisis, 808
  World War I, 604, 605, 607, 608, 611, 616
  World War II, 712*i*, 713, 714–715, 722–724, 731–732, 743
  Yalta Conference, 754
Great Depression; *see also* New Deal
  beginning of, 649–653
  culture, 660–667
  and global depression, 656–657
  historical debate on causes of, 652–653
  Hoover administration, 667–673
  society, 654–660
  World War II, 727
Great Depression, The (Bernstein, 1987), 652–653
Great Frontier, The (Webb, 1952), 444
Great Gatsby, The (Fitzgerald, 1925), 638
Great Lakes, shipping and steel industry, 460
Great Migrations, 619, 620*m*, 655, 658*i*, 732
Great Plains
  agriculture, 451
  Dust Bowl, 655
Great Plains, The (Webb, 1931), 444
Great Society, 817, 819
"Great White Fleet", 594
Greece, 756–757

INDEX